A PROBLEM BOOK IN MATHEMATICAL ANALYSIS

GN BERMAN

CLASSIC
TEXTS
SERIES...

A PROBLEM BOOK IN
MATHEMATICAL ANALYSIS

GN BERMAN

arihant
Arihant Prakashan (Series), Meerut

arihant
Arihant Prakashan (Series), Meerut

Administrative & Production Offices

Regd. Office
'Ramchhaya' 4577/15, Agarwal Road, Darya Ganj, New Delhi -110002
Tele: 011- 47630600, 43518550

Head Office
Kalindi, TP Nagar, Meerut (UP) - 250002
Tel: 0121-7156203, 7156204

Sales & Support Offices
Agra, Ahmedabad, Bengaluru, Bareilly, Chennai, Delhi, Guwahati, Hyderabad, Jaipur, Jhansi, Kolkata, Lucknow, Nagpur & Pune.

ISBN 978-93-88127-32-5

PO No : TXT-XX-XXXXXXX-X-XX

Published by Arihant Publications (India) Ltd.

For further information about the books published by Arihant, log on to www.arihantbooks.com or e-mail at info@arihantbooks.com

Follow us on

PREFACE

This collection of problems is designed for students studying mathematical analysis in higher technical educational institutions. Problems and exercises are systematically selected and arranged in compliance with the major sections of the course in mathematical analysis.

Theoretical information is not included in this book. The reader will find it in the corresponding sections of the textbook Mathematical Analysis (A Brief Course for Engineering Students) by A.F. Bermant and I.G. Aramanovich brought out in English by Mir Publishers of Moscow in 1975. For convenience, most sections of the present book are subdivided into parts. Necessary information is given before problems on physics. More difficult problems (indicated by an asterisk) are supplied with hints for their solution to be found in the Answers.

Tables of the values of basic elementary functions compiled by A.T. Tsvetkov are presented in the Appendix. The tables are borrowed from Problems in Higher Mathematics by V.P. Minorsky (Mir Publishers, Moscow, 1975).

The first edition to the present book came out in 1947. All subsequent editions, including two major revisions, were published without Georgii Nikolaevich Berman, who died February 9, 1949 after a long and severe illness acquired when he was wounded at the front during the Great Patriotic War. The work was undertaken jointly by Berman's colleagues I.G. Aramanovich, A.F. Bermant, B.A. Kordemsky, R.I. Pozoisky, and M.G. Shestopal.

Our collective lost its co-author and the editor of the first edition of the present book, Professor Anisim Fedorovich Bermant, who died suddenly May 26, 1959.

Georgii Nikolaevich and Anisim Fedorovich were esteemed colleagues, Cultured men, and talented progressive teachers. They leave a lasting impression.

I.G. Aramanovich
B.A. Kordemsky
R.I. Pozoisky
M.G. Shestopal

CONTENTS

1

Function

1. Preliminaries

Representation of functions

1. The sum of the interior angles of a plane convex polygonal is a function of the number of its sides. Represent this function analytically. What values can the argument attain?
2. A function y of x is specified by the following table:

Independent variable x	0	0.5	1	1.5	2	3
Function y	−1.5	−1	0	3.2	2.6	0

Independent variable x	4	5	6	7	8	9	10
Function y	−1.8	−2.8	0	1.1	1.4	1.9	2.4

Plot the graph of the function $y(x)$ by joining the points with a smooth line, and, using the graph thus obtained, make the given table "denser" by determining the values of the function for $x = 2.5, 3.5, 4.5, 5.5, 6.5, 7.5, 8.5, 9.5$.

3. A function is represented by the graph shown in Fig. 1. Draw the graph to a given scale on the graph paper. Take from the graph the values of the function corresponding to the chosen values of the independent variable, and tabulate these values.
4. A function is specified by the graph shown in Fig. 2. Taking advantage of the graph, answer the following questions:

   (a) At what values of the independent variable does the function vanish?

   (b) For what values of the independent variable is the function positive?

(c) For what values of the independent variable is the function negative?

5. The force F of electrostatic interaction of two point electric charges e_1 and e_2 is related to the distance r between them by the formula (Coulomb's law)

$$F = \frac{e_1 \cdot e_2}{\varepsilon \cdot r^2}.$$

Putting $e_1 = e_2 = 1$ and $\varepsilon = 1$, make a table of values of the given function for $r = 1, 2, 3, \ldots, 10$, and plot it joining the found points with a smooth line.

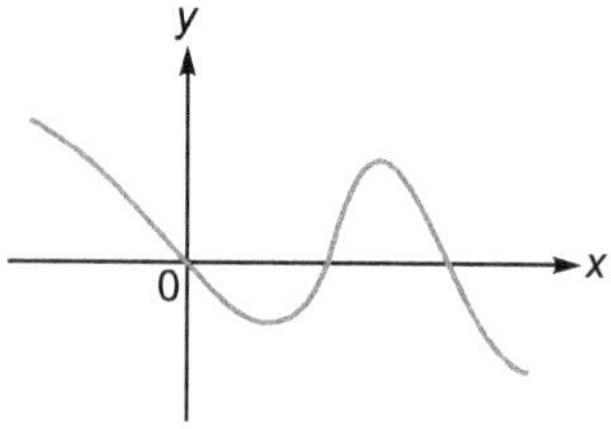

Fig. 1

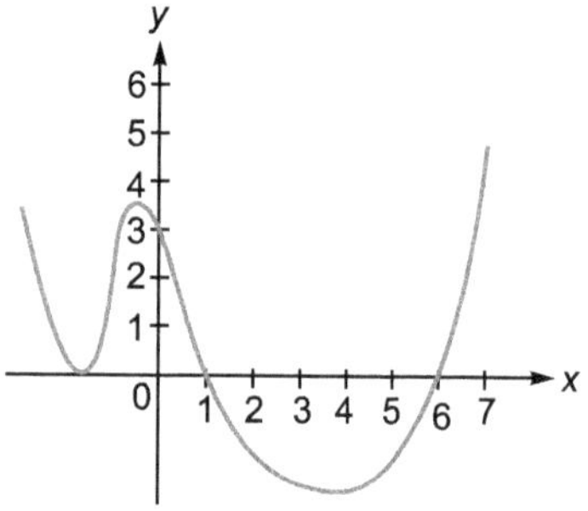

Fig. 2

6. Write the function expressing the relationship between the radius r of the cylinder base and its height h for a given volume $V = 1$. Compute the respective values of r for the following values of h : 0.5, 1, 1.5, 2, 2.5, 3, 3.5, 4, 4.5, 5. Plot the graph of the function.

7. Express the area of an isosceles trapezium with the bases a and b as a function of the angle α at the base a. Plot the graph of the function for $a = 2, b = 1$.

8. Express the length b of one side of a right-angled triangle as a function of the length a of the other at a constant hypotenuse $c = 5$. Graph this function.

9. Given the functions $f(x) = \dfrac{x-2}{x+1}$ and $\varphi(x) = \dfrac{|x-2|}{x+1}$.

Find : $f(0), f(1), f(2), f(-2), f\left(-\frac{1}{2}\right), f(\sqrt{2}), \left|f\left(\frac{1}{2}\right)\right|; \varphi(0), \varphi(1), \varphi(2),$ $\varphi(-2), \varphi(4)$. Are $f(-1)$ and $\varphi(-1)$ existant?

10. Given the function $f(u) = u^3 - 1$.

Find : $f(1), f(a), f(a+1), f(a-1), 2f(2a)$.

11. Given the functions $F(z) = 2^{z-2}$ and $\varphi(z) = 2|z|^{-2}$.

Find : $F(0), F(2), F(3), F(-1), F(2.5), F(-1.5)$ and $\varphi(0), \varphi(2), \varphi(-1), \varphi(x), \varphi(-1) + F(1)$.

12. Given the function $\psi(t) = t \cdot a^t$. Find $\psi(0), \psi(1), \psi(-1), \psi\left(\frac{1}{a}\right), \psi(a), \psi(-a)$.

13. $\varphi(t) = t^3 + 1$. Find $\varphi(t^2)$ and $[\varphi(t)]^2$.

14. $F(x) = x^4 - 2x^2 + 5$. Prove that $F(a) = F(-a)$.

15. $\phi(z) = z^3 - 5z$. Prove that $\phi(-z) = -\phi(z)$.

16. $f(t) = 2t^2 + \frac{2}{t^2} + \frac{5}{t} + 5t$. Prove that $f(t) = f\left(\frac{1}{t}\right)$.

17. $f(x) = \sin x - \cos x$. Prove that $f(1) > 0$.

18. $\psi(x) = \log_{10} x$. Prove that $\psi(x) + \psi(x+1) = \psi[x(x+1)]$.

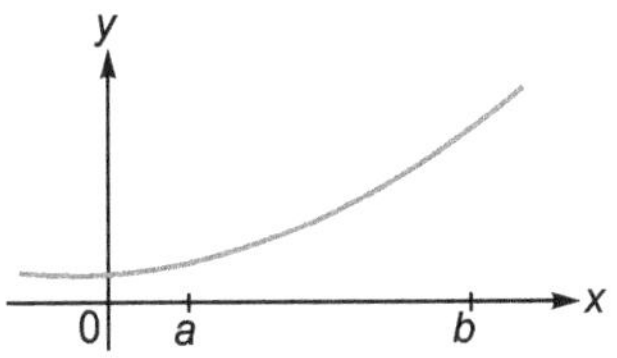

Fig. 3

19. $F(z) = a^z$.

(1) Prove that the following relationship holds true for any z

$$F(-z) \cdot F(z) - 1 = 0.$$

(2) Prove that

$$F(x) \cdot F(y) = F(x + y).$$

20. Given : the graph of the function $y = f(x)$ and the values a and b of the independent variable x (Fig. 3). Construct the ordinates for $f(a)$ and $f(b)$. Give the geometrical meaning of the ratio $\frac{f(b) - f(a)}{b - a}$.

21. Show that if any chord on the graph of the function $y = f(x)$ lies higher than the subtended arc, then there exists the following inequality:

$$\frac{f(x_1) + f(x_2)}{2} > f\left(\frac{x_1 + x_2}{2}\right)$$

for all $x_1 \neq x_2$.

22. Given : $f(x) = x^2 - 2x + 3$. Find all roots of the equation

(a) $f(x) = f(0)$; (b) $f(x) = f(-1)$.

23. Given : $f(x) = 2x^3 - 5x^2 - 23x$. Find all roots of the equation $f(x) = f(-2)$.

24. Given : the function $f(x)$. Find at least one root of the equation $f(x) = f(a)$.

25. Find two roots of the equation $f(x) = f\left(\frac{x+8}{x-1}\right)$, if it is known that the function $f(x)$ is defined on the interval $[-5, 5]$. Find all roots of the given equation for the case when $f(x) = x^2 - 12x + 3$.

26. $F(x) = x^2 + 6$; $\varphi(x) = 5x$. Find all roots of the equation $F(x) = |\varphi(x)|$.

27. $f(x) = x + 1$; $\varphi(x) = x - 2$. Solve the equation

$$|f(x) + \varphi(x)| = |f(x)| + |\varphi(x)|.$$

28. In the expression of the function $f(x) = ax^2 + bx + 5$ find the values of a and b for which the identity $f(x+1) - f(x) \equiv 8x + 3$ is true.

29. Let $f(x) = a \cdot \cos(bx + c)$. For what values of the constants a, b and c is the identity $f(x+1) - f(x) \equiv \sin x$ fulfilled?

Composite functions

30. Given : $y = z^2$, $z = x + 1$. Express y as a function of x.

31. Given : $y = \sqrt{z+1}$, $z = \tan^2 x$. Express y as a function of x.

32. Given : $y = z^2$, $z = \sqrt[3]{x+1}$, $x = a^t$. Express y as a function of t.

33. Given : $y = \sin x$, $v = \log_{10} y$, $u = \sqrt{1+v^2}$. Express v as a function of x.

34. Given : $y = 1 + x$, $z = \cos y$, $v = \sqrt{1 - z^2}$. Express v as a function of x.

35. Represent the following composite functions by means of chains made of basic elementary functions:

(1) $y = \sin^3 x$; (2) $y = \sqrt[3]{(1+x)^2}$; (3) $y = \log_{10}\tan x$;

(4) $y = \sin^3(2x+1)$; (5) $y = 5^{(3x+1)2}$.

36. $f(x) = x^3 - x$; $\varphi(x) = \sin 2x$. Find : (a) $f\left[\varphi\left(\frac{\pi}{12}\right)\right]$; (b) $\varphi[f(1)]$;

(c) $\varphi[f(2)]$; (d) $f[\varphi(x)]$; (e) $f[f(x)]$; (f) $\{f[f(1)]\}$; (g) $\varphi[\varphi(x)]$.

37. Prove the validity of the following method of constructing the graph of the composite function $y = f[\varphi(x)] = F(x)$ given the graphs of its components: $y = f(x)$, $y = \varphi(x)$. From point A of the graphs of the function $\varphi(x)$ (see Fig. 4) corresponding to the given value of the independent variable x draw a straight line parallel to the x-axis to intersect the bisector of the first and third quadrants at point B. From the point B draw a straight line parallel to the y-axis to intersect the graph of the function $f(x)$ at point C. If now a straight line is drawn from the point C and parallel to the x-axis, then point D at which it intersects the straight line NN' will be the point on the curve for the function $F(x)$ corresponding to the taken value of x.

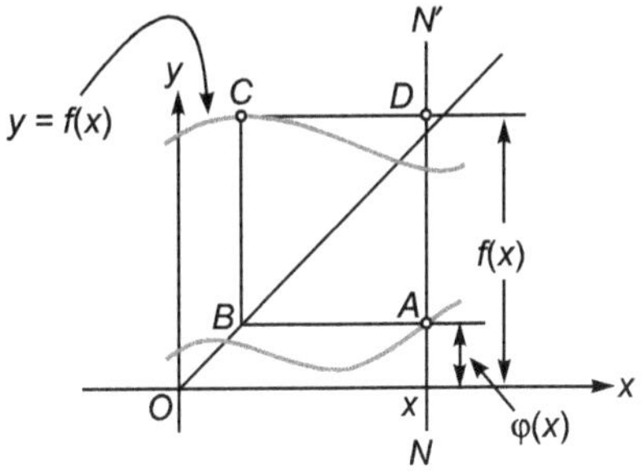

Fig. 4

Implicit functions

38. Write the explicit form of the function y represented implicitly by the following equations:

(1) $x^2 + y^2 = 1$; (2) $\frac{x^2}{a^2} - \frac{y^2}{b^2} = 1$; (3) $x^3 + y^3 = a^3$;

(4) $xy = C$; (5) $2^{xy} = 5$;

(6) $\log_{10} x + \log_{10}(y + 1) = 4$;

(7) $2^{x+y}(x^2 - 2) = x^3 + 7$;

(8) $(1 + x)\cos y - x^2 = 0$.

39*. Show that for $x > 0$ the equation $y + |y| - x - |x| = 0$ defines the function whose graph is the bisector of the first quadrant, and for $x \le 0$ the given equation is satisfied by the coordinates of all points of the third quadrant (including its boundary points).

2. Simplest Properties of Functions

Domain of definition of a function

40. Tabulate the values of the function of an integral argument $y = \frac{1}{x!}$ for $1 \le x \le 6$.

41. The value of the function of an integral argument $u = f(n)$ is equal to the number of simple numbers not exceeding n. Compile a table of values of u for $1 \le n \le 20$.

42. The value of the function of an integral argument $u = f(n)$ is equal to the number of integral devisors, different from 1 and n, of the argument. Make a table of the values of u for $1 \le n \le 20$.

43. A bar (Fig. 5) is made up of three parts whose lengths are equal to 1, 2, 1 length units, their weights being equal to 2, 3, 1 weight units, respectively. The weight of the variable part AM (Fig. 5) is a function of its length x. For what values of x is this function defined? Express it analytically and sketch its graph.

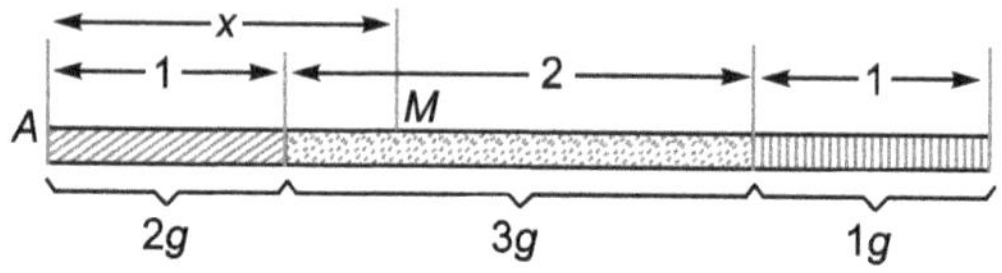

Fig. 5

44. A tower has the following shape : a truncated right circular cone with the radii $2R$ (the lower base) and R (the upper base), and the height R bears a right circular cylinder whose radius is R, the height being $2R$. Finally, a semisphere of radius R is mounted on the cylinder. Express the cross-sectional area S of the tower as a function of the distance x of the cross-section from the lower base of the cone. Draw the graph of the function $S = f(x)$.

45. A cylinder is inscribed in a sphere of radius R. Express the volume V of the cylinder as a function of its height x. Indicate the domain of definition of this function.

46. A right cone is inscribed in a sphere of radius R. Find the functional relationship between the lateral surface area S of the cone and its generatrix x. Indicate the domain of definition of this function.

In Problems 47 and 48 find the domains of definition of the given functions.

47. (1) $y = 1 - \log_{10} x$; (2) $y = \log_{10}(x+3)$;

(3) $y = \sqrt{5-2x}$; (4) $y = \sqrt{-px}\ (p > 0)$;

(5) $y = \dfrac{1}{x^2-1}$; (6) $y = \dfrac{1}{x^2+1}$;

(7) $y = \dfrac{1}{x^3-x}$; (8) $y = \dfrac{2x}{x^2-3x+2}$;

(9) $y = 1 - \sqrt{1-x^2}$; (10) $y = \dfrac{1}{\sqrt{x^2-4x}}$;

(11) $y = \sqrt{x^2-4x+3}$; (12) $y = \dfrac{x}{\sqrt{x^2-3x+2}}$;

(13) $y = \arcsin \dfrac{x}{4}$; (14) $y = \arcsin (x-2)$;

(15) $y = \arccos(1 - 2x)$; (16) $y = \arccos \frac{1-2x}{4}$;

(17) $y = \arcsin \sqrt{2x}$; (18) $y = \sqrt{1 - |x|}$;

(19) $y = \frac{1}{\sqrt{|x| - x}}$; (20) $y = \frac{1}{\sqrt{x - |x|}}$;

(21) $y = \sqrt{\log_{10}\left(\frac{5x - x^2}{4}\right)}$; (22) $y = \log_{10} \sin x$;

(23) $y = \arccos \frac{2}{2 + \sin x}$; (24) $y = \log_x 2$.

48. (1) $y = \frac{1}{\log_{10}(1-x)} + \sqrt{x+2}$;

(2) $y = \sqrt{3-x} + \arcsin \frac{3-2x}{5}$;

(3) $y = \arcsin \frac{x-3}{2} - \log_{10}(4-x)$;

(4) $y = \sqrt{x} + \sqrt[3]{\frac{1}{x-2}} - \log_{10}(2x-3)$;

(5) $y = \sqrt{x-1} + 2\sqrt{1-x} + \sqrt{x^2+1}$;

(6) $y = \frac{3}{4-x^2} + \log_{10}(x^3 - x)$;

(7) $y = \log_{10} \sin(x-3) + \sqrt{16-x^2}$;

(8) $y = \sqrt{\sin x} + \sqrt{16 - x^2}$;

(9) $y = \frac{1}{\sqrt{\sin x}} + \sqrt[3]{\sin x}$;

(10) $y = \log_{10} \frac{x-5}{x^2 - 10x + 24} - \sqrt[3]{x+5}$;

(11) $y = \sqrt{\frac{x-2}{x+2}} + \sqrt{\frac{1-x}{1+x}}$;

(12) $y = \sqrt{x^2 - 3x + 2} + \frac{1}{\sqrt{3 + 2x - x^2}}$;

(13) $y = (x^2 + x + 1)^{-\frac{3}{2}}$;

(14) $y = \log_{10}(\sqrt{x-4} + \sqrt{6-x})$;

(15) $y = \log_{10}[1 - \log_{10}(x^2 - 5x + 16)]$.

49. Are the following functions identical?

(1) $f(x) = \frac{x}{x^2}$ and $\varphi(x) = \frac{1}{x}$; (2) $f(x) = \frac{x^2}{x}$ and $\varphi(x) = x$;

(3) $f(x) = x$ and $\varphi(x) = \sqrt{x^2}$;

(4) $f(x) = \log_{10} x^2$ and $\varphi(x) = 2\log_{10} x$.

50. Give an example of an analytically represented function:

(1) defined only on the interval $-2 \le x \le 2$;

(2) defined only on the interval $-2 < x < 2$ and not defined at $x = 0$;

(3) defined for all real values of x, except for $x = 2$, $x = 3$, $x = 4$.

51. Find the domains of definition of the single-valued branches of the function $y = \varphi(x)$ specified by the equation:

(1) $y^2 - 1 + \log_2 (x-1) = 0$; (2) $y^4 - 2xy^2 + x^2 - x = 0$.

Characteristics of behaviour of functions

52. $f(x) = \dfrac{x^2}{1+x^2}$; indicate the domain of definition of the function $f(x)$ and make sure that this function is nonnegative.

53. Find the intervals of constant sign and the roots of the functions:

(1) $y = 3x - 6$; (2) $y = x^2 - 5x + 6$; (3) $y = 2^{x-1}$;

(4) $y = x^3 - 3x^2 + 2x$; (5) $y = |x|$.

54. Which of the below functions are even, which are odd, and which are neither even nor odd?

(1) $y = x^4 - 2x^2$; (2) $y = x - x^2$; (3) $y = \cos x$;

(4) $y = 2^x$; (5) $y = x - \dfrac{x^3}{6} + \dfrac{x^5}{120}$; (6) $y = \sin x$;

(7) $y = \sin x - \cos x$; (8) $y = 1 - x^2$; (9) $y = \tan x$;

(10) $y = 2^{-x^2}$; (11) $y = \dfrac{a^x + a^{-x}}{2}$; (12) $y = \dfrac{a^x - a^{-x}}{2}$;

(13) $y = \dfrac{x}{a^x - 1}$; (14) $y = \dfrac{a^x + 1}{a^x - 1}$; (15) $y = x \cdot \dfrac{a^x - 1}{a^x + 1}$;

(16) $y = 2^{x - x^4}$; (17) $y = \ln \dfrac{1-x}{1+x}$.

55. Represent each of the following functions in the form of a sum of an even and an odd function:

(1) $y = x^2 + 3x + 2$; (2) $y = 1 - x^3 - x^4 - 2x^5$;

(3) $y = \sin 2x + \cos \dfrac{x}{2} + \tan x$.

56. Prove that $f(x) + f(-x)$ is an even function, and $f(x) - f(-x)$ is an odd one.

57. Represent the following functions as a sum of an even and an odd function:

(1) $y = a^x$; (2) $y = (1+x)^{100}$ (see Problem 56).

58. Prove that the product of two even functions is an even function, the product of two odd functions is an even function and the product of an even function by an odd one is an odd function.

59. Which of the following functions are periodic?

(1) $y = \sin^2 x$; (2) $y = \sin x^2$; (3) $y = x \cdot \cos x$;

(4) $y = \sin \frac{1}{x}$; (5) $y = 1 + \tan x$; (6) $y = 5$;

(7) $y = [x]$; (8) $y = x - [x]$.

The function $[x]$ is determined in the following way: if x is an integer, then $[x] = x$. If x is not an integer, then $[x]$ equals the largest integer less than x. Hence, $[2] = 2$; $[3.25] = 3$; $[-1.37] = -2$.

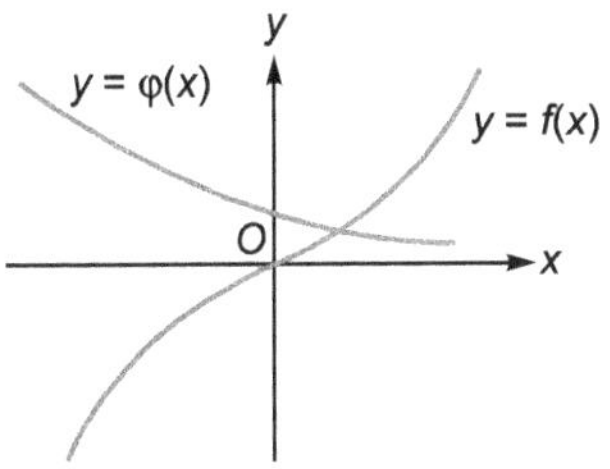

Fig. 6

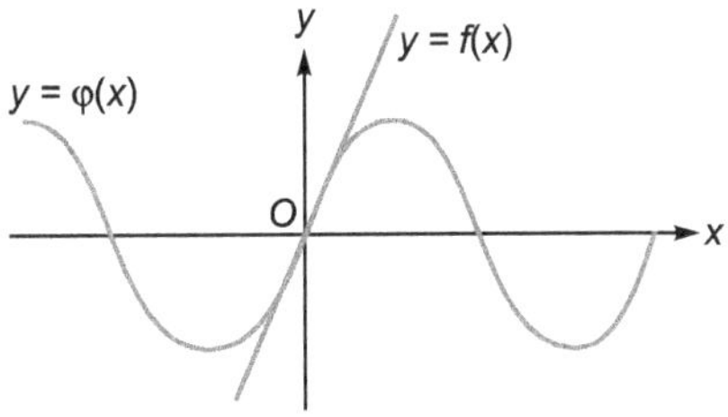

Fig. 7

60. Construct the graph of a periodic function with period $T = 1$, which on the half-open interval $[0.1)$ is specified by the formula:

(1) $y = x$; (2) $t = x^2$.

61. For the functions

(1) $y = |x|$; (2) $y = |x| - x$

indicate the intervals of increase and decrease and also the intervals where the functions are constant.

62. Find the greatest and the least values of the following functions:

(1) $y = \sin^2 x$; (2) $y = \cos x^3$;

(3) $y = 1 - \sin x$; (4) $y = 2^{x^2}$.

63. Construct the graph of the function $y = f(x) + \varphi(x)$ adding graphically the curves shown (1) in Fig. 6; (2) in Fig. 7.

64. Knowing the graph of the function $y = f(x)$, construct the graphs of the functions:

(1) $y = |f(x)|$;

(2) $y = \frac{1}{2}[|f(x)| + f(x)]$;

(3) $y = \frac{1}{2}[|f(x)| - f(x)]$.

3. Basic Elementary Functions

Linear function

65. Given that at a voltage $V = 2.4$ V the current $I = 0.8$ A. Using Ohm's law, express analytically the relationship between the current intensity and voltage; construct the graph of the found function.

66. A vessel of an arbitrary shape is filled with liquid. At the depth of $h = 25.3$ cm the pressure of this liquid $p = 18.4\ \text{gf/cm}^2$.

(a) Write the function expressing the dependence of pressure on depth.

(b) Determine the pressure at the depth $h = 14.5$ cm.

(c) At what depth will the pressure become equal to 26.5 gf/cm^2?

67. A body is in rectilinear motion under the action of force F. Proceeding from Newton's law, express the force F and acceleration w, if it is known that when the body moves with the acceleration 12 m/s^2, over the distance of $s = 15$ m the work $A = 32$ J is done.

68. Determine the linear function $y = ax + b$, given the following:

(1)

x	y
0	4
3	6

(2)

x	y
2	4.3
−1.6	0

(3)

x	y
2.5	7.2
3.2	6.8

69. A certain amount of gas at 20°C occupied the volume of 107 cm^3, whereas at 40°C its volume became equal to 114 cm^3.

(a) Taking advantage of the Gay-Lussac law, write the volume V as a function of temperature t.

(b) What will the volume be at 0°C?

70. A point moving uniformly in a straight line was at a distance of +32.7 cm from a certain point on this line in 12 s after its start; in 20 s after the point started the corresponding distance was equal to +43.4 cm. Express the distance s as a function of time t.

71. Voltage in a circuit drops uniformly (according to the linear law). At the beginning of the experiment which lasted during 8 s the voltage was 12 V, and at the end of it the voltage dropped to the value of 6.4 V. Express the voltage V as a function of t and plot the graph of this function.

72. Find the increment of the linear function $y = 2x - 7$ as the independent variable x passes from the value $x_1 = 3$ to the value $x_2 = 6$.

73. Find the increment of the linear function $y = -3x + 1$ corresponding to the increment of the independent variable $\Delta x = 2$.

74. The function $y = 2.5x + 4$ gained an increment $\Delta y = 10$. Find the increment of the argument.

75. Given the function $y = \dfrac{x - a}{a^2 - b^2}$ and the initial value of the independent variable $x_1 = a - b$. At what terminal value x_2 of the independent variable x is the increment Δy equal to $\dfrac{1}{a - b}$?

76. The function $\varphi(x)$ is specified as follows: $\varphi(x) = \dfrac{1}{2}x + 2$ for $-\infty < x \le 2$; $\varphi(x) = 5 - x$ for $2 \le x < +\infty$. Find analytically and graphically the roots of the equation $\varphi(x) = 2x - 4$.

77. Graph the following functions:

(1) $y = |x + 1| + |x - 1|$; (2) $y = |x + 1| - |x - 1|$;

(3) $y = |x - 3| - 2|x + 1| + 2|x| - x + 1$.

78*. For what values of x is the inequality $|f(x) + \varphi(x)| < |f(x)| + |\varphi(x)|$ true if $f(x) = x - 3$, and $\varphi(x) = 4 - x$?

79. For what values of x is the inequality $|f(x) - \varphi(x)| > |f(x)| - |\varphi(x)|$ true if $f(x) = x$, and $\varphi(x) = x - 2$?

80. The function $f(x)$ is defined as follows: on each of the intervals $n \le x < n + 1$, where n is a positive integer, $f(x)$ varies linearly, and $f(n) = -1$, $f\left(n + \dfrac{1}{2}\right) = 0$. Draw the graph of the function.

Quadratic function

81. Construct the graphs and indicate the intervals on which the given functions increase and decrease.

(1) $y = \dfrac{1}{2}x^2$; (2) $y = x^2 - 1$; (3) $y = |x^2 - 1|$;

(4) $y = 1 - x^2$; (5) $y = x^2 - x + 4$; (6) $y = x - x^2$;

(7) $y = |x - x^2|$; (8) $y = 2x^2 + 3$; (9) $y = 2x^2 - 6x + 4$;

(10) $y = -3x^2 + 6x - 1$; (11) $y = |-3x^2 + 6x - 1|$; (12) $y = -x|x|$.

82. Express analytically the single-valued function defined on the interval $(-\infty, 6]$, if it is known that its graph consists of the points of the x-axis with abscissas less than -3, of the points of a parabola symmetrical about the y-axis and passing through the points $A(-3, 0)$, $B(0, 5)$ and of the points of the line segment CD with the end-points $C(3, 0)$ and $D(6, 2)$.

83. Find the greatest values of the functions:

(1) $y = -2x^2 + x - 1$; (2) $y = -x^2 - 3x + 2$;

(3) $y = 5 - x^2$; (4) $y = -2x^2 + ax - a^2$;

(5) $y = a^2x - b^2x^2$.

84. Find the least values of the functions:

(1) $y = x^2 + 4x - 2$; (2) $y = 2x^2 - 1.5x + 0.6$;

(3) $y = 1 - 3x + 6x^2$; (4) $y = a^2x^2 + a^4$;

(5) $y = (ax + b)(ax - 2b)$.

85. Represent the number a as a sum of two terms so that their product is the greatest number.

86. Represent the number a as a sum of two numbers such that the sum of their squares is the least possible number.

87. A rectangular area is to be fenced off near the stone wall. The total length of the fence is 8 metres. What must the length of the side parallel to the wall be to yield the greatest area?

88. In a triangle the sum of the sides forming the given angle equals 100 cm. What must the length of the sides be to obtain a triangle of the greatest possible area?

89. Which of the cylinders with the given perimeter, $P = 100$ cm, of the axial section has the greatest possible area of the lateral surface?

90. Which of the cones, with the perimeter P of the axial section, has the greatest possible area of the lateral surface?

91. A solid is made up of a right circular cylinder and a cone (with the same base) mounted on it. The angle at the vertex of the cone is 60°. The perimeter of axial section of the solid equals 100 cm. What radius of the base circle must the cylinder have to yield the greatest possible area of the lateral surface of the body?

92. A rectangle is inscribed in an isosceles triangle with base a and height h (see Fig. 8). What height must the triangle have to yield the greatest possible area?

93. A cylinder is inscribed in a given right cone so that the planes and the centres of the circular bases of the cylinder and the cone coincide. At what ratio of the radii of the bases of the cylinder and the cone will the cylinder have the greatest possible lateral surface area?

94. Given a right circular cone of height H whose base has a radius R. A cylinder is inscribed in the cone so that the planes and the centres of the base circles coincide. What must the radius of the cylinder be to yield the total surface of the greatest area? Consider the cases $H > 2R$ and $H \leq 2R$.

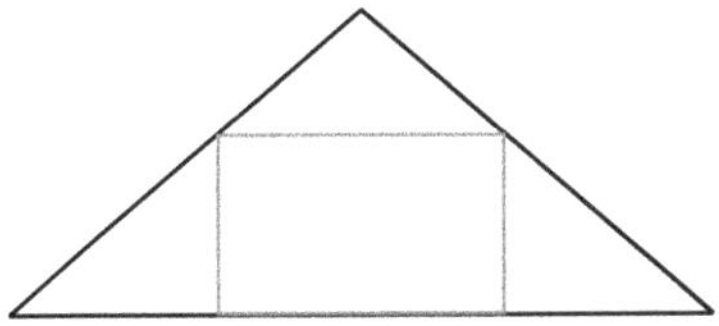

Fig. 8

95. What must the radius of a circle be for the sector whose perimeter is equal to the given number P to have the greatest possible area?

96. A window has the shape of a rectangle with a regular triangle on it. The perimeter of the window is P. What must the base a of the rectangle be to obtain a window of the greatest area?

97. An arched window of perimeter 2 m has the shape of a rectangle with a semicircular head. What must the base of the rectangle be to obtain a window of the greatest area?

98. To make a box from a sheet of cardboard 30×50 cm^2 size it is necessary to cut small squares out of its corners and to bend the sheet along the dashed line as is shown in Fig. 9. Find the side of the cut-out squares.

99. Given a piece of wire 120 cm long. It is required to make a model of a right parallelopiped with a square base. What must the side of the base be to construct a parallelopiped of the greatest possible area of the total surface?

100. A piece of wire of length a must be cut into two parts to make a square and a regular triangle. How must the wire be cut to obtain the least possible sum of the surface areas of the figures thus obtained?

101. On the straight line $y = x$ find the point for which the sum of the squared distances from the points $(-a, 0)$, $(a, 0)$, and $(0, b)$ would be the least possible.

102. On the straight line $y = x + 2$ find the point for which the sum of the squared distances from the straight lines $3x - 4y + 8 = 0$ and $3x - y - 1 = 0$ would be the least possible.

103. Electric current I is distributed between two branches of the circuit with resistances r_1 and r_2 (Fig. 10). Show that the least losses of energy due to heating the conductor per unit time correspond to the currents in the branches which are inversely proportional to the resistances of the branches. (Take advantage of the following law: the amount of heat emitted $Q = 0.24 . I^2RT$.)

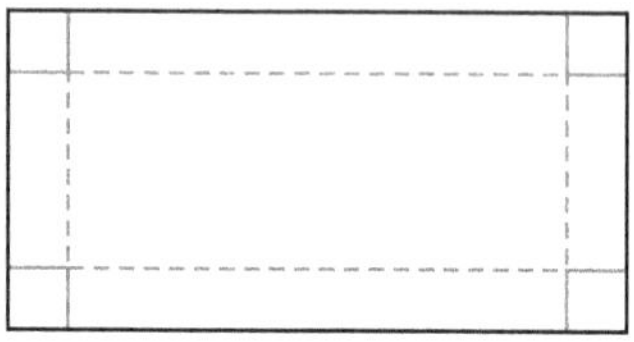

Fig. 9

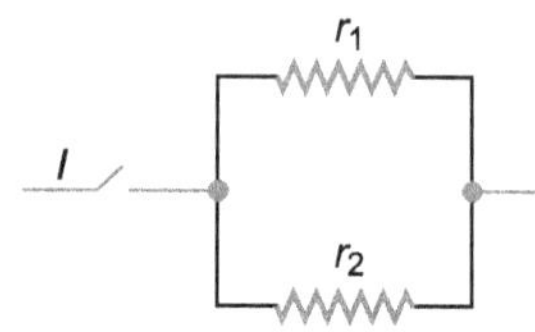

Fig. 10

104. Draw the parabola $y = x^2$ and use it for graphical solution of the following equations:

(1) $x^2 - x - 2.25 = 0$; (2) $2x^2 - 3x - 5 = 0$;

(3) $3.1x^2 - 14x + 5.8 = 0$; (4) $4x^2 - 12x + 9 = 0$;

(5) $3x^2 - 8x + 7 = 0$.

105. Function $\varphi(x)$ is specified as follows: $\varphi(x) = \frac{1}{2}x - \frac{1}{2}$ for $-\infty < x \le \frac{11}{3}$; $\varphi(x) = 1 + x$ for $\frac{11}{3} \le x < +\infty$. Find analytically and graphically all real roots of the equation $[\varphi(x)]^2 = 7x + 25$.

106. Indicate the domain of definition of the function

$$y = \log(ax^2 + bx + c).$$

107. Find $f(x + 1)$, if it is given that $f(x - 1) = 2x^2 - 3x + 1$.

108*. Show that the function $f(x) = \dfrac{x^2 + 2x + c}{x^2 + 4x + 3c}$ attains any real value if $0 < c \le 1$.

Linear-fractional function

109. Taking advantage of the Boyle-Mariotte law, find the function expressing the relationship between the volume of the gas and its pressure at t = const, if it is known that at the pressure of 760 mm Hg its volume is equal to 2.31. Draw the graph of this function.

110. A variable x is inversely proportional to y, y is inversely proportional to z, z is, in its turn, inversely proportional to v. What is the relationship between x and v?

111. A variable x is inversely proportional to y, y is directly proportional to z, z is directly proportional to u, and u is inversely proportional to v. What is the relationship between x and v?

112. In the process of electrolysis the amount of substance deposited on the electrode is proportional to current intensity, current intensity is proportional to conductivity of the electrolyte, the conductivity is proportional to concentration of the electrolyte, and the concentration at a given amount of substance is inversely proportional to the volume of solvent. Find the dependence of the amount of the substance deposited on the electrode on the volume of the solvent.

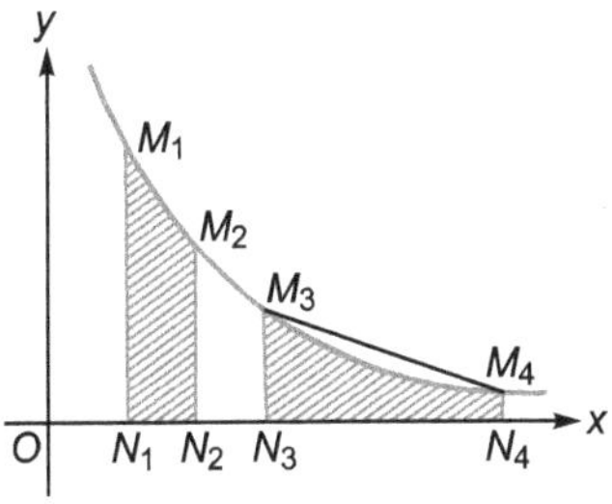

Fig. 11

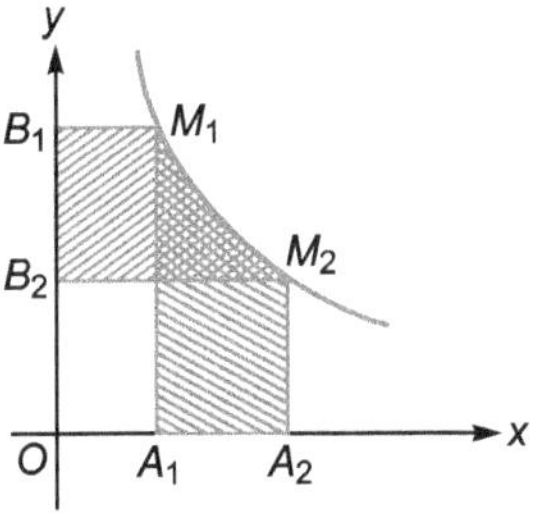

Fig. 12

113. Construct the graphs of the given linear-fractional functions:

(1) $y = \dfrac{x-1}{x-2}$; (2) $y = \dfrac{2x}{3-x}$; (3) $y = \dfrac{2x-5}{3x-7.5}$;

(4) $y = \dfrac{x}{1-\frac{1}{2}x}$; (5) $y = \dfrac{4-3x}{3-2.25x}$.

114. Using the graphs find the greatest and the least values of the linear-fractional functions on the given interval:

(1) $y = \dfrac{4}{x}$ [1, 5]; (2) $y = \dfrac{x}{2x-5}$ [−1, 2];

(3) $y = \dfrac{1-x}{1+x}$ [0, 4].

115. Prove that (1) if the abscissas of the four points $M_1(x_1, y_1)$, $M_2(x_2, y_2)$, $M_3(x_3, y_3)$, $M_4(x_4, y_4)$ on the graph representing the function $y = \dfrac{k}{x}$ (Fig. 11) are in the following interrelation $\dfrac{x_1}{x_2} = \dfrac{x_3}{x_4}$, then the rectilinear trapeziums $M_1M_2N_2N_1$ and $M_3M_4N_4N_3$ are equal; (2) if the points M_1 and M_2 lie on the graph of the function $y = \frac{k}{x}$ (Fig. 12), then the areas of the figures $A_1M_1M_2A_2$ and $B_1M_1M_2B_2$ are equal to each other.

116. Graph the function $y = \frac{x^2 + 1}{x}$ with the aid of graphical addition.

4. Inverse Function. Power, Exponential and Logarithmic Functions

Inverse function

117. Find the inverses to the given functions:

(1) $y = x$; (2) $y = 2x$; (3) $y = 1 - 3x$;

(4) $y = x^2 + 1$; (5) $y = \frac{1}{x}$; (6) $y = \frac{1}{1 - x}$;

(7) $y = x^2 - 2x$; (8) $y = \sqrt[3]{x^2 + 1}$; (9) $y = 10^{x+1}$;

(10) $y = 1 + \log(x + 2)$; (11) $y = \log_x 2$;

(12) $y = \frac{2^x}{1 + 2^x}$; (13) $y = \frac{10^x - 10^{-x}}{10^x + 10^{-x}} + 1$;

(14) $y = 2 \sin 3x$; (15) $y = 1 + 2 \sin \frac{x - 1}{x + 1}$;

(16) $y = 4 \arcsin \sqrt{1 - x^2}$.

118. Prove that the inverse to the linear-fractional function $y = \frac{ax + b}{cx + d}$ $(ad - bc \neq 0)$ is also a linear-fractional function.

119. Under what condition does the linear-fractional function of Problem 118 coincide with its inverse?

120. Show that if $f(x) = \sqrt[n]{a - x^n}$, $x > 0$, then $f[f(x)] = x$. Find the function inverse to $f(x)$.

121. What is the peculiarity of the graph of a function identical with its inverse?

122. A function y of x is represented by the equation

$$y^2 - 1 + \log_2(x - 1) = 0.$$

Find the domain of definition of the given function and write its inverse.

123. A function y of x is specified by the equation

$$y^2 + \sin^3 x - y + 2 = 0.$$

Find the inverse of the given function.

Power function

124. Graph the given functions:

(1) $y = \frac{1}{3}x^3$; (2) $y = -\frac{1}{2}x^3$; (3) $y = x^3 + 3x^2$;

(4) $y = x^3 - x + 1$; (5) $y = -x^3 + 2x - 2$; (6) $y = 2x^{3/2}$;

(7) $y = \frac{1}{2}x^{5/4}$; (8) $y = x^{0.3}$; (9) $y = x^{2.1}$;

(10) $y = x^{0.62}$; (11) $y = \frac{1}{2}x^{-0.2}$; (12) $y = 5x^{-2.5}$;

(13) $y = 1 - \sqrt{|x|}$.

125. Find graphically the approximate values of the real roots of the equation $x + 3 = 4\sqrt[3]{x^2}$.

126*. Draw the cubical parabola $y = x^3$ and use it for a graphical solution of the following equations:

(1) $x^3 + x - 4 = 0$; (2) $x^3 - 3x^2 - x + 3 = 0$;

(3) $x^3 - 6x^2 + 9x - 4 = 0$; (4) $x^3 + 3x^2 + 6x + 4 = 0$.

127. Derive the equations and solve them graphically:

(1) The square of what number is equal to the sum of the number itself and its inverse?

(2) A wooden sphere whose radius is 10 cm and density is 0.8 g/cm^3 floats on the water surface. Find the altitude of the spherical segment submerged in the water.

(3) The total weight of a wooden cube and a pyramid with a square base amounts to 0.8 kgf. The edge of the cube is equal to the side of the pyramid base, the altitude of the pyramid is 45 cm. Find the edge of the cube. Specific weight of wood is 0.8 gf/cm^3.

128. Given a function $y = x^n$, $x > 0$. For what values of x does the function attain values exceeding the values of its inverse, and for what values of x are its values less than those of its inverse?

Exponential and hyperbolic functions

129. Graph the functions:

(1) $y = -2^x$; (2) $y = 2^{x+3}$; (3) $y = \frac{1}{3}\cdot 3^x$;

(4) $y = 1 - 3^{x-3}$; (5) $y = \left(\frac{1}{2}\right)^{|x|}$; (6) $y = 2^{-x^2}$.

130. Taking advantage of the graph of the function $y = 2^x$, graph (without further calculations) the following functions:

(1) $y = 2^{x-1}$; (2) $y = \frac{1}{12} \cdot 2^{x/2}$; (3) $y = \frac{1}{3} \cdot 2^{(x-1)/2} + 1$.

131. Show that the graph of the function $y = k + a^x (k > 0)$ is the same curve as for the function $y = a^x$ but translated with respect to the ordinate axis.

132. With the aid of a graphical addition construct the graphs of the given functions:

(1) $y = x^2 + 2^x$; (2) $y = x^2 - 2^x$.

133. Solve graphically the equation: $2^x - 2x = 0$.

134. Construct the figure bounded by the following lines $y = 2^x$, $y = \frac{1+x}{x}$, and $x = 3$. Using the drawing, find approximately the coordinates of the points of intersection of the lines.

135. Find the greatest possible value of n at which $2^x > x^n$ for all $x \geq 100$ (n is an integer).

136. Prove that $y = \sinh x$ and $y = \tanh x$ are odd functions, and $y = \cosh x$ is an even one. Are these functions periodic?

137. Prove that the following equalities hold true:

(1) $\cosh^2 x - \sinh^2 x = 1$; (2) $\cosh^2 x + \sinh^2 x = \cosh 2x$;

(3) $2 \sinh x \cdot \cosh x = \sinh 2x$;

(4) $\sinh(\alpha \pm \beta) = \sinh \alpha \cdot \cosh \beta \pm \sinh \beta \cdot \cosh \alpha$;

(5) $\cosh(\alpha \pm \beta) = \cosh \alpha \cdot \cosh \beta \pm \sinh \alpha \cdot \sinh \beta$;

(6) $1 - \tanh^2 x = \frac{1}{\cosh^2 x}$; (7) $1 - \coth^2 x = -\frac{1}{\sinh^2 x}$.

Logarithmic function

138. Graph the given functions:

(1) $y = -\log_2 x$; (2) $y = \log_{10} \frac{10}{x}$; (3) $y = |\log_{10} x|$;

(4) $y = \log_2 |x|$; (5) $y = 1 + \log_{10}(x + 2)$;

(6) $y = \log_2 |1 - x|$; (7) $y = a^{\log_a x}$; (8) $y = \log_x 2$.

139. Using the graph of the function $y = \log_{10} x$, graph the functions:

(1) $y = \frac{1}{2} \log_{10}(x + 1)$; (2) $y = 2 \log_{10} \left(\frac{x+1}{2}\right)$.

140. Given a function $y = x + \log_{10} \frac{1}{x}$. With the aid of graphical addition construct the graph of the given function. Using the graph thus, obtained, find the least value of this function in the interval (0.2].

141. Show that the graph of the function $y = \log_a (x + \sqrt{x^2 + 1})$ is symmetric about the origin. Find the inverse function.

142. Prove that the ordinate of the graph $y = \log_a x$ is equal to the corresponding ordinate of the graph $y = \log_{a^n} x$ multiplied by n.

5. Trigonometric and Inverse Trigonometric Functions

Trigonometric functions

143. Indicate the amplitudes and periods of the harmonics:

(1) $y = \sin 3x$; (2) $y = 5 \cos 2x$; (3) $y = 4 \sin \pi x$;

(4) $y = 2 \sin \frac{x}{2}$; (5) $y = \sin \frac{3\pi x}{4}$; (6) $y = 3 \sin \frac{5x}{8}$.

144. Indicate the amplitudes, periods, frequencies and initial phases of the harmonics:

(1) $y = 2 \sin (3x + 5)$; (2) $y = - \cos \frac{x-1}{2}$;

(3) $y = \frac{1}{3} \sin 2\pi \left(\omega - \frac{1}{6}\right)$; (4) $y = \sin \frac{2t + 3}{6\pi}$.

145. Graph the functions:

(1) $y = - \sin x$; (2) $y = 1 - \sin x$; (3) $y = 1 - \cos x$;

(4) $y = \sin 2x$; (5) $y = \sin \frac{x}{2}$; (6) $y = -2 \sin \frac{x}{3}$;

(7) $y = \cos 2x$; (8) $y = 2 \sin \left(x - \frac{\pi}{3}\right)$;

(9) $y = 2 \sin \left(3x + \frac{3\pi}{4}\right)$; (10) $y = \frac{1}{2} \sin (2\pi x - 1.2)$;

(11) $y = 2 + 2 \sin \left(\frac{\pi x}{2} + \frac{\pi}{6}\right)$; (12) $y = 2 \cos \frac{x - \pi}{3}$;

(13) $y = |\sin x|$; (14) $y = |\cos x|$;

(15) $y = |\tan x|$; (16) $y = |\cot x|$;

(17) $y = \sec x$; (18) $y = \operatorname{cosec} x$;

(19) $y = \begin{cases} \cos x & \text{for } -\pi \le x \le 0, \\ 1 & \text{for } 0 < x < 1, \\ \frac{1}{x} & \text{for } 1 \le x \le 2 \end{cases}$

146. The sides of a triangle are equal to 1 cm and 2 cm. Construct the graph for the relationship between the area of the triangle and the angle x formed by the given sides. Find the domain of definition of this function and the value of the argument x for which the area of the triangle will be the greatest possible.

147. A point moves uniformly anticlockwise with velocity v cm/s along a circle of radius R. The centre of the circle is in the origin. At the starting instant the abscissa of the point was a.

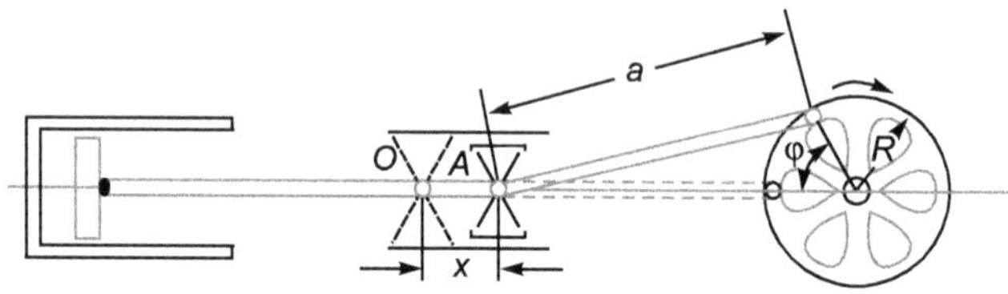

Fig. 13

Derive the equation of harmonic oscillation of the abscissa of the given point.

148. A point moves uniformly in the circle $x^2 + y^2 = 1$. At the instant t_0 its ordinate was y_0, at t_1, y_1. Find the dependence of ordinate of the point on time, the period and the initial phase of oscillation.

149. Figure 13, illustrates a crank gear. The radius of the flywheel is R, the length of the connecting rod is a. The flywheel rotates uniformly clockwise at a speed of n revolutions per second. At the instant $t = 0$, when the connecting rod and the crank formed a straight line (so-called "dead" position), the crosshead A was found at the point O. Find the dependence of the displacement x of the crosshead A on time t.

150. With the aid of graphical addition graph the functions:

(1) $y = \sin x + \cos x$; (2) $y = \sin 2\pi x + \sin 3\pi x$;

(3) $y = 2\sin\dfrac{x}{2} + 3\sin\dfrac{x}{3}$; (4) $y = x + \sin x$;

(5) $y = x - \sin x$; (6) $y = -2^x + \cos x$.

151. Solve graphically the given equations:

(1) $x = 2\sin x$; (2) $x = \tan x$; (3) $x - \cos x = 0$;

(4) $4\sin x = 4 - x$; (5) $2^{-x} = \cos x$.

152. Find the periods of the composite harmonics:

(1) $y = 2\sin 3x + 3\sin 2x$; (2) $y = \sin t + \cos 2t$;

(3) $y = \sin\dfrac{\pi t}{3} + \sin\dfrac{\pi t}{4}$;

(4) $y = \sin\left(2\pi t + \dfrac{\pi}{3}\right) + 2\sin\left(3\pi t + \dfrac{\pi}{4}\right) + 3\sin 5\pi t$.

153. Represent the following as one simple harmonic:

(1) $y = \sin x + \cos x$; (2) $y = \sin x + 2\sin\left(x + \frac{\pi}{6}\right)$.

154. Substantiate the following graphical method for adding harmonic oscillations. Let be given the following harmonics:

$A_1 \sin(\omega x + \varphi_1)$ and $A_2 \sin(\omega x + \varphi_2)$.

Construct vectors A_1 and A_2 whose lengths are A_1 and A_2, respectively, at angles φ_1 and φ_2 to the horizontal axis (Fig. 14). Add the vector A_1 to A_2 to get vector A of length A and inclined to the horizontal axis at an angle φ; A and φ will be, respectively, the amplitude and the initial phase of the sum

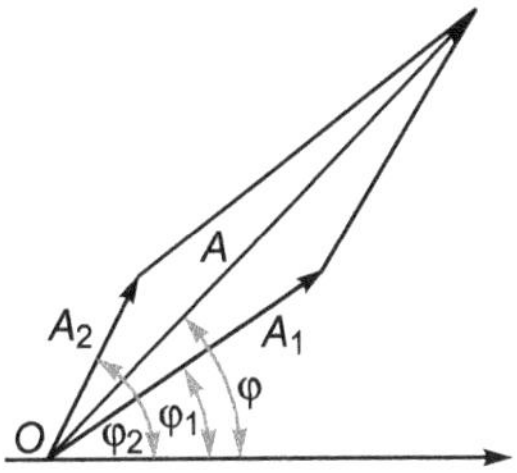

Fig. 14

$$A_1 \sin(\omega x + \varphi_1) + A_2 \sin(\omega x + \varphi_2) = A \sin(\omega x + \varphi).$$

155*. Indicate the periods of the functions and graph them:

(1) $y = |\sin x| + |\cos x|$; (2) $y = \frac{1}{2}\left(\frac{|\sin x|}{\cos x} + \frac{\sin x}{|\cos x|}\right)$.

156. Find the domains of the functions and find out the character of graphs:

(1) $y = \log \sin x$; (2) $y = \sqrt{\log \sin x}$;

(3) $y = \sqrt{\log \frac{1}{|\sin x|}}$.

Inverse trigonometric functions

157. Graph the given functions:

(1) $y = \operatorname{arccot} x$; (2) $y = 2\arcsin \frac{x}{2}$; (3) $y = 1 + \arctan 2x$;

(4) $y = \frac{\pi}{2} - \arccos 2x$; (5) $y = \arcsin \frac{1-x}{4}$.

158. A cone is made from a circular sector whose central angle is α. Find the dependence of the angle ω at the vertex of the cone on the angle α and draw its graph.

159. A picture of height a hangs on a wall in an inclined position, forming a dihedral angle φ with the wall. The lower edge of the picture is higher than the level of the observer's eye by b, the distance between him and the wall being l. Find the relationship between the angle γ, at which the observer sees the picture, and φ.

160. Find the relationship between the angle α and the displacement x of the crosshead for the crank gear shown in Fig. 13. (see Problem 149).

161. Find out for what interval of variation of x the following identities are true:

(1) $\arcsin x + \arccos x = \frac{\pi}{2}$; (2) $\arcsin \sqrt{x} + \arccos \sqrt{x} = \frac{\pi}{2}$;

(3) $\arccos \sqrt{1 - x^2} = \arcsin x$; (4) $\arccos \sqrt{1 - x^2} = -\arcsin x$;

(5) $\arctan x = \operatorname{arccot} \frac{1}{x}$; (6) $\arctan x = \operatorname{arccot} \frac{1}{x} - \pi$;

(7) $\arccos \frac{1 - x^2}{1 + x^2} = 2 \arctan x$; (8) $\arccos \frac{1 - x^2}{1 + x^2} = -2 \arctan x$;

(9) $\arctan x + \arctan 1 = \arctan \frac{1 + x}{1 - x}$;

(10) $\arctan x + \arctan 1 = \pi + \arctan \frac{1 + x}{1 - x}$.

162. Using the identities of Problem 161, find the domains of definition of the given functions and graph them:

(1) $y = \arccos \sqrt{1 - x^2}$; (2) $y = \arcsin \sqrt{1 - x} + \arcsin \sqrt{x}$;

(3) $y = \arccos \frac{1 - x^2}{1 + x^2}$; (4) $y = \arctan x - \operatorname{arccot} \frac{1}{x}$.

163*. Graph the function $y = \arcsin (\sin x)$. Prove that this function is a periodic one and find its period.

164. Graph the function $y = \arccos (\cos x)$.

165. Graph the function $y = \arctan (\tan x)$.

166. Graph the functions:

(1) $y = x - \arctan (\tan x)$;

(2) $y = x - \arcsin (\sin x)$;

(3) $y = x \arcsin (\sin x)$;

(4) $y = \arccos (\cos x) - \arcsin (\sin x)$.

6. Computational Problems

167. Plot the graph of the function $y = x^3 + 2x^2 - 4x + 7$ for the interval $[-4, 2]$, using the values of x spaced at 0.2; along the ordinate axis choose a scale 20 times smaller than that along the abscissa axis. Taking advantage of the graph, find the greatest and the least values of the function in the interval $[-3, 2]$. At what point does the function pass over from increasing to decreasing? Find the root of the function in the interval [−4, 2]. Computational accuracy is 0.1.

168. In studying the laws of scattering of shrapnel-filled shells it is required to graph the function $y = e^{A\cos^2\alpha}$; $e \approx 2.718$. Carry out the plotting at $A = 2$, taking for α the values from 0° to 90° spaced at 5°. Perform computations accurate to 0.01.

169. Given three points: $M_1(1, 8)$; $M_2(5, 6)$; $M_3(9, 3)$. Pass through them the parabola $y = ax^2 + bx + c$. Find the roots of the function $ax^2 + bx + c$. Carry out the computations accurate to 0.01.

170. To make a box from sheet metal having the shape of a square (30×30 cm^2) it is necessary to cut small squares out of its corners. How long must the side x of the cut-out squares be to bend a box of capacity 1600 cm^3? Carry out the computations accurate to 0.01.

171. Check to see that if in the equation $x^4 + px^2 + qx + s = 0$ we put, $x^2 = y$, then this equation is replaced by the system

$$\begin{cases} x^2 = y \\ (y - y_0)^2 + (x - x_0)^2 = r^2, \end{cases}$$

where $y_0 = \dfrac{1-p}{2}$, $x_0 = -\dfrac{q}{2}$ and $r^2 = y_0^2 + x_0^2 - s$.

Using this method, solve graphically the equation

$$x^4 - 3x^2 - 8x - 29 = 0$$

accurate to 0.1.

172*. Taking advantage of the method mentioned in Problem 171, prove that with the aid, of an additional substitution of the variable $x = x' + \alpha$, the real roots of the fourth-degree equation $x^4 + ax^3 + bx^2 + cx + d = 0$ can be determined graphically as the points of intersection of a circle and the parabola $y = x^2$. Applying this method, solve graphically the equation $x^4 + 1.2x^3 - 22x^2 - 39x + 31 = 0$ accurate to 0.1.

173. Find graphically the roots of the equation $e^x \sin x = 1$, $e \approx 2.718$, lying between 0 and 10; give an approximate formula for the values of the remaining roots. Carry out the computations accurate to 0.01.

174. Solve graphically the system

$$x + y^2 = 1,\ 16x^2 + y = 4$$

accurate to 0.01.

175. Graph the given functions (in polar coordinates) using the values of the polar angle φ spaced at $\frac{\pi}{12}$[1]:

(1) $\rho = a\varphi$ (spiral of Archimedes);

(2) $\rho = \frac{a}{\varphi}$ (hyperbolic spiral);

(3) $\rho = e^{a\varphi}$ $(e \approx 2.718)$ (logarithmic spiral);

(4) $\rho = a \sin 3\varphi$ (three-leafed rose);

(5) $\rho = a \cos 2\varphi$ (two-leafed rose);

(6) $\rho = a(1 - \cos \varphi)$ (cardioid).

Carry out all the computations accurate to 0.01. The constant $a > 0$ is chosen arbitrarily.

[1] It is maintained here that if $\rho(\varphi) < 0$, then there is no point of the graph on the corresponding ray.

2

Limit Continuity

1. Basic Definitions

Functions of an integral argument

176. A function of an integral argument attains the values

$$u_1 = 0.9, u_2 = 0.99, u_3 = 0.999, \ldots, u_n = \underbrace{0.999\ldots 9}_{n \text{ times}}, \ldots$$

What is the $\lim_{n \to \infty} u_n$ equal to? What must the value of n be for the absolute value of the difference between u_n and its limit not to exceed 0.0001?

177. The function u_n takes on the values

$$u_1 = 1,\ u_2 = \frac{1}{4},\ u_3 = \frac{1}{9}, \ldots,\ u_n = \frac{1}{n^2}, \ldots$$

Find $\lim_{n \to \infty} u_n$. What must the value of n be for the difference between u_n and its limit to be less than the given positive number ε?

178. Prove that $u_n = \dfrac{n-1}{n+1}$ tends to 1 as n increases indefinitely. Beginning with what value of n does the absolute value of the difference between u_n and 1 not exceed 10^{-4}?

179. A function v_n attains the values

$$v_1 = \frac{\cos\frac{\pi}{2}}{1},\ v_2 = \frac{\cos \pi}{2},\ v_3 = \frac{\cos\frac{3\pi}{2}}{3}, \ldots,\ v_n = \frac{\cos\frac{n\pi}{2}}{n}, \ldots$$

Find $\lim_{n \to \infty} v_n$. What must the value of n be for the absolute value of the difference between v_n and its limit not to exceed 0.001? Does v_n take on the value of its limit?

180. The general term u_n of the sequence $u_1 = \frac{1}{2}, u_2 = \frac{5}{4}, u_3 = \frac{7}{8}, u_4 = \frac{17}{16}, \ldots$ has the form $\frac{2^n - 1}{2^n}$ if n is odd, and $\frac{2^n + 1}{2^n}$ if n is even.

Find $\lim_{n \to \infty} u_n$. What must the value of n be for the absolute value of the difference between u_n and its limit not to exceed 10^{-4}; a given positive number ε?

181. Prove that the sequence $u_n = \frac{4n^2 + 1}{3n^2 + 2}$ tends to the limit equal to $\frac{4}{3}$ increasing monotonically as n increases indefinitely. Beginning with what value of n does the magnitude $\frac{4}{3} - u_n$ not exceed a given positive number ε?

182. Prove that $u_n = \frac{\sqrt{n^2 + a^2}}{n}$ has the limit equal to 1 as n increases indefinitely. Beginning with what value of n does the magnitude $|1 - u_n|$ not exceed a given positive number ε?

What character has the passage to the limit of the variable u_n?

183. The function v_n takes on the values of binomial coefficients:

$$v_1 = m,\ v_2 = \frac{m(m-1)}{1 \cdot 2},\ v_3 = \frac{m(m-1)(m-2)}{1 \cdot 2 \cdot 3}, \ldots,$$

$$v_n = \frac{m(m-1)(m-2)\ldots[m-(n-1)]}{1 \cdot 2 \cdot 3 \ldots n}, \ldots,$$

where m is a positive integer. Find $\lim_{n \to \infty} v_n$.

184. Prove that the sequence $u_n = 1 + (-1)^n$ has no limit as n increases without bound.

185. Prove that, as n increases infinitely, the sequence $u_n = \frac{2^n + (-2)^n}{2^n}$ has no limit, and $v_n = \frac{2^n + (-2)^n}{3^n}$ has a limit. What is the limit?

186. Have the given sequences limits?

(1) $u_n = n \sin \frac{n\pi}{2}$;

(2) $u_n = \frac{\sin \frac{n\pi}{2}}{\log n}$ $(n > 1)$.

187. Prove the theorem : if the sequences $u_1, u_2, \ldots, u_n, \ldots$ and $v_1, v_2, \ldots, v_n, \ldots$ tend to a common limit a, then the sequence $u_1, v_1, u_2, v_2, \ldots, u_n, v_n, \ldots$ tends to the same limit.

188. Prove the theorem: if the sequence $u_1, u_2, \ldots, u_n, \ldots$ tends to the limit a, then any of its infinite subsequences (say, $u_1, u_3, u_5, \ldots$) tends to the same limit.

189. The sequence $u_1, u_2, \ldots, u_n, \ldots$ has a limit $a \neq 0$. Prove that

$$\lim_{n \to \infty} \frac{u_{n+1}}{u_n} = 1.$$

What can be said about this limit if $a = 0$? (Give examples).

Functions of continuous argument

190. Given $y = x^2$. As $x \to 2$, $y \to 4$. What must the value of δ be for which from $|x - 2| < \delta$ it follows that $|y - 4| < \varepsilon = 0.001$?

191. Let $y = \dfrac{x^2 - 1}{x^2 + 1}$. As $x \to 2$, we have $y \to \dfrac{3}{5}$. What must the value of δ be for which from $|x - 2| < \delta$ it follows that $\left| y - \dfrac{3}{5} \right| < 0.1$?

192. Let $y = \dfrac{x - 1}{2(x + 1)}$. As $x \to 3$, we have $y \to \dfrac{1}{4}$. What must the value of δ be for which from $|x - 3| < \delta$ it follows that $\left| \dfrac{1}{4} - y \right| < 0.01$?

193. Prove that $\sin x$ tends to unity as $x \to \dfrac{\pi}{2}$. What conditions must x satisfy in the neighbourhood of the point $x = \dfrac{\pi}{2}$ for the inequality $1 - \sin x < 0.01$ to be valid?

194. As x increases without bound, the function $y = \dfrac{1}{x^2 + 1}$ tends to zero, $\lim\limits_{x \to \infty} \dfrac{1}{x^2 + 1} = 0$. What must the value of N be for which from $|x| > N$ it follows that $y < \varepsilon$?

195. As $x \to \infty$, $y = \dfrac{x^2 - 1}{x^2 + 3} \to 1$. What must the value of N be for which from $|x| > N$ it follows that $|y - 1| < \varepsilon$?

2. Infinite Magnitudes. Tests for the Existence of the Limit

Infinite magnitudes

196. The function u_n attains the following values

$$u_1 = 3,\ y_2 = 5,\ u_3 = 7, \ldots,\ u_n = 2n + 1, \ldots$$

Prove that u_n is an infinitely large magnitude as $n \to \infty$. Beginning with what n does the magnitude u_n become larger than N?

197. Prove that the general term of any arithmetic progression is an infinitely large magnitude as $n \to \infty$. (When will it be positive and when negative?) Is this assertion true for an arbitrary geometric progression?

198. As $x \to 0$, we have $y = \dfrac{1 + 2x}{x} \to \infty$. What conditions must be satisfied by x for the inequality $|y| > 10^4$ to take place?

199. Prove that the function $y = \dfrac{x}{x - 3}$ is infinitely large as $x \to 3$. Of what value must x be for the magnitude $|y|$ to exceed 1000?

200. As $x \to 1$, the function $y = \dfrac{1}{(x - 1)^2}$ increases without bound. What must the value of δ be such that from $|x - 1| < \delta$ it follows that $\dfrac{1}{(x - 1)^2} > N = 10^4$?

201. The function $y = \dfrac{1}{2^x - 1}$ is infinitely large as $x \to 0$. What inequalities must be satisfied by x to get $|y|$ exceeding 100?

202. As $x \to \infty$, we have $y = \log_{10} x \to \infty$. What must the value of M be for $y > N = 100$ to follow from $x > M$.

203. Which of the basic elementary functions are bounded throughout the whole domain of their definition?

204. Prove that the function $y = \dfrac{x^2}{1 + x^4}$ is bounded throughout the number scale.

205. Is the function $y = \dfrac{x^2}{1 + x^5}$ bounded throughout the number scale? Is it bounded in the interval $(0, \infty)$?

206. Is the function $y = \log \sin x$ bounded within the whole domain of its existence?

The same question about the function $y = \log \cos x$.

207. Given the functions $y = x \sin x$ and $y = x \cos x$.

(1) Prove that the functions are not bounded as $x \to \infty$ (indicate for each of them at least one sequence x_n for which $y_n \to \infty$).

(2) Are the functions infinitely large?

(3) Graph the functions.

208. Graph the functions $f(x) = 2^{x \sin x}$ and $f(x) = 2^{-x \sin x}$. For each of them indicate two sequences x_n and x'_n such that

$$\lim_{n \to \infty} f(x_n) = \infty, \quad \text{and} \quad \lim_{n \to \infty} f(x'_n) = 0.$$

209. For what values of a is the function $y = a^x \sin x$ unbounded as

$$x \to +\infty \ (x \to -\infty)?$$

210. Will the given functions be infinitely large:

(1) $f(x) = \frac{1}{x} \cos \frac{1}{x}$ as $x \to 0$;

(2) $f(x) = x \arctan x$ as $x \to \infty$;

(3) $f(x) = 2^x \arcsin(\sin x)$ as $x \to +\infty$;

(4) $f(x) = (2 + \sin x) \log x$ as $x \to +\infty$;

(5) $f(x) = (1 + \sin x) \log x$ as $x \to +\infty$?

211. The function u_n attains the following values

$$u_1 = 2, \ u_2 = \frac{3}{4}, \ u_3 = \frac{4}{9}, \ \ldots, \ u_n = \frac{n+1}{n^2}, \ \ldots$$

Prove that u_n is an infinitesimal as $n \to \infty$.

212. The function u_n takes on the following values

$$u_1 = 7, \ u_2 = -\frac{1}{2}, \ u_3 = \frac{1}{27}, \ u_4 = \frac{1}{8}, \ldots, \ u_n = \frac{n^2 - 8}{n^3}, \ldots$$

Prove that u_n is an infinitesimal as $n \to \infty$.

213. Prove that $y = \frac{x}{x+1} \to 0$ as $x \to 0$. What conditions must be satisfied by x for the inequality $|y| < 10^{-4}$ to be valid?

214. Show that the function $y = \sqrt{x+1} - \sqrt{x}$ tends to zero as $x \to \infty$. What must N be to ensure $y < \varepsilon$ for $x > N$?

215. Prove that if the limit of the function $f(x)$ is equal to a as $x \to \infty$, then $f(x)$ is representable as a sum $f(x) = a + \varphi(x)$, where $\varphi(x)$ is an infinitesimal as $x \to \infty$.

Represent the following functions in the form of such sums:

(1) $y = \frac{x^3}{x^3 - 1}$; (2) $y = \frac{x^2}{2x^2 + 1}$; (3) $y = \frac{1 - x^2}{1 + x^2}$.

Tests for the existence of the limit

216*. The function u_n takes on the following values:

$$u_1 = \frac{1}{4},\ u_2 = \frac{1}{4} + \frac{1}{10},\ \ldots,$$

$$u_n = \frac{1}{3+1} + \frac{1}{3^2+1} + \ldots + \frac{1}{3^n+1}, \ldots$$

Prove that u_n tends to a certain limit as $n \to \infty$.

217. The function u_n attains the values

$$u_1 = \frac{1}{2},\ u_2 = \frac{1}{2} + \frac{1}{2\cdot 4},\ u_3 = \frac{1}{2} + \frac{1}{2\cdot 4} + \frac{1}{2\cdot 4\cdot 6}, \ldots,$$

$$u_n = \frac{1}{2} + \frac{1}{2\cdot 4} + \ldots + \frac{1}{2\cdot 4\ldots(2n)}, \ldots$$

Prove that u_n tends to a certain limit as $n \to \infty$.

218. Prove the theorem : if the difference between two functions for one and the same variation of the independent variable is an infinitesimal, one of them increasing, the other decreasing at the same time, then both functions tend to one and the same limit.

219. Given two numbers: u_0 and $v_0 (u_0 < v_0)$. The terms of the sequences u_n and v_n are specified by the formulas

$$u_1 = \frac{u_0 + v_0}{2},\ v_1 = \frac{u_0 + 2v_0}{3};\ u_2 = \frac{u_1 + v_1}{2},\ v_2 = \frac{u_1 + 2v_1}{3}$$

in general

$$u_n = \frac{u_{n-1} + v_{n-1}}{2},\ v_n = \frac{u_{n-1} + 2v_{n-1}}{3}.$$

Taking advantage of the theorem of Problem 218, prove that both sequences u_n and v_n tend to one and the same limit lying between u_0 and v_0.

220. Given a sequence u_n of numbers

$$u_1 = \sqrt{6},\ u_2 = \sqrt{6 + u_1},\ \ldots,\ u_n = \sqrt{6 + u_{n-1}},\ \ldots$$

Prove that the sequence possesses a limit, and find it.

3. Continuous Functions

221. A function y is defined in the following way:

$y = 0$ for $x < 0$;

$y = x$ for $0 \le x < 1$;

$y = -x^2 + 4x - 2$ for $1 \le x < 3$;

$y = 4 - x$ for $x \ge 3$.

Will this function be continuous?

222. Three cylinders having the radii of the base circles equal to 3, 2, and 1 m, respectively, and equal altitudes (5 m) are mounted on each other to form a single solid. Express the cross-sectional area of the solid thus obtained as a function of the distance between the cross-section and the lower base of the lower cylinder. Will this function be continuous? Draw the graph.

223. Let

$$f(x)=\begin{cases} x+1 & \text{if } x\le 1; \\ 3-ax^2 & \text{if } x>1. \end{cases}$$

For what a will the function $f(x)$ be continuous? (Draw its graph.)

224. Let

$$f(x)=\begin{cases} -2\sin x & \text{if } x\le -\frac{\pi}{2}; \\ A\sin x+B & \text{if } -\frac{\pi}{2}<x<\frac{\pi}{2}; \\ \cos x & \text{if } x\ge \frac{\pi}{2}. \end{cases}$$

Choose the numbers A and B so as to make the function $f(x)$ continuous; graph it.

225. At what points do the functions $y=\frac{1}{x-2}$ and $y=\frac{1}{(x+2)^2}$ suffer discontinuities? Draw the graphs of both functions. Find out the difference in the behaviour of the functions near the points of discontinuity.

226. The function $f(x)=\frac{x^2-1}{x^3-1}$ is not defined for $x=1$. What must the value of $f(1)$ be for the function extended by this value to be continuous for $x=1$?

227. What kind of discontinuities have the functions $y=\frac{\sin x}{x}$ and $y=\frac{\cos x}{x}$ at $x=0$? Indicate the character of the graphs of the functions in the neighbourhood of the point $x=0$.

228. Test for continuity the function specified as follows: $y=\frac{|x|}{x}$ for $x\ne 0$, $y=0$ for $x=0$. Draw the graph of this function.

229. How many points of discontinuity (and of what kind) has the function $y=\frac{1}{\log|x|}$? Draw its graph.

230. The function $y=\arctan\frac{1}{x}$ is not defined at the point $x=0$. Is it possible to define the function $f(x)$ at the point $x=0$ so as to make the function continuous at this point? Draw the graph of this function.

231. Test for continuity the function specified in the following way

$$f(x) = \sin\frac{\pi}{2x} \text{ for } x \neq 0,\ f(0) = 1.$$

Draw the graph of this function.

232. Graph the function $f(x) = x\sin\frac{\pi}{x}$. What value must $f(0)$ have for the function $f(x)$ to be continuous everywhere?

233. Prove that the function $y = \dfrac{1}{1 + 2^{1/x}}$ has a discontinuity of the first kind at the point $x = 0$. Sketch the graph of this function in the vicinity of the point $x = 0$.

234. Determine the kind of discontinuity of the function $y = 2^{-2^{1/1-x}}$ at the point $x = 1$. Is it possible to define y for $x = 1$ so as the function becomes continuous at $x = 1$?

235. Determine the kind of discontinuity of the function $y = -\dfrac{2^{1/x} - 1}{2^{1/x} + 1}$ at the point $x = 0$.

236. The function $f(x)$ is defined in the following way: $f(x) = (x+1)2^{-\left(\frac{1}{|x|}+\frac{1}{x}\right)}$ for $x \neq 0$ and $f(0) = 0$. Prove that on the interval $-2 \leq x \leq 2$ the function $f(x)$ attains all the values (without any exception) lying between $f(-2)$ and $f(2)$, and that it is still discontinuous (at what point?). Sketch its graph.

237. Test the function $y = \dfrac{1}{1 + 2^{\tan x}}$ for continuity. Find out the character of its graph.

238. The function is defined as follows: if x is a rational number, then $f(x) = 0$; if x is an irrational number, then $f(x) = x$. For what value of x is the function continuous?

239. Test the following functions for continuity and plot their graphs:

(1) $y = x - [x]$; (2) $y = \dfrac{1}{x - [x]}$; (3) $y = (-1)^{[x]}$.

(The function $[x]$ is equal to the greatest integer not exceeding x, see Problem 59).

240. Taking advantage of the properties of continuous function, make sure that the equation $x^5 - 3x = 1$ has at least one root lying between 1 and 2.

241*. Show that:

(a) a polynomial of an odd degree has at least one real root;

(b) a polynomial of an even degree has at least two real roots if it attains at least one value opposite in sign to the coefficient of its highest-degree term.

242. Show that the equation $x \cdot 2^x = 1$ has at least one positive root not exceeding 1.

243. Show that the equation $x = a \sin x + b$, where $0 < a < 1$, $b > 0$, has at least one positive root which does not exceed $b + a$.

244. Show that the equation

$$\frac{a_1}{x - \lambda_1} + \frac{a_2}{x - \lambda_2} + \frac{a_3}{x - \lambda_3} = 0,$$

where $a_1 > 0, a_2 > 0, a_3 > 0$ and $\lambda_1 < \lambda_2 < \lambda_3$, has two real roots lying in the intervals (λ_1, λ_2) and (λ_2, λ_3).

4. Finding Limits. Comparison of Infinitesimals

Functions of an integral argument

In Problems 245 to 267 find the limits.

245. $\lim\limits_{n\to\infty} \frac{n+1}{n}$.

246. $\lim\limits_{n\to\infty} \frac{(n+1)^2}{2n^2}$.

247. $\lim\limits_{n\to\infty} \frac{(n+1)^3 - (n-1)^3}{(n+1)^2 + (n-1)^2}$.

248. $\lim\limits_{n\to\infty} \frac{n^3 - 100n^2 + 1}{100n^2 + 15n}$.

249. $\lim\limits_{n\to\infty} \frac{1000n^3 + 3n^2}{0.001n^4 - 100n^3 + 1}$.

250. $\lim\limits_{n\to\infty} \frac{(n+1)^4 - (n-1)^4}{(n+1)^4 + (n-1)^4}$.

251. $\lim\limits_{n\to\infty} \frac{(2n+1)^4 - (n-1)^4}{(2n+1)^4 + (n-1)^4}$.

252. $\lim\limits_{n\to\infty} \frac{\sqrt[3]{n^3 + 2n - 1}}{n + 2}$.

253. $\lim\limits_{n\to\infty} \frac{\sqrt[3]{n^2 + n}}{n+1}$.

254. $\lim\limits_{n\to\infty} \frac{(\sqrt{n^2+1} + n)^2}{\sqrt[3]{n^6 + 1}}$.

255. $\lim\limits_{n\to\infty} \frac{\sqrt{n^3 - 2n^2 + 1} + \sqrt[3]{n^4 + 1}}{\sqrt[4]{n^6 + 6n^5 + 2} - \sqrt[5]{n^7 + 3n^3 + 1}}$.

256. $\lim\limits_{n\to\infty} \frac{\sqrt[4]{n^5 + 2} - \sqrt[3]{n^2 + 1}}{\sqrt[5]{n^4 + 2} - \sqrt{n^3 + 1}}$.

257. $\lim\limits_{n\to\infty} \frac{n!}{(n+1)! - n!}$.

258. $\lim\limits_{n\to\infty} \frac{(n+2)! + (n+1)!}{(n+3)!}$.

259. $\lim\limits_{n\to\infty} \frac{(n+2)! + (n+1)!}{(n+2)! - (n+1)!}$.

260. $\lim\limits_{n\to\infty} \frac{1 + \frac{1}{2} + \frac{1}{4} + \ldots + \frac{1}{2^n}}{1 + \frac{1}{3} + \frac{1}{9} + \ldots + \frac{1}{3^n}}$.

261. $\lim\limits_{n\to\infty} \frac{1}{n^2}(1 + 2 + 3 + \ldots + n)$.

262. $\lim\limits_{n\to\infty}\left(\dfrac{1+2+3+\ldots+n}{n+2}-\dfrac{n}{2}\right)$. **263.** $\lim\limits_{n\to\infty}\left(\dfrac{1-2+3-4+\ldots-2n}{\sqrt{n^2+1}}\right)$.

264. $\lim\limits_{n\to\infty}\left(\dfrac{1}{1\cdot 2}+\dfrac{1}{2\cdot 3}+\ldots+\dfrac{1}{(n-1)n}\right)$.

265. $\lim\limits_{n\to\infty}\left(\dfrac{1}{1\cdot 3}+\dfrac{1}{3\cdot 5}+\ldots+\dfrac{1}{(2n-1)(2n+1)}\right)$.

266. $\lim\limits_{n\to\infty}\dfrac{2^n-1}{2^n+1}$. **267.** $\lim\limits_{n\to\infty}\dfrac{2^{1/n}-1}{2^{1/n}+1}$.

Functions of the continuous argument

In Problems 268 to 304 find the limits.

268. $\lim\limits_{x\to 2}\dfrac{x^2+5}{x^2-3}$. **269.** $\lim\limits_{x\to 0}\left(\dfrac{x^3-3x+1}{x-4}+1\right)$.

270. $\lim\limits_{x\to 1}\dfrac{x}{1-x}$. **271.** $\lim\limits_{x\to\sqrt{3}}\dfrac{x^2-3}{x^4+x^2+1}$.

272. $\lim\limits_{x\to 1}\dfrac{x^2-2x+1}{x^3-x}$. **273.** $\lim\limits_{x\to -2}\dfrac{x^3+3x^2+2x}{x^2-x-6}$.

274. $\lim\limits_{x\to 1}\dfrac{(x-1)\sqrt{2-x}}{x^2-1}$. **275.** $\lim\limits_{x\to\frac{1}{2}}\dfrac{8x^3-1}{6x^2-5x+1}$.

276. $\lim\limits_{x\to 1}\dfrac{x^3+x-2}{x^3-x^2-x+1}$. **277.** $\lim\limits_{x\to 1}\left(\dfrac{1}{1-x}-\dfrac{3}{1-x^3}\right)$.

278. $\lim\limits_{x\to 2}\left[\dfrac{1}{x(x-2)^2}-\dfrac{1}{x^2-3x+2}\right]$.

279. $\lim\limits_{x\to 1}\left[\dfrac{x+2}{x^2-5x+4}+\dfrac{x-4}{3(x^2-3x+2)}\right]$.

280. $\lim\limits_{x\to 1}\dfrac{x^m-1}{x^n-1}$ (m and n integers).

281. $\lim\limits_{x\to\infty}\dfrac{x^3+x}{x^4-3x^2+1}$. **282.** $\lim\limits_{x\to\infty}\dfrac{x^4-5x}{x^2-3x+1}$.

283. $\lim\limits_{x\to\infty}\dfrac{x^2-1}{2x^2+1}$. **284.** $\lim\limits_{x\to\infty}\dfrac{1+x-3x^3}{1+x^2+3x^3}$.

285. $\lim\limits_{x\to\infty}\left(\dfrac{x^3}{x^2+1}-x\right)$. **286.** $\lim\limits_{x\to\infty}\left(\dfrac{x^3}{2x^2-1}-\dfrac{x^2}{2x+1}\right)$.

287. $\lim_{x \to \infty} \left[\frac{3x^2}{2x+1} - \frac{(2x-1)(3x^2+x+2)}{4x^2} \right]$.

288. $\lim_{x \to \infty} \frac{(x+1)^{10} + (x+2)^{10} + \ldots + (x+100)^{10}}{x^{10} + 10^{10}}$.

289. $\lim_{x \to +\infty} \frac{\sqrt{x^2+1} + \sqrt{x}}{\sqrt[4]{x^3+x} - x}$.

290. $\lim_{x \to \infty} \frac{\sqrt{x^2+1} - \sqrt[3]{x^2+1}}{\sqrt[4]{x^4+1} - \sqrt[5]{x^4+1}}$.

291. $\lim_{x \to +\infty} \frac{\sqrt[6]{x^7+3} + \sqrt[4]{2x^3-1}}{\sqrt[6]{x^8+x^7+1} - x}$.

292. $\lim_{x \to \infty} \frac{\sqrt[3]{x^4+3} - \sqrt[5]{x^3+4}}{\sqrt[3]{x^7+1}}$.

293. $\lim_{x \to 0} \frac{\sqrt{1+x^2} - 1}{x}$.

294. $\lim_{x \to 0} \frac{\sqrt{1+x} - 1}{x^2}$.

295. $\lim_{x \to 0} \frac{\sqrt{x^2+1} - 1}{\sqrt{x^2+16} - 4}$.

296. $\lim_{x \to 5} \frac{\sqrt{x-1} - 2}{x-5}$.

297. $\lim_{x \to 1} \frac{x^2 - \sqrt{x}}{\sqrt{x} - 1}$.

298. $\lim_{h \to 0} \frac{\sqrt{x+h} - \sqrt{x}}{h}$.

299. $\lim_{x \to 0} \frac{\sqrt[3]{1+x^2} - 1}{x^2}$.

300. $\lim_{x \to 0} \frac{\sqrt[3]{1+x} - \sqrt[3]{1-x}}{x}$.

301. $\lim_{x \to a} \frac{\sqrt{x-b} - \sqrt{a-b}}{x^2 - a^2}$ $(a > b)$.

302. $\lim_{x \to 1} \frac{\sqrt[n]{x} - 1}{\sqrt[m]{x} - 1}$ (m and n integers).

303*. $\lim_{x \to 0} \frac{\sqrt[3]{1+x^2} - \sqrt[4]{1-2x}}{x + x^2}$.

304. $\lim_{x \to 1} \frac{\sqrt[3]{7+x^3} - \sqrt{3+x^2}}{x-1}$.

305. How do the roots of the equation $ax^2 + bx + c = 0$ change when b and c retain constant values $(b \neq 0)$ and a tends to zero?

In Problems 306 to 378 find the limits.

306. $\lim_{x \to \infty} (\sqrt{x+a} - \sqrt{x})$.

307. $\lim_{x \to \infty} (\sqrt{x^2+1} - \sqrt{x^2-1})$.

308. $\lim_{x \to \pm\infty} (\sqrt{x^2+1} - x)^1$.

309. $\lim_{x \to \pm\infty} x(\sqrt{x^2+1} - x)$.

310. $\lim_{x \to \pm\infty} (\sqrt{(x+a)(x+b)} - x)$.

311. $\lim_{x \to \pm\infty} (\sqrt{x^2 - 2x - 1} - \sqrt{x^2 - 7x + 3})$.

312. $\lim_{x \to \infty} (\sqrt[3]{(x+1)^2} - \sqrt[3]{(x-1)^2})$.

313. $\lim_{x \to \infty} x^{3/2} (\sqrt{x^3+1} - \sqrt{x^3-1})$.

314. $\lim_{x \to 0} \frac{\sin 3x}{x}$.

315. $\lim_{x \to 0} \frac{\tan kx}{x}$.

316. $\lim_{x \to 0} \frac{\sin \alpha x}{\sin \beta x}$.

---

*In problems where it is given $x \to \pm\infty$, consider separately the cases $x \to +\infty$ and $x \to -\infty$.

317. $\lim_{x \to 0} \frac{\tan 2x}{\sin 5x}$.

318. $\lim_{\alpha \to 0} \frac{\sin (\alpha^n)}{(\sin \alpha)^m}$ (m and n positive integers).

319. $\lim_{x \to 0} \frac{2 \arcsin x}{3x}$.

320. $\lim_{x \to 0} \frac{2x - \arcsin x}{2x + \arctan x}$.

321. $\lim_{x \to 0} \frac{1 - \cos x}{x^2}$.

322. $\lim_{x \to 0} \frac{1 - \cos^3 x}{x \sin 2x}$.

323. $\lim_{\alpha \to 0} \frac{\tan \alpha}{\sqrt[3]{(1 - \cos \alpha)^2}}$.

324. $\lim_{x \to 0} \frac{1 + \sin x - \cos x}{1 - \sin x - \cos x}$.

325. $\lim_{\alpha \to 0} \frac{\tan \alpha - \sin \alpha}{\alpha^3}$.

326. $\lim_{\alpha \to 0} \frac{(1 - \cos \alpha)^2}{\tan^3 \alpha - \sin^3 \alpha}$.

327. $\lim_{x \to 0} \left(\frac{1}{\sin x} - \frac{1}{\tan x} \right)$.

328. $\lim_{x \to \frac{\pi}{2}} \frac{1 - \sin x}{\left(\frac{\pi}{2} - x \right)^2}$.

329. $\lim_{x \to \frac{\pi}{2}} \frac{\cos x}{\sqrt[3]{(1 - \sin x)^2}}$.

330. $\lim_{x \to \pi} \frac{\sin 3x}{\sin 2x}$.

331. $\lim_{x \to \frac{\pi}{2}} \left(\frac{\pi}{2} - x \right) \tan x$.

332. $\lim_{\alpha \to \pi} \frac{\sin \alpha}{1 - \frac{a^2}{\pi^2}}$.

333. $\lim_{z \to 1} (1 - z) \tan \frac{\pi z}{2}$.

334. $\lim_{y \to a} \left(\sin \frac{y - a}{2} \cdot \tan \frac{\pi y}{2a} \right)$.

335. $\lim_{x \to \frac{\pi}{4}} \frac{\cos x - \sin x}{\cos 2x}$.

336. $\lim_{x \to \frac{\pi}{6}} \frac{\sin \left(x - \frac{\pi}{6} \right)}{\frac{\sqrt{3}}{2} - \cos x}$.

337. $\lim_{x \to \pi} \frac{1 - \sin \frac{x}{2}}{\cos \frac{x}{2} \left(\cos \frac{x}{4} - \sin \frac{x}{4} \right)}$.

338. $\lim_{x \to \frac{\pi}{2}} \left(2x \tan x - \frac{\pi}{\cos x} \right)$.

339. $\lim_{x \to 0} \frac{\cos (a + x) - \cos (a - x)}{x}$.

340. $\lim_{x \to 0} \frac{\cos \alpha x - \cos \beta x}{x^2}$.

341. $\lim_{x \to 0} \frac{\sin (a + x) - \sin (a - x)}{\tan (a + x) - \tan (a - x)}$.

342. $\lim_{\alpha \to \beta} \frac{\sin^2 \alpha - \sin^2 \beta}{\alpha^2 - \beta^2}$.

343. $\lim_{h \to 0} \frac{\sin (a + 2h) - 2 \sin (a + h) + \sin a}{h^2}$.

344. $\lim_{h \to 0} \frac{\tan (a + 2h) - 2 \tan (a + h) + \tan a}{h^2}$.

345. $\lim_{x \to 0} \frac{\sqrt{2} - \sqrt{1 + \cos x}}{\sin^2 x}$.

346. $\lim_{x \to 0} \frac{\sqrt{1 + \sin x} - \sqrt{1 - \sin x}}{\tan x}$.

347. $\lim\limits_{x\to 0} \dfrac{\sqrt{1+x\sin x}-\sqrt{\cos 2x}}{\tan^2 \dfrac{x}{2}}$. **348.** $\lim\limits_{x\to 0} \dfrac{1-\cos x\sqrt{\cos 2x}}{x^2}$.

349. $\lim\limits_{x\to 0} \dfrac{\sqrt[3]{1+\arctan 3x}-\sqrt[3]{1-\arcsin 3x}}{\sqrt{1-\arcsin 2x}-\sqrt{1+\arctan 2x}}$.

350*. $\lim\limits_{x\to -1} \dfrac{\sqrt{\pi}-\sqrt{\arccos x}}{\sqrt{x+1}}$. **351.** $\lim\limits_{x\to\infty} \left(\dfrac{x}{1+x}\right)^x$. **352.** $\lim\limits_{t\to\infty} \left(1-\dfrac{1}{t}\right)^t$.

353. $\lim\limits_{x\to\infty} \left(1+\dfrac{1}{x}\right)^{\frac{x+1}{x}}$. **354.** $\lim\limits_{x\to\infty} \left(1+\dfrac{k}{x}\right)^{mx}$.

355. $\lim\limits_{x\to\infty} \left(\dfrac{x+1}{x-2}\right)^{2x-1}$. **356.** $\lim\limits_{x\to\infty} \left(\dfrac{3x-4}{3x+2}\right)^{\frac{x+1}{3}}$. **357.** $\lim\limits_{x\to\infty} \left(\dfrac{x^2+1}{x^2-1}\right)^{x^2}$.

358. $\lim\limits_{x\to\pm\infty} \left(\dfrac{x+1}{2x-1}\right)^x$. **359.** $\lim\limits_{x\to\pm\infty} \left(\dfrac{2x+1}{x-1}\right)^x$.

360. $\lim\limits_{x\to\infty} \left(1+\dfrac{1}{x^2}\right)^x$. **361.** $\lim\limits_{x\to\pm\infty} \left(1+\dfrac{1}{x}\right)^{x^2}$.

362. $\lim\limits_{x\to\infty} \left(\dfrac{x^2-2x+1}{x^2-4x+2}\right)^x$. **363.** $\lim\limits_{x\to 0} (1+\sin x)^{\operatorname{cosec} x}$.

364. $\lim\limits_{x\to 0} (1+\tan^2\sqrt{x})^{1/2x}$. **365.** $\lim\limits_{x\to 0} \dfrac{\ln(1+kx)}{x}$.

366. $\lim\limits_{x\to 0} \dfrac{\ln(a+x)-\ln a}{x}$. **367.** $\lim\limits_{x\to\infty} \{x[\ln(x+a)-\ln x]\}$.

368. $\lim\limits_{x\to e} \dfrac{\ln x-1}{x-e}$. **369.** $\lim\limits_{h\to 0} \dfrac{a^h-1}{h}$.

370. $\lim\limits_{x\to 0} \dfrac{e^{2x}-1}{3x}$. **371.** $\lim\limits_{x\to 1} \dfrac{e^x-e}{x-1}$.

372*. $\lim\limits_{x\to 0} \dfrac{e^{x^2}-\cos x}{x^2}$. **373.** $\lim\limits_{x\to 0} \dfrac{e^x-e^{-x}}{\sin x}$.

374. $\lim\limits_{x\to 0} \dfrac{e^{\sin 2x}-e^{\sin x}}{x}$. **375.** $\lim\limits_{x\to 0} \dfrac{e^{ax}-e^{bx}}{x}$.

376. $\lim\limits_{x\to\infty} x(e^{1/x}-1)$. **377.** $\lim\limits_{x\to\pm\infty} (\cosh x-\sinh x)$. **378.** $\lim\limits_{x\to\pm\infty} \tanh x$.

Various limits

In Problems 379 to 401 find the limits.

379. $\lim\limits_{x\to\infty} \dfrac{(ax+1)^n}{x^n+A}$. Consider separately the cases when n is (1) positive integer, (2) negative integer, (3) zero.

380. $\lim\limits_{x\to\pm\infty} x(\sqrt{x^2+\sqrt{x^4+1}}-x\sqrt{2})$.

381. $\lim\limits_{x\to\pm\infty} \frac{a^x}{a^x+1}$ $(a>0)$.

382. $\lim\limits_{x\to\pm\infty} \frac{a^x-a^{-x}}{a^x+a^{-x}}$ $(a>0)$.

383. $\lim\limits_{x\to\infty} \frac{\sin x}{x}$.

384. $\lim\limits_{x\to\infty} \frac{\arctan x}{x}$.

385. $\lim\limits_{x\to\infty} \frac{x+\sin x}{x+\cos x}$.

386. $\lim\limits_{x\to 1} \frac{\arcsin x}{\tan \frac{\pi x}{2}}$.

387. $\lim\limits_{h\to 0} \frac{\sin(a+3h)-3\sin(a+2h)+3\sin(a+h)-\sin a}{h^3}$.

388. $\lim\limits_{x\to\frac{\pi}{2}} \tan^2 x(\sqrt{2\sin^2 x+3\sin x+4}-\sqrt{\sin^2 x+6\sin x+2})$.

389. $\lim\limits_{x\to 0} \frac{1-\cos(1-\cos x)}{x^4}$.

390*. $\lim\limits_{n\to\infty} \left(\cos\frac{x}{2}\cdot\cos\frac{x}{4}\ldots\cos\frac{x}{2^n}\right)$.

391. $\lim\limits_{x\to\infty} x^2\left(1-\cos\frac{1}{x}\right)$.

392. $\lim\limits_{x\to\infty} (\cos\sqrt{x+1}-\cos\sqrt{x})$.

393*. $\lim\limits_{x\to\infty} x\left(\arctan\frac{x+1}{x+2}-\frac{\pi}{4}\right)$.

394. $\lim\limits_{x\to\infty} x\left(\arctan\frac{x+1}{x+2}-\arctan\frac{x}{x+2}\right)$.

395*. $\lim\limits_{x\to 0} \frac{\arcsin x-\arctan x}{x^3}$.

396. $\lim\limits_{x\to+\infty} \left(1+\frac{1}{x^n}\right)^x$ $(n>0)$.

397*. $\lim\limits_{x\to 0} (\cos x)^{1/\sin x}$.

398. $\lim\limits_{x\to 0} \frac{\ln\cos x}{x^2}$.

399. $\lim\limits_{x\to 0} \left(\frac{\sin x}{x}\right)^{\frac{\sin x}{x-\sin x}}$.

400. $\lim\limits_{x\to 0} (\cos x+\sin x)^{1/x}$.

401. $\lim\limits_{x\to 0} (\cos x+a\sin bx)^{1/x}$.

Comparison of infinitesimals

402. The infinitesimal u_n takes on the values

$$u_1=1,\ u_2=\frac{1}{2},\ u_3=\frac{1}{3},\ \ldots,\ u_n=\frac{1}{n},\ \ldots,$$

and the infinitesimal v_n attains the values

$$v_1=1,\ v_2=\frac{1}{2!},\ v_3=\frac{1}{3!},\ldots,\ v_n=\frac{1}{n!},\ldots$$

Compare the infinitesimals u_n and v_n, which of them is of higher order?

403. The function u_n takes on the values

$$u_1 = 0,\ u_2 = \frac{3}{8},\ u_3 = \frac{8}{27},\ \ldots,\ u_n = \frac{n^2-1}{n^3},\ \ldots,$$

and the function v_n, respectively,

$$v_1 = 2,\ v_2 = \frac{5}{8},\ v_3 = \frac{10}{27},\ldots,\ v_n = \frac{n^2+1}{n^3},\ldots$$

Compare these infinitesimals.

404. The infinitesimal u_n attains the values

$$u_1 = 0,\ u_2 = \frac{1}{4},\ u_3 = \frac{2}{9},\ldots,\ u_n = \frac{n-1}{n^2},\ldots,$$

and the infinitesimal v_n, respectively, the values

$$v_1 = 3,\ v_2 = \frac{5}{4},\quad v_3 = \frac{7}{9},\ldots,\ v_n = \frac{2n+1}{n^2},\ldots$$

Make sure that u_n and v_n are infinitesimals of one and the same order but not equivalent.

405. As $x \to 1$ the functions $y = \frac{1-x}{1+x}$ and $y = 1-\sqrt{x}$ are infinitesimals.

Which of them is of the higher order?

406. Given the function $y = x^3$. Show that Δy and Δx are infinitesimals of the same order as $\Delta x \to 0$ and for $x \neq 0$.

Check to see that for $x = 0$ the magnitude Δy is an infinitesimal of higher order, than Δx. For what x will the increments Δx and Δy be equivalent?

407. Make sure that as $x \to 1$ the infinitesimals $1 - x$ and $1 - \sqrt[3]{x}$ will be of the same order. Will they be equivalent?

408. Let $x \to 0$. Then $\sqrt{a + x^3} - \sqrt{a}(a > 0)$ will be an infinitesimal. Determine its order with respect to x.

409. Determine the order (with respect to x) of the function which is an infinitesimal as $x \to 0$:

(1) $x^3 + 1000x^2$; (2) $\sqrt[3]{x^2} - \sqrt{x}$; (3) $\frac{x(x+1)}{1+\sqrt{x}}$; (4) $\frac{7x^{10}}{x^3+1}$.

410. Prove that the increments of the functions $u = a\sqrt{x}$ and $v = bx^2$ for $x > 0$ as the total increment $\Delta x \to 0$, will be infinitesimals of the same order. For what value of x will they be equivalent (a and b being different from zero)?

411. Show that as $x \to 1$ the infinitesimals $1 - x$ and $a(1 - \sqrt[k]{x})$, where $a \neq 0$ and k is a positive integer, will be of the same order. For what a will they be equivalent?

412. Prove that as $x \to \frac{\pi}{2}$ the functions $\sec x - \tan x$ and $\pi - 2x$ will be infinitesimals of the same order. Will they be equivalent?

413. Prove that the infinitesimals $e^{2x} - e^x$ and $\sin 2x - \sin x$ will be equivalent as $x \to 0$.

414. Determine the order (with respect to x) of the function which is an infinitesimal as $x \to 0$

(1) $\sqrt[3]{1 + \sqrt[3]{x}} - 1$; (2) $\sqrt{1 + 2x} - 1 - \sqrt{x}$;

(3) $e^{\sqrt{x}} - 1$; (4) $e^{\sin x} - 1$;

(5) $\ln (1 + \sqrt{x \sin x})$; (6) $\sqrt{1 + x^2} \tan \dfrac{\pi x}{2}$;

(7) $e^x - \cos x$; (8) $e^{x^2} - \cos x$;

(9) $\cos x - \sqrt[3]{\cos x}$; (10) $\sin (\sqrt{1 + x} - 1)$;

(11) $\ln (1 + x^2) - 2\sqrt[3]{(e^x - 1)^2}$; (12) $\arcsin (\sqrt{4 + x^2} - 2)$.

Some geometrical problems

415. Given a regular triangle with the side a; a new regular triangle is formed by its altitudes, this procedure being repeated n times. Find the limit of the sum of areas of all the triangles as $n \to \infty$.

416. Inscribed in a circle of radius R is a square, a circle is inscribed in the square, a new square in the circle, and so on for n times. Find the limit of the sum of areas of all the circles and the limit of the sum of areas of all the squares as $n \to \infty$.

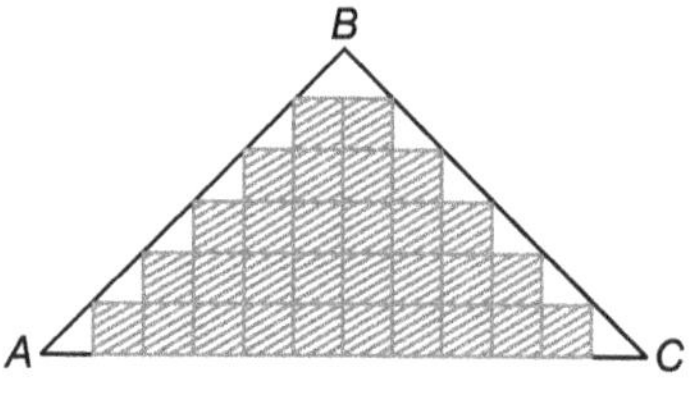

Fig. 15

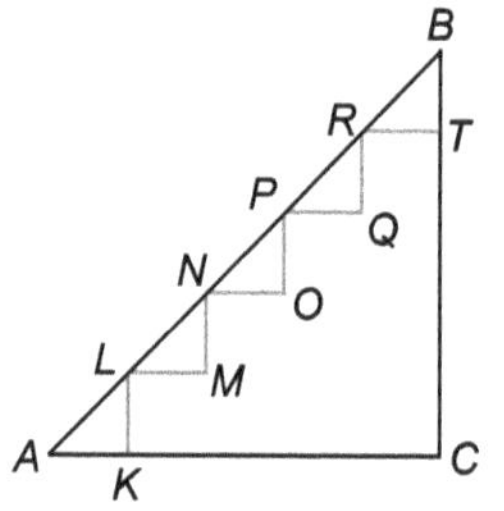

Fig. 16

417. A step-like figure is inscribed in an isosceles right-angled triangle whose base is divided into $2n$ equal parts (Fig. 15). Prove that the difference between the area of the triangle and that of the inscribed figure is an infinitesimal as n increases without bound.

418. In an isosceles right-angled triangle whose side is equal to a, the hypotenuse is divided into n equal parts and straight lines parallel to the sides are drawn from the points of division to form a polygonal line *AKLMNOPQRTB* (see Fig. 16).

The length of this line is equal to $2a$ for any n, hence the limit of its length is $2a$. But on the other hand, the polygonal line approaches without bound the hypotenuse of the triangle. Hence, the length of the hypotenuse is equal to the sum of the lengths of the sides. Find the error in reasoning.

419. The segment AB of length a is divided into equal parts by n points from which rays are drawn at an angle of $\frac{\pi}{2\pi}$ (Fig. 17).

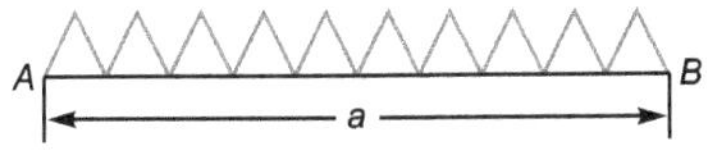

Fig. 17

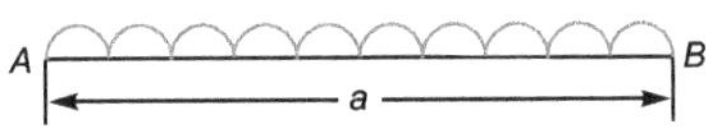

Fig. 18

Find the limit of the length of the polygonal line thus obtained as n tends to infinity. Compare the results of Problems 418 and 419.

420. The segment AB of length a is divided into n equal parts. Each small segment thus obtained subtends a circular arc equal to $\frac{\pi}{n}$ radians (Fig. 18). Find the length of the obtained line as $n \to \infty$. How will the result change if the arcs are replaced by semicircles?

421. A circle of radius R is divided into equal parts by n points: $M_1, M_2, \ldots, M_n$. From each point of division as from a centre a circular arc of radius r is drawn to intersect the arcs constructed at the neighbouring points (Fig. 19). Find the limit of the length of the closed line thus obtained as n increases without bound.

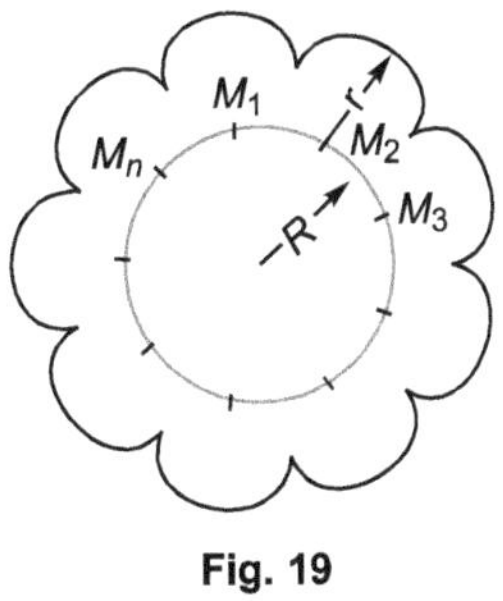

Fig. 19

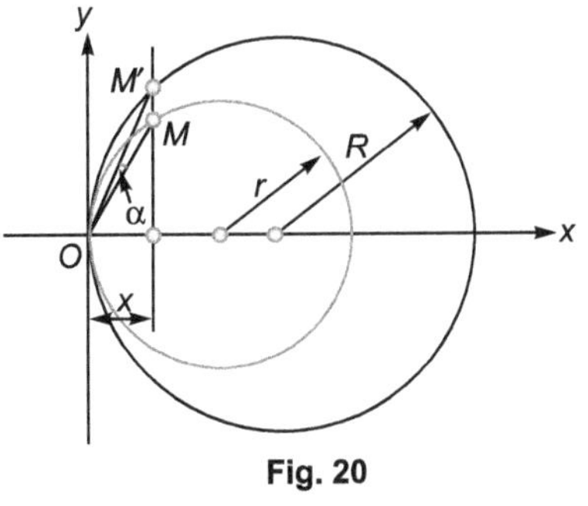

Fig. 20

422. Two circles of radii R and r $(R > r)$ are tangent to the y-axis at the origin and are situated to its right (Fig. 20). What order, with respect to x, will the infinitely small segment MM' and the infinitely small angle α be as $x \to 0$?

423. The centre of a circle is joined by a straight line OP with the point P found outside the circle. From the point P a tangent line is drawn to the circle and from the point T a perpendicular TN is dropped onto the straight line OP. Prove that the segments AP and AN, where A is the point of intersection of the straight line OP and the circle, are equivalent infinitesimals as $P \to A$.

424. At the end-points and the midpoint of a circular arc AB tangent lines are drawn, and the points A and B are joined with a chord. Prove that the ratio of the areas of the two triangles thus formed tends to 4 as the arc AB decreases infinitely.

Computational problems

425. Proceeding from the fact that the functions $\sqrt{1+x}-1$ and $\frac{1}{2}x$ are equivalent as $x \to 0$, compute approximately:

(1) $\sqrt{105}$; (2) $\sqrt{912}$; (3) $\sqrt{260}$;
(4) $\sqrt{1632}$; (5) $\sqrt{0.31}$; (6) $\sqrt{0.021}$.

426. Show that the functions $\sqrt[n]{1+x}-1$ and $\frac{x}{n}$ are equivalent infinitesimals as $x \to 0$. Take advantage of this fact for approximate computation of the following roots:

(1) $\sqrt[3]{1047}$; (2) $\sqrt[3]{8144}$; (3) $\sqrt[5]{1.1}$; $\sqrt[5]{1080}$.

Find the values of the same roots with the aid of the logarithmic tables. Compare the results.

427. Take advantage of the equivalence of $\ln(1+x)$ and x, as $x \to 0$ for approximate computation of the natural logarithms of the following numbers: 1.01, 1.02, 1.1, 1.2. Find the common logarithms of the same numbers and compare the results with the tabular values.

3

Derivative and Differential. Differential Calculus

1. Derivative. The Rate of Change of a Function

Some physical problems

428. Given the equation of rectilinear motion of a point $s = 5t + 6$. Determine the average velocity of motion : (a) for the first six seconds, (b) for the time interval from the end of the 3rd to the end of the 6th second.

429. Point M moves off a fixed point A so that the distance AM increases proportional to the squared time. In two minutes after its start the distance AM was equal to 12 m. Find the average velocity of motion : (a) for the first five minutes, (b) for the time interval from $t = 4$ min to $t = 7$ min, (c) for the time interval from $t = t_1$ to $t = t_2$.

430. Given the equation of rectilinear motion : $s = t^3 + \frac{3}{t}$. Find the average velocity of motion for the time interval from $t = 4$ to $t = 4 + \Delta t$, putting $\Delta t = 2, 1, 0.1, 0.03$.

431. A freely falling body moves according to the law $s = \frac{gt^2}{2}$, where $g \left(= 9.80 \frac{\text{m}}{\text{s}^2}\right)$ is the acceleration of gravity. Find the average velocity of motion for the time interval from $t = 5$ s to $(t + \Delta t)$ s, putting $\Delta t = 1$ s, 0.1 s, 0.05 s, 0.001 s, find the velocity of the falling body at the end of the 5th second, at the end of the 10th second. Derive the formula for determining the velocity of a falling body at any instant of time t.

432. There is a thin nonhomogeneous rod AB. Its length $L = 20$ cm. The mass of the portion AM increases directly proportional to the squared distance between the points A and M, and it is known that the mass of the portion $AM = 2$ cm equals 8 g. Find : (a) the mean mass density of the portion $AM = 2$ cm; (b) the same of the whole rod; (c) mass density of the rod at the point M.

433. In a thin nonhomogeneous rod AB 30 cm long the mass (in g) is distributed according to the law $m = 3l^2 + 5l$, where l is the length of a portion of the rod as measured from the point A. Find : (1) the mean mass density of the rod; (2) the linear mass density : (a) at the point 5 cm (l) distant from the point A, (b) at the point A itself, (c) at the end-point of the rod.

434. The quantity of heat Q (in calories) required for heating 1 g of water from 0° to t°C is determined by the formula

$$Q = t + 0.00002t^2 + 0.0000003t^3.$$

Compute the heat capacity of water for $t = 30°C$, $t = 100°C$.

435*. The angular velocity of uniform rotation is defined as the ratio of the angle of rotation to the corresponding time interval. Give the definition for the angular velocity of nonuniform rotation.

436. If the process of radioactive decay proceeded uniformly, then the rate of decay would be understood as the amount of substance decayed during unit time. But in reality this process is nonuniform. Give the definition for the rate of radioactive decay.

437. Intensity of direct current is defined as the quantity of electricity flowing through the cross section of a conductor in unit time. Give the definition for the intensity of alternating current.

438. Linear (thermal) expansion coefficient of a rod is defined as the change in length per unit length per degree (°C) in temperature if thermal expansion is assumed to be a uniform process. In reality it is a nonuniform process. Let $l = f(t)$, where l is the length of the rod, and t, temperature. Give the definition for the linear expansion coefficient.

439. Extension coefficient of a spring is defined as elongation per unit length of the spring under the action of unit force acting on each square centimetre of the cross section of the spring. It is obvious that extension is proportional to the tensile force (Hooke's law). Give the definition of the extension coefficient k for the case of deviation from Hooke's law. (Let l be the length of the spring; S, the cross-sectional area, P, tensile force, and $l = \varphi(P)$.)

The derivative of a function

440. Find the increment of the function $y = x^3$ at the point $x_1 = 2$, putting the increment Δx of the independent variable equal to : (1) 2; (2) 1; (3) 0.5; (4) 0.1.

441. Find the ratio $\frac{\Delta y}{\Delta x}$ for the functions:

(1) $y = 2x^3 - x^2 + 1$ for $x = 1$, $\Delta x = 0.1$;

(2) $y = \frac{1}{x}$ for $x = 2$, $\Delta x = 0.01$;

(3) $y = \sqrt{x}$ for $x = 4$, $\Delta x = 0.4$.

Show that as $\Delta x \to 0$, the limit of this ratio in the first case is equal to 4, in the second to $\left(-\frac{1}{4}\right)$, in the third to $\frac{1}{4}$.

442. Given the function $y = x^2$. Find the approximate values of the derivative at the point $x = 3$, putting Δx successively equal to : (a) 0.5; (b) 0.1; (c) 0.01; (d) 0.001.

443. $f(x) = x^2$. Find : $f'(5)$, $f'(-2)$, $f'\left(-\frac{3}{2}\right)$.

444. $f(x) = x^3$. Find : $f'(1)$, $f'(0)$, $f'(-\sqrt{2})$, $f'\left(\frac{1}{3}\right)$.

445. $f(x) = x^2$. At what point is $f(x) = f'(x)$?

446. Check to see that for the function $f(x) = x^2$ the relationship $f'(a+b) = f'(a) + f'(b)$ is valid. Will this identity be valid for the function $f(x) = x^3$?

447. Find the derivative of the function $y = \sin x$ at $x = 0$.

448. Find the derivative of the function $y = \log x$ at $x = 1$.

449. Find the derivative of the function $y = 10^x$ at $x = 0$.

450. It is known that $f(0) = 0$ and there exists a limit of the expression $\frac{f(x)}{x}$ as $x \to 0$. Prove that the limit is equal to $f'(0)$.

451. Prove the theorem : if $f(x)$ and $\varphi(x)$ are equal to zero for $x = 0$ $[f(0) = 0, \varphi(0) = 0]$ and have derivatives at $x = 0$, $\varphi'(0)$ being not equal to zero, then $\lim\limits_{x \to 0} \frac{f(x)}{\varphi(x)} = \frac{f'(0)}{\varphi'(0)}$.

452. Prove that if $f(x)$ has a derivative at $x = a$, then

$$\lim_{x \to a} \frac{xf(a) - af(x)}{x - a} = f(a) - af'(a).$$

453. Prove that a derivative of an even function is an odd function, and that of an odd function is an even function.

Geometrical meaning of the derivative

454. Find the slope of the tangent line drawn to the parabola $y = x^2$: (1) at the origin of coordinates, (2) at the point (3, 9), (3) at the point (– 2, 4), (4) at the points of intersection of the parabola with the straight line $y = 3x - 2$.

455. At what points is the slope of the tangent line to the cubical parabola $y = x^3$ equal to 3?

456. At what point is the tangent line to the parabola $y = x^3$: (1) parallel to the x-axis, (2) at an angle of 45° to the x-axis?

457. Is it possible for the tangent line to the cubical parabola $y = x^3$ to form an obtuse angle with the x-axis?

458. At what angles do the parabola $y = x^2$ and the straight line $3x - y - 2 = 0$ intersect?

459. At what angles do the parabolas $y = x^2$ and $y^2 = x$ intersect?

460. Determine the angle of intersection of the hyperbola $y = \frac{1}{x}$ and the parabola $y = \sqrt{x}$.

461. Write the equations of the tangent and the normal drawn to the curve $y = x^3$ at the point whose abscissa is equal to 2. Find the subtangent and subnormal.

462. For what value of the independent variable are the tangent lines to the curves $y = x^2$ and $y = x^3$ parallel?

463. At what point is the tangent to the parabola $y = x^2$: (1) parallel to the straight line $y = 4x - 5$; (2) perpendicular to the straight line $2x - 6y + 5 = 0$; (3) at an angle of 45° to the straight line $3x - y + 1 = 0$?

464. Prove that the subnormal corresponding to any point of the parabola $y = ax^2$ is equal to half the abscissa of the tangency point. Making use of this fact, give the method of constructing a line tangent to the parabola at a given point.

465. Prove that a normal to a parabola at any of its points serves as a bisector of the angle formed by the focal radius of the point and the straight line parallel to the parabola axis and passing through the given point.

2. Differentiating Functions

Power functions

In the problems of this section x, y, z, t, u, v, s denote independent variables, a, b, c, d, m, n, p, q, constants.

466. Differentiate the functions:

(1) $3x^2 - 5x + 1$; (2) $x^4 - \frac{1}{3}x^3 + 2.5x^2 - 0.3x + 0.1$; (3) $ax^2 + bx + c$;

(4) $\sqrt[3]{x} + \sqrt[3]{2}$; (5) $2\sqrt{x} - \frac{1}{x} + \sqrt[4]{3}$; (6) $0.8\sqrt[4]{y} - \frac{y^3}{0.3} + \frac{1}{5y^2}$;

(7) $\frac{x}{n} + \frac{n}{x} + \frac{x^2}{m^2} + \frac{m^2}{x^2}$; (8) $\frac{mx^2}{\sqrt{x}} + \frac{nx\sqrt{x}}{\sqrt[3]{x}} - \frac{p\sqrt{x}}{x}$; (9) $\frac{mz^2 + nz + 4p}{p + q}$;

(10) $0.1\,t^{-\frac{2}{3}} - \frac{5.2}{t^{1.4}} + \frac{2.5}{\sqrt[5]{t}}$; (11) $(x-0.5)^2$; (12) $\sqrt{x}\,(x^3 - \sqrt{x} + 1)$;

(13) $(v+1)^2\,(v-1)$; (14) $0.5 - 3\,(a-x)^2$;

(15) $\frac{ax^3 + bx^2 + c}{(a+b)\,x}$; (16) $\left(\frac{mu+n}{p}\right)^3$.

467. $f(x) = 3x - 2\sqrt{x}$. Find : $f(1)$, $f'(1)$, $f(4)$, $f'(4)$, $f(a^2)$, $f'(a^2)$.

468. $f(t) = \frac{t^2 - 5t - 1}{t^3}$. Find : $f(-1)$, $f'(-1)$, $f'(2)$, $f'\left(\frac{1}{a}\right)$.

469. $f(z) = \frac{2z^3 - 3z + \sqrt{z} - 1}{z}$. Find $f'\left(\frac{1}{4}\right)$.

470. $f(x) = 4 - 5x + 2x^3 - x^5$. Show that $f'(a) = f'(-a)$.

In Problems 471 to 489 differentiate the given functions.

471. (1) $y = (x^2 - 3x + 3)(x^2 + 2x - 1)$; (2) $y = (x^3 - 3x + 2)(x^4 + x^2 - 1)$;

(3) $y = (\sqrt{x} + 1)\left(\frac{1}{\sqrt{x}} - 1\right)$; (4) $y = \left(\frac{2}{\sqrt{x}} - \sqrt{3}\right)\left(4x\sqrt[3]{x} + \frac{\sqrt[3]{x^2}}{3x}\right)$;

(5) $y = (\sqrt[3]{x} + 2x)(1 + \sqrt[3]{x^2} + 3x)$; (6) $y = (x^2 - 1)(x^2 - 4)(x^2 - 9)$;

(7) $y = (1 + \sqrt{x})(1 + \sqrt{2x})(1 + \sqrt{3x})$.

472. $y = \frac{x+1}{x-1}$.

473. $y = \frac{x}{x^2+1}$.

474. $s = \frac{3t^2 + 1}{t - 1}$.

475. $u = \frac{v^3 - 2v}{v^2 + v + 1}$.

476. $y = \frac{ax+b}{cx+d}$.

477. $z = \frac{x^2+1}{3(x^2-1)} + (x^2-1)(1-x)$.

478. $u = \frac{v^5}{v^3 - 2}$.

479. $y = \frac{1 - x^3}{1 + x^3}$.

480. $y = \frac{2}{x^3 - 1}$.

481. $u = \frac{v^2 - v + 1}{a^2 - 3}$.

482. $y = \frac{1 - x^3}{\sqrt{\pi}}$.

483. $z = \frac{1}{t^2 + t + 1}$.

484. $s = \frac{1}{t^2 - 3t + 6}$.

485. $y = \frac{2x^4}{b^2 - x^2}$.

486. $y = \frac{x^2 + x - 1}{x^3 + 1}$.

487. $y = \frac{3}{(1 - x^2)(1 - 2x^3)}$.

488. $y = \frac{ax + bx^2}{am + bm^2}$.

489. $y = \frac{a^2b^2c^2}{(x-a)(x-b)(x-c)}$.

490. $f(x) = (x^2 + x + 1)(x^2 - x + 1)$. Find $f'(0)$ and $f'(1)$.

491. $F(x) = (x - 1)(x - 2)(x - 3)$. Find $F'(0)$, $F'(1)$ and $F'(2)$.

492. $F(x) = \dfrac{1}{x + 2} + \dfrac{3}{x^2 + 1}$. Find $F'(0)$ and $F'(-1)$.

493. $s(t) = \dfrac{3}{5 - t} + \dfrac{t^2}{5}$. Find $s'(0)$ and $s'(2)$.

494. $y(x) = (1 + x^3)\left(5 - \dfrac{1}{x^2}\right)$. Find $y'(1)$ and $y'(a)$.

495. $\rho(\varphi) = \dfrac{\varphi}{1 - \varphi^2}$. Find $\rho'(2)$ and $\rho'(0)$.

496. $\varphi(z) = \dfrac{a - z}{1 + z}$. Find $\varphi'(1)$.

497. $z(t) = (\sqrt{t^3} + 1)t$. Find $z'(0)$.

In Problems 498 to 513 differentiate the given functions.

498. (1) $(x - a)(x - b)(x - c)(x - d)$; (2) $(x^2 + 1)^4$; (3) $(1 - x)^{20}$; (4) $(1 + 2x)^{30}$; (5) $(1 - x^2)^{10}$; (6) $(5x^3 + x^2 - 4)^5$; (7) $(x^3 - x)^6$; (8) $\left(7x^2 - \dfrac{4}{x} + 6\right)^6$; (9) $s = \left(t^3 - \dfrac{1}{t^3} + 3\right)^4$; (10) $y = \left(\dfrac{x + 1}{x - 1}\right)^2$; (11) $y = \left(\dfrac{1 + x^2}{1 + x}\right)^5$; (12) $y = (2x^3 + 3x^2 + 6x + 1)^4$.

499. $v = \dfrac{(s + 4)^2}{s + 3}$. **500.** $s = \dfrac{t^3}{(1 - t)^2}$. **501.** $y = \dfrac{1 + \sqrt{x}}{1 + \sqrt{2x}}$.

502. $y = \dfrac{1 - \sqrt[3]{2x}}{1 + \sqrt[3]{2x}}$. **503.** $y = \sqrt{1 - x^2}$. **504.** $y = (1 - 2x^{1/2})$.

505. $u = \left(\dfrac{v}{1 - v}\right)^m$. **506.** $y = \dfrac{2}{(x^2 - x + 1)^2}$. **507.** $y = \dfrac{1}{\sqrt{a^2 - x^2}}$.

508. $y = \sqrt[3]{\dfrac{1}{1 + x^2}}$. **509.** $y = \dfrac{1}{\sqrt{1 - x^4 - x^8}}$. **510.** $y = \dfrac{1 + x}{\sqrt{1 - x}}$.

511. $y = \dfrac{x^2}{\sqrt{x^2 + a^2}}$. **512.** $u = \dfrac{1}{v - \sqrt{a^2 + v^2}}$.

513. $y = \dfrac{1}{\sqrt[3]{2x - 1}} + \dfrac{5}{\sqrt[4]{(x^2 + 2)^3}}$. **514.** $u(v) = (v^2 + v + 2)^{3/2}$. Find $u'(1)$.

515. $y(x) = \sqrt{\dfrac{x + 1}{x - 1}}$. Find $y'(2)$. **516.** $y(x) = \sqrt{\dfrac{1 - x^2}{1 + x^2}}$. Find $y'(0)$.

Trigonometric functions

In Problems 517 to 546 differentiate the given functions.

517. $y = \sin x + \cos x.$

518. $y = \dfrac{x}{1 - \cos x}.$

519. $y = \dfrac{\tan x}{x}.$

520. $\rho = \varphi \sin \varphi + \cos \varphi.$

521. $z = \dfrac{\sin \alpha}{\alpha} + \dfrac{\alpha}{\sin \alpha}.$

522. $s = \dfrac{\sin t}{1 + \cos t}.$

523. $y = \dfrac{x}{\sin x + \cos x}.$

524. $y = \dfrac{x \sin x}{1 + \tan x}.$

525. $y = \cos^2 x.$

526. $y = \dfrac{1}{4} \tan^4 x.$

527. $y = \cos x - \dfrac{1}{3} \cos^3 x.$

528. $y = 3 \sin^2 x - \sin^3 x.$

529. $y = \dfrac{1}{3} \tan^3 x - \tan x + x.$

530. $y = x \sec^2 x - \tan x.$

531. $y = \sec^2 x + \operatorname{cosec}^2 x.$

532. $y = \sin 3x.$

533. $y = a \cos \dfrac{x}{3}.$

534. $y = 3 \sin (3x + 5).$

535. $y = \tan \dfrac{x + 1}{2}.$

536. $y = \sqrt{1 + 2 \tan x}.$

537. $y = \sin \dfrac{1}{x}.$

538. $y = \sin (\sin x).$

539. $y = \cos^3 4x.$

540. $y = \sqrt{\tan \dfrac{x}{2}}.$

541. $y = \sin \sqrt{1 + x^2}.$

542. $y = \cot \sqrt[3]{1 + x^2}.$

543. $y = (1 + \sin^2 x)^4.$

544. $y = \sqrt{1 + \tan \left(x + \dfrac{1}{x}\right)}.$

545. $y = \cos^2 \dfrac{1 - \sqrt{x}}{1 + \sqrt{x}}.$

546. $y = \sin^2 (\cos 3x).$

547. Deduce the following formulas

$$(\sin^n x \cos nx)' = n \sin^{n-1} x \cos (n + 1) x;$$
$$(\sin^n x \sin nx)' = n \sin^{n-1} x \sin (n + 1) x;$$
$$(\cos^n x \sin nx)' = n \cos^{n-1} x \cos (n + 1) x;$$
$$(\cos^n x \cos nx)' = - n \cos^{n-1} x \sin (n + 1) x.$$

Inverse trigonometric functions

In Problems 548 to 572 differentiate the given functions.

548. $y = x \arcsin x.$

549. $y = \dfrac{\arcsin x}{\arccos x}.$

550. $y = (\arcsin x)^2.$

551. $y = x \arcsin x + \sqrt{1 - x^2}.$

552. $y = \dfrac{1}{\arcsin x}$.

553. $y = x \sin x \arctan x$.

554. $y = \dfrac{\arccos x}{x}$.

555. $y = \sqrt{x} \cdot \arctan x$.

556. $y = (\arccos x + \arcsin x)^n$.

557. $y = \operatorname{arcsec} x$.

558. $y = \dfrac{x}{1 + x^2} - \arctan x$.

559. $y = \dfrac{\arcsin x}{\sqrt{1 - x^2}}$.

560. $y = \dfrac{x^2}{\arctan x}$.

561. $y = \arcsin (x - 1)$.

562. $y = \arccos \dfrac{2x - 1}{\sqrt{3}}$.

563. $y = \arctan x^2$.

564. $y = \arcsin \dfrac{2}{x}$.

565. $y = \arcsin (\sin x)$.

566. $y = \arctan^2 \dfrac{1}{x}$.

567. $y = \sqrt{1 - (\arccos x)^2}$.

568. $y = \arcsin \sqrt{\dfrac{1 - x}{1 + x}}$.

569. $y = \dfrac{1}{2} \sqrt[4]{\arcsin \sqrt{x^2 + 2x}}$.

570. $y = \arcsin \dfrac{\sin \alpha \sin x}{1 - \cos \alpha \sin x}$.

571. $y = \arccos \dfrac{b + a \cos x}{a + b \cos x}$.

572. $y = \arctan (x - \sqrt{1 + x^2})$.

Logarithmic functions

In Problems 573 to 597 differentiate the given functions.

573. $y = x^2 \log_3 x$.

574. $y = \ln^2 x$.

575. $y = x \log_{10} x$.

576. $y = \sqrt{\ln x}$.

577. $y = \dfrac{x - 1}{\log_2 x}$.

578. $y = x \sin x \ln x$.

579. $y = \dfrac{1}{\ln x}$.

580. $y = \dfrac{\ln x}{x^n}$.

581. $y = \dfrac{1 - \ln x}{1 + \ln x}$.

582. $y = \dfrac{\ln x}{1 + x^2}$.

583. $y = x^n \ln x$.

584. $y = \sqrt{1 + \ln^2 x}$.

585. $y = \ln (1 - 2x)$.

586. $y = \ln (x^2 - 4x)$.

587. $y = \ln \sin x$.

588. $y = \log_3 (x^2 - 1)$.

589. $y = \ln \tan x$.

590. $y = \ln \arccos 2x$.

591. $y = \ln^4 \sin x$.

592. $y = \arctan [\ln (ax + b)]$.

593. $y = (1 + \ln \sin x)^n$.

594. $y = \log_2 [\log_3 (\log_5 x)]$.

595. $y = \ln \arctan \sqrt{1 + x^2}$.

596. $y = \arcsin^2 [\ln (a^3 + x^3)]$.

597. $y = \sqrt[3]{\ln \sin \dfrac{x + 3}{4}}$.

Exponential functions

In Problems 598 to 633 differentiate the given functions.

598. $y = 2^x$. **599.** $y = 10^x$. **600.** $y = \dfrac{1}{3^x}$.

601. $y = \dfrac{x}{4^x}$. **602.** $y = x \cdot 10^x$. **603.** $y = xe^x$.

604. $y = \dfrac{x}{e^x}$. **605.** $y = \dfrac{x^3 + 2^x}{e^x}$. **606.** $y = e^x \cos x$.

607. $y = \dfrac{e^x}{\sin x}$. **608.** $y = \dfrac{\cos x}{e^x}$. **609.** $y = 2^{\frac{x}{\ln x}}$.

610. $y = x^3 - 3^x$. **611.** $y = \sqrt{1 + e^x}$.

612. $y = (x^2 - 2x + 3)\, e^x$. **613.** $y = \dfrac{1 + e^x}{1 - e^x}$.

614. $y = \dfrac{1 - 10^x}{1 + 10^x}$. **615.** $y = \dfrac{e^x}{1 + x^2}$.

616. $y = xe^x (\cos x + \sin x)$. **617.** $y = e^{-x}$.

618. $y = 10^{2x - 3}$. **619.** $y = e^{\sqrt{x + 1}}$.

620. $y = \sin (2^x)$. **621.** $y = 3^{\sin x}$.

622. $y = a^{\sin 3^x}$. **623.** $y = e^{\arcsin^2 x}$.

624. $y = 2^{3^x}$. **625.** $y = e^{\sqrt{\ln x}}$.

626. $y = \sin (e^{x^2 + 3x - 2})$. **627.** $y = 10^{1 - \sin^4 3x}$.

628. $y = e^{\sqrt{\ln (ax^2 + bx + c)}}$. **629.** $y = \ln \sin \sqrt[3]{\arctan e^{3x}}$.

630. $y = ae^{-b^2x^2}$. **631.** $y = x^2 e^{-\frac{x^2}{a^2}}$.

632. $y = Ae^{-k^2x} \sin (\omega x + \alpha)$. **633.** $y = a^x x^a$.

Hyperbolic functions

In Problems 634 to 649 differentiate the given functions.

634. $y = \sinh^3 x$. **635.** $y = \ln \cosh x$.

636. $y = \arctan (\tanh x)$. **637.** $y = \tanh (1 - x^2)$.

638. $y = \sinh^2 x - \cosh^2 x$. **639.** $y = \cosh (\sinh x)$.

640. $y = \sqrt{\cosh x}$. **641.** $y = e^{\cosh^2 x}$.

642. $y = \tanh (\ln x)$. **643.** $y = x \sinh x - \cosh x$.

644. $y = \sqrt[4]{(1 + \tanh^2 x)^3}$. **645.** $y = \dfrac{1}{2} \tanh \dfrac{x}{2} - \dfrac{1}{6} \tanh^3 \dfrac{x}{2}$.

646. $y = \sqrt[4]{\frac{1 + \tanh x}{1 - \tanh x}}$. **647.** $y = \frac{1}{2} \tanh x + \frac{\sqrt{2}}{8} \ln \frac{1 + \sqrt{2} \tanh x}{1 - \sqrt{2} \tanh x}$.

648. $y = \frac{1}{x} \cosh 2x + \sqrt{x} \sinh 2x$. **649.** $y = x^2 e^{3x} \cosh x$.

Logarithmic differentiation

In Problems 650 to 666 differentiate the given functions using the rules for logarithmic differentiation.

650. $y = x^{x^2}$. **651.** $y = x^{x^x}$.

652. $y = (\sin x)^{\cos x}$. **653.** $y = (\ln x)^x$.

654. $y = (x + 1)^{2/x}$. **655.** $y = x^3 e^{x^2} \sin 2x$.

656. $y = \frac{(x - 2)^2 \sqrt[3]{x + 1}}{(x - 5)^3}$. **657.** $y = x^{\ln x}$.

658. $y = \frac{(x + 1)^3 \sqrt[4]{x - 2}}{\sqrt[5]{(x - 3)^2}}$. **659.** $y = \sqrt{x \sin x \sqrt{1 - e^x}}$.

660. $y = \sqrt{\frac{1 - \arcsin x}{1 + \arcsin x}}$. **661.** $y = x^{1/x}$.

662. $y = x^{\sin x}$. **663.** $y = \left(\frac{x}{1 + x}\right)^x$.

664. $y = 2x^{\sqrt{x}}$. **665.** $y = (x^2 + 1)^{\sin x}$.

666. $y = \sqrt[3]{\frac{x\,(x^2 + 1)}{(x^2 - 1)^2}}$.

Miscellaneous functions

In Problems 667 to 770 differentiate the given functions.

667. $y = (1 + \sqrt[3]{x})^3$. **668.** $y = a \tan\left(\frac{x}{k} + b\right)$.

669. $y = \sqrt{1 + \sqrt{2px}}$. **670.** $y = \arctan (x^2 - 3x + 2)$.

671. $y = \log_{10} (x - \cos x)$. **672.** $y = 3 \cos^2 x - \cos^3 x$.

673. $y = 5 \tan \frac{x}{5} + \tan \frac{\pi}{8}$. **674.** $y = \frac{1}{\sqrt[3]{x + \sqrt{x}}}$.

675. $y = \sin \frac{x}{2} \sin 2x$. **676.** $y = \sin x \cdot e^{\cos x}$.

677. $y = x^5 \sqrt[3]{x^6 - 8}$. **678.** $y = e^{-x^2} \ln x$.

679. $y = \left(\sqrt{x} + \frac{1}{\sqrt{x}}\right)^{10}$. **680.** $y = \arctan \frac{x + 1}{x - 1}$.

681. $y = e^{2x+3}\left(x^2 - x + \frac{1}{2}\right)$.

682. $y = \frac{2\sin^2 x}{\cos 2x}$.

683. $y = \frac{1}{\sqrt{3}} \arctan \frac{x\sqrt{3}}{1 - x^2}$.

684. $y = \frac{\tan \frac{x}{2} + \cot \frac{x}{2}}{x}$.

685. $y = \sin^2 \frac{x}{3} \cot \frac{x}{2}$.

686. $y = \frac{\sqrt[9]{4x^5 + 2}}{3x^4}$.

687. $\ln (x + \sqrt{a^2 + x^2})$.

688. $y = x \arctan \sqrt{x}$.

689. $y = \sqrt{1 + \tan^2 x + \tan^4 x}$.

690. $y = \cos 2x \ln x$.

691. $y = \frac{2}{3} \arctan x + \frac{1}{3} \arctan \frac{x}{1 - x^2}$.

692. $y = \arcsin (n \sin x)$.

693. $y = \arcsin \sqrt{\sin x}$.

694. $y = \frac{1}{18} \sin^6 3x - \frac{1}{24} \sin^8 3x$.

695. $y = x - \sqrt{1 - x^2} \arcsin x$.

696. $y = \cos \frac{\arcsin x}{2}$.

697. $y = \sqrt{x + \sqrt{x + \sqrt{x}}}$.

698. $y = \arccos \sqrt{1 - 3x}$.

699. $y = \sin^2 \left(\frac{1 - \ln x}{x}\right)$.

700. $y = \log_3 (x^2 - \sin x)$.

701. $y = \arctan \sqrt{\frac{1 - x}{1 + x}}$.

702. $y = \ln \frac{x + \sqrt{1 - x^2}}{x}$.

703. $y = x \arcsin (\ln x)$.

704. $y = \tan \frac{1 - e^x}{1 + e^x}$.

705. $y = \cos x \sqrt{1 + \sin^2 x}$.

706. $y = 0.4\left(\cos \frac{2x + 1}{2} - \sin 0.8\, x\right)^2$.

707. $y = x \cdot 10^{\sqrt{x}}$.

708. $y = \frac{1}{\tan^2 2x}$.

709. $y = \ln \arctan \frac{1}{1 + x}$.

710. $y = \ln \frac{1}{x + \sqrt{x^2 - 1}}$.

711. $y = \sqrt[3]{1 + x\sqrt{x + 3}}$.

712. $y = x^2 \sqrt{1 + \sqrt{x}}$.

713. $y = \frac{1}{\sqrt{1 + \sin^2 x}}$.

714. $y = x^3 \arctan x^3$.

715. $y = \frac{\ln \sin x}{\ln \cos x}$.

716. $y = \arcsin x + \sqrt{1 - x^2}$.

717. $y = \frac{\arcsin 4x}{1 - 4x}$.

718. $y = e^{\frac{1}{\ln x}}$.

719. $y = \frac{1 - e^x}{e^x}$.

720. $y = 10^{x \tan x}$.

721. $y = \sin^2 x \cdot \sin x^2$.

722. $y = \frac{2 \cos x}{\sqrt{\cos 2x}}$.

723. $y = x \sqrt{\frac{1 - x}{1 + x^2}}$.

724. $y = \frac{1}{4} \ln \frac{1 + x}{1 - x} - \frac{1}{2} \arctan x$.

725. $y = 2^{\frac{x}{\ln x}}$.

726. $y = \sqrt{(a - x)(x - b)} - (a - b) \arctan \sqrt{\frac{a - x}{x - b}}$.

727. $y = \frac{\sin 3x}{2 \sin^2 x \cos x}$.

728. $y = e^{\sqrt{\frac{1 - x}{1 + x}}}$.

729. $y = \sqrt{a^2 - x^2} - a \arccos \frac{x}{a}$.

730. $y = \sqrt{x^2 + 1} - \ln \left(\frac{1}{x} + \sqrt{1 + \frac{1}{x^2}} \right)$.

731. $y = \frac{\sin^2 x}{1 + \cot x} + \frac{\cos^2 x}{1 + \tan x}$.

732. $y = \ln (x + \sqrt{x^2 - 1}) - \frac{x}{\sqrt{x^2 - 1}}$.

733. $y = e^{ax} (a \sin x - \cos x)$.

734. $y = xe^{1 - \cos x}$.

735. $y = \frac{1}{\arctan e^{-2x}}$.

736. $y = e^x (\sin 3x - 3 \cos 3x)$.

737. $y = 3x^3 \arcsin x + (x^2 + 2) \sqrt{1 - x^2}$.

738. $y = \frac{1}{\sqrt{1 + e^{-\sqrt{x}}}}$.

739. $y = 2 \arcsin \frac{x - 2}{\sqrt{6}} - \sqrt{2 + 4x - x^2}$.

740. $y = \ln (e^x \cos x + e^{-x} \sin x)$.

741. $y = \frac{1 + x \arctan x}{\sqrt{1 + x^2}}$.

742. $y = \frac{1}{\cos (x - \cos x)}$.

743. $y = e^x \sin x \cos^3 x$.

744. $y = \sqrt[11]{9 + 6 \sqrt[5]{x^9}}$.

745. $y = x - \ln (2e^x + 1 + \sqrt{e^{2x} + 4e^x + 1})$.

746. $y = e^{\arctan \sqrt{1 + \ln (2x + 3)}}$.

747. $y = \frac{e^{x^2}}{e^x + e^{-x}}$.

748. $y = \ln \tan \frac{x}{2} - \cot x \ln (1 + \sin x) - x$.

749. $y = 2 \ln (2x - 3\sqrt{1 - 4x^2}) - 6 \arcsin 2x$.

750. $y = \frac{3x^2 - 1}{3x^3} + \ln \sqrt{1 + x^2} + \arctan x$.

751. $y = \frac{1}{2} (3 - x) \sqrt{1 - 2x - x^2} + 2 \arcsin \frac{x + 1}{\sqrt{2}}$.

752. $y = \ln (x \sin x \sqrt{1 - x^2})$.

753. $y = x\sqrt{1 + x^2} \sin x$.

754. $y = \dfrac{\sqrt{x+2}\,(3-x)^4}{(x+1)^5}$.

755. $y = \sqrt[5]{(1 + xe^{\sqrt{x}})^3}$.

756. $y = \dfrac{1}{\sqrt{x}} e^{x^2 - \arctan x + \frac{1}{2}\ln x + 1}$.

757. $y = \dfrac{\sin x}{4\cos^4 x} + \dfrac{3\sin x}{8\cos^2 x} + \dfrac{3}{8}\ln \dfrac{1 + \tan\frac{x}{2}}{1 - \tan\frac{x}{2}}$.

758. $y = \dfrac{xe^x \arctan x}{\ln^5 x}$.

759. $y = \dfrac{(1 - x^2)\,e^{3x-1}\cos x}{(\arccos x)^3}$.

760. $y = x\sqrt{(x^2 + a^2)^3} + \dfrac{3a^2 x}{2}\sqrt{x^2 + a^2} + \dfrac{3a^4}{2}\ln (x + \sqrt{x^2 + a^2})$.

761. $y = x(\arcsin x)^2 - 2x + 2\sqrt{1 - x^2}\arcsin x$.

762. $y = \ln\cos\left(\arctan \dfrac{e^x - e^{-x}}{2}\right)$.

763. $y = \dfrac{-1}{m\sqrt{ab}}\arctan\left(e^{mx}\sqrt{\dfrac{a}{b}}\right)$.

764. $y = \dfrac{1}{3}\ln \dfrac{x+1}{\sqrt{x^2 - x + 1}} + \dfrac{1}{\sqrt{3}}\arctan \dfrac{2x-1}{\sqrt{3}}$.

765. $y = \ln \dfrac{\sqrt{1+x} - \sqrt{1-x}}{\sqrt{1+x} + \sqrt{1-x}} + 2\arctan\sqrt{\dfrac{1-x}{1+x}}$.

766. $y = (\tan 2x)^{\cot \frac{x}{2}}$.

767. $y = \sqrt[3]{\dfrac{x-5}{\sqrt[5]{x^2+4}}}$.

768. $y = \ln\sqrt[4]{\dfrac{x^2 + x + 1}{x^2 - x + 1}} + \dfrac{1}{2\sqrt{3}}\left(\arctan \dfrac{2x+1}{\sqrt{3}} + \arctan \dfrac{2x-1}{\sqrt{3}}\right)$.

769. $y = \arccos \dfrac{x^{2n} - 1}{x^{2n} + 1}$.

770. $y = -\dfrac{x}{1 + 8x^3} + \dfrac{1}{12}\ln \dfrac{(1+2x)^2}{1 - 2x + 4x^2} + \dfrac{\sqrt{3}}{6}\arctan \dfrac{4x-1}{\sqrt{3}}$.

771. Prove that the function $y = \ln \dfrac{1}{1+x}$ satisfies the relationship

$$xy' + 1 = e^y.$$

772. Prove that the function $y = \dfrac{x^2}{2} + \dfrac{1}{2}x\sqrt{x^2+1} + \ln\sqrt{x + \sqrt{x^2+1}}$ satisfies the relationship $2y = xy' + \ln y'$.

773. Prove that the function $y = \dfrac{\arcsin x}{\sqrt{1 - x^2}}$ satisfies the relationship $(1 - x^2)y' - xy = 1$.

774*. Compute the sums

(a) $1 + 2x + 3x^2 + \ldots + nx^{n-1}$;

(b) $2 + 2 \cdot 3x + 3 \cdot 4x^2 + \ldots + n(n-1)x^{n-2}$.

Inverse functions

775. Suppose that the rule for differentiating a power function is established only for positive integral exponents. Derive the formula for differentiating a root, using the rule for differentiating inverse function.

776. $x = e^{\arcsin y}$. Find the expression for $\frac{dy}{dx}$ in terms of y, in terms of x.

777. $t = 2 - 3s + s^3$. Express $\frac{ds}{dt}$ in terms of s.

778. $u = \frac{1}{2} \ln \frac{1+v}{1-v}$. Check the relation $\frac{du}{dv} \cdot \frac{dv}{du} = 1$.

779. Knowing that $\arcsin \sqrt{x}$ and $\sin^2 x$ are mutually inverse functions and that $(\sin^2 x)' = \sin 2x$, find $(\arcsin \sqrt{x})'$.

780. Let us denote the inverse of the function $y = x^x$ as $\alpha(x)$, i.e., let us suppose that from $y = x^x$ it follows that $x = \alpha(y)$. Find the formula for the derivative of the function $y = \alpha(x)$.

781. The inverse functions of the corresponding hyperbolic functions are denoted as $\sinh^{-1} x$, $\cosh^{-1} x$, $\tanh^{-1} x$. Find the derivatives of these functions.

782. $s = te^{-t}$. Find $\frac{dt}{ds}$.

783. $y = \frac{1 - x^4}{1 + x^4}$. Express $\frac{dx}{dy}$ in terms of x, in terms of y. Show that the relation $\frac{dy}{dx} \cdot \frac{dx}{dy} = 1$ is valid.

784. $x = y^3 - 4y + 1$. Find $\frac{dy}{dx}$.

785. $t = \arcsin 2^s$. Find the expression for $\frac{ds}{dt}$ in terms of s; in terms of t.

786. Verify the validity of the relationship $\frac{dy}{dx} \cdot \frac{dx}{dy} = 1$ if x and y are related in the following way:

(1) $y = x^2 + ax + b$; (2) $y = x^{-n}$; (3) $y = \ln(x^2 - 1)$.

Implicit functions

787. Make sure by differentiation that the derivatives of both members of the equality $\sin^2 x = 1 - \cos^2 x$ are identically equal to each other.

788. Make sure by differentiation that the derivatives of both members of the equality

$$\frac{2\sin^2 x - 1}{\cos x} + \frac{\cos x\,(2\sin x + 1)}{1 + \sin x} = \tan x$$

are identically equal to each other.

789. What is the slope of the tangent line drawn to the ellipse

$$\frac{x^2}{2} + \frac{y^2}{4} = 1 \text{ at the point } (1, \sqrt{2})?$$

790. What is the slope of the tangent line drawn to the hyperbola $xy = a\ (a \neq 0)$ at the point $(a, 1)$?

791. What is the slope of the tangent line drawn to the circle $(x-1)^2 + (y+3)^2 = 17$ at the point $(2, 1)$?

In Problems 792 to 812 find the derivatives of the implicit functions.

792. $\frac{x^2}{a^2} + \frac{y^2}{b^2} = 1.$

793. $x^{1/2} + y^{1/2} = a^{1/2}.$

794. $x^3 + y^3 - 3axy = 0.$

795. $y^2 \cos x = a^2 \sin 3x.$

796. $y^3 - 3y + 2ax = 0.$

797. $y^2 - 2xy + b^2 = 0.$

798. $x^4 + y^4 = x^2y^2.$

799. $x^3 + ax^2y + bxy^2 + y^3 = 0.$

800. $\sin(xy) + \cos(xy) = \tan(x+y).$

801. $2^x + 2^y = 2^{x+y}.$

802. $2y \ln y = x.$

803. $x - y = \arcsin x - \arcsin y.$

804. $x^y = y^x.$

805. $y = \cos(x+y).$

806. $\cos(xy) = x.$

807. $x^{2/3} + y^{2/3} = a^{2/3}.$

808. $y = 1 + xe^y.$

809. $x \sin y - \cos y + \cos 2y = 0.$

810. $\tan\frac{y}{2} = \sqrt{\frac{1-k}{1+k}}\tan\frac{x}{2}.$

811. $y \sin x - \cos(x-y) = 0.$

812. $y = x + \arctan y.$

813. Make sure that the function y defined by the equation $xy - \ln y = 1$ also satisfies the relationship

$$y^2 + (xy - 1)\frac{dy}{dx} = 0.$$

Applications of the derivative

814. Two points with the abscissas $x_1 = 1$ and $x_2 = 3$ are taken on the parabola $y = x^2$. A secant is drawn through these points. At what point of the parabola will the tangent to it be parallel to the secant?

815. Drawn through the focus of a parabola is a chord perpendicular to the axis of the parabola. Two tangent lines are drawn through the points of intersection of the chord and the parabola. Prove that the tangents intersect at right angles.

816. Derive the equations of the tangent and the normal to the hyperbola $y = \frac{1}{x}$ at the point $x = -\frac{1}{2}$. Find the subtangent and the subnormal.

817. Show that the segment of a tangent to the hyperbola $y = \frac{a}{x}$ contained between the axes of coordinates is bisected at the point of tangency.

818. Show that for the hyperbola $xy = a$ the area of the triangle formed by any tangent and the axes of coordinates equals the square of the semiaxis of the hyperbola.

819. A point moves in a straight line so that its distance from the start in t second is equal to $s = \frac{1}{4}t^4 - 4t^3 + 16t^2$.

(a) At what times was the point at the start?

(b) At what times is its velocity equal to zero?

820. A body whose mass is 3 kg performs rectilinear motion according to the formula $s = 1 + t + t^2$, where s is measured in centimetres, and t in seconds. Determine the kinetic energy $\left(\frac{mv^2}{2}\right)$ of the body in 5 s after its start.

821. The angle α through which a pulley turns with time t is specified by the function $\alpha = t^2 + 3t - 5$. Find the angular velocity for $t = 5$ s.

822. A wheel rotates so that the angle of rotation is proportional to the square of time. The first revolution was performed by the wheel for 8 s. Find the angular velocity ω in 32 s after the wheel started.

823. The angle θ through which a wheel turns for t second is equal to $\theta = at^2 - bt + c$, where a, b, c are positive constants. Find the angular velocity ω of the moving wheel. At what instant will the angular velocity be equal to zero?

824. The charge flowing through a conductor beginning with time $t = 0$ is given by the formula

$$Q = 2t^2 + 3t + 1 \text{ (coulombs)}.$$

Find the current intensity at the end of the fifth second.

825. On the curve $y = x^2 (x - 2)^2$ find the points at which the tangents are parallel to the x-axis.

826. Show that the curve $y = x^5 + 5x - 12$ at all its points is inclined to the x-axis at an acute angle.

827. At what points of the curve $y = x^3 + x - 2$ is its tangent parallel to the straight line $y = 4x - 1$?

828. Derive the equations of the tangents to the curve $y = x - \frac{1}{x}$ at the points of its intersection with the x-axis.

829. Derive the equation of the tangent to the curve $y = x^3 + 3x^2 - 5$ perpendicular to the straight line $2x - 6y + 1 = 0$.

In Problems 830 to 833 derive the equations of the tangent and the normal to the given curves.

830. $y = \sin x$ at the point $M\ (x_0, y_0)$.

831. $y = \ln x$ at the point $M\ (x_0, y_0)$.

832. $y = \dfrac{8a^3}{4a^2 + x^2}$ at the point with the abscissa $x = 2a$.

833. $y^2 = \dfrac{x^3}{2a - x}$ (cissoid) at the point $M\ (x_0, y_0)$.

834. Show that the subtangent to the parabola of the nth order $y = x^n$ is n times less than the abscissa of the point of tangency.

Give the method of constructing a tangent to the curve $y = x^n$.

835. Find the subtangents and the subnormals to the curves $y = x^3$, $y^2 = x^3$, $xy^2 = 1$. Give the method of constructing tangents to these curves.

836. Derive the equations of the tangent and the normal to the parabola $x^2 = 4ay$ at the point (x_0, y_0); show that the tangent at the point with the abscissa $x_0 = 2am$ has the equation $x = \frac{y}{m} + am$.

837. A chord of the parabola $y = x^2 - 2x + 5$ joins the points with the abscissas $x_1 = 1$, $x_2 = 3$. Derive the equation of the tangent to the parabola parallel to the chord.

838. Derive the equation of the normal to the curve $y = \dfrac{x^2 - 3x + 6}{x^2}$ at the point with the abscissa $x = 3$.

839. Derive the equation of the normal to the curve $y = -\sqrt{x} + 2$ at the point of its intersection with the bisector of the first quadrant.

840. Derive the equation of the normal to the parabola $y = x^2 - 6x + 6$ perpendicular to the straight line joining the origin to the vertex of the parabola.

841. Show that the normals to the curve $y = x^2 - x + 1$, drawn at the points with the abscissas $x_1 = 0$, $x_2 = -1$ and $x_3 = \frac{5}{2}$, intersect at one point.

842. At the points of intersection of the straight line $x - y + 1 = 0$ and the parabola $y = x^2 - 4x + 5$ normals are drawn to the parabola.

Find the area of the triangle formed by the normals and the chord joining the mentioned points of intersection.

843. Show that the tangents drawn to the hyperbola $y = \frac{x-4}{x-2}$ at the points of its intersection with the axes of coordinates are parallel to each other.

844. Draw a tangent to the hyperbola $y = \frac{x+9}{x+5}$ so that it passes through the origin.

845. On the curve $y = \frac{1}{1+x^2}$ find a point at which the tangent is parallel to the axis of abscissas.

846. Find the equation of the tangent to the curve $x^2(x+y) = a^2(x-y)$ at the origin.

847. Prove that the tangents to the curve $y = \frac{1+3x^2}{3+x^2}$, drawn at the points for which $y = 1$, intersect at the origin.

848. Draw a normal to the curve $y = x \ln x$ parallel to the straight line $2x - 2y + 3 = 0$.

849. Find the distance between the origin and the normal to the curve $y = e^{2x} + x^2$ drawn at the point $x = 0$.

850. Draw the graph of the function $y = \sin\left(2x - \frac{\pi}{3}\right)$ and find the point of intersection of the tangents to the curve drawn at the points with the abscissas $x_1 = 0$ and $x_2 = \frac{5\pi}{12}$.

851. Show that the subtangent to the curve $y = ae^{bx}$ (a and b are constants) has a constant length at all its points.

852. Show that the subnormal at any point of the curve $y = x \ln(cx)$ (c is an arbitrary constant) is the fourth proportional for the abscissa, ordinate and the sum of the abscissa and the ordinate of this point.

853. Show that any tangent to the curve $y = \frac{1}{2}\sqrt{x - 4x^2}$ intersects with the y-axis at a point equidistant from the point of tangency and the origin.

854. Show that the tangent to the ellipse $\frac{x^2}{a^2} + \frac{y^2}{b^2} = 1$ at the point $M(x_0, y_0)$ has the equation $\frac{xx_0}{a^2} + \frac{yy_0}{b^2} = 1$.

855. Show that the tangent to the hyperbola $\frac{x^2}{a^2} - \frac{y^2}{b^2} = 1$ at the point $M(x_0, y_0)$ has the equation $\frac{xx_0}{a^2} - \frac{yy_0}{b^2} = 1$.

856. Prove that a normal to an ellipse at any point bisects the angle between the focal radii of this point (Fig. 21). Taking this fact into consideration, develop a method of constructing a tangent and a normal to an ellipse.

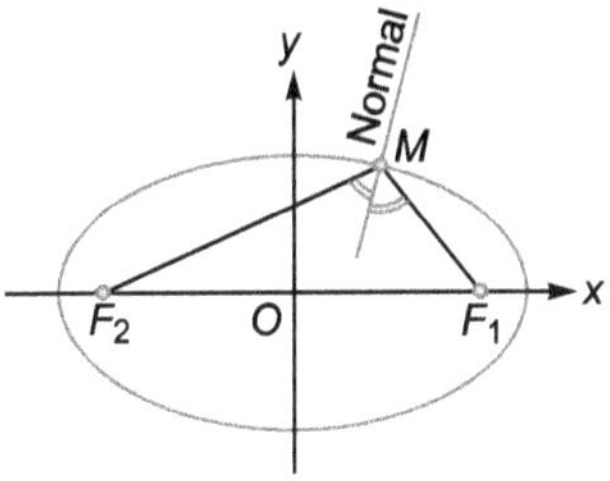

Fig. 21

857. Derive the equation of the tangents to the hyperbola $\frac{x^2}{2} - \frac{y^2}{7} = 1$ perpendicular to the straight line $2x + 4y - 3 = 0$.

858. A straight line is drawn through the origin and parallel to the tangent to a curve at an arbitrary point M. Find the locus of the points P of intersection of this straight line and the straight line parallel to the y-axis and passing through the point M.

Find such loci for (a) parabola $y^2 = 2px$, (b) logarithmic curve $y = \log_b x$, (c) circle $x^2 + y^2 = a^2$, (d) tractrix

$$y = \sqrt{a^2 - x^2} - a \ln \frac{a + \sqrt{a^2 - x^2}}{x}.$$

In Problems 859 to 864 find the angles at which the given lines intersect.

859. (1) $y = \frac{x+1}{x+2}$ and $y = \frac{x^2 + 4x + 8}{16}$;

(2) $y = (x-2)^2$ and $y = 4x - x^2 + 4$.

860. (1) $x^2 + y^2 = 8$ and $y^2 = 2x$;

(2) $x^2 + y^2 - 4x = 1$ and $x^2 + y^2 + 2y = 9$.

861. $x^2 - y^2 = 5$ and $\frac{x^2}{18} + \frac{y^2}{8} = 1$.

862. $x^2 + y^2 = 8ax$ and $y^2 = \frac{x}{2a - x}$.

863. $x^2 = 4ay$ and $y = \frac{8a^3}{x^2 + 4a^2}$.

864. $y = \sin x$ and $y = \cos x$ $(0 \le x \le \pi)$.

865. Derive the equations of the tangent and normal to the curve

$$\left(\frac{x}{a}\right)^n + \left(\frac{y}{b}\right)^n = 2$$

at the point with the abscissa equal to a.

866. Prove that the sum of the segments cut off the axes of coordinates by the tangent to the curve $x^{1/2} + y^{1/2} = a^{1/2}$ is equal to a for all of its points.

867. Show that the segment of the tangent to the astroid $x^{2/3} + y^{2/3} = a^{2/3}$, contained between the axes of coordinates, has a constant length equal to a.

868. Prove that the segment of the tangent to the tractrix

$$y = \frac{a}{2} \ln \frac{a + \sqrt{a^2 - x^2}}{a - \sqrt{a^2 - x^2}} - \sqrt{a^2 - x^2}$$

contained between the y-axis and the point of tangency has a constant length.

869. Show that for any point $M\,(x_0, y_0)$ of the equilateral hyperbola $x^2 - y^2 = a^2$ the segment of the normal from the point M to the point of intersection with the x-axis is equal to the polar radius of the point M.

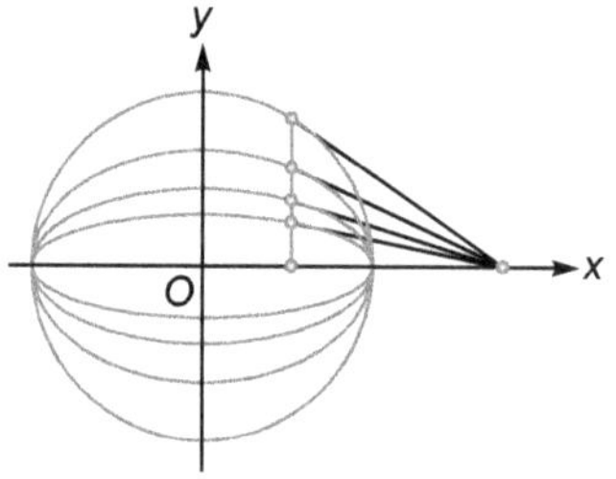

Fig. 22

870. Show that the x-intercept of the tangent at an arbitrary point of the curve $\frac{a}{x^2} + \frac{b}{y^2} = 1$ is proportional to the cube of the abscissa of the point of tangency.

871. Prove that the ordinate of any point of the curve $2x^2y^2 - x^4 = c$ (c constant) is the mean proportional between the abscissa and the difference between the abscissa and subnormal drawn to the curve at the same point.

872. Prove that in the ellipses $\frac{x^2}{a^2} + \frac{y^2}{b^2} = 1$, whose axis $2a$ is common and axes $2b$ are different (Fig. 22), tangents drawn at the points with equal abscissas intersect at one point lying on the x-axis. Taking advantage of this fact, give a simple method of constructing a tangent to the ellipse.

873. Show that the curve $y = e^{kx} \sin mx$ touches each of the curves $y = e^{kx}$ and $y = -e^{kx}$ at all common points.

874. To construct a tangent to the catenary $y = a \cosh \frac{x}{a}$ the following method is used. A semicircle is drawn with the ordinate MN of the point M as the diameter (Fig. 23) and the chord $NP = a$ is marked off, then MP is the required tangent. Prove it.

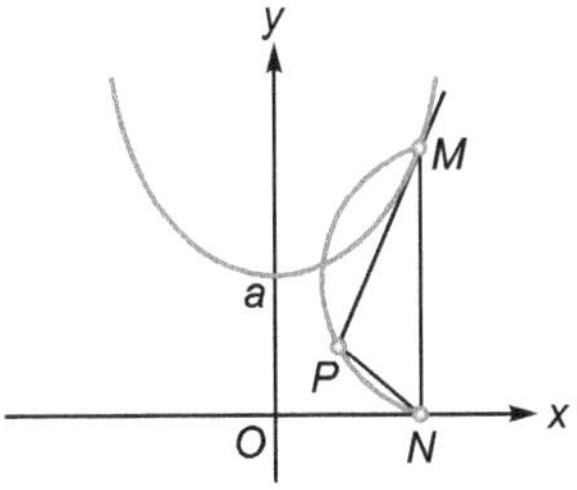

Fig. 23

Graphical differentiation

875. With an electric motor switched on, the temperature of the winding of the electromagnet was measured each five minutes during an hour. The results of the measurements are tabulated below.

Time t min ...	0	5	10	15	20	25
Temperature 0°C ...	20	26	32.5	41	46	49
Time t min ...	30	35	40	45	50	55
Temperature 0°C ...	52.5	54.5	56.5	58	59.5	61

Plot an approximate graph of continuous dependence of the temperature on time. Construct the graph of the rate of change in the temperature with time by graphical differentiation.

876. Figure 24 illustrates the curve of the lift of the inlet valve of the cylinder of a low-pressure steam machine. Construct the curve of the rate by graphical differentiation.

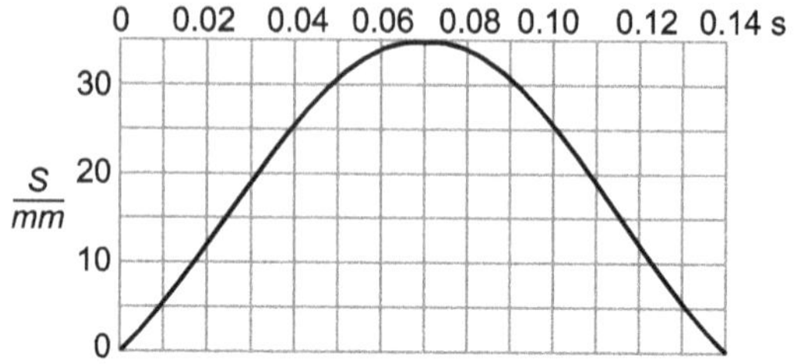

Fig. 24

3. Differential. Differentiability of a Function

Differential

877. Find the increment of the function $y = x^2$ corresponding to the increment Δx of the independent variable. Compute Δy if $x = 1$ and $\Delta x = 0.1, 0.01$. What will the error (absolute and relative) in the value of Δy be to the term with Δx in the first power?

878. Find the increment Δv of the volume v of a sphere with the radius $R = 2$ changing by ΔR. Compute Δv if $\Delta R = 05, 0.1, 0.01$. What will the error in the value of Δv be to the term with ΔR in the first power?

879. Given a function $y = x^3 + 2x$. Find the values of the increment and its principal linear part corresponding to the variation of x from $x = 2$ to $x = 2.1$.

880. What increment does the function $y = 3x^2 - x$ receive when the independent variable passes from the value $x = 1$ to the value $x = 1.02$? What is the value of the corresponding principal linear part? Find the ratio of the second magnitude to the first one.

881. Given a function $y = f(x)$, and the increment $\Delta x = 0.2$ for some point x; the corresponding principal part of the increment of the function turned out to be equal to 0.8. Find the derivative at the point x.

882. Given a function $f(x) = x^2$. The principal part of the increment of the function $df(x) = -0.8$ is known to correspond, at a certain point, to the increment of the independent variable $\Delta x = 0.2$. Find the initial value of the independent variable.

883. Find the increment and the differential of the function $y = x^2 - x$ at $x = 10$ and $\Delta x = 0.1$. Compute the absolute and relative errors due to replacing the increment by the differential. Make the drawing.

884. Find the increment and differential of the function $y = \sqrt{x}$ at $x = 4$ and $\Delta x = 0.41$. Compute the absolute and relative errors. Make the drawing.

885. $y = x^3 - x$. For $x = 2$ compute Δy and dy assigning to Δx the following values : $\Delta x = 1$, $\Delta x = 0.1$, $\Delta x = 0.01$. Find the corresponding values of the relative error $\delta = \frac{|\Delta y - dy|}{|\Delta y|}$.

886. Find graphically (sketching a drawing on squared paper to a large scale) the increment and differential, and compute the absolute and relative errors due to replacing the increment by the differential for the function $y = 2^x$ at $x = 2$ and $\Delta x = 0.4$.

887. The side of a square is equal to 8 cm. What will the increase in its area be if each of its sides is increased by : (a) 1 cm; (b) 0.5 cm; (c) 0.1 cm. Find the principal linear part of the increment of the area of this square and estimate the relative error (in per cent) resulting from the replacement of the increment by its principal part.

888. It is known, that with an increase in the side of a given square by 0.3 cm the principal linear part of the increment of the area amounts to 2.4 cm^2. Find the principal linear part of the increment of the area corresponding to the increase in each side by : (a) 0.6 cm; (b) 0.75 cm; (c) 1.2 cm.

889. Find the differentials of the functions:

(1) $0.25\sqrt{x}$; (2) $\frac{\sqrt[3]{x}}{0.2}$; (3) $\frac{1}{0.5x^2}$;

(4) $\frac{1}{4x^4}$; (5) $\frac{1}{2\sqrt{x}}$; (6) $\frac{1}{n\sqrt[3]{x}}$;

(7) $\frac{\sqrt{x}}{a+b}$; (8) $\frac{p}{q^x}$; (9) $\frac{m-n}{x^{0.2}}$;

(10) $\frac{m+n}{\sqrt{x}}$; (11) $(x^2 + 4x + 1)(x^2 - \sqrt{x})$;

(12) $\frac{x^3+1}{x^3-1}$; (13) $\frac{1}{1-t^2}$; (14) $(1 + x - x^2)^3$;

(15) $\tan^2 x$; (16) $5^{\ln \tan x}$; (17) $2^{-\frac{1}{\cos x}}$;

(18) $\ln \tan\left(\frac{\pi}{2} - \frac{x}{4}\right)$; (19) $\frac{\cos x}{1-x^2}$;

(20) $\sqrt{\arcsin x} + (\arctan x)^2$;

(21) $3 \arcsin x - 4 \arctan x + \frac{1}{2} \arccos x - \frac{7}{2} \arctan x$;

(22) $3^{-\frac{1}{x^2}} + 3x^3 - 4\sqrt{x}$.

890. Compute the values of the differentials of the functions:

(1) $y = \frac{1}{(\tan x + 1)^2}$ with the independent variable changing from $x = \frac{\pi}{6}$ to $x = \frac{61\,\pi}{360}$;

(2) $y = \cos^2 \varphi$, with φ changing from 60° to 60°30′;

(3) $y = \sin 2\varphi$ with φ changing from $\frac{\pi}{6}$ to $\frac{61\,\pi}{360}$;

(4) $y = \sin 3\varphi$ with φ changing from $\frac{\pi}{6}$ to $\frac{61\,\pi}{360}$;

(5) $y = \sin \frac{\theta}{3}$ with θ changing from $\frac{\pi}{6}$ to $\frac{61\,\pi}{360}$.

891. Find the approximate value of the increment of the function $y = \sin x$ for x varying from 30° to 30°1′. Compute sin 30°1′.

892. Find the approximate value of the increment of the function $y = \tan x$ for x varying from 45° to 45°10′.

893. Find the approximate value of the increment of the function $y = \frac{1 + \cos x}{1 - \cos x}$ for x changing from $\frac{\pi}{3}$ to $\frac{\pi}{3} + \frac{1}{100}$.

894. $\rho = k\sqrt{\cos 2\varphi}$. Find $d\rho$.

895. $y = 3^{1/x} + \frac{1}{2^{2x}} + 6^{\sqrt{x}}$. Compute dy for $x = 1$ and $dx = 0.2$.

896. Compute approximately sin 60°3′, sin 60°18′. Compare the obtained results with the tabular values.

897. Check to see that the function $y = \frac{1 + \ln x}{x - x \ln x}$ satisfies the relationship $2x^2 dy = (x^2 y^2 + 1)\,dx$.

898. Check to see that the function y, specified by the equation $\arctan \frac{y}{x} = \ln \sqrt{x^2 + y^2}$, satisfies the relationship $x\,(dy - dx) = y\,(dy + dx)$.

899. $f(x) = e^{0.1\,x\,(1 - x)}$. Compute approximately $f\,(1.05)$.

900. Compute arctan 1.02, arctan 0.97.

901. Compute approximately $\sqrt{\frac{(2.037)^2 - 3}{(2.037)^2 + 5}}$.

902. Compute approximately arcsin 0.4983.

903. If the length of a heavy thread (wire, chain) (see Fig. 25) is equal to $2S$, half-span to l, and the sag to f, then the approximate equality $S = l\left(1 + \frac{2}{3}\frac{f^2}{l^2}\right)$ is valid.

(a) Compute the change occurring in the length of the thread when the sag changes by df.

(b) If the change in the length of the wire (dS) (due to a change in temperature or load) is taken into account, then what will change in the sag be?

904. Compare the errors resulting from finding an angle by its tangent and by its sine with the aid of logarithmic tables, i.e., compare the accuracies of finding the angle x by the formulas $\log_{10} \sin x = y$ and $\log_{10} \tan x = z$, if y and z are given with equal errors.

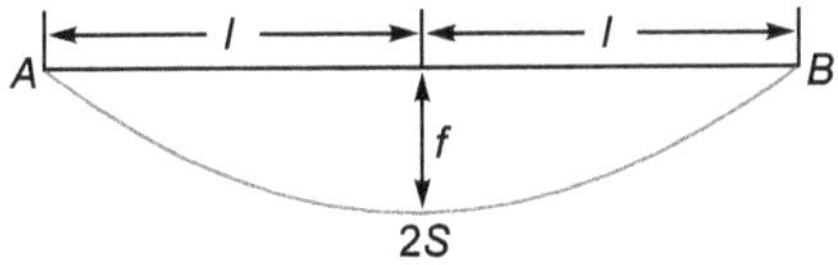

Fig. 25

905. In engineering calculations π and $\sqrt{g}$ (g is the acceleration or gravity) are often reduced when one of them is in the numerator, the other in the denominator. What relative error is introduced by such a reduction?

906. Express the differentials of composite functions in terms of the independent variable and its differential:

(1) $y = \sqrt[3]{x^2 + 5x},\ x = t^3 + 2t + 1;$

(2) $s = \cos^2 z,\ z = \dfrac{t^2 - 1}{4};$

(3) $z = \arctan v,\ v = \dfrac{1}{\tan s};$

(4) $v = 3^{-\frac{1}{x}},\ x = \ln \tan s;$

(5) $s = e^z,\ z = \dfrac{1}{2} \ln t,\ t = 2u^2 - 3u + 1;$

(6) $y = \ln \tan \dfrac{u}{2},\ u = \arcsin v,\ v = \cos 2s.$

Differentiability of functions

907. The function $y = |x|$ is continuous for any x. Make sure that at $x = 0$ it is not differentiable.

908. Test the function $y = |x^3|$ for continuity and differentiability at $x = 0$.

909. The function $f(x)$ is defined as follows : $f(x) = 1 + x$ for $x \le 0$, $f(x) = x$ for $0 < x < 1$; $f(x) = 2 - x$ for $1 \le x \le 2$, and $f(x) = 3x - x^2$ for $x > 2$. Test $f(x)$ for continuity and find out the existence and continuity of $f'(x)$.

910. The function $y = |\sin x|$ is continuous for any x. Make sure that it is not differentiable at $x = 0$. Are there any other values of the independent variable at which the function is not differentiable?

911. Test the function $y = e^{-|x|}$ for continuity and differentiability at $x = 0$.

912. $f(x) = x^2 \sin \frac{1}{x}$ for $x \neq 0$, $f(0) = 0$. Is the function $f(x)$ differentiable at $x = 0$?

913. $f(x) = \frac{\sqrt{x+1} - 1}{\sqrt{x}}$ for $x \neq 0$, $f(0) = 0$. Is the function $f(x)$ continuous and differentiable at $x = 0$?

914. Given the function $f(x) = 1 + \sqrt[3]{(x-1)^2}$. Show that at $x = 1$ it is impossible to single out the principal linear part and therefore $f(x)$ has no derivative at $x = 1$. Give the geometrical meaning of the result obtained.

915. $f(x) = x \arctan \frac{1}{x}$ for $x \neq 0$, $f(0) = 0$. Will the function $f(x)$ be, at $x = 0$, continuous? Differentiable? Give the geometrical meaning of the result obtained.

916. $f(x) = \frac{1}{1 + e^{1/x}}$ for $x \neq 0$ and $f(0) = 0$. Will the function $f(x)$ be, at $x = 0$, continuous? Differentiable?

4. The Derivative as the Rate of Change

Relative velocity

917. A point moves in a spiral of Archimedes $\rho = a\varphi$. Find the rate of change of the polar radius ρ with respect to the polar angle φ.

918. A point moves in a logarithmic spiral $\rho = e^{a\varphi}$. Find the rate of change of the polar radius if it is known that it turns with an angular velocity ω.

919. A point moves in a circle $\rho = 2r \cos \varphi$. Find the rates of change of the abscissa and ordinate of the point if the polar radius turns with an angular velocity ω. The polar axis serves as the x-axis, the pole being the origin of the Cartesian coordinates.

920. A circle of radius R rolls without sliding along a straight line. The centre of the circle moves with a constant velocity v. Find the rates of change of the abscissa x and ordinate y for a point lying on the circumference of the circle.

921. Barometric pressure p changes with altitude h in accordance with the law $\ln\frac{p}{p_0} = ch$, where p_0 denotes normal pressure, and c is a constant. At the altitude 5540 m the pressure turns out to be equal to half the value of the normal pressure. Find the rate of change of barometric pressure with altitude.

922. y is related with x as follows : $y^2 = 12x$. The argument x increases uniformly at a rate of two units per second. What is the rate of increase in y for $x = 3$?

923. The ordinate of a point describing the circle $x^2 + y^2 = 25$ decreases at a rate of $1.5\,\frac{\text{cm}}{\text{s}}$. What is the rate of change of the abscissa of the point when the ordinate becomes equal to 4 cm?

924. At what point of the ellipse $16x^2 + 9y^2 = 400$ does the ordinate decrease at the same rate at which the abscissa increases?

925. The side of a square increases at a rate v. What is the rate of change in the perimeter and area of the square at the instant its side is equal to a.

926. The radius of a circle changes at a rate v. What is the rate of change in the length of circumference and the area of the circle at the instant its radius is equal to r?

927. The radius of a sphere changes at a rate v. What is the rate of change in the volume and the surface of the sphere?

928. At what value of an angle its sine changes at half the rate of change in the argument?

929. At what value of an angle the rates of change in sine and tangent of one and the same angle are equal to each other?

930. The rate of growth in sine increases n times. How many times does the rate of increase in tangent change?

931. Assuming that the volume of the trunk of a tree is proportional to the cube of its diameter and that the latter increases uniformly from year to year, show that the rate of increase in the volume when the diameter is equal to 90 cm is 25 times the rate when it is 18 cm.

Functions represented parametrically

932. Check to see whether a point specified in the Cartesian coordinates lies on a line whose equation is represented parametrically.

(a) Is the point (5, 1) on the circle $x = 2 + 5\cos t$, $y = -3 + 5\sin t$?

(b) Is the point $(2, \sqrt{3})$ on the circle $x = 2\cos t$, $y = 2\sin t$?

933. Graph the functions represented parametrically:

(a) $x = 3\cos t,\ y = 4\sin t$; (b) $x = t^2 - 2t,\ y = t^2 + 2t$;

(c) $x = \cos t,\ y = t + 2\sin t$; (d) $x = 2^{t-1},\ y = \frac{1}{4}(t^3 + 1)$.

934. Eliminate the parameter from the equations represented parametrically:

(1) $x = 3t,\ y = 6t - t^2$; (2) $x = \cos t,\ y = \sin 2t$;

(3) $x = t^3 + 1,\ y = t^2$; (4) $x = \varphi - \sin\varphi,\ y = 1 - \cos\varphi$;

(5) $x = \tan t,\ y = \sin 2t + 2\cos 2t$.

935. Find the value of the parameter corresponding to the given coordinates of a point on a curve whose equation is represented parametrically :

(1) $x = 3(2\cos t - \cos 2t),\ y = 3(2\sin t - \sin 2t),\ (-9, 0)$;

(2) $x = t^2 + 2t,\ y = t^3 + t,\ (3, 2)$;

(3) $x = 2\tan t,\ y = 2\sin^2 t + \sin 2t,\ (2, 2)$;

(4) $x = t^2 - 1,\ y = t^3 - t,\ (0, 0)$.

In Problems 936 to 945 find the derivatives of y with respect to x.

936. $x = a\cos\varphi,\ y = b\sin\varphi$.

937. $x = a\cos^3\varphi,\ y = b\sin^3\varphi$.

938. $x = a(\varphi - \sin\varphi),\ y = a(1 - \cos\varphi)$.

939. $x = 1 - t^2,\ y = t - t^3$.

940. $x = \dfrac{t+1}{t},\ y = \dfrac{t-1}{t}$.

941. $x = \ln(1 + t^2),\ y = t - \arctan t$.

942. $x = \varphi(1 - \sin\varphi),\ y = \varphi\cos\varphi$.

943. $x = \dfrac{1+t^3}{t^2-1},\ y = \dfrac{1}{t^2-1}$.

944. $x = e^t\sin t,\ y = e^t\cos t$.

945. $x = \dfrac{3at}{1+t^3},\ y = \dfrac{3at^2}{1+t^3}$.

In Problems 946 to 949 find the angular coefficients of the tangents to the given curves.

946. $x = 3\cos t,\ y = 4\sin t$ at the point $(3\sqrt{2}/2, 2\sqrt{2})$.

947. $x = t - t^4,\ y = t^2 - t^3$ at the point $(0, 0)$.

948. $x = t^3 + 1,\ y = t^2 + t + 1$ at the point $(1, 1)$.

949. $x = 2\cos t,\ y = \sin t$ at the point $(1, -\sqrt{3}/2)$.

950. For the curve represented parametrically indicate the relation between the parameter t and the angle α between the tangent to the given curve and the x-axis.

$$(1)\begin{cases} x = \cos t + t\sin t - \dfrac{t^2}{2}\cos t, \\ y = \sin t - t\cos t - \dfrac{t^2}{2}\sin t; \end{cases}$$

(2) $x = a\cos^3 t$, $y = a\sin^3 t$;

(3) $x = a\cos t\sqrt{2\cos 2t}$, $y = a\sin t\sqrt{2\cos 2t}$.

951. Make sure that the function represented parametrically by the equations

$$x = 2t + 3t^2,\ y = t^2 + 2t^3$$

satisfies the relationship

$$y = y'^2 + 2y'^3$$

(where $y' = \dfrac{dy}{dx}$, i.e., differentiation with respect to x).

952. Make sure that the function represented parametrically by the equations

$$x = \frac{1+t}{t^3},\ \ y = \frac{3}{2t^2} + \frac{2}{t}$$

satisfies the relationship

$$xy'^3 = 1 + y'\left(y' = \frac{dy}{dx}\right).$$

953. Make sure that the function represented parametrically by the equations

$$xy = \cosh 2t,\ y = \sinh 2t$$

satisfies the relationship

$$yy' - x = 0\left(y' = \frac{dy}{dx}\right).$$

954. Make sure that the function represented parametrically by the equations

$$x = \frac{1}{\sqrt{1+t^2}} - \ln\frac{1+\sqrt{1+t^2}}{t},\ \ y = \frac{t}{\sqrt{1+t^2}}$$

satisfies the relationship

$$y\sqrt{1+y'^2} = y'\left(y' = \frac{dy}{dx}\right).$$

955. Make sure that the function represented parametrically by the equations

$$x = \frac{1+\ln t}{t^2},\ \ y = \frac{3+2\ln t}{t}$$

satisfies the relationship

$$yy' = 2xy'^2 + 1 \left(y' = \frac{dy}{dx} \right).$$

956. Find the angles at which the given curves intersect:

(1) $y = x^2$ and $\begin{cases} x = \frac{5}{3} \cos t, \\ y = \frac{5}{4} \sin t; \end{cases}$

(2) $\begin{cases} x = a \cos \varphi, \\ y = a \sin \varphi \end{cases}$ and $\begin{cases} x = \frac{at^2}{1+t^2}, \\ y = \frac{at\sqrt{3}}{1+t^2}. \end{cases}$

957. Show that at any position of the generating circle of the cycloid the tangent and the normal at the corresponding point of the cycloid pass through its upmost and lowest points.

958. Find the lengths of the tangent normal, subtangent and subnormal to the cardioid

$$x = a(2\cos t - \cos 2t),\ y = a(2\sin t - \sin 2t)$$

at an arbitrary point.

959. Find the lengths of the tangent, normal, subtangent and subnormal to the astroid

$$x = a\sin^3 t,\ y = a\cos^3 t$$

at an arbitrary point.

960. Prove that a tangent to the circle $x^2 + y^2 = a^2$ serves as a normal to the evolute of a circle

$$x = a(\cos t + t\sin t),\ y = a(\sin t - t\cos t).$$

961. Find the lengths of the tangent, normal, subtangent and subnormal to the evolute of a circle from the previous problem.

962. Prove that the segment of the normal to the curve $x = 2a\sin t + a\sin t\cos^2 t,\ y = -a\cos^3 t$ contained between the coordinate axes is equal to $2a$.

In Problems 963 to 966 derive the equations of the tangent and the normal to the following curves at the given points.

963. $x = 2e^t;\ y = e^{-t}$ at $t = 0$.

964. $x = \sin t,\ y = \cos 2t$ at $t = \pi/6$.

965. $x = 2\ln\cot t + 1,\ y = \tan t + \cot t$ at $t = \pi/4$.

966. (1) $x = \frac{3at}{1+t^2}$, $y = \frac{3at^2}{1+t^2}$ at $t = 2$;

(2) $\begin{cases} x = t\,(t\cos t - 2\sin t), \\ y = t\,(t\sin t + 2\cos t), \end{cases}$ at $t = \frac{\pi}{4}$;

(3) $x = \sin t$, $y = a^t$ at $t = 0$.

967. Show that at two points of the cardioid (see Problem 958), which correspond to the values of the parameter t differing from each other by $\frac{2}{3}\pi$, the tangents are parallel.

968. Prove that if OT and ON are perpendiculars dropped from the origin to the tangent and the normal to the astroid at any of its points (see Problem 959), then

$$4\,OT^2 + ON^2 = a^2.$$

969. Find the length of the perpendicular dropped from the origin to the tangent to the curve

$$2x = a\,(3\cos t + \cos 3t),\ 2y = a\,(3\sin t + \sin 3t).$$

Show that $4\rho^2 = 3p^2 + 4a^2$, where ρ is the polar radius of the given point and p is the length of the mentioned perpendicular.

The rate of change of the polar radius

970. Given a circle $\rho = 2r\sin\varphi$. Find the angle θ between the polar radius and the tangent, and the angle α between the polar axis and the tangent.

971. Prove that in the parabola $\rho = a\sec^2\frac{\varphi}{2}$ the sum of the angles formed by the tangent with the polar radius and with the polar axis is equal to 180°. Make use of this property when constructing a tangent to the parabola.

972. Given the curve $\rho = a\sin^3\frac{\varphi}{3}$, show that $\alpha = 4\theta$ (notation is the same as in Problem 970).

973. Show that the two parabolas, $\rho = a\sec^2\frac{\varphi}{2}$ and $\rho = b\sec^2\frac{\varphi}{2}$, intersect at right angles.

974. Find the tangent of the angle between the polar axis and the tangent line to the curve $\rho = a\sec^2\varphi$ for the points at which $\rho = 2a$.

975. Find the tangent of the angle between the polar axis and the tangent line at the origin : (1) to the curve $\rho = \sin^3\varphi$, (2) to the curve $\rho = \sin 3\varphi$.

976. Show that the two cardioids $\rho = a(1 + \cos\varphi)$ and $\rho = a(1 - \cos\varphi)$ intersect at right angles.

977. The equation of a curve in polar coordinates is represented parametrically : $\rho = f_1(t)$, $\varphi = f_2(t)$. Express the tangent of the angle θ between the tangent line and the polar radius as a function of t.

978. A curve is specified by the equations $\rho = at^3$ and $\varphi = bt^2$. Find the angle between the polar radius and the tangent to the curve.

979. Given an ellipse $x = a\cos t$, $y = b\sin t$. Express the polar radius ρ and the polar angle φ as functions of the parameter t. Use the obtained form of specifying an ellipse for computing the angle between the tangent line and the polar radius.

The **polar subtangent** is the term of the projection of the segment of the tangent line, from the point of tangency to the point of its intersection with the perpendicular, erected to the polar radius at the pole, on the perpendicular. The **polar subnormal** is defined analogously. Remembering this,

solve Problems 980 to 984.

980. Derive the formula for the polar subtangent and the polar subnormal to the curve $\rho = f(\varphi)$.

981. Show that the length of the polar subtangent to the hyperbolic spiral $\rho = \dfrac{a}{\varphi}$ is a constant.

982. Show that the length of the polar subnormal to the spiral of Archimedes $\rho = \alpha\varphi$ is a constant.

983. Find the length of the polar subtangent to the logarithmic spiral $\rho = a^{\varphi}$.

984. Find the length of the polar subnormal to the logarithmic spiral $\rho = a^{\varphi}$.

The rate of change in length

In Problems 985 to 999 denotes the arc length of the given curves.

985. Straight line $y = ax + b$. $\dfrac{ds}{dx} = ?$

986. Circle $x^2 + y^2 = r^2$. $\dfrac{ds}{dx} = ?$

987. Ellipse $\dfrac{x^2}{a^2} + \dfrac{y^2}{b^2} = 1$. $\dfrac{ds}{dy} = ?$

988. Parabola $y^2 = 2px$. $ds = ?$

989. Semicubical parabola $y^2 = ax^3$. $\frac{ds}{dy} = ?$

990. Sinusoid $y = \sin x$. $ds = ?$

991. Catenary $y = \frac{e^x + e^{-x}}{2}$ $(y = \cosh x)$. $\frac{ds}{dx} = ?$

992. Circle $x = r\cos t,\ y = r\sin t$. $\frac{ds}{dt} = ?$

993. Cycloid $x = a(t - \sin t),\ y = a(1 - \cos t)$. $\frac{ds}{dt} = ?$

994. Astroid $x = a\cos^3 t,\ y = a\sin^3 t$. $ds = ?$

995. Spiral of Archimedes $x = at\sin t,\ y = at\cos t$. $ds = ?$

996. Cardioid $\begin{cases} x = a(2\cos t - \cos 2t), \\ y = a(2\sin t - \sin 2t), \end{cases}$ $ds = ?$

997. Tractrix

$$x = a\left(\cos t + \ln\tan\frac{t}{2}\right),\ y = a\sin t.\ ds = ?$$

998. Involute of a circle $x = a(\cos t + t\sin t),\ y = a(\sin t - t\cos t)$. $\frac{ds}{dt} = ?$

999. Hyperbola $x = a\cosh t,\ y = a\sinh t$. $ds = ?$

Motion speed

1000. A ladder 10 m long is lined up with one end against a vertical wall, the other resting on the floor. The lower end moves away from the wall at a rate of $2\frac{\text{m}}{\text{min}}$. At what rate is the upper end of the ladder falling when its base lies 6 m away from the wall? What is the direction of the velocity vector?

1001. A train and a balloon leave a given point at the same time. The train moves uniformly at a speed of 50 km/h while the balloon rises (also uniformly) at an average speed of 10 km/h. At what speed are they moving apart? What is the direction of the velocity vector?

1002. A man 1.7 m tall walks away from a source of light 3 m high at a speed of 6.34 km/h. What is the velocity of motion of the shadow of his head?

1003. A horse runs around a circle at 20 km/h. A lantern is placed in the centre of the circle, and a partition is placed along a tangent to the circle at the point from which the horse begins to run. At what rate is the horse's shadow moving along the fence at the movement when the horse has run around 1/8th of the circle?

1004. Figure 26 presents a schematic diagram of the crank gear of a steam engine. A is the crosshead, BB' are the guide bars, AP is the connecting

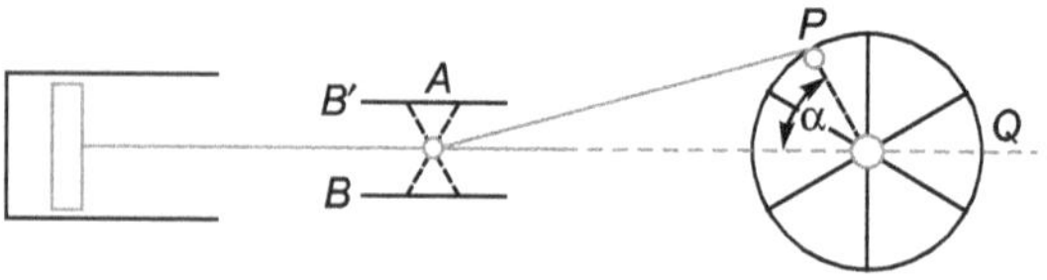

Fig. 26

rod, P is the crank's cog, and Q is the flywheel. The flywheel rotates uniformly at an angular velocity ω, its radius is R, and the length of the connecting rod is l. At what rate is the crosshead moving when the flywheel is turned through the angle α?

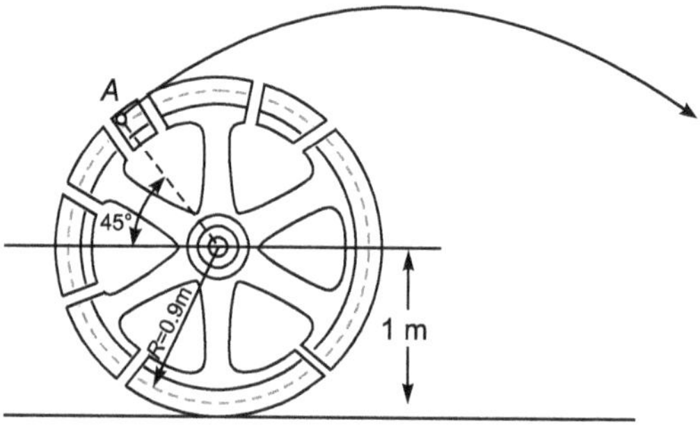

Fig. 27

1005. A flywheel, moving at 80 rpm, breaks. The radius of the wheel is 0.9 m, its centre being set 1 m above the ground. What will the speed of a fragment indicated in Fig. 27 by the letter A be, as it is falling to the ground?

5. Repeated Differentiation

Explicit functions

1006. $y = x^2 - 3x + 2.\ y'' = ?$

1007. $y = 1 - x^2 - x^4.\ y''' = ?$

1008. $f(x) = (x + 10)^6.\ f'''(2) = ?$

1009. $f(x) = x^6 - 4x^3 + 4.\ f^{IV}(1) = ?$

1010. $y = (x^2 + 1)^3.\ y'' = ?$

1011. $y = \cos^2 x.\ y''' = ?$

1012. $f(x) = e^{2x-1}.\ f''(0) = ?$

1013. $f(x) = \arctan x.\ f''(1) = ?$

1014. $f(x) = \dfrac{1}{1-x}.\ f^{V}(x) = ?$

1015. $y = x^3 \ln x.\ y^{IV} = ?$

1016. $f(x) = \frac{a}{x^n}$. $y''(x) = ?$

1017. $\rho = a \sin 2\varphi$. $\frac{d^4\rho}{d\varphi^4} = ?$

1018. $y = \frac{1 - x}{1 + x}$. $y^{(n)} = ?$

In Problems 1019 to 1028 find the second derivatives of the given functions.

1019. $y = xe^{x^2}$.

1020. $y = \frac{1}{1 + x^3}$.

1021. $y = (1 + x^2) \arctan x$.

1022. $y = \sqrt{a^2 - x^2}$.

1023. $y = \ln (x + \sqrt{1 + x^2})$.

1024. $y = \frac{1}{a + \sqrt{x}}$.

1025. $y = e^{\sqrt{x}}$.

1026. $y = \sqrt{1 - x^2} \arcsin x$.

1027. $y = \arcsin (a \sin x)$.

1028. $y = x^x$.

In Problems 1029 to 1040 find the general expressions for derivatives of order n of the following functions.

1029. $y = e^{ax}$.

1030. $y = e^{-x}$.

1031. $y = \sin ax + \cos bx$.

1032. $y = \sin^2 x$.

1033. $y = xe^x$.

1034. $y = x \ln x$.

1035. $y = \frac{1}{ax + b}$.

1036. $y = \ln (ax + b)$.

1037. $y = \log_a x$.

1038. $y = \frac{x}{x^2 - 1}$.

1039. $y = \frac{1}{x^2 - 3x + 2}$.

1040. $y = \sin^4 x + \cos^4 x$.

1041. Prove that the function $y = (x^2 - 1)^n$ satisfies the relationship

$$(x^2 - 1) y^{(n+2)} + 2xy^{(n+1)} - n(n + 1) y^{(n)} = 0.$$

1042. Prove that the function $y = e^x \sin x$ satisfies the relationship $y'' - 2y' + 2y = 0$, $y = e^{-x} \sin x$, the relationship $y'' + 2y' + 2y = 0$.

1043. Prove that the function $y = \frac{x - 3}{x + 4}$ satisfies the relationship

$$2y'^2 = (y - 1) y''.$$

1044. Prove that the function $y = \sqrt{2x - x^2}$ satisfies the relationship

$$y^3 y'' + 1 = 0.$$

1045. Prove that the function $y = e^{4x} + 2e^{-x}$ satisfies the relationship

$$y''' - 13y' - 12y = 0.$$

1046. Prove that the function $y = e^{\sqrt{x}} + e^{-\sqrt{x}}$ satisfies the relationship

$$xy'' + \frac{1}{2}y' - \frac{1}{4}y = 0.$$

1047. Prove that the function $y = \cos e^x + \sin e^x$ satisfies the relationship

$$y'' - y' + ye^{2x} = 0.$$

1048. Prove that the function

$$y = A\sin(\omega t + \omega_0) + B\cos(\omega t + \omega_0)$$

(A, B, ω, ω_0 constants) satisfies the relationship

$$\frac{d^2y}{dt^2} + \omega^2 y = 0.$$

1049. Prove that the function

$$a_1 e^{nx} + a_2 e^{-nx} + a_3\cos nx + a_4\sin nx$$

(a_1, a_2, a_3, a_4, n constants) satisfies the relationship $\frac{d^4y}{dx^4} = n^4 y$.

1050. Prove that the function $y = \sin(n\arcsin x)$ satisfies the relationship

$$(1 - x^2)y'' - xy' + n^2 y = 0.$$

1051. Prove that the function $e^{a\arcsin x}$ satisfies the relationship

$$(1 - x^2)y'' - xy' - \alpha^2 y = 0.$$

1052. Prove that the function $y = (x + \sqrt{x^2 + 1})^k$ satisfies the relationship

$$(1 + x^2)y'' + xy' - k^2 y = 0.$$

1053. Prove that the expression $S = \frac{y'''}{y'} - \frac{3}{2}\left(\frac{y''}{y'}\right)^2$ remains unchanged if y is replaced by $\frac{1}{y}$, i.e., if we put $y = \frac{1}{y_1}$, then $\frac{y_1'''}{y_1'} - \frac{3}{2}\left(\frac{y_1''}{y_1'}\right)^2 = S$.

1054. Given $y = f(x)$. Express $\frac{d^2x}{dy^2}$ in terms of $\frac{dy}{dx}$ and $\frac{d^2y}{dx^2}$. Show that the formula $R = \frac{(1 + y'^2)^{3/2}}{y''}$ can be reduced to the form

$$R^{2/3} = \frac{1}{\left(\frac{d^2y}{dx^2}\right)^{2/3}} + \frac{1}{\left(\frac{d^2x}{dy^2}\right)^{2/3}}.$$

1055. Given $F(x) = f(x)\cdot\varphi(x)$, and $f'(x)\varphi'(x) = C$. Prove that

$$\frac{F''}{F} = \frac{f''}{f} + \frac{\varphi''}{\varphi} + \frac{2C}{f\cdot\varphi} \text{ and } \frac{F'''}{F} = \frac{f'''}{f} + \frac{\varphi'''}{\varphi}.$$

Implicit functions

1056. $b^2x^2 + a^2y^2 = a^2b^2$. $\frac{d^2y}{dx^2} = ?$

1057. $x^2 + y^2 = r^2$. $\frac{d^3y}{dx^3} = ?$

1058. $y = \tan(x + y)$. $\frac{d^3y}{dx^3} = ?$

1059. $s = 1 + te^s$. $\frac{d^2s}{dt^2} = ?$

1060. $y^3 + x^3 - 3axy = 0$. $y'' = ?$

1061. $y = \sin(x + y)$. $y'' = ?$

1062. $e^{x+y} = xy$. $y'' = ?$

1063. Deduce the formula for the second derivative of the function inverse to $y = f(x)$.

1064. $e^y + xy = e$. Find $y''(x)$ for $x = 0$.

1065. $y^2 = 2px$. Define the expression $k = \frac{y''}{\sqrt{(1 + y'^2)^3}}$.

1066. Make sure that from $y^2 + x^2 = R^2$ it follows that $k = \frac{1}{R}$, where $k = \frac{|y''|}{\sqrt{(1 + y'^2)^3}}$.

1067. Prove that if

$$ax^2 + 2bxy + cy^2 + 2gx + 2fy + h = 0,$$

then $\frac{dy}{dx} = -\frac{ax + by + g}{bx + cy + f}$ and $\frac{d^2y}{dx^2} = \frac{A}{(bx + cy + f)^3}$,

where A is a constant (independent of x and y).

1068. Prove that if $(a + bx)e^{y/x} = x$, then

$$x^3 \frac{d^2y}{dx^2} = \left(x\frac{dy}{dx} - y\right)^2.$$

Functions represented parametrically

1069. $x = at^2$, $y = bt^3$. $\frac{d^2x}{dy^2} = ?$

1070. $x = a\cos t$, $y = a\sin t$. $\frac{d^2y}{dx^2} = ?$

1071. $x = a\cos t$, $y = b\sin t$. $\frac{d^3y}{dx^3} = ?$

1072. $x = a(\varphi - \sin\varphi)$, $y = a(1 - \cos\varphi)$. $\frac{d^2y}{dx^2} = ?$

1073. (1) $x = a\cos^3 t$, $y = a\sin^3 t$. $\frac{d^3y}{dx^3} = ?$

(2) $x = a\cos^2 t$, $y = a\sin^2 t$. $\frac{d^2y}{dx^2} = ?$

1074. (1) $x = \ln t, \quad y = t^2 - 1. \; \dfrac{d^2y}{dx^2} = ?$

(2) $x = \arcsin t, \quad y = \ln (1 - t^2). \; \dfrac{d^2y}{dx^2} = ?$

1075. $x = at \cos t, \quad y = at \sin t. \; \dfrac{d^2y}{dx^2} = ?$

1076. Prove that the function $y = f(x)$, represented parametrically by the equations $y = e^t \cos t$, $x = e^t \sin t$, satisfies the relationship

$$y'' (x + y)^2 = 2 (xy' - y).$$

1077. Prove that the function $y = f(x)$, represented parametrically by the equations $y = 3t - t^3$, $x = 3t^2$, satisfies the relation

$$36y'' (y - \sqrt{3x}) = x + 3.$$

1078. Prove that the function, represented parametrically by the equations

$$x = \sin t, \; y = \sin kt,$$

satisfies the relation

$$(1 - x^2) \frac{d^2y}{dx^2} - x \frac{dy}{dx} + k^2 y = 0.$$

1079. Prove that if

$$x = f(t) \cos t - f'(t) \sin t, \; y = f(t) \sin t + f'(t) \cos t,$$

then $ds^2 = dx^2 + dy^2 = [f(t) + f''(t)]^2 \, dt^2$.

Acceleration of motion

1080. A point is in rectilinear motion, $s = \dfrac{4}{3} t^3 - t + 5$. Find the acceleration a at the end of the 2nd second (s is expressed in metres, t in seconds).

1081. Rectilinear motion is performed in accordance with the formula $s = t^2 - 4t + 1$. Find the velocity and acceleration.

1082. A point is in rectilinear motion, $s = \dfrac{2}{9} \sin \dfrac{\pi t}{2} + s_0$. Find the acceleration at the end of the first second (s is expressed in centimetres, t in seconds).

1083. A point moves in a straight line, $s = \sqrt{t}$. Prove that the motion is decelerated and that the acceleration a is proportional to the cube of the velocity v.

1084. A heavy beam 13 m long is lowered to the ground so that its lower end is fastened to a truck and the upper end is held by a rope wound on a windlass (Fig. 28). The rope is unwound from the drum at a rate of

2 m/min. At what acceleration does the truck rolls away at the moment when it is at a distance of 5 m from the point O?

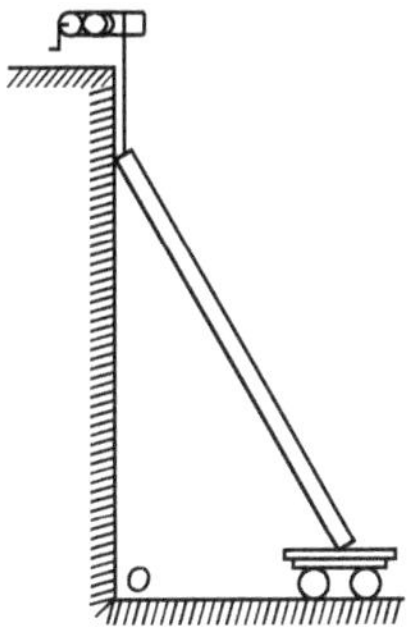

Fig. 28

1085. A barge whose deck is 4 m lower than the level of the wharf is hauled up to the latter with the aid of a rope wound on a windlass at a rate of 2 m/s. At what acceleration does the barge move at the moment when it is 8 m distant from the wharf (as measured along the horizontal).

1086. A point performs rectilinear motion so that its velocity changes proportionally to the square of the path covered. Show that the motion takes place under the action of a constant force.

1087. Given that the force acting on a material point is inversely proportional to the velocity of the moving point. Prove that the kinetic energy of the point is a linear function of time.

Leibniz formula

1088. Use the Leibniz formula for computing the following derivatives :

(1) $[(x^2+1)\sin x]^{(20)}$; (2) $(e^x \sin x)^{(n)}$; (3) $(x^3 \sin \alpha x)^{(n)}$.

1089. Show that if $y = (1-x)^{-\alpha} e^{-\alpha x}$, then

$$(1-x)\frac{dy}{dx} = \alpha xy.$$

Using the Leibniz formula, show that

$$(1-x)\,y^{(n+1)} - (n+\alpha x)\,y^{(n)} - n\alpha y^{(n-1)} = 0.$$

1090. The function $y = e^{\alpha \arcsin x}$ satisfies the relation

$$(1-x^2)\,y'' - xy' - \alpha^2 y = 0 \text{ (see Problem 1051).}$$

Using the Leibniz formula and differentiating this equality n times, show that

$$(1-x^2)\,y^{(n+2)} - (2n+1)\,xy^{(n+1)} - (n^2+\alpha^2)\,y^{(n)} = 0.$$

1091. Show that

$$(e^{ax}\cos bx)^{(n)} = r^n e^{ax}\cos(bx + n\varphi),$$

where $r = \sqrt{a^2 + b^2}$, $\tan\varphi = \frac{b}{a}$.

Using the Leibniz formula, obtain the following relations:

$$r^n \cos n\psi = a^n - C_n^2\, a^{n-2}\, b^2 + C_n^4\, a^{n-4}\, b^4 - \ldots,$$

$$r^n \sin n\varphi = C_n^1\, a^{n-1}\, b - C_n^3\, a^{n-3}\, b^3 + C_a^5\, a^{n-5}\, b^5 - \ldots$$

1092. Prove that $(x^{n-1}\, e^{1/x})^{(n)} = (-1)^n \dfrac{e^{1/x}}{x^{n+1}}$.

1093. Show that the function $y = \arcsin x$ satisfies the relation $(1 - x^2)\, y'' = xy'$. Applying the Leibniz formula to both sides of this equation, find $y^{(n)}(0)$ $(n \ge 2)$.

1094. Applying the Leibniz formula n times, show that the function $y = \cos(m \arcsin x)$ satisfies the relation

$$(1 - x^2)\, y^{(n+2)} - (2n + 1)\, xy^{(n+1)} + (m^2 - n^2)\, y^{(n)} = 0.$$

1095. If $y = (\arcsin x)^2$, then

$$(1 - x^2)\, y^{(n+1)} - (2n - 1)\, xy^{(n)} - (n - 1)^2\, y^{(n-1)} = 0.$$

Find $y'(0), y''(0), \ldots, y^{(n)}(0)$.

Differentials of higher orders

1096. $y = \sqrt[3]{x^2}$. $d^2y = ?$

1097. $y = x^m$. $d^3y = ?$

1098. $y = (x + 1)^3 (x - 1)^2$. $d^2y = ?$

1099. $y = 4^{-x^2}$. $d^2y = ?$

1100. $y = \arctan\left(\frac{b}{a}\tan x\right)$. $d^2y = ?$

1101. $y = \sqrt{\ln^2 x - 4}$. $d^2y = ?$

1102. $y = \sin^2 x$. $d^3y = ?$

1103. $\rho^2 \cos^3\varphi - a^2 \sin^3\varphi = 0$. $d^2\rho = ?$

1104. $x^{2/3} + y^{2/3} = a^{2/3}$. $d^2y = ?$

1105. $y = \ln\dfrac{1 - x^2}{1 + x^2}$, $x = \tan t$. Express d^2y in terms of:

(1) x and dx; (2) t and dt.

1106. $y = \sin z$, $z = a^x$, $x = t^3$. Express d^2y in terms of:

(1) z and dz; (2) x and dx; (3) t and dt.

4

Investigating Functions and Their Graphs

1. Behaviour of a Function

1107. Show that the point $x = 0$ is a point of minimum of the function

$$y = 3x^4 - 4x^3 + 12x^2 + 1.$$

1108. Proceeding directly from the definition of an increasing and a decreasing function and that of points of maximum and minimum, show that the function $y = x^3 - 3x + 2$ increases at the point $x_1 = 2$, decreases at the point $x_2 = 0$, reaches its maximum at the point $x_3 = -1$ and minimum at the point $x_4 = 1$.

1109. As in Problem 1108, show that the function $y = \cos 2x$ increases at the point $x_1 = \frac{3\pi}{4}$, decreases at the point $x_2 = \frac{\pi}{6}$, reaches its maximum at the point $x_3 = 0$ and minimum at the point $x_4 = \frac{\pi}{2}$.

1110. Without resorting to the notion of the derivative, find out the behaviour of the given functions at the point $x = 0$

(1) $y = 1 - x^4$; (2) $y = x^5 - x^3$; (3) $y = \sqrt[3]{x}$;

(4) $y = \sqrt[3]{x^2}$; (5) $y = 1 - \sqrt[5]{x^4}$; (6) $y = |\tan x|$;

(7) $y = |\ln (x + 1)|$; (8) $y = e^{-|x|}$; (9) $y = \sqrt{x^3 + x^2}$.

1111. Show that the function $y = \ln (x^2 + 2x - 3)$ increases at the point $x_1 = 2$, decreases at the point $x_2 = -4$ and has no stationary points.

1112. Find out the behaviour of the function $y = \sin x + \cos x$ at the points $x_1 = 0$, $x_2 = 1$, $x_3 = -\frac{\pi}{3}$, and $x_4 = 2$.

1113. Find out the behaviour of the function $y = x - \ln x$ at the points $x_1 = \frac{1}{2}$, $x_2 = 2$, $x_3 = e$ and $x_4 = 1$ and show that if the given function increases at the point $x = a > 0$, then it decreases at the point $x = \frac{1}{a}$.

1114. Find out the behaviour of the function $y = x \arctan x$ at the points $x_1 = 1$, $x_2 = -1$ and $x_3 = 0$.

1115. Find out the behaviour of the function

$$y = \begin{cases} \dfrac{\sin x}{x} & \text{for } x \neq 0, \\ 1 & \text{for } x = 0 \end{cases}$$

at the points $x_1 = \frac{1}{2}$, $x_2 = -\frac{1}{2}$ and $x_3 = 0$.

2. Application of the First Derivative

Rolle's and Lagrange's theorems

1116. Check the validity of Rolle's theorem for the function $y = x^3 + 4x^2 - 7x - 10$ in the interval $[-1, 2]$.

1117. Check the validity of Rolle's theorem for the function $y = \ln \sin x$ in the interval $\left[\frac{\pi}{6}, \frac{5\pi}{6}\right]$.

1118. Check the validity of Rolle's theorem for the function $y = 4^{\sin x}$ in the interval $[0, \pi]$.

1119. Check the validity of Rolle's theorem for the function $y = \sqrt[3]{x^2 - 3x + 2}$ in the interval $[1, 2]$.

1120. The function $y = \dfrac{2 - x^2}{x^4}$ takes on equal values at the end-points of the interval $[-1, 1]$. Make sure that the derivative of this function does not vanish at any point of the interval $[-1, 1]$ and explain this deviation from Rolle's theorem.

1121. The function $y = |x|$ attains equal values at the end-points of the interval $[-a, a]$. Make sure that the derivative of this function vanishes at no point within the interval $[-a, a]$ and explain this deviation from Rolle's theorem.

1122. Prove the following theorem : if the equation

$$a_0 x^n + a_1 x^{n-1} + \ldots + a_{n-1}\, x = 0$$

has a positive root $x = x_0$, then the equation

$$n a_0 x^{n-1} + (n-1) a_1 x^{n-2} + \ldots + a_{n-1} = 0$$

also has a positive root which is smaller than x_0.

1123. Given the function $f(x) = 1 + x^m (x - 1)^n$, where m and n are positive integers. Without computing the derivative, show that the equation $f'(x) = 0$ has at least one root in the interval $(0, 1)$.

1124. Show that the equation $x^3 - 3x + c = 0$ cannot have two different roots in the interval $(0, 1)$.

1125. Without finding the derivative of the function

$$f(x) = (x - 1)(x - 2)(x - 3)(x - 4),$$

find out how many real roots the equation $f'(x) = 0$ has, and indicate the intervals in which they lie.

1126. Show that the function $f(x) = x^n + px + q$ cannot have more than two real roots if n is even and more than three if n is odd.

1127. Write Lagrange's formula for the function $y = \sin 3x$ in the interval $[x_1, x_2]$.

1128. Write Lagrange's formula for the function $y = x(1 - \ln x)$ in the interval $[a, b]$.

1129. Write Lagrange's formula for the function $y = \arcsin 2x$ in the interval $[x_0, x_0 + \Delta x]$.

1130. Prove the validity of Lagrange's theorem for the function $y = x^n$ in the interval $[0, a]$; $n > 0$, $a > 0$.

1131. Prove the validity of Lagrange's theorem for the function $y = \ln x$ in the interval $[1, e]$.

1132. With the aid of Lagrange's formula prove the inequalities

$$\frac{a-b}{a} \le \ln\frac{a}{b} \le \frac{a-b}{b},$$

for the condition $0 < b \le a$.

1133. With the aid of Lagrange's formula prove the inequalities $\frac{\alpha - \beta}{\cos^2\beta} \le \tan\alpha - \tan\beta \le \frac{\alpha-\beta}{\cos^2\alpha}$, for the condition $0 < \beta \le \alpha < \frac{\pi}{2}$.

1134. With the aid of Lagrange's formula prove the validity for $a > b$ of the inequalities

$$nb^{n-1}(a - b) < a^n - b^n < na^{n-1}(a - b)$$

if $n > 1$, and the inequalities of the opposite sense if $n < 1$.

1135. Consider the function

$$f(x) = \begin{cases} x^2 \sin\dfrac{1}{x} & \text{for } x \ne 0, \\ 0 & \text{for } x = 0. \end{cases}$$

This function is differentiable for any x. Write Lagrange's formula in the interval $[0, x]$:

$$f(x) - f(0) = xf'(\xi) \quad (0 < \xi < x).$$

We have
$$x^2 \sin \frac{1}{x} = x\left(2\xi \sin \frac{1}{\xi} - \cos \frac{1}{\xi}\right),$$

whence $\cos \frac{1}{\xi} = 2\xi \sin \frac{1}{\xi} - x \sin \frac{1}{\xi}$. Make x tend to zero, then ξ will tend to zero as well, and we obtain : $\lim_{\xi \to 0} \cos \frac{1}{\xi} = 0$. Explain this.

1136. Applying to the function $f(x) = \arctan x$ the formula

$$f(x_0 + \Delta x) \approx f(x_0) + f'\left(x_0 + \frac{\Delta x}{2}\right) \Delta x$$

in the interval $[1, 1.1]$ find the approximate value of arctan 1.1.

In Problems 1137 to 1141 using the formula

$$f(x_0 + \Delta x) \approx f(x_0) + f'\left(x_0 + \frac{\Delta x}{2}\right) \Delta x$$

compute the approximate values of the given expressions.

1137. arcsin 0.54.

1138. $\log_{10} 11$. Compare the result with the tabular value.

1139. $\ln (x + \sqrt{1 + x^2})$ for $x = 0.2$.

1140. $\log_{10} 7$, knowing that $\log_{10} 2 = 0.3010$ and $\log_{10} 3 = 0.4771$. Compare the result with the tabular value.

1141. $\log_{10} 61$. Compare the result with the tabular value.

1142. Make sure that, using the formula

$$f(b) = f(a) + (b - a)\, f'\left(\frac{a + b}{2}\right)$$

for computing the logarithm of $N + 0.01\,N$, *ie*, putting

$$\log_{10} (N + 0.01\,N) \log_{10} N + \frac{0.43429}{N + \frac{0.01}{2} N} 0.01\,N$$

$$= \log_{10} N + \frac{0.43429}{100.5},$$

we make an error less than 0.00001, i.e., we obtain five correct digits after the decimal point provided $\log_{10} N$ is given five correct digits.

Behaviour of functions in an interval

1143. Show that the function $y = 2x^3 + 3x^2 - 12x + 1$ decreases in the interval $(-2, 1)$.

1144. Show that the function $y = \sqrt{2x - x^2}$ increases in the interval $(0, 1)$ and decreases in the interval $(1, 2)$. Construct the graph of the given function.

1145. Show that the function $y = x^3 + x$ increases everywhere.

1146. Show that the function $y = \arctan x - x$ decreases everywhere.

1147. Show that the function $y = \dfrac{x^2 - 1}{x}$ increases in any interval not containing the point $x = 0$.

1148. Show that the function $y = \dfrac{\sin(x + a)}{\sin(x + b)}$ changes monotonically in any interval having no points of discontinuity of the function.

1149*. Prove the inequality $\dfrac{\tan x_2}{\tan x_1} > \dfrac{x_1}{x_2}$ for the condition $0 < x_1 < x_2 < \dfrac{\pi}{2}$.

1150. Find the intervals of monotonicity of the function $y = x^3 - 3x^2 - 9x + 14$ and plot its graph on the interval $(-2, 4)$.

1151. Find the intervals of monotonicity of the function $y = x^4 - 2x^2 - 5$.

In Problems 1152 to 1164 find the intervals of monotonicity of the given functions.

1152. $y = (x - 2)^5 (2x + 1)^4$.

1153. $y = \sqrt[3]{(2x - a)(a - x)^2} \quad (a > 0)$.

1154. $y = \dfrac{1 - x + x^2}{1 + x + x^2}$.

1155. $y = \dfrac{10}{4x^3 - 9x^2 + 6x}$.

1156. $y = x - e^x$.

1157. $y = x^2 e^{-x}$.

1158. $y = \dfrac{x}{\ln x}$.

1159. $y = 2x^2 - \ln x$.

1160. $y = x - 2\sin x \ (0 \le x \le 2\pi)$.

1161. $y = 2\sin x + \cos 2x \ (0 \le x \le 2\pi)$.

1162. $y = x + \cos x$.

1163. $y = \ln(x + \sqrt{1 + x^2})$.

1164. $y = x\sqrt{ax - x^2} \ (a > 0)$.

In Problems 1165 to 1184 find the extrema of the given functions.

1165. $y = 2x^3 - 3x^2$.

1166. $y = 2x^3 - 6x^2 - 18x + 7$.

1167. $y = \dfrac{3x^2 + 4x + 4}{x^2 + x + 1}$.

1168. $y = \sqrt[3]{x^3 - 3x^2 + 8^2}$.

1169. $y = \dfrac{1}{\ln(x^4 + 4x^3 + 30)}$.

1170. $y = -x^2\sqrt{x^2 + 2}$.

1171. $y = \dfrac{2}{3}x^2\sqrt[3]{6x - 7}$.

1172. $y = \dfrac{4\sqrt{3}}{9x\sqrt{1 - x}}$.

1173. $y = \dfrac{1 + 3x}{\sqrt{4 + 5x^2}}$.

1174. $y = \sqrt[3]{(x^2 - a^2)^2}$.

1175. $y = x - \ln(1 + x)$.

1176. $y = x - \ln(1 + x^2)$.

1177. $y = (x - 5)^2\sqrt[3]{(x + 1)^2}$.

1178. $y = (x^2 - 2x)\ln x - \dfrac{3}{2}x^2 + 4x$.

1179. $y = \dfrac{1}{2}(x^2 + 1)\arctan x - \dfrac{\pi}{8}x^2 - \dfrac{x - 1}{2}$.

1180. $y = \dfrac{1}{2}\left(x^2 - \dfrac{1}{2}\right)\arcsin x + \dfrac{1}{4}x\sqrt{1 - x^2} - \dfrac{\pi}{12}x^2$.

1181. $y = x\sin x + \cos x - \dfrac{1}{4}x^2\left(-\dfrac{\pi}{2} \le x \le \dfrac{\pi}{2}\right)$.

1182. $y = \left(\dfrac{1}{2} - x\right)\cos x + \sin x - \dfrac{x^2 - x}{4}\left(0 \le x \le \dfrac{\pi}{2}\right)$.

1183. $y = \dfrac{2 - x}{\pi}\cos\pi(x + 3) + \dfrac{1}{\pi^2}\sin\pi(x + 3)\,(0 < x < 4)$.

1184. $y = ae^{px} + be^{-px}$.

In Problems 1185 to 1197 find the greatest and the least values of the functions on the given intervals.

1185. $y = x^4 - 2x^2 + 5\,[-2, 2]$.

1186. $y = x + 2\sqrt{x}\ [0, 4]$.

1187. $y = x^5 - 5x^4 + 5x^3 + 1\,[-1, 2]$.

1188. $y = x^3 - 3x^2 + 6x - 2\ [-1, 1]$.

1189. $y = \sqrt{100 - x^2}\ [-6, 8]$.

1190. $y = \dfrac{1 - x + x^2}{1 + x - x^2}\ [0, 1]$.

1191. $y = \dfrac{x - 1}{x + 1}\ [0, 4]$.

1192. $y = \dfrac{a^2}{x} + \dfrac{b^2}{1 - x}(0, 1)\ (a > 0,\ b > 0)$.

1193. $y = \sin 2x - x\left[-\dfrac{\pi}{2}, \dfrac{\pi}{2}\right]$.

1194. $y = 2\tan x - \tan^2 x\left[0, \dfrac{\pi}{2}\right)$.

1195. $y = x^x\ [0.1, \infty)$.

1196. $y = \sqrt[3]{(x^2 - 2x)^2}\ [0, 3]$.

1197. $y = \arctan\dfrac{1 - x}{1 + x}\ [0, 1]$.

Inequalities

In Problems 1198 to 1207 prove that the given inequalities are true.

1198. $2\sqrt{x} > 3 - \frac{1}{x}\ (x > 1)$.

1199. $e^x > 1 + x\ (x \neq 0)$.

1200. $x > \ln(1 + x)\ (x > 0)$.

1201. $\ln x > \frac{2(x-1)}{x+1}\ (x > 1)$.

1202. $2x \arctan x \geq \ln(1 + x^2)$.

1203. $1 + x \ln(x + \sqrt{1 + x^2}) \geq \sqrt{1 + x^2}$.

1204. $\ln(1 + x) > \frac{\arctan x}{1 + x}\ (x > 0)$.

1205. $\sin x < x - \frac{x^3}{6} + \frac{x^5}{120}\ (x > 0)$.

1206. $\sin x + \tan x > 2x \left(0 < x < \frac{\pi}{2}\right)$.

1207. $\cosh x > 1 + \frac{x^2}{2}\ (x \neq 0)$.

Problems on finding the greatest and the least values of functions

1208. Break up the number 8 into two summands such that the sum of their cubes is the least possible.

1209. What positive number added to its reciprocal yields the least possible sum?

1210. Decompose the number 36 into two factors such that the sum of their squares is the least possible.

1211. A covered box of volume 72 cm^3 and the base sides in a ratio of 1 : 2 is to be made. What must the lengths of all sides be so that the total surface area is the least possible?

1212. Equal squares must be cut out of the corners of a square piece of cardboard 18 cm by 18 cm in order to fold the cardboard along the dashed line (Fig. 29) and make a box of the greatest possible capacity. What must the side of the cut-out square be?

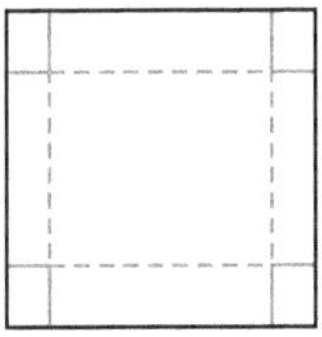

Fig. 29

1213. Solve the previous problem for a rectangular piece of cardboard 8 cm by 5 cm.

1214. The volume of a regular triangular prism is v. What must the side of the base be so that the total surface area is the least possible?

1215. An open cylindrical tub has a given volume v. What must the radius of the base and the altitude of the cylinder be to yield the least possible surface area?

1216. Determine the relationship between the radius R and the altitude H of a cylinder which has the least possible total surface area at the given volume.

1217. A conic funnel with the generatrix 20 cm long must be made. What must the height of the funnel be to yield the greatest possible volume?

1218. A sector with a central angle α is cut out of a circle to make a cone. What value of the angle α will yield the greatest possible volume of the cone?

1219. The perimeter of an isosceles triangle is equal to $2p$. What must its sides be so that the volume of the solid generated by revolving the triangle about its base is the greatest possible?

1220. The perimeter of an isosceles triangle is equal to $2p$. What must its sides be so that the volume of the solid generated by revolving the triangle about the altitude dropped on the base is the greatest possible?

1221. Determine the altitude of a cylinder of the greatest possible volume which can be inscribed in a sphere with a radius R.

1222. Determine the altitude of a cone with the greatest possible volume which can be inscribed in a sphere of radius R.

1223. A raindrop with an initial mass of m_0 is falling under the force of gravity. The loss in mass, due to evaporation, is proportional to time (the proportionality factor is equal to k). How many seconds will it take the kinetic energy to attain its greatest value after it begins to fall? What will its kinetic energy be? (Ignore the resistance of the air.)

1224. A lever of the second kind has a point of support A; a weight P is hung at point B ($AB = a$). The weight of the unit length of the lever is equal to k. What must the length of the lever be so that the weight P is balanced with the least force? (The torque of the balancing force must equal the sum of the torques of the weight P and the lever).

1225. Fuel expenditures for a steamship are proportional to the cube of its speed. As is known, at a speed of 10 km/h fuel costs are 30 roubles per hour and other expenses (independent of the speed) amount of 480 roubles per hour. At what speed of the ship will the sum of expenses per kilometre of travel be the best? What will the total sum of expenditures per hour be?

1226. Three points A, B and C are situated so that the angle ABC is equal to 60°. A car leaves point A, while simultaneously a train leaves point B.

The car travels toward B at a speed of 80 km/h, while the train travels toward C at 50 km/h. At what time (from the beginning of travel) is the distance between the train and the car the smallest if $AB = 200$ km?

1227. A point is given on the circumference of a circle. Draw a chord BC parallel to the tangent at point A so that the area of the triangle ABC is the greatest.

1228. Find the sides of a rectangle with the greatest possible perimeter inscribed in a semicircle of radius R.

1229. In a given segment of a circle inscribe a rectangle of the greatest possible area.

1230. About a given cylinder circumscribe a cone of the least possible volume (the planes of the bases of the cylinder and cone must coincide).

1231. Find the altitude of a right circular cone having the least volume circumscribed about a sphere of radius R.

1232. Find the angle at the vertex of an axial section of a cone with the least lateral surface circumscribed around a given sphere.

1233. What must the angle at the vertex of an isosceles triangle of a given area be such that the radius of the circle inscribed in this triangle is the greatest?

1234. Find the altitude of a cone of the least volume which can be drawn around a hemisphere of radius R (the centre of the base of the cone falls on the centre of the sphere).

1235. What must be the altitude of a cone inscribed in a sphere of radius R such that its lateral surface area is the greatest?

1236. Prove that a conical tent of a given volume requires the least amount of material when its height is $\sqrt{2}$ times the radius of the base.

1237. Through a given point P (1, 4) draw a straight line so that the sum of its positive intercepts on the coordinate axes is the smallest.

1238. Find the sides of a rectangle with the greatest area which can be inscribed in the ellipse $\frac{x^2}{a^2} + \frac{y^2}{b^2} = 1$.

1239. Find the ellipse having the least area which can be circumscribed about a given rectangle (the area of the ellipse with semiaxes a and b equals πab).

1240. At which point on the ellipse $\frac{x^2}{8} + \frac{y^2}{18} = 1$ must a tangent be drawn such that the area of the triangle formed by this tangent and the coordinate axes is the smallest?

1241. Two points A (1, 4) and B (3, 0) are given on the ellipse $2x^2 + y^2 = 18$. Find a third point C on the ellipse such that the area of the ΔABC is the greatest.

1242. A point is given on the axis of the parabola $y^2 = 2px$ at a distance a from its vertex. Determine the abscissa x of the point on the curve closest to the given point.

1243. An iron band of width a must be bent into an open cylinderical groove (the cross section of the groove is in the form of an arc of the circular segment). Find the value of the central angle subtended by this arc which yields the greatest capacity of the groove.

1244. A log 20 m long has the form of a truncated cone whose bases have diameteres of 2 m and 1 m. A beam of the square cross section and the greatest volume is to be cut from the log. The axis of the beam and the axis of the log must coincide. Find the dimensions of the beam.

1245. A series of trials resulted in n distinct values : $x_1, x_2, \ldots, x_n$ of a magnitude A. A value of x is often used for A such that the sum of the squares of its deviations from $x_1, x_2, \ldots, x_n$ is the least possible. Find the value of x which satisfies this requirement.

1246. A torpedo-boat is anchored 9 km away from the nearest point on shore. A messenger must be sent from the torpedo-boat to a camp, 15 km from the point on shore closest to the torpedo-boat. If the messenger can walk at a speed of 5 km per hour and can row at 4 km per hour, then at what point on shore must he land in order to reach the camp in the shortest possible time?

1247. A lantern must be hanged directly above a circular plaza of radius R. At what height must it be installed to provide the best lighting for the road around the plaza? (The intensity of illumination of a surface is directly proportional to the cosine of the angle of incidence of the rays and indirectly proportional to the square of the distance from the source of light).

1248. Two sources of light with candlepowers I_1 and I_2 are separated from one another by a length l. Find the least illuminated point.

1249. A picture 1.4 m high is hung on a wall so that its lower edge is 1.8 m above the line of the observer's eye. At what distance from the wall must the observer stand to occupy a most favourable position for examining the picture (i.e., to ensure the greatest angle of view)?

1250. A load of weight P lying on a horizontal plane must be displaced by a force F applied to it. The frictional force is directly proportional to the force pressing the load against the plane and is directed against the displacing force. The proportionality factor (coefficient of friction) is equal to k. At what angle φ to the horizontal must the force F be applied so that its value turns out to be the least possible? Determine the least value of the displacing force.

1251. The rate of flow of water through a round pipe is directly proportional to the so-called hydraulic radius R computed by the formula $R = \frac{S}{p}$, where S is the cross- sectional area of the water flow in the pipe and p is the wetted perimeter of the cross section of the pipe. The degree to what the pipe is filled with water is characterized by a central angle resting on the horizontal surface of running water. At what degree of filling the pipe will the rate of flow of water be the greatest? (Find graphically the roots of the transcendental equation obtained in solving the problem.)

1252. In a printed book the text must occupy S square centimetres of each page. The top and bottom margins must be a cm each, and the right-hand and left-hand margins b cm each. If we are interested only in saving the paper, then what must the size of the printed page be?

1253*. A conic funnel of the base radius R and the altitude H is filled with water . A heavy ball is dropped in the funnel . What must the radius of the ball be to obtain the greatest possible volume of the water displaced from the funnel by the sunken portion of the ball?

1254. The vertex of a parabola lies on a circle of radius R, its axis is directed along the diameter. What must the parameter of the parabola be so that the area of the segment bounded by the parabola and the chord (common with the circle) is the greatest? [The area of a symmetric parabolic segment is equal to two thirds of the product of its base (the chord) by the altitude (the distance from the vertex to the chord).]

1255. A cone of altitude H and the base radius R is cut by a plane parallel to the generatrix. What must be the distance between the line of intersection (of this plane and the plane of the cone base) and the centre of the cone base so that the area of the section is the greatest? (see the previous problem.)

1256. For what point P of the parabola $y^2 = 2px$ has the segment of the inner normal at P the smallest length?

1257. Show that a tangent to an ellipse whose segment intercepted by the axes is the shortest is divided, at the point of tangency, into two parts respectively equal to the semiaxes of the ellipse.

1258. Prove that in an ellipse the distance between the centre and any normal does not exceed the difference between the semiaxes. (Make use of a parametric representation of the ellipse).

1259. Given in a rectangular coordinate system xOy : a point (a, b) and a curve $y = f(x)$. Show that the distance between the fixed point (a, b)

and a variable point $(x, f(x))$ can reach an extremum only in the direction of the normal to the curve $y = f(x)$.

The *antiderivative* (or *primitive*) of a function $f(x)$ is defined as a function $F(x)$ whose derivative is equal to the given function: $F'(x) = f(x)$.

In Problem 1260 to 1262 show (with the aid of differentiation and without it) that the given functions are antiderivatives of one and the same function .

1260. $y = \ln ax$ and $y = \ln x$.

1261. $y = 2\sin^2 x$ and $y = -\cos 2x$.

1262. $y = (e^x + e^{-x})^2$ and $y = (e^x - e^{-x})^2$.

1263*. Show that the function

$$y = \cos^2 x + \cos^2\left(\frac{\pi}{3} + x\right) - \cos x \cos\left(\frac{\pi}{3} + x\right)$$

is a constant (i.e., is independent of x). Find the value of this constant.

1264. Show that the function $y = 2\arctan x + \arcsin\dfrac{2x}{1+x^2}$ is a constant for $x \geq 1$. Find the value of this constant.

1265. Show that the function

$$y = \arccos\frac{a\cos x + b}{a + b\cos x} - 2\arctan\left(\sqrt{\frac{a-b}{a+b}}\tan\frac{x}{2}\right),$$

where $0 < b \leq a$, is a constant for $x \geq 0$. Find the value of this constant.

1266. Make sure that the functions $\frac{1}{2}e^{2x}$, $e^x \sinh x$ and $e^x \cosh x$ differ from one another by a constant. Show that each of the given functions is an antiderivative of the function e^{2x}.

3. Application of the Second Derivative

Extrema

In Problems 1267 to 1275 find the extrema of the given functions taking advantage of the second derivative.

1267. $y = x^3 - 2ax^2 + a^2x$ $(a > 0)$.

1268. $y = x^2(a - x)^2$.

1269. $y = x + \dfrac{a^2}{x}$ $(a > 0)$.

1270. $y = x + \sqrt{1 - x}$.

1271. $y = x\sqrt{2 - x^2}$.

1272. $y = \cosh ax$.

1273. $y = x^2 e^{-x}$.

1274. $y = \dfrac{x}{\ln x}$.

1275. $y = x^{1/x}$.

1276. For what a does the function

$$f(x) = a \sin x + \frac{1}{3} \sin 3x$$

have an extremum at $x = \dfrac{\pi}{3}$? Will it be a maximum or a minimum?

1277. Find the values of a and b for which the function

$$y = a \ln x + bx^2 + x$$

has extrema at the points $x_1 = 1$ and $x_2 = 2$. Show that for the found values of a and b the given function has a minimum at the point x_1 and a maximum at x_2.

Convexity, concavity, points of inflection

1278. Find out whether the curve $y = x^5 - 5x^3 - 15x^2 + 30$ is convex or concave in the neighbourhoods of the points (1, 11) and (3, 3).

1279. Find out whether the curve $y = \arctan x$ is convex or concave in the neighbourhoods of the points $\left(1, \dfrac{\pi}{4}\right)$ and $\left(-1, -\dfrac{\pi}{4}\right)$.

1280. Find out whether the curve $y = x^2 \ln x$ is convex or concave in the neighbourhoods of the points (1, 0) and $\left(\dfrac{1}{e^2}, -\dfrac{2}{e^4}\right)$.

1281. Show that the graph of the function $y = x \arctan x$ is concave everywhere.

1282. Show that the graph of the function $y = \ln(x^2 - 1)$ is convex everywhere.

1283. Prove that if the graph of a function is everywhere convex or everywhere concave, then this function cannot have more than one extremum.

1284. Let $P(x)$ be a polynomial with positive coefficients and even exponents. Show that the graph of the function $y = P(x) + ax + b$ is concave everywhere.

1285. The curves $y = \varphi(x)$ and $y = \psi(x)$ are concave on an interval (a, b). Prove that in the given interval : (a) the curve $y = \varphi(x) + \psi(x)$ is concave; (b) if $\varphi(x)$ and $\psi(x)$ are positive and have a common point of minimum, then the curve $y = \varphi(x)\,\psi(x)$ is concave.

1286. Find out the shape of the graph of the function if it is known that in the interval (a, b):

(1) $y > 0,\ y' > 0,\ y'' < 0$; (2) $y > 0,\ y' < 0,\ y'' > 0$;

(3) $y < 0,\ y' > 0,\ y'' > 0$; (4) $y > 0,\ y' < 0,\ y'' < 0$.

In Problems 1287 to 1300 find the points of inflection and the intervals of concavity and convexity of the graphs of the given functions.

1287. $y = x^3 - 5x^2 + 3x - 5$. **1288.** $y = (x+1)^4 + e^x$.

1289. $y = x^4 - 12x^3 + 48x^2 - 50$. **1290.** $y = x + 36x^2 - 2x^3 - x^4$.

1291. $y = 3x^5 - 5x^4 + 3x - 2$. **1292.** $y = (x+2)^6 + 2x + 2$.

1293. $y = \dfrac{x^3}{x^2 + 3a^2}\ (a > 0)$. **1294.** $y = a - \sqrt[3]{x - b}$.

1295. $y = e^{\sin x}\left(-\dfrac{\pi}{2} \le x \le \dfrac{\pi}{2}\right)$. **1296.** $y = \ln(1 + x^2)$.

1297. $y = \dfrac{a}{x}\ln\dfrac{x}{a}\ (a > 0)$. **1298.** $y = a - \sqrt[5]{(x-b)^2}$.

1299. $y = e^{\arctan x}$. **1300.** $y = x^4(12\ln x - 7)$.

1301. Show that the curve $y = \dfrac{x+1}{x^2+1}$ has three points of inflection which lie on one straight line.

1302. Show that the points of inflection of the curve $y = x \sin x$ lie on the curve $y^2(4 + x^2) = 4x^2$.

1303. Show that the points of inflection of the curve $y = \dfrac{\sin x}{x}$ lie on the curve $y^2(4 + x^4) = 4$.

1304. Make sure that the graphs of the functions $y = \pm e^{-x}$ and $y = e^{-x}\sin x$ (the curve of damped oscillations) have common tangents at the points of inflection of the curve $y = e^{-x}\sin x$.

1305. At what values of a and b does the point $(1, 3)$ serve as the point of inflection of the curve $y = ax^3 + bx^2$?

1306. Choose α and β such that the point $A\,(2, 2.5)$ becomes a point of inflection of the curve $x^2y + \alpha x + \beta y = 0$. Will it have some more points of inflection? What are they?

1307. At what values of a has the graph of the function $y = e^x + ax^3$ points of inflection?

1308. Prove that the abscissa of an inflection point of the graph of a function cannot coincide with a point of extremum of this function.

1309. Prove that in any twice differentiable function between two points of extremum there lies at least one abscissa of the inflection point of the graph of the function.

1310. Taking the function $y = x^4 + 8x^3 + 18x^2 + 8$ as an example, verify that between the abscissas of the inflection points of the graph of a function can be no points of extremum (cf. the previous problem).

1311. Using the graph of a function (Fig. 30), find out the shape of the graphs of its first and second derivatives.

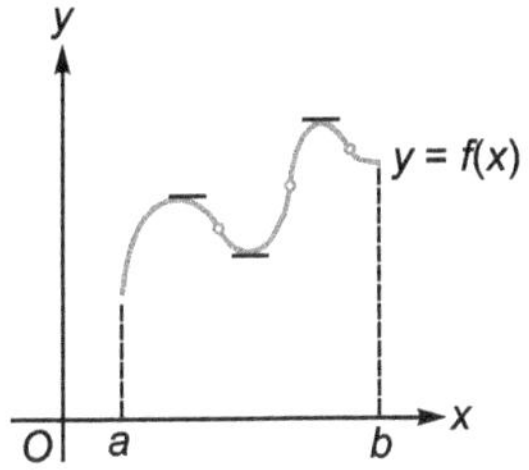

Fig. 30

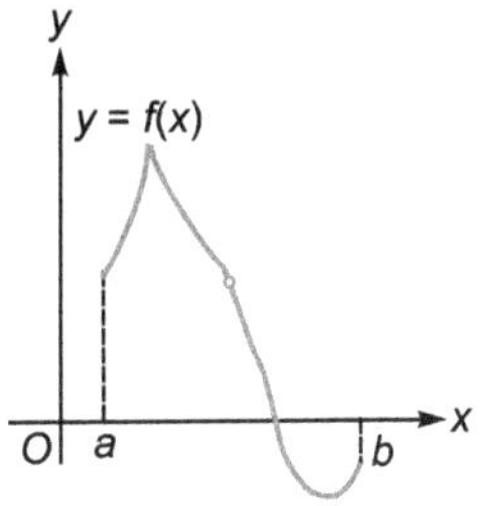

Fig. 31

1312. Using the graph of a function (Fig. 31), find out the shape of the graphs of its first and second derivatives.

1313. Find out the shape of the graph of a function using the given graph of its derivative (Fig. 32).

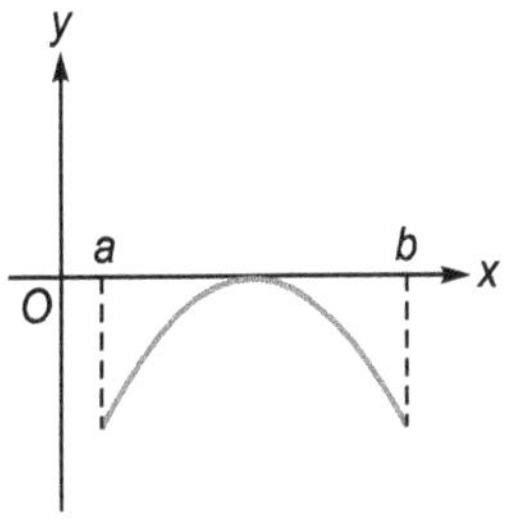

Fig. 32

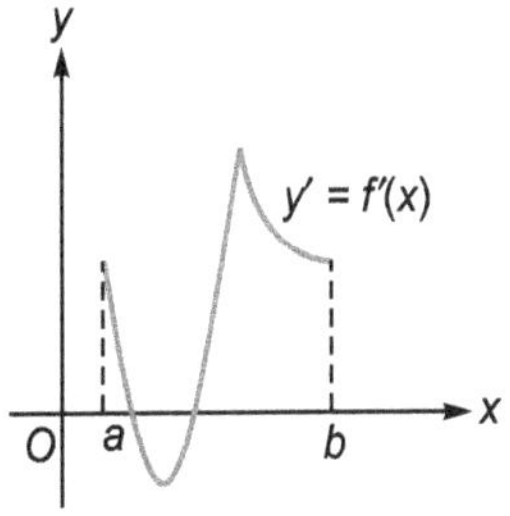

Fig. 33

1314. Find out the shape of the graph of a function using the given graph of its derivative (Fig. 33).

1315. A curve is represented parametrically by the equations $x = \varphi(t)$, $y = \psi(t)$. Make sure that to the values of t at which the expression $\dfrac{\varphi' \psi'' - \psi' \varphi''}{\varphi'}$ changes sign (the prime denotes differentiation with respect to t) and $\varphi'(t) \neq 0$, there correspond the points of inflection of the curve.

1316. Find the points of inflection of the curve $x = t^2$, $y = 3t + t^3$.

1317. Find the points of inflection of the curve $x = e^t$, $y = \sin t$.

4. Additional Items. Solving Equations

Cauchy's formula and L'Hospital's rule

1318. Write Cauchy's formula for the functions $f(x) = \sin x$ and $\varphi(x) = \ln x$ in the interval $[a, b]$, $0 < a < b$.

1319. Write Cauchy's formula for the functions $f(x) = e^{2x}$ and $\varphi(x) = 1 + e^x$ in the interval $[a, b]$.

1320. Check the validity of Cauchy's formula for the functions $f(x) = x^3$ and $\varphi(x) = x^2 + 1$ in the interval $[1, 2]$.

1321. Check the validity of Cauchy's formula for the functions $f(x) = \sin x$ and $\varphi(x) = x + \cos x$ in the interval $\left[0, \frac{\pi}{2}\right]$.

1322. Prove that if the relationship $|f'(x)| \geq |\varphi'(x)|$ is valid in the interval $[a, b]$ and $\varphi'(x)$ does not vanish, then the relationship $|\Delta f(x)| \geq |\Delta\varphi(x)|$ is also valid, where $\Delta f(x) = f(x + \Delta x) - f(x)$, $\Delta\varphi(x) = \varphi(x + \Delta x) - \varphi(x)$, and x and $x + \Delta x$ are arbitrary points of the interval $[a, b]$.

1323. Prove that in the interval $\left[x, \frac{1}{2}\right]$ $(x \geq 0)$ the increment of the function $y = \ln(1 + x^2)$ is smaller than that of the function $y = \arctan x$, and in the interval $\left[\frac{1}{2}, x\right]$ vice-versa : $\Delta \arctan x < \Delta \ln(1 + x^2)$. Using the latter relationship, show that in the interval $\left[\frac{1}{2}, 1\right]$.

$$\arctan x - \ln(1 + x^2) \geq \frac{\pi}{4} - \ln 2.$$

In Problems 1324 to 1364 find the limits.

1324. $\lim\limits_{x \to a} \dfrac{\sqrt[3]{x} - \sqrt[3]{a}}{\sqrt{x} - \sqrt{a}}$.

1325. $\lim\limits_{x \to 0} \dfrac{\ln \cos x}{x}$.

1326. $\lim\limits_{x \to 0} \dfrac{e^x - 1}{\sin x}$.

1327. $\lim\limits_{x \to 0} \dfrac{e^{\alpha x} - \cos \alpha x}{e^{\beta x} - \cos \beta x}$.

1328. $\lim\limits_{x \to 0} \dfrac{x - \arctan x}{x^3}$.

1329. $\lim\limits_{x \to 0} \dfrac{e^{\alpha\sqrt{x}} - 1}{\sqrt{\sin bx}}$.

1330. $\lim\limits_{x \to 0} \dfrac{x - \sin x}{x - \tan x}$.

1331. $\lim\limits_{x \to \infty} \dfrac{\pi - 2\arctan x}{\ln\left(1 + \frac{1}{x}\right)}$.

1332. $\lim\limits_{x \to a} \dfrac{x^m - a^m}{x^n - a^n}$.

1333. $\lim\limits_{x \to 0} \dfrac{a^x - b^x}{c^x - d^x}$.

1334. $\lim\limits_{x \to 0} \dfrac{e^{x^2} - 1}{\cos x - 1}$.

1335. $\lim\limits_{x \to 0} \dfrac{e^x - e^{-x}}{\sin x \cos x}$.

1336. $\lim\limits_{x \to 0} \dfrac{a^x - b^x}{x\sqrt{1 - x^2}}$.

1337. $\lim\limits_{x \to a} \dfrac{\cos x \ln (x - a)}{\ln (e^x - e^a)}$.

1338. $\lim\limits_{x \to 0} \dfrac{e^x - e^{-x} - 2x}{x - \sin x}$.

1339. $\lim\limits_{x \to 0} \dfrac{e^{\tan x} - e^x}{\tan x - x}$.

1340. $\lim\limits_{x \to 0} \dfrac{e^x - \dfrac{x^3}{6} - \dfrac{x^2}{2} - x - 1}{\cos x + \dfrac{x^2}{2} - 1}$.

1341. $\lim\limits_{x \to 0} \dfrac{e^{x^3} - 1 - x^3}{\sin^6 2x}$.

1342. $\lim\limits_{x \to 0} \dfrac{\ln (1 + x)^4 - 4x + 2x^2 - \dfrac{4}{3}x^3 + x^4}{6 \sin x - 6x + x^3}$.

1343. $\lim\limits_{x \to 0} \dfrac{\ln \sin 2x}{\ln \sin x}$.

1344. $\lim\limits_{x \to 0} \dfrac{\ln x}{\ln \sin x}$.

1345. $\lim\limits_{x \to 1} \dfrac{\ln (1 - x) + \tan \dfrac{\pi x}{2}}{\cot \pi x}$.

1346. $\lim\limits_{x \to +\infty} (x^n e^{-x})$.

1347. $\lim\limits_{x \to \infty} [(\pi - 2 \arctan x) \ln x]$.

1348. $\lim\limits_{x \to \infty} \left[x \sin \dfrac{a}{x}\right]$.

1349. $\lim\limits_{x \to 1} \left[\dfrac{x}{x - 1} - \dfrac{1}{\ln x}\right]$.

1350. $\lim\limits_{\varphi \to a} \left[(a^2 - \varphi^2) \tan \dfrac{\pi\varphi}{2a}\right]$.

1351. $\lim\limits_{x \to 1} \left(\dfrac{1}{\ln x} - \dfrac{x}{\ln x}\right)$.

1352. $\lim\limits_{x \to 0} \left(\cot x - \dfrac{1}{x}\right)$.

1353. $\lim\limits_{x \to 1} \dfrac{1}{\cos \dfrac{\pi x}{2} \ln (1 - x)}$.

1354. $\lim\limits_{x \to \infty} [\sqrt[3]{(a + x)(b + x)(c + x)} - x]$.

1355. $\lim\limits_{x \to \infty} [x (e^{1/x} - 1)]$.

1356. $\lim\limits_{x \to 0} [x^2 e^{1/x^2}]$.

1357. $\lim\limits_{x \to \frac{\pi}{2}} (\tan x)^{2x - \pi}$.

1358. $\lim\limits_{x \to 0} x^{\sin x}$.

1359. $\lim\limits_{x \to 0} x^{\frac{1}{\ln (e^x - 1)}}$.

1360. $\lim\limits_{x \to 0} \left(\dfrac{1}{x}\right)^{\tan x}$.

1361. $\lim\limits_{x \to 0} (e^x + x)^{1/x}$.

1362. $\lim\limits_{x \to a} \left(2 - \dfrac{x}{a}\right)^{\tan \frac{\pi x}{2a}}$.

1363. $\lim\limits_{x \to \infty} \left(1 + \frac{1}{x^2}\right)^x$. **1364.** $\lim\limits_{x \to 0} \left[\frac{\ln (1 + x)^{1+x}}{x^2} - \frac{1}{x}\right]$.

1365. Verify that $\lim\limits_{x \to \infty} \frac{x - \sin x}{x + \sin x}$ exists but cannot be computed by L' Hospital's rule.

1366. The values of which function (for sufficiently large values of x) are greater : $a^x x^a$ or x^x?

1367. The values of which function (for sufficiently large values of x) are greater : $f(x)$ or $\ln f(x)$, provided $f(x) \to \infty$ as $x \to \infty$.

1368. Let $x \to 0$. Prove that $e - (1 + x)^{1/x}$ is an infinitesimal of the first order with respect to x.

1369. Let $x \to 0$. Prove that $\ln (1 + x) - e \ln \ln (e + x)$ is an infinitesimal of the second order with respect to x.

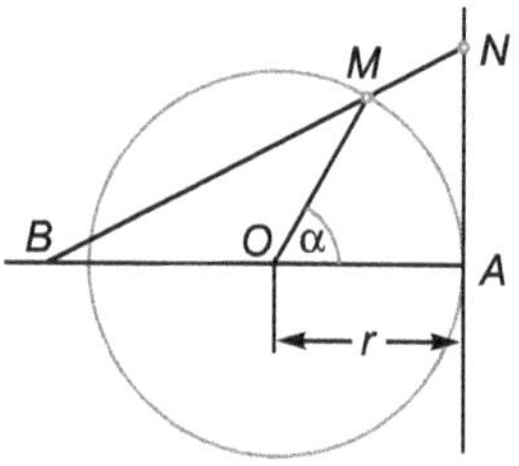

Fig. 34

1370. A tangent line is drawn to a circle of radius r at point A (Fig. 34), and a segment AN is laid off whose length is equal to that of the arc AM. A straight line MN is drawn to intersect the extension of the diameter AO at point B. Prove that

$$OB = \frac{r\,(\alpha \cos \alpha - \sin \alpha)}{\sin \alpha - \alpha},$$

where α is a radian measure of the central angle corresponding to the arc AM and show that $\lim\limits_{\alpha \to 0} OB = 2r$.

Asymptotic behaviour of functions and asymptotes of curves

1371. Proceeding directly from the definition, verify that the straight line $y = 2x + 1$ is the asymptote of the curve $y = \frac{2x^3 + x^3 + 1}{x^3}$.

1372. Proceeding directly from the definition, verify that the straight line $x + y = 0$ is the asymptote of the curve $x^2y + xy^2 = 1$.

1373. Show that the curves $y = \sqrt[3]{x^3 + 3x^2}$ and $y = \frac{x^2}{x-1}$ approach each other asymptotically as $x \to \pm\infty$.

1374. Prove that the functions

$$f(x) = \sqrt{x^6 + 2x^4 + 7x^2 + 1} \text{ and } \varphi(x) = x^3 + x$$

are asymptotically equal to each other as $x \to \infty$. Taking advantage of this fact carry out approximate calculation of $f(115)$ and $f(120)$. What will the error be if we put $f(100) = \varphi(100)$?

In Problems 1375 to 1391 find the asymptotes of the given curves.

1375. $\frac{x^2}{a^2} - \frac{y^2}{b^2} = 1.$

1376. $xy = a.$

1377. $y = \frac{1}{x^2 - 4x + 5}.$

1378. $y = c + \frac{a^3}{(x-b)^2}.$

1379. $2y(x+1)^2 = x^3.$

1380. $y^3 = a^3 - x^3.$

1381. $y^3 = 6x^2 + x^3.$

1382. $y^2(x^2+1) = x^2(x^2-1).$

1383. $xy^2 + x^2y = a^3.$

1384. $y(x^2 - 3bx + 2b^2) = x^3 - 3ax^2 + a^3.$

1385. $(y + x + 1)^2 = x^2 + 1.$

1386. $y = x \ln\left(e + \frac{1}{x}\right).$

1387. $y = xe^x.$

1388. $y = xe^{2/x} + 1.$

1389. $y = x \operatorname{arcsec} x.$

1390. $y = 2x + \arctan\frac{x}{2}.$

1391. $y = \frac{xf(x) + a}{f(x)}$, where $f(x)$ is a polynomial $(a \neq 0)$.

1392. A curve is represented parametrically by the equations $x = \varphi(t)$, $y = \varphi(t)$. Prove that the asymptotes not parallel to the axes of coordinates can exist only at the values of $t = t_0$ for which simultaneously

$$\lim_{t \to t_0} \varphi(t) = \infty \quad \text{and} \quad \lim_{t \to t_0} \psi(t) = \infty.$$

and if the equation of the asymptote is $y = ax + b$, then

$$a = \lim_{t \to t_0} \frac{\psi(t)}{\varphi(t)}, \; b = \lim_{t \to t_0} [\psi(t) - a\varphi(t)].$$

How are the asymptotes parallel to the coordinate axes found?

1393. Find the asymptotes of the curve: $x = \frac{1}{t}$, $y = \frac{t}{t+1}.$

1394. Find the asymptotes of the curve: $x = \frac{2e^t}{t-1}$, $y = \frac{te^t}{t-1}.$

1395. Find the asymptotes of the curve: $x = \dfrac{2t}{1 - t^2}$, $y = \dfrac{t^2}{1 - t^2}$.

1396. Find the asymptotes of the folium of Descartes: $x = \dfrac{3at}{1 + t^3}$, $y = \dfrac{3at^2}{1 + t^3}$.

1397. Find the asymptotes of the curve: $x = \dfrac{t - 8}{t^2 - 4}$, $y = \dfrac{3}{t\,(t^2 - 4)}$.

General investigation of functions and curves

In Problems 1398 to 1464 carry out complete investigation of the given functions and graph them.

1398. $y = \dfrac{x}{1 + x^2}$.

1399. $y = \dfrac{1}{1 - x^2}$.

1400. $y = \dfrac{x}{x^2 - 1}$.

1401. $y\,(x - 1)(x - 2)(x - 3) = 1$.

1402. $y = \dfrac{x^2}{x^2 - 1}$.

1403. $y = (x^2 - 1)^3$.

1404. $y = 32x^2\,(x^2 - 1)^3$.

1405. $y = \dfrac{1}{x} + 4x^2$.

1406. $y = x^2 + \dfrac{1}{x^2}$.

1407. $y = \dfrac{2x - 1}{(x - 1)^2}$.

1408. $y = \dfrac{x^3}{3 - x^2}$.

1409. $y = \dfrac{x^3}{2\,(x + 1)^2}$.

1410. $y\,(x - 1) = x^3$.

1411. $y\,(x^3 - 1) = x^4$.

1412. $y = \dfrac{(x - 1)^2}{(x + 1)^3}$.

1413. $y = \dfrac{x^3 + 2x^2 + 7x - 3}{2x^2}$.

1414. $xy = (x^2 - 1)(x - 2)$.

1415. $(y - x)\,x^4 + 8 = 0$.

1416. $y = \dfrac{x}{e^x}$.

1417. $y = x^2 e^{-x}$.

1418. $y = \dfrac{e^x}{x}$.

1419. $y = x - \ln\,(x + 1)$.

1420. $y = \ln\,(x^2 + 1)$.

1421. $y = x^2 e^{-x^2}$.

1422. $y = x^3 e^{-x}$.

1423. $y = xe^{-\frac{x^2}{2}}$.

1424. $y = \dfrac{1}{e^x - 1}$.

1425. $y = x + \dfrac{\ln x}{x}$.

1426. $y = \left(1 + \dfrac{1}{x}\right)^x$.

1427. $y = x + \sin x$.

1428. $y = x \sin x$.

1429. $y = \ln \cos x$.

1430. $y = \cos x - \ln \cos x$. **1431.** $y = x - 2 \arctan x$.

1432. $y = e^{\frac{1}{x^2 - 4x + 3}}$ (without finding the inflection points).

1433. $y = e^{\sin x} - \sin x$ (without finding the inflection points).

1434. $y = \sqrt[3]{x^2} - x$. **1435.** $y^3 = x^2 (x^2 - 4)^3$.

1436. $(3y + x)^3 = 27x$. **1437.** $y = \sqrt[3]{(x+1)^2} - \sqrt[3]{x^2} = 1$.

1438. $y = (x - 1)^{2/3} (x + 1)^3$. **1439.** $y^3 = 6x^2 - x^3$.

1440. $(y - x)^2 = x^5$. **1441.** $(y - x^2)^2 = x^5$.

1442. $y^2 = x^3 + 1$. **1443.** $y^2 = x^3 - x$.

1444. $y^2 = x(x - 1)^2$. **1445.** $y^2 = x^2 (x - 1)$.

1446. $y^2 = \dfrac{x^3 - 2}{3x}$. **1447.** $x^2y + xy^2 = 2$.

1448. $y^2 = x^2 \dfrac{a + x}{a - x}$ (strophoid) $(a > 0)$.

1449. $9y^2 = 4x^3 - x^4$. **1450.** $25y^2 = x^2 (4 - x^2)^3$.

1451. $y^2 = x^2 - x^4$. **1452.** $x^2y^2 = 4(x - 1)$.

1453. $y^2 (2a - x) = x^3$ (cissoid) $(a > 0)$.

1454. $x^2y^2 = (x - 1)(x - 2)$.

1455. $x^2y^2 = (a + x)^3 (a - x)$ (conchoid) $(a > 0)$.

1456. $16y^2 = (x^2 - 4)^2 (1 - x^2)$. **1457.** $y^2 = (1 - x^2)^3$.

1458. $y^2x^4 = (x^2 - 1)^3$. **1459.** $y^2 = 2exe^{-2x}$.

1460. $y = e^{1/x} - x$. **1461.** $y = e^{\tan x}$.

1462. $f(x) = \dfrac{\sin x}{x}$, $f(0) = 1$.

1463. $y = 1 - xe^{-\frac{1}{|x|} - \frac{1}{x}}$ for $x \neq 0$, $y = 1$ at $x = 0$.

1464. $y = x^2 - 4|x| + 3$.

In Problems 1465 to 1469 analyze the functions represented parametrically and graph them.

1465. $x = t^3 + 3t + 1$, $y = t^3 - 3t + 1$.

1466. $x = t^3 - 3\pi$, $y = t^3 - 6 \arctan t$. **1467.** $x = \dfrac{3t}{1 + t^3}$, $y = \dfrac{3t^2}{1 + t^3}$.

1468. $x = te^t$, $y = te^{-t}$.

1469. $x = 2a \cos t - a \cos 2t$, $y = 2a \sin t - a \sin 2t$ (cardioid).

In Problems 1470 to 1477 analyze the curves whose equations are given in polar coordinates (see the footnote on page 31).

1470. $\rho = a \sin 3\varphi$ (three-leafed rose). **1471.** $\rho = a \tan \varphi$.

1472. $\rho = a(1 + \tan \varphi)$. **1473.** $\rho = a(1 + \cos \varphi)$ (cardioid).

1474. $\rho = a(1 + b \cos \varphi)$ $(a > 0,\ b > 1)$. **1475.** $\rho = \sqrt{\dfrac{\pi}{\varphi}}$.

1476. $\rho = \dfrac{2}{\pi} \arctan \dfrac{\varphi}{\pi}$.

1477. $\rho = \sqrt{1 - t^2},\ \varphi = \arcsin t + \sqrt{1 - t^2}$.

In Problems 1478 to 1481 investigate the functions and construct the curves in polar coordinates.

1478. $(x^2 + y^2)^3 = 4a^2x^2y^2$. **1479.** $(x^2 + y^2)\,x = a^2y$.

1480. $x^4 + y^4 = a^2(x^2 + y^2)$. **1481.** $(x^2 + y^2)(x^2 - y^2)^2 = 4x^2y^2$.

Solving equations

1482. Check to see that the equation $x^3 - x^2 - 8x + 12 = 0$ has one simple root $x_1 = -3$ and one double root $x_2 = 2$.

1483. Check to see that the equation $x^4 + 2x^3 - 3x^2 - 4x + 4 = 0$ has two double roots $x_1 = 1$ and $x_2 = -2$.

1484. Make sure that the equation $x \arcsin x = 0$ has only one real root $x = 0$ which is a double one.

1485. Show that the roots of the equation $x \sin x = 0$ have the form $y = k\pi$ $(k = 0, \pm 1, \pm 2, \ldots)$, a double root corresponding to the value $k = 0$. What is the multiplicity of the remaining roots?

1486. Show that the equation $x^3 - 3x^2 + 6x - 1 = 0$ has the only real simple root belonging to the interval (0, 1), and find this root to within 0.1, using the trial-and-error method.

1487. Show that the equation $x^4 + 3x^2 - x - 2 = 0$ has two (and only two) real simple roots each belonging to one of the following intervals (–1, 0) and (0, 1). Find these roots with the aid of the trial-and-error method to within 0.1.

1488. Show that the equation $f(x) = a \neq 0$, where $f(x)$ is a polynomial with positive coefficients all terms of which have odd exponents, has one and only one real root (which can be multiple as well). Consider the case when $a = 0$. Find (to within 0.01) the root of the equation $x^3 + 3x - 1 = 0$, using the trial-and-error method combined with the method of chords.

1489. Prove the theorem : for the equation $x^3 + px + q = 0$ to have three simple real roots it is necessary and sufficient that p and q satisfy the inequality $4p^3 + 27q^2 < 0$. Find (to within 0.01) all the roots of the equation $x^3 - 9x + 2 = 0$, using the trial-and-error method combined with the method of chords.

1490. Show that the equation $x^4 + 2x^2 - 6x + 2 = 0$ has two (and only two) real simple roots, each belonging to one of the two intervals (0, 1) and (1, 2). Using the method of chords combined with the method of tangents, find these roots to within 0.01.

1491. Show that the equation $x^5 + 5x + 1 = 0$ has one real simple root belonging to the interval $(-1, 0)$, and find this root to within 0.01, using the method of chords combined with the method of tangents.

In Problems 1492 to 1497 find the approximate values of the roots of the given equations using a combination of three methods : the trial-and-error method, the method of chords and the method of tangents. (If necessary, use the tables of values of the functions entering the given equation).

1492. Show that the equation $xe^x = 2$ has only one real root which belongs to the interval (0, 1), and find this root to within 0.01.

1493. Show that the equation $x \ln x = a$ has no real roots for $a < -\frac{1}{e}$, has one real double root for $a = -\frac{1}{e}$, two real simple roots for $-\frac{1}{e} < a < 0$ and one real simple root for $a \geq 0$.

Find the root of the equation $x \ln x = 0.8$ accurate to 0.01.

1494. Show that the so-called Kepler's equation $x = \varepsilon \sin x + a$, where $0 < \varepsilon < 1$, has one simple real root and find this root to within 0.001 if $\varepsilon = 0.538$ and $a = 1$.

1495. Show that the equation $a^x = ax$ for $a > 1$ always has two (and only two) real and positive roots, one of them being equal to unity, the other less than, greater than, or equal to, unity depending on whether a is more than, less than, or equal to e.

Find (to within 0.001) the second root of this equation for $a = 3$.

1496. Show that the equation $x^2 \arctan x = a$, where $a \neq 0$, has one real root. Find (to within 0.001) the root of this equation for $a = 1$.

1497. At what base a of a system of logarithms are there numbers equal to their logarithms? How many such numbers can be? Find such a number (to within 0.01) if $a = \frac{1}{2}$.

5. Taylor's Formula and Its Application

Taylor's formula for polynomials

1498. Expand the polynomial $x^4 - 5x^3 + x^2 - 3x + 4$ into a series in powers of the binomial $x - 4$.

1499. Expand the polynomial $x^3 + 3x^2 - 2x + 4$ into a series in powers of the binomial $x + 1$.

1500. Expand the polynomial $x^{10} - 3x^5 + 1$ into a series in powers of the binomial $x - 1$.

1501. Using Taylor's formula, expand the function $f(x) = (x^2 - 3x + 1)^3$ into a series in powers of x.

1502. $f(x)$ is a polynomial of the 4th degree. Knowing that $f(2) = -1$, $f'(2) = 0$, $f''(2) = 2$, $f'''(2) = -12$, $f^{IV}(2) = 24$, compute $f(-1)$, $f'(0)$, $f''(1)$.

Taylor's formula

1503. Write Taylor's formula of the nth order for the function $y = \dfrac{1}{x}$ at $x_0 = -1$.

1504. Write Taylor's formula (Maclaurin's formula) of the nth order for the function $y = xe^x$ at $x_0 = 0$.

1505. Write Taylor's formula of the nth order for the function $y = \sqrt{x}$ at $x_0 = 4$.

1506. Write Taylor's formula of the $2n$th order for the function $y = \dfrac{e^x + e^{-x}}{2}$ at $x_0 = 0$.

1507. Write Taylor's formula of the nth order for the function $y = x^3 \ln x$ at $x_0 = 1$.

1508. Write Taylor's formula of the $2n$th order for the function $y = \sin^2 x$ at $x_0 = 0$.

1509. Write Taylor's formula of the third order for the function $y = \dfrac{x}{x-1}$ at $x_0 = 2$. Draw the graphs of the given function and its Taylor's polynomial of the 3rd degree.

1510. Write Taylor's formula of the second order for the function $y = \tan x$ at $x_0 = 0$. Draw the graphs of the given function and its Taylor polynomial of the second degree.

1511. Write Taylor's formula of the third order for the function $y = \arcsin x$ at $x_0 = 0$ and construct the graphs of the given function and its Taylor polynomial of the third degree.

1512. Write Taylor's formula of the third order for the function $y = \frac{1}{\sqrt{x}}$ at $x_0 = 1$ and graph the given function and its Taylor polynomial of the third degree.

1513*. Prove that the number θ in the remainder in Taylor's formula of the first order $f(a+h) = f(a) + hf'(a) + \frac{h^2}{2} f''(a+\theta h)$ tends to $\frac{1}{3}$ as $h \to 0$, if $f'''(x)$ is continuous at $x = a$ and $f'''(a) \neq 0$.

Some applications of taylor's formula

In Problems 1514 to 1519 find out the behaviour of the given functions at the indicated points.

1514. $y = 2x^6 - x^3 + 3$ at $x = 0$.

1515. $y = x^{11} + 3x^6 + 1$ at $x = 0$.

1516. $y = 2\cos x + x^2$ at $x = 0$.

1517. $y = 6\ln x - 2x^3 + 9x^2 - 18x$ at $x = 1$.

1518. $y = 6\sin x + x^2$ at $x = 0$.

1519. $y = 24e^x - 24x - 12x^2 - 4x^3 - x^4 - 20$ at $x = 0$.

1520. $f(x) = x^{10} - 3x^6 + x^2 + 2$. Find the first three terms of the expansion by Taylor's formula at $x_0 = 1$. Compute approximately $f(1.03)$.

1521. $f(x) = x^8 - 2x^7 + 5x^6 - x + 3$. Find the first three terms of the expansion by Taylor's formula at $x_0 = 2$. Compute approximately $f(2.02)$ and $f(1.97)$.

1522. $f(x) = x^{80} - x^{40} + x^{20}$. Find the first three terms of the expansion of $f(x)$ in powers of $x - 1$ and find approximately $f(1.005)$.

1523. $f(x) = x^5 - 5x^3 + x$. Find the first three terms of the expansion in powers of $x - 2$. Compute approximately $f(2.1)$. Find the exact value of $f(2.1)$, the absolute and relative errors.

1524. Check to see that in evaluating the function e^x for $0 < x \leq \frac{1}{2}$ by the approximate formula

$$e^x \approx 1 + x + \frac{x^2}{2} + \frac{x^3}{6}$$

the permissible error is less than 0.01. This taken into account, find $\sqrt{e}$ with three correct digits.

1525. Using the approximate formula $e^x \approx 1 + x + \frac{x^2}{2}$, find $\frac{1}{\sqrt[4]{e}}$ and estimate the error.

1526. Verify that for angles smaller than 28° the error introduced by replacing $\sin x$ by the expression $x - \frac{x^3}{3!} + \frac{x^5}{5!}$ will be less than 0.000001. Then, compute $\sin 20°$ with six correct digits.

1527. Find $\cos 10°$ to within 0.001. Make sure that to achieve the indicated accuracy it is sufficient to use the corresponding Taylor's formula of the second order.

1528. Using the approximate formula

$$\ln(1 + x) \approx x - \frac{x^2}{2} + \frac{x^3}{3} - \frac{x^4}{4},$$

find $\ln 1.5$ and estimate the error.

6. Curvature

In Problems 1529 to 1536 find the curvature of the given curves.

1529. Hyperbola $xy = 4$ at the point $(2, 2)$.

1530. Ellipse $\frac{x^2}{a^2} + \frac{y^2}{b^2} = 1$ at the vertices.

1531. $y = x^4 - 4x^3 - 18x^2$ at the origin.

1532. $y^2 = 8x$ at the point $\left(\frac{9}{8}, 3\right)$.

1533. $y = \ln x$ at the point $(1, 0)$.

1534. $y = \ln(x + \sqrt{1 + x^2})$ at the origin.

1535. $y = \sin x$ at the points of extremum.

1536. Folium of Descartes $x^3 + y^3 = 3axy$ at the point $\left(\frac{3}{2}a, \frac{3}{2}a\right)$.

In Problems 1537 to 1542 find the curvature of the given curves at an arbitrary point (x, y).

1537. $y = x^3$.

1538. $\frac{x^2}{a^2} - \frac{y^2}{b^2} = 1$.

1539. $y = \ln(\sec x)$.

1540. $x^{2/3} + y^{2/3} = a^{2/3}$.

1541. $\frac{x^m}{a^m} + \frac{y^m}{b^m} = 1$.

1542. $y = a \cosh \frac{x}{a}$.

In Problems 1543 to 1549 find the curvature of the given curves.

1543. $x = 3t^2$, $y = 3t - t^3$ at $t = 1$.

1544. $x = a\cos^3 t$, $y = a\sin^3 t$ at $t = t_1$.

1545. $x = a(\cos t + t\sin t)$, $y = a(\sin t - t\cos t)$ at $t = \frac{\pi}{2}$.

1546. $x = 2a\cos t - a\cos 2t,\ y = 2a\sin t - a\sin 2t$ at an arbitrary point.

1547. $\rho = a^{\varphi}$ at the point $\rho = 1,\ \varphi = 0$.

1548. $\rho = a\varphi$ at an arbitrary point.

1549. $\rho = a\varphi^k$ at an arbitrary point.

1550. Find the radius of curvature of the ellipse $\frac{x^2}{a^2} + \frac{y^2}{b^2} = 1$ at the point of contact in which the intercepted segment of the tangent is bisected.

1551. Show that the radius of curvature of a parabola equals twice the segment of the normal contained between the points of intersection of the normal with the parabola and its directrix.

1552. Show that the radius of curvature of a cycloid at any point is twice the length of the normal at the same point.

1553. Show that the radius of curvature of the lemniscate $\rho^2 = a^2\cos 2\varphi$ is inversely proportional to the corresponding polar radius.

1554. Find the circle of curvature of the parabola $y = x^2$ at the point (1, 1).

1555. Find the circle of curvature of the hyperbola $xy = 1$ at the point (1, 1).

1556. Find the circle of curvature of the curve $y = e^x$ at the point (0, 1).

1557. Find the circle of curvature of the curve $y = \tan x$ at the point $\left(\frac{\pi}{4}, 1\right)$.

1558. Find the circle of curvature of the cissoid $(x^2 + y^2)x - 2ay^2 = 0$ at the point (a, a).

In Problems 1559 to 1562 find the vertices (the points at which the curvature has an extremum) of the given curves.

1559. $\sqrt{x} + \sqrt{y} = \sqrt{a}$.

1560. $y = \ln x$.

1561. $y = e^x$.

1562. $x = a(3\cos t + \cos 3t),\ y = a(3\sin t + \sin 3t)$.

1563. Find the greatest value of the radius of curvature of the curve $\rho = a\sin^3\frac{\varphi}{3}$.

1564. Show that the curvature of the curve $y = f(x)$ at point P is equal to $|y''\cos^3\alpha|$, where α is the angle between the positive x-axis and the tangent to the curve at the point P.

1565. Show that the curvature of a curve at an arbitrary point can be represented by the expression $k = \left|\frac{d\sin\alpha}{dx}\right|$, where α has the same meaning as in the previous problem.

1566. A function $f(x)$ is defined as follows : $f(x)=x^3$ in the interval $-\infty < x \le 1$, $f(x)=ax^2+bx+c$ in the interval $1 < x < \infty$. What must a, b, c be so that the curvature of curve $y=f(x)$ is continuous everywhere?

1567. Given (Fig. 35) : a circular arc AM with the point (0, 5) as centre and the radius equal to 5, and a segment BC of a straight line which joins the point B (1, 3) to the point C (11, 66). Required : join M to B by an arc of a parabola so that the line $AMBC$ has a continuous curvature. Find the equation of the required parabola (take a parabola of the fifth order).

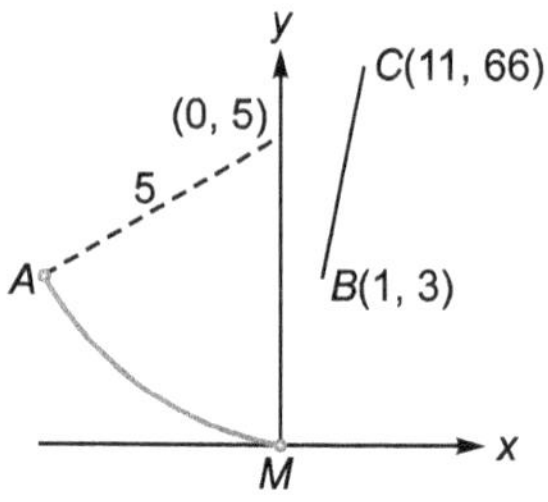

Fig. 35

In Problems 1568 to 1574 find the coordinates of the centres of curvature and the equations of the evolutes for the given curves.

1568. Parabola of the nth order $y=x^n$.

1569. Hyperbola $\dfrac{x^2}{a^2}-\dfrac{y^2}{b^2}=1$.

1570. Astroid $x^{2/3}+y^{2/3}=a^{2/3}$.

1571. Semicubical parabola $y^3=ax^2$.

1572. Parabola $x=3t,\ y=t^2-6$.

1573. Cissoid $y^2=\dfrac{x^3}{2a-x}$.

1574. Curve $\begin{cases} x = a(1+\cos^2 t)\sin t, \\ y = a\sin^2 t\cos t. \end{cases}$

1575. Show that the evolute of the tractrix

$$x=-a\left(\ln\tan\frac{t}{2}+\cos t\right),\ y=a\sin t$$

is a catenary.

1576. Show that the evolute of the logarithmic spiral $\rho=a^{\varphi}$ represents just the same spiral but turned through a certain angle. Is it possible to choose a such that the evolute coincides with the given spiral?

1577. Show that any involute of a circle can be obtained by turning one of them through an appropriate angle.

1578. Show that the distance between an arbitrary point of a cycloid and the centre of curvature corresponding to the point of the evolute equals twice the diameter of the generating circle.

1579. The semicubical parabola $py^2 = \frac{4}{27}(x-2p)^3$ serves as the evolute of the parabola $y^2 = 4px$. Find the arc length of the semicubical parabola beginning with the cusp to the point (x, y).

1580. Find the length of the evolute of an ellipse whose semiaxes are equal to a and b.

1581. Show that the evolute of the astroid $x = a\cos^3 t$, $y = a\sin^3 t$ is an astroid turned through 45° whose linear dimensions are twice the linear dimensions of the given astroid. Bearing this in mind, compute the arc length of the given astroid.

1582*. Show that the evolute of the cardioid

$$x = 2a\cos t - a\cos 2t, \quad y = 2a\sin t - a\sin 2t$$

is also a cardioid similar to the given one. Taking this into consideration, find the arc length of the entire cardioid.

1583*. Prove the theorem: if the curvature of an arc of a certain curve either only increases, or only decreases, then the circles of curvature corresponding to various points of this arc do not intersect and lie one inside another.

7. Computational Problems

1584. Find the minimum of the function $y = x^4 + x^2 + x + 1$ to within 0.001.

1585. Find the maximum of the function $y = x + \ln x - x^3$ to within 0.001.

1586. Find the greatest and the least value of the function $y = x^2 + 3\cos x$ in the interval $\left(0, \frac{\pi}{2}\right)$ to within 0.01.

1587. Find the greatest and the least value of the function $y = x - e^{x^2}$ in the interval (0.2, 0.5) to within 0.001.

1588. Find the coordinates of the inflection point of the curve $y = \frac{e^x}{10}(x^3 - 6x^2 + 19x - 30)$ to within 0.01.

1589. Find the coordinates of the inflection point of the curve $y = 6x^2 \ln x + 2x^3 - 9x^2$ to within 0.01.

1590. Find (to within 0.01) the curvature of the curve $y = \frac{1}{x^2}$ at the point of its intersection with the straight line $y = x - 1$.

1591. On the curve $y = \ln x$ find (to within 0.001) the coordinates of the point at which the radius of curvature of the given curve is three times the abscissa of this point.

5

The Definite Integral

1. The Definite Integral and Its Simplest Properties

1592. Express with the aid of an integral the area of a figure bounded by:

(1) the coordinate axes, the straight line $x = 3$ and the parabola $y = x^2 + 1$;

(2) the x-axis, the straight lines $x = a$, $x = b$ and the curve $y = e^x + 2\,(b > a)$;

(3) the x-axis and an arc of the sinusoid $y = \sin x$ corresponding to the first half-period;

(4) the parabolas $y = x^2$ and $y = 8 - x^2$;

(5) the parabolas $y = x^2$ and $y = \sqrt{x}$;

(6) the curves $y = \ln x$ and $y = \ln^2 x$.

1593. A figure is bounded by the x-axis and the straight lines $y = 2x$, $x = 4$, $x = 6$. Subdividing the interval [4, 6] into equal parts, find the areas of the n-step figures. Make sure that the both obtained expressions tend to one and the same limit S—the area of the figure—as n increases infinitely. Find the absolute and relative errors introduced by replacing the area of the given figure by the sum of areas of the n-step figures.

1594. A curvilinear trapezium with the base [2, 3] is bounded by the parabola $y = x^2$. Find the absolute and relative errors introduced by replacing the area of the given figure by the area of the 10 stepped "stairs".

1595. Compute the area of a figure bounded by the parabola $y = \dfrac{x^2}{2}$, the straight lines $x = 3$, $x = 6$ and the x-axis.

1596. Compute the area of the parabolic segment cut by the straight line $y = 2x + 3$ off the parabola $y = x^2$.

1597. Compute the area of a parabolic segment with the base $a = 10$ cm and altitude $h = 6$ cm. (The base is a chord perpendicular to the axis of the parabola, Fig. 36).

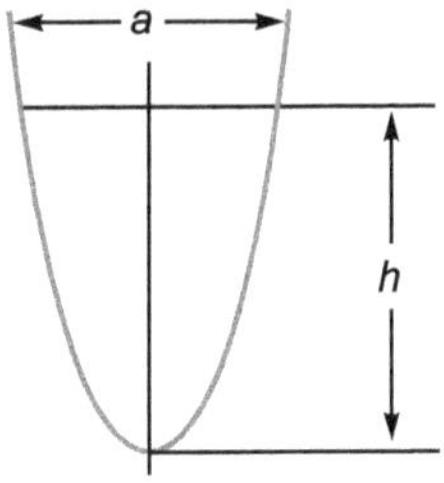

Fig. 36

1598. Compute the area of the figure bounded by the parabola $y = x^2 - 4x + 5$, the x-axis and the straight lines $x = 3$, $x = 5$.

1599. Find the area of the figure bounded by arcs of the parabola $y = \frac{1}{4}x^2$ and $y = 3 - \frac{x^2}{2}$.

1600. Compute the area of the figure bounded by the parabola $y = x^2 - 6x + 10$ and $y = 6x - x^2$.

1601. Compute the area contained between the parabola $y = x^2 - 2x + 2$, the tangent to it at the point (3, 5), the y-axis and the x-axis.

1602. A material point moves at a velocity of $v = 2t + 4$ cm/s. Find the path covered by the point in the first 10 s.

1603. Free-fall velocity $v = gt$. Find the distance travelled in the first five seconds of free fall.

1604. After four seconds of motion the speed, which is proportional to the square of the time, is equal to 1 cm/s. What is the distance travelled in the first ten seconds?

1605. It is known that the force opposing the expansion of a spring varies in proportion to its elongation (Hooke's law). Expanding a spring by 4 cm involves 100 J of work. How much work must be performed to expand the spring by 10 cm?

1606. To expand a spring by 2 cm it is needed to perform work of 20 J. By how much will the spring be expanded if a work of 80 J is performed?

1607. The rate of radioactive decay is a given function of time: $v = v(t)$. Express the quantity m of radioactive substance decayed during the interval from the time T_0 to the time T_1: (a) approximately, with the aid of a sum, (b) exactly, by an integral.

1608. The rate of heating a body is a specified function of time $\psi(t)$. By how many degrees θ is the body heated during the time interval $T_0 - T_1$? Express the solution : (a) approximately, by a sum, (b) exactly, by an integral.

1609. Alternating current I is a defined function of time : $I = I(t)$. Express (approximately, by a sum and exactly, by an integral) the quantity Q of electricity flown through the cross-section of a conductor during the time T as measured from the beginning of the experiment.

1610. The voltage E of alternating current is a specified function of time : $E = \varphi(t)$; current I is also a defined function of time : $I = \psi(t)$. Express the work A of the current performed from the time T_0 to the time T_1: (a) approximately, by a sum, (b) exactly, by an integral.

1611. An electric circuit is fed by a storage battery. During 10 min the terminal voltage drops uniformly from $E_0 = 60$ V to $E = 40$ V. The circuit resistance $R = 20\ \Omega$. Find the electric charge flown through the circuit during 10 min.

1612. The voltage in an electric circuit drops uniformly at a rate of $a = 1.5$ V per minute. The initial voltage in the circuit $E_0 = 120$ V; the resistance of the circuit $R = 60\ \Omega$. Find the work of the current during 5 minutes. Inductance and capacitance may be neglected.

1613. A circuit is uniformly supplied with voltage. At the beginning of the experiment the voltage is equal to zero. In one minute it reaches 120 V. The resistance of the circuit is equal to 100 Ω. Inductance and capacitance may be neglected. Find the work of the current during one minute.

1614. A rectangular wall of an aquarium, filled with water to the brim, has the base a and altitude b. Express the force P with which the water presses on the entire wall : (a) approximately, with the aid of a sum, (b) exactly, by an integral.

1615. (a) Determine the force P with which the water in the aquarium presses on one of its walls. The wall has the form of a rectangle whose length $a = 60$ cm, and altitude $b = 25$ cm.

(b) Divide the wall of the aquarium into two parts by a horizontal straight line so that the forces acting on each part are equal.

Evaluating integrals by summation

1616. Evaluate the integral $\int_0^1 e^x\, dx$ by direct summation and subsequent passage to the limit. (Divide the interval of integration into n equal parts).

1617. Using the method of direct summation and subsequent passage to the limit, evaluate the integral $\int_a^b x^k\, dx$, where k is a positve integer (subdivide the interval of integration into parts so that the abscissas of the division points form a geometric progression).

1618. With the aid of the formula obtained in the previous problem, evaluate the following integrals:

(1) $\int_0^{10} x\,dx$; (2) $\int_{a-2}^{a+2} x\,dx$;

(3) $\int_{a/2}^{a} x^2\,dx$; (4) $\int_a^{2a} \frac{b^2x^2}{a^2}\,dx$;

(5) $\int_0^a (3x^2 - x + 1)\,dx$; (6) $\int_0^m \frac{x^2 + m^2}{m^2}\,dx$;

(7) $\int_1^{2.5} (2x + 1)^2\,dx$; (8) $\int_a^b (x - a)(x - b)\,dx$;

(9) $\int_{-a}^{0} \frac{(a + x)^2}{a}\,dx$; (10) $\int_0^1 \left(\frac{ax - b}{a - b}\right)^2 dx$;

(11) $\int_0^2 x^3\,dx$; (12) $\int_1^3 \frac{x^4}{3}\,dx$;

(13) $\int_0^1 \left(\frac{x^5}{7} - \frac{x^6}{6}\right) dx$.

1619*. Find $\lim_{n\to\infty}\left(\frac{1^k + 2^k + \ldots + n^k}{n^{k+1}}\right)$ for $k > 0$. Approximate $1^5 + 2^5 + \ldots + 100^5$.

1620. Evaluate the integral $\int_1^2 \frac{dx}{x}$ with the aid of direct summation and subsequent passage to the limit. (Divide the interval of integration so that the abscissas of the division points form a geometric progression.)

1621. For the integral $\int_1^2 \frac{dx}{x}$ form an integral sum by dividing the interval of integration into n equal parts. Comparing it with the result of the previous problem, compute

$$\lim_{n\to\infty}\left(\frac{1}{n} + \frac{1}{n+1} + \frac{1}{n+2} + \ldots + \frac{1}{2n}\right).$$

1622*. Compute $\lim_{n\to\infty}\left(\frac{1}{n} + \frac{1}{n+1} + \frac{1}{n+2} + \ldots + \frac{1}{an}\right)$ (a an integer). Calculate approximately $\left(\frac{1}{100} + \frac{1}{101} + \frac{1}{102} + \ldots + \frac{1}{300}\right)$.

1623*. With the aid of direct summation and subsequent passage to the limit evaluate the following integrals:

(1) $\int_0^a xe^x\,dx$; (2) $\int_1^a \ln x\,dx$;

(3) $\int_a^b \frac{\ln x}{x}\,dx$.

[In (1) divide the interval of integration into equal parts, in (2) and (3) as in problem 1620.]

2. Basic Properties of the Definite Integral

Geometric interpretation of the definite integral

1624. With the aid of a definite integral express the area of the figure bounded by the arc of a sinusoid corresponding to the interval $0 \le x \le 2\pi$ and the x-axis.

1625. Find the area of the figure bounded by the cubical parabola $y = x^3$ and straight line $y = x$.

1626. Compute the area of the figure bounded by the parabolas $y = x^2 - 2x - 3$ and $y = -x^2 + 6x - 3$.

1627. Evaluate the area of the figure bounded by the curves $y = x^3 - x$ and $y = x^4 - 1$.

Estimating the definite integral

1628. Prove that the integral $\int_0^{10} \frac{x\,dx}{x^3 + 16}$ is less than $\frac{5}{6}$.

1629. Prove that the integral $\int_0^2 e^{x^2 - x}\,dx$ is contained between $\frac{2}{\sqrt[4]{e}}$ and $2e^2$.

In Problems 1630 to 1635 estimate the integrals.

1630. $\int_{1.5}^{3.5} \frac{x^2\,dx}{x - 1}$.

1631. $\int_0^2 \frac{x^2 + 5}{x^2 + 2}\,dx$.

1632. $\int_{\pi/4}^{5\pi/4} (1 + \sin^2 x)\,dx$.

1633. $\int_{1/2}^{5/2} \frac{x}{1 + x^2}\,dx$.

1634. $\int_{\sqrt{3}/3}^{\sqrt{3}} x \arctan x \, dx.$

1635. $\int_{1/e}^{e} x^2 e^{-x^2} \, dx.$

1636. Find out (without evaluating) which integral is greater :

(1) $\int_0^1 x^2 \, dx$ or $\int_0^1 x^3 \, dx$?

(2) $\int_1^2 x^2 \, dx$ or $\int_1^2 x^3 \, dx$?

1637. Find out which integral is greater :

(1) $\int_0^1 2^{x^2} \, dx$ or $\int_0^1 2^{x^3} \, dx$?

(2) $\int_1^2 2^{x^2} \, dx$ or $\int_1^2 2^{x^3} \, dx$?

(3) $\int_1^2 \ln x \, dx$ or $\int_1^2 (\ln x)^2 \, dx$?

(4) $\int_3^4 \ln x \, dx$ or $\int_3^4 (\ln x)^2 \, dx$?

1638. Prove that $\int_0^1 \sqrt{1 + x^3} \, dx < \frac{\sqrt{5}}{2}$, using the Cauchy-Bunyakovsky inequality:

$$\left| \int_a^b f_1(x) \, f_2(x) \, dx \right| \le \sqrt{\int_a^b [f_1(x)]^2 \, dx} \sqrt{\int_a^b [f_2(x)]^2 \, dx}.$$

Make sure that the use of the general rule yields a less accurate estimate.

1639. Proceeding from geometrical reasoning, prove the following propositions:

(a) If the function $f(x)$ increases in the interval $[a, b]$ and has a concave graph, then

$$(b - a) \, f(a) < \int_a^b f(x) \, dx < (b - a) \frac{f(a) + f(b)}{2};$$

(b) If the function $f(x)$ increases in the interval $[a, b]$ and has a convex graph, then

$$(b - a) \frac{f(a) + f(b)}{2} < \int_a^b f(x) \, dx < (b - a) \, f(b).$$

1640. Estimate the integral $\int_2^3 \frac{x^2 \, dx}{1 + x^2}$ using the result of Problem 1639.

1641. Estimate the integral $\int_0^1 \sqrt{1+x^4}\,dx$, making use of the

(a) main theorem on estimating an integral,

(b) result of Problem 1639,

(c) Cauchy-Bunyakovsky inequality (see Problem 1638).

Mean value of a function

1642. Compute the mean value of the linear function $y = kx + b$ in the interval $[x_1, x_2]$. Find the point at which the function attains this value.

1643. Compute the mean value of the quadratic function $y = ax^2$ in the interval $[x_1, x_2]$. At how many points of the interval does the function attain this value?

1644. Compute the mean value of the function $y = 2x^2 + 3x + 3$ in the interval $[1, 4]$.

1645. Proceeding from geometrical reasoning, compute the mean value of the function $y = \sqrt{a^2 - x^2}$ on the interval $[-a, a]$.

1646. Proceeding from geometrical reasoning, indicate the mean value of a continuous odd function on an interval symmetrical with respect to the origin.

1647. The cross-section of a trough has the form of a parabolic segment. Its base $a = 1$ m, depth $h = 1.5$ m (see Fig. 36). Find the mean depth of the trough.

1648. The voltage in an electric circuit increases uniformly from $E_0 = 100$ V to $E_1 = 120$ V during one minute. Find the mean current intensity during this time. The resistance of the circuit is 10 Ω.

1649. The voltage in an electric circuit drops uniformly at a rate of 0.4 V per minute. The initial voltage in the circuit is 100 V, the resistance being equal to 5 Ω. Find the mean wattage during the first hour of operation.

Integral with a variable limit

1650. Compute the integrals with a variable upper limit:

(1) $\int_0^x x^2\,dx$; (2) $\int_a^x x^5\,dx$;

(3) $\int_1^x \left(\frac{x^3}{5} - \frac{x^4}{4}\right) dx$.

1651. The speed of motion of a body is proportional to the square of time. Find the relation between the travelled distance s and the time t, if it is known that in the first 3 seconds the body covered a path 18 cm long and the motion began at the time $t = 0$.

1652. A force acting on a material point varies uniformly over the distance travelled. When the point started the force equalled 100 N, and when it covered the path equal to 10 m, the force increased up to 600 N. Find the function determining the dependence of the work on the distance travelled.

1653. The voltage of an electric circuit changes uniformly. At $t = t_1$ it equals E_1, at $t = t_2$ it is E_2. The resistance R is constant, self-inductance and capacitance may be neglected. Express the work of the current as a function of the time t from the beginning of the experiment.

1654. Heat capacity of a body depends on temperature as follows: $c = c_0 + \alpha t + \beta t^2$. Find the function determining the dependence of the quantity of heat, received by the body when heated from zero to t, on temperature t.

1655. A curvilinear trapezium is bounded by the parabola $y = x^2$, the x-axis and a moving ordinate. Find the values of the increment ΔS and the differential dS of the area of the trapezium for $x = 10$ and $\Delta x = 0.1$.

1656. A curvilinear trapezium is bounded by the curve $y = \sqrt{x^2 + 16}$, the coordinate axes and a moving ordinate. Find the value of the differential dS of the area of the trapezium for $x = 3$ and $\Delta x = 0.2$.

1657. A curvilinear trapezium is bounded by the curve $y = x^3$, the x-axis and a moving ordinate. Find the values of the increment ΔS of the area, its differential dS, absolute (α) and relative $\left(\delta = \frac{\alpha}{\Delta S}\right)$ errors due to replacing the increment by the differential, if $x = 4$ and Δx attains the values 1, 0.1 and 0.01.

1658. Find the derivative of the function

$$y = \int_0^x \frac{1 - t + t^2}{1 + t + t^2}\, dt \text{ at } x = 1.$$

1659. Find the derivative of the function

$$y = \int_0^x \sin x\, dx \text{ at } x = 0,\ x = \frac{\pi}{4} \text{ and } x = \frac{\pi}{2}.$$

1660. What is the derivative of an integral with a variable lower limit and fixed upper limit with respect to the lower limit?

1661. Find the derivative of the function

$$y = \int_x^5 \sqrt{1 + x^2}\, dx \text{ at } x = 0 \text{ and } x = \frac{3}{4}.$$

1662. Find the derivative of the function $y = \int_0^{2x} \frac{\sin x}{x}\, dx$ with respect to x.

1663. Find the derivatives with respect to x of the functions

(1) $\int_2^{e^x} \frac{\ln z}{z}\, dz$;

(2) $\int_{x^2}^1 \ln x\, dx$.

1664*. Find the derivative with respect to x of the function

$$\int_x^{2x} \ln^2 x\, dx.$$

1665. Find the derivative with respect to x of the function y specified implicitly

$$\int_0^y e^t\, dt + \int_0^x \cos t\, dt = 0.$$

1666. Find the derivative with respect to x of the function y represented parametrically

(1) $x = \int_0^t \sin t\, dt, \quad y = \int_0^t \cos t\, dt$;

(2) $x = \int_1^{t^2} t \ln t\, dt, \quad y = \int_{t^2}^1 t^2 \ln t\, dt$.

1667. Find the second derivative with respect to z of the function

$$y = \int_0^{z^2} \frac{dx}{1 + x^3} \text{ for } z = 1.$$

1668. At what value of x does the function $I(x) = \int_0^x xe^{-x^2}\, dx$ have an extremum? What is it equal to?

1669. At point (0, 0) find the curvature of the curve specified by the equation

$$y = \int_0^x (1 + t) \ln (1 + t)\, dt.$$

1670. Find the points of extremum and the points of inflection of the graph of the function $y = \int_0^x (x^2 - 3x + 2)\,dx$. Plot the graph of this function.

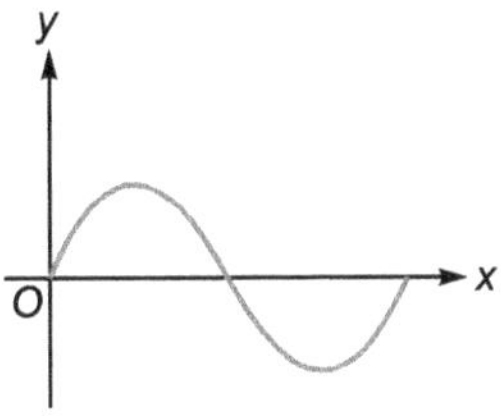

Fig. 37

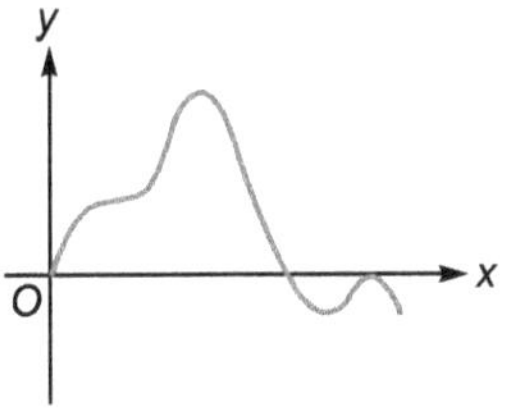

Fig. 38

1671. Given the graphs of functions (Figs. 37 and 38), find out the shape of the graphs of their antiderivatives.

The Newton-Leibniz formula

1672. Compute the integrals:

(1) $\int_1^4 \frac{dx}{x^2}$;

(2) $\int_4^1 \frac{dx}{x^3}$;

(3) $\int_1^9 3\sqrt{x}\,dx$;

(4) $\int_1^2 \left(x + \frac{1}{x}\right)^2 dx$;

(5) $\int_4^9 \sqrt{x}\,(1 + \sqrt{x})\,dx$;

(6) $\int_1^2 (\sqrt{x} - \sqrt[3]{x})\,dx$;

(7) $\int_a^{2a} \frac{dx}{\sqrt{2ax}}$;

(8) $\int_1^4 \frac{1+t}{\sqrt{t}}\,dt$;

(9) $\int_a^b \frac{dx}{\sqrt[3]{x^4}}$ $(a > 0,\ b > 0)$;

(10) $\int_{z_0}^{z_1} (\sqrt{z} - 1)^2\,dz$.

1673. Compute the integrals:

(1) $\int_0^{\pi} \sin x\,dx$;

(2) $\int_0^{\pi} \cos x\,dx$;

(explain the geometrical meaning of the result obtained),

(3) $\int_0^3 e^x\, dx$;

(4) $\int_0^{\pi/4} \sec^2 x\, dx$;

(5) $\int_0^1 \frac{dx}{1+x^2}$;

(6) $\int_1^{\sqrt{3}/2} \frac{dx}{\sqrt{1-x^2}}$.

1674. The function $f(x)$ has equal values at the points $x = a$ and $x = b$ and a continuous derivative. What is $\int_a^b f'(x)\, dx$ equal to?

1675. The tangent to the graph of the function $y = f(x)$ at the point with abscissa $x = a$ forms with the x-axis an angle of $\frac{\pi}{3}$ and at the point with abscissa $x = b$ an angle of $\frac{\pi}{4}$. Compute $\int_a^b f''(x)\, dx$ and $\int_a^b f'(x) f''(x)\, dx$; $f''(x)$ is supposed to be continuous.

6

Indefinite Integral. Integral Calculus

1. Simplest Integration Rules

In Problems 1676 to 1702 find the integrals by using the basic table of integrals and simplest rules of integration.

1676. $\int \sqrt{x}\, dx$.

1677. $\int \sqrt[m]{x^n}\, dx$.

1678. $\int \frac{dx}{x^2}$.

1679. $\int 10^x\, dx$.

1680. $\int a^x e^x\, dx$.

1681. $\int \frac{dx}{2\sqrt{x}}$.

1682. $\int \frac{dh}{\sqrt{2gh}}$.

1683. $\int 3.4x^{-0.17}\, dx$.

1684. $\int (1 - 2u)\, du$.

1685. $\int (\sqrt{x} + 1)(x - \sqrt{x} + 1)\, dx$.

1686. $\int \frac{\sqrt{x} - x^3 e^x + x^2}{x^3}\, dx$.

1687. $\int (2x^{-1.2} + 3x^{-0.8} - 5^{0.38})\, dx$.

1688. $\int \left(\frac{1-z}{z}\right)^2 dz$.

1689. $\int \frac{(1-x)^2}{x\sqrt{x}}\, dx$.

1690. $\int \frac{(1+\sqrt{x})^3}{\sqrt[3]{x}}\, dx$.

1691. $\int \frac{\sqrt[3]{x^2} - \sqrt[4]{x}}{\sqrt{x}}\, dx$.

1692. $\int \frac{dx}{\sqrt{3 - 3x^2}}$.

1693. $\int \frac{3 \cdot 2^x - 2 \cdot 3^x}{2^x}\, dx$.

1694. $\int \frac{1 + \cos^2 x}{1 + \cos 2x}\, dx$.

1695. $\int \frac{\cos 2x}{\cos^2 x \cdot \sin^2 x}\, dx$.

1696. $\int \tan^2 x\, dx$.

1697. $\int \cot^2 x\, dx$.

1698. $\int 2\sin^2 \frac{x}{2}\, dx$.

1699. $\int \frac{(1 + 2x^2)dx}{x^2(1 + x^2)}$.

1700. $\int \frac{(1+x)^2\, dx}{x(1 + x^2)}$.

1701. $\int \frac{dx}{\cos 2x + \sin^2 x}$.

1702. $\int (\arcsin x + \arccos x)\, dx$.

In Problems 1703 to 1780 find the integrals by using the theorem on the invariance of integration formulas.

1703. $\int \sin x \, d(\sin x)$.

1704. $\int \tan^3 x \, d(\tan x)$.

1705. $\int \frac{d(1+x^2)}{\sqrt{1+x^2}}$.

1706. $\int (x+1)^{15} \, dx$.

1707. $\int \frac{dx}{(2x-3)^5}$.

1708. $\int \frac{dx}{(a+bx)^c}$, $(c \neq 1)$.

1709. $\int \sqrt[5]{(8-3x)^6} \, dx$.

1710. $\int \sqrt{8-2x} \, dx$.

1711. $\int \frac{m}{\sqrt[3]{(a+bx)^2}} \, dx$.

1712. $\int 2x\sqrt{x^2+1} \, dx$.

1713. $\int x\sqrt{1-x^2} \, dx$.

1714. $\int x^2 \sqrt[5]{x^2+2} \, dx$.

1715. $\int \frac{x \, dx}{\sqrt{x^2+1}}$.

1716. $\int \frac{x^4 \, dx}{\sqrt{4+x^5}}$.

1717. $\int \frac{x^3 \, dx}{\sqrt[3]{x^4+1}}$.

1718. $\int \frac{(6x-5) \, dx}{2\sqrt{3x^2-5x+6}}$.

1719. $\int \sin^3 x \cos x \, dx$.

1720. $\int \frac{\sin x \, dx}{\cos^2 x}$.

1721. $\int \frac{\cos x \, dx}{\sqrt[3]{\sin^2 x}}$.

1722. $\int \cos^3 x \sin 2x \, dx$.

1723. $\int \frac{\sqrt{\ln x}}{x} \, dx$.

1724. $\int \frac{(\arctan x)^2 \, dx}{1+x^2}$.

1725. $\int \frac{dx}{(\arcsin x)^3 \sqrt{1-x^2}}$.

1726. $\int \frac{dx}{\cos^2 x\sqrt{1+\tan x}}$.

1727. $\int \cos 3x \, d(3x)$.

1728. $\int \frac{d(1+\ln x)}{\cos^2(1+\ln x)}$.

1729. $\int \cos 3x \, dx$.

1730. $\int (\cos\alpha - \cos 2x) \, dx$.

1731. $\int \sin(2x-3) \, dx$.

1732. $\int \cos(1-2x) \, dx$.

1733. $\int \left[\cos\left(2x - \frac{\pi}{4}\right)\right]^{-2} dx$.

1734. $\int e^x (\sin e^x) \, dx$.

1735. $\int \frac{d(1+x^2)}{1+x^2}$.

1736. $\int \frac{d(\arcsin x)}{\arcsin x}$.

1737. $\int \frac{(2x-3) \, dx}{x^2-3x+8}$.

1738. $\int \frac{dx}{2x-1}$.

1739. $\int \frac{dx}{cx+m}$.

1740. $\int \frac{x \, dx}{x^2+1}$.

1741. $\int \frac{x^2\,dx}{x^3+1}$. **1742.** $\int \frac{e^x\,dx}{e^x+1}$. **1743.** $\int \frac{e^{2x}\,dx}{e^{2x}+a^2}$.

1744. $\int \tan x\,dx$. **1745.** $\int \cot x\,dx$. **1746.** $\int \tan 3x\,dx$.

1747. $\int \cot(2x+1)\,dx$. **1748.** $\int \frac{\sin 2x}{1+\cos^2 x}\,dx$.

1749. $\int \frac{dx}{x\ln x}$. **1750.** $\int \frac{(\ln x)^m}{x}\,dx$. **1751.** $\int e^{\sin x}\,d(\sin x)$.

1752. $\int e^{\sin x}\cos x\,dx$. **1753.** $\int a^{3x}\,dx$. **1754.** $\int a^{-x}\,dx$.

1755. $\int e^{-3x+1}\,dx$. **1756.** $\int e^{x^2}x\,dx$. **1757.** $\int e^{-x^3}x^2\,dx$.

1758. $\int \frac{d\left(\frac{x}{3}\right)}{\sqrt{1-\left(\frac{x}{3}\right)^2}}$. **1759.** $\int \frac{dx}{\sqrt{1-25x^2}}$. **1760.** $\int \frac{dx}{1+9x^2}$.

1761. $\int \frac{dx}{\sqrt{4-x^2}}$. **1762.** $\int \frac{dx}{2x^2+9}$.

1763. $\int \frac{dx}{\sqrt{4-9x^2}}$. **1764.** $\int \frac{x\,dx}{x^4+1}$.

1765. $\int \frac{x\,dx}{\sqrt{a^2-x^4}}$. **1766.** $\int \frac{x^2\,dx}{x^6+4}$.

1767. $\int \frac{x^3\,dx}{\sqrt{1-x^8}}$. **1768.** $\int \frac{e^x\,dx}{e^{2x}+4}$.

1769. $\int \frac{2^x\,dx}{\sqrt{1-4^x}}$. **1770.** $\int \frac{\cos\alpha\,d\alpha}{a^2+\sin^2\alpha}$.

1771. $\int \frac{e^{2x}-1}{e^x}\,dx$. **1772.** $\int (e^x+1)^3\,dx$.

1773. $\int \frac{1+x}{\sqrt{1-x^2}}\,dx$. **1774.** $\int \frac{3x-1}{x^2+9}\,dx$.

1775. $\int \sqrt{\frac{1-x}{1+x}}\,dx$. **1776.** $\int \frac{x(1-x^2)}{1+x^4}\,dx$.

1777. $\int \frac{1+x-x^2}{\sqrt{(1-x^2)^3}}\,dx$. **1778.** $\int \frac{dx}{(x+\sqrt{x^2-1})^2}$.

1779. $\int \frac{2x-\sqrt{\arcsin x}}{\sqrt{1-x^2}}\,dx$. **1780.** $\int \frac{x+(\arccos 3x)^2}{\sqrt{1-9x^2}}\,dx$.

In Problems 1781 to 1790 find the integrals by separating the integer part of the integrand fraction.

1781. $\int \frac{x}{x+4}\,dx.$

1782. $\int \frac{x}{2x+1}\,dx.$

1783. $\int \frac{Ax}{a+bx}\,dx.$

1784. $\int \frac{3+x}{3-x}\,dx.$

1785. $\int \frac{(2x-1)\,dx}{x-2}.$

1786. $\int \frac{x+2}{2x-1}\,dx.$

1787. $\int \frac{(1+x)^2}{x^2+1}\,dx.$

1788. $\int \frac{x^2-1}{x^2+1}\,dx.$

1789. $\int \frac{x^4}{1-x}\,dx.$

1790. $\int \frac{x^4\,dx}{x^2+1}.$

In Problems 1791 to 1807 find the integrals by splitting the integrand and separating a complete square.

1791. $\int \frac{dx}{x(x-1)}.$

1792. $\int \frac{dx}{x(x+1)}.$

1793. $\int \frac{dx}{(x+1)(2x-3)}.$

1794. $\int \frac{dx}{(a-x)(b-x)}.$

1795. $\int \frac{x^2+1}{x^2-1}\,dx.$

1796. $\int \frac{dx}{x^2-7x+10}.$

1797. $\int \frac{dx}{x^2+3x-10}.$

1798. $\int \frac{dx}{4x^2-9}.$

1799. $\int \frac{dx}{2-3x^2}.$

1800. $\int \frac{dx}{(x-1)^2+4}.$

1801. $\int \frac{dx}{x^2+2x+3}.$

1802. $\int \frac{dx}{x-x^2-2.5}.$

1803. $\int \frac{dx}{4x^2+4x+5}.$

1804. $\int \frac{dx}{\sqrt{1-(2x+3)^2}}.$

1805. $\int \frac{dx}{\sqrt{4x-3-x^2}}.$

1806. $\int \frac{dx}{\sqrt{8+6x-9x^2}}.$

1807. $\int \frac{dx}{\sqrt{2-6x-9x^2}}.$

In Problems 1808 to 1831 find the integrals by using the trigonometric formulas for reducing the integrand.

1808. $\int \cos^2 x\,dx.$

1809. $\int \sin^2 x\,dx.$

1810. $\int \frac{dx}{1-\cos x}.$

1811. $\int \frac{dx}{1+\sin x}.$

1812. $\int \frac{1-\cos x}{1+\cos x}\,dx.$

1813. $\int \frac{1+\sin x}{1-\sin x}\,dx.$

1814. $\int (\tan^2 x + \tan^4 x)\,dx.$

1815. $\int \frac{\cos 2x\,dx}{1 + \sin x \cos x}.$

1816. $\int \cos x \sin 3x\,dx.$

1817. $\int \cos 2x \cos 3x\,dx.$

1818. $\int \sin 2x \sin 5x\,dx.$

1819. $\int \cos x \cos 2x \cos 3x\,dx.$

1820. $\int \frac{dx}{\cos x}.$

1821. $\int \frac{1 - \sin x}{\cos x}\,dx.$

1822. $\int \frac{\sin^3 x}{\cos x}\,dx.$

1823. $\int \frac{\cos^3 x\,dx}{\sin^4 x}.$

1824. $\int \frac{\sin^3 \alpha}{\sqrt{\cos \alpha}}\,d\alpha.$

1825. $\int \frac{dx}{\cos^4 x}.$

1826. $\int \cos^3 x\,dx.$

1827. $\int \tan^4 x\,dx.$

1828. $\int \sin^5 x\,dx.$

1829. $\int \sin^4 x\,dx.$

1830. $\int \tan^3 x\,dx.$

1831. $\frac{dx}{\sin^6 x}.$

2. Basic Methods of Integration

Integration by parts

In Problems 1832 to 1868 find the integrals.

1832. $\int x \sin 2x\,dx.$

1833. $\int x \cos x\,dx.$

1834. $\int xe^{-x}\,dx.$

1835. $\int x3^x\,dx.$

1836. $\int x^n \ln x\,dx, (n \neq -1).$

1837. $\int x \arctan x\,dx.$

1838. $\int \arccos x\,dx.$

1839. $\int \arctan \sqrt{x}\,dx.$

1840. $\int \frac{\arcsin x}{\sqrt{x+1}}\,dx.$

1841. $\int x \tan^2 x\,dx.$

1842. $\int x \cos^2 x\,dx.$

1843. $\int \frac{\log x}{x^3}\,dx.$

1844. $\int \frac{x \arctan x}{\sqrt{1 + x^2}}\,dx.$

1845. $\int \frac{\arcsin \sqrt{x}}{\sqrt{1 - x}}\,dx.$

1846. $\int \ln (x^2 + 1)\,dx.$

1847. $\int \frac{x^2\,dx}{(1 + x^2)^2}.$

1848. $\int \frac{x^3\,dx}{\sqrt{1 + x^2}}.$

1849. $\int x^2 \ln (1 + x)\,dx.$

1850. $\int x^2e^{-x}\,dx.$

1851. $\int x^3e^x\,dx.$

1852. $\int x^2a^x\,dx.$

1853. $\int x^3 \sin x\,dx.$

1854. $\int x^2 \cos^2 x\,dx.$

1855. $\int \ln^2 x\,dx.$

1856. $\int \frac{\ln^3 x}{x^2}\,dx.$

1857. $\int \frac{\ln^2 x}{\sqrt{x^5}}\,dx.$

1858. $\int (\arcsin x)^2\,dx.$

1859. $\int (\arctan x)^2 x\,dx.$

1860. $\int e^x \sin x\,dx.$

1861. $\int e^{3x}(\sin 2x - \cos 2x)\,dx.$

1862. $\int e^{ax}\cos nx\,dx.$

1863. $\int \sin(\ln x)\,dx.$

1864. $\int \cos(\ln x)\,dx.$

1865*. $\int \frac{x^2\,dx}{\sqrt{1-x^2}}.$

1866*. $\int \sqrt{a^2+x^2}\,dx.$

1867. $\int \frac{x^2e^x\,dx}{(x+2)^2}.$

1868. $\int x^2e^x \sin x\,dx.$

Integration by change of variable

In Problems 1869 to 1904 find the integrals.

1869. $\int \frac{dx}{1+\sqrt{x+1}}$ (apply the substitution $x+1=z^2$).

1870. $\int \frac{x^3\,dx}{\sqrt{x-1}}.$

1871. $\int \frac{4x+3}{(x-2)^3}\,dx.$

1872. $\int \frac{dx}{x\sqrt{x+1}}.$

1873. $\int \frac{x+1}{x\sqrt{x-2}}\,dx.$

1874. $\int \frac{dx}{1+\sqrt{x}}.$

1875. $\int \frac{\sqrt{x}}{x(x+1)}\,dx.$

1876. $\int \frac{\sqrt{x}}{x+1}\,dx.$

1877. $\int \frac{dx}{1+\sqrt[3]{x+1}}.$

1878. $\int \frac{dx}{\sqrt{ax+b}+m}.$

1879. $\int \frac{\sqrt{x}\,dx}{\sqrt{x}-\sqrt[3]{x}}$ (apply the substitution $x=z^6$).

1880. $\int \frac{dx}{\sqrt[3]{x}(\sqrt[3]{x}-1)}.$

1881. $\int \frac{dx}{\sqrt{x}+\sqrt[4]{x}}.$

1882. $\int \frac{\sqrt{x}}{\sqrt[3]{x^2}-\sqrt[4]{x}}\,dx.$

1883. $\int \frac{e^{2x}\,dx}{\sqrt[4]{e^x + 1}}$ (apply the substitution $e^x + 1 = z^4$).

1884. $\int \frac{dx}{\sqrt{1 + e^x}}$.

1885. $\int \frac{\sqrt{1 + \ln x}}{x \ln x}\,dx$.

1886. $\int \sqrt{1 + \cos^2 x} \cdot \sin 2x \cdot \cos 2x\,dx$.

1887. $\int \frac{\ln(\tan x)}{\sin x \cdot \cos x}\,dx$.

1888. $\int \frac{x^5\,dx}{\sqrt{a^3 - x^3}}$.

1889. $\int \frac{x^5\,dx}{(x^2 - 4)^2}$.

1890. $\int \frac{dx}{x^2\sqrt{x^2 + a^2}}$ (apply the substitution $x = \frac{1}{z}$ or $x = a \tan z$ or $x = a \sinh z$).

1891. $\int \frac{x^2\,dx}{\sqrt{a^2 - x^2}}$ (apply the substitution $x = a \sin z$).

1892. $\int \frac{dx}{x\sqrt{x^2 - a^2}}$ (apply the substitution $x = \frac{1}{z}$ or $x = \frac{a}{\cos z}$ or $x = a \cosh z$).

1893. $\int \frac{\sqrt{1 + x^2}}{x^4}\,dx$.

1894. $\int \frac{\sqrt{1 - x^2}}{x^2}\,dx$.

1895. $\int \frac{dx}{\sqrt{(a^2 + x^2)^3}}$.

1896. $\int \frac{\sqrt{(9 - x^2)^3}}{x^6}\,dx$.

1897. $\int \frac{dx}{x^2\sqrt{x^2 - 9}}$.

1898. $\frac{dx}{x\sqrt{1 + x^2}}$.

1899. $\int \frac{dx}{\sqrt{(x^2 - a^2)^3}}$.

1900. $\int x^2\sqrt{4 - x^2}\,dx$.

1901. $\int \frac{dx}{(x^2 + 4)\sqrt{4x^2 + 1}}$.

1902*. $\int \sqrt{\frac{x - 1}{x + 1}}\,\frac{dx}{x^2}$.

1903*. $\int \frac{dx}{\sqrt{x - x^2}}$.

1904*. $\int \frac{(x + 1)\,dx}{x(1 + xe^x)}$.

In Problems 1905 to 1909 find the integrals first changing the variable and then integrating by parts.

1905. $\int e^{\sqrt{x}}\,dx$.

1906. $\int \sin \sqrt[3]{x}\,dx$.

1907. $\int \frac{\arcsin x}{\sqrt{(1 - x^2)^3}}\,dx$.

1908. $\int \frac{x^2 \arctan x}{1 + x^2}\,dx$.

1909. $\int \frac{\arctan x}{x^2(1 + x^2)}\,dx$.

Miscellaneous problems

In Problems 1910 to 2011 evaluate the integrals.

1910. $\int (x+1)\sqrt{x^2+2x}\,dx.$

1911. $\int (1+e^{3x})^2 e^{3x}\,dx.$

1912. $\int \frac{e^{\sqrt{x}}}{\sqrt{x}}\,dx.$

1913. $\int \frac{\sin x}{e^{\cos x}}\,dx.$

1914. $\int \sqrt{1-e^x}\,e^x\,dx.$

1915. $\int x\cos x^2\,dx.$

1916. $\int (2-3x^{4/3})^{1/5}x^{1/3}\,dx.$

1917. $\int \frac{2x^5-3x^2}{1+3x^3-x^6}\,dx.$

1918. $\int \frac{\sqrt{x}\,dx}{1+x^{3/2}}.$

1919. $\int \frac{dx}{e^x(3+e^{-x})}.$

1920. $\int \frac{dx}{e^x\sqrt{1-e^{-2x}}}.$

1921. $\int \frac{2x+3}{\sqrt{1+x^2}}\,dx.$

1922. $\int \frac{2x-1}{\sqrt{9x^2-4}}\,dx.$

1923. $\int \frac{\cos\sqrt{x}}{\sqrt{x}}\,dx.$

1924. $\int \frac{dx}{x\sqrt{3-\ln^2 x}}.$

1925. $\int \frac{\ln x\,dx}{x(1-\ln^2 x)}.$

1926. $\int \frac{x^2-x+1}{\sqrt{(x^2+1)^3}}\,dx.$

1927. $\int \frac{(\arctan x)^n}{1+x^2}\,dx.$

1928. $\int \frac{d\varphi}{\sin^2\varphi\cos^2\varphi}.$

1929. $\int \frac{\cos 2x}{\cos^2 x}\,dx.$

1930. $\int \frac{\sin^4 x\,dx}{\cos^6 x}.$

1931. $\int \sqrt{\tan^3 x}\,\sec^4 x\,dx.$

1932. $\int (1-\tan 3x)^2\,dx.$

1933. $\int \frac{x^3\,dx}{x+1}.$

1934. $\int \frac{x\,dx}{(x-1)^3}.$

1935. $\int \frac{x\,dx}{\sqrt{2+4x}}.$

1936. $\int \frac{x\,dx}{\sqrt{1+2x}}.$

1937. $\int x\sqrt{a+x}\,dx.$

1938. $\int (\sqrt{\sin x}+\cos x)^2\,dx.$

1939. $\int a^{mx}b^{nx}\,dx.$

1940. $\int \frac{dx}{\sqrt{5-2x+x^2}}.$

1941. $\int \frac{dx}{\sqrt{9x^2-6x+2}}.$

1942. $\int \frac{dx}{\sqrt{12x-9x^2-2}}.$

1943. $\int \frac{(8x-11)\,dx}{\sqrt{5+2x-x^2}}.$

1944. $\int \frac{(x+2)\,dx}{x^2+2x+2}.$

1945. $\int \frac{(x-3)\,dx}{\sqrt{3-2x-x^2}}.$

1946. $\int \frac{(3x-1)\,dx}{4x^2-4x+17}.$

1947. $\int \frac{(3x-1)\,dx}{\sqrt{x^2+2x+2}}.$

1948. $\int \frac{(x-2)\,dx}{x^2-7x+12}$.

1949. $\int \frac{2x+5}{\sqrt{9x^2+6x+2}}\,dx$.

1950. $\int \frac{3-4x}{2x^2-3x+1}\,dx$.

1951. $\int \frac{(4-3x)\,dx}{5x^2+6x+18}$.

1952. $\int \frac{(2-5x)\,dx}{\sqrt{4x^2+9x+1}}$.

1953. $\int \frac{x\,dx}{\sqrt{3x^2-11x+2}}$.

1954. $\int \frac{\sqrt{x}\,dx}{\sqrt{2x+3}}$.

1955. $\int \sqrt{\frac{a-x}{x-b}}\,dx$.

1956. $\int \arctan x\,dx$.

1957. $\int x \sin x \cos x\,dx$.

1958. $\int x^2 \cos \omega x\,dx$.

1959. $\int e^{2x} x^3\,dx$.

1960. $\int \frac{\ln(\cos x)}{\cos^2 x}\,dx$.

1961. $\int \frac{\cot x}{\ln(\sin x)}\,dx$.

1962. $\int \frac{x^7\,dx}{(1+x^4)^2}$.

1963. $\int \frac{\cos^2 3x}{\sin 3x}\,dx$.

1964. $\int \frac{dx}{1-\sin 3x}$.

1965. $\int \frac{\sin 2x\,dx}{4-\cos^2 2x}$.

1966. $\int \frac{dx}{e^x+1}$.

1967. $\int \frac{e^x-1}{e^x+1}\,dx$.

1968. $\int e^{e^x+x}\,dx$.

1969. $\int e^{2x^2+\ln x}\,dx$.

1970. $\int \frac{3+x^3}{\sqrt{2+2x^2}}\,dx$.

1971. $\int \frac{x \arcsin x}{\sqrt{1-x^2}}\,dx$.

1972. $\int \frac{x \cos x}{\sin^3 x}\,dx$.

1973. $\int e^x \sin^2 x\,dx$.

1974. $\int \frac{(1+\tan x)\,dx}{\sin 2x}$.

1975. $\int \frac{1-\tan x}{1+\tan x}\,dx$.

1976. $\int \frac{d\varphi}{\sqrt{3}\cos\varphi+\sin\varphi}$.

1977. $\int \frac{\sin x\,dx}{1+\sin x}$.

1978. $\int \frac{\sin^2 x \cos x}{(1+\sin^2 x)}\,dx$.

1979. $\int \frac{\sqrt{1+\cos x}}{\sin x}\,dx$.

1980. $\int \frac{\ln(\ln x)}{x}\,dx$.

1981. $\int x^3 e^{x^2}\,dx$.

1982. $\int e^{-x^2} x^5\,dx$.

1983. $\int \frac{x^3\,dx}{\sqrt{1+2x^2}}$.

1984. $\int \frac{x^4\,dx}{\sqrt{(1-x^2)^3}}$.

1985. $\int \frac{\sqrt{(x^2-a^2)^5}}{x}\,dx$.

1986. $\int \frac{dx}{x^4\sqrt{x^2+4}}$.

1987. $\int \frac{\sqrt{x^2-8}}{x^4}\,dx$.

1988. $\int \frac{\sqrt{4+x^2}}{x^6}\,dx$.

1989. $\int \frac{dx}{x^4\sqrt{x^2-3}}$.

1990. $\int \frac{\sqrt{x}\,dx}{\sqrt[4]{x^3}+1}$.

1991. $\int \frac{\sqrt{x+1}+1}{\sqrt{x+1}-1}\,dx$.

1992. $\int \frac{dx}{(2+x)\sqrt{1+x}}$.

1993. $\int \frac{\sqrt[3]{x}\,dx}{x(\sqrt{x}+\sqrt[3]{x})}$.

1994. $\int \frac{\sqrt{x^2+2x}}{x}\,dx$.

1995*. $\int \frac{x^7\,dx}{(1-x^2)^5}$.

1996. $\int \frac{dx}{(ax+b)\sqrt{x}}$.

1997. $\int \frac{\sqrt{1+x^8}}{x^{13}}\,dx$.

1998. $\int \frac{x\,dx}{(1-x^4)^{3/2}}$.

1999. $\int \frac{x^5\,dx}{\sqrt{x^4+4}}$.

2000. $\int \frac{dx}{\sqrt{x(x-1)}}$.

2001. $\int \frac{\sqrt{1-x^3}}{x^2\sqrt{x}}\,dx$.

2002. $\int \frac{x^4\,dx}{(1+x^2)^3}$.

2003. $\int \frac{3x^2-1}{2x\sqrt{x}} \arctan x\,dx$.

2004. $\int \frac{e^x(1+e^x)\,dx}{\sqrt{1-e^{2x}}}$.

2005. $\int \sqrt{e^x-1}\,dx$.

2006*. $\int \frac{\ln(x+1)-\ln x}{x(x+1)}\,dx$.

2007. $\int \frac{dx}{x^6+x^4}$.

2008. $\int \arccos\sqrt{\frac{x}{x+1}}\,dx$.

2009. $\int \ln(x+\sqrt{1+x^2})\,dx$.

2010. $\int \sqrt[3]{\frac{\sin^2 x}{\cos^{14} x}}\,dx$.

2011. $\int \frac{dx}{\cos^3 x\sqrt{\sin 2x}}$.

3. Basic Classes of Integrable Functions

Rational-fractional functions

In Problems 2012 to 2067 evaluate the integrals.

(1) The denominator has only different real roots.

2012. $\int \frac{x\,dx}{(x+1)(2x+1)}$.

2013. $\int \frac{x\,dx}{2x^2-3x-2}$.

2014. $\int \frac{2x^2+41x-91}{(x-1)(x+3)(x-4)}\,dx$.

2015. $\int \frac{dx}{6x^3-7x^2-3x}$.

2016. $\int \frac{x^5+x^4-8}{x^3-4x}\,dx$.

2017. $\int \frac{x^3-1}{4x^3-x}\,dx$.

2018. $\int \frac{32x\,dx}{(2x-1)(4x^2-16x+15)}$.

2019. $\int \frac{x\,dx}{x^4-3x^2+2}$.

2020. $\int \frac{(2x^2-5)\,dx}{x^4-5x^2+6}$.

2021. $\int \frac{x^6-2x^4+3x^3-9x^2+4}{x^5-5x^3+4x}\,dx$.

(2) The denominator has only real roots; some roots are multiple.

2022. $\int \frac{(x^2 - 3x + 2)\,dx}{x(x^2 + 2x + 1)}$.

2023. $\int \left(\frac{x+2}{x-1}\right)^2 \frac{dx}{x}$.

2024. $\int \frac{x^2\,dx}{x^2 + 5x^2 + 8x + 4}$.

2025. $\int \frac{x^3+1}{x^3 - x^2}\,dx$.

2026. $\int \frac{x^3 - 6x^2 + 11x - 5}{(x-2)^4}\,dx$.

2027. $\int \frac{dx}{x^4 - x^2}$.

2028. $\int \frac{x^2\,dx}{(x+2)^2(x+4)^2}$.

2029. $\int \frac{x^3 - 6x^2 + 9x + 7}{(x-2)^3(x-5)}\,dx$.

2030. $\int \frac{1}{8}\left(\frac{x-1}{x+1}\right)^4 dx$.

2031. $\int \frac{x^5\,dx}{(x-1)^2(x^2-1)}$.

2032. $\int \frac{(x^2 - 2x + 3)\,dx}{(x-1)(x^3 - 4x^2 + 3x)}$.

2033. $\int \frac{(7x^3 - 9)\,dx}{x^4 - 5x^3 + 6x^2}$.

2034. $\int \frac{x^3 - 2x^2 + 4}{x^3(x-2)^2}\,dx$.

2035. $\int \frac{3x^2+1}{(x^2-1)^3}\,dx$.

(3) The denominator has different complex roots.

2036. $\int \frac{dx}{x(x^2+1)}$.

2037. $\int \frac{dx}{1+x^3}$.

2038. $\int \frac{x\,dx}{x^3 - 1}$.

2039. $\int \frac{(2x^2 - 3x - 3)\,dx}{(x-1)(x^2 - 2x + 5)}$.

2040. $\int \frac{(x^4+1)\,dx}{x^3 - x^2 + x - 1}$.

2041. $\int \frac{x^2\,dx}{1 - x^4}$.

2042. $\int \frac{dx}{(x^2+1)(x^2+x)}$.

2043. $\int \frac{dx}{(x+1)^2(x^2+1)}$.

2044. $\int \frac{(3x^2 + x + 3)\,dx}{(x-1)^3(x^2+1)}$.

2045. $\int \frac{x^5 + 2x^3 + 4x + 4}{x^4 + 2x^3 + 2x^2}\,dx$.

2046. $\int \frac{(x^3 - 6)\,dx}{x^4 + 6x^2 + 8}$.

2047*. $\int \frac{dx}{1+x^4}$.

(4) The denominator has complex multiple roots.

2048. $\int \frac{x^3 + x - 1}{(x^2+2)^2}\,dx$.

2049. $\int \frac{dx}{x(4+x^2)^2(1+x^2)}$.

2050. $\int \frac{(5x^2 - 12)\,dx}{(x^2 - 6x + 13)^2}$.

2051. $\int \frac{(x+1)^4\,dx}{(x^2 + 2x + 2)^3}$.

2052. $\int \frac{dx}{(x^2+9)^3}$.

2053. $\int \frac{2x\,dx}{(1+x)(1+x^2)^2}$.

2054. $\int \frac{dx}{(1+x^2)^4}$.

2055. $\int \frac{x^9\,dx}{(x^4-1)^2}$.

(5) Ostrogradsky's method.

2056. $\int \frac{x^7 + 2}{(x^2 + x + 1)^2}\,dx$.

2057. $\int \frac{(4x^2 - 8x)\,dx}{(x-1)^2(x^2+1)^2}$.

2058. $\int \frac{x^2 + x + 1}{x^5 - 2x^4 + x^3}\,dx.$

2059. $\int \frac{x^6 + x^4 - 4x^2 - 2}{x^3(x^2 + 1)^2}\,dx.$

2060. $\int \frac{(x^2 - 1)^2\,dx}{(1 + x)(1 + x^2)^3}.$

2061. $\int \frac{dx}{x^4(x^3 + 1)^2}.$

2062. $\int \frac{dx}{(x^2 + 2x + 10)^3}.$

2063. $\int \frac{(x + 2)\,dx}{(x^2 + 2x + 2)^3}.$

2064. $\int \frac{x^5 - x^4 - 26x^2 - 24x - 25}{(x^2 + 4x + 5)^2(x^2 + 4)^2}\,dx.$

2065. $\int \frac{3x^4 + 4}{x^2(x^2 + 1)^3}\,dx.$

2066. $\int \frac{5 - 3x + 6x^2 + 5x^3 - x^4}{x^5 - x^4 - 2x^3 + 2x^2 + x - 1}\,dx.$

2067. $\int \frac{9\,dx}{5x^2(3 - 2x^2)^3}.$

Some irrational functions

In Problems 2068 to 2089 evaluate the integrals.

(1) Functions of the form $R\left(x, \sqrt[m]{\frac{ax + b}{a_1x + b_1}}, \sqrt[p]{\frac{ax + b}{a_1x + b_1}}, \dots\right).$

2068. $\int \frac{dx}{x(\sqrt{x} + \sqrt[5]{x^2})}.$

2069. $\int \frac{dx}{\sqrt{x} + \sqrt[3]{x} + 2\sqrt[4]{x}}.$

2070. $\int \frac{x\,dx}{(x + 1)^{1/2} + (x + 1)^{1/3}}.$

2071. $\int \sqrt{\frac{1 - x}{1 + x}}\,\frac{dx}{x}.$

2072. $\int \sqrt{\frac{1 - \sqrt{x}}{1 + \sqrt{x}}}\,dx.$

2073. $\int \frac{x^2 + \sqrt{1 + x}}{\sqrt[3]{1 + x}}\,dx.$

2074. $\int \sqrt[3]{\frac{1 - x}{1 + x}}\,\frac{dx}{x}.$

2075*. $\int \frac{dx}{\sqrt[4]{(x - 1)^3(x + 2)^5}}.$

(2) Differential binomials $x^m(a + bx^n)^p\,dx$.

2076. $\int \sqrt{x}\,(1 + \sqrt[3]{x})^4\,dx.$

2077. $\int x^{-1}\,(1 + x^{1/3})^{-3}\,dx.$

2078. $\int \frac{dx}{x\sqrt[3]{x^2 + 1}}.$

2079. $\int x^5\,\sqrt[3]{(1 + x^3)^2}\,dx.$

2080. $\int \frac{dx}{\sqrt[3]{1 + x^3}}.$

2081. $\int \frac{dx}{\sqrt[4]{1 + x^4}}.$

2082. $\int \frac{\sqrt{1 - x^4}}{x^5}\,dx.$

2083. $\int \frac{\sqrt[3]{1 + \sqrt[4]{x}}}{\sqrt{x}}\,dx.$

2084. $\int \frac{\sqrt{1 + \sqrt{x}}}{x}\,dx.$

2085. $\int \frac{dx}{x\sqrt[3]{1 + x^5}}.$

2086. $\int \frac{\sqrt[3]{1 + x^3}}{x^2}\,dx.$

2087. $\int \frac{dx}{x^{11}\sqrt{1 + x^4}}.$

2088. $\int \sqrt[3]{x(1 - x^2)}\,dx.$

2089. $\int \sqrt[3]{1 + \sqrt[4]{x}}\,dx.$

Trigonometric functions

In Problems 2090 to 2131 find the integrals.

2090. $\int \sin^3 x \cos^2 x \, dx.$ **2091.** $\int \frac{\sin^3 x}{\cos^4 x} dx.$

2092. $\int \frac{dx}{\cos x \cdot \sin^3 x}.$ **2093.** $\int \frac{\sin^4 x}{\cos^2 x} dx.$

2094. $\int \frac{dx}{\cos^3 x \cdot \sin^3 x}.$ **2095.** $\int \frac{dx}{\sin^4 x \cdot \cos^4 x}.$

2096. $\int \frac{\sin x \, dx}{(1 - \cos x)^2}.$ **2097.** $\int \frac{\cos x \, dx}{(1 - \cos x)^2}.$

2098. $\int \cos^6 x \, dx.$ **2099.** $\int \cot^4 x \, dx.$

2100. $\int \tan^5 x \, dx.$ **2101.** $\int \frac{dx}{\tan^8 x}.$

2102. $\int \frac{dx}{\sin^3 x}.$ **2103.** $\int \frac{\cos^4 x + \sin^4 x}{\cos^2 x - \sin^2 x} dx.$

2104. $\int \frac{dx}{(\sin x + \cos x)^2}.$ **2105.** $\int \frac{dx}{\sin x + \cos x}.$

2106. $\int \frac{dx}{a \cos x + b \sin x}.$ **2107.** $\int \frac{dx}{\tan x \cdot \cos 2x}.$

2108. $\int \frac{\cos^2 x \, dx}{\sin x \cdot \cos 3x}.$ **2109.** $\int \frac{dx}{1 + \tan x}.$ **2110.** $\int \frac{dx}{5 - 3 \cos x}.$

2111. $\int \frac{dx}{5 + 4 \sin x}.$ **2112.** $\int \frac{2 - \sin x}{2 + \cos x} dx.$ **2113.** $\int \frac{\sin^2 x \, dx}{1 - \tan x}.$

2114. $\int \frac{dx}{4 + \tan x + 4 \cot x}.$ **2115.** $\int \frac{dx}{(\sin x + 2 \sec x)^2}.$

2116. $\int \frac{dx}{5 - 4 \sin x + 3 \cos x}.$ **2117.** $\int \frac{dx}{4 - 3 \cos^2 x + 5 \sin^2 x}.$

2118. $\int \frac{dx}{1 + \sin^2 x}.$ **2119.** $\int \frac{dx}{1 - \sin^4 x}.$

2120. $\int \frac{dx}{a^2 \sin^2 x + b^2 \cos^2 x}.$ **2121.** $\int \frac{dx}{\sin^2 x + \tan^2 x}.$

2122. $\int \frac{\cos x \, dx}{\sin^3 x - \cos^3 x}.$ **2123.** $\int \sqrt{1 + \sin x} \, dx.$

2124. $\int \frac{\sqrt{\tan x}}{\sin x \cos x} dx.$ **2125*.** $\int \frac{\sqrt{\sin^3 2x}}{\sin^5 x} dx.$ **2126.** $\int \frac{dx}{\sqrt[4]{\sin^3 x \cos^5 x}}.$

2127. $\int \frac{dx}{\sqrt{1 - \sin^4 x}}.$ **2128.** $\int \sqrt{1 + \cos x} \, dx.$ **2129.** $\int \frac{(\cos 2x - 3) \, dx}{\cos^4 x \sqrt{4 - \cot^2 x}}.$

2130. $\int \frac{dx}{\sin \frac{x}{2} \sqrt{\cos^3 \frac{x}{2}}}.$ **2131.** $\int \sqrt{\tan x} \, dx.$

Hyperbolic functions

In Problems 2132 to 2150 evaluate the integrals.

2132. $\int \cosh x\, dx.$

2133. $\int \sinh x\, dx.$

2134. $\int \frac{dx}{\cosh^2 x}.$

2135. $\int \frac{e^x\, dx}{\cosh x + \sinh x}.$

2136. $\int (\cosh^2 ax + \sinh^2 ax)\, dx.$

2137. $\int \sinh^2 x\, dx.$

2138. $\int \tanh^2 x\, dx.$

2139. $\int \coth^2 x\, dx.$

2140. $\int \sinh^3 x\, dx.$

2141. $\int \cosh^3 x\, dx.$

2142. $\int \tanh^4 x\, dx.$

2143. $\int \sinh^2 x \cosh^3 x\, dx.$

2144. $\int \coth^5 x\, dx.$

2145. $\int \frac{dx}{\sinh x \cosh x}.$

2146. $\int \frac{dx}{\sinh x}.$

2147. $\int \frac{dx}{(1 + \cosh x)^2}.$

2148. $\int \sqrt{\tanh x}\, dx.$

2149. $\int \frac{x\, dx}{\cosh^2 x}.$

2150. $\int \frac{e^{2x}\, dx}{\sinh^4 x}.$

Rational functions of x and $\sqrt{ax^2 + bx + c}$

In Problems 2151 to 2174 evaluate the integrals.

2151*. $\int \frac{dx}{x\sqrt{x^2 + x + 1}}.$

2152. $\int \frac{dx}{x\sqrt{x^2 + 4x - 4}}.$

2153. $\int \frac{dx}{x\sqrt{x^2 + 2x - 1}}.$

2154. $\int \frac{dx}{x\sqrt{2 + x - x^2}}.$

2155. $\int \frac{\sqrt{2x + x^2}}{x^2}\, dx.$

2156. $\int \frac{dx}{(x - 1)\sqrt{x^2 + x + 1}}.$

2157. $\int \frac{dx}{(2x - 3)\sqrt{4x - x^2}}.$

2158. $\int \sqrt{x^2 - 2x - 1}\, dx.$

2159. $\int \sqrt{3x^2 - 3x + 1}\, dx.$

2160. $\int \sqrt{1 - 4x - x^2}\, dx.$

2161. $\int \frac{dx}{x - \sqrt{x^2 - x + 1}}.$

2162. $\int \frac{dx}{x^2 (x + \sqrt{1 + x^2})}.$

2163. $\int \frac{dx}{1 + \sqrt{x^2 + 2x + 2}}.$

2164. $\frac{x^2\, dx}{\sqrt{1 - 2x - x^2}}.$

2165. $\int \frac{(2x^2 - 3x)\,dx}{\sqrt{x^2 - 2x + 5}}$.

2166. $\int \frac{3x^2 - 5x}{\sqrt{3 - 2x - x^2}}\,dx$.

2167. $\int \frac{3x^3\,dx}{\sqrt{x^2 + 4x + 5}}$.

2168. $\int \frac{x^3 - x + 1}{\sqrt{x^2 + 2x + 2}}\,dx$.

2169. $\int \frac{3x^3 - 8x + 5}{\sqrt{x^2 - 4x - 7}}\,dx$.

2170. $\int \frac{x^4\,dx}{\sqrt{x^2 + 4x + 5}}$.

2171. $\int \frac{dx}{(x^3 + 3x^2 + 3x + 1)\sqrt{x^2 + 2x - 3}}$.

2172. $\int \frac{\sqrt{1 + x^2}}{2 + x^2}\,dx$.

2173. $\int \frac{(x - 1)\,dx}{x^2\sqrt{2x^2 - 2x + 1}}$.

2174. $\int \frac{(2x + 3)\,dx}{(x^2 + 2x + 3)\sqrt{x^2 + 2x + 4}}$.

Miscellaneous functions

In Problems 2175 to 2230 find the integrals.

2175. $\int \frac{x^3\,dx}{(x - 1)^{12}}$.

2176. $\int \frac{x\,dx}{x - \sqrt{x^2 - 1}}$.

2177. $\int x\sqrt[3]{a + x}\,dx$.

2178. $\int \frac{dx}{ae^{mx} + be^{-mx}}$.

2179. $\int \frac{x\sqrt{1 + x}}{\sqrt{1 - x}}\,dx$.

2180. $\int \frac{x^4\,dx}{(x^2 - 1)(x + 2)}$.

2181. $\int \frac{dx}{1 - x^4}$.

2182. $\int \frac{dx}{(x^4 - 1)^2}$.

2183. $\int \frac{\ln(x + 1)\,dx}{\sqrt{x + 1}}$.

2184. $\int (x^2 + 3x + 5)\cos 2x\,dx$.

2185. $\int x^2 \sinh x\,dx$.

2186. $\int \arctan(1 + \sqrt{x})\,dx$.

2187. $\int \frac{\arcsin x\,dx}{x^2}$.

2188. $\int e^{\sqrt[3]{x}}\,dx$.

2189. $\int xe^{\sqrt[3]{x}}\,dx$.

2190. $\int (x^3 - 2x^2 + 5)e^{3x}\,dx$.

2191. $\int \sin\sqrt{x}\,dx$.

2192. $\int \frac{dx}{x^3(x - 1)^{1/2}}$.

2193. $\int \frac{dx}{x - \sqrt{x^2 - 1}}$.

2194. $\int \frac{\sqrt{(1 + x^2)^5}}{x^6}\,dx$.

2195. $\int \frac{x^4\,dx}{\sqrt{x^2 + 1}}$.

2196. $\int \sqrt{\frac{1 - \sqrt[3]{x}}{1 + \sqrt[3]{x}}}\,\frac{dx}{x}$.

2197. $\frac{dx}{x^3\sqrt{(1 + x)^3}}$.

2198. $\int \frac{\sqrt{2x + 1}}{x^2}\,dx$.

2199. $\int \frac{x^4\,dx}{x^{15}-1}$.

2200. $\int \frac{dx}{\sin 2x - 2\sin x}$.

2201. $\int \frac{dx}{1+\cos^2 x}$.

2202. $\int \frac{dx}{a^2 - b^2\cos^2 x}$.

2203. $\int x \ln(1+x^3)\,dx$.

2204. $\int \frac{(\ln x - 1)\,dx}{\ln^2 x}$.

2205. $\int \frac{x \ln x}{\sqrt{(x^2-1)^3}}\,dx$.

2206. $\int x^e e^x \cos x\,dx$.

2207. $\int x e^{x^2}(x^2+1)\,dx$.

2208. $\int \frac{dx}{\sqrt{\sin^3 x \cos^5 x}}$.

2209. $\int \frac{dx}{\sin^5 x \cos^5 x}$.

2210. $\int \frac{\sin 2x\,dx}{\cos^4 x + \sin^4 x}$.

2211. $\int \frac{dx}{1+\sin x + \cos x}$.

2212. $\int \sqrt{\tan^2 x + 2}\,dx$.

2213. $\int \frac{(x^2-1)\,dx}{x\sqrt{x^4+3x^2+1}}$.

2214. $\int \frac{dx}{(2x-3)\sqrt{4x-x^2}}$.

2215. $\int \frac{xe^x\,dx}{(1+x)^2}$.

2216. $\int \frac{xe^x\,dx}{\sqrt{1+e^x}}$.

2217. $\int \frac{\arctan x\,dx}{x^4}$.

2218. $\int \frac{x \arctan x}{(1+x^2)^2}\,dx$.

2219. $\int \frac{\arctan x}{(1+x)^3}\,dx$.

2220. $\int \frac{dx}{(1-2^x)^4}$.

2221. $\int \frac{(e^{3x}+e^x)\,dx}{e^{4x}-e^{2x}+1}$.

2222. $\int \frac{dx}{\sqrt{1+e^x+e^{2x}}}$.

2223. $\int \frac{\tan x\,dx}{1+\tan x + \tan^2 x}$.

2224. $\int \sin^8 x\,dx$.

2225. $\int \frac{(3+x^2)^2\,x^3\,dx}{(1+x^2)^3}$.

2226. $\frac{x^2-8x+7}{(x^2-3x-10)^2}\,dx$.

2227. $\int \frac{dx}{\sin^4 x + \cos^4 x}$.

2228. $\int \frac{(x+\sin x)\,dx}{1+\cos x}$.

2229*. $\int \frac{x^2-1}{x^2+1} \cdot \frac{dx}{\sqrt{1+x^4}}$.

2230. $\int e^{\sin x}\,\frac{x\cos^3 x - \sin x}{\cos^2 x}\,dx$.

7

Methods for Evaluating Definite Integrals. Improper Integrals

1. Methods for Exact Evaluation of Integrals

Direct application of the Newton-Leibniz formula

In Problems 2231 to 2258 compute the integrals.

2231. $\int_0^1 \sqrt{1+x}\,dx.$

2232. $\int_{-2}^{-1} \frac{dx}{(11+5x)^3}.$

2233. $\int_2^{-13} \frac{dx}{\sqrt[5]{(3-x)^4}}.$

2234. $\int_4^9 \frac{y-1}{\sqrt{y}+1}\,dy.$

2235. $\int_0^{T/2} \sin\left(\frac{2\pi t}{T} - \varphi_0\right) dt.$

2236. $\int_0^{16} \frac{dx}{\sqrt{x+9}-\sqrt{x}}.$

2237. $\int_0^1 (e^x-1)^4 e^x\,dx.$

2238. $\int_0^{2a} \frac{3\,dx}{2b-x}$ $(b > a > 0).$

2239. $\int_0^1 \frac{x\,dx}{(x^2+1)^2}.$

2240. $\int_1^e \frac{dx}{x\sqrt{1-(\ln x)^2}}.$

2241. $\int_1^e \frac{1+\log_{10} x}{x}\,dx.$

2242. $\int_1^2 \frac{e^{1/x}\,dx}{x^2}.$

2243. $\int_0^{\sqrt[n]{a/2}} \frac{x^{n-1}\,dx}{\sqrt{a^2-x^{2n}}}.$

2244. $\int_1^{e^3} \frac{dx}{x\sqrt{1+\ln x}}.$

2245. $\int_{1/2}^{\sqrt{3}/2} \frac{x^3\,dx}{\left(\frac{5}{8} - x^4\right)\sqrt{\frac{5}{8} - x^4}}$.

2246. $\int_0^{a/2} \frac{a\,dx}{(x-a)(x-2a)}$.

2247. $\int_2^3 \frac{dx}{2x^2 + 3x - 2}$.

2248. $\int_0^1 \frac{dx}{x^2 + 4x + 5}$.

2249. $\int_1^2 \frac{dx}{x + x^3}$.

2250. $\int_{-0.5}^1 \frac{dx}{\sqrt{8 + 2x - x^2}}$.

2251. $\int_{-\pi/2}^{\pi/2} \frac{dx}{1 + \cos x}$.

2252. $\int_0^{\pi/2} \cos^5 x \cdot \sin 2x\,dx$.

2253. $\int_{-\pi/2}^{\pi/2} \sqrt{\cos x - \cos^3 x}\,dx$.

2254. $\int_0^{\pi/\omega} \sin^2(\omega x + \varphi_0)\,dx$.

2255. $\int_{-\pi/2}^{-\pi/4} \frac{\cos^3 x\,dx}{\sqrt[3]{\sin x}}$.

2256. $\int_\alpha^{\pi/4} \cot^4 \varphi\,d\varphi$.

2257. $\int_{1/\pi}^{2/\pi} \frac{\sin \frac{1}{x}}{x^2}\,dx$.

2258. $\int_{-\pi/2}^{\pi/2} \cos t \cdot \sin\left(2t - \frac{\pi}{4}\right) dt$.

In Problems 2259 to 2268 find the integrals using the method of integration by parts.

2259. $\int_0^1 xe^{-x}\,dx$.

2260. $\int_0^{\pi/2} x \cos x\,dx$.

2261. $\int_{\pi/4}^{\pi/3} \frac{x\,dx}{\sin^2 x}$.

2262. $\int_0^{\pi} x^3 \sin x\,dx$.

2263. $\int_1^2 x \log_2 x\,dx$.

2264. $\int_0^{e-1} \ln(x+1)\,dx$.

2265. $\int_0^{a\sqrt{7}} \frac{x^3\,dx}{\sqrt[3]{a^2+x^2}}$.

2266. $\int_0^a \sqrt{a^2-x^2}\,dx$.

2267. $\int_0^{\pi/2} e^{2x}\cos x\,dx$.

2268. $\int_1^e \ln^3 x\,dx$.

2269. Derive recurrence formulas for computing the integrals $\int_0^{\pi/2} \cos^n x\,dx$ and $\int_0^{\pi/2} \sin^n x\,dx$ (n a positive integer or zero) and compute the integrals :

(a) $\int_0^{\pi/2} \sin^5 x\,dx$;

(b) $\int_0^{\pi/2} \cos^8 x\,dx$;

(c) $\int_0^{\pi/2} \sin^{11} x\,dx$.

2270. Derive a recurrence formula for computing the integral $\int_0^{\pi/2} \sin^m x\cos^n x\,dx$ (m and n positive integers or zeros). Investigate particular cases of even and odd values of m and n).

2271. Derive a recurrence formula and compute the integral $\int_{-1}^0 x^n e^x\,dx$ (n a positive integer).

2272. Prove the recurrence formula

$$\int \frac{dx}{(1+x^2)^n} = \frac{x}{2(n-1)(1+x^2)^{n-1}} + \frac{2n-3}{2(n-1)}\int \frac{dx}{(1+x^2)^{n-1}}$$

(n a positive integer) and with the aid of it compute the integral $\int_0^1 \frac{dx}{(1+x^2)^4}$.

2273. Prove that if $J_m = \int_1^e \ln^m x\,dx$, then $J_m = e - mJ_{m-1}$ (m a positive integer).

2274*. Find $\int_0^1 x^p(1-x)^q\,dx$ (p and q positive integers).

Change of variable in the definite integral

In Problems 2275 to 2295 compute the integrals.

2275. $\int_4^9 \frac{\sqrt{x}}{\sqrt{x}-1}\,dx.$

2276. $\int_0^1 \frac{\sqrt{x}\,dx}{1+x}.$

2277. $\int_3^8 \frac{x\,dx}{\sqrt{1+x}}.$

2278. $\int_0^1 \frac{x\,dx}{1+\sqrt{x}}.$

2279. $\int_0^1 \frac{\sqrt{e^x}\,dx}{\sqrt{e^x+e^{-x}}}.$

2280. $\int_3^{29} \frac{\sqrt[3]{(x-2)^2}\,dx}{3+\sqrt[3]{(x-2)^2}}.$

2281*. $\int_0^{\pi} \sin^6 \frac{x}{2}\,dx.$

2282*. $\int_0^{\pi/4} \cos^7 2x\,dx.$

2283. $\int_0^1 \frac{x^2\,dx}{(1+x^2)^3}.$

2284. $\int_1^{\sqrt{3}} \frac{\sqrt{1+x^2}}{x^2}\,dx.$

2285. $\int_{\sqrt{2}/2}^1 \frac{\sqrt{1-x^2}}{x^6}\,dx.$

2286. $\int_1^2 \frac{\sqrt{x^2-1}}{x}\,dx.$

2287. $\int_{\sqrt{2}}^2 \frac{dx}{x^5\sqrt{x^2-1}}.$

2288. $\int_0^1 \sqrt{(1-x^2)^3}\,dx.$

2289. $\int_0^1 x^2\sqrt{1-x^2}\,dx.$

2290. $\int_0^{-\ln 2} \sqrt{1-e^{2x}}\,dx.$

2291. $\int_0^a \frac{dx}{x+\sqrt{a^2-x^2}}.$

2292. $\int_0^3 \frac{dx}{(x^2+3)^{5/2}}.$

2293. $\int_{2.5}^5 \frac{(\sqrt{25-x^2})^3}{x^4}\,dx.$

2294. $\int_0^{1/\sqrt{3}} \frac{dx}{(2x^2+1)\sqrt{x^2+1}}.$

2295. $\int_{\sqrt{8/3}}^{2\sqrt{2}} \frac{dx}{x\sqrt{(x^2-2)^5}}.$

Miscellaneous problems

2296. Compute the mean value of the function $y = \sqrt{x} + \frac{1}{\sqrt{x}}$ on the interval $[1, 4]$.

2297. Compute the mean value of the function $f(x) = \frac{1}{x^2 + x}$ on the interval $[1, 1.5]$.

2298. Compute the mean value of the functions $f(x) = \sin x$ and $f(x) = \sin^2 x$ on the interval $[0, \pi]$.

2299. Find the mean value of the function $f(x) = \frac{2}{e^x + 1}$ on the interval $[0, 2]$.

2300. For what a the mean value of the function $y = \ln x$ on the interval $[1, a]$ is equal to the average rate of change of the function in this interval?

In Problems 2301 to 2317 compute the integrals.

2301. $\int_1^2 \frac{dx}{x + x^3}$.

2302. $\int_0^{\sqrt[5]{2}} \frac{x^9\,dx}{(1 + x^5)^3}$.

2303. $\int_0^{1/2} \frac{x^3\,dx}{x^2 - 3x + 2}$.

2304. $\int_0^{\sqrt[4]{2}} \frac{x^{15}\,dx}{(1 + x^8)^{2/5}}$.

2305. $\int_0^2 \frac{dx}{\sqrt{x + 1} + \sqrt{(x + 1)^3}}$.

2306. $\int_{-a}^{+a} \frac{x^2\,dx}{\sqrt{a^2 + x^2}}$.

2307. $\int_0^1 \sqrt{2x + x^2}\,dx$.

2308. $\int_0^{\sqrt{3}} x^5 \sqrt{1 + x^2}\,dx$.

2309. $\int_0^{\ln 5} \frac{e^x \sqrt{e^x - 1}}{e^x + 3}\,dx$.

2310. $\int_1^3 \frac{dx}{x\sqrt{x^2 + 5x + 1}}$.

2311. $\int_0^{\pi/4} \frac{x \sin x}{\cos^3 x}\,dx$.

2312. $\int_0^{\pi/2} \frac{dx}{2 \cos x + 3}$.

2313. $\int_0^{\pi/2} \frac{dx}{1 + \frac{1}{6}\sin^2 x}$.

2314. $\int_0^1 (\arcsin x)^4\,dx$.

2315. $\int_1^{16} \arctan \sqrt{\sqrt{x} - 1}\, dx.$

2316. $\int_0^1 \frac{(3x + 2)\, dx}{(x^2 + 4x + 1)^{5/2}}.$

2317. $\int_0^{\pi/2} \frac{\sin x \cos x\, dx}{a^2 \cos^2 x + b^2 \sin^2 x}.$

2318. Show that $\int_0^{\pi/2} \frac{|ab|\, dx}{a^2 \cos^2 x + b^2 \sin^2 x} = \frac{\pi}{2}$, where a and b are any real numbers different from zero.

2319. Solve the equation $\int_{\sqrt{2}}^{x} \frac{dx}{x\sqrt{x^2 - 1}} = \frac{\pi}{12}.$

2320. Solve the equation $\int_{\ln 2}^{x} \frac{dx}{\sqrt{e^x - 1}} = \frac{\pi}{6}.$

2321. Make sure that the inequalities $\frac{x}{e} > \ln x > 1$ hold true for $x > e$, and show that the integral $\int_3^4 \frac{dx}{\sqrt[3]{\ln x}}$ is less than unity, but more than 0.92.

2322*. Show that

$$\frac{\pi}{6} \approx 0.523 < \int_0^1 \frac{dx}{\sqrt{4 - x^2 - x^3}} < \frac{\pi}{4\sqrt{2}} \approx 0.555.$$

2323*. Show that

$$0.5 < \int_0^{0.5} \frac{dx}{\sqrt{1 - x^{2n}}} \le \frac{\pi}{6} \approx 0.523\ (n \ge 1).$$

2324. Using the inequality $\sin x > x - \frac{x^3}{6}$, true for $x > 0$, and the Cauchy-Bunyakovsky inequality (see Problem 1638), estimate the integral $\int_0^{\pi/2} \sqrt{x \sin x}\, dx.$

2325*. Show that

$$0.78 < \int_0^1 \frac{dx}{\sqrt{1 + x^4}} < 0.93.$$

2326. Find the greatest and least values of the function $I(x) = \int_0^x \frac{2t+1}{t^2 - 2t + 2}\, dt$ on the interval $[-1, 1]$.

2327. Find the point of extremum and the points of inflection on the graph of the function $y = \int_0^x (t-1)(t-2)^2\, dt$.

In Problems 2328 to 2331, prove without computing the integrals, that the following equalities are true.

2328. $\int_{-\pi/8}^{\pi/8} x^{10} \sin^9 x\, dx = 0.$

2329. $\int_{-1}^{1} \frac{x^7 - 3x^5 + 7x^3 - x}{\cos^2 x}\, dx = 0.$

2330. $\int_{-1}^{1} e^{\cos x}\, dx = 2\int_0^1 e^{\cos x}\, dx.$

2331. $\int_{-1/2}^{1/2} \cos x \ln \frac{1+x}{1-x}\, dx = 0.$

2332*. (a) Show that if $f(t)$ is an odd function, then $\int_a^x f(t)\, dt$ is an even function, i.e., that $\int_a^{-x} f(t)\, dt = \int_a^x f(t)\, dt$.

(b) Will $\int_a^x f(t)\, dt$ be an odd function if $f(t)$ is an even function?

2333*. Prove the validity of the equality

$$\int_x^1 \frac{dt}{1+t^2} = \int_1^{1/x} \frac{dt}{1+t^2} \; (x > 0).$$

2334. Prove the identity $\int_{1/e}^{\tan x} \frac{t\, dt}{1+t^2} + \int_{1/e}^{\cot x} \frac{dt}{t(1+t^2)} \equiv 1.$

2335. Prove the identity

$$\int_0^{\sin^2 x} \arcsin \sqrt{t}\, dt + \int_0^{\cos^2 x} \arccos \sqrt{t}\, dt \equiv \frac{\pi}{4}.$$

2336. Prove the validity of the equality

$$\int_0^1 x^m (1-x)^n \, dx = \int_0^1 x^n (1-x)^m \, dx.$$

2337. Prove the validity of the equality

$$\int_a^b f(x)\, dx = \int_a^b f(a+b-x)\, dx.$$

2338. Prove that $\int_0^{\pi/2} f(\cos x)\, dx = \int_0^{\pi/2} f(\sin x)\, dx$. Apply the obtained result in computing the integrals $\int_0^{\pi/2} \cos^2 x \, dx$ and $\int_0^{\pi/2} \sin^2 x \, dx$.

2339*. Prove that

$$\int_0^{\pi} xf(\sin x)\, dx = \frac{\pi}{2}\int_0^{\pi} f(\sin x)\, dx = \frac{\pi}{2}\cdot 2 \times \int_0^{\pi/2} f(\sin x)\, dx$$
$$= \pi \int_0^{\pi/2} f(\sin x)\, dx.$$

Apply the obtained result to the computation of the integral

$$\int_0^{\pi} \frac{x \sin x}{1+\cos^2 x}\, dx.$$

2340*. Show that if $f(x)$ is a periodic function with the period T, then $\int_a^{a+T} f(x)\, dx$ is independent of a.

2341*. It is known that $f(x)$ is an odd function in the interval $\left[-\frac{T}{2}, \frac{T}{2}\right]$ and has a period equal to T. Prove that $\int_a^x f(t)\, dt$ is also a periodic function with the same period.

2342. Compute the integral $\int_0^1 (1-x^2)^n \, dx$, where n is a positive integer, using two methods : (1) expanding the integrand by the binomial formula; (2) by the substitution $x = \sin \varphi$. Comparing the results thus obtained, get the following summation formula (C_n^k binomial coefficients) :

$$C_n^0 - \frac{C_n^1}{3} + \frac{C_n^2}{5} - \frac{C_n^3}{7} + \ldots + \frac{(-1)^n C_n^n}{2n+1} = \frac{2 \times 4 \times 6 \ldots 2n}{1 \times 3 \times 5 \ldots (2n+1)}.$$

2343. The integral $\int_0^{2\pi} \frac{dx}{5 - 3\cos x}$ is readily taken with the aid of the substitution $\tan \frac{x}{2} = z$.

We have
$$\int_0^{2\pi} \frac{dx}{5 - 3\cos x} = \int_0^0 \frac{2\,dz}{(1 + z^2)\left(5 - 3\frac{1 - z^2}{1 + z^2}\right)} = 0.$$

On the other hand, $-3 < -3\cos x < +3$, therefore,
$$2 < 5 - 3\cos x < 8 \quad \text{and} \quad \frac{1}{2} > \frac{1}{5 - 3\cos x} > \frac{1}{8}.$$

Hence,
$$\int_0^{2\pi} \frac{1}{2}\,dx > \int_0^{2\pi} \frac{dx}{5 - 3\cos x} > \int_0^{2\pi} \frac{1}{8}\,dx,$$

and therefore, $\int_0^{2\pi} \frac{dx}{5 - 3\cos x} > \frac{\pi}{4}$. Find the mistake in reasoning.

2344*. Let $I_n = \int_0^{\pi/4} \tan^n x\,dx$ ($n > 1$ and is an integer). Check to see that $I_n + I_{n-2} = \frac{1}{n - 1}$. Prove that $\frac{1}{2n + 2} < I_n < \frac{1}{2n - 2}$.

2345*. Prove the validity of the equality
$$\int_0^x e^{zx} e^{-z^2}\,dz = e^{x^2/4} \int_0^x e^{-z^2/4}\,dz.$$

2346*. Prove that
$$\lim_{\omega \to \infty} \frac{e^{k\omega^2 x^2}}{\int_a^b e^{k\omega^2 x^2}\,dx} = \begin{cases} 0 & \text{if } x < b \\ \infty & \text{if } x = b \end{cases} \quad (\omega > 0,\ k > 0,\ b > a > 0).$$

2. Approximate Methods

In Problems 2347 to 2349 carry out computations to within 0.001.

2347. The area of a quarter of a circle whose radius equals to unity is $\frac{\pi}{4}$. On the other hand, taking a unit circle $x^2 + y^2 = 1$ with the origin as centre, and applying integration for computing the area of a quarter of the circle, we get

$$\frac{\pi}{4} = \int_0^1 \sqrt{1 - x^2}\, dx, \quad \text{i.e.,} \quad \pi = 4\int_0^1 \sqrt{1 - x^2}\, dx.$$

Using the rectangle, trapezoid and Simpson's rules, compute approximately the number π, dividing the interval of integration [0, 1] into 10 parts. Compare the results obtained, and also compare them with the tabular value of the number π.

2348. Knowing that $\int_0^1 \frac{dx}{1 + x^2} = \frac{\pi}{2}$, compute approximately the number π.

Compare the results obtained by applying various rules when the interval of integration is divided into 10 parts. Also, compare the results with those of the previous problem.

2349. Compute $\ln 10 = \int_1^{10} \frac{dx}{x}$ using Simpson's rule for $n = 10$. Find the modulus of natural logarithms with respect to common logarithms. Compare the results with the tabular value.

In Problems 2350 to 2355 evaluate approximately (using Simpson's rule) the integrals which cannot be found in the final form with the aid of elementary functions. The number n of subintervals is specified in parentheses.

2350. $\int_0^1 \sqrt{1 - x^3}\, dx \ (n = 10)$.

2351. $\int_0^1 \sqrt{1 + x^4}\, dx \ (n = 10)$.

2352. $\int_2^5 \frac{dx}{\ln x} \ (n = 6)$.

2353. $\int_0^{\pi/3} \sqrt{\cos \varphi}\, d\varphi \ (n = 10)$.

2354. $\int_0^{\pi/2} \sqrt{1 - 0.1 \sin^2 \varphi}\, d\varphi \ (n = 6)$.

2355. $\int_0^{\pi/3} \frac{\sin x}{x}\, dx \ (n = 10)$.

2356. Using Simpson's formula, evaluate the integral $\int_{1.05}^{1.35} f(x)\, dx$, with the aid of the following table of values of $f(x)$:

x	1.05	1.10	1.15	1.20	1.25	1.30	1.35
$f(x)$	2.36	2.50	2.74	3.04	3.46	3.98	4.60

2357. A straight line touches the riverside at points A and B. To measure the area of the surface contained between the riverside and the straight line AB eleven perpendiculars are set up from the river to AB spaced at each 5 m (which means that the straight line AB is 60 m long). The lengths of the perpendiculars turn out to be equal to 3.28, 4.02, 4.64, 5.26, 4.98, 3.62, 3.82, 4.68, 5.26, 3.82, 3.24 m. Compute the approximate value of the mentioned area.

2358. Compute the cross-sectional area of a ship (Fig. 39) if

$$AA_1 = A_1A_2 = A_2A_3 = A_3A_4 = A_4A_5$$
$$= A_5A_6 = A_6A_7 = 0.4 \text{ m},$$

$AB = 3$ m, $A_1B_1 = 2.92$ m,

$A_2B_2 = 2.75$ m, $A_3B_3 = 2.52$ m,

$A_4B_4 = 2.30$ m, $A_5B_5 = 1.84$ m,

$A_6B_6 = 0.92$ m.

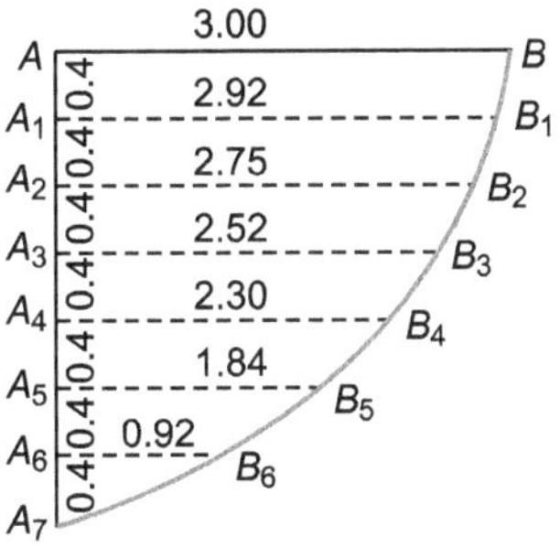

Fig. 39

2359. To compute the work of steam in the cylinder of a steam engine it is necessary to calculate the area of the indicator diagram which is a graphical representation of the relationship between the pressure of

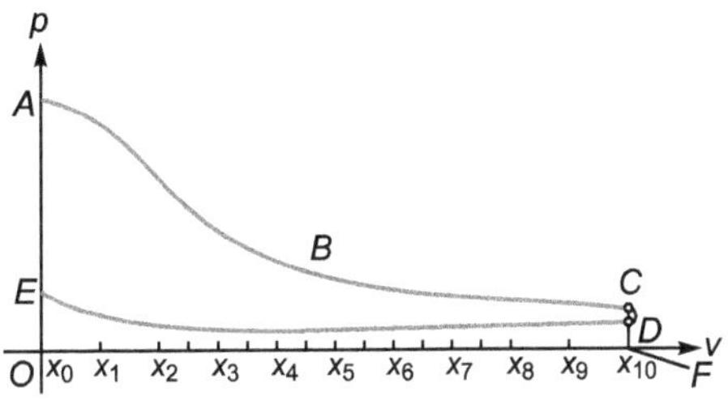

Fig. 40

the steam in the cylinder and the piston stroke. Figure 40 illustrates the indicator diagram of a steam engine. The ordinates of the points of the lines *ABC* and *ED* corresponding to the abscissas $x_0, x_1, x_2, \ldots, x_{10}$ are tabulated below :

Abscissas ...	x_0	x_1	x_2	x_3	x_4	x_5
Ordinates of line *ABC* ...	60.6	53.0	32.2	24.4	19.9	17.0
Ordinates of line *ED* ...	5.8	1.2	0.6	0.6	0.7	0.8
Abscissas ...	x_6	x_7	x_8	x_9	x_{10}	
Ordinates of line *ABC* ...	15.0	13.3	12.0	11.0	6.2	
Ordinates of line *ED* ...	0.9	1.0	1.3	1.8	5.7	

Compute the area *ABCDE* with the aid of Simpson's formula. The ordinates are given in millimetres. The length $OF = 88.7$ mm (point F is a common projection of the points C and D on the x-axis).

In Problems 2360 to 2363 use the methods of approximate solution of the equation to find the limits of integration.

2360. Find the area of the figure bounded by arcs of the parabolas $y = x^3 - 7$ and $y = -2x^2 + 3x$ and the y-axis.

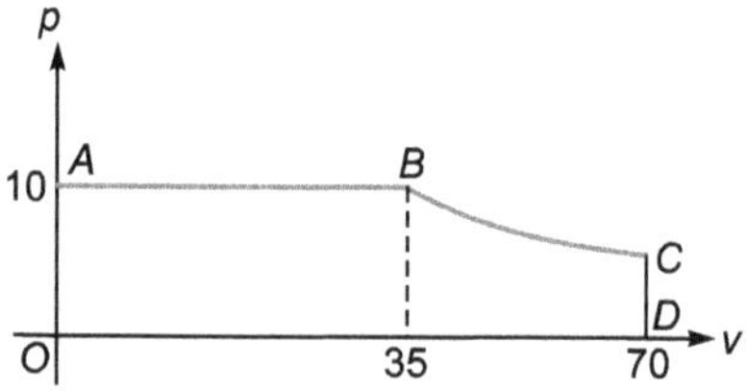

Fig. 41

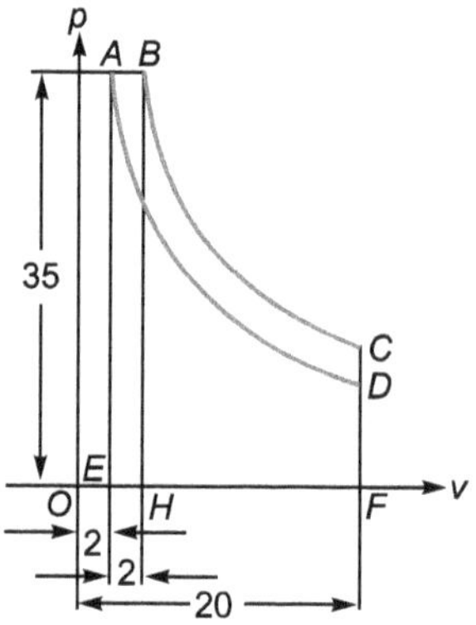

Fig. 42

2361. Find the area of the figure bounded by the parabola $y = x^3$ and the straight line $y = 7(x + 1)$.

2362. Find the area of the figure bounded by the parabola $y = 16 - x^2$ and semicubical parabola $y = -\sqrt[3]{x^2}$.

2363. Find the area of the figure bounded by the curves $y = 4 - x^4$ and $y = \sqrt[3]{x}$.

2364. Figure 41 illustrates a simplified indicator diagram of a steam engine. Proceeding from the given dimensions (in mm), compute the area

ABCDO if the equation of the line *BC* is known : $pv^{\gamma} = \text{const}$ (this line is called the adiabat), $\gamma = 1.3$, *AB* is a straight line parallel to the axis *Ov*.

2365. Figure 42 represents an indicator diagram of a diesel engine. The segment *AB* corresponds to the process of combustion of the fuel mixture, the adiabat *BC* to the expansion, the segment *CD* to the release and the adiabat *DA* to the compression. The equations of the adiabats *BC* and *AD* are : $pv^{1.3} = \text{const}$ and $pv^{1.35} = \text{const}$, respectively. Proceeding from the given dimensions (in mm), determine the area *ABCD*.

3. Improper Integrals

Integrals with infinite limits

In Problems 2366 to 2385 compute the improper integrals (or prove their divergence).

2366. $\int_1^{\infty} \frac{dx}{x^4}$.

2367. $\int_1^{\infty} \frac{dx}{\sqrt{x}}$.

2368. $\int_0^{\infty} e^{-ax}\,dx \quad (a > 0)$.

2369. $\int_{-\infty}^{\infty} \frac{2x\,dx}{x^2+1}$.

2370. $\int_{-\infty}^{\infty} \frac{dx}{x^2+2x+2}$.

2371. $\int_2^{\infty} \frac{\ln x}{x}\,dx$.

2372. $\int_1^{\infty} \frac{dx}{x^2(x+1)}$.

2373. $\int_0^{\infty} \frac{dx}{(1+x)^3}$.

2374. $\int_{\sqrt{2}}^{\infty} \frac{dx}{x\sqrt{x^2-1}}$.

2375. $\int_{a^2}^{\infty} \frac{dx}{x\sqrt{1+x^2}}$.

2376. $\int_0^{\infty} xe^{-x^2}\,dx$.

2377. $\int_0^{\infty} x^3 e^{-x^2}\,dx$.

2378. $\int_0^{\infty} x \sin x\,dx$.

2379. $\int_0^{\infty} e^{-\sqrt{x}}\,dx$.

2380. $\int_0^\infty e^{-x} \sin x \, dx.$

2381. $\int_0^\infty e^{-ax} \cos bx \, dx.$

2382. $\int_1^\infty \frac{\arctan x}{x^2} \, dx.$

2383. $\int_0^\infty \frac{dx}{1 + x^3}.$

2384. $\int_{-\infty}^\infty \frac{dx}{(x^2 + 1)^2}.$

2385. $\int_1^\infty \frac{\sqrt{x}}{(1 + x)^2} \, dx.$

In Problems 2386 to 2393 test the integrals for convergence.

2386. $\int_0^\infty \frac{x}{x^3 + 1} \, dx.$

2387. $\int_1^\infty \frac{x^3 + 1}{x^4} \, dx.$

2388. $\int_0^\infty \frac{x^{13}}{(x^5 + x^3 + 1)^3} \, dx.$

2389. $\int_1^\infty \frac{\ln (x^2 + 1)}{x} \, dx.$

2390. $\int_0^\infty \sqrt{x} \, e^{-x} \, dx.$

2391. $\int_0^\infty \frac{x \arctan x}{\sqrt[3]{1 + x^4}} \, dx.$

2392. $\int_{e^2}^\infty \frac{dx}{x \ln (\ln x)}.$

2393. $\int_e^\infty \frac{dx}{x (\ln x)^{3/2}}.$

Integrals of functions with infinite discontinuities

In Problems 2394 to 2411 compute the improper integrals (or prove their divergence).

2394. $\int_0^1 \frac{dx}{\sqrt{1 - x^2}}.$

2395. $\int_0^2 \frac{dx}{x^2 - 4x + 3}.$

2396. $\int_1^2 \frac{x \, dx}{\sqrt{x - 1}}.$

2397. $\int_0^1 x \ln x \, dx.$

2398. $\int_0^{1/e} \frac{dx}{x \ln^2 x}.$

2399. $\int_1^2 \frac{dx}{x \ln x}.$

2400. $\int_1^e \frac{dx}{x \sqrt{\ln x}}.$

2401. $\int_a^b \frac{dx}{\sqrt{(x - a)(b - x)}} \; (a < b).$

2402. $\int_a^b \frac{x\,dx}{\sqrt{(x-a)(b-x)}}$ $(a<b)$.

2403. $\int_3^5 \frac{x^2\,dx}{\sqrt{(x-3)(5-x)}}$.

2404. $\int_0^1 \frac{dx}{1-x^2+2\sqrt{1-x^2}}$.

2405. $\int_{-1}^1 \frac{dx}{(2-x)\sqrt{1-x^2}}$.

2406. $\int_{-1}^1 \frac{3x^2+2}{\sqrt[3]{x^2}}\,dx$.

2407. $\int_{-1}^1 \frac{x+1}{\sqrt[5]{x^3}}\,dx$.

2408. $\int_{-1}^1 \frac{x-1}{\sqrt[3]{x^5}}\,dx$.

2409. $\int_{-1}^1 \frac{\ln(2+\sqrt[3]{x})}{\sqrt[3]{x}}\,dx$.

2410. $\int_{-1}^0 \frac{e^{1/x}}{x^3}\,dx$.

2411. $\int_0^1 \frac{e^{1/x}}{x^3}\,dx$.

In Problems 2412 to 2417 test the integrals for convergence.

2412. $\int_0^1 \frac{\sqrt{x}}{\sqrt{1-x^4}}\,dx$.

2413. $\int_0^1 \frac{x^2\,dx}{\sqrt[3]{(1-x^2)^5}}$.

2414. $\int_0^1 \frac{dx}{e^{\sqrt{x}}-1}$.

2415. $\int_0^1 \frac{\sqrt{x}\,dx}{e^{\sin x}-1}$.

2416. $\int_0^1 \frac{dx}{e^x-\cos x}$.

2417. $\int_0^{\pi/2} \frac{\ln \sin x}{\sqrt{x}}\,dx$.

Miscellaneous problems

2418. A function $f(x)$ is continuous in the interval $[a, \infty]$ and $f(x) \to A \neq 0$ as $x \to \infty$. Can the integral $\int_a^\infty f(x)\,dx$ converge?

2419. For what values of k is the integral $\int_1^\infty x^k \frac{x+\sin x}{x-\sin x}\,dx$ convergent?

2420. For what k's are the integrals $\int_2^\infty \frac{dx}{x^k \ln x}$ and $\int_2^\infty \frac{dx}{x(\ln x)^k}$ convergent?

2421. For what values of k is the integral $\int_a^b \frac{dx}{(b-x)^k}$ $(b < a)$ convergent?

2422. Is it possible to find a k such that the integral $\int_0^\infty x^k\, dx$ is convergent?

2423. For what values of k and t is the integral $\int_0^\infty \frac{x^k}{1+x^t}\, dx$ convergent?

2424. For what values of m is the integral $\int_0^{\pi/2} \frac{1-\cos x}{x^m}\, dx$ convergent?

2425. For what values of k is the integral $\int_0^\pi \frac{dx}{\sin^k x}$ convergent?

In Problems 2426 to 2435 compute the improper integrals.

2426. $\int_1^\infty \frac{dx}{x\sqrt{x-1}}$.

2427*. $\int_{-1}^1 \ln\frac{1+x}{1-x}\frac{x^3\, dx}{\sqrt{1-x^2}}$.

2428. $\int_0^\infty \frac{\arctan(x-1)\, dx}{\sqrt[3]{(x-1)^4}}$.

2429. $\int_0^\infty \frac{dx}{(a^2+r^2)^n}$ (n a positive integer).

2430. $\int_0^\infty x^n e^{-x}\, dx$ (n a positive integer).

2431. $\int_0^\infty x^{2n+1} e^{-x^2}\, dx$ (n a positive integer).

2432. $\int_0^1 (\ln x)^n\, dx$ (n a positive integer).

2433*. $\int_0^1 \frac{x^m\, dx}{\sqrt{1-x^2}}$ for m : (a) even, (b) odd $(m > 0)$.

2434*. $\int_0^1 \frac{(1-x)^n}{\sqrt{x}}\, dx$ (n a positive integer).

2435. $\int_1^\infty \frac{dx}{(x-\cos\alpha)\sqrt{x^2-1}}$ $(0<\alpha<2\pi)$.

2436*. Prove that $\int_0^\infty \frac{dx}{1+x^4} = \int_0^\infty \frac{x^2\,dx}{1+x^4} = \frac{\pi}{2\sqrt{2}}$.

2437*. Prove that $\int_0^\infty \frac{x\ln x}{(1+x^2)^2}\,dx = 0$.

2438. Compute the integral $\int_1^\infty \frac{x^2-2}{x^3\sqrt{x^2-1}}\,dx$.

In Problems 2439 to 2448 compute the integrals using Poisson's integral $\int_0^\infty e^{-x^2}\,dx = \frac{\sqrt{\pi}}{2}$ and Dirichlet's integral $\int_0^\infty \frac{\sin x}{x}\,dx = \frac{\pi}{2}$.

2439. $\int_0^\infty e^{-ax^2}\,dx$ $(a>0)$.

2440. $\int_0^\infty \frac{e^{-x}}{\sqrt{x}}\,dx$.

2441*. $\int_0^\infty x^2 e^{-x^2}\,dx$.

2442. $\int_0^\infty x^{2n} e^{-x^2}\,dx$ (n a positive integer).

2443. $\int_0^\infty \frac{\sin 2x}{x}\,dx$.

2444. $\int_0^\infty \frac{\sin ax}{x}\,dx$.

2445. $\int_0^\infty \frac{\sin ax\cos bx}{x}\,dx$ $(a>0,\ b>0)$.

2446*. $\int_0^\infty \frac{\sin^2 x}{x^2}\,dx$.

2447*. $\int_0^\infty \frac{\sin^3 x}{x}\,dx$.

2448*. $\int_0^\infty \frac{\sin^4 x}{x^2}\,dx$.

2449*. Put $\varphi(x) = -\int_0^x \ln\cos y\,dy$. (This integral is called Lobachevsky's integral). Prove the relationship

$$\varphi(x) = 2\varphi\left(\frac{\pi}{4} + \frac{x}{2}\right) - 2\varphi\left(\frac{\pi}{4} - \frac{x}{2}\right) - x\ln 2.$$

With the aid of the found relationship compute the following

$$\varphi\left(\frac{\pi}{2}\right) = -\int_0^{\pi/2} \ln\cos y\,dy$$

(Euler was the first to calculate it).

In Problems 2450 to 2454 compute the integrals.

2450. $\int_0^{\pi/2} \ln\sin x\,dx.$

2451. $\int_0^{\pi} x\ln(\sin x)\,dx.$

2452*. $\int_0^{\pi/2} x\cot x\,dx.$

2453*. $\int_0^1 \frac{\arcsin x}{x}\,dx.$

2454. $\int_0^1 \frac{\ln x\,dx}{\sqrt{1-x^2}}.$

8

Application of Integral Calculus

1. Some Problems in Geometry and Statics

The area of a figure

2455. Compute the area of the figure bounded by the curves $y^2 = 2x + 1$ and $x - y - 1 = 0$.

2456. Compute the area of the figure contained between the parabola $y = -x^2 + 4x - 3$ and the tangents to it at the points $(0, -3)$ and $(3, 0)$.

2457. Compute the area of the figure bounded by the parabola $y^2 = 2px$ and a normal to it inclined at an angle of 135° to the x-axis.

2458. Compute the area of the figure bounded by the parabolas $y = x^2$ and $y = \sqrt{x}$.

2459. Compute the area of the figure bounded by the parabolas $y^2 + 8x = 16$ and $y^2 - 24x = 48$.

2460. Compute the area of the figure bounded by the parabolas $y = x^2$ and $y = \frac{x^3}{3}$.

2461. The circle $x^2 + y^2 = 8$ is divided into two parts by the parabola $y = \frac{x^2}{2}$. Find the areas of both parts.

2462. Find the areas of the figures into which the parabola $y^2 = 6x$ divides the circle $x^2 + y^2 = 16$.

2463. An ellipse is cut out of a circle whose radius is a. The major axis of the ellipse coincides with one of the diameteres of the circle, while the minor axis is equal to $2b$. Prove that the area of the remaining part equals that of the ellipse with the semiaxes a and $a - b$.

2464. Find the area of the figure bounded by an arc of a hyperbola and its chord drawn from the focus and perpendicular to the real axis.

2465. The circle $x^2 + y^2 = a^2$ is divided into three parts by the hyperbola $x^2 - 2y^2 = \frac{a^2}{4}$. Determine the areas of these parts.

2466. Compute the areas of the curvilinear figures formed by intersection of the ellipse $\frac{x^2}{4} + y^2 = 1$ and the hyperbola $\frac{x^2}{2} - y^2 = 1$.

2467. Compute the area of the figure contained between the curve $y = \frac{1}{1 + x^2}$ and the parabola $y = \frac{x^2}{2}$.

2468. Compute the area of the figure bounded by the curve $y = x(x-1)^2$ and the x-axis.

2469. Find the area of the figure bounded by the y-axis and the curve $x = y^2(y-1)$.

2470. For the figure bounded by the curves $y^m = x^n$ and $y^n = x^m$, where m and n are positive integers, find the area of the portion situated in the first quadrant. Consider the area of the entire figure depending on whether the numbers m and n are even or odd.

2471. (a) Compute the area of the curvilinear trapezium bounded by the x-axis and the curve $y = x - x^2\sqrt{x}$.

(b) Compute the area of the figure bounded by two branches of the curve $(y - x)^2 = x^5$ and the straight line $x = 4$.

2472. Compute the area of the figure bounded by the curve $(y - x - 2)^2 = 9x$ and the coordinate axes.

2473. Find the area of a loop of the line $y^2 = x(x-1)^2$.

2474. Find the area of the figure enclosed by the curve $y^2 = (1 - x^2)^3$.

2475. Find the area of the figure enclosed by the curve $y^2 = x^2 - x^4$.

2476. Find the area of the figure enclosed by the curve $x^4 - ax^3 + a^2y^2 = 0$.

2477. Find the area of the finite portion of the figure bounded by the curve $x^2y^2 = 4(x-1)$ and the straight line passing through its points of inflection.

2478. Find the area of the figure bounded by the curves $y = e^x$, $y = e^{-x}$ and the straight line $x = 1$.

2479. Find the area of the curvilinear trapezium bounded by the curve $y = (x^2 + 2x)e^{-x}$ and the x-axis.

2480. Compute the area of the curvilinear trapezium bounded by the curve $y = e^{-x}(x^2 + 3x + 1) + e^2$, the x-axis and two straight lines parallel to the y-axis drawn through the points of extremum of the function y.

2481. Find the area of the finite portion of the figure bounded by the curves $y = 2x^2e^x$ and $y = -x^3e^x$.

2482. (a) Compute the area of the curvilinear trapezium with the base $[a, b]$ bounded by the curve $y = \ln x$.

(b) Compute the area of the figure bounded by the curve $y = \ln x$, the y-axis and the straight lines $y = \ln a$ and $y = \ln b$.

2483. Compute the area of the figure bounded by the curves $y = \ln x$ and $y = \ln^2 x$.

2484. Compute the area of the figure bounded by the curves $y = \dfrac{\ln x}{4x}$ and $y = x \ln x$.

2485. Compute the area of one of the curvilinear triangles bounded by the x-axis and the curves $y = \sin x$ and $y = \cos x$.

2486. Compute the area of the curvilinear triangle bounded by the y-axis and the curves $y = \tan x$ and $y = \dfrac{2}{3} \cos x$.

2487. Find the area of the figure bounded by the curve $y = \sin^3 x + \cos^3 x$ and the segment of the x-axis joining two successive points of intersection of the curve with the x-axis.

2488. Compute the area of the figure bounded by the x-axis and the curves $y = \arcsin x$ and $y = \arccos x$.

2489. Find the area of the figure enclosed by the curve $(y - \arcsin x)^2 = x - x^2$.

2490. Find the area of the figure bounded by one arc of the cycloid $x = a(t - \sin t)$, $y = a(1 - \cos t)$ and the x-axis.

2491. Compute the area of the figure enclosed by the astroid $x = a\cos^3 t$, $y = a \sin^3 t$.

2492. Find the area of the figure enclosed by the cardioid $x = 2a\cos t - a\cos 2t$, $y = 2a \sin t - a \sin 2t$.

2493. Find the area of the figure enclosed by :

(1) The epicycloid

$$x = (R + r)\cos t - r\cos \frac{R + r}{r} t,$$

$$y = (R + r)\sin t - r\sin \frac{R + r}{r} t;$$

(2) The hypocycloid

$$x = (R - r)\cos t + r\cos \frac{R - r}{r} t,$$

$$y = (R - r)\sin t - r\sin \frac{R - r}{r} t,$$

where $R = nr$ (n an integer). Here R is the radius of the fixed circle and r is the radius of the movable circle; the centre of the fixed circle coincides with the origin, and t denotes the angle of rotation of the radius drawn from the centre of the fixed circle to the point of tangency.

2494. Find the area of the loop of the curve :
(1) $x = 3t^2, y = 3t - t^3$; (2) $x = t^2 - 1,\ y = t^3 - t$.

2495. (a) Compute the area described by the polar radius of the spiral of Archimedes $\rho = a\varphi$ for one its turn if at the start $\varphi = 0$.
(b) Compute the area of the figure bounded by the second and third turns of the spiral and the segment of the polar axis.

2496. Find the area of the figure bounded by the line $\rho = a \sin 2\varphi$ (two-leafed rose).

2497. Find the area of the figure bounded by the curve $\rho = a \cos 5\varphi$.

2498. Find the area of the figure bounded by Pascal's limacon $\rho = 2a\,(2 + \cos\varphi)$.

2499. Find the area of the figure bounded by the curve $\rho = a \tan\varphi\ (a > 0)$ and the straight line $\varphi = \frac{\pi}{4}$.

2500. Find the area of the common part of the figures bounded by the curves $\rho = 3 + \cos 4\varphi$ and $\rho = 2 - \cos 4\varphi$.

2501. Find the area of the portion of the figure bounded by the curve $\rho = 2 + \cos 2\varphi$, situated outside the curve $\rho = 2 + \sin\varphi$.

2502. Find the area of the figure bounded by the curve $\rho^2 = a^2 \cos n\varphi$ (n a positive integer).

2503. Show that the area of the figure bounded by any two polar radii of the hyperbolic spiral $\rho\varphi = a$ and its arc is proportional to the difference of these radii.

2504. Show that the area of the figure bounded by any polar radii of the logarithmic spiral $\rho = ae^{m\varphi}$ and its arc is proportional to the difference of the squares of these radii.

2505*. Find the area of the figure contained between the outside and inside portions of the curve $\rho = a \sin^3 \frac{\varphi}{3}$.

2506. Compute the area of the figure bounded by the curve $\rho = \sqrt{1 - t^2}$, $\varphi = \arcsin t + \sqrt{1 - t^2}$.

In Problems 2507 to 2511 it is convenient to pass over to polar coordinates.

2507. Find the area of the figure bounded by the lemniscate of Bernoulli $(x^2 + y^2)^2 = a^2\,(x^2 - y^2)$.

2508. Find the area of the portion of the figure bounded by the lemniscate of Bernoulli (see Problem 2507) lying inside the circle $x^2 + y^2 = \frac{a^2}{2}$.

2509. Find the area of the figure bounded by the curve $(x^2 + y^2)^2 - a^2x^2 - b^2y^2 = 0$.

2510. Find the area of the figure bounded by the curve $(x^2 + y^2)^3 = 4a^2xy\,(x^2 - y^2)$.

2511. Compute the area of the figure bounded by the curve $x^4 + y^4 = x^2 + y^2$.

2512. Compute the area of the figure contained between the curve $y = \dfrac{1}{1 + x^2}$ and its asymptote.

2513. Find the area of the figure lying between the curve $y = xe^{-\frac{x^2}{2}}$ and its asymptote.

2514. Find the area of the figure situated between the cissoid $y^2 = \dfrac{x^3}{2a - x}$ and its asymptote.

2515. Find the area of the figure contained between the curve $xy^2 = 8 - 4x$ and its asymptote.

2516*. (1) Compute the area of the figure bounded by the curve $y = x^2e^{-x^2}$ and its asymptote.

(2) Compute the area of the figure bounded by the curve $y^2 = xe^{-2x}$.

2517. Find the area of the figure contained between the tractrix $x = a\left[\cos t + \ln\left(\tan\dfrac{t}{2}\right)\right]$, $y = a\sin t$ and the x-axis.

2518. For the curve $\rho = \dfrac{\cos 2\varphi}{\cos\varphi}$ find the area of the loop and the area of the figure contained between the curve and its asymptote.

Arc length[1]

2519. Compute the arc length of the catenary $y = a\cosh\dfrac{x}{a}$ (from $x_1 = 0$ to $x_2 = b$).

2520. Find the arc length of the parabola $y^2 = 2px$ from the vertex to the point $M\,(x, y)$. (Take y as the independent variable).

2521. Find the arc length of the curve $y = \ln x$ (from $x_1 = \sqrt{3}$ to $x_2 = \sqrt{8}$).

2522. Find the arc length of the curve $y = \ln(1 - x^2)$ (from $x_1 = 0$ to $x_2 = \dfrac{1}{2}$).

[1]In problems on computing the arc lengths the interval of variation of the independent variable corresponding to the rectified arc is given in parentheses whenever it is necessary.

2523. Find the arc length of the curve $y = \ln \dfrac{e^x + 1}{e^x - 1}$ (from $x_1 = a$ to $x_2 = b$).

2524. Compute the arc length of the semicubical parabola $y^2 = \dfrac{2}{3}(x-1)^3$ situated inside the parabola $y^2 = \dfrac{x}{3}$.

2525. Compute the arc length of the semicubical parabola $5y^3 = x^2$ contained inside the circle $x^2 + y^2 = 6$.

2526. Compute the length of the loop of the curve $9ay^2 = x(x-3a)^2$.

2527. Find the perimeter of one of the curvilinear triangles bounded by the x-axis and the curves $y = \ln(\cos x)$ and $y = \ln(\sin x)$.

2528. Find the arc length of the curve $x = \dfrac{x^2}{4} - \dfrac{\ln x}{2}$ between its lowest point and the vertex (the point with the extremum curvature).

2529. Find the length of the curve $y = \sqrt{x - x^2} + \arcsin\sqrt{x}$.

2530. Find the length of the curve $(y - \arcsin x)^2 = 1 - x^2$.

2531. On the cycloid $x = a(t - \sin t)$, $y = a(1 - \cos t)$ find the point which divides the length of the first arc of the cycloid in the ratio 1 : 3.

2532. Given the astroid $x = R\cos^3 t$, $y = R\sin^3 t$ and two its points : $A(R, 0)$ and $B(0, R)$. On the arc $\overset{\frown}{AB}$ find a point M such that the arc length of $\overset{\frown}{AM}$ is equal to a quarter of the arc length of $\overset{\frown}{AB}$.

2533*. Find the length of the curve $\left(\dfrac{x}{a}\right)^{2/3} + \left(\dfrac{y}{b}\right)^{2/3} = 1$.

2534. Find the length of the curve $x = a\cos^5 t$, $y = a\sin^5 t$.

2535. Find the arc length of the tractrix

$$x = a\left[\cos t + \ln\left(\tan\frac{t}{2}\right)\right],\ y = a\sin t$$

from the point $(0, a)$ to the point (x, y).

2536. Find the arc length of the evolvent of the circle

$$x = R(\cos t + t\sin t),\ \ y = R(\sin t - t\cos t)$$

from $t_1 = 0$ to $t_2 = \pi$.

2537. Compute the arc length of the curve

$$x = (t^2 - 2)\sin t + 2t\cos t,\ y = (2 - t^2)\cos t + 2t\sin t$$

from $t_1 = 0$ to $t_2 = \pi$.

2538. Find the length of the loop of the curve $x = t^2$, $y = t - \dfrac{t^3}{3}$.

2539. Along a circle of radius a, outside and inside it, two circles of equal radii b are rolling (without sliding) with equal angular velocities. At the time

$t = 0$ they touch the point M on the fixed circle with their points M_1 and M_2. Show that the ratio of the paths covered by the points M_1 and M_2 during an arbitrary interval of time t is constant and equals $\frac{a+b}{a-b}$ (see Problem 2493).

2540. Show that the arc length of the curve

$$x = f''(t)\cos t + f'(t)\sin t, \quad y = -f''(t)\sin t + f'(t)\cos t,$$

corresponding to the interval (t_1, t_2), is equal to $[f(t) + f''(t)]\big|_{t_1}^{t_2}$.

2541. Apply the result of the previous problem to computing the arc length of the curve $x = e^t(\cos t + \sin t)$, $y = e^t(\cos t - \sin t)$ from $t_1 = 0$ to $t_2 = t$.

2542. Prove that the arcs of the curves

$$x = f(t) - \varphi'(t), \quad y = \varphi(t) + f'(t)$$

and $x = f'(t)\sin t - \varphi'(t)\cos t$, $y = f'(t)\cos t + \varphi'(t)\sin t$, corresponding to one and the same interval of variation of the parameter t, have equal lengths.

2543. Find the arc length of the spiral of Archimedes $\rho = a\varphi$ from the beginning to the end of the first turn.

2544. Prove that the arc of the parabola $y = \frac{1}{2p}x^2$, corresponding to the interval $0 \le x \le a$, has the same length as the arc of the spiral $\rho = p\varphi$, correspoding to the interval $0 \le \rho \le a$.

2545. Compute the arc length of the hyperbolic spiral $\rho\varphi = 1$ $\left(\text{from } \varphi_1 = \frac{3}{4} \text{ to } \varphi_2 = \frac{4}{3}\right)$.

2546. Find the length of the cardioid $\rho = a(1 + \cos\varphi)$.

2547. Find the length of the curve $\rho = a\sin^3\frac{\varphi}{3}$ (see Problem 2505).

2548. Prove that the length of the curve $\rho = a\sin^m\frac{\varphi}{m}$ (m an integer) is commensurable with a at an even m and with the length of the circumference of a circle of radius a at an odd m.

2549. For what values of k ($k \ne 0$) is the arc length of the curve $y = ax^k$ expressed in terms of elementary functions? (Apply Chebyshev's theorem on the conditions of integrability of a differential binomial.)

2550. Find the length of the curve specified by the equation

$$y = \int_{-\frac{\pi}{2}}^{x} \sqrt{\cos x}\, dx.$$

2551. Compute the arc length of the curve

$$x = \int_1^t \frac{\cos z}{z}\,dz, \quad y = \int_1^t \frac{\sin z}{z}\,dz$$

between the origin and the nearest point having a vertical tangent.

2552. Prove that the arc length of the sinusoid $y = \sin x$, corresponding to the period of the sine, is equal to the length of the ellipse whose semiaxes are $\sqrt{2}$ and 1.

2553. Show that the arc length of the curtate or prolate cycloid $x = mt - n \sin t$, $y = m - n \cos t$ (m and n positive numbers) in the interval from $t_1 = 0$ to $t_2 = 2\pi$ equals the length of the ellipse with the semiaxes $a = m + n$, $b = |m - n|$.

2554*. Prove that the length of the ellipse with the semiaxes a and b satisfies the inequalities $\pi(a + b) < L < \pi\sqrt{2} \times \sqrt{a^2 + b^2}$ (Bernoulli's problem).

Volume of a solid

2555. Compute the volume of the solid bounded by the surface generated by revolving the parabola $y^2 = 4x$ about its axis (a paraboloid of revolution) and a plane perpendicular to its axis, the distance between the plane and the vertex of the parabola being equal to unity.

2556. An ellipse whose major axis is equal to $2a$ and minor axis to $2b$ revolves : (1) about the major axis, (2) about the minor axis. Find the volume of the ellipsoids of revolution thus obtained. As a particular case, find the volume of a sphere.

2557. A symmetric parabolic segment whose base is a and altitude h rotates about the base. Compute the volume of the solid of revolution thus generated.

2558. A figure bounded by the hyperbola $x^2 - y^2 = a^2$ and the straight line $x = a + h$ $(h > 0)$ rotates about the x-axis. Find the volume of the solid of revolution.

2559. A curvilinear trapezium bounded by the curve $y = xe^x$ and the straight lines $x = 1$ and $y = 0$ rotates about the x-axis. Find the volume of the solid thus obtained.

2560. A catenary $y = \cosh x$ rotates about the x-axis to generate a catenoid. Find the volume of the solid bounded by the catenoid and two planes a and b distant from the origin and perpendicular to the x-axis.

2561. A figure bounded by arcs of the parabolas $y = x^2$ and $y^2 = x$ rotates about the x-axis. Compute the volume of the solid thus generated.

2562. Find the volume of the solid obtained by revolving, about the x-axis, a trapezium situated above the x-axis and bounded by the curve $(x-4)\,y^2 = x\,(x-3)$.

2563. Find the volume of the solid obtained by revolving a curvilinear trapezium bounded by the curve $y = \arcsin x$ with the base $[0, 1]$ about the x-axis.

2564. Compute the volume of the solid obtained by revolving, about the y-axis, a figure bounded by the parabola $y = 2x - x^2$ and the x-axis.

2565. Compute the volume of the solid generated by revolving, about the y-axis, a curvilinear trapezium bounded by the arc of the sinusoid $y = \sin x$ corresponding to the half-period.

2566. The lemniscate $(x^2 + y^2)^2 = a^2\,(x^2 - y^2)$ rotates about the x-axis. Find the volume of the solid bounded by the surface generated.

2567. Compute the volume of the solid generated by revolving, about the x-axis, a figure bounded by the curve:

(1) $x^4 + y^4 = a^2x^2$; (2) $x^4 + y^4 = x^3$.

2568. One arc of the cycloid $x = a\,(t - \sin t)$, $y = a\,(1 - \cos t)$ rotates about its base. Compute the volume of the solid bounded by the surface thus generated.

2569. A figure bounded by an arc of the cycloid (see the previous problem) and its base rotates about a straight line perpendicular to the base at its mid point (the axis of symmetry). Find the volume of the solid thus obtained.

2570. Find the volume of the solid obtained by revolving the astroid $x^{2/3} + y^{2/3} = a^{2/3}$ about its axis of symmetry.

2571. A figure bounded by the arc of the curve $x = \dfrac{c^2}{a}\cos^3 t$, $y = \dfrac{c^2}{b}\sin^3 t$ (evolute of ellipse) situated in the first quadrant, and the coordinate axes, rotates about the x-axis. Find the volume of the solid thus obtained.

2572. Compute the volume of the solid bounded by the infinite spindle-shaped surface generated by revolving the curve $y = \dfrac{1}{1+x^2}$ about its asymptote.

2573. The curve $y^2 = 2exe^{-2x}$ rotates about its asymptote. Find the volume of the solid bounded by the surface thus obtained.

2574*. (1) A figure bounded by the curve $y = e^{-x^2}$ and its asymptote rotates about the y-axis. Compute the volume of the solid thus generated.

(2) The same figure rotates about the x-axis. Find the volume of the obtained solid.

2575*. Compute the volume of the solid bounded by the surface generated by revolving the curve $y = x^2e^{-x^2}$ about its asymptote.

2576*. A figure bounded by the curve $y = \dfrac{\sin x}{x}$ and the x-axis rotates about the x-axis. Compute the volume of the solid thus obtained.

2577*. Find the volume of the solid bounded by the surface generated by revolving the cissoid $y^2 = \dfrac{x^3}{2a - x}$ $(a > 0)$ about its asymptote.

2578. Find the volume of the solid bounded by the surface obtained by revolving the tractrix $x = a\left[\cos t + \ln\left(\tan\dfrac{t}{2}\right)\right]$, $y = a\sin t$ about its asymptote.

2579*. Compute the volume of the solid enclosed by the ellipsoid $\dfrac{x^2}{a^2} + \dfrac{y^2}{b^2} + \dfrac{z^2}{c^2} = 1.$

2580. (1) Compute the volume of the solid bounded by the elliptic paraboloid $z = \dfrac{x^2}{4} + \dfrac{y^2}{2}$ and the plane $z = 1$.

(2) Find the volume of the solid bounded by the hyperboloid of one sheet $\dfrac{x^2}{4} + \dfrac{y^2}{9} - z^2 = 1$ and the planes $z = -1$ and $z = 2$.

2581. Compute the volumes of the solids bounded by the paraboloid $z = x^2 + 2y^2$ and the ellipsoid $x^2 + 2y^2 + z^2 = 6$.

2582. Find the volumes of the solids formed by intersection of the hyperboloid of two sheets $\dfrac{x^2}{3} - \dfrac{y^2}{4} - \dfrac{z^2}{9} = 1$ and the ellipsoid $\dfrac{x^2}{6} + \dfrac{y^2}{4} + \dfrac{z^2}{9} = 1.$

2583. Find the volume of the solid bounded by the conic surface $(z - 2)^2 = \dfrac{x^2}{3} + \dfrac{y^2}{2}$ and the plane $z = 0$.

2584. Compute the volume of the solid bounded by the paraboloid $2z = \dfrac{x^2}{4} + \dfrac{y^2}{9}$ and the cone $\dfrac{x^2}{4} + \dfrac{y^2}{9} = z^2$.

2585*. Find the volume of the solid cut off a circular cylinder by a plane passing through the diameter of the base (the cylindrical segment shown in Fig. 43). In particular, put $R = 10$ cm and $H = 6$ cm.

2586. A parabolic cylinder is cut by two planes one of which is perpendicular to the generatrix. The solid thus obtained is illustrated in Fig. 44. The common base of the parabolic segments $a=10$ cm, the altitude of the base segment $H = 8$ cm, the altitude of the solid $h = 6$ m. Compute the volume of the solid.

2587. A cylinder whose base is an ellipse is cut by an inclined plane passing through the minor axis of the ellipse. Compute the volume of the solid thus obtained. The linear dimensions are given in Fig. 45.

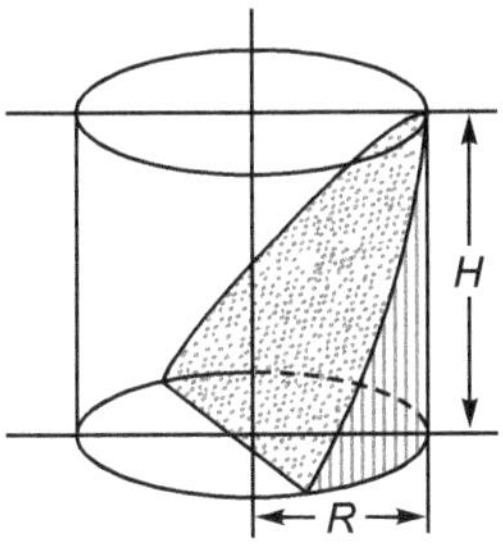

Fig. 43

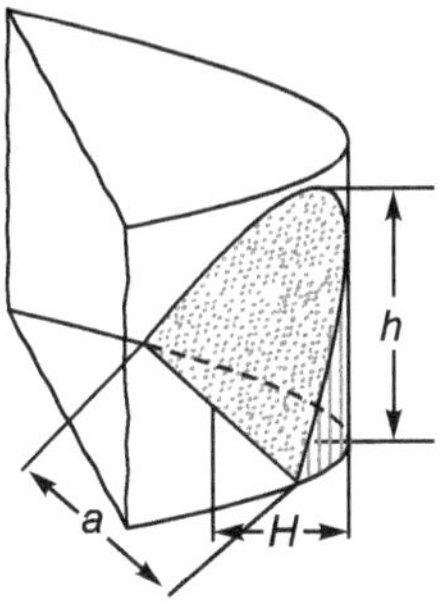

Fig. 44

2588*. Constructed on all chords of a circle of radius R parallel to one and the same direction are symmetric parabolic segments of a constant altitude H. The planes containing the segments are perpendicular to the plane of the circle. Find the volume of the solid thus obtained.

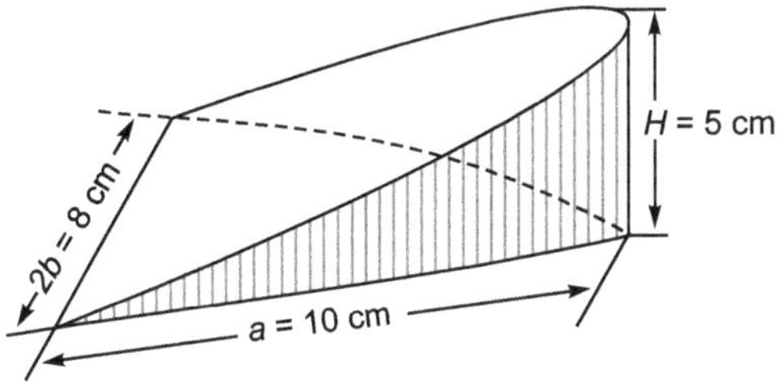

Fig. 45

2589*. A right circular cone of radius R and altitude H is cut into two parts by a plane passing through the centre of the base parallel to the generatrix (Fig. 46). Find the volumes of both parts of the cone. (The sections of the cone yielded by planes parallel to the generatrix are parabolic segments.)

2590. The centre of a square of variable size moves along the diameter of a circle of radius a, the plane of the square remaining perpendicular to the plane containing the circle, and two opposite vertices of the square travel along the circumference of the circle. Find the volume of the solid generated by the moving square.

2591. A circle of variable radius is displaced so that one of the points on its circumference remains on the x-axis, the centre moves along the circle $x^2 + y^2 = r^2$ and the plane containing this circle is perpendicular to the x-axis. Find the volume of the solid thus obtained.

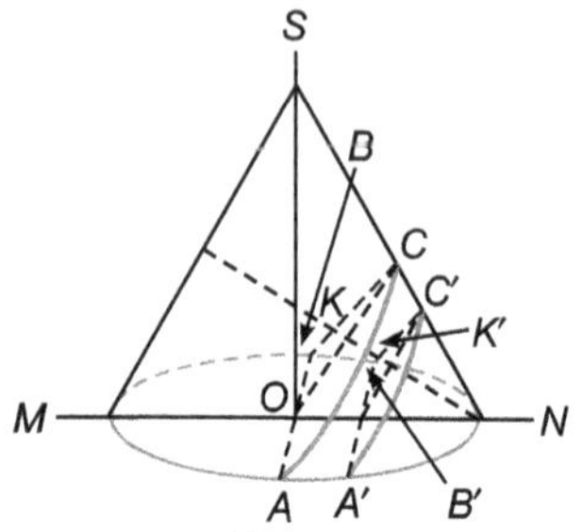

Fig. 46

2592. The axes of two equal cylinders intersect at right angles. Find the volume of the solid constituting the common portion of the cylinders (Fig. 47 shows one-eighth of the solid). (Consider the sections yielded by the planes parallel to the axes of both cylinders.)

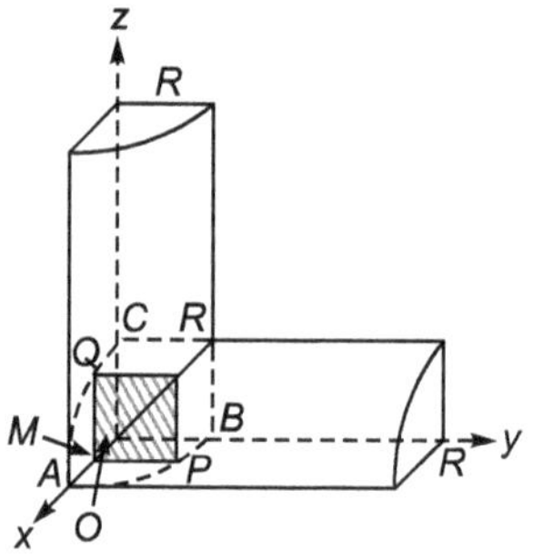

Fig. 47

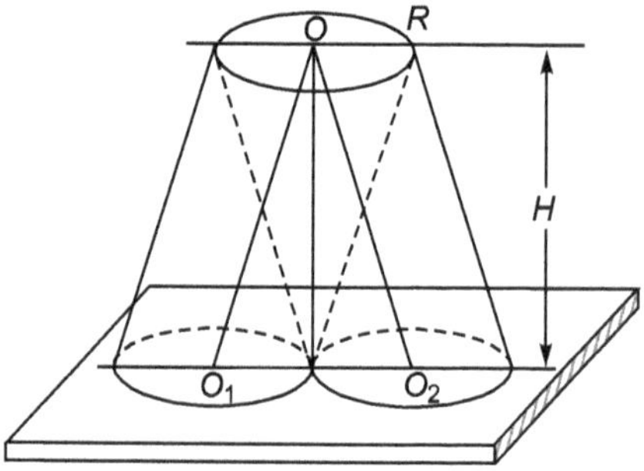

Fig. 48

2593. Two inclined cylinders have one and the same altitude H and a common upper base of radius R and their lower bases touch each other (see Fig. 48). Find the volume of the common portion of the cylinders.

The area of a surface of revolution

2594. Find the area of a surface obtained by revolving the parabola $y^2 = 4ax$ about the x-axis (the segment from the vertex to the point with the abscissa $x = 3a$).

2595. Compute the area of a surface generated by revolving the cubical parabola $3y - x^3 = 0$ about the x-axis (from $x_1 = 0$ to $x_2 = a$).

2596. Compute the surface area of the catenoid, i.e., of the surface generated by revolving the catenary $y = a \cosh \frac{x}{a}$ about the x-axis (from $x_1 = 0$ to $x_2 = a$).

2597. The surface generated by revolving an ellipse about the major axis is called the prolate spheroid, when the ellipse rotates about the minor axis the obtained surface is called the oblate spheroid. Find the surface areas of the prolate and oblate spheroids.

2598. Compute the area of a spindle-shaped surface generated by revolving one arc of the sinusoid $y = \sin x$ about the x-axis.

2599. An arc of the tangent curve $y = \tan x$ from the point $(0, 0)$ to the point $\left(\frac{\pi}{4}, 1\right)$ rotates about the x-axis. Compute the area of the surface thus obtained.

2600. Find the area of a surface generated by revolving, about the x-axis, the loop of the curve $9ay^2 = x(3a - x)^2$.

2601. The arc of the circle $x^2 + y^2 = a^2$ situated in the first quadrant rotates about the chord which subtends it. Compute the area of the obtained surface.

2602. Find the area of a surface generated by revolving, about the x-axis, an arc of the curve $x = e^t \sin t$, $y = e^t \cos t$ from $t_1 = 0$ to $t_2 = \frac{\pi}{2}$.

2603. Find the area of a surface generated by revolving the astroid $x = a\cos^3 t,\ y = a\sin^3 t$ about the x-axis.

2604. An arc of a cycloid rotates about its axis of symmetry. Find the area of the surface thus obtained. (See Problem 2568.)

2605. Find the area of a surface generated by revolving the cardioid $\rho = a(1 + \cos\varphi)$ about the polar axis.

2606. The circle $\rho = 2r \sin\varphi$ rotates about the polar axis. Find the area of the surface thus obtained.

2607. The lemniscate $\rho^2 = a^2 \cos 2\varphi$ rotates about the polar axis. Find the area of the surface thus generated.

2608. An endless arc of the curve $y = e^{-x}$, corresponding to the positive values of x, rotates about the x-axis. Compute the area of the surface thus obtained.

2609. The tractrix $x = a\left[\cos t + \ln\left(\tan\frac{t}{2}\right)\right]$, $y = a \sin t$ rotates about the x-axis. Find the area of the endless surface thus generated.

Moments and the centre of gravity[1]

2610. Compute the static moment of a rectangle with the base a and altitude h about its base.

2611. Compute the static moment of a right-angled isosceles triangle with the sides equal to a about each of its sides.

2612. Prove that the following formula is true :

$$\int_a^b (ax+b)\,f(x)\,dx = (a\xi + b)\int_a^b f(x)\,dx,$$

where ξ is the abscissa of the centre of gravity of a curvilinear trapezium with the base $[a, b]$ bounded by the curve $y = f(x)$.

2613. Find the centre of gravity of a symmetric parabolic segment with the base a and altitude h.

2614. A rectangle with the sides a and b is divided into two parts by an arc of a parabola whose vertex coincides with one of the vertices of the rectangle and which passes through its opposite vertex (Fig. 49). Find the centres of gravity of both parts (S_1 and S_2) of the rectangle.

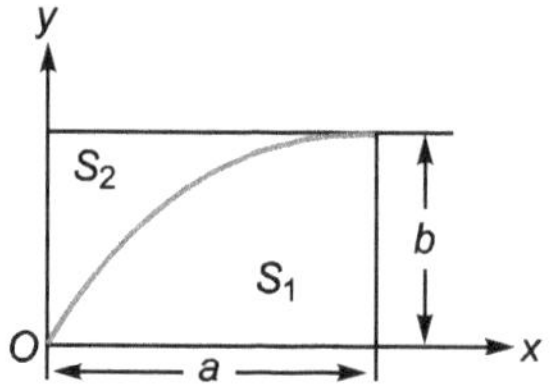

Fig. 49

2615. Find the coordinates of the centre of gravity of the semicircle $y = \sqrt{r^2 - x^2}$.

2616. Find the coordinates of the centre of gravity of a figure bounded by the x-axis and the semicircle $y = \sqrt{r^2 - x^2}$.

2617. Find the centre of gravity of a circular arc of radius R subtending the central angle α.

2618. Find the coordinates of the centre of gravity of a figure bounded by the coordinates axes and the parabola $\sqrt{x} + \sqrt{y} = \sqrt{a}$.

2619. Find the coordinates of the centre of gravity of a figure bounded by the coordinate axes and the arc of the ellipse $\dfrac{x^2}{a^2} + \dfrac{y^2}{b^2} = 1$ situated in the first quadrant.

2620. Find the static moment of the arc of the ellipse $\dfrac{x^2}{a^2} + \dfrac{y^2}{b^2} = 1$, situated in the first quadrant, about the x-axis.

---

[1]In Problems 2610 to 2662 density is assumed to be equal to unity.

2621. Find the coordinates of the centre of gravity of a figure bounded by an arc of the sinusoid $y = \sin x$ and the segment of the x-axis (from $x_1 = 0$ to $x_2 = \pi$).

In Problems 2622 to 2624 find the static moment about the x-axis of a figure bounded by the curves.

2622. $y = \dfrac{2}{1 + x^2}$ and $y = x^2$.

2623. $y = \sin x$ and $y = \dfrac{1}{2}$ (for one segment).

2624. $y = x^2$ and $y = \sqrt{x}$.

2625. Find the coordinates of the centre of gravity of a figure enclosed by the curve $y^2 = ax^3 - x^4$.

2626. Find the coordinates of the centre of gravity of the arc of the catenary $y = a \cosh \dfrac{x}{a}$ contained between the points with the abscissas $x_1 = -a$ and $x_2 = a$.

2627. Prove that the static moment of an arbitrary arc of a parabola about the axis of the parabola is proportional to the difference of the radii of curvature at the end-points of the arc. The proportionality factor is equal to $\dfrac{p}{3}$, where p is the parameter of the parabola.

2628. Find the coordinates of the centre of gravity of the first arc of the cycloid $x = a(t - \sin t)$, $y = a(1 - \cos t)$.

2629. Find the coordinates of the centre of gravity of a figure bounded by the first arc of a cycloid and the x-axis.

2630. Find the coordinates of the centre of gravity of the arc of the astroid $x = a \cos^3 t$, $y = a \sin^3 t$ located in the first quadrant.

2631. Find the coordinates of the centre of gravity of a figure bounded by the coordinated axes and an arc of an astroid (in the first quadrant).

2632. Prove that the abscissa and ordinate of the centre of gravity of a sector bounded by two polar radii and a line whose equation is given in polar coordinates $\rho = \rho(\varphi)$ are expressed as follows :

$$x = \frac{2}{3} \frac{\int_{\varphi_1}^{\varphi_2} \rho^3 \cos \varphi \, d\varphi}{\int_{\varphi_1}^{\varphi_2} \rho^2 \, d\varphi}, \quad y = \frac{2}{3} \frac{\int_{\varphi_1}^{\varphi_2} \rho^3 \sin \varphi \, d\varphi}{\int_{\varphi_1}^{\varphi_2} \rho^2 \, d\varphi}.$$

2633. Find the Cartesian coordinates of the centre of gravity of a sector bounded by one half-turn of the spiral of Archimedes $\rho = a\varphi$ (from $\varphi_1 = 0$ to $\varphi_2 = \pi$).

2634. Find the centre of gravity of a circular sector of radius R with a central angle 2α.

2635. Find the Cartesian coordinates of the centre of gravity of a figure enclosed by the cardioid $\rho = a(1 + \cos\varphi)$.

2636. Find the Cartesian coordinates of the centre of gravity of a figure bounded by the right-hand loop of Bernoulli's lemniscate $\rho^2 = a^2 \cos 2\varphi$.

2637. Show that the Cartesian coordinates of the centre of gravity of an arc of the curve, whose equation is given in polar coordinates $\rho = \rho(\varphi)$, are expressed as follows

$$y = \frac{\int_{\varphi_1}^{\varphi_2} \rho \cos\varphi \sqrt{\rho^2 + \rho'^2}\, d\varphi}{\int_{\varphi_1}^{\varphi_2} \sqrt{\rho^2 + \rho'^2}\, d\varphi}, \qquad y = \frac{\int_{\varphi_1}^{\varphi_2} \rho \sin\varphi \sqrt{\rho^2 + \rho'^2}\, d\varphi}{\int_{\varphi_1}^{\varphi_2} \sqrt{\rho^2 + \rho'^2}\, d\varphi}.$$

2638. Find the Cartesian coordinates of the centre of gravity of the arc of the logarithmic spiral $\rho = ae^{\varphi}$ from $\varphi_1 = \frac{\pi}{2}$ to $\varphi_2 = \pi$.

2639. Find the Cartesian coordinates of the centre of gravity of the arc of the cardioid $\rho = a(1 + \cos\varphi)$ from $\varphi_1 = 0$ to $\varphi_2 = \pi$.

2640. At what distance from the geometric centre is the centre of gravity of a hemisphere of radius R located?

2641. Find the centre of gravity of the surface of a hemisphere.

2642. Given a right circular cone, the radius of its base is R, the altitude is H. Find the distances between the base of the cone and centres of gravity of its lateral surface, total surface and volume.

2643. What is the distance between the base and the centre of gravity of a solid bounded by a paraboloid of revolution and a plane perpendicular to its axis? The altitude of the solid is h.

2644. Find the moment of inertia of the segment $AB = l$ about an axis which is situated in the same plane, knowing that the end-point A of the segment is a units and the end-points B is b units distant from the axis.

2645. Find the moment of inertia of a semicircle of radius R with respect to its diameter.

2646. Find the moment of inertia of an arc of the curve $y = e^x \left(0 \le x \le \frac{1}{2}\right)$ with respect to the x-axis.

2647. Compute the moments of inertia of one arc of the cycloid $x = a(t - \sin t)$, $y = a(1 - \cos t)$ with respect to both coordinate axes.

2648. Find the moment of inertia of a rectangle with the sides a and b with respect to the side a.

2649. Find the moment of inertia of a triangle with the base a and altitude h with respect to :

(1) the base;

(2) the straight line parallel to the base and passing through the vertex;

(3) the straight line parallel to the base and passing through the centre of gravity of the triangle.

2650. Find the moment of inertia of a semicircle of radius R with respect to its diameter.

2651. Find the moment of inertia of a circle of radius R with respect to its centre.

2652. Find the moment of inertia of an ellipse with the semiaxes a and b with respect to its axes.

2653. Find the moment of inertia of a cylinder, whose base radius is R and altitude is H, with respect to its axis.

2654. Find the moment of inertia of a cone, the base radius of which is R, the altitutde is H, with respect to its axis.

2655. Find the moment of inertia of a sphere of radius R with respect to its diameter.

2656. An ellipse rotates about one of its axes. Find the moment of inertia of the solid thus generated (ellipsoid of revolution) with respect to the axis of revolution.

2657. Find the moment of inertia of a paraboloid of revolution, the base radius of which is R and the altitude is H, with respect to the axis of revolution.

2658. Compute the moment of inertia with respect to the z-axis of the solid bounded by the hyperboloid of one sheet $\frac{x^2}{2}+\frac{y^2}{2}-z^2=1$ and the planes $z=0$ and $z=1$.

2659. A curvilinear trapezoid bounded by the curves $y=e^x$, $y=0$, $x=0$ and $x=1$ rotates about

(1) the x-axis, (2) the y-axis.

Compute the moment of inertia of the obtained solid with respect to the axis of revolution.

2660. Find the moment of inertia of the lateral surface of a cylinder (the radius of its base is R, altitude H) with respect to its axis.

2661. Find the moment of inertia of the lateral surface of a cone (the radius of the base is R, the altitude H) with respect to its axis.

2662. Find the moment of inertia of the surface of a sphere of radius R with respect to its diameter.

Guldin's theorem

2663. A regular hexagon with the side a rotates about one of the sides. Find the volume of the solid thus generated.

2664. An ellipse with the axes $AA_1 = a_2$ and $BB_1 = 2b$ rotates about a straight line which is parallel to the axis AA_1 and $3b$ distant from it. Find the volume of the solid thus generated.

2665. An astroid rotates about a straight line passing through two neighbouring cusps. Find the volume and the surface of the solid thus generated (see Problem 2630).

2666. A figure formed by the first arcs of the cycloids

$$x = a(t - \sin t),\ y = a(1 - \cos t)$$

and

$$x = a(t - \sin t),\quad y = -a(1 - \cos t)$$

rotates about the y-axis. Find the volume and the surface of the solid thus generated.

2667. A square rotates about a straight line which lies in its plane and passes through one of its vertices. At what position of the straight line relative to the square will the volume of the obtained solid be the greatest possible? The same question for a triangle.

2. Some Physics Problems

2668. The speed of a solid is given by the formula $v = \sqrt{1+t}$ m/s. Find the distance travelled by the solid during the first 10 seconds after the start.

2669. In harmonic oscillatory motion of a point along the x-axis about the origin the velocity $\frac{dx}{dt}$ is specified by the formula

$$\frac{dx}{dt} = \frac{2\pi}{T}\cos\left(\frac{2\pi t}{T} + \varphi_0\right)$$

(t time, T period of oscillation, φ_0 initial phase). Find the position of the point at the time t_2 if it is known that at the time t_1 it was at the point $x = x_1$.

The force f of interaction of two point masses is determined by the formula $f = k\frac{mM}{r^2}$, where m and M are the point masses, r is the distance between them, and k is the proportionality factor equal to $6.67 \times 10^{-11}\frac{\text{m}^3}{\text{kg-s}^2}$ (Newton's law).

Taking this into consideration, solve Problems 2670 to 2678. (Density is assumed to be constant.)

2670. A rod AB whose length is l, mass M, attracts a point C of mass m which lies on its extension at a distance a from the nearest end B of the rod. Find the force of interaction between the rod and the point. What point mass must be placed at A so that it acts on C with the same force as the rod AB does? What work will be performed by the attracting force by the time when the point r_1 distant from the rod approaches it at the distance r_2 moving along the straight line which is the extension of the rod?

2671. With what force is a semiring of radius r and mass M acting on a material point of mass m located at its centre?

2672. With what force is a wire ring of mass M and radius R acting on a material point C of mass m which lies on a straight line passing through the centre of the ring perpendicular to its plane. The distance between the point and the centre of the ring is equal to a. What work will be performed by the attracting force when bringing the point from infinity to the centre of the ring?

2673. Using the result of the preceeding problem, compute the force with which a flat disk whose radius is R and mass M acts on a material point of mass m which lies on its axis at a distance a from the centre.

2674. Using the result of the previous problem compute the force with which an infinite plane carrying a uniformly distributed mass with surface density σ acts on a material point m. The distance between the point and the plane is equal to a.

2675. The radii of the bases of a truncated right circular cone are R and r, altitude is h and density is γ. What is the force with which the cone acts on a material point of mass m placed at its vertex?

2676. What is the force with which the material polygonal line $y = |x| + 1$ attracts a material point of mass m situated at the origin? (Linear density is equal to γ).

2677. Prove that the material polygonal line $y = a|x| + 1$ $(a \geq 0)$ attracts a material point located at the origin with one and the same force independent of a, i.e., without regard to the magnitude of the angle between the segments of the polygonal line.

2678*. Two equal rods (each of length l and mass M) lie on one straight line at a distance l from each other. Compute the force of mutual attraction.

2679. A drop with the initial mass M falls under the action of the force of gravity and evaporates uniformly lossing a mass m each second. What is the work performed by the force of gravity during the time interval from the start to the complete evaporation of the drop? (Air resistance may be neglected.)

2680. What work must be performed to pour a heap of sand in the form of a truncated cone of height H having the radii of the bases R and r $(r < R)$? The specific weight is equal to d (the sand is lifted from the surface of the ground on which the larger base of the cone rests).

2681. The approximate dimensions of the Great pyramid of Cheops are as follows : the altitude is 140 m, the edge of the base (square) is 200 m. Specific weight of the stone it is made of is approximately equal to 2.5 gf/cm^3. Compute the work performed during its construction to overcome the force of gravity.

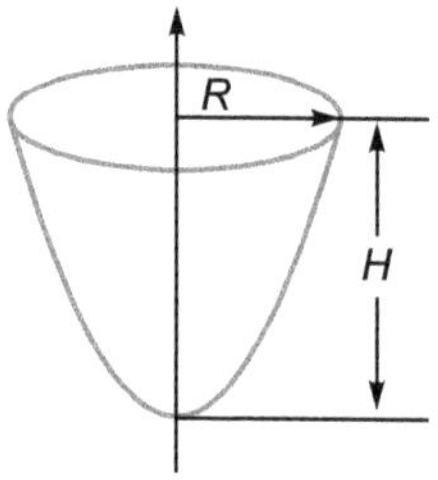

Fig. 50

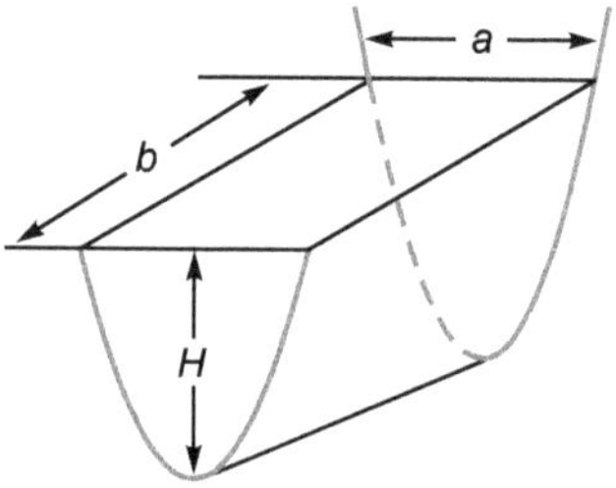

Fig. 51

2682. Compute the work which must be done to pump the water out of a cylinderical reservoir whose altitude $H = 5$ m and the radius R of the base circle is equal to 3 m.

2683. Compute the work which must be perfomed to pump a liquid of specific weight d out of a reservoir having the form of a cone with the vertex downward. The altitude of the cone is H, and the radius of the base is R. How will the result change in case of a cone with the vertex upward?

2684. Compute the work which must be performed to pump the water out of a hemispherical reservoir of radius $R = 0.6$ m.

2685. A boiler has the form of a paraboloid of revolution (see Fig. 50). The radius of the base $R = 2$ m, the height of the boiler $H = 4$ m. The boiler is filled with a liquid whose specific weight $d = 0.8$ gf / cm^3. Compute the work which must be performed to pump the liquid out of the boiler.

2686. Compute the work which must be performed to pump the water out of the tank which has the following dimensions (Fig. 51) : $a = 0.75$ m $b = 1.2$ m, $H = 1$ m. The lateral surface of the tank has the shape of a parabolic cylinder. Kinetic energy of a body revolving about a fixed axis is equal to $\frac{1}{2} I\omega^2$ where ω is the angular velocity, and I the moment of inertia with respect to the axis of revolution.

Knowing this, solve Problems 2687 to 2692.

2687. The rod AB (Fig. 52) revolves in a horizontal plane about the axis OO' with an angular velocity $\omega = 10\pi\ \text{s}^{-1}$. The cross-sectional area of the rod $S = 4\ \text{cm}^2$, its length $l = 20$ cm, the density $\gamma = 7.8\ \text{g/cm}^3$. Find the kinetic energy of the rod.

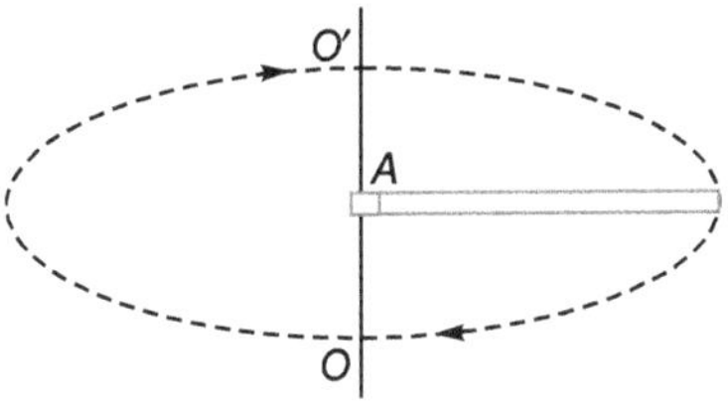

Fig. 52

2688. A rectangular plate whose sides are $a = 50$ cm and $b = 40$ cm, rotates about the side a with a constant angular velocity ω equal to $3\pi\ \text{s}^{-1}$. Find the kinetic energy of the plate. The thickness of the plate $d = 0.3$ cm, density is 8 g/cm^3.

2689. A triangular plate, whose base is $a = 40$ cm and height $h = 30$ cm, rotates about its base with a constant angular velocity $\omega = 5\pi\ \text{s}^{-1}$. Find the kinetic energy of the plate if its thickness $d = 0.2$ cm and the density $\gamma = 2.2\ \text{g/cm}^3$.

2690. A plate which has the shape of a parabolic segment (Fig. 53) rotates about the axis of the parabola with a constant angular velocity $\omega = 4\pi\ \text{s}^{-1}$. The base of the segment $a = 20$ cm, altitude $h = 30$ cm, thickness of the plate $d = 0.3$ cm, density $\gamma = 7.8\ \text{g/cm}^3$. Find the kinetic energy of the plate.

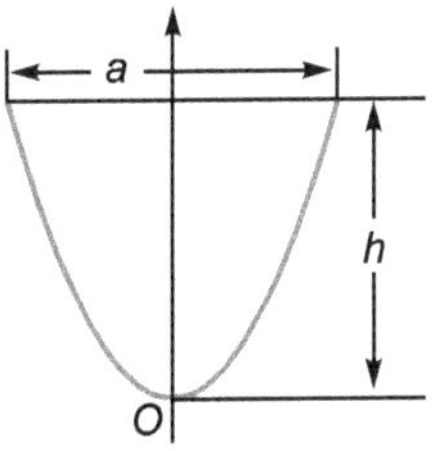

Fig. 53

2691. A circular cylinder, the radius of the base of which is R and altitude H, rotates about its axis with a consant angular velocity ω. The density is equal to γ. Find the kinetic energy of the cylinder.

2692. A thin wire of mass M is bent to form a semicircle of radius R and rotates about the axis passing through the end-points of the semicircle at a rate of n revolutions per minute. Compute its kinetic energy.

Compute the kinetic energy of revolution about the tangent at the mid-point of the semicircle.

2693. A plate having the shape of a triangle is submerged vertically into water so that its base lies on the surface of the water. The base of the plate is a, the height h.

(a) Compute the pressure force of the water on each side of the plate.

(b) How many times will the pressure increase if the plate is turned over so that the vertex is found on the water surface and the base is parallel to the latter?

2694. A square plate is submerged vertically into water so that one of the vertices of the square lies on the water surface, and one of the diagonals is parallel to it. The side of the square is equal to a. What is the force with which the water presses on each side of the plate?

2695. Compute the force with which the water presses on the dam having the shape of an equilateral trapezoid whose upper base $a = 6.4$ m, lower base $b = 4.2$ m and altitude $H = 3$ m.

2696. A plate having the shape of an ellipse is half submerged vertically into the liquid so that one of the axes (of length $2b$) lies on the surface. What is the pressure force of the liquid on each of the sides of the plate if the length of the submerged semiaxis is equal to a and specific weight of the liquid to d?

2697. A rectangular plate with the sides a and b $(a > b)$ is submerged into the liquid at an angle α to its surface. The longer side of the plate is parallel to the surface and lies at a depth h. Compute the liquid pressure on each side of the plate if specific weight of the liquid is d.

2698. A rectangular vessel is filled with water and oil in equal proportion (by volume), the oil being twice lighter than water. Show that the pressure on each wall of the vessel will be reduced by one fifth if the vessel is filled only with oil. (Take into consideration the fact that the oil is found at the top of the vessel).

In solving Problems 2699 and 2700 proceed from Archimedes' principle : a body immersed in a fluid is acted on by a buoyancy force, made evident by a loss of weight, equal to the weight of displaced fluid.

2699. A cylindrical wooden float whose base area $S = 4000\ \text{cm}^2$ and the altitude $H = 50$ cm drifts on the water surface. Specific weight of wood $d = 0.8\ \text{gf}/\text{cm}^3$. (a) What work must be performed to take the float out of the water? (b) Compute the work to be performed to submerge completely the float into the water.

2700. A sphere of radius R whose specific weight is unity is submerged into the water so that it touches the surface. What work must be performed to take the sphere out of the water?

Problems 2701 to 2706 are related with the phenomenon of liquid efflux from an orifice. The efflux rate is determined according to the Torricelli law : $v = \sqrt{2gh}$, where h is the height of the liquid column above the orifice, g acceleration due to gravity[1].

2701. The bottom of a cylindrical container filled with water (the area of its base 100 cm^2, altitutde 30 cm) has an opening.

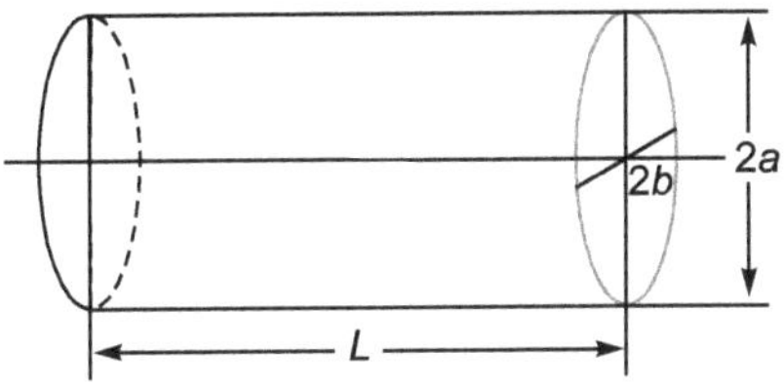

Fig. 54

Compute the area of the opening if it is known that the container can be emptied through this opening in two minutes.

2702. A conical funnel whose height $H = 20$ cm is filled with water. The radius of the upper opening $R = 12$ cm. The lower opening through which the water begins to flow out of the funnel has the radius $r = 0.3$ cm. (a) In what time is the water level in the funnel lowered by 5 cm? (b) When will the funnel be emptied?

2703. A hole (its area $S = 0.2$ cm^2) has appeared in the bottom of a boiler having the shape of a hemisphere of radius $R = 43$ cm. In what time will the water contained in the boiler flow out from the hole?

2704. A boiler has the shape of an elliptical cylinder with a horizontal axis. The semiaxes of an elliptic section (perpendicular to the axis of the cylinder) are equal to b (the horizontal one) and a (the vertical one), the generatrix of the cylinder is L (Fig. 54). The boiler is half filled with water . In what time will the water run out of the boiler through an opening (area S) in its bottom?

---

[1]This form of the Torricelli law is applicable only to an ideal liquid. The answers to the problems are given for such an ideal liquid. (In practice the following formula is used: $v = \mu\sqrt{2gh}$, where μ is the coefficeint depending on viscosity of liquid and the character of the efflux orifice. For water in the simplest case $\mu = 0.6$).

2705. The vertical wall of a prismatic vessel filled with water is provided with a vertical rectangular slit whose height is h and width b. The upper edge of the slit parallel to the water surface is situated at a distance H from the surface. What quantity of water will run out of the vessel during 1 second if the water level is supposed to be kept at one and the same height all the time? Consider the case $H = 0$ (the problem of spillway).

2706. A vessel, filled with water to the brim, has the shape of a parallelopiped whose base area is 100 cm^2. Its lateral wall is provided with narrow slit 20 cm high and 0.1 cm wide (Fig. 55). During what time will the level of the water in the vessel be lowered by

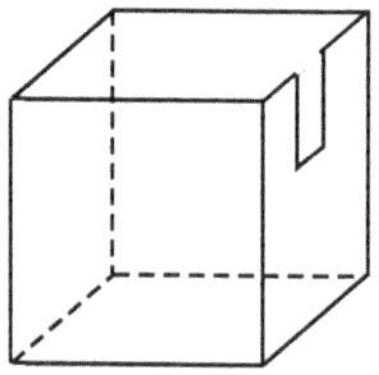

Fig. 55

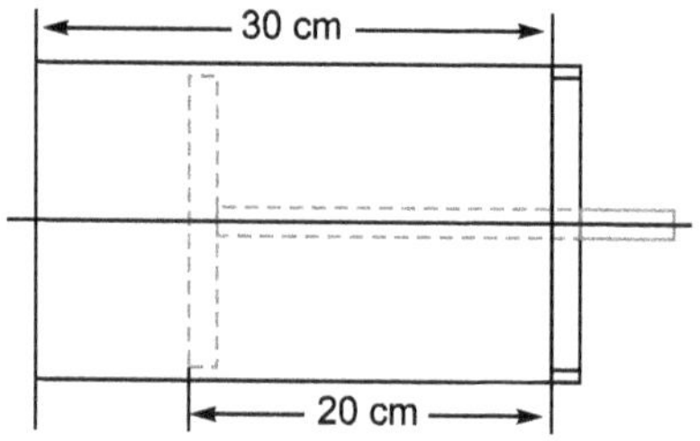

Fig. 56

(a) 5 cm? (b) 10 cm? (c) 19 cm?

(d) 20 cm? (Use the result of the previous problem.)

The ideal gas equation of state has the form $pv = RT$, where p is pressure, v volume, T absolute temperature and R constant for a given mass of gas.

Solve Problems 2707 to 2709 considering the gases to be ideal.

2707. A cylinder, whose base area is equal to 10 cm^2 and altitude to 30 cm, contains atmospheric air. What work must be performed to push in the piston by 20 cm, i.e., to push it in so that it stops at a distance of 10 cm from the bottom of the cylinder (Fig. 56)? Atmospheric pressure is equal to 1.033 kgf/cm^2. The process is assumed to be isothermal, i.e., the temperature reamains unchanged. (To obtain the work in kgf-m the pressure should be measured in kgf/m^2 and the volume in m^3.)

2708. A cylindrical vessel, whose cross-sectional area is equal to 100 cm^2, contains air at atmospheric pressure. The vessel is provided with a piston. Its initial distance from the bottom of the vessel equals 0.1 m.

Then, the cylinder is placed in a vacuum and therefore, the air contained in it begins to expand thus pushing out the piston.

(1) Compute the work performed by the air in the cylinder when it raises the piston to a height of (a) 0.2 m, (b) 0.5 m, (c) 1 m.

(2) Can this work increase infinitely as the gas expands infinitely? (As in the previous problem, the process goes on isothermically.)

2709. A cylindrical vessel, whose volume is $v_0 = 0.1\ \text{m}^3$, contains air at atmospheric pressure ($1.033\ \text{kgf/cm}^2$) which is rapidly compressed by adiabatically pushing in the piston. Find the work to be performed to compress the air in the vessel to the volume $v = 0.03\ \text{m}^3$. In adiabatic process the air pressure and volume are related by the Poisson equation: $pv^\gamma = p_0 v_0^\gamma$. For diatomic gases (and also for air) $\gamma \approx 1.40$.

According to Newton's law of cooling, the rate at which the body looses heat is proportional to the temperature difference between the body and the surrounding air. Proceeding from this law,

solve Problems 2710 and 2711.

2710. A body whose temperature is 25°C is immeresed in a thermostat kept at 0°C. In what time will the temperature of the body reach 10°C if during 20 minutes it is cooled to the temperature 20°C?

2711. A body whose temperature was 30°C after being held in a thermostat (kept at 0°C) has been cooled to 22.5°C. What will the temperature of the body be in three hours after the beginning of the experiment?

According to the Coulomb law, the force of interaction between two point charges in free space is a pure attraction or repulsion, and is given in rationalized mksa units by $F = \dfrac{q_1 q_2}{4\pi\varepsilon_0 \varepsilon r^2}$ newtons where q_1 and q_2 are the magnitudes of the charges in coulombs, r is their separation in metres, electric constant $\varepsilon_0 = 8.85 \times 10^{-12}$ farad per metre $(4\pi\varepsilon_0 = 1.11 \times 10^{-10})$ and ε is the relative electric permittivity (for air $\varepsilon \approx 1$). Proceeding from this law, solve problems 2712 to 2714.

2712. An endless straight line is uniformly positively charged (linear electric denisity σ). What is the force with which this straight line acts on the unit charge located at point A a distant from it. The relative electric permittivity is equal to unity.

2713. Two electric charges $q_1 = 6.67 \times 10^{-9}$ C and $q_2 = 10 \times 10^{-9}$ C are situated 10 cm apart. The separation medium is air. First both charges are fixed, then the charge q_2 is set free and under the action of the repulsion force begins to move away from the charge q_1. What work will the repulsion force perform when the charge (a) moves 30 cm away? (b) moves away to infinity?

2714. Two electric charges $q_1 = 33.3 \times 10^{-9}$C and $q_2 = 40 \times 10^{-9}$C are 20 cm apart. What will the distance between the charges be if the second charge is brought to the first one, the work thus performed being equal to 18×10^{-5} J. (The charges are separated by air.)

2715. The voltage across the terminals of an electric circuit is $V = 120$ V. Resistance is introduced uniformly into the circuit at a rate of 0.1 ohm per second. Besides, the circuit is provided with a constant resistance $r = 10$ ohms. What charge will flow through the circuit during two minutes?

2716. The voltage across the terminals of an electric circuit originally equal to 120 V reduces uniformly decreasing at a rate of 0.01 V per second. At the same time resistance is introduced into the circuit also at a consant rate, viz. 0.1 ohm per second. Besides, the circuit is provided with a constant resistance equal to 12 ohms. What charge will flow through the circuit during 3 min?

2717. At ordinary temperatures resistance of metal conductors changes with temperature according to the law $R = R_0\,(1 + 0.004\,\theta)$, where R_0 is the resistance at 0°C and θ is the temperature in degrees centigrade. (This law is valid for the majority of pure metals.) A conductor whose resistance is equal to 10 ohms at 0°C is uniformly heated from $\theta_1 = 20$°C to $\theta_2 = 200$°C during ten minutes. At this time current of voltage 120 V flows through it. What charge will flow through the conductor during this time?

2718. The law of variation of the voltage of a sinusoidal current having frequency ω is given by the following formula $E = E_0 \times \sin\,(\omega t + \varphi)$, where E_0 is the maximum voltage, φ the phase and t the time. Find the root-mean-square voltage for one period. Show that, with a constant resistance during one period, alternating current generates the same quantity of heat as direct current whose voltage is equal to $\sqrt{(E^2)_{\text{mean}}}$. (Therefore, the expression $\sqrt{(E^2)_{\text{mean}}}$ is called the effective voltage of the alternating current.)

2719. Sinusoidal voltage is given by the formula

$$E = E_0 \sin\left(\frac{2\pi}{T}t\right),$$

and sinusoidal current by the formula

$$I = I_0 \sin\left(\frac{2\pi t}{T} - \varphi_0\right),$$

where E_0 and I_0 are constants (the greatest values of voltage and current), T is the period and φ_0 is the so-called phase difference. Compute the work performed by the current during the time from $t_1 = 0$ to $t_2 = T$, and show that the work will attain the greatest value when the phase difference φ_0 is equal to zero.

2720. Find the time during which 1 kg of water is heated by an electric heater from 20°C to 100°C if the voltage is 120 V, the resistance of the coil 14.4 ohms, the ambient temperature 20°C and if it is known that 1 kg of water cools from 40°C to 30°C during 10 min. (According to the Joule-Lenz law $Q = I^2Rt$, where Q is the quantity of heat in joules, I the current in amperes, R the resistance in ohms and t the time in seconds; the specific heat of water is equal to 4190 $\frac{\text{J}}{\text{kg}\cdot\text{deg}}$. Also, make use of the Newton law of cooling; see Problem 2710.)

2721. The air in a vessel of 3 litres capacity contains 20 per cent of oxygen. The vessel is fitted with two tubes : one for pure oxygen inlet, the other for the air outlet, the quantity of the oxygen entering the vessel being equal to that of the air leaving it. What amount of oxygen is contained in the vessel after 10 litres of the gas has flown through it?

2722. Air containing a per cent (= 8%) of CO_2 passes through a cylindrical vessel with an adsorbent. A thin layer of the filtering mass adsorbs a quantity of the gas proportional to its concentration and thickness of the layer. (a) If the air, on passing the layer H cm (= 10 cm) thick, contains b per cent (= 2%) of CO_2, then what thickness (H_1) must the adsorbing layer have so that the air leaving the adsorbent contains only c per cent (=1%) of CO_2? (b) How much carbonic acid gas (in per cent) remains in the air after its passage through the absorbent if the adsorbing layer is 30 cm thick?

2723. If as a result of passing through a 3 m thick layer of water the initial quantity of light is half absorbed, then what portion of this quantity will reach the depth of 30 m? The quantity of light absorbed during the passage through a thin layer of water is proportional to the thickness of the layer and the quantity of light received by its surface.

2724. If the initial mass of ferment of 1 g becomes equal to 1.2 g after an hour of fermentation, then what will it be equal to after five hours of fermentation, assuming the rate of the ferment growth to be proportional to its available amount?

2725. If after two hours of fermentation the available amount of the ferment turns out to be equal to 2 g, and after three hours of fermentation to 3 g, then what was its initial amount? (See the previous problem.)

2726. Two kilograms of salt is to be dissolved in thirty litres of water. In five minutes half of this quantity is dissolved. In what time will 99 per cent of the initial quantity of salt be dissolved? (The rate of dissolution is proportional to the quantity of the undissolved salt and the difference between the concentration of a saturated solution, which is 1 kg per 3 litres and that of the solution at a given time.)

9

Series

1. Numerical Series

Convergence of a numerical series

In Problems 2727 to 2736 for each of the series (1) find the sum (S_n) of first n terms of the series, (2) prove convergence of the series making direct use of the definition of convergence, (3) find the sum (S) of the series.

2727. $\frac{1}{1\times 2}+\frac{1}{2\times 3}+\ldots+\frac{1}{n(n+1)}+\ldots.$

2728. $\frac{1}{1\times 3}+\frac{1}{3\times 5}+\ldots+\frac{1}{(2n-1)(2n+1)}+\ldots.$

2729. $\frac{1}{1\times 4}+\frac{1}{4\times 7}+\ldots+\frac{1}{(3n-2)(3n+1)}+\ldots.$

2730. $\frac{1}{1\times 4}+\frac{1}{2\times 5}+\ldots+\frac{1}{n(n+3)}+\ldots.$

2731. $\frac{1}{1\times 7}+\frac{1}{3\times 9}+\ldots+\frac{1}{(2n-1)(2n+5)}+\ldots.$

2732. $\frac{1}{1\times 2\times 3}+\frac{1}{2\times 3\times 4}+\ldots+\frac{1}{n(n+1)(n+2)}+\ldots.$

2733. $\frac{5}{6}+\frac{13}{36}+\ldots+\frac{3^n+2^n}{6^n}+\ldots.$

2734. $\frac{3}{4}+\frac{5}{36}+\ldots+\frac{2n+1}{n^2(n+1)^2}+\ldots.$

2735. $\frac{1}{9}+\frac{2}{225}+\ldots+\frac{1}{(2n-1)^2(2n+1)^2}+\ldots.$

2736. $\arctan\frac{1}{2}+\arctan\frac{1}{8}+\ldots+\arctan\frac{1}{2\times n^2}+\ldots.$

Positive series

In Problems 2737 to 2753 find out whether the given series is convergent or divergent with the aid of comparison tests.

2737. $\frac{1}{1\times 2}+\frac{1}{3\times 2^3}+\ldots+\frac{1}{(2n-1)\times 2^{2n-1}}+\ldots.$

2738. $\sin\frac{\pi}{2} + \sin\frac{\pi}{4} + \ldots + \sin\frac{\pi}{2^n} + \ldots.$

2739. $1 + \frac{1+2}{1+2^2} + \ldots + \frac{1+n}{1+n^2} + \ldots.$

2740. $\frac{1}{2\times 5} + \frac{1}{3\times 6} + \ldots + \frac{1}{(n+1)(n+4)} + \ldots.$

2741. $\frac{2}{3} + \frac{3}{8} + \ldots + \frac{n+1}{(n+2)n} + \ldots.$

2742. $\tan\frac{\pi}{4} + \tan\frac{\pi}{8} + \ldots + \tan\frac{\pi}{4n} + \ldots.$

2743. $\frac{1}{2} + \frac{1}{5} + \ldots + \frac{1}{n^2+1} + \ldots.$

2744. $\frac{1}{2} + \frac{1}{5} + \ldots + \frac{1}{3n-1} + \ldots.$

2745. $\frac{1}{\ln 2} + \frac{1}{\ln 3} + \ldots + \frac{1}{\ln(n+1)} + \ldots.$

2746. $\sum_{n=1}^{\infty} \frac{1}{n^2 - 4n + 5}.$

2747. $\sum_{n=1}^{\infty} \left(\frac{1+n^2}{1+n^3}\right)^2.$

2748. $\sum_{n=1}^{\infty} \frac{1}{\sqrt{n^2+2n}}.$

2749. $\sum_{n=1}^{\infty} \frac{\ln n}{\sqrt[4]{n^5}}.$

2750. $\sum_{n=1}^{\infty} (\sqrt{n} - \sqrt{n-1}).$

2751. $\sum_{n=1}^{\infty} \sqrt{\frac{1}{n^4+1}}.$

2752. $\sum_{n=1}^{\infty} \frac{1}{n}(\sqrt{n+1} - \sqrt{n-1}).$

2753. $\sum_{n=1}^{\infty} \frac{1}{n}(\sqrt{n^2+n+1} - \sqrt{n^2-n+1}).$

In Problems 2754 to 2762 prove convergence of the given series with the aid of d'Alembert's test.

2754. $\frac{1}{3!} + \frac{1}{5!} + \ldots + \frac{1}{(2n+1)!} + \ldots.$

2755. $\frac{1}{2} + \frac{2}{2^2} + \ldots + \frac{n}{2^n} + \ldots.$

2756. $\tan\frac{\pi}{4} + 2\tan\frac{\pi}{8} + \ldots + n\tan\frac{\pi}{2^{n+1}} + \ldots.$

2757. $\frac{2}{1} + \frac{2\times 5}{1\times 5} + \ldots + \frac{2\times 5\times\ldots\times(3n-1)}{1\times 5\times\ldots\times(4n-3)} + \ldots.$

2758. $\frac{1}{3} + \frac{4}{9} + \ldots + \frac{n^2}{3^n} + \ldots.$

2759. $\frac{1}{3} + \frac{1 \times 3}{3 \times 6} + \ldots + \frac{1 \times 3 \times \ldots \times (2n-1)}{3^n \times n!} + \ldots .$

2760. $\sin \frac{\pi}{2} + 4 \sin \frac{\pi}{4} + \ldots + n^2 \sin \frac{\pi}{2^n} + \ldots .$

2761. $\frac{1}{2!} + \frac{2}{3!} + \ldots + \frac{n}{(n+1)!} + \ldots .$

2762. $\frac{2}{2} + \frac{2 \times 3}{2 \times 4} + \ldots + \frac{(n+1)!}{2^n \times n!} + \ldots .$

In Problems 2763 to 2766 prove convergence of the given series with the aid of Cauchy's root test.

2763. $\frac{1}{\ln 2} + \frac{1}{\ln^2 3} + \ldots + \frac{1}{\ln^2 (n+1)} + \ldots .$

2764. $\frac{1}{3} + \left(\frac{2}{5}\right)^2 + \ldots + \left(\frac{n}{2n+1}\right)^n + \ldots .$

2765. $\arcsin 1 + \arcsin^2 \frac{1}{2} + \ldots + \arcsin \frac{1}{n} + \ldots .$

2766. $\frac{2}{3} + \frac{\left(\frac{3}{2}\right)^4}{9} + \ldots + \frac{\left(\frac{n+1}{n}\right)^{n^2}}{3^n} + \ldots .$

In Problems 2767 to 2770 find out whether the given series is convergent or divergent with the aid of Cauchy's integral test.

2767. $\frac{1}{2 \ln^2 2} + \frac{1}{3 \ln^2 3} + \ldots + \frac{1}{(n+1) \ln^2 (n+1)} + \ldots .$

2768. $\frac{1}{2 \ln 2} + \frac{1}{3 \ln 3} + \ldots + \frac{1}{n \ln n} + \ldots .$

2769. $\left(\frac{1+1}{1+1^2}\right)^2 + \left(\frac{1+2}{1+2^2}\right)^2 + \ldots + \left(\frac{1+n}{1+n^2}\right)^2 + \ldots .$

2770. $\sum_{n=2}^{\infty} \frac{1}{\sqrt{n}} \ln \frac{n+1}{n-1}.$

In Problems 2771 to 2784 find out which of the given series are convergent and which are divergent.

2771. $\frac{1}{2\sqrt{2}} + \frac{1}{3\sqrt{3}} + \frac{1}{(n+1)\sqrt{n+1}} + \ldots .$

2772. $1 + \frac{2}{3} + \ldots + \frac{n}{2n-1} + \ldots .$

2773. $\sqrt{2} + \sqrt{\frac{3}{2}} + \ldots + \sqrt{\frac{n+1}{n}} + \ldots .$

2774. $1 + \frac{4}{1 \times 2} + \ldots + \frac{n^2}{n!} + \ldots .$

2775. $2+\frac{5}{8}+\ldots+\frac{n^2+1}{n^3}+\ldots.$

2776. $\frac{1}{1001}+\frac{2}{2001}+\ldots+\frac{n}{1000n+1}+\ldots.$

2777. $\frac{1}{1+1^2}+\frac{2}{1+2^2}+\ldots+\frac{n}{1+n^2}+\ldots.$

2778. $\frac{1}{3}+\frac{3}{3^2}+\ldots+\frac{2n-1}{3^n}+\ldots.$

2779. $\arctan 1+\arctan^2\frac{1}{2}+\ldots+\arctan^n\frac{1}{n}+\ldots.$

2780. $2+\frac{4}{16}+\ldots+\frac{2n}{n^4}+\ldots.$

2781. $\frac{1}{1\times 3}+\frac{1}{6\times 7}+\ldots+\frac{1}{(5n-4)(4n-1)}+\ldots.$

2782. $\frac{3}{2}+\frac{9}{8}+\ldots+\frac{3^n}{n\times 2^n}+\ldots.$

2783. $1+\frac{1\times 2}{2^2}+\ldots+\frac{n!}{n^n}+\ldots.$

2784*. $\sin\frac{\pi}{2}+\sin\frac{\pi}{4}+\ldots+\sin\frac{\pi}{2n}+\ldots.$

In Problems 2785 to 2789 prove each of the relationships with the aid of a series whose general term is the given function.

2785. $\lim_{n\to\infty}\frac{a^n}{n!}=0.$

2786. $\lim_{n\to\infty}\frac{(2n)!}{a^{n!}}=0\ (a>1).$

2787. $\lim_{n\to\infty}\frac{n^n}{(2n)!}=0.$

2788. $\lim_{n\to\infty}\frac{n^n}{(n!)^2}=0.$

2789. $\lim_{n\to\infty}\frac{(n!)^n}{n^{n^2}}=0.$

Series with arbitrary terms. Absolute convergence

In Problems 2790 to 2799 find out which of the given series are absolutely convergent, which are conditionally convergent, and which are divergent.

2790. $1-\frac{1}{3}+\ldots+(-1)^{n+1}\frac{1}{2n-1}+\ldots.$

2791. $1-\frac{1}{3^3}+\ldots+(-1)^{n+1}\frac{1}{(2n-1)^3}+\ldots.$

2792. $\frac{1}{\ln 2}-\frac{1}{\ln 3}+\ldots+(-1)^{n+1}\frac{1}{\ln(n+1)}+\ldots.$

2793. $\frac{\sin\alpha}{1}+\frac{\sin 2\alpha}{4}+\ldots+\frac{\sin n\alpha}{n^2}+\ldots.$

2794. $\frac{1}{2}-\frac{1}{2}\times\frac{1}{2^2}+\ldots+(-1)^{n+1}\frac{1}{n}\times\frac{1}{2^n}+\ldots.$

2795. $2-\frac{3}{2}+\ldots+(-1)^{n+1}\frac{n+1}{n}+\ldots.$

2796. $-1+\frac{1}{\sqrt{2}}-\ \ldots+(-1)^n\frac{1}{\sqrt{n}}+\ldots.$

2797. $\frac{1}{2}-\frac{8}{4}+\ldots+(-1)^{n+1}\frac{n^3}{2^n}+\ldots.$

2798. $\sum_{n=1}^{\infty}\frac{(-1)^n}{n-\ln n}.$

2799. $\sum_{n=1}^{\infty}(-1)^{n+1}\frac{2n^2}{n!}.$

2800. Show that if $\sum_{n=1}^{\infty} a_n^2$ and $\sum_{n=1}^{\infty} b_n^2$ are convergent series, then $\sum_{n=1}^{\infty} a_n b_n$ is an absolutely convergent series.

2801. Show that if the series $\sum_{n=1}^{\infty} a_n$ is absolutely convergent, then the series $\sum_{n=1}^{\infty}\frac{n+1}{n}a_n$ is also absolutely convergent.

2. Functional Series

Convergence of functional series

In Problems 2802 to 2816 determine the domains of convergence of the given series.

2802. $1+x+\ldots+x^n+\ldots.$

2803. $\ln x+\ln^2 x+\ldots+\ln^n x+\ldots.$

2804. $x+x^4+\ldots+x^{n^2}+\ldots.$

2805. $x+\frac{x^2}{2^2}+\ldots+\frac{x^n}{n^2}+\ldots.$

2806. $x+\frac{x^2}{\sqrt{2}}+\ldots+\frac{x^n}{\sqrt{n}}+\ldots.$

2807. $\frac{1}{1+x}+\frac{1}{1+x^2}+\ldots+\frac{1}{1+x^n}+\ldots.$

2808. $2x+6x^2+\ldots+n(n+1)x^n+\ldots.$

2809. $\frac{x}{2}+\frac{x^2}{2+\sqrt{2}}+\ldots+\frac{x^n}{n+\sqrt{n}}+\ldots.$

2810. $\frac{x}{1+x^2}+\frac{x^2}{1+x^4}+\ldots+\frac{x^n}{1+x^{2n}}+\ldots.$

2811. $\sin\frac{x}{2}+\sin\frac{x}{4}+\ldots+\sin\frac{x}{2^{2n}}+\ldots.$

2812. $x\tan\frac{x}{2}+x^2\tan\frac{x}{4}+\ldots+x^n\tan\frac{x}{2^n}+\ldots.$

2813. $\sin x+\frac{\sin 2x}{2^2}+\ldots+\frac{\sin nx}{n^2}+\ldots.$

2814. $\frac{\cos x}{e^x}+\frac{\cos 2x}{e^{2x}}+\ldots+\frac{\cos nx}{e^{nx}}+\ldots.$

2815. $e^{-x}+e^{-4x}+\ldots+e^{-n^2x}+\ldots.$

2816. $\frac{x}{e^x}+\frac{2x}{e^{2x}}+\ldots+\frac{nx}{e^{nx}}+\ldots.$

Uniform (regular) convergence

In Problems 2817 to 2820 prove that the given series are uniformly (regularly) convergent throughout the x-axis.

2817. $1+\frac{\sin x}{1!}+\ldots+\frac{\sin nx}{n!}+\ldots.$ **2818.** $\sum_{n=1}^{\infty}\frac{1}{n^2[1+(nx)^2]}.$

2819. $\sum_{n=1}^{\infty}\frac{\sin nx}{2^n}.$ **2820.** $\sum_{n=1}^{\infty}\frac{e^{-n^2x^2}}{n^2}.$

2821. Show that the series

$$\frac{1}{1+[\varphi(x)]^2}+\frac{1}{4+[\varphi(x)]^2}+\ldots+\frac{1}{n^2+[\varphi(x)]^2}+\ldots$$

is uniformly (regularly) convergent on any interval in which the function $\varphi(x)$ is defined.

2822. Show that the series

$$\frac{1}{\sqrt{1+x}}+\frac{1}{2\sqrt{1+2x}}+\ldots+\frac{1}{2^{n-1}\sqrt{1+nx}}+\ldots$$

is uniformly (regularly) convergent throughout the positive x-axis. How many terms must be taken so that for any non-negative x the sum of the series can be computed to within 0.001?

2823*. Show that the series

$$\frac{\ln(1+x)}{x}+\frac{\ln(1+2x)}{2x^2}+\ldots+\frac{\ln(1+nx)}{nx^n}+\ldots$$

is uniformly convergent in the interval $1+\omega\le x<\infty$, where ω is any positive number. Make sure that for any x from the interval

$(2 \le x \le 100)$ it is sufficient to take eight terms to obtain the sum of the series to within 0.01.

2824. Show that the series

$\sum_{n=1}^{\infty} x^n (1-x)$ converges nonuniformly in the interval $[0, 1]$.

2825. A function $f(x)$ is defined by the equality

$$f(x) = \sum_{n=1}^{\infty} \frac{\cos nx}{10^n}.$$

Show that the function $f(x)$ is defined and continuous for any x. Find $f(0)$, $f\left(\frac{\pi}{2}\right)$ and $f\left(\frac{\pi}{3}\right)$. Make sure that it is sufficient to take three terms of the series to compute approximate values of the function $f(x)$ for any x to within 0.001. Find $f(1)$ and $f(-0.2)$ with the indicated accuracy.

2826. The function $f(x)$ is defined by the equality

$$f(x) = \frac{1}{1+x^2} + \sum_{n=1}^{\infty} \frac{1}{1+(x+n\omega)^2} + \sum_{n=1}^{\infty} \frac{1}{1+(x-n\omega)^2} \quad (\omega > 0).$$

Show that the function $f(x)$ is defined and continuous for any x. Make sure that $f(x)$ is a periodic function with period ω.

Integrating and differentiating series

2827. Show that the series $x^2 + x^6 + \ldots + x^{4n-2} + \ldots$ converges uniformly in the interval $-1 + \omega \le x \le 1 - \omega$, where ω is any positive number less than 1. Integrating the given series, find in the interval $(-1, 1)$ the sum of the series

$$\frac{x^3}{3} + \frac{x^7}{7} + \ldots + \frac{x^{4n-1}}{4n-1} + \ldots.$$

2828. Find the sum of the series

$$x + \frac{x^5}{5} + \ldots + \frac{x^{4n-3}}{4n-3} + \ldots.$$

2829. Find the sum of the series

$$\frac{x^2}{1\times 2} - \frac{x^3}{2\times 3} + \ldots + (-1)^{n+1} \frac{x^{n+1}}{n(n+1)} + \ldots.$$

2830. The function $f(x)$ is defined by the equality

$$f(x) = e^{-x} + 2e^{-2x} + \ldots + ne^{-nx} + \ldots.$$

Show that the function $f(x)$ is continuous throughout the entire positive axis. Evaluate $\int_{\ln 2}^{\ln 3} f(x)\,dx$.

2831. The function $f(x)$ is defined by the equality

$$f(x) = 1 + 2\times 3x + \ldots + n3^{n-1}x^{n-1} + \ldots.$$

Show that the function $f(x)$ is continuous in the interval $\left(-\frac{1}{3}, \frac{1}{3}\right)$.

Evaluate $\int_0^{0.125} f(x)\,dx$.

2832*. The function $f(x)$ is defined by the equality

$$f(x) = \frac{1}{2}\tan\frac{x}{2} + \frac{1}{4}\tan\frac{x}{4} + \ldots + \frac{1}{2^n}\tan\frac{x}{2^n} + \ldots.$$

Make sure that the function $f(x)$ is continuous in the given interval of integration and evaluate $\int_{\pi/6}^{\pi/2} f(x)\,dx$.

2833*. The function $f(x)$ is defined by the series $f(x) = \sum_{n=1}^{\infty} \frac{1}{n^4 + x^2}$. Show that the function $f(x)$ is continuous throughout the number scale. Evaluate $\int_0^{\infty} f(x)\,dx$.

2834. Proceeding from the relationship $\int_0^1 x^n\,dx = \frac{1}{n+1}$, find the sum of the series

(1) $1 - \frac{1}{4} + \ldots + \frac{(-1)^{n+1}}{3n-2} + \ldots$,

(2) $1 - \frac{1}{5} + \ldots + \frac{(-1)^{n+1}}{4n-3} + \ldots$.

2835. Proceeding from the relationship $\int_2^{\infty} \frac{dx}{x^{n+1}} = \frac{1}{n2^n}$, find the sum of the series $\frac{1}{1\times 2} + \frac{1}{2\times 2^2} + \ldots + \frac{1}{n2^n} + \ldots$.

2836. Proceeding from the relationship

$$\int_0^{\pi/2} \cos^{2n} x\,dx = \frac{\pi}{2}\cdot\frac{(2n-1)(2n-3)\ldots 3\times 1}{2n(2n-2)\ldots 4\times 2},$$

find the sum of the series

$$\frac{1}{2} - \frac{1\times 3}{2\times 4} + \ldots + (-1)^{n+1}\frac{1\times 3\ldots(2n-1)}{2\times 4\ldots 2n} + \ldots.$$

2837. Prove that the series

$$\frac{\sin 2\pi x}{2} + \frac{\sin 4\pi x}{4} + \ldots + \frac{\sin 2^n \pi x}{2^n} + \ldots.$$

converges uniformly throughout the entire number scale. Show that this series cannot be differentiated termwise in any interval.

2838. Proceeding from the equality $1 + x + x^2 + \ldots = \frac{1}{1-x}$ $(|x| < 1)$, sum up the series $1 + 2x + 3x^2 + \ldots + nx^{n-1} + \ldots$ and $1 + 3x + \ldots + \frac{n(n+1)}{2} x^{n-1} + \ldots$ and show that the series $1 + 2x + \ldots + nx^{n-1} + \ldots$ converges uniformly in the interval $[-\rho, \rho]$ where $|\rho| < 1$.

2839. Show the validity of the equality

$$\frac{1}{1+x} + \frac{2x}{1+x^2} + \ldots + \frac{mx^{m-1}}{1+x^m} + \ldots = \frac{1}{1-x},$$

where $m = 2^{n-1}$ and $-1 < x < 1$.

2840. Make sure that the function $y = f(x)$ defined by the series

$$x + x^2 + \frac{x^3}{2!} + \ldots + \frac{x^n}{(n-1)!} + \ldots$$

satisfies the relationship $xy' = y(x + 1)$.

3. Power Series

Expanding functions into power series

2841. Expand the function $y = \ln x$ into Taylor's series in the neighbourhood of the point $x = 1$ (at $x_0 = 1$).

2842. Expand the function $y = \sqrt{x^3}$ into Taylor's series in the neighbourhood of the point $x = 1$.

2843. Expand the function $y = \frac{1}{x}$ into Taylor's series in the neighbourhood of the point $x = 3$.

2844. Expand the function $y = \sin \frac{\pi x}{4}$ into Taylor's series in the neighbourhood of the point $x = 2$.

In Problems 2845 to 2849 expand the given functions into Taylor's series in the neighbourhood of the point $x = 0$ (Maclaurin's series).

2845. $y = \cosh x$.

2846. $y = x^2 e^x$.

2847. $y = \cos(x + \alpha)$.

2848. $y = e^x \sin x$.

2849. $y = \cos x \cosh x$.

In Problems 2850 to 2854 find the first five terms of Taylor's series for the given functions in the neighbourhood of the point $x = 0$.

2850. $y = \ln(1 + e^x)$.

2851. $y = e^{\cos x}$.

2852. $y = \cos^n x$.

2853. $y = -\ln(\cos x)$.

2854. $y = (1 + x)^x$.

In Problems 2855 to 2868 expand the given functions in the neighbourhood of the point $x = 0$, using the formulas for expanding into Maclaurin's series the functions e^x, $\sin x$, $\cos x$, $\ln(1 + x)$ and $(1 + x)^m$.

2855. $y = e^{2x}$.

2856. $y = e^{-x^2}$.

2857. $y = \begin{cases} \dfrac{e^x - 1}{x} & \text{for } x \neq 0, \\ 1 & \text{for } x = 0. \end{cases}$

2858. $y = \begin{cases} \dfrac{e^{x^3} - e^{-x^3}}{2x^3} & \text{for } x \neq 0, \\ 1 & \text{for } x = 0. \end{cases}$

2859. $y = \sin \dfrac{x}{2}$.

2860. $y = \cos^2 x$.

2861. $y = \begin{cases} \dfrac{\sin x}{x} & \text{for } x \neq 0, \\ 1 & \text{for } x = 0. \end{cases}$

2862. $y = (x - \tan x)\cos x$.

2863. $y = \ln(10 + x)$.

2864. $y = x\ln(1 + x)$.

2865. $y = \sqrt{1 + x^2}$.

2866. $y = \sqrt[3]{8 - x^3}$.

2867. $y = \dfrac{1}{\sqrt[3]{1 + x^3}}$.

2868. $y = \dfrac{x^2}{\sqrt{1 - x^2}}$.

2869. Expand the function $y = \dfrac{1 + x}{(1 - x)^3}$ into Taylor's series in the neighbourhood of the point $x = 0$. Using this expansion, find the sum of the series

$$1 + \frac{4}{2} + \ldots + \frac{n^2}{2^{n-1}} + \ldots.$$

2870. Using the expansion of the function into Taylor's series, find the value of the

(1) seventh derivative of the function $y = \dfrac{x}{1 + x^2}$ at $x = 0$,

(2) fifth derivative of the function $y = x^2\sqrt[4]{1 + x}$ at $x = 0$,

(3) tenth derivative of the function $y = x^6 e^x$ at $x = 0$,

(4) curvature of the curve $y = x[\sqrt[3]{(1 + x)^4} - 1]$ at the origin.

In Problems 2871 to 2877 using the expansions of the functions into Taylor's series, compute the limits.

2871. $\lim\limits_{x\to 0} \dfrac{x + \ln(\sqrt{1+x^2} - x)}{x^3}$. **2872.** $\lim\limits_{x\to 0} \dfrac{2(\tan x - \sin x) - x^3}{x^5}$.

2873. $\lim\limits_{x\to 0} \dfrac{\ln(1 + x + x^2) + \ln(1 - x + x^2)}{x(e^x - 1)}$.

2874. $\lim\limits_{x\to\infty} \left[x - x^2 \ln\left(1 + \dfrac{1}{x}\right)\right]$. **2875.** $\lim\limits_{x\to 0} \left(\dfrac{1}{x^2} - \cot^2 x\right)$.

2876. $\lim\limits_{x\to 0} \left(\dfrac{1}{x^2} - \dfrac{\cot x}{x}\right)$. **2877.** $\lim\limits_{x\to 0} \left(\dfrac{2 + \cos x}{x^3 \sin x} - \dfrac{3}{x^4}\right)$.

Interval of convergence

In Problems 2878 to 2889 find the intervals of convergence of the power series.

2878. $10x + 100x^2 + \ldots + 10^n x^n + \ldots.$

2879. $x - \dfrac{x^2}{2} + \ldots + (-1)^{n+1} \dfrac{x^n}{n} + \ldots.$

2880. $x + \dfrac{x^2}{20} + \ldots + \dfrac{x^n}{n \cdot 10^{n-1}} + \ldots.$ **2881.** $1 + x + \ldots + n!\,x^n + \ldots.$

2882. $1 + 2x^2 + \ldots + 2^{n-1} x^{2(n-1)} + \ldots.$

2883. $x - \dfrac{x^3}{3 \cdot 3!} + \ldots + (-1)^{n+1} \dfrac{x^{2n-1}}{(2n-1)(2n-1)!} + \ldots.$

2884. $1 + 3x + \ldots + (n-1)3^{n-1} x^{n-1} + \ldots.$

2885. $\dfrac{x}{1 \times 2} + \dfrac{x^2}{2 \times 3} + \ldots + \dfrac{x^n}{n(n+1)} + \ldots.$

2886. $x + \dfrac{(2x)^2}{2!} + \ldots + \dfrac{(nx)^n}{n!} + \ldots$ When testing for convergence at the right-hand end-point of the interval, take into account that the factorials of large numbers can be expressed approximately by Stirling's formula

$$n! \approx \left(\frac{n}{e}\right)^n \sqrt{2\pi n}.$$

2887. $x + 4x^2 + \ldots + (nx)^n + \ldots.$

2888. $\dfrac{\ln 2}{2} x^2 + \dfrac{\ln 3}{3} x^3 + \ldots + \dfrac{\ln(n+1)}{n+1} x^{n+1} + \ldots.$

2889. $2x + \left(\dfrac{9}{4} x\right)^2 + \ldots + \left[\left(\dfrac{n+1}{n}\right)^n x\right]^n + \ldots.$

2890. Expand the function $y = \ln(x + \sqrt{1 + x^2})$ into Taylor's series in the neighbourhood of the point $x = 0$, proceeding from the relationship

$$\ln(x + \sqrt{1 + x^2}) = \int_0^x \frac{dx}{\sqrt{1 + x^2}},$$

and indicate the interval of convergence of the obtained series.

2891. Expand the function $y = \ln\sqrt{\frac{1 + x}{1 - x}}$ into Taylor's series in the neighbourhood of the point $x = 0$, proceeding from the relationship

$$\ln\sqrt{\frac{1 + x}{1 - x}} = \int_0^x \frac{dx}{1 - x^2},$$

and indicate the interval of convergence of the series obtained.

2892. Expand the function $y = \ln[(1 + x)^{1 + x}] + \ln[(1 - x)^{1 - x}]$ into Taylor's series in the neighbourhood of the point $x = 0$ and indicate the interval of convergence of the series, thus obtained.

2893. Expand the function $y = (1 + x)e^{-x} - (1 - x)e^x$ into Taylor's series in the neighbourhood of the point $x = 0$ and indicate the interval of convergence of the obtained series. Using the expansion, find the sum of the series

$$\frac{1}{3!} + \frac{2}{5!} + \ldots + \frac{n}{(2n + 1)!} + \ldots.$$

4. Some Applications of Taylor's Series

Approximate computation of values of functions

2894. Compute approximation to the value of $\sqrt[3]{e}$, taking three terms of the expansion of the function $f(x) = e^x$ into Maclaurin's series, and estimate the error.

2895. Compute approximation to the value of $\sin 18°$, taking three terms of the expansion of the function $f(x) = \sin x$ into Maclaurin's series and estimate the error.

2896. Compute approximation to the value $\sqrt[3]{10} = 2\sqrt[3]{1.25}$, taking four terms of the expansion of the function $f(x) = (1 + x)^m$ into Maclaurin's series, and estimate the error.

In Problems 2897 to 2904, using the Maclaurin series expansions of the functions e^x, $\sin x$ and $\cos x$, compute the expressions.

2897. e^2 to within 0.001.

2898. $\sqrt{e}$ to within 0.001.

2899. $\frac{1}{e}$ to within 0.0001.

2900. $\frac{1}{\sqrt[4]{e}}$ to within 0.0001.

2901. sin 1° to within 0.0001.

2902. cos 1° to within 0.001.

2903. sin 10° to within 0.00001.

2904. cos 10° to within 0.0001.

In Problems 2905 to 2911, using the Maclaurin series expansion of the function $(1 + x)^m$, compute the indicated roots to within 0.001.

2905. $\sqrt[3]{30}$.

2906. $\sqrt[3]{70}$.

2907. $\sqrt[3]{500}$.

2908. $\sqrt[3]{1.015}$.

2909. $\sqrt[5]{250}$.

2910. $\sqrt[3]{129}$.

2911. $\sqrt[10]{1027}$.

In Problems 2912 to 2914 using the formula for expanding the function $\ln \frac{1+x}{1-x}$ into Maclaurin's series compute the given expressions.

2912. ln 3 to within 0.0001.

2913. $\log_{10} e = \frac{1}{\ln 10}$ to within 0.000001.

2914. $\log_{10} 5$ to within 0.0001.

Solving equations

2915. Given the equation $xy + e^x + y$. Using the method of undetermined coefficients, expand the function y into Taylor's series in powers of x. Solve the problem finding the coefficients of Taylor's series by successive differentiation.

2916. Given the equation $y = \ln(1 + x) - xy$. Using the method of undetermined coefficients expand the function y into Taylor's series in powers of x. Solve the problem finding the coefficients of Taylor's series by successive differentiation.

In Problems 2917 to 2919 solve the equations with respect to y (find the explicit expression for y) with the aid of Taylor's series using two methods : the method of undetermined coefficients and that of successive differentiation.

2917. $y^3 + xy = 1$ (find three terms of the expansion).

2918. $2 \sin x + \sin y = x - y$ (find two terms of the expansion).

2919. $e^x - e^y = xy$ (find three terms of the expansion).

Integrating functions

In Problems 2920 to 2929 express the integrals in the form of series using the series expansions of the integrands, indicate the domains of convergence of the obtained series.

2920. $\int \frac{\sin x}{x}\, dx.$

2921. $\int \frac{\cos x}{x}\, dx.$

2922. $\int \frac{e^x}{x}\, dx.$

2923. $\int \frac{e^x}{x^2}\, dx.$

2924. $\int_0^x e^{-x^2}\, dx.$

2925. $\int_0^x \frac{\arctan x}{x}\, dx.$

2926. $\int_0^x \frac{dx}{\sqrt{1-x^4}}.$

2927. $\int_0^x \sqrt{1+x^3}\, dx.$

2928. $\int_0^x \frac{dx}{1-x^9}.$

2929. $\int_0^x \frac{\sqrt[4]{1+x^4}-1}{x^2}\, dx.$

In Problems 2930 to 2934 compute the approximate values of the definite integrals, taking the indicated number of terms of the series expansions of the integrands, indicate the error.

2930. $\int_{\pi/6}^{\pi/4} \frac{\cos x}{x}\, dx$ (3 terms).

2931. $\int_0^{1/4} e^{-x^2}\, dx$ (3 terms).

2932. $\int_0^{1/2} \frac{dx}{\sqrt{1+x^4}}$ (2 terms).

2933. $\int_{0.1}^{1} \frac{e^x}{x}\, dx$ (6 terms).

2934. $\int_0^{\sqrt{3}/3} x^3 \arctan x\, dx$ (2 terms).

In Problems 2935 to 2938 evaluate the given integrals to within 0.001.

2935. $\int_{0.1}^{0.2} \frac{e^{-x}}{x^3}\, dx.$

2936. $\int_0^{0.5} \frac{\arctan x}{x}\, dx.$

2937. $\int_0^{0.8} x^{10} \sin x \, dx.$

2938. $\int_0^{0.5} \frac{dx}{1 + x^4}.$

2939. Show that in the interval $(-0.1, 0.1)$ the function $\int_0^x e^{-x^2} dx$ differs from the function $\arctan x - \frac{x^5}{10}$ by not more than 0.0000001.

2940. Taking into consideration the identity

$$\frac{\pi}{4} = 4 \arctan \frac{1}{5} - \arctan \frac{1}{239},$$

evaluate π with 10 correct digits.

2941. Expand the function $y = e^{x^2} \int_0^x e^{-x^2} dx$ into Taylor's series by two methods : by direct computation of successive derivatives at $x = 0$ and by multiplication of the series.

2942*. Evaluate the integral $\int_0^1 x^x \, dx.$

2943. Compute $\int_0^{0.5} e^{\sin x} dx$ to within 0.0001.

2944. Compute $\int_0^{\pi/6} \sqrt{\cos x} \, dx$ to within 0.001.

Miscellaneous problems

2945. Compute the area bounded by the curve $y^2 = x^3 + 1$, the y-axis and the straight line $x = \frac{1}{2}$ accurate to 0.001.

2946*. Compute the area of the oval $x^4 + y^4 = 1$ accurate to 0.01.

2947. Compute the arc length of the curve $25y^2 = 4x^5$ between the cusp and the point of intersection with the parabola $5y = x^2$ to within 0.0001.

2948. Compute the arc length of the sinusoid $y = \sin x$ for one half period to within 0.001.

2949. A figure bounded by the curve $y = \arctan x$, the x-axis and the straight line $x = \frac{1}{2}$ rotates about the x-axis. Compute the volume of the solid of revolution thus generated to within 0.001.

2950. A figure bounded by the curves $y^3 - x^3 = 1$, $4y + x^3 = 0$, the straight line $y = \frac{1}{2}$ and the y-axis rotates about the y-axis. Compute the volume of the obtained solid of revolution accurate to 0.001.

2951. Compute (to within 0.001) the coordinates of the centre of gravity of an arc of the hyperbola $y = \frac{1}{x}$ between the points with the abscissas $x_1 = \frac{1}{4}$ and $x_2 = \frac{1}{2}$.

2952. Compute (to within 0.01) the coordinates of the centre of gravity of a curvilinear trapezoid bounded by the curve $y = \frac{1}{\ln x}$, the straight lines $x = 1.5$ and $x = 2$ and the x-axis.

10

Functions of Several Variables. Differential Calculus

1. Functions of Several Variables

2953. Express the volume z of a cone as a function of its element x and altitude y.

2954. Express the area S of a triangle as a function of its three sides x, y, z.

2955. Compile a table of values of the function $z = 2x - 3y + 1$ giving the independent variables the values from 0 to 5 spaced at unity.

2956. Compile a table of values of the function $z = \sqrt{x^2 + y^2}$, taking the values of the independent variables from 0 to 1 spaced at 0.1. Compute the values of the function to within 0.01.

2957. Find the values of the functions :

(1) $z = \left(\dfrac{\arctan(x+y)}{\arctan(x-y)}\right)^2$ for $x = \dfrac{1+\sqrt{3}}{2}$, $y = \dfrac{1-\sqrt{3}}{2}$;

(2) $z = e^{\sin(x+y)}$ for $x = y = \dfrac{\pi}{2}$;

(3) $z = y^{x^2-1} + x^{y^2-1}$ for $x = 2, y = 2$; $x = 1, y = 2$; $x = 2, y = 1$.

2958. Given the function

$$F(x, y) = \frac{\varphi(x)\psi(y) - \psi(x)\varphi(y)}{\varphi(xy)\psi(xy)}$$

Find $F(a, 1/a)$. In particular, put $\varphi(u) = u^3$, $\psi(u) = u^2$ and compute $F(a, 1/a)$.

2959. Given the function $F(x, y) = y^x - \dfrac{1}{2}x^y$. If x and y vary at an equal rate, then which of the functions increases more rapidly for $x = 3, y = 2$: the one obtained with a fixed y (when only x varies), or the one obtained for a fixed x with y as a variable?

2960. Given the function

$$\varphi(x, y, z) = y^2 - (y \cos z + z \cos y)x + x^{\frac{y+z}{y-z}}.$$

The variables y and z retain the fixed values y_0, z_0, and $y_0 = 3z_0$. What is the graph of the function $v = \varphi(x, y_0, z_0)$? Is $\varphi(x, y, z)$: (1) a rational function of y? of z? (2) an integral function of x?

2961*. A function $z = f(x, y)$, satisfying identically the relationship $f(mx, my) = m^k f(x, y)$ for any m is called the homogeneous function of the kth order. Show that a homogeneous function of the kth order $z = f(x, y)$ can always be represented in the form $z = x^k F\left(\frac{y}{x}\right)$.

2962. Whether a function of any number of independent variables is homogeneous or not is determined analogously as in the case of a function of two variables : for instance $f(x, y, z)$ is a homogeneous function of the order k if

$$f(mx, my, mz) = m^k f(x, y, z) \text{ for any } m.$$

The following property is also valid :

$$f(x, y, z) = x^k F\left(\frac{y}{x}, \frac{z}{x}\right);$$

prove it.

2963. Check to see that the function $z = F(x, y) = xy$ satisfies the functional equation

$$F(ax + bu, cy + dv) = acF(x, y) + bcF(u, y) + ad\,F(x, v) + bd\,F(u, v).$$

2964. Check to see that the function $z = F(x, y) = \ln x \ln y$ satisfies the functional equation

$$F(xy, uv) = F(x, u) + F(x, v) + F(y, u) + F(y, v) \quad (x, y, u, v \text{ positive}).$$

2965. From the equation $\frac{x^2}{a^2} + \frac{y^2}{b^2} + \frac{z^2}{c^2} = 1$ define z as an explicit function of x and y. Will this function be single-valued?

2966. Given a composite function $z = u^v$, where $u = x + y$, $v = x - y$. Find the value of the function :

(1) for $x = 0, y = 1$; (2) for $x = 1, y = 1$;

(3) for $x = 2, y = 3$; (4) for $x = 0, y = 0$;

(5) for $x = -1, y = -1$.

2967. $z = \frac{u + v}{uv}$, $u = w^t$, $v = w^{-t}$, $w = \sqrt{x + y}$, $t = 2(x - y)$. Express z directly as a function of x and y. Is z a rational function of u and v? of w and t? of x and y?

2968. Given a composite function $z = u^w + w^{u+v}$ where $u = x + y$, $v = x - y$, $w = xy$. Express z directly as a function of x and y.

2969. $u = (\xi + \eta)^2 - \xi^3 - \eta^3; \xi = \dfrac{e^{\omega} + e^{\varphi}}{2}, \eta = \dfrac{e^{\omega} - e^{\varphi}}{2}; \omega = \ln(x^2 + y^2 + z^2)$, $\varphi = 2\ln(x + y + z)$. Express u directly as a function of x, y and z. Is u an integral rational function of ξ and η? of ω and φ? of x, y, z?

2970. Represent the composite function

$$z = \left(\frac{x^2 + xy + y^2}{x^2 - xy + y^2}\right)^{xy} + x^2 + y^2$$

in the form of a "chain" of dependences made up of two "links".

2971. Investigate the graph of the function $z = \frac{1}{2}(x^2 - y^2)$ using the method of parallel sections. What are the sections by the planes $x = \text{const}$? $y = \text{const}$? $z = \text{const}$?

2972. Investigate the graph of the function $z = xy$ using the method of parallel sections. What are the sections by the planes $x = \text{const}$? $y = \text{const}$? $z = \text{const}$?

2973. Investigate the graph of the function $z = y^2 - x^3$ using the method of parallel sections.

2974. Investigate the graph of the function $z^3 = ax^2 + b\,(a > 0, b > 0)$ using the method of parallel sections.

2. Simplest Properties of Functions

Domain of definition

2975. A domain is enclosed by a parallelogram whose sides are $y = 0$, $y = 2$, $y = \frac{1}{2}x$, $y = \frac{1}{2}x - 1$; the boundary is excluded. Specify the domain by inequalities.

2976. The domain is a figure bounded by the parabolas $y = x^2$ and $x = y^2$ (including the boundaries). Specify this domain by inequalities.

2977. Specify with the aid of inequalities an open domain which is a regular triangle with a vertex at the origin, and the sides equal to a, one of them being directed along the positive x-axis (the triangle lies in the first quadrant).

2978. A domain is bounded by an endless circular cylinder of radius R (the boundaries are excluded) with an axis parallel to the z-axis and passing through the point (a, b, c). Specify this domain with the aid of an inequality.

2979. Write with the aid of an inequality the domain bounded by a sphere of radius R with the point (a, b, c) as centre (including the boundary).

2980. The vertices of a right-angled triangle lie inside a circle of radius R. The area S of the triangle is a function of its sides x and y : $S = \varphi(x, y)$. What is the domain of definition of the function $S = \varphi(x, y)$?

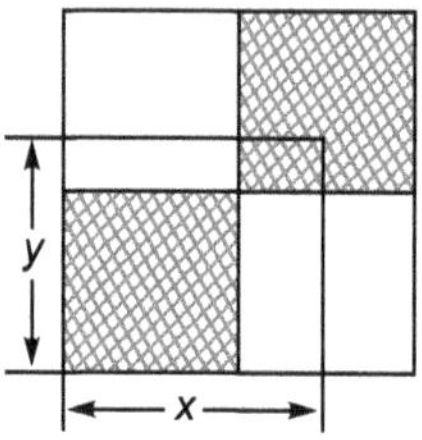

Fig. 57

2981. Inscribed in a sphere of radius R is a pyramid with a rectangular base whose vertex is projected orthogonally in the point of intersection of the diagonals of the base. The volume V of the pyramid is a function of the sides x and y of its base. Will this function be single-valued? Express it analytically. Find the domain of definition of the function.

2982. Figure 57 illustrates a square board consisting of four equal squares with the unit side two black and two white. Consider a rectangle whose sides x and y are parallel to the sides of the board and one of the angles coincides with one of the black angles. The area of the black portion of the rectangle will be a function of x and y. What is the domain of definition of this function? Express this function analytically.

In Problems 2983 to 3002 find the domains of definition of the given functions.

2983. $z = \sqrt{1 - \frac{x^2}{a^2} - \frac{y^2}{b^2}}$.

2984. $z = \ln(y^2 - 4x + 8)$.

2985. $z = \frac{1}{R^2 - x^2 - y^2}$.

2986. $z = \sqrt{x + y} + \sqrt{x - y}$.

2987. $z = \frac{1}{\sqrt{x + y}} + \frac{1}{\sqrt{x - y}}$.

2988. $z = \arcsin \frac{y - 1}{x}$.

2989. $z = \ln xy$.

2990. $z = \sqrt{x - \sqrt{y}}$.

2991. $z = \arcsin \dfrac{x^2 + y^2}{4} + \operatorname{arcsec}(x^2 + y^2)$.

2992. $z = \dfrac{\sqrt{4x - y^2}}{\ln(1 - x^2 - y^2)}$.

2993. $z = \sqrt{\dfrac{x^2 + 2x + y^2}{x^2 - 2x + y^2}}$.

2994. $z = xy\sqrt{\ln \dfrac{R^2}{x^2 + y^2}} + \sqrt{x^2 + y^2 - R^2}$.

2995. $z = \cot \pi (x + y)$.

2996. $z = \sqrt{\sin \pi (x^2 + y^2)}$.

2997. $z = \sqrt{x \sin y}$.

2998. $z = \ln x - \ln \sin y$.

2999. $z = \ln [x \ln (y - x)]$.

3000. $z = \arcsin [2y(1 + x^2) - 1]$.

3001. $u = \dfrac{1}{\sqrt{x}} + \dfrac{1}{\sqrt{y}} + \dfrac{1}{\sqrt{z}}$.

3002. $u = \sqrt{R^2 - x^2 - y^2 - z^2} + \dfrac{1}{\sqrt{x^2 + y^2 + z^2 - r^2}}$ $(R > r)$.

Limit. Continuity of a function

In Problems 3003 to 3008 find the limits of the given functions supposing that the independent variables tend to their limiting values in an arbitrary way.

3003. $\lim\limits_{\substack{x \to 0 \\ y \to 0}} \dfrac{x^2 + y^2}{\sqrt{x^2 + y^2 + 1} - 1}$.

3004. $\lim\limits_{\substack{x \to 0 \\ y \to 0}} \dfrac{\sqrt{x^2y^2 + 1} - 1}{x^2 + y^2}$.

3005. $\lim\limits_{\substack{x \to 0 \\ y \to 0}} \dfrac{\sin(x^3 + y^3)}{x^2 + y^2}$.

3006. $\lim\limits_{\substack{x \to 0 \\ y \to 0}} \dfrac{1 - \cos(x^2 + y^2)}{(x^2 + y^2)x^2y^2}$.

3007. $\lim\limits_{\substack{x \to 0 \\ y \to 0}} \dfrac{e^{-\frac{1}{x^2 + y^2}}}{x^4 + y^4}$.

3008. $\lim\limits_{\substack{x \to 0 \\ y \to 0}} (1 + x^2y^2)^{-\frac{1}{x^2 + y^2}}$.

3009. Make sure that the function $u = \dfrac{x + y}{x - y}$ as $x \to 0$, $y \to 0$ can tend to any limit (depending on how x and y tend to zero). Give examples of variation of x and y such that : (a) $\lim u = 1$, (b) $\lim u = 2$.

3010. Find the points of discontinuity of the function $z = \dfrac{2}{x^2 + y^2}$. Investigate the behaviour of the function in the neighbourhood of the point of discontinuity.

3011. Find the points of discontinuity of the function $z = \dfrac{1}{\sin^2 \pi x + \sin^2 \pi y}$.

3012. Where is the function $z = \dfrac{1}{x - y}$ discontinuous?

3013. Where is the function $z = \dfrac{1}{\sin \pi x} + \dfrac{1}{\sin \pi y}$ discontinuous?

3014. Where is the function $z = \dfrac{y^2 + 2x}{y^2 - 2x}$ discontinuous?

3015*. Test the following functions for continuity at $x = 0, y = 0$:

(1) $f(x, y) = \dfrac{x^2 y^2}{x^2 + y^2}$; $f(0, 0) = 0$. (2) $f(x, y) = \dfrac{xy}{x^2 + y^2}$; $f(0, 0) = 0$.

(3) $f(x, y) = \dfrac{x^3 y^3}{x^2 + y^2}$; $f(0, 0) = 0$. (4) $f(x, y) = \dfrac{1}{x^2 + y^2}$; $f(0, 0) = 0$.

(5) $f(x, y) = \dfrac{x^4 - y^4}{x^4 + y^4}$; $f(0, 0) = 0$. (6) $f(x, y) = \dfrac{x^2 y^2}{x^4 + y^4}$; $f(0, 0) = 0$.

Level lines and surfaces

3016. Given the function $z = f(x, y) = \dfrac{1}{x^2 + y^2}$. Construct the level lines of this function for $z = 1, 2, 3, 4$.

3017. The function $z = f(x, y)$ is specified in the following way : at point $P\ (x, y)$ its value is equal to the angle at which a segment AB given in the Oxy-plane is seen from this point.

Find the level lines of the function $f(x, y)$.

In Problems 3018 to 3021 draw the level lines of the given functions taking the values of z from -5 to $+5$ spaced at 1.

3018. $z = xy$.

3019. $z = x^2 y + x$.

3020. $z = y\,(x^2 + 1)$.

3021. $z = \dfrac{xy - 1}{x^2}$.

3022. Construct the level lines of the function $z = (x^2 + y^2)^2 - 2\,(x^2 - y^2)$, taking the values of z from -1 to $\dfrac{3}{2}$ spaced at $\dfrac{1}{2}$.

3023. Construct the level lines of the function z represented implicitly by the equation $\left(\dfrac{3}{2}\right)^z [(x - 5)^2 + y^2] = \left(\dfrac{2}{3}\right)^z [(x + 5)^2 + y^2]$ varying z from -4 to 4 spaced at 1.

3024. Construct the level lines of the function z represented implicitly by the equation $y^2 = 2^{-z}\,(x - z)$ taking the values of z from -3 to 3 spaced at 1.

3025. Find the level lines of the function z represented implicitly by the equation $z + x \ln z + y = 0$.

3026. Given in space is point A. The distance between a variable point M and the point A is a function of the coordinates of the point M. Find the level surfaces of this function corresponding to the distances equal to 1, 2, 3, 4.

3027. The function $u = f(x, y, z)$ is specified in the following way : at point $P(x, y, z)$ its value equals the sum of the distances between this point and each of the two given points :

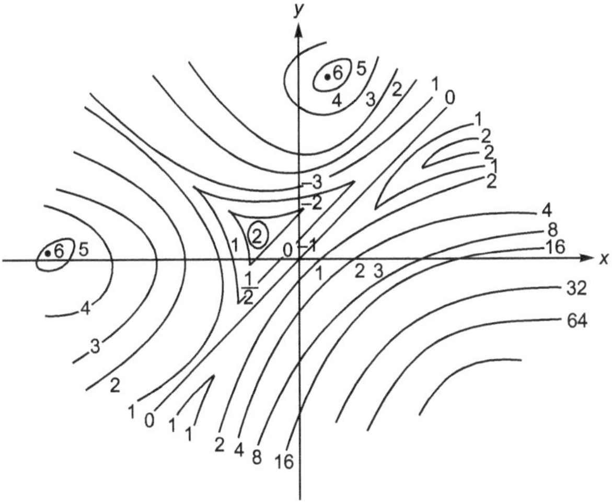

Fig. 58

$A(x_1, y_1, z_1)$, $B(x_2, y_2, z_2)$. Indicate the level surfaces of the function $f(x, y, z)$.

3028. Find the level surfaces of the function

$$u = \ln \frac{1 + \sqrt{x^2 + y^2 + z^2}}{1 - \sqrt{x^2 + y^2 + z^2}}.$$

3029. Find the level surfaces of the function $u = \dfrac{x^2 + y^2}{z}$.

3030. Find the level surfaces of the functions :

(1) $u = 5^{2x + 3y - z}$; (2) $u = \tan(x^2 + y^2 - 2z^2)$.

3031. Figure 58 illustrates the level lines of the function $z = f(x, y)$. Construct the graphs of the functions :

(1) $z = f(x, 0)$; (2) $z = f(x, 4)$; (3) $z = f(1, y)$;

(4) $z = f(-5, y)$; (5) $z = f(x, 3x)$; (6) $z = f(x, x^2)$.

3. Derivatives and Differentials of Functions of Several Variables

Partial derivatives

3032. The volume of gas v is a function of its temperature and pressure, $v = f(p, T)$. The expression $\frac{v_2 - v_1}{v_1 (T_2 - T_1)}$ is called the mean expansion coefficient at constant pressure and temperature changing from T_1 to T_2. What is the expansion coefficient at constant pressure and given temperature T_0?

3033. The temperature at a given point A of the rod Ox is a function of the abscissa x of the point A and the time t, $\theta = f(x, t)$. What physical meaning have the partial derivatives $\frac{\partial \theta}{\partial t}$ and $\frac{\partial \theta}{\partial x}$?

3034. The area S of a rectangle is expressed in terms of the base b and altitude h by the formula $S = bh$. Find $\frac{\partial S}{\partial h}, \frac{\partial S}{\partial b}$ and find out the geometrical meaning of the results obtained.

3035. Given two functions : $u = \sqrt{a^2 - x^2}$ (a is a constant) and $z = \sqrt{y^2 - x^2}$. Find $\frac{du}{dx}$ and $\frac{\partial z}{\partial x}$. Compare the results.

In Problems 3036 to 3084 find the partial derivatives of the given functions with respect to each of the independent variables (x, y, z, u, v, t, φ and ψ are variables).

3036. $z = x - y$.

3037. $z = x^3 y - y^3 x$.

3038. $\theta = axe^{-t} + bt$ (a, b constants).

3039. $z = \frac{u}{v} + \frac{v}{u}$.

3040. $z = \frac{x^3 + y^3}{x^2 + y^2}$.

3041. $z = (5x^2 y - y^3 + 7)^3$.

3042. $z = x\sqrt{y} + \frac{y}{\sqrt[3]{x}}$.

3043. $z = \ln (x + \sqrt{x^2 + y^2})$.

3044. $z = \arctan \frac{x}{y}$.

3045. $z = \frac{1}{\arctan \frac{y}{x}}$.

3046. $z = x^y$.

3047. $z = \ln (x^2 + y^2)$.

3048. $z = \ln \frac{\sqrt{x^2 + y^2} - x}{\sqrt{x^2 + y^2} + x}$.

3049. $z = \arcsin \frac{\sqrt{x^2 - y^2}}{\sqrt{x^2 + y^2}}$.

3050. $z = \ln \left(\tan \frac{x}{y} \right)$.

3051. $z = e^{-\frac{x}{y}}$.

3052. $z = \ln (x + \ln y)$.

3053. $u = \arctan \frac{v + w}{v - w}$.

3054. $z = \sin\frac{x}{y}\cos\frac{y}{x}$.

3055. $z = \left(\frac{1}{3}\right)^{y/x}$.

3056. $z = (1 + xy)^y$.

3057. $z = xy\ln(x + y)$.

3058. $z = x^{xy}$.

3059. $u = xyz$.

3060. $u = xy + yz + zx$.

3061. $u = \sqrt{x^2 + y^2 + z^2}$.

3062. $u = x^3 + yz^2 + 3yx - x + z$.

3063. $w = xyz + yzv + zvx + vxy$.

3064. $u = e^{x(x^2 + y^2 + z^2)}$.

3065. $u = \sin(x^2 + y^2 + z^2)$.

3066. $u = \ln(x + y + z)$.

3067. $u = x^{y/z}$.

3068. $u = x^{y^z}$.

3069. $f(x, y) = x + y - \sqrt{x^2 + y^2}$ at the point (3, 4).

3070. $z = \ln\left(x + \frac{y}{2x}\right)$ at the point (1, 2).

3071. $z = (2x + y)^{2x + y}$.

3072. $z = (1 + \log_u x)^3$.

3073. $z = xye^{\sin \pi xy}$.

3074. $z = (x^2 + y^2)\frac{1 - \sqrt{x^2 + y^2}}{1 + \sqrt{x^2 + y^2}}$.

3075. $z = \arctan\sqrt{x^y}$.

3076. $z = 2\sqrt{\frac{1 - \sqrt{xy}}{1 + \sqrt{xy}}}$.

3077. $z = \ln[xy^2 + yx^2 + \sqrt{1 + (xy^2 + yx^2)^2}]$.

3078. $z = \sqrt{1 - \left(\frac{x + y}{xy}\right)^2} + \arcsin\frac{x + y}{xy}$.

3079. $z = \arctan\left(\arctan\frac{y}{x}\right) - \frac{1}{2}\frac{\arctan\frac{y}{x} - 1}{\arctan\frac{y}{x} + 1} - \arctan\frac{y}{x}$.

3080. $u = \frac{k}{(x^2 + y^2 + z^2)^2}$.

3081. $u = \arctan(x - y)^z$.

3082. $u = (\sin x)^{yz}$.

3083. $u = \ln\frac{1 - \sqrt{x^2 + y^2 + z^2}}{1 + \sqrt{x^2 + y^2 + z^2}}$.

3084. $w = \frac{1}{2}\tan^2(x^2y^2 + z^2v^2 - xyzv) + \ln[\cos(x^2y^2 + z^2v^2 - xy\,zv)]$.

3085. $u = \frac{\cos(\varphi - 2\psi)}{\cos(\varphi + 2\psi)}$. Find $\left(\frac{\partial u}{\partial \psi}\right)_{\substack{\varphi = \frac{\pi}{4} \\ \psi = \pi}}$.

3086. $u = \sqrt{az^3 - bt^3}$. Find $\frac{\partial u}{\partial z}$ and $\frac{\partial u}{\partial t}$ for $z = b$, $t = a$.

3087. $z = \frac{x\cos y - y\cos x}{1 + \sin x + \sin y}$. Find $\frac{\partial z}{\partial x}$ and $\frac{\partial z}{\partial y}$ for $x = y = 0$.

3088. $u = \sqrt{\sin^2 x + \sin^2 y + \sin^2 z}$. Find $\left(\dfrac{\partial u}{\partial z}\right)_{\substack{x=0\\ y=0\\ z=\frac{\pi}{4}}}$.

3089. $u = \ln(1 + x + y^2 + z^3)$. Find $u'_x + u'_y + u'_z$ for $x = y = z = 1$.

3090. $f(x, y) = x^3y - y^3x$. Find $\left(\dfrac{\dfrac{\partial f}{\partial x} + \dfrac{\partial f}{\partial y}}{\dfrac{\partial f}{\partial x} \cdot \dfrac{\partial f}{\partial y}}\right)_{\substack{x=1\\ y=2}}$.

3091. What angle is formed between the positive direction of the x-axis and the tangent to the curve

$$\begin{cases} z = \dfrac{x^2 + y^2}{4} \\ y = 4 \end{cases}, \text{ at the point } (2, 4, 5)?$$

3092. What angle is formed between the positive direction of the y-axis and the tangent to the curve

$$\begin{cases} z = \sqrt{1 + x^2 + y^2} \\ x = 1 \end{cases}, \text{ at the point } (1, 1, \sqrt{3})?$$

3093. What is the angle of intersection of plane curves obtained as a result of cutting the surfaces $z = x^2 + \dfrac{y^2}{6}$ and $z = \dfrac{x^2 + y^2}{3}$ by the plane $y = 2$?

Differentials. Approximate calculations

In Problems 3094 to 3097 find the partial differentials of the given functions with respect to each of the independent variables.

3094. $z = xy^3 - 3x^2y^2 + 2y^4$.

3095. $z = \sqrt{x^2 + y^2}$.

3096. $z = \dfrac{xy}{x^2 + y^2}$.

3097. $u = \ln(x^3 + 2y^3 - z^3)$.

3098. $z = \sqrt[3]{x^2 + y^2}$. Find $d_y z$ for $x = 2$, $y = 5$, $\Delta y = 0.01$.

3099. $z = \sqrt{\ln xy}$. Find $d_x z$ for $x = 1$, $y = 1.2$, $\Delta x = 0.016$.

3100. $u = p - \dfrac{qr}{p} + \sqrt{p + q + r}$. Find $d_p u$ for $p = 1$, $q = 3$, $r = 5$, $\Delta_p = 0.01$.

In Problems 3101 to 3109 find the total differentials of the functions.

3101. $z = x^2y^4 - x^3y^3 + x^4y^2$.

3102. $z = \dfrac{1}{2}\ln(x^2 + y^2)$.

3103. $z = \frac{x+y}{x-y}$.

3104. $z = \arcsin \frac{x}{y}$.

3105. $z = \sin (xy)$.

3106. $z = \arctan \frac{x+y}{1-xy}$.

3107. $z = \frac{x^2+y^2}{x^2-y^2}$.

3108. $z = \arctan (xy)$.

3109. $u = x^{yz}$.

Applying differentials to calculations

3110. Evaluate the total differential of the function $z = x + y - \sqrt{x^2+y^2}$ for $x = 3$, $y = 4$, $\Delta x = 0.1$, $\Delta y = 0.2$.

3111. Evaluate the total differential of the function $z = e^{xy}$ for $x = 1$, $y = 1$, $\Delta x = 0.15$, $\Delta y = 0.1$.

3112. Find the value of the total differential of the function $z = \frac{xy}{x^2-y^2}$ for $x = 2$, $y = 1$, $\Delta x = 0.01$, $\Delta y = 0.03$.

3113. Compute approximately the change of the function $z = \frac{x+3y}{y-3x}$ as x varies from $x_1 = 2$ to $x_2 = 2.5$ and y from $y_1 = 4$ to $y_2 = 3.5$.

3114. Compute approximately $\ln (\sqrt[3]{1.03} + \sqrt[4]{0.98} - 1)$.

3115. Compute approximately $1.04^{2.02}$.

3116. Find the length of the segment of the straight line $x = 2$, $y = 3$ contained between the surface $z = x^2 + y^2$ and its tangent plane at the ponit (1, 1, 2).

3117. A body was weighed in air (4.1 ± 0.1 gf) and in water (1.8 ± 0.2 gf). Find the specific weight of the body and indicate the error of the calculations.

3118. The radius of the base of a cone is equal to 10.2 ± 0.1 cm, the generatrix to 44.6 ± 0.1 cm. Find the volume of the cone and indicate the error of the computations.

3119. Given the side a and angles B and C the area S of a triangle is usually computed by the formula

$$S = \frac{1}{2} a^2 \frac{\sin B \sin C}{\sin (B+C)}.$$

Find the relative error δ_S in computing S, if the relative errors of the given elements are equal to δ_a, δ_B, δ_C, respectively.

3120. One side of a triangle is 2.4 m long and increases at a rate of 10 cm/s; the other is 1.5 m long and decreases at a rate of 5 cm/s. The angle of 60° formed by these sides increases at a rate of 2° per second. How and at what rate does the area of the triangle change?

3121. In a truncated cone the radii of the bases $R = 30$ cm, $r = 20$ cm, the altitude $h = 40$ cm. How will the volume of the cone change if R is increased by 3 mm, r by 4 mm and h by 2 mm?

3122. Show that in computing the oscillation period T of a pendulum by the formula $T = \pi\sqrt{\frac{l}{g}}$ (where l is the length of the pendulum and g the acceleration due to gravity) the relative error equals half the sum of the relative errors introduced in determining l and g (all the errors are assumed to be sufficiently small).

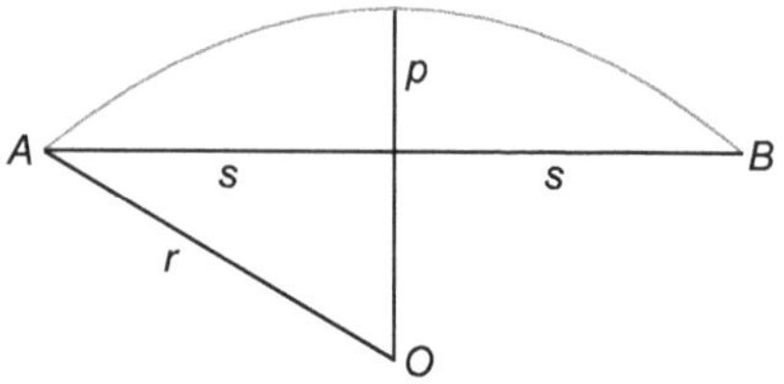

Fig. 59

3123. Express the error of computing the radius r of the circular arc AB (Fig. 59) by the chord $2s$ and sagitta p in terms of the errors ds and dp. Compute dr for $2s = 19.45$ cm ± 0.5 mm, $p = 3.62$ cm ± 0.3 mm.

4. Differentiating Functions

Composite function

3124. $u = e^{x-2y}$, where $x = \sin t$, $y = t^3$; $\frac{du}{dt} = ?$

3125. $u = z^2 + y^2 + zy$, $z = \sin t$, $y = e^t$; $\frac{du}{dt} = ?$

3126. $z = \arcsin(x - y)$, $x = 3t$, $y = 4t^3$; $\frac{dz}{dt} = ?$

3127. $z = x^2y - y^2x$, where $x = u\cos v$, $y = u\sin v$; $\frac{\partial z}{\partial u} = ?$ $\frac{\partial z}{\partial v} = ?$

3128. $z = x^2\ln y$, $x = \frac{u}{v}$, $y = 3u - 2v$; $\frac{\partial z}{\partial u} = ?$ $\frac{\partial z}{\partial v} = ?$

3129. $u = \ln(e^x + e^y)$; $\frac{\partial u}{\partial x} = ?$ Find $\frac{du}{dx}$ if $y = x^3$.

3130. $z = \arctan(xy)$. Find $\frac{dz}{dx}$ if $y = e^x$.

3131. $u = \arcsin\frac{x}{z}$, where $z = \sqrt{x^2 + 1}$; $\frac{du}{dx} = ?$

3132. $z = \tan(3t + 2x^2 - y)$, $x = \frac{1}{t}$, $y = \sqrt{t}$; $\frac{dz}{dt} = ?$

3133. $u = \frac{e^{ax}(y - z)}{a^2 + 1}$, $y = a\sin x$, $z = \cos x$, $\frac{du}{dx} = ?$

3134. $z = \dfrac{xy \ \arctan\,(xy + x + y)}{x + y}$; $dz = ?$

3135. $z = (x^2 + y^2)\,e^{\frac{x^2+y^2}{xy}}$; $\dfrac{\partial z}{\partial x} = ?\ \dfrac{\partial z}{\partial y} = ?\ dz = ?$

3136. $z = f(x^2 - y^2, e^{xy})$; $\dfrac{\partial z}{\partial x} = ?\ \dfrac{\partial z}{\partial y} = ?$

3137. Show that the function $z = \arctan \dfrac{x}{y}$, where $x = u + v,\ y = u - v$, satisfies the relationship $\dfrac{\partial z}{\partial u} + \dfrac{\partial z}{\partial v} = \dfrac{u - v}{v^2 + u^2}$.

3138. Show that the function $z = \varphi\,(x^2 + y^2)$, where $\varphi\,(u)$ is a differentiable function, satisfies the relationship $y\,\dfrac{\partial z}{\partial x} - x\,\dfrac{\partial z}{\partial y} = 0$.

3139. $u = \sin\,x + F(\sin\,y - \sin\,x)$; make sure that

$$\frac{\partial u}{\partial y}\cos x + \frac{\partial u}{\partial x} \times \cos y = \cos x \cos y,$$

whatever the differentiable function F is.

3140. $z = \dfrac{y}{f(x^2 - y^2)}$; make sure that $\dfrac{1}{x}\dfrac{\partial z}{\partial x} + \dfrac{1}{y}\dfrac{\partial z}{\partial y} = \dfrac{z}{y^2}$, whatever the differentiable function f is.

3141. Show that the homogeneous differentiable function of the zeroth order $z = F\left(\dfrac{y}{x}\right)$ (see Problem 2961) satisfies the relationship

$$x\,\frac{\partial z}{\partial x} + y\,\frac{\partial z}{\partial y} = 0.$$

3142. Show that the homogeneous function of the kth order $u = x^k F\left(\dfrac{z}{x};\ \dfrac{y}{x}\right)$, where F is a differentiable function, satisfies the relationship

$$x\,\frac{\partial u}{\partial x} + y\,\frac{\partial u}{\partial y} + z\,\frac{\partial u}{\partial z} = ku.$$

3143. Check on the proposition of Problem 3142 for the function

$$u = x^5 \sin \frac{z^2 + y^2}{x^2}.$$

3144. Given a differentiable function $f(x, y)$. Prove that if the variables x and y are replaced by homogeneous linear functions of X and Y, then the obtained function $F(X, Y)$ is related with the given function as follows:

$$x\,\frac{\partial f}{\partial x} + y\,\frac{\partial f}{\partial y} = X\,\frac{\partial F}{\partial X} + Y\,\frac{\partial F}{\partial Y}.$$

Functions represented implicitly and parametrically

In Problems 3145 to 3155 find the derivative $\frac{dy}{dx}$ of the functions represented implicitly.

3145. $x^3y - y^3x = a^4$.

3146. $x^2y^2 - x^4 - y^4 = a^4$.

3147. $xe^y + ye^x - e^{xy} = 0$.

3148. $(x^2 + y^2)^2 - a^2(x^2 - y^2) = 0$.

3149. $\sin(xy) - e^{xy} - x^2y = 0$.

3150. $x^{\frac{2}{3}} + y^{\frac{2}{3}} = a^{\frac{2}{3}}$.

3151. $xy - \ln y = a$.

3152. $\arctan\frac{x+y}{a} - \frac{y}{a} = 0$.

3153. $yx^2 = e^y$.

3154. $ye^x + e^y = 0$.

3155. $y^x = x^y$.

3156. $F(x, y) = F(y, x)$. Show that the derivative of y with respect to x can be expressed with the aid of a fraction whose numerator is obtained from the denominator by transposing the letters y and x.

3157. $x^2 + y^2 - 4x - 10y + 4 = 0$; find $\frac{dy}{dx}$ at $x = 6$, $y = 2$ and at $x = 6$, $y = 8$. Give a geometrical interpretation of the obtained results.

3158. $x^4y + xy^4 - ax^2y^2 = a^5$. Find $\frac{dy}{dx}$ at $x = y = a$.

3159. Prove that from $x^2y^2 + x^2 + y^2 - 1 = 0$ it follows that :

$$\frac{dx}{\sqrt{1-x^4}} + \frac{dy}{\sqrt{1-y^4}} = 0.$$

3160. Prove that from $a + b(x + y) + cxy = m(x - y)$ it follows that

$$\frac{dx}{a + 2bx + cx^2} = \frac{dy}{a + 2by + cy^2}.$$

3161. $\frac{x^2}{a^2} + \frac{y^2}{b^2} + \frac{z^2}{c^2} = 1$; $\frac{\partial z}{\partial x} = ?$ $\frac{\partial z}{\partial y} = ?$

3162. $x^2 - 2y^2 + z^2 - 4x + 2z - 5 = 0$; $\frac{\partial z}{\partial x} = ?$ $\frac{\partial z}{\partial y} = ?$

3163. $z^3 + 3xyz = a^3$; $\frac{\partial z}{\partial x} = ?$ $\frac{\partial z}{\partial y} = ?$

3164. $e^z - xyz = 0$; $\frac{\partial z}{\partial x} = ?$ $\frac{\partial z}{\partial y} = ?$

3165. Show that whatever the differentiable function φ is, the relationship $\varphi(cx - az, cy - bz) = 0$ implies that

$$a\frac{\partial z}{\partial x} + b\frac{\partial z}{\partial y} = c.$$

3166. $F(x, y, z) = 0$. Prove that

$$\frac{\partial x}{\partial y}\cdot\frac{\partial y}{\partial x} = 1; \quad \frac{\partial y}{\partial z}\cdot\frac{\partial z}{\partial x}\cdot\frac{\partial x}{\partial y} = -1.$$

3167. Find the total differential of the function z specified by the equation $\cos^2 x + \cos^2 y + \cos^2 z = 1$.

3168. Function z is represented parametrically : $x = u + v$, $y = u - v$, $z = uv$. Express z as an explicit function of x and y.

3169. $x = u + v$, $y = u^2 + v^2$, $z = u^3 + v^3$. Express z as an explicit function of x and y.

3170. $x = u \cos v$, $y = u \sin v$, $z = kv$. Express z as an explicit function of x and y.

In Problems 3171 to 3175 express dz in terms of x, y, z, dx and dy of the functions represented parametrically.

3171. $x = \dfrac{u^2 + v^2}{2}$, $y = \dfrac{u^2 - v^2}{2}$, $z = uv$.

3172. $x = \sqrt{a}\,(\sin u + \cos v)$, $y = \sqrt{a}\,(\cos u - \sin v)$, $z = 1 + \sin(u - v)$.

3173. $x = u + v$, $y = u - v$, $z = u^2 v^2$.

3174. $x = u \cos v$, $y = u \sin v$, $z = u^2$.

3175. $x = v \cos u - u \cos u + \sin u$, $y = v \sin u - u \sin u - \cos u$, $z = (u - v)^2$.

3176. $x = e^u \cos v$, $y = e^u \sin v$, $z = uv$. Express dz in terms of u, v, dx and dy.

3177. The relationships $u = f(x, y)$, $v = F(x, y)$, where f and F are differentiable functions of x and y, specify x and y as differentiable functions of u and v. Prove that

$$\left(\frac{\partial u}{\partial x}\frac{\partial v}{\partial y} - \frac{\partial u}{\partial y}\frac{\partial v}{\partial x}\right)\left(\frac{\partial x}{\partial u}\frac{\partial y}{\partial v} - \frac{\partial x}{\partial v}\frac{\partial y}{\partial u}\right) = 1.$$

3178. u and v are functions of x, y, z, satisfying the relationships $uv = 3x - 2y + z$, $v^2 = x^2 + y^2 + z^2$. Show that

$$x\frac{\partial u}{\partial x} + y\frac{\partial u}{\partial y} + z\frac{\partial u}{\partial z} = 0.$$

3179. Let $y = f(x, t)$, $F(x, y, t) = 0$. Check to see that

$$\frac{dy}{dx} = \frac{\dfrac{\partial f}{\partial x}\dfrac{\partial F}{\partial t} - \dfrac{\partial f}{\partial t}\dfrac{\partial F}{\partial x}}{\dfrac{\partial f}{\partial t}\dfrac{\partial F}{\partial y} + \dfrac{\partial F}{\partial t}}.$$

3180. Let $f(x, y, z) = 0$, $F(x, y, z) = 0$. Check to see that

$$\frac{dy}{dx} = -\frac{\dfrac{\partial f}{\partial x}\dfrac{\partial F}{\partial z} - \dfrac{\partial F}{\partial x}\dfrac{\partial f}{\partial z}}{\dfrac{\partial f}{\partial y}\dfrac{\partial F}{\partial z} - \dfrac{\partial F}{\partial y}\dfrac{\partial f}{\partial z}}.$$

5. Repeated Differentiation

3181. $x = x^3 + xy^2 - 5xy^3 + y^5$. Show that $\dfrac{\partial^2 z}{\partial x\,\partial y} = \dfrac{\partial^2 z}{\partial y\,\partial x}$.

3182. $z = x^y$. Show that $\dfrac{\partial^2 z}{\partial x\,\partial y} = \dfrac{\partial^2 z}{\partial y\,\partial x}$.

3183. $z = e^x(\cos y + x\sin y)$. Show that $\dfrac{\partial^2 z}{\partial x\,\partial y} = \dfrac{\partial^2 z}{\partial y\,\partial x}$.

3184. $z = \arctan\dfrac{y}{x}$. Show that $\dfrac{\partial^3 z}{\partial y^2\,\partial x} = \dfrac{\partial^3 z}{\partial x\,\partial y^2}$.

In Problems 3185 to 3192 find $\dfrac{\partial^2 z}{\partial x^2}$, $\dfrac{\partial^2 z}{\partial x\,\partial y}$ and $\dfrac{\partial^2 z}{\partial y^2}$ of the given functions.

3185. $z = \dfrac{1}{3}\sqrt{(x^2+y^2)^3}$.

3186. $z = \ln(x + \sqrt{x^2+y^2})$.

3187. $z = \arctan\dfrac{x+y}{1-xy}$.

3188. $z = \sin^2(ax+by)$.

3189. $z = e^{xe^y}$.

3190. $z = \dfrac{x-y}{x+y}$.

3191. $z = y^{\ln x}$.

3192. $z = \arcsin(xy)$.

3193. $u = \sqrt{x^2+y^2+z^2-2xz}$; $\dfrac{\partial^2 u}{\partial y\partial z} = ?$

3194. $z = e^{xy^2}$; $\dfrac{\partial^3 z}{\partial x^2\partial y} = ?$

3195. $z = \ln(x^2+y^2)$; $\dfrac{\partial^3 z}{\partial x\,\partial y^2} = ?$

3196. $z = \sin xy$; $\dfrac{\partial^3 z}{\partial x\partial y^2} = ?$

3197. $w = e^{xyz}$; $\dfrac{\partial^3 w}{\partial x\,\partial y\,\partial z} = ?$

3198. $v = x^m y^n z^p$; $\dfrac{\partial^6 v}{\partial x\,\partial y^3\,\partial z^2} = ?$

3199. $z = \ln(e^x + e^y)$. Make sure that $\dfrac{\partial z}{\partial x} + \dfrac{\partial z}{\partial y} = 1$ and that

$$\frac{\partial^2 z}{\partial x^2}\frac{\partial^2 z}{\partial y^2} - \left(\frac{\partial^2 z}{\partial x\,\partial y}\right)^2 = 0.$$

3200. $u = e^x(x\cos y - y\sin y)$. Show that $\dfrac{\partial^2 u}{\partial x^2} + \dfrac{\partial^2 u}{\partial y^2} = 0$.

3201. $u = \ln\dfrac{1}{\sqrt{x^2+y^2}}$. Show that $\dfrac{\partial^2 u}{\partial x^2} + \dfrac{\partial^2 u}{\partial y^2} = 0$.

3202. $u = \dfrac{1}{\sqrt{x^2+y^2+z^2}}$. Show that $\dfrac{\partial^2 u}{\partial x^2} + \dfrac{\partial^2 u}{\partial y^2} + \dfrac{\partial^2 u}{\partial z^2} = 0$.

3203. $r = \sqrt{x^2+y^2+z^2}$. Show that

$$\frac{\partial^2 r}{\partial x^2} + \frac{\partial^2 r}{\partial y^2} + \frac{\partial^2 r}{\partial z^2} = \frac{2}{r},\quad \frac{\partial^2(\ln r)}{\partial x^2} + \frac{\partial^2(\ln r)}{\partial y^2} + \frac{\partial^2(\ln r)}{\partial z^2} = \frac{1}{r^2}.$$

3204. At what value of the constant a does the function $v = x^3 + axy^2$ satisfy the equation $\frac{\partial^2 v}{\partial x^2} + \frac{\partial^2 v}{\partial y^2} = 0$?

3205. $z = \frac{y}{y^2 - a^2x^2}$. Show that $\frac{\partial^2 z}{\partial x^2} = a^2 \frac{\partial^2 z}{\partial y^2}$.

3206. $v = \frac{1}{x - y} + \frac{1}{y - z} + \frac{1}{z - x}$. Show that

$$\frac{\partial^2 v}{\partial x^2} + \frac{\partial^2 v}{\partial y^2} + \frac{\partial^2 v}{\partial z^2} + 2\left(\frac{\partial^2 v}{\partial x\, \partial y} + \frac{\partial^2 v}{\partial y\, \partial z} + \frac{\partial^2 v}{\partial z\, \partial x}\right) = 0.$$

3207. $z = f(x, y)$, $\xi = x + y$, $\eta = x - y$. Check to see that

$$\frac{\partial^2 z}{\partial x^2} - \frac{\partial^2 z}{\partial y^2} = 4 \frac{\partial^2 z}{\partial \xi\, \partial \eta}.$$

3208. $v = x \ln(x + r) - r$, where $r^2 = x^2 + y^2$. Show that

$$\frac{\partial^2 v}{\partial x^2} + \frac{\partial^2 v}{\partial y^2} = \frac{1}{x + r}.$$

3209. Find the expression for the second derivative $\frac{d^2 y}{dx^2}$ of the function y specified implicitly by the expression $f(x, y) = 0$.

3210. $y = \varphi(x - at) + \psi(x + at)$. Show that $\frac{\partial^2 y}{\partial t^2} = a^2 \frac{\partial^2 y}{\partial x^2}$, whatever the twice differentiable functions φ and ψ are.

3211. $u = \varphi(x) + \psi(y) + (x - y)\psi'(y)$. Check to see that

$$(x - y)\frac{\partial^2 u}{\partial x\, \partial y} = \frac{\partial u}{\partial y}$$

(φ and ψ are twice differentiable functions).

3212. $z = y\varphi(x^2 - y^2)$. Check to see that $\frac{1}{x}\frac{\partial z}{\partial x} + \frac{1}{y}\frac{\partial z}{\partial y} = \frac{z}{y^2}$ (φ is a differentiable function).

3213. $r = x\varphi(x + y) + y\psi(x + y)$. Show that

$$\frac{\partial^2 r}{\partial x^2} - 2\frac{\partial^2 r}{\partial x\, \partial y} + \frac{\partial^2 r}{\partial y^2} = 0.$$

(φ and ψ are twice differentiable functions).

3214. $u = \frac{1}{y}[\varphi(ax + y) + \psi(ax - y)]$. Show that $\frac{\partial^2 u}{\partial x^2} = \frac{a^2}{y^2} \cdot \frac{\partial}{\partial y}\left(y^2 \frac{\partial u}{\partial y}\right)$.

3215. $u = \frac{1}{x}[\varphi(x - y) + \psi(x + y)]$. Show that

$$\frac{\partial}{dx}\left(x^2 \frac{\partial u}{\partial x}\right) = x^2 \frac{\partial^2 u}{\partial y^2}.$$

3216. $u = xe^y + ye^x$. Show that

$$\frac{\partial^3 u}{\partial x^3} + \frac{\partial^3 u}{\partial y^3} = x \frac{\partial^3 u}{\partial x\, \partial y^2} + y \frac{\partial^3 u}{\partial x^2\, \partial y}.$$

3217. $u = e^{xyz}$. Show that

$$\frac{\partial^3 u}{\partial x\,\partial y\,\partial z} = xy\frac{\partial^2 u}{\partial x\,\partial y} + 2x\frac{\partial u}{\partial x} + u.$$

3218. $u = \ln\frac{x^2 - y^2}{xy}$. Show that

$$\frac{\partial^3 u}{\partial x^3} + \frac{\partial^3 u}{\partial x^2\,\partial y} - \frac{\partial^3 u}{\partial x\,\partial y^2} - \frac{\partial^3 u}{\partial y^3} = 2\left(\frac{1}{y^3} - \frac{1}{x^3}\right).$$

In Problems 3219 to 3224 find the differentials of the second order of the given functions.

3219. $z = xy^2 - x^2y$.

3220. $z = \ln(x - y)$.

3221. $z = \frac{1}{2(x^2 + y^2)}$.

3222. $z = x\sin^2 y$.

3223. $z = e^{xy}$.

3224. $u = xyz$.

3225. $z = \sin(2x + y)$. Find d^3z at the points $(0, \pi)$, $\left(-\frac{\pi}{2}, \frac{\pi}{2}\right)$.

3226. $u = \sin(x + y + z)$; $d^2u = ?$

3227. $\frac{x^2}{a^2} + \frac{y^2}{b^2} + \frac{z^2}{c^2} = 1$; $d^2z = ?$

3228. $z^3 - 3xyz = a^3$; $d^2z = ?$

3229. $3x^2y^2 + 2z^2xy - 2zx^3 + 4zy^3 - 4 = 0$. Find d^2z at the point $(2, 1, 2)$.

Change of variables

3230. Transform the differential expression

$$x^4\frac{d^2y}{dx^2} + 2x^3\frac{dy}{dx} + y,$$

putting $x = \frac{1}{t}$.

3231. Transform the differential expression

$$x^2y'' - 4xy' + y,$$

putting $x = e^z$.

3232. Transform the differential expression

$$(1 - x^2)\frac{d^2y}{dx^2} - x\frac{dy}{dx} + ay,$$

putting $x = \sin t$.

3233. Transform the differential expression $\frac{y''}{y'^2} + y$ assuming y as the independent variable and x as its function.

3234. Transform the expression $y'\,y''' - 3y''^2$ taking y for the independent variable.

3235. Transform the expression $yy'' - 2(y^2 + y'^2)$ to a new function v, putting $y = \frac{1}{v}$.

3236. Transform the equation $\frac{dy}{dx} = \frac{x+y}{x-y}$ to polar coordinates. The latter are related with the Cartesian coordinates by the formulas $x = \rho \cos \varphi$, $y = \rho \sin \varphi$.

3237. Transform the expression $k = \frac{y''}{(1 + y'^2)^{3/2}}$ to the polar coordinates ρ, φ.

3238. The function z depends on x and y. In the expression $y \frac{\partial z}{\partial x} - x \frac{\partial z}{\partial y}$ change the independent variables with the aid of the formulas $x = u \cos v$; $y = u \sin v$.

3239. Transform the Laplacian operator $\frac{\partial^2 u}{\partial x^2} + \frac{\partial^2 u}{\partial y^2}$ to the polar coordinates.

3240. Transform the expression $\frac{\partial^2 z}{\partial x^2} + \frac{\partial^2 z}{\partial y^2} + kz$ to the polar coordinates assuming that $z = \omega(\rho)$ depends only on ρ and is independent of φ.

3241. In the expression $\frac{\partial^2 z}{\partial x^2} + 2\frac{\partial^2 z}{\partial x\, \partial y} + \frac{\partial^2 z}{\partial y^2}$ substitute u and v for the independent variables x and y, and the variable w for the function z, assuming that these variables are related as follows:

$$x = \frac{u+v}{2},\ y = \frac{u-v}{2};\ z = \frac{u^2 - v^2}{4} - w.$$

11

Applications of Differential Calculus of Functions of Several Variables

1. Taylor's Formula. Extrema of Functions of Several Variables

Taylor's formula

3242. $f(x, y) = x^3 + 2y^3 - xy$. Expand the function $f(x+h, y+k)$ in powers of h and k.

3243. $f(x, y) = x^3 + y^2 - 6xy - 39x + 18y + 4$. Find the increment gained by the function when the independent variables pass from the values $x = 5$, $y = 6$ to the values $x = 5 + h$, $y = 6 + k$.

3244. $f(x, y) = \frac{xy^3}{4} - yx^3 + \frac{x^2y^2}{2} - 2x + 3y - 4$. Find the increment gained by the function when the independent variables pass from the values $x = 1$, $y = 2$ to the values $x = 1 + h$, $y = 2 + k$. Compute $f(1.02, 2.03)$ up to the second order terms (included).

3245. $f(x, y, z) = Ax^2 + By^2 + Cz^2 + Dxy + Eyz + Fzx$.

Expand $f(x+h, y+k, z+l)$ in powers of h k and l.

3246. Expand $z = \sin x \sin y$ in powers of $\left(x - \frac{\pi}{4}\right)$, and $\left(y - \frac{\pi}{4}\right)$. Find the terms of the first and second orders and R_2 (the remainder of the second order).

3247. Expand the function $z = x^y$ in powers of $(x-1)$, $(y-1)$, finding the terms up to the third order included. Use the result to compute (without tables) $1.1^{1.02}$.

3248. $f(x, y) = e^x \sin y$. Expand $f(x+h, y+k)$ in powers of h and k, confining to the terms of the third order with respect to h and k. Use the result to compute $e^{0.1} \sin 0.49\pi$.

3249. Find first several terms of the expansion of the function $e^x \sin y$ into Taylor's series in the neighbourhood of the point $(0, 0)$.

3250. Find first several terms of the expansion of the function $e^x \ln(1+y)$ into Taylor's series in the neighbourhood of the point (0, 0).

In Problems 3251 to 3256 expand the given functions into Taylor's series at $x_0 = 0$, $y_0 = 0$.

3251. $z = \dfrac{1}{1 - x - y + xy}$.

3252*. $z = \arctan \dfrac{x - y}{1 + xy}$.

3253. $z = \ln(1 - x)\ln(1 - y)$.

3254. $z = \ln \dfrac{1 - x - y + xy}{1 - x - y}$.

3255. $z = \sin(x^2 + y^2)$.

3256. $z = e^x \cos y$.

3257. Find first several terms of the expansion in powers of $x - 1$, $y - 1$ of the function z represented implicitly by the equation

$$z^3 + yz - xy^2 - x^3 = 0$$

and equal to unity at $x = 1$, $y = 1$.

3258. Derive the approximate formula

$$\frac{\cos x}{\cos y} \approx 1 - \frac{1}{2}(x^2 - y^2)$$

for sufficiently small values of $|x|, |y|$.

Extrema

In Problems 3259 to 3267 find the stationary points of the functions.

3259. $z = 2x^3 + xy^2 + 5x^2 + y^2$.

3260. $z = e^{2x}(x + y^2 + 2y)$.

3261. $z = xy(a - x - y)$.

3262. $z = (2ax - x^2)(2by - y^2)$.

3263. $z = \sin x + \sin y + \cos(x + y)\left(0 \le x \le \dfrac{\pi}{4}, 0 \le y \le \dfrac{\pi}{4}\right)$.

3264. $z = \dfrac{a + bx + cy}{\sqrt{1 + x^2 + y^2}}$.

3265. $z = y\sqrt{1 + x} + x\sqrt{1 + y}$.

3266. $u = 2x^2 + y^2 + 2z - xy - xz$.

3267. $u = 3\ln x + 2\ln y + 5\ln z + \ln(22 - x - y - z)$.

3268. Figure 60 illustrates the level lines of the function $z = f(x, y)$. What singularities has the function at points A, B, C, D and along the line EF?

3269. A function z is specified implicitly $2x^2 + 2y^2 + z^2 + 8xz - z + 8 = 0$. Find its stationary points.

3270. A function z is specified implicitly

$$5x^2 + 5y^2 + 5z^2 - 2xy - 2xz - 2yz - 72 = 0.$$

Find its stationary points.

3271. Find the points of extremum of the function $z = 2xy - 3x^2 - 2z^2 + 10$.

3272. Find the points of extremum of the function $z = 4(x - y) - x^2 + y^2$.

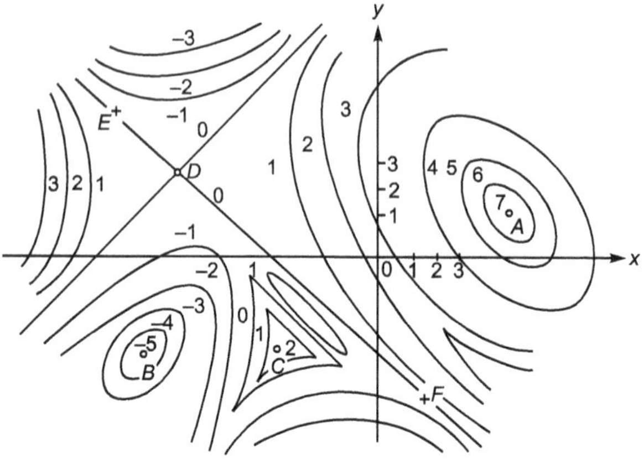

Fig. 60

3273. Find the points of extremum of the function

$$z = x^2 + xy + y^2 + x - y + 1.$$

3274. Make sure that the function $z = x^2 + xy + y^2 + \frac{a^3}{x} + \frac{a^2}{y}$ has a minimum at the point $x = y = \frac{a}{\sqrt[3]{3}}$.

3275. Make sure that at $x = \sqrt{2}$, $y = \sqrt{2}$ and at $x = -\sqrt{2}$, $y = -\sqrt{2}$ the function $z = x^4 + y^4 - 2x^2 - 4xy - 2y^2$ has a minimum.

3276. Make sure that the function $z = x^3 + y^2 - 6xy - 39x + 18y + 20$ has a minimum at $x = 5$, $y = 6$.

3277. Find the stationary points of the function $z = x^3y^2(12 - x - y)$ which satisfy the condition $x > 0$, $y > 0$, and investigate their character.

3278. Find the stationary points of the function $z = x^3 + y^3 - 3xy$ and investigate their character.

The greatest and least values

3279. Find the greatest and the least value of the function $z = x^2 - y^2$ within the circle $x^2 + y^2 \leq 4$.

3280. Find the greatest and the least value of the function $z = x^2 + 2xy - 4x + 8y$ in the rectangle bounded by the straight lines $x = 0$, $y = 0$, $x = 1$, $y = 2$.

3281. Find the greatest and the least value of the function $z = x^2y(4 - x - y)$ within the triangle bounded by the straight lines $x = 0$, $y = 0$, $x + y = 6$.

3282. Find the greatest and the least value of the function $z = e^{-x^2 - y^2}(2x^2 + 3y^2)$ inside the circle $x^2 + y^2 \le 4$.

3283. Find the greatest and the least values of the function $z = \sin x + \sin y + \sin(x + y)$ inside the rectangle $0 \le x \le \frac{\pi}{2}$; $0 \le y \le \frac{\pi}{2}$.

3284. Split a positive number a into three positive addends so that their product is the greatest possible.

3285. Represent a positive number a in the form of a product of four positive factors so that their sum is the least possible.

3286. On the plane Oxy find the point for which the sum of its squared distances from the three straight lines $x = 0$, $y = 0$, $x + 2y - 16 = 0$ is the least possible.

3287. Through the point (a, b, c) pass a plane so that the volume of the tetrahedron cut by it from the coordinate trihedral angle is the least possible.

3288. Given n points : $A_1(x_1, y_1, z_1), \ldots, A_n(x_n, y_n, z_n)$. On the plane Oxy find a point for which the sum of its squared distances from all the given points is the least possible.

3289. Given three points : $A(0, 0, 12)$, $B(0, 0, 4)$ and $C(8, 0, 8)$. On the plane Oxy find a point D such that the sphere passing through A, B, C and D has the least possible radius.

3290. In a given sphere of diameter $2R$ inscribe a rectangular parallelepiped of the greatest volume.

Relative extrema

In Problems 3291 to 3296 investigate the functions for extremum.

3291. $z = x^m + y^m$ $(m > 1)$ for $x + y = 2$ $(x \ge 0, y \ge 0)$.

3292. $z = xy$ for $x^2 + y^2 = 2a^2$.

3293. $z = \frac{1}{x} + \frac{1}{y}$ for $\frac{1}{x^2} + \frac{1}{y^2} = \frac{1}{a^2}$.

3294. $z = a\cos^2 x + b\cos^2 y$ for $y - x = \frac{\pi}{4}$.

3295. $u = x + y + z$ for $\frac{1}{x} + \frac{1}{y} + \frac{1}{z} = 1$.

3296. $u = xyz$ for $\begin{cases} (1)\ x + y + z = 5; \\ (2)\ xy + xz + yz = 8. \end{cases}$

3297*. Prove the validity of the relationship

$$\frac{x_1^2 + x_2^2 + \ldots + x_n^2}{n} \geq \left(\frac{x_1 + x_2 + \ldots + x_n}{n}\right)^2.$$

3298. $f(x, y) = x^3 - 3xy^2 + 18y$, and $3x^2y - y^3 - 6x = 0$. Prove that the function $f(x, y)$ reaches an extremum at points $x = y = \pm\sqrt{3}$.

3299. Find the minimum of the function $u = ax^2 + by^2 + cz^2$, where a, b, c are positive constants and x, y, z enter the relationship $x + y + z = 1$.

3300. Find the greatest and the least value of the function $u = y^2 + 4z^2 - 4yz - 2xz - 2xy$, provided $2x^2 + 3y^2 + 6z^2 = 1$.

3301. On the plane $3x - 2z = 0$ find the point, such that the sum of its squared distances from the points $A(1, 1, 1)$ and $B(2, 3, 4)$ is the least possible.

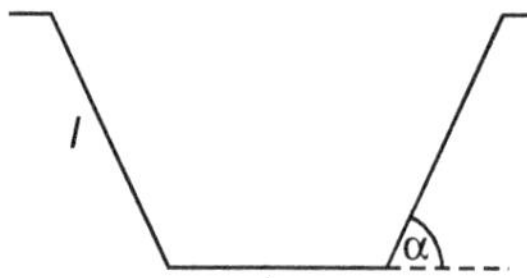

Fig. 61

3302. On the plane $x + y - 2z = 0$ find the point, such that the sum of its squared distances from the planes $x + 3z = 6$ and $y + 3z = 2$ is the least possible.

3303. Given the points : $A(4, 0, 4)$, $B(4, 4, 4)$, $C(4, 4, 0)$. On the surface of the sphere $x^2 + y^2 + z^2 = 4$ find the point S such that the volume of the pyramid $SABC$ is : (a) the greatest, (b) the least possible, Check the answer geometrically.

3304. Find a rectangular parallelepiped of a given volume V having the least surface.

3305. Find a rectangular parallelepiped of a given surface S having the greatest volume.

3306. Find the volume of the greatest rectangular parallelepiped which can be inscribed in an ellipsoid with the semiaxes a, b and c.

3307. A tent has the shape of a cylinder with a conic top mounted on it. What must the relationship among the linear dimensions be so that to spend the least possible amount of the material to construct the tent of a given volume?

3308. The cross section of a canal has the form of an equilateral trapezoid of a given area. What must its dimensions be to obtain the least possible wetted surface (Fig. 61)?

3309. Of all rectangular parallelepipeds having a given diagonal find the one with the greatest volume.

3310. Indicate the outer dimensions of an open (without a cover) box, having the form of a rectangular parallelepiped with a given wall thickness

α and volume V, which will make it possible to construct it from the least possible amount of the material.

3311. Find the greatest volume of a parallelepiped with the given sum $12a$ of all its edges.

3312. About a given ellipse describe a triangle with the base parallel to the major axis and of the least possible area.

3313. On the ellipse $\frac{x^2}{4} + \frac{y^2}{9} = 1$ find the points least distant and most distant from the straight line $3x + y - 9 = 0$.

3314. On the parabola $x^2 + 2xy + y^2 + 4y = 0$ find the point least distant from the straight line $3x - 6y + 4 = 0$.

3315. On the parabola $2x^2 - 4xy + 2y^2 - x - y = 0$ find the point nearest to the straight line $9x - 7y + 16 = 0$.

3316. Find the points on the surface $2x^2 + 3y^2 + 2z^2 + 2xz = 6$ which are most distant from the plane $z = 0$.

3317. Find the sides of a right-angled triangle having the least perimeter at a given area S.

3318. Inscribed in a right elliptic cone, whose base semiaxes are equal to a and b, and the altitude to H, is a prism with a rectangular base so that the sides of the base are parallel to the axes, and the point at which the diagonals of the base intersect lies in the centre of the ellipse. What must the sides of the base and the altitude of the prism be to obtain the greatest volume? What is this volume?

3319. Find the regular triangular pyramid of a given volume having the least sum of edges.

3320. Given two points on an ellipse; find a third point on the same ellipse such that the area of the triangle specified by these three points is the greatest possible.

3321. To the ellipse $\frac{x^2}{a^2} + \frac{y^2}{b^2} = 1$ draw the normal most distant from the origin.

3322. On the ellipsoid of revolution $\frac{x^2}{96} + y^2 + z^2 = 1$ find the points least distant and most distant from the plane $3x + 4y + 12z = 288$.

3323. Given the plane curves $f(x, y) = 0$ and $\varphi(x, y) = 0$. Show that the distance between the points (α, β) and (ξ, η) lying respectively on these curves reaches its extremum if the following condition is fulfilled:

$$\frac{\alpha - \xi}{\beta - \eta} = \frac{\left(\frac{\partial f}{\partial x}\right)_{\substack{x = \alpha \\ y = \beta}}}{\left(\frac{\partial f}{\partial y}\right)_{\substack{x = \alpha \\ y = \beta}}} = \frac{\left(\frac{\partial \varphi}{\partial x}\right)_{\substack{x = \xi \\ y = \eta}}}{\left(\frac{\partial \varphi}{\partial y}\right)_{\substack{x = \xi \\ y = \eta}}}.$$

Taking advantage of this fact, find the shortest distance between the ellipse $x^2 + 2xy + 5y^2 - 16y = 0$ and the straight line $x + y - 8 = 0$.

2. Plane Curves

Tangents and normals

In Problems 3324 to 3327 write the equations of the tangent and normal to the lines at the indicates points.

3324. $x^3y + y^3x = 3 - x^2y^2$ at the point $(1, 1)$.

3325. $a^2(x^4 + y^4) - x^3y^3 = 9a^6$ at the point $(a, 2a)$.

3326. $\cos xy = x + 2y$ at the point $(1, 0)$.

3327. $2x^3 - x^2y + 3x^2 + 4xy - 5x - 3y + 6 = 0$ at the point of intersection with the y-axis.

Singular points

In Problems 3328 to 3340 find singular points of the curves.

3328. $y^2 = x^2(x - 1)$.

3329. $a^2x^2 = (x^2 + y^2)y^2$.

3330. $y^2 = ax^2 + bx^5$.

3331. $y^2 = x(x - a)^2$.

3332. $x^{2/3} + y^{2/3} = a^{2/3}$.

3333. $x^4 + y^4 - 8x^2 - 10y^2 + 16 = 0$.

3334. $x^4 + 12x^3 - 6y^3 + 36x^2 + 27y^2 - 81 = 0$.

3335. $x^3 + y^3 + 3axy = 0$.

3336. $x^2 + y^2 = x^4 + y^4$.

3337. $y = x \ln x$.

3338. $y^2 = \sin^3 x$.

3339. $y^2 = (x - a)^3$.

3340. $x^5 = (y - x^2)^2$.

Envelopes

3341. Find the equation of the envelope of the family of straight lines $y = ax + f(a)$. In particular, put $f(a) = \cos a$.

3342. Find the envelope of the family of straight lines $y = 2mx + m^4$.

3343. A pencil of straight lines is drawn through the point $A\ (a, 0)$. Find the envelope of the family of normals drawn to the straight lines of this pencil at the points of their intersection with the y-axis.

3344. Find the envelope of the family of parabolas $y^2 = a\,(x - a)$.

3345. Find the envelope of the family of parabolas $ax^2 + a^2y = 1$.

3346. Find the envelope of the family of parabolas $y = a^2\ (x - a)^2$.

3347. Find the envelope of the family of semicubical parabolas $(y - a)^2 = (x - a)^3$.

3348. Find the envelope of the family of curves $x^2 + ay^2 = a^3$.

3349. Find the envelope of the family of ellipses $\frac{x^2}{a^2} + \frac{y^2}{b^2} = 1$, provided the sum of the semiaxes of each ellipse is equal to d.

3350. The radii of a circle are projected on its two mutually perpendicular diameters and on the projections, as on the semiaxes, ellipses are constructed. Find the envelope of the family of ellipses thus obtained.

3351. Find the envelope of the family of circles with the centres on the parabola $y = bx^2$ and passing through its vertex.

3352. A straight line moves so that the sum of the lengths of the x- and y-intercepts remains constant and equals a. Find the envelope of the obtained family of straight lines.

3353. Find the envelope of the diameter of a circle rolling (without sliding) along a given straight line(the radius of the circle is R).

3354. On the chords of a circle (or radius R) parallel to a given direction, as on the diameters, circles are described. Find the envelope of this family of circles.

3355. A straight line moves so that the product of the x- and y-intercepts is equal to a constant a. Find the envelope of these straight lines.

3356. Show that any curve is the envelope of the family of its tangents.

3357. Show that the evolute of a curve is the envelope of its normals. Find the evolute of the parabola $y^2 = 2px$ as the locus of the centres of curvature and as the envelope of the family of normals. Compare the results.

3358. Prove the theorem : if the curve (A) is the envelope of the family of straight lines $x \cos t + y \sin t - f(t) = 0$, then the evolute of the curve (A) is the envelope of the family of straight lines $-x \sin t + y \cos t - f'(t) = 0$.

3359. The radius vector $\overline{OM}$ of an arbitrary point M of the equilateral hyperbola $xy = 1$ is projected on the asymptotes of the hyperbola. Find the envelope of the ellipses constructed on the projections of $\overline{OM}$ as on the semiaxes.

3. Vector Function of a Scalar Argument. Space Curves. Surfaces

Vector function of a scalar argument

3360. Prove the differentiation formulas

$$\frac{d}{dt}(\mathbf{u}\,\mathbf{v}) = \mathbf{u}\frac{d\mathbf{v}}{dt} + \mathbf{v}\frac{d\mathbf{u}}{dt},\quad \frac{d}{dt}(\mathbf{u}\times\mathbf{v}) = \mathbf{u}\frac{d\mathbf{v}}{dt} + \frac{d\mathbf{u}}{dt}\times\mathbf{v}.$$

Here **u** and **v** are vector functions of the scalar argument t.

3361. Given $\mathbf{r} = \mathbf{r}(t)$. Find the derivatives.

(a) $\frac{d}{dt}(\mathbf{r}^2)$; (b) $\frac{d}{dt}\left(\mathbf{r}\,\frac{d\mathbf{r}}{dt}\right)$; (c) $\frac{d}{dt}\left(\mathbf{r}\times\frac{d\mathbf{r}}{dt}\right)$; (d) $\frac{d}{dt}\left(\mathbf{r}\,\frac{d\mathbf{r}}{dt}\,\frac{d^2\mathbf{r}}{dt^2}\right)$.

3362. Given that for all values of t the vectors $\mathbf{r}(t)$ and $\frac{d\mathbf{r}}{dt}$ are collinear. Prove that the vectors $\frac{d^2\mathbf{r}}{dt^2}, \frac{d^3\mathbf{r}}{dt^3}, \ldots, \frac{d^n\mathbf{r}}{dt^n}$ are also collinear to the vector $\mathbf{r}(t)$.

3363. Prove that if the absolute value $|\mathbf{r}|$ of the function $\mathbf{r}(t)$ remains unchanged for all values of t, then $\frac{d\mathbf{r}}{dt}\perp\mathbf{r}$. What is the geometrical meaning of this fact? Is the converse theorem true?

3364. Given $\mathbf{r} = \mathbf{a}\cos\omega t + \mathbf{b}\sin\omega t$, where **a** and **b** are constant vectors. Prove that

(1) $\mathbf{r}\times\frac{d\mathbf{r}}{dt} = \omega\mathbf{a}\times\mathbf{b}$ and (2) $\frac{d^2\mathbf{r}}{dt^2} + \omega^2\mathbf{r} = 0$.

3365. Prove that if **e** is a unit vector of the direction of the vector **E**, then

$$\mathbf{e}\times d\,\mathbf{e} = \frac{\mathbf{E}\times d\,\mathbf{E}}{E^2}.$$

3366. Prove that if $\mathbf{r} = \mathbf{a}\,e^{\omega t} + \mathbf{b}\,e^{-\omega t}$, where **a** and **b** are constant vectors, then

$$\frac{d^2\mathbf{r}}{dt^2} - \omega^2\mathbf{r} = 0.$$

3367. $\mathbf{u} = \alpha(x, y, z, t)\,\mathbf{i} + \beta(x, y, z, t)\,\mathbf{j} + \gamma(x, y, z, t)\,\mathbf{k}$, where x, y, z are functions of t. Prove that

$$\frac{d\mathbf{u}}{dt} = \frac{\partial\mathbf{u}}{dt} + \frac{\partial\mathbf{u}}{dx}\frac{dx}{dt} + \frac{\partial\mathbf{u}}{\partial y}\frac{dy}{dt} + \frac{\partial\mathbf{u}}{dz}\frac{dz}{dt}.$$

3368. Given : $\mathbf{r} = \mathbf{r}(u)$, $u = \varphi(x)$. Express the derivatives $\frac{d\mathbf{r}}{dx}, \frac{d^2\mathbf{r}}{dx^2}, \frac{d^3\mathbf{r}}{dx^3}$ in terms of $\frac{d\mathbf{r}}{du}, \frac{d^2\mathbf{r}}{du^2}, \frac{d^3\mathbf{r}}{du^3}$.

3369. Prove that if for the vector function $\mathbf{r} = \mathbf{r}(t)$ the relationship $\frac{d\mathbf{r}}{dt} = \alpha \cdot \mathbf{r}$, ($\alpha = \text{const}$) is valid, then the hodograph of the function $\mathbf{r}(t)$ is a ray emanating from the pole.

3370. Let the function $\mathbf{r}(t)$ be defined, continuous and differentiable in the interval, (t_1, t_2), and $\mathbf{r}(t_1) = \mathbf{r}(t_2)$. Apply Rolle's theorem to the function $\mathbf{a} \cdot \mathbf{r}$, where $\mathbf{a}$ is an arbitrary constant vector. Explain the result geometrically.

3371. Given the radius vector $\mathbf{r}\{a \sin t, -a \cos t, bt^2\}$ (t time, a and b constants) of a point moving in space. Find the hodographs of velocity and acceleration.

3372. Find the path of motion for which the radius vector of the moving point satisfies the condition $\frac{d\mathbf{r}}{dt} = \mathbf{a} \times \mathbf{r}$, where $\mathbf{a}$ is a constant vector.

3373. A material point moves according to the law $\mathbf{r} = \mathbf{v}_0 t + \frac{1}{2} \mathbf{g} t^2$ ($\mathbf{r}$ is the radius vector of this point at the time t, $\mathbf{v}_0$ and $\mathbf{g}$ are the given vectors). Show that : (1) the kinetic energy of the material point is a quadratic function of time; (2) $\mathbf{v}_0$ is the initial velocity (i.e., the value of the velocity vector at the time $t = 0$); (3) the motion is performed with a constant acceleration equal to the vector $\mathbf{g}$; (4) the point moves in a parabola (if only the vectors $\mathbf{v}_0$ and $\mathbf{g}$ are not collinear) whose axis is parallel to the vector $\mathbf{g}$.

3374. The law of motion of a material point is specified by the formula $\mathbf{r} = \mathbf{a} \cos t + \mathbf{b} \sin t + \mathbf{c}$, where the vectors $\mathbf{a}$ and $\mathbf{b}$ are mutually perpendicular. Determine the path of motion. At what times will the velocity attain the extreme value? At what moments will the acceleration attain the extreme value?

3375. The formulas for transforming the Cartesian coordinates to spherical coordinates have the form $x = \rho \sin\theta \cos\varphi$, $y = \rho \sin\theta \sin\varphi$, $z = \rho \cos\theta$, where ρ is the distance of a given point from the pole, θ its latitude, φ the azimuth or longitude. Find the components of the velocity of a material point in the directions of the orthogonal unit vectors $\mathbf{e}_\rho$, $\mathbf{e}_\theta$, $\mathbf{e}_\varphi$.

Space curves

In Problems 3376 to 3383 derive the equations of the tangent line and normal plane to the given curves at the indicated points.

3376. $\mathbf{r}\left(\frac{t^4}{4}, \frac{t^3}{3}, \frac{t^2}{2}\right)$, i.e., $x = \frac{t^4}{4}, y = \frac{t^3}{3}, z = \frac{t^2}{2}$, at an arbitrary point.

3377. $x = a\cos\varphi,\ y = a\sin\varphi,\ z = \frac{k}{2\pi}\varphi$ at the point $\left(\frac{a\sqrt{2}}{2}, \frac{a\sqrt{2}}{2}, \frac{k}{8}\right)$. Prove that the tangent forms one and the same angle with the z-axis at all points of the curve.

3378. $x = at,\ y = \frac{1}{2}at^2,\ z = \frac{1}{3}at^3$ at the point $(6a, 18a, 72a)$.

3379. $x = t - \sin t,\ y = 1 - \cos t,\ z = 4\sin\frac{t}{2}$ at the point $\left(\frac{\pi}{2} - 1, 1, 2\sqrt{2}\right)$.

3380. $y^2 + z^2 = 25,\ x^2 + y^2 = 10$ at the point $(1, 3, 4)$.

3381. $2x^2 + 3y^2 + z^2 = 47,\ x^2 + 2y^2 = z$ at the point $(-2, 1, 6)$.

3382. $x^2 + y^2 = z^2,\ x = y$ at the point (x_0, y_0, z_0).

3383. $x^3 + z^3 = a^3,\ y^3 + z^3 = b^3$ at an arbitrary point.

3384. On the curve $\mathbf{r}\{\cos t, \sin t, e^t\}$ find the point at which the tangent is parallel to the plane

$$\sqrt{3}\,x + y - 4 = 0$$

In Problems 3385 to 3387 derive the equations of the osculating plane, principal normal and binormal to the given curves at the indicated points.

3385. $y^2 = x,\ x^2 = z$ at the point $(1, 1, 1)$.

3386. $x^2 = 2az,\ y^2 = 2bz$ at an arbitrary point.

3387. $\mathbf{r}\{e^t, e^{-t}, t\sqrt{2}\}$ at the point $(e, e^{-1}, \sqrt{2})$.

3388. Show that the tangents, principal normals and binormals to the line $\mathbf{r}\{e^t\cos t, e^t\sin t, e^t\}$ form constant angles with the z-axis.

In Problems 3389 to 3392 derive the equations of the tangent line, normal plane, binormal, osculating plane, principal normal and rectifying plane to the given curves at the indicated points.

3389. $x = t^2,\ y = 1 - t,\ z = t^3$ at point $(1, 0, 1)$.

3390. $x^2 + y^2 + z^2 = 3,\ x^2 + y^2 = 2$ at point $(1, 1, 1)$.

3391. $\mathbf{r}\{\sin t, \cos t, \tan t\}$ at the point $\left(\frac{\sqrt{2}}{2}, \frac{\sqrt{2}}{2}, 1\right)$.

3392. $\mathbf{r}\{t^3 - t^2 - 5, 3t^2 + 1, 2t^3 - 16\}$ at the point corresponding to the value of the parameter $t = 2$.

3393. Show that the curve $\mathbf{r}\{2t + 3, 3t - 1, t^2\}$ has one and the same osculating plane at all points.

3394. Prove that the curve

$$\mathbf{r}\{a_1t^2 + b_1t + c_1,\ a_2t^2 + b_2t + c_2,\ a_3t^2 + b_3t + c_3\}$$

is a plane one and derive the equation of the plane it is contained in.

3395. Find the radius of twist of the curve $\mathbf{r}\ \{\cos t, \sin t, \cosh t\}$.

3396. Find the radius of curvature of the curve $\mathbf{r}\ \{\ln \cos t, k \ln \sin t, \sqrt{2}t\}$, $0 < t < \frac{\pi}{2}$. Show that the twist at any of its points is equal to the curvature at this point.

3397. Show that for the line $\mathbf{r}\ \{e^t \cos t, e^t \sin t, e^t\}$ (see Problem 3388) the ratio of the curvature to twist remains constant for all the points of the curve.

3398. What is the expression for the curvature of the space curve specified by the equations $y = \varphi(x)$, $z = \psi(x)$?

3399. Express the vectors τ_1, ν_1, β_1 in terms of the derivatives of the radius vector of a point on the curve $\mathbf{r} = \mathbf{r}(t)$.

3400. Express each of the vectors τ_1, ν_1, β_1 in terms of the other two.

3401. Find the vector $\omega(s)$ satisfying the conditions

$$\frac{d\tau_1}{ds} = \omega \times \tau_1; \frac{d\nu_1}{ds} = \omega \times \nu_1; \frac{d\beta_1}{ds} = \omega \times \beta_1.$$

Arc length of a space curve

In Problems 3402 to 3409 find the arc lengths of the given curves.

3402. $\mathbf{r}\ \{2t, \ln t, t^2\}$ from $t = 1$ to $t = 10$.

3403. $\mathbf{r}\ \{a \cos t, a \sin t, a \ln \cos t\}$ from the point $(a, 0, 0)$ to the point $\left(\frac{a\sqrt{2}}{2}, \frac{a\sqrt{2}}{2}, -\frac{a}{2}\ln 2\right)$.

3404. $\mathbf{r}\ \{e^t \cos t, e^t \sin t, e^t\}$ from the point $(1, 0, 1)$ to the point corresponding to the parameter t.

3405. $x^2 = 3y$, $2xy = 9z$ from the point $(0, 0, 0)$ to the point $(3, 3, 2)$.

3406. $z^2 = 2ax$, $9y^2 = 16xz$ from the point $(0, 0, 0)$ to the point $(2a, 8a/3, 2a)$.

3407. $4ax = (y + z)^2$, $4x^2 + 3y^2 = 3z^2$ from the origin to the point (x, y, z).

3408. $y = \sqrt{2ax - x^2}$, $z = a \ln \dfrac{2a}{2a - x}$ from the origin to the point (x, y, z).

3409. $y = a \arcsin \dfrac{x}{a}$, $z = \dfrac{1}{4} a \ln \dfrac{a + x}{a - x}$ from the origin to the point $\left(\frac{a}{2}, \frac{a\pi}{6}, \frac{a}{4}\ln 3\right)$.

Surfaces

In Problems 3410 to 3419 find the equations of the tangent planes and normals at the indicated points.

3410. $z = 2x^2 - 4y^2$ at the point (2, 1, 4).

3411. $z = xy$ at the point (1, 1, 1).

3412. $z = \dfrac{x^3 - 3axy + y^3}{a^2}$ at the point $(a, a, -a)$.

3413. $z = \sqrt{x^2 + y^2} - xy$ at the point $(3, 4, -7)$.

3414. $z = \arctan \dfrac{y}{x}$ at the point $\left(1, 1, \dfrac{\pi}{4}\right)$.

3415. $\dfrac{x^2}{a^2} + \dfrac{y^2}{b^2} + \dfrac{z^2}{c^2} = 1$ at the point $\left(\dfrac{a\sqrt{3}}{3}, \dfrac{b\sqrt{3}}{3}, \dfrac{c\sqrt{3}}{3}\right)$.

3416. $x^3 + y^3 + z^3 + xyz - 6 = 0$ at the point $(1, 2, -1)$.

3417. $3x^4 - 4y^3z + 4z^2xy - 4z^3x + 1 = 0$ at the point (1, 1, 1).

3418. $(z^2 - x^2)\,xyz - y^5 = 5$ at the point (1, 1, 2).

3419. $4 + \sqrt{x^2 + y^2 + z^2} = x + y + z$ at the point (2, 3, 6).

3420. Show that the equation $\dfrac{x_0x}{a^2} + \dfrac{y_0y}{b^2} + \dfrac{z_0z}{c^2} = 1$ is that of the tangent plane to the ellipsoid $\dfrac{x^2}{a^2} + \dfrac{y^2}{b^2} + \dfrac{z^2}{c^2} = 1$ at any of its points $M_0\,(x_0, y_0, z_0)$.

3421. Draw the tangent plane to the ellipsoid $x^2 + 2y^2 + z^2 = 1$ parallel to the plane $x - y + 2z = 0$.

3422. Draw the tangent plane to the ellipsoid $\dfrac{x^2}{a^2} + \dfrac{y^2}{b^2} + \dfrac{z^2}{c^2}$ cutting equal intercepts off the positive axes of coordinates.

3423. Show that the surfaces $x + 2y - \ln z + 4 = 0$ and $x^2 - xy - 8x + z + 5 = 0$ touch each other (i.e., have a common tangent plane) at the point $(2, -3, 1)$.

3424. Prove that all the planes tangent to the surface $z = xf\left(\dfrac{y}{x}\right)$ intersect at one point.

3425. Write the equations of the tangent plane and the normal to the sphere $\mathbf{r}\,\{u \cos v, u \sin v, \sqrt{a^2 - u^2}\}$ at the point $\mathbf{r}_0\,\{x_0, y_0, z_0\}$.

3426. Write the equations of the tangent plane and the normal to the hyperbolic paraboloid $\mathbf{r}\,\{a\,(u + v), b\,(u - v), uv\}$ at an arbitrary point $\{x_0, y_0, z_0\}$.

3427. Prove that the surfaces $x^2 + y^2 + z^2 = ax$ and $x^2 + y^2 + z^2 = by$ are orthogonal to each other.

3428. Show that the tangent plane to the surface $xyz = a^3$ at any points forms with the planes of coordinates a tetrahedron of a constant volume. Find the volume.

3429. Show that the tangent planes to the surface $\sqrt{x} + \sqrt{y} + \sqrt{z} = \sqrt{a}$ cut off the coordinate axes intercepts whose sum is equal to a.

3430. For the surface $z = xy$ write the equation of the tangent plane perpendicular to the straight line $\frac{x+2}{2} = \frac{y+2}{2} = \frac{z-1}{-1}$.

3431. Show that for the surface $x^2 + y^2 + z^2 = y$ the length of the segment of the normal contained between the surface and the plane xOy is equal to the distance between the origin and the trace of the normal on this plane.

3432. Prove that the normal to the surface of the ellipsoid of revolution $\frac{x^2 + z^2}{9} + \frac{y^2}{25} = 1$ at any point P (x, y, z) forms equal angles with the straight lines PA and PB if A $(0, -4, 0)$ and B $(0, 4, 0)$.

3433. Prove that all the normals to the surface of revolution $z = f(\sqrt{x^2 + y^2})$ intersect with the axis of revolution.

3434. To the surface $x^2 - y^2 - 3z = 0$ draw the tangent plane passing through the point A $(0, 0, -1)$ parallel to the straight line $\frac{x}{2} = \frac{y}{1} = \frac{z}{2}$.

3435. On the surface $x^2 + y^2 + z^2 - 6y + 4z = 12$, find the points at which the tangent planes are parallel to the planes of coordinates.

3436. Derive the equation of the tangent plane to the surface $x = u + v$, $y = u^2 + v^2$, $z = y^3 + v^3$ at an arbitrary point. Express the coefficients of this equation in terms of:

(a) the values of the parameters u_0 and v_0,

(b) the coordinates x_0, y_0, z_0 of the point of tendency.

3437. Find the locus of the feet of the perpendiculars dropped from the origin on the tangent planes to the paraboloid of revolution $2pz = x^2 + y^2$.

3438. Find the locus of the feet of the perpendiculars dropped from the origin on the tangent planes to the surface $xyz = a^3$.

4. Scalar Field. Gradient. Directional Derivative

Gradient

3439. (1) $\psi(x, y) = x^2 - 2xy + 3y - 1$. Find the projections of the gradient at the point (1, 2).

(2) $u = 5x^2y - 3xy^3 + y^4$. Find the projections of the gradient at an arbitrary point.

3440. (1) $z=x^2+y^2$. Find grad z at the point (3, 2).

(2) $z=\sqrt{4+x^2+y^2}$. Find grad z at the point (2, 1).

(3) $z=\arctan\frac{y}{x}$. Find grad z at the point (x_0, y_0).

3441. (1) Find the steepest gradient of the surface $z=\ln(x^2+4y^2)$ at the point (6, 4, ln 100).

(2) Find the steepest gradient of the surface $z=x^y$ at the point (2, 2, 4).

3442. What is the direction of maximum variation of the function $\varphi(x, y, z)=x\sin z-y\cos z$ at the origin?

3443. (1) $z=\arcsin\frac{x}{x+y}$. Find the angle between the gradients of this function at the points (1, 1) and (3, 4).

(2) Given the functions $z=\sqrt{x^2+y^2}$ and $z=x-3y+\sqrt{3xy}$. Find the angle between the gradients of these functions at the point (3, 4).

3444. (1) Find the point at which the gradient of the function $z=\ln\left(x+\frac{1}{y}\right)$ is equal to $\mathbf{i}-\frac{16}{9}\mathbf{j}$.

(2) Find the points at which the modulus of the gradient of the function $z=(x^2+y^2)^{3/2}$ is equal to 2.

3445. Prove the following relationships (φ and ψ differentiable functions, c constant):

$$\text{grad}(\varphi+\psi)\ \text{grad}\,\varphi+\text{grad}\,\psi,\ \text{grad}(c+\varphi)=\text{grad}\,\varphi,$$
$$\text{grad}(c\varphi)=c\,\text{grad}\,\varphi,\ \text{grad}(\varphi\psi)=\varphi\,\text{grad}\,\psi+\psi\,\text{grad}\,\varphi,$$
$$\text{grad}(\varphi^n)=n\varphi^{n-1}\,\text{grad}\,\varphi,\ \text{grad}[\varphi(\psi)]=\varphi'(\psi)\,\text{grad}\,\psi.$$

3446. $z=\varphi(u, v), u=\psi(x, y), v=\zeta(x, y)$. Show that

$$\text{grad}\,z=\frac{\partial\varphi}{\partial u}\text{grad}\,u+\frac{\partial\varphi}{\partial v}\text{grad}\,v.$$

3447. (1) $u(x, y, z)=x^2y^2z$. Find the projections of grad u at the point (x_0, y_0, z_0).

(2) $u(x, y, z)=\sqrt{x^2+y^2+z^2}$. Find grad u.

3448. Show that the function $u=\ln(x^2+y^2+z^2)$ satisfies the relationship $u=2\ln 2-\ln(\text{grad}\,u)^2$.

3449. Prove that if x, y, z are functions of t, then $\frac{d}{dt}f(x, y, z)=\text{grad}\,f\cdot\frac{d\mathbf{r}}{dt}$, where $\mathbf{r}=x\mathbf{i}+y\mathbf{j}+z\mathbf{k}$.

3450. Use the relationship proved in the previous problem to find the gradients of the functions

(1) $f=\mathbf{r}^2$; (2) $f=|\mathbf{r}|$; (3) $f=F(\mathbf{r}^2)$; (4) $f=(\mathbf{ar})(\mathbf{br})$;

(5) $f=(\mathbf{abr})$; where **a** and **b** are constant vectors.

Directional derivative

3451. (1) Find the derivative of the function $z = x^3 - 3x^2y + 3xy^2 + 1$ at the point M (3, 1) in the direction leading from this point to the point (6, 5).

(2) Find the derivative of the function $z = \arctan xy$ at the point (1, 1) in the direction of the bisector of the first coordinate angle.

(3) Find the derivative of the function $z = x^2y^2 - xy^3 - 3y - 1$ at the point (2, 1) in the direction leading from this point to the origin.

(4) Find the derivative of the function $z = \ln (e^x + e^y)$ at the origin in the direction of the ray forming an angle α with the x-axis.

3452. Find the derivative of the function $z = \ln (x + y)$ at the point (1, 2), belonging to the parabola $y^2 = 4x$, in the direction of this parabola.

3453. Find the derivative of the function $z = \arctan \dfrac{y}{x}$ at the point $\left(\dfrac{1}{2}, \dfrac{\sqrt{3}}{2}\right)$, belonging to the circle $x^2 + y^2 - 2x = 0$ in the direction of this circle.

3454. Prove that the derivative of the function $z = \dfrac{y^2}{x}$ at any point of the ellipse $2x^2 + y^2 = 1$ in the direction of the normal to the ellipse is equal to zero.

3455. (1) Find the derivative of the function $u = xy^2 + z^3 - xyz$ at the point M (1, 1, 2) in the direction forming with the coordinate axes angles of 60°, 45°, 60°, respectively.

(2) Find the derivative of the function $w = xyz$ at the point A (5, 1, 2) in the direction leading from this point to the point B (9, 4, 14).

3456. Find the derivative of the function $u = x^2y^2z^2$ at the point A (1, – 1, 3) in the direction leading from this point to the point B (0, 1, 1).

3457. Prove that the derivative of the function $u = \dfrac{x^2}{a^2} + \dfrac{y^2}{b^2} + \dfrac{z^2}{c^2}$ at any point M (x, y, z) in the direction leading from this point to the origin is equal to $-\dfrac{2u}{r}$, where $r = \sqrt{x^2 + y^2 + z^2}$.

3458. Prove that the derivative of the function $u = f(x, y, z)$ in the direction of its gradient equals the modulus of the gradient.

3459. Find the derivative of the function

$$u = \frac{1}{r}, \text{ where } r^2 = x^2 + y^2 + z^2$$

in the direction of its gradient.

12

Multiple Integrals

1. Double and Triple Integrals

3460. A thin plate (its thickness is neglected) lies in the plane xOy occupying the domain D. The density of the plate is a function of the point $\gamma = \gamma(P) = \gamma(x, y)$. Find the mass of the plate.

3461. On the plate from Problem 3460 an electric charge is distributed with the surface density $\sigma = \sigma(P) = \sigma(x, y)$. Derive the expression for the total charge of the plate.

3462. The plate (Problem 3460) rotates about the x-axis with an angular velocity ω. Derive the expression for the kinetic energy of the plate.

3463. The specific heat of the plate (Problem 3460) changes according to the law $c = c(P) = c(x, y)$. Find the amount of heat received by the plate when heated from the temperature t_1 to temperature t_2.

3464. A solid occupies the space domain Ω; its density is a function of the point $\gamma = \gamma(P) = \gamma(x, y, z)$. Find the mass of the solid.

3465. An electric charge is uniformly distributed in the solid of Problem 3464; the charge density is a function of the point $\delta = \delta(x, y, z)$. Find the total charge of the solid.

In Problems 3466 to 3476 estimate the integrals.

3466. $\iint\limits_D (x + y + 10)\, d\sigma$, where D is a circle $x^2 + y^2 \leq 4$.

3467. $\iint\limits_D (x^2 + 4y^2 + 9)\, d\sigma$, where D is a circle $x^2 + y^2 \leq 4$.

3468. $\iint\limits_D (x + y + 1)\, d\sigma$, where D is a rectangle $0 \leq x \leq 1$, $0 \leq y \leq 2$

3469. $\iint\limits_D (x + xy - x^2 - y^2)\, d\sigma$, where D is a rectangle $0 \le x \le 1, 0 \le y \le 2$.

3470. $\iint\limits_D xy\,(x + y)\, d\sigma$, where D is a square $0 \le x \le 2, 0 \le y \le 2$.

3471. $\iint\limits_D (x + 1)^y\, d\sigma$, where D is a square $0 \le x \le 2, 0 \le y \le 2$.

3472. $\iint\limits_D (x^2 + y^2 - 2\sqrt{x^2 + y^2} + 2)\, d\sigma$, where D is a square $0 \le x \le 2$, $0 \le y \le 2$.

3473. $\iint\limits_D (x^2 + y^2 - 4x - 4y + 10)\, d\sigma$, where D is a domain enclosed by the ellipse $x^2 + 4y^2 - 2x - 16y + 13 = 0$ (the boundary included).

3474. $\iiint\limits_\Omega (x^2 + y^2 + z^2)\, dv$, where Ω is a sphere $x^2 + y^2 + z^2 \le R^2$.

3475. $\iiint\limits_\Omega (x + y + z)\, dv$, where Ω is a cube $x \ge 1, y \ge 1, z \ge 1$, $x \le 3, y \le 3, z \le 3$.

3476. $\iiint\limits_\Omega (x + y - z + 10)\, dv$, where Ω is a sphere $x^2 + y^2 + z^2 \le 3$.

2. Multiple Integration

Double integral. A rectangular domain

In Problems 3477 to 3484 evaluate the double integrals taken over rectangular domains of integration D specified by the conditions in parentheses.

3477. $\iint\limits_D xy\, dx\, dy$ $\quad (0 \le x \le 1, 0 \le y \le 2)$.

3478. $\iint\limits_D e^{x+y}\, dx\, dy$ $\quad (0 \le x \le 1, 0 \le y \le 1)$.

3479. $\iint\limits_D \frac{x^2}{1 + y^2}\, dx\, dy$ $\quad (0 \le x \le 1, 0 \le y \le 1)$.

3480. $\iint\limits_D \frac{dx\, dy}{(x + y + 1)^2}$ $\quad (0 \le x \le 1, 0 \le y \le 1)$.

3481. $\iint\limits_D \frac{y\,dx\,dy}{(1+x^2+y^2)^{3/2}}$ $(0 \le x \le 1, 0 \le y \le 1)$.

3482. $\iint\limits_D x \sin(x+y)\,dx\,dy$ $\left(0 \le x \le \pi, 0 \le y \le \frac{\pi}{2}\right)$.

3483. $\iint\limits_D x^2 y e^{xy}\,dx\,dy$ $(0 \le x \le 1, 0 \le y \le 2)$.

3484. $\iint\limits_D x^2 y \cos(xy^2)\,dx\,dy$ $\left(0 \le x \le \frac{\pi}{2}, 0 \le y \le 2\right)$.

Double integral. Arbitrary domain

In Problems 3485 to 3497 find the limits of the double integral $\iint\limits_D f(x, y)\,dx, dy$ over the given (finite) domains of integration D.

3485. Parallelogram with the sides

$$x = 3,\ x = 5,\ 3x - 2y + 4 = 0,\ 3x - 2y + 1 = 0.$$

3486. Triangle with the sides $x = 0$, $y = 0$, $x + y = 2$.

3487. $x^2 + y^2 \le 1$, $x \ge 0$, $y \ge 0$.

3488. $x + y \le 1$, $x - y \le 1$, $x \ge 0$.

3489. $y \ge x^2$, $y \le 4 - x^2$.

3490. $\frac{x^2}{4} + \frac{y^2}{9} \le 1$.

3491. $(x-2)^2 + (y-3)^2 \le 4$.

3492. D is bounded by the parabolas $y = x^2$ and $y = \sqrt{x}$.

3493. Triangle with the sides $y = x$, $y = 2x$ and $x + y = 6$.

3494. Parallelogram with the sides $y = x$, $y = x + 3$, $y = -2x + 1$, $y = -2x + 5$.

3495. $y - 2x \le 0$, $2y - x \ge 0$, $xy \le 2$.

3496. $y^2 \le 8x$, $y \le 2x$, $y + 4x - 24 \le 0$.

3497. D is bounded by the hyperbola $y^2 - x^2 = 1$ and the circle $x^2 + y^2 = 9$ (a domain containing the origin is meant.)

In Problems 3498 to 3503 change the order of integration.

3498. $\int_0^1 dy \int_y^{\sqrt{y}} f(x, y)\,dx$.

3499. $\int_{-1}^1 dx \int_0^{\sqrt{1-x^2}} f(x, y)\,dy$.

3500. $\int_0^r dx \int_x^{\sqrt{2rx - x^2}} f(x, y)\,dy$.

3501. $\int_{-2}^2 dx \int_{-\frac{1}{\sqrt{2}}\sqrt{4-x^2}}^{\frac{1}{\sqrt{2}}\sqrt{4-x^2}} f(x, y)\,dy$.

3502. $\int_1^2 dx \int_x^{2x} f(x, y)\, dy.$

3503. $\int_0^2 dx \int_{2x}^{6-x} f(x, y)\, dy.$

3504. Changing the order of integration, write the given expression in the form of one twofold iterated integral:

(1) $\int_0^1 dx \int_0^x f(x, y)\, dy + \int_1^2 dx \int_0^{2-x} f(x, y)\, dy;$

(2) $\int_0^1 dx \int_0^{x^2} f(x, y)\, dy + \int_1^3 dx \int_0^{\frac{3-x}{2}} f(x, y)\, dy;$

(3) $\int_0^1 dx \int_0^{x^{2/3}} f(x, y)\, dy + \int_1^2 dx \int_0^{1-\sqrt{4x-x^2-3}} f(x, y)\, dy.$

3505. Represent the double integral $\iint\limits_D f(x, y)\, dx\, dy$, where D are the domains shown in Figs. 62, 63, 64, 65, as a sum of twofold iterated integrals (with a least number of summands). The regions shown in Figs. 64 and 65 are made up of straight lines and circular arcs.

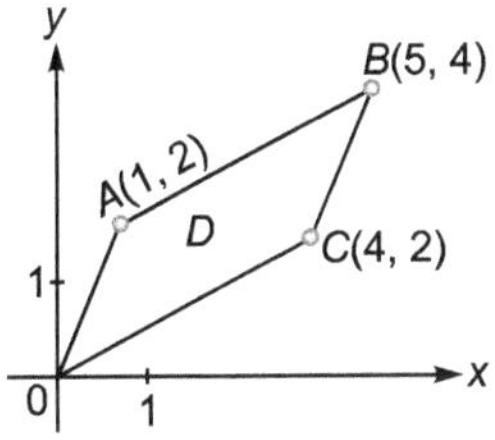

Fig. 62

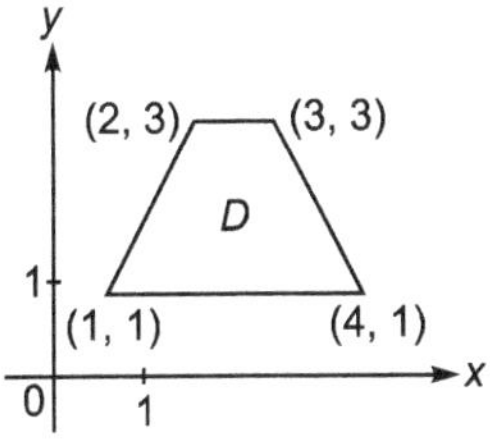

Fig. 63

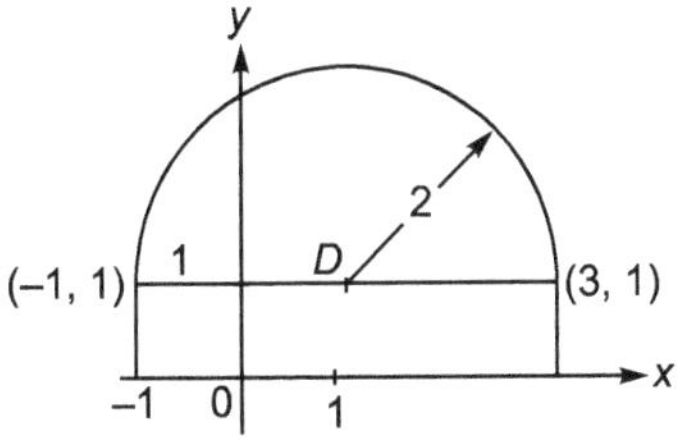

Fig. 64

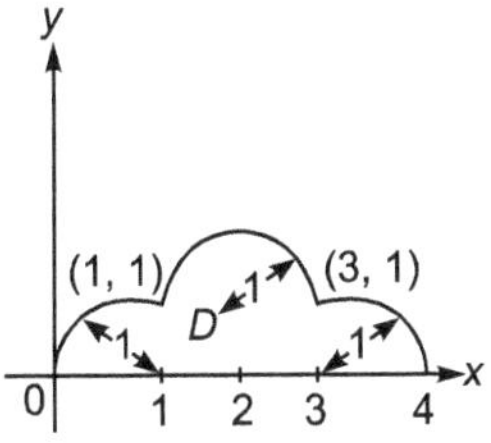

Fig. 65

In Problems 3506 to 3512 evaluate the given integrals.

3506. (1) $\int_0^a dx \int_0^{\sqrt{x}} dy$; (2) $\int_2^4 dx \int_x^{2x} \frac{y}{x}\, dy$; (3) $\int_1^2 dy \int_0^{\ln y} e^x\, dx$.

3507. $\iint\limits_D x^3y^2\, dx\, dy$, D is a circle $x^2 + y^2 \le R^2$.

3508. $\iint\limits_D (x^2 + y^2)\, dx\, dy$, D is a domain bounded by the parabolas $y = x^2$ and $y^2 = x$.

3509. $\iint\limits_D \frac{x^2}{y^2}\, dx\, dy$, D is a domain bounded by the straight line $x = 2$, $y = x$ and the hyperbola $xy = 1$.

3510. $\iint\limits_D \cos(x + y)\, dx\, dy$, D is a domain bounded by the straight lines $x = 0$, $y = \pi$ and $y = x$.

3511. $\iint\limits_D \sqrt{1 - x^2 - y^2}\, dx\, dy$, D is the quarter of the circle $x^2 + y^2 \le 1$, lying in the first quadrant.

3512. $\iint\limits_D x^2y^2\sqrt{1 - x^3 - y^3}\, dx\, dy$, D is the domain bounded by the curve $x^3 + y^3 = 1$ and the coordinate axes.

3513. Find the mean value of the function $z = 12 - 2x - 3y$ in the domain bounded by the straight lines $12 - 2x - 3y = 0$, $x = 0$, $y = 0$.

3514. Find the mean value of the function $z = 2x + y$ in the triangle bounded by the coordinate axes and straight line $x + y = 3$.

3515. Find the mean value of the function $z = x + 6y$ in the triangle bounded by the straight lines $y = x$, $y = 5x$ and $x = 1$.

3516. Find the mean value of the function $z = \sqrt{R^2 - x^2 - y^2}$ in the circle $x^2 + y^2 \le R^2$.

Triple integral

In Problems 3517 to 3524 compute the given threefold iterated integrals.

3517. $\int_0^1 dx \int_0^2 dy \int_0^3 dz$.

3518. $\int_0^a dx \int_0^b dy \int_0^c (x + y + z)\, dz$.

3519. $\int_0^a dx \int_0^x dy \int_0^y xyz\, dz.$

3520. $\int_0^a dx \int_0^x dy \int_0^{xy} x^3y^3z\, dz.$

3521. $\int_0^{e-1} dx \int_0^{e-x-1} dy \int_e^{x+y+e} \frac{\ln(z-x-y)}{(x-e)(x+y-e)}\, dz.$

3522. $\iiint\limits_\Omega \frac{dx\, dy\, dz}{(x+y+z+1)^3}$, Ω is the domain bounded by the planes $x=0,\ y=0,\ z=0,\ x+y+z=1.$

3523. $\iiint\limits_\Omega xy\, dx\, dy\, dz$, Ω is the domain bounded by the hyperbolic paraboloid $z = xy$ and the planes $x + y = 1$ and $z = 0$ $(z \geq 0)$.

3524. $\iiint\limits_\Omega y\cos(z+x)\, dx\, dy\, dz$, Ω is the domain bounded by the cylinder $y = \sqrt{x}$ and the planes $y = 0$, $z = 0$ and $x + z = \frac{\pi}{2}$.

3. Integrals in Polar, Cylindrical and Spherical Coordinates

Double integral

In Problems 3525 to 3531 in the double integral $\iint\limits_D f(x, y)\, dx\, dy$ pass over to the polar coordinates ρ and φ $(x = \rho\cos\varphi,\ y = \rho\sin\varphi)$, and indicate the limits of integration.

3525. D is a circle: (1) $x^2 + y^2 \leq R^2$; (2) $x^2 + y^2 \leq ax$; (3) $x^2 + y^2 \leq by$.

3526. D is the domain bounded by the circles $x^2 + y^2 = 4x$, $x^2 + y^2 = 8x$ and the straight lines $y = x$ and $y = 2x$.

3527. D is the domain which is the common part of two circles $x^2 + y^2 \leq ax$ and $x^2 + y^2 \leq by$.

3528. D is the domain bounded by the straight lines

$$y = x,\quad y = 0 \text{ and } x = 1.$$

3529. D is the smaller of the two segments into which the straight line cuts the circle $x^2 + y^2 \leq 4$.

3530. D is the interior part of the right-hand loop of the Bernoulli lemniscate $(x^2 + y^2)^2 = a^2(x^2 - y^2)$.

3531. D is the domain specified by the inequalities $x \geq 0$, $y \geq 0$, $(x^2 + y^2)^3 \leq 4a^2x^2y^2$.

In Problems 3532 to 3535 transform the twofold iterated integrals to the polar coordinates.

3532. $\int_0^R dx \int_0^{\sqrt{R^2 - x^2}} f(x, y)\, dy.$

3533. $\int_{R/2}^{2R} dy \int_0^{\sqrt{2Ry - y^2}} f(x, y)\, dx.$

3534. $\int_0^R dx \int_0^{\sqrt{R^2 - x^2}} f(x^2 + y^2)\, dy.$

3535. $\int_0^{R/\sqrt{1+R^2}} dx \int_0^{Rx} f\left(\frac{x}{y}\right) dy + \int_{R/\sqrt{1+R^2}}^{R} dx \int_0^{\sqrt{R^2 - x^2}} f\left(\frac{y}{x}\right) dy.$

In Problems 3536 to 3540 compute the double integrals by passing over to polar coordinates.

3536. $\int_0^R dx \int_0^{\sqrt{R^2 - x^2}} \ln(1 + x^2 + y^2)\, dy.$

3537. $\iint_D \sqrt{\frac{1 - x^2 - y^2}{1 + x^2 + y^2}}\, dx\, dy$, where the domain D is specified by the inequalities $x^2 + y^2 \leq 1$, $x \geq 0$, $y \geq 0$.

3538. $\iint_D (h - 2x - 3y)\, dx\, dy$, where D is a circle $x^2 + y^2 \leq R^2$.

3539. $\iint_D \sqrt{R^2 - x^2 - y^2}\, dx\, dy$, where D is a circle $x^2 + y^2 \leq Rx$.

3540. $\iint_D \arctan \frac{y}{x}\, dx\, dy$, where D is a portion of a ring:

$$x^2 + y^2 \geq 1,\ x^2 + y^2 \leq 9,\ y \geq \frac{x}{\sqrt{3}},\ y \leq x\sqrt{3}.$$

3541. Proceeding from geometric reasoning, show that if the Cartesian coordinates are transformed by the formulas $x = a\rho \cos\varphi$, $y = b\rho \sin\varphi$ (a and b constants), then the element of the area will be $d\sigma = ab\rho\, d\rho\, d\varphi$.

In Problems 3542 to 3544, using the result of the previous problem and choosing suitably a and b, transform the double integrals.

3542. $\iint\limits_D f(x, y)\,dx\,dy$, where the domain D is bounded by the ellipse $\frac{x^2}{4} + \frac{y^2}{9} = 1.$

3543. $\iint\limits_D f(x, y)\,dx\,dy$, where D is the domain bounded by the curve $\left(x^2 + \frac{y^2}{3}\right)^2 = x^2 y.$

3544. $\iint\limits_D f\left(\sqrt{4 - \frac{x^2}{a^2} - \frac{y^2}{b^2}}\right) dx\,dy$, where D is a part of the elliptic ring bounded by the ellipses $\frac{x^2}{a^2} + \frac{y^2}{b^2} = 1$, $\frac{x^2}{4a^2} + \frac{y^2}{4b^2} = 1$ and situated in the first quadrant.

3545. Evaluate the integral $\iint\limits_D xy\,dx\,dy$, where D is the domain bounded by the ellipse $\frac{x^2}{a^2} + \frac{y^2}{b^2} = 1$ and situated in the first quadrant.

3546. Evaluate the integral $\iint\limits_D \sqrt{xy}\,dx\,dy$, where D is the domain bounded by the curve $\left(\frac{x^2}{2} + \frac{y^2}{3}\right)^4 = \frac{xy}{\sqrt{6}}$ and situated in the first quadrant.

Triple integral

In Problems 3547 to 3551 in the triple integral $\iiint\limits_\Omega f(x, y, z)\,dx\,dy$ pass over to cylindrical coordinates ρ, φ, z ($x = \rho\cos\varphi$, $y = \rho\sin\varphi$, $z = z$) or to spherical coordinates ρ, θ, φ ($x = \rho\cos\varphi\sin\theta$, $y = \rho\sin\varphi\sin\theta$, $z = \rho\cos\theta$) and indicate the limits of integration.

3547. Ω is the domain situated in the first octant and bounded by the cylinder $x^2 + y^2 = R^2$ and the planes $z = 0$, $z = 1$, $y = x$ and $y = x\sqrt{3}$.

3548. Ω is the domain bounded by the cylinder $x^2 + y^2 = 2x$, plane $z = 0$ and paraboloid $z = x^2 + y^2$.

3549. Ω is the part of the sphere $x^2 + y^2 + z^2 \le R^2$, lying in the first octant.

3550. Ω is the part of the sphere $x^2 + y^2 + z^2 \le R^2$, lying inside the cylinder $(x^2 + y^2)^2 = R^2(x^2 - y^2)\ (x \ge 0)$.

3551. Ω is the common portion of the two spheres

$$x^2 + y^2 + z^2 \le R^2 \text{ and } x^2 + y^2 + (z - R)^2 \le R^2.$$

In Problems 3552 to 3558 compute the integrals by passing over to cylindrical or spherical coordinates.

3552. $\int_0^1 dx \int_{-\sqrt{1-x^2}}^{\sqrt{1-x^2}} dy \int_0^a dz.$

3553. $\int_0^2 dx \int_0^{\sqrt{2x-x^2}} dy \int_0^a z\sqrt{x^2+y^2}\, dz.$

3554. $\int_{-R}^{R} dx \int_{-\sqrt{R^2-x^2}}^{\sqrt{R^2-x^2}} dy \int_0^{\sqrt{R^2-x^2-y^2}} (x^2+y^2)\, dz.$

3555. $\int_0^1 dx \int_0^{\sqrt{1-x^2}} dy \int_0^{\sqrt{1-x^2-y^2}} \sqrt{x^2+y^2+z^2}\, dz.$

3556. $\iiint\limits_{\Omega} (x^2 + y^2)\, dx\, dy\, dz$, where the domain Ω is specified by the inequalities $z \ge 0$, $r^2 \le x^2 + y^2 + z^2 \le R^2$.

3557. $\iiint\limits_{\Omega} \dfrac{dx\, dy\, dz}{\sqrt{x^2 + y^2 + (z-2)^2}}$, where Ω is the sphere $x^2 + y^2 + z^2 \le 1$.

3558. $\iiint\limits_{\Omega} \dfrac{dx\, dy\, dz}{\sqrt{x^2 + y^2 + (z-2)^2}}$, where Ω is the cylinder $x^2 + y^2 \le 1$, $-1 \le z \le 1$.

4. Application of Double and Triple Integrals

Volume of a solid. I

In Problems 3559 to 3596 by means of double integrals find the volumes of the solids bounded by[1].

3559. The planes of coordinates, planes $x = 4$ and $y = 4$ and paraboloid of revolution $z = x^2 + y^2 + 1$.

[1]The parameters are assumed to be positive.

3560. The planes of coordinates, planes $x = a$, $y = b$ and elliptic paraboloid $z = \frac{x^2}{2p} + \frac{y^2}{2q}$.

3561. The plane $\frac{x}{a} + \frac{y}{b} + \frac{z}{c} = 1$ and coordinate planes (a pyramid).

3562. The planes $y = 0$, $z = 0$, $3x + y = 6$, $3x + 2y = 12$ and $x + y + z = 6$.

3563. The paraboloid of revolution $z = x^2 + y^2$, coordinate planes and the plane $x + y = 1$.

3564. The paraboloid of revolution $z = x^2 + y^2$ and the planes $z = 0$, $y = 1$, $y = 2x$ and $y = 6 - x$.

3565. The cylinders $y = \sqrt{x}$, $y = 2\sqrt{x}$ and the planes $z = 0$ and $x + z = 6$.

3566. The planes of coordinates, plane $2x + 3y - 12 = 0$ and cylinder $z = \frac{y^2}{2}$.

3567. The cylinder $z = 9 - y^2$, coordinate planes and plane $3x + 4y = 12\ (y \geq 0)$.

3568. The cylinder $z = 4 - x^2$, coordinate planes and plane $2x + y = 4\ (x \geq 0)$.

3569. The cylinder $2y^2 = x$, planes $\frac{x}{4} + \frac{y}{2} + \frac{z}{4} = 1$ and $z = 0$.

3570. The circular cylinder of radius r, whose axis coincides with the y-axis, coordinate planes and plane $\frac{x}{r} + \frac{y}{a} = 1$.

3571. The elliptic cylinder $\frac{x^2}{4} + y^2 = 1$, planes $z = 12 - 3x - 4y$ and $z = 1$.

3572. The cylinders $x^2 + y^2 = R^2$ and $x^2 + z^2 = R^2$.

3573. The cylinders $z = 4 - y^2$, $y = \frac{x^2}{2}$ and plane $z = 0$.

3574. The cylinders $x^2 + y^2 = R^2$, $z = \frac{x^3}{a^2}$ and plane $z = 0\ (x \geq 0)$.

3575. The hyperbolic paraboloid $z = x^2 - y^2$ and planes $z = 0$, $x = 3$.

3576. The hyperbolic paraboloid $z = xy$, cylinder $y = \sqrt{x}$ and planes $x + y = 2$, $y = 0$ and $z = 0$.

3577. The paraboloid $z = x^2 + y^2$, cylinder $y = x^2$ and planes $y = 1$ and $z = 0$.

3578. The elliptic cylinder $\frac{x^2}{a^2} + \frac{z^2}{c^2} = 1$ and planes $y = \frac{b}{a}x$, $y = 0$ and $z = 0$ $(x \geq 0)$.

3579. The paraboloid $z = \frac{a^2 - x^2 - 4y^2}{a}$ and plane $z = 0$.

3580. The cylinders $y = e^x$, $x = e^{-x}$, $z = e^2 - y^2$ and plane $z = 0$.

3581. The cylinders $y = \ln x$ and $y = \ln^2 x$ and planes $z = 0$ and $y + z = 1$.

3582*. The cylinders $z = \ln x$ and $z = \ln y$ and planes $z = 0$ and $x + y = 2e$ $(x \geq 1)$.

3583. The cylinders $y = x + \sin x$, $y = x - \sin x$ and $z = \frac{(x+y)^2}{4}$ (a parabolic cylinder whose elements are parallel to the straight line $x - y = 0$, $z = 0$) and plane $z = 0$ $(0 \leq x \leq \pi, y = 0)$.

3584. The conic surface $z^2 = xy$ (Fig. 66), cylinder $\sqrt{x} + \sqrt{y} = 1$ and plane $z = 0$.

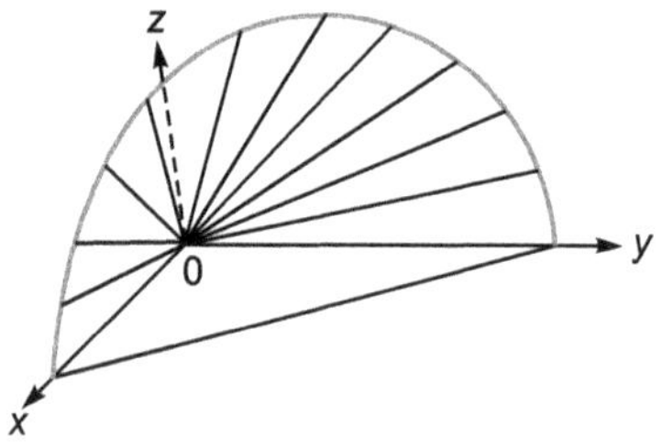

Fig. 66

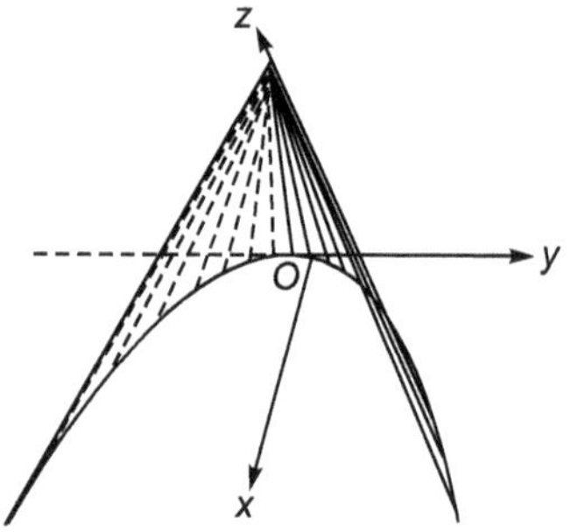

Fig. 67

3585. The conic surface $4y^2 = x(2 - z)$ (a parabolic cone, see Fig. 67) and planes $z = 0$ and $x + z = 2$.

3586. The surface $z = \cos x \cdot \cos y$ and planes $x = 0$, $y = 0$, $z = 0$ and $x + y = \frac{\pi}{2}$.

3587. The cylinder $x^2 + y^2 = 4$, planes $z = 0$ and $z = x + y + 10$.

3588. The cylinder $x^2 + y^2 = 2x$, planes $2x - z = 0$ and $4x - z = 0$.

3589. The cylinder $x^2 + y^2 = R^2$, paraboloid $Rz = 2R^2 + x^2 + y^2$ and plane $z = 0$.

3590. The cylinder $x^2 + y^2 = 2ax$, paraboloid $z = \frac{x^2 + y^2}{a}$ and plane $z = 0$.

3591. The sphere $x^2 + y^2 + z^2 = a^2$ and cylinder $x^2 + y^2 = ax$ (Viviani's problem).

3592. The hyperbolic paraboloid $z = \frac{xy}{a}$, cylinder $x^2 + y^2 = ax$ and plane $z = 0$ $(x \geq 0, y \geq 0)$.

3593. The cylinders $x^2 + y^2 = x$ and $x^2 + y^2 = 2x$, paraboloid $z = x^2 + y^2$ and planes $x + y = 0$, $x - y = 0$, $z = 0$.

3594. The cylinders $x^2 + y^2 = 2x$, $x^2 + y^2 = 2y$ and planes $z = x + 2y$ and $z = 0$.

3595. The conic surface $z^2 = xy$ and cylinder

$$(x^2 + y^2)^2 = 2xy \ (x \geq 0,\ y \geq 0,\ z \geq 0).$$

3596. The helicoid $z = h \arctan \dfrac{y}{x}$, cylinder $x^2 + y^2 = R^2$ and planes $x = 0$ and $z = 0\ (x \geq 0,\ y \geq 0)$.

Area of a plane figure

In Problems 3597 to 3608 using double integration, find the areas of the indicated domains.

3597. The domain bounded by the straight lines $x = 0$, $y = 0$, $x + y = 1$.

3598. The domain bounded by the straight lines $y = x$, $y = 5x$, $x = 1$.

3599. The domain enclosed by the ellipse $\dfrac{x^2}{a^2} + \dfrac{y^2}{b^2} = 1$.

3600. The domain contained between the parabola $y^2 = \dfrac{b^2}{a} x$ and straight line $y = \dfrac{b}{a} x$.

3601. The domain bounded by the parabolas $y = \sqrt{x}$, $y = 2\sqrt{x}$ and straight line $x = 4$.

3602*. The domain enclosed by the curve $(x^2 + y^2)^2 = 2ax^3$.

3603. The domain enclosed by the curve $(x^2 + y^2)^3 = x^4 + y^4$.

3604. The domain enclosed by the curve $(x^2 + y^2)^2 = 2a^2 (x^2 - y^2)$ (Bernoulli's lemniscate).

3605. The domain enclosed by the loop of the curve $x^3 + y^3 = 2xy$ lying in the first quadrant.

3606. The domain enclosed by the loop of the curve $(x + y)^3 = xy$ lying in the first quadrant.

3607. The domain enclosed by the loop of the curve $(x + y)^5 = x^2y^2$ lying in the first quadrant.

3608*. The domain enclosed by the curve

(1) $\left(\dfrac{x^2}{a^2} + \dfrac{y^2}{b^2}\right) = \dfrac{xy}{c^2}$; (2) $\left(\dfrac{x^2}{4} + \dfrac{y^2}{9}\right)^2 = \dfrac{x^2 + y^2}{25}$.

Volume of a solid. II

In Problems 3609 to 3625, using triple integrals, compute the volumes of the solids bounded by[1].

3609. The cylinders $z = 4 - y^2$ and $z = y^2 + 2$, and planes $x = -1$ and $x = 2$

[1]The parameters are assumed to be positive.

3610. The paraboloids $z = x^2 + y^2$ and $z = x^2 + 2y^2$, and planes $y = x$, $y = 2x$, $x = 1$.

3611. The paraboloids $z = x^2 + y^2$ and $z = 2x^2 + 2y^2$, cylinder $y = x^2$, and plane $y = x$.

3612. The cylinders $z = \ln(x + 2)$ and $z = \ln(6 - x)$, and planes $x = 0$, $x + y = 2$, $x - y = 2$.

3613*. The paraboloid $(x - 1)^2 + y^2 = z$ and plane $2x + z = 2$.

3614*. The paraboloid $z = x^2 + y^2$ and plane $z = x + y$.

3615*. The sphere $x^2 + y^2 + z^2 = 4$ and paraboloid $x^2 + y^2 = 3z$.

3616. The sphere $x^2 + y^2 + z^2 = R^2$ and paraboloid

$$x^2 + y^2 = R(R - 2z)\ (z \geq 0).$$

3617. The paraboloid $z = x^2 + y^2$ and cone $z^2 = xy$.

3618. The sphere $x^2 + y^2 + z^2 = 4Rz - 3R^2$ and cone $z^2 = 4(x^2 + y^2)$ (i.e., the portion of the sphere lying inside the cone).

3619*. $(x^2 + y^2 + z^2)^2 = a^3x$.

3620. $(x^2 + y^2 + z^2)^2 = axyz$.

3621. $(x^2 + y^2 + z^2)^3 = a^2z^4$.

3622. $(x^2 + y^2 + z^2)^3 = \dfrac{a^6z^2}{x^2 + y^2}$.

3623. $(x^2 + y^2 + z^2)^3 = a^2(x^2 + y^2)^2$.

3624. $(x^2 + y^2)^2 + z^4 = a^3z$.

3625. $x^2 + y^2 + z^2 = 1$, $x^2 + y^2 + z^2 = 16$, $z^2 = x^2 + y^2$, $x = 0$, $y = 0$, $z = 0$ $(x \geq 0, y \geq 0, z \geq 0)$.

Area of a surface

3626. Compute the area of the part of the plane $6x + 3y + 2z = 12$ contained in the first octant.

3627. Compute the area of the part of the surface $z^2 = 2xy$ located above the rectangle situated in the plane $z = 0$ and bounded by the straight lines $x = 0$, $y = 0$, $x = 3$, $y = 6$.

3628. Find the area of the portion of the cone $z^2 = x^2 + y^2$ situated above the xy-plane and cut off by the plane $z = \sqrt{2}\left(\dfrac{x}{2} + 1\right)$.

In Problems 3629 to 3639 find the areas of the indicated parts of the given surfaces.

3629. The part of $z^2 = x^2 + y^2$ cut off by the cylinder $z^2 = 2py$.

3630. The part of $y^2 + z^2 = x^2$ found inside the cylinder $x^2 + y^2 = R^2$.

3631. The part of $y^2 + z^2 = x^2$ cut off by the cylinder $x^2 - y^2 = a^2$ and planes $y = b$ and $y = -b$.

3632. The part of $z^2 = 4x$ cut off by the cylinder $y^2 = 4x$ and plane $x = 1$.

3633. The part of $z = xy$ cut off by the cylinder $x^2 + y^2 = R^2$.

3634. The part of $2z = x^2 + y^2$ cut off by the cylinder $x^2 + y^2 = 1$.

3635. The part of $x^2 + y^2 + z^2 = a^2$ cut off by the cylinder $x^2 + y^2 = R^2$ $(R \le a)$.

3636. The part of $x^2 + y^2 + z^2 = R^2$ cut off by the cylinder $x^2 + y^2 = Rx$.

3637. The part of $x^2 + y^2 + z^2 = R^2$ cut off by the surface $(x^2 + y^2)^2 = R^2(x^2 - y^2)$.

3638. The part of $z = \dfrac{x + y}{x^2 + y^2}$ cut off by the surfaces $x^2 + y^2 = 1$, $x^2 + y^2 = 4$ and situated in the first octant.

3639. The part of $(x \cos\alpha + y \sin\alpha)^2 + z^2 = a^2$ lying in the first octant $\left(\alpha < \dfrac{\pi}{2}\right)$.

3640*. Compute the area of the part of the Earth's surface (considering it as a sphere of radius $R \approx 6400$ km) contained between the meridians $\varphi = 30°$, $\varphi = 60°$ and parallels $\theta = 45°$ and $\theta = 60°$.

3641. Compute the total surface area of the solid bounded by the sphere $x^2 + y^2 + z^2 = 3a^2$ and paraboloid $x^2 + y^2 = 2az$ $(z \ge 0)$.

3642. The axes of two equal cylinders of radius R intersect at right angles. Find the area of the part of the surface of one of the cylinders found in the other.

Moments and centre of gravity

In Problems 3643 to 3646, using double integrals, find the static moments of homogeneous plane figures (density $\gamma = 1$).

3643. A rectangle with the sides a and b about the side a.

3644. A semi-circle about its diameter.

3645. A circle about its tangent.

3646. A regular hexagon about its side.

3647. Prove that the static moment of a triangle with the base a about this base depends only on the altitude of the triangle.

In Problems 3648 to 3652, using double integrals, find the centres of gravity of homogeneous plane figures.

3648. A figure bounded by the upper half of the ellipse subtended by the major axis.

3649. A figure bounded by the sinusoid $y = \sin x$, x-axis and straight line $x = \dfrac{\pi}{4}$.

3650. A circular sector corresponding to the central angle α (the radius of the circle is R).

3651. A circular segment corresponding to the central angle α (the radius of the circle is R).

3652. A figure enclosed by the curve $y^2 = x^2 - x^4 (x \geq 0)$.

In Problems 3653 to 3659 find the moments of inertia of homogeneous plane figures (density $\gamma = 1$).

3653. A circle of radius R about the tangent.

3654. A square with the side a about a vertex.

3655. An ellipse about the centre.

3656. A rectangle with the sides a and b about the point of intersection of the diagonals.

3657. An isosceles triangle with the base a and height h about the vertex.

3658. A circle of radius R about a point lying on the circumference.

3659. A parabolic segment with the chord perpendicular to the axis, about the vertex of the parabola (the length of the chord is a, altitude is h).

3660. Prove that the moment of inertia of circular ring with respect to the centre is twice the moment of inertia about any axis passing through the centre of the ring and lying in its plane.

3661. Prove that the sum of the moments of inertia of a plane figure F about any pair of mutually perpendicular axes, lying in the same plane with this figure and passing through a fixed point O, is a constant.

3662*. Prove that the moment of inertia of a plane figure about an axis is equal to $Md^2 + I_c$, where M is the mass distributed on the figure, d the distance between the axis and the centre of gravity of the figure and I_c the moment of inertia about the axis parallel to the given one and passing through the centre of gravity of the figure (Steiner' s theorem).

In Problems 3663 to 3665 find the static moments of homogeneous solids (density $\gamma = 1$).

3663. A rectangular parallelopiped with the edges a, b and c about its faces.

3664. A right circular cone (the radius of the base is R, the altitude H) with respect to the plane passing through the vertex parallel to the base.

3665. A solid bounded by the ellipsoid $\frac{x^2}{a^2} + \frac{y^2}{b^2} + \frac{z^2}{c^2} = 1$ and plane Oxy with respect to this plane.

In Problems 3666 to 3672 find the centres of gravity of homogeneous solids bounded by the given surfaces.

3666. The planes $x = 0, y = 0, z = 0, x = 2, y = 4$ and $x + y + z = 8$ (truncated parallelopiped).

3667. The ellipsoid $\frac{x^2}{a^2}+\frac{y^2}{b^2}+\frac{z^2}{c^2}=1$ and coordinate planes (i.e., a solid situated in the first octant).

3668. The cylinder $z=\frac{y^2}{2}$ and planes $x=0$, $y=0$, $z=0$, $2x+3y-12=0$.

3669. The cylinders $y=\sqrt{x}$, $y=2\sqrt{x}$ and planes $z=0$ and $x+z=6$.

3670. The paraboloid $z=\frac{x^2+y^2}{2a}$ and sphere $x^2+y^2+z^2=3a^2$ $(z\geq 0)$.

3671. The sphere $x^2+y^2+z^2=R^2$ and cone $z\tan\alpha=\sqrt{x^2+y^2}$ (a spherical sector).

3672. $(x^2+y^2+r^2)^2=a^3z$.

In Problems 3673 to 3674 find the centres of gravity of homogeneous surfaces .

3673. The part of a sphere located in the first octant.

3674. The part of the paraboloid $x^2+y^2=2z$ cut away by the plane $z=1$.

In Problems 3675 to 3680 find the moments of inertia of homogeneous solids with a mass equal to M.

3675. A rectangular parallelepiped with the edges a, b and c about each of the edges and with respect to the centre of gravity.

3676. A sphere about a straight line tangent to it.

3677. The ellipsoid $\frac{x^2}{a^2}+\frac{y^2}{b^2}+\frac{z^2}{c^2}=1$ about each of its three axes.

3678. A right circular cylinder (the radius of the base R, the altitude H) about the diameter of the base and with respect to the diameter of its mid-section.

3679. A hollow sphere of outer radius R and inner radius r about the diameter.

3680. A paraboloid of revolution (the radius of the base R, altitude H) about the axis passing through its centre of gravity perpendicular to the axis of revolution (the equatorial moment).

In Problems 3681 to 3683 compute the moments of intertia of the indicated parts of homogeneous surfaces (the mass of each part is equal to M).

3681. The lateral surface of a cylinder (the radius of the base R, altitude H) about the axis passing through its centre of gravity and perpendicular to the axis of the cylinder.

3682. The part of the paraboloid $x^2 + y^2 = 2cz$, cut away by the plane $z = c$, about the axis Oz.

3683. The lateral surface of a truncated cone (the radii of the bases R and r, altitude H) about its axis.

Miscellaneous problems

3684. Find the mass of a square plate with the side $2a$ if the density of the material is proportional to the square of the distance from the point of intersection of the diagonals and is equal to unity at the corners of the square.

3685. A flat ring is bounded by two concentric circles whose radii are equal to R and r $(R > r)$. Knowing that the density of the material is inversely proportional to the distance from the centre of the circles, find the mass of the ring. The density on the circumference of the inner circle is equal to unity.

3686. On the figure bounded by the ellipse with the semiaxes a and b the mass is distributed so that its density is proportional to the distance from the major axis, being equal to γ at the unit distance from this axis. Find the total mass.

3687. A solid is bounded by two concentric spherical surfaces whose radii are equal to r and R $(R > r)$. Knowing that the density of the material is inversely proportional to the distance from the centre of the spheres, equalling γ at a unit distance, find the total mass of the solid.

3688. Compute the mass of the solid bounded by a right circular cylinder of radius R and altitude H if its density at any point is numerically equal to the square of the distance between this point and the centre of the base of the cylinder.

3689*. A solid is bounded by a circular cone whose altitude is h and the angle between the axis and generatrix is equal to α. Compute the mass of the solid if its density is proportional to the nth power of the distance from the plane drawn through the vertex of the cone and parallel to the base, being equal to γ at the unit distance $(n > 0)$.

3690. Find the mass of a sphere of radius R if the density is proportional to the cube of the distance from the centre and is equal to γ at the unit distance.

3691. Compute the mass of the solid bounded by the paraboloid $x^2 + y^2 = 2az$ and sphere $x^2 + y^2 + z^2 = 3a^2$ $(z > 0)$ if the density at each point is equal to the sum of the squares of the coordinates.

3692*. The density of the sphere $x^2 + y^2 + z^2 \leq 2Rz$ at any of its points is numerically equal to the square of the distance of this point from the origin. Find the coordinates of the centre of gravity of the sphere.

3693*. Find the static moment of the common portion of the spheres $x^2+y^2+z^2 \le R^2$ and $x^2+y^2+z^2 \le 2Rz$ with respect to the xy- plane. The density at any point of the solid is numerically equal to the distance of this point from the xy- plane.

3694*. Prove that the moment of inertia of a solid about some axis equals $Md^2 + I_C$, where M is the mass of the solid, d the distance between the axis and the centre of gravity of the solid and I_c the moment of inertia about the axis parallel to the given one and passing through the centre of gravity of the solid (Steiner's theorem ; cf. Problem 3662).

Proceeding from Newton's law of universal gravitation (see the hint to Problem 2670), solve Problem 3695 to 3698.

3695. Given a homogeneous sphere of radius R whose density is γ. Compute the force with which it attracts a material point of mass m located at a distance $a(a > R)$ from its cantre. Make sure that the force of interaction is such as if the total mass of the sphere was concentrated at its centre.

3696*. Prove that Newton's force of interaction between two homogeneous spheres is such as if the masses of the spheres were concentrated at its centres.

3697. Given a non-homogeneous solid sphere $x^2+y^2+z^2 \le R^2$ whose density changes according to the law $\gamma = \lambda z^2$. Compute the force with which it attracts a material point of mass m if it is situated on the z-axis at a distance $2R$ from the centre of the sphere.

3698. Given a homogeneous solid bounded by two concentric spheres (a spherical layer). Prove that the force with which this layer attracts a point found in the inner hollow of the solid is equal to zero.

The centre of pressure is the term for the point of application of the resultant of all the pressure forces acting on a given plane figure (all the pressure forces are perpendicular to the plane containing the figure). In determining the coordinates of the centre of pressure we usually proceed from the fact that the static moment of the resultant (i.e., the pressure on the total area) about any axis is equal to the sum of the static moments of individual forces with respect to the same axis. Remembering this, solve Problems 3699 to 3701.

3699. Find the centre of pressure of a rectangle with the sides a and b $(a > b)$ whose larger side is situated along the free surface of a liquid, and the plane of the rectangle is perpendicular to this surface.

Show that the position of the centre of pressure with respect to the rectangle remains unchanged if the plane of the rectangle is inclined to the surface of the liquid at an angle α ($\alpha \neq 0$). How will the obtained results change if the longer side a is situated not on the surface of the liquid but at a depth h (remaining parallel to the surface)?

3700. A triangle whose altitude is h is contained in the plane inclined at an angle α to the free surface of a liquid. At what depth is the centre of pressure of this triangle located if

(a) the base of the triangle lies on the surface of the liquid?

(b) the vertex lies on the surface, and the base is parallel to it?

3701. Find the centre of pressure of a figure bounded by an ellipse with the semiaxes a and b ($a > b$), if the longer of the axes is perpendicular to the surface of the liquid and the upper end of this axis is found at a distance h from the surface.

3702*. Prove that the pressure of a liquid on a flat plate submerged arbitrarily into the liquid is equal to the weight of a cylindrical column of this liquid situated above the plate, provided it lies horizontally at the depth of its centre of gravity.

5. Improper Integrals. Integrals Dependent on Parameters

Improper double and triple integrals

In Problems 3703 to 3711 compute the improper integrals or establish their divergence.

3703. $\displaystyle\int_{-\infty}^{\infty}\int_{-\infty}^{\infty}\frac{dx\,dy}{1+x^2+y^2}.$

3704. $\displaystyle\int_{-\infty}^{\infty}\int_{-\infty}^{\infty}\frac{dx\,dy}{(1+x^2+y^2)^{3/2}}.$

3705. $\displaystyle\int_{0}^{\infty}\int_{0}^{\infty}\frac{dx\,dy}{(x^2+y^2+a^2)^2}.$

3706. $\displaystyle\int_{-\infty}^{\infty}\int_{-\infty}^{\infty} e^{-|x|-|y|}\,dx\,dy.$

3707. $\displaystyle\int_{0}^{\infty}\int_{0}^{\infty}(x+y)\,e^{-(x+y)}\,dx\,dy.$

3708. $\displaystyle\int_{0}^{\infty}\int_{0}^{\infty} xye^{-x^2-y^2}\,dx\,dy.$

3709*. $\int_0^{\infty}\int_0^{\infty} e^{-(x^2 + 2xy\cos\alpha + y^2)}\,dx\,dy.$

3710*. $\int_0^{\infty} dx \int_x^{\infty} e^{-y^2}\,dy.$

3711*. $\int_0^{\infty} dx \int_{2x}^{\infty} xe^{-y}\frac{\sin y}{y^2}\,dy.$

In Problems 3712 to 3715 find out which of the improper integrals taken round the circle of radius R with centre at the origin are convergent.

3712. $\iint\limits_D \ln\sqrt{x^2 + y^2}\,dx\,dy.$

3713. $\iint\limits_D \frac{e^{-x^2 - y^2}}{x^2 + y^2}\,dx\,dy.$

3714. $\iint\limits_D \frac{\sin(x^2 + y^2)}{\sqrt{(x^2 + y^2)^3}}\,dx\,dy.$

3715. $\iint\limits_D \frac{\cos(x^2 + y^2)}{x^2 + y^2}\,dx\,dy.$

3716. Is it possible to choose the number m so that the improper integral $\iint \frac{dx\,dy}{\sqrt{(x^2 + y^2)^m}}$, spread over the entire plane, is convergent?

In Problems 3717 to 3719 compute the given improper integrals.

3717. $\int_0^{\infty}\int_0^{\infty}\int_0^{\infty} \frac{dx\,dy\,dz}{\sqrt{(1 + x + y + z)^7}}.$

3718. $\int_0^{\infty}\int_0^{\infty}\int_0^{\infty} \frac{xy\,dx\,dy\,dz}{(1 + x^2 + y^2 + z^2)^3}.$

3719*. $\int_{-\infty}^{\infty}\int_{-\infty}^{\infty}\int_{-\infty}^{\infty} e^{-x^2 - y^2 - z^2}\,dx\,dy\,dz.$

In Problems 3720 to 3722 find out whether the given improper integrals, taken over the sphere Ω of radius R with centre at the origin, are convergent.

3720. $\iiint\limits_{\Omega} \frac{dx\,dy\,dz}{\sqrt{(x^2 + y^2 + z^2)^3}\,\ln\sqrt[3]{x^2 + y^2 + z^2}}.$

3721. $\iiint\limits_{\Omega} \frac{\ln\sqrt{x^2 + y^2 + z^2}}{x^2 + y^2 + z^2}\,dx\,dy\,dz.$

3722. $\iiint\limits_{\Omega} \frac{xyz}{(x^2 + y^2 + z^2)^3}\,dx\,dy\,dz.$

3723. Evaluate the integral $\iiint\limits_{\Omega} \ln(x^2 + y^2 + z^2)\,dx\,dy\,dz$, where the domain Ω is a sphere of radius R with centre at the origin.

3724*. Compute the volume of the solid bounded by the surface $z = (x^2 + y^2)\, e^{-(x^2 + y^2)}$ and the plane $z = 0$.

3725. Compute the volume of the solid bounded by the surface $z = x^2 y^2 e^{-(x^2 + y^2)}$ and the plane $z = 0$.

3726. Compute the volume of the solid bounded by the plane $z = 0$ and the part of the surface $z = xe^{-(x^2 + y^2)}$ situated above this plane.

3727. Given a homogeneous solid bounded by a right circular cylinder (the radius of the base R, altitute H, density γ). Find the force acting on the mass point m situated at the centre of the base of the cylinder.

3728. Given a homogeneous solid bounded by a right circular cone (the radius of the base R, altitude H, density γ). Compute the force with which the solid attracts the mass point m placed at the vertex of the cone.

3729. Given a non-homogeneous solid sphere of radius R, whose density γ is related with the distance from the centre r as follows : $\gamma = a - br\ (a > 0,\ b > 0)$.

(a) Find the constants a and b if it is known that the mean density of the sphere is equal to γ_{mean} and the density on the surface of the sphere to γ_0.

(b) Compute the force with which the sphere attracts the mass point m situated on its surface.

Integrals dependent on a parameter. Leibniz' rule

3730. Find the domain of definition of the function $f(x) = \int_0^1 \frac{dz}{\sqrt{x^2 + z^2}}$.

3731. Find the curvature of the curve $y = \int_{\pi}^{2\pi} \frac{\sin \alpha x}{\alpha}\, d\alpha$ at the point with the abscissa $x = 1$.

3732. Using the equality $\int_0^b \frac{dx}{1 + ax} = \frac{1}{a} \ln (1 + ab)$, obtain the following formula by differentiating with respect to the parameter.

$$\int_0^b \frac{x\,dx}{(1 + ax)^2} = \frac{1}{a^2} \ln (1 + ab) - \frac{b}{a\,(1 + ab)}.$$

3733. Proceeding from the equality $\int_0^b \frac{dx}{a^2 + x^2} = \frac{1}{a} \arctan \frac{b}{a}$, compute the integral $\int_0^b \frac{dx}{(x^2 + a^2)^3}$.

3734. Proceeding from the equality $\int_0^\infty \frac{dx}{a^2 + x^2} = \frac{\pi}{2a}$, compute $\int_0^\infty \frac{dx}{(x^2 + a^2)^n}$ (n a positive integer).

3735. Evaluate the integral $\int_0^\infty e^{-ax} x^{n-1}\, dx$ (n a positive integer) for $a > 0$, first finding $\int_0^\infty e^{-ax}\, dx$.

3736*. Proceeding from the equality (see Problem 2318)

$$\int_0^{\pi/2} \frac{dx}{a^2 \cos^2 x + b^2 \sin^2 x} = \frac{\pi}{2|ab|},$$

find $\int_0^{\pi/2} \frac{dx}{(a^2 \cos^2 x + b^2 \sin^2 x)^2}$.

In Problems 3737 to 3749 compute the integrals with the aid of differentiation with respect to the parameter.

3737. $\int_0^\infty \frac{1 - e^{-ax}}{xe^x}\, dx$ ($a > -1$).

3738. $\int_0^\infty \frac{1 - e^{-ax^2}}{xe^{x^2}}\, dx$ ($a > -1$).

3739. $\int_0^1 \frac{\arctan ax}{x\sqrt{1 - x^2}}\, dx$.

3740. $\int_0^1 \frac{\ln(1 - a^2x^2)}{x^2\sqrt{1 - x^2}}\, dx$ ($a^2 < 1$).

3741. $\int_0^\infty \frac{\arctan ax}{x(1 + x^2)}\, dx$.

3742. $\int_0^1 \frac{\ln(1 - a^2x^2)}{\sqrt{1 - x^2}}\, dx$ ($a^2 < 1$).

3743. $\int_0^\pi \frac{\ln(1 + a\cos x)}{\cos x}\, dx$ ($a^2 < 1$).

3744. $\int_0^{\pi/2} \ln\left(\frac{1 + a\sin x}{1 - a\sin x}\right) \frac{dx}{\sin x}$ ($a^2 < 1$).

3745. $\int_0^{\infty} \frac{1-e^{-ax^2}}{x^2}\,dx$ $(a > 0)$, knowing that

$$\int_0^{\infty} e^{-ax^2}\,dx = \frac{1}{2}\sqrt{\frac{\pi}{a}} \quad (a > 0) \qquad \text{(see Problem 2439).}$$

3746*. $\int_0^{\infty} \frac{e^{-ax^2} - e^{-bx^2}}{x^2}\,dx$ $(a > 0,\ b > 0)$.

3747*. $\int_0^{\infty} e^{-ax} \frac{\sin bx - \sin cx}{x}\,dx$ $(a > 0)$.

3748. $\int_0^{\infty} e^{-ax} \frac{\cos bx - \cos cx}{x}\,dx$ $(a > 0)$.

3749*. $\int_0^{\pi/2} \ln\,(a^2 \cos^2 x + b^2 \sin^2 x)\,dx$.

3750. Computing the integral $\int_0^{\pi/2} \frac{\arctan\,(a \tan x)}{\tan x}\,dx$, find $\int_0^{\pi/2} \frac{x}{\tan x}\,dx$.

3751. Using the equation $\int_0^1 x^n\,dx = \frac{1}{n+1}$, compute the integral

$$\int_0^1 \frac{x^{\beta} - x^{\alpha}}{\ln x}\,dx \quad (\alpha > -1,\ \beta > -1).$$

3752. Using the equation $2a\int_0^{\infty} e^{-a^2x^2}\,dx = \sqrt{\pi}$ (see Problem 2439), compute the integral $\int_0^{\infty} (e^{-a^2/x^2} - e^{-b^2/x^2})\,dx$.

3753. From the relationship $\int_0^{\infty} e^{-z^2}\,dz = \frac{\sqrt{\pi}}{2}$ (Poisson's integral) derive the equality $\frac{1}{\sqrt{x}} = \frac{2}{\sqrt{\pi}}\int_0^{\infty} e^{-z^2x}\,dz$ $(x > 0)$ and use it for computing the below integrals (diffraction integrals):

(a) $\int_0^{\infty} \frac{\cos x\,dx}{\sqrt{x}}$;

(b) $\int_0^{\infty} \frac{\sin x\,dx}{\sqrt{x}}$.

Miscellaneous problems

3754. Let the function $f(x)$ be continuous for $x \geq 0$ and for $x \to \infty$. Prove that if $a > 0$ and $b > 0$, then

$$\int_0^{\infty} \frac{f(ax) - f(bx)}{x}\,dx = [f(\infty) - f(0)] \ln \frac{a}{b}$$

In Problems 3755 to 3756 compute the integrals taking advantage of the result of Problem 3754.

3755. $\int_0^{\infty} \frac{\arctan ax - \arctan bx}{x}\,dx.$

3756. $\int_0^{\infty} \frac{e^{-ax^n} - e^{-bx^n}}{x}\,dx \ (n > 0).$

3757*. Let the function $f(x)$ be continuous for $x \geq 0$ and $\int_A^{\infty} \frac{f(x)}{x}\,dx$ be convergent for any $A > 0$. Prove that if $a > 0$ and $b > 0$, then $\int_0^{\infty} \frac{f(ax) - f(bx)}{x}\,dx = f(0) \ln \frac{b}{a}$. (Cf. Problem 3754.)

In Problems 3758 to 3762 compute the integrals using the result of Problem 3757 ($a > 0$, $b > 0$).

3758. $\int_0^{\infty} \frac{e^{-ax} - e^{-bx}}{x}\,dx.$

3759. $\int_0^{\infty} \frac{\cos ax - \cos bx}{x}\,dx.$

3760. $\int_0^{\infty} \frac{\sin ax \cdot \sin bx}{x}\,dx.$

3761. $\int_0^{\infty} \frac{b \sin ax - a \sin bx}{x^2}\,dx.$

3762*. $\int_0^{\infty} \frac{\sin^3 x}{x^2}\,dx.$

3763*. Laplace's function $\Phi(x)$ is defined as follows : $\Phi(x) = \frac{2}{\sqrt{\pi}} \int_0^x e^{-t^2}\,dt$ (this function plays an important role in the theory of probability). Prove the following relationships:

(1) $\int_0^x \Phi(az)\,dz = \frac{e^{-a^2x^2} - 1}{a\sqrt{\pi}} + x\Phi(ax);$

(2) $\int_0^{\infty} [1 - \Phi(x)]\,dx = \frac{1}{\sqrt{\pi}}.$

3764*. The functions Si (x) and Ci (x) are usually defined as: $\text{Si}\,(x) = -\int_x^{\infty} \frac{\sin t}{t}\,dt$ (sine integral) and $\text{Ci}\,(x) = -\int_x^{\infty} \frac{\cos t}{t}\,dt$ (cosine integral). Prove that

$$\int_0^{\infty} \sin x \,\text{Si}\,(x)\,dx = \int_0^{\infty} \cos x \,\text{Ci}\,(x)\,dx = -\frac{\pi}{4}.$$

3765*. The function $J_0(x)$ defined by the equality

$$J_0(x) = \frac{2}{\pi}\int_0^{\pi/2} \cos\,(x \sin\theta)\,d\theta$$

is called Bessel's function of the zeroth order. Prove that:

(1) $\int_0^{\infty} e^{-ax} J_0(x)\,dx = \frac{1}{\sqrt{1+a^2}}$ $(a > 0)$;

(2) $\int_0^{\infty} \frac{\sin ax}{x} J_0(x)\,dx = \begin{cases} \frac{\pi}{2} & \text{for } a \geq 1; \\ \arcsin a & \text{for } |a| \leq 1; \\ -\frac{\pi}{2} & \text{for } a \leq -1. \end{cases}$

3766. Prove that the function $y = \int_0^{\infty} \frac{e^{-xz}}{1+z^2}\,dz$ satisfies the differential equation $y'' + y = \frac{1}{x}$.

3767*. Prove that the function $y = \int_{-1}^{1} (z^2-1)^{n-1} e^{xz}\,dz$ satisfies the differential equation $xy'' + 2ny' - xy = 0$.

3768*. Prove that the function $y = \int_0^{\infty} \frac{e^{-xz}}{(1+z^2)^{n+1}}\,dz$ satisfies the differential equation $xy'' - 2ny' + xy = 1$.

3769*. Prove that Bessel's function of the zeroth order $J_0(x) = \frac{2}{\pi}\int_0^{\pi/2} \cos\,(x\sin\theta)\,d\theta$ satisfies the differential equation $J_0''(x) + \frac{J_0'(x)}{x} + J_0(x) = 0.$

13

Line Integrals and Surface Integrals

1. Line Integrals with Respect to Arc Length

Evaluating integrals

In Problems 3770 to 3775 evaluate the line integrals.

3770. $\int\limits_L \frac{ds}{x-y}$, where L is the segment of the straight line $y = \frac{1}{2}x - 2$, contained between the points $A\,(0, -2)$ and $B\,(4, 0)$.

3771. $\int\limits_L xy\, ds$, where L is the contour of the rectangle with the vertices $A\,(0, 0)$, $B\,(4, 0)$, $C\,(4, 2)$ and $D\,(0, 2)$.

3772. $\int\limits_L y\, ds$, where L is the arc of the parabola $y^2 = 2px$ cut off by the parabola $x^2 = 2py$.

3773. $\int\limits_L (x^2 + y^2)^n\, ds$, where L is the circle $x = a\cos t$, $y = a\sin t$.

3774. $\int\limits_L xy\, ds$, where L is the quarter of the ellipse $\frac{x^2}{a^2} + \frac{y^2}{b^2} = 1$, lying in the first quadrant.

3775. $\int\limits_L \sqrt{2y}\, ds$, where L is the first arc of the cycloid $x = a\,(t - \sin t)$, $y = a\,(1 - \cos t)$.

3776. Derive the formula for computing the integral $\int\limits_L F\,(x, y)\, ds$ in polar coordinates if the curve L is specified by the equation $\rho = \rho\,(\varphi)\ (\varphi_1 \le \varphi \le \varphi_2)$.

3777*. Evaluate $\int\limits_L (x - y)\, ds$, where L is the circle $x^2 + y^2 = ax$.

3778. Evaluate $\int_L x\sqrt{x^2 - y^2}\, ds$, where L is the curve specified by the equation $(x^2 + y^2)^2 = a^2(x^2 - y^2)$ $(x \geq 0)$ (half of the lemniscate).

3779. Compute $\int_L \arctan \frac{y}{x}\, ds$, where L is the part of spiral of Archimedes $\rho = 2\varphi$, contained inside a circle of radius R with the centre at the origin (in the pole).

3780. Compute the integral $\int_L \frac{z^2\, ds}{x^2 + y^2}$, where L is the first turn of the helix $x = a\cos t$, $y = a\sin t$, $z = at$.

3781. Evaluate $\int_L xyz\, ds$, where L is the quarter of the circle $x^2 + y^2 + z^2 = R^2$, $x^2 + y^2 = \frac{R^2}{4}$, lying in the first octant.

3782. Evaluate $\int_L (2z - \sqrt{x^2 + y^2})\, ds$, where L is the first turn of the conical helix $x = t\cos t$, $y = t\sin t$, $z = t$.

3783. Compute $\int_L (x + y)\, ds$, where L is the quarter of the circle $x^2 + y^2 + z^2 = R^2$, $y = x$, lying in the first octant.

Applications of integrals

3784. Find the mass of the segment of the curve $y = \ln x$ connecting the points x_1 and x_2 if the density at each point is equal to the square of the abscissa of the point.

3785. Find the mass of the segment of the catenary $y = a\cosh \frac{x}{a}$ between the points with the abscissas $x_1 = 0$ and $x_2 = a$ if the density of the curve at each of its points is inversely proportional to the ordinate of this point. The density equals δ at the point $(0, a)$.

3786. Find the mass of the quarter of the ellipse $x = a\cos t$, $y = b\sin t$ situated in the first quadrant if the density at each point is equal to the ordinate of this point.

3787. Find the mass of the first turn of the helix $x = a\cos t$, $y = a\sin t$, $z = bt$ whose density at each point is equal to the square of the polar radius of this point.

3788. Find the mass of the arc of the curve $x = e^t\cos t$, $y = e^t\sin t$, $z = e^t$ connecting the point corresponding to $t = 0$ and an arbitrary point if the density of the arc is inversely proportional to the square of the polar radius and is equal to unity at the point $(1, 0, 1)$.

3789. Find the coordinates of the centre of gravity of the first half-turn of the helix $x = a\cos t,\ y = a\sin t,\ z = bt$, assuming the density to be constant.

3790. Compute the static moment of the first turn of the conical helix $x = t\cos t,\ y = t\sin t,\ z = t$ with respect to the *xy*-plane, assuming the density to be proportional to the square of the distance from this plane $\rho = kz^2$.

3791. Compute the moments of inertia about the coordinate axes of the first turn of the helix $x = a\cos t,\ y = a\sin t,\ z = \frac{h}{2\pi}t$.

In Problems 3792 to 3797 compute the areas of the parts of the cylindrical surfaces contained between the *xy*-plane and the indicated surfaces.

3792. $x^2 + y^2 = R^2,\ z = R + \frac{x^2}{R}$.

3793. $y^2 = 2px,\ \ z = \sqrt{2px - 4x^2}$.

3794. $y^2 = \frac{4}{9}(x-1)^3,\ \ z = 2 - \sqrt{x}$.

3795. $x^2 + y^2 = R^2,\ \ 2Rz = xy$.

3796. $\frac{x^2}{a^2} + \frac{y^2}{b^2} = 1,\ \ z = kx$ and $z = 0$ $(z \geq 0)$ (a "cylindrical horse shoe").

3797. $y = \sqrt{2px},\ \ z = y$ and $x = \frac{8}{9}p$.

3798. Compute the area of the surface cut from a circular cylinder of radius R by an equal cylinder if the axes of these cylinders intersect at right angles (cf. the solution of Problem 3642).

3799. Find the area of the part of the surface of the cylinder $x^2 + y^2 = Rx$ contained inside the sphere $x^2 + y^2 + z^2 = R^2$. According to the Biot-Savart law, a current element acts on a magnet mass m with a force equal to $\frac{mI\sin\alpha\, ds}{r^2}$, where I denotes the current, ds the element of the conductor length, r the distance between the current element and magnetic mass, α the angle between the direction of the straight line, connecting the magnetic mass and the current element, and the direction of the current element itself. This force is directed along the normal to the plane containing the current element and the point in which the magnetic mass is placed; the direction of the force is established by the right hand rule.

Proceeding from this law, solve Problems 3800 to 3805.

3800. Find the force with which current I flowing in an endless rectilinear conductor acts on a magnetic mass point m located at a distance a from the conductor.

3801. Current I flows in a circuit having the shape of a square with the side a. What is the force with which the current acts on a magnetic mass point m situated at the centre of the square?

3802. Show that current I flowing in the arc of the curve, whose equation in polar coordinates has the form $\rho = \rho(\varphi)$, acts on a magnetic mass located in the pole with the force $f = mI\int_{\varphi_1}^{\varphi_2}\frac{d\varphi}{\rho}$.

3803. What is the force with which current I flowing in the closed elliptic circuit acts on a magnetic mass point m located at one of the foci of the ellipse?

3804. What is the force with which current I flowing in an endless parabolic circuit acts on a magnetic mass m placed at the focus of the parabola? The distance between the vertex and focus is equal to $\frac{p}{2}$.

3805. What is the force, with which current I, flowing in a circular circuit of radius R, acts on a magnetic mass point m placed at the point P lying on the perpendicular erected at the centre of the circle and at the distance h from the plane containing the circle?

For what value of R will this force be the greatest at a given h?

2. Line Integrals with Respect to Coordinates

Evaluating integrals

In Problems 3806 to 3821 evaluate the line integrals.

3806. $\int_L x\,dy$, where L is the contour of the triangle formed by the coordinate axes and the straight line $\frac{x}{2}+\frac{y}{3}=1$, in the positive direction, i.e., anticlockwise.

3807. $\int_L x\,dy$, where L is the segment of the straight line $\frac{x}{a}+\frac{y}{b}=1$ joining the end-points of the x- and y- intercepts.

3808. $\int\limits_L (x^2 - y^2)\,dx$, where L is the arc of the parabola $y = x^2$ connecting its points (0, 0) and (2, 4).

3809. $\int\limits_L (x^2 + y^2)\,dy$, where L is the contour of the quadrilateral with the vertices at the points A (0, 0), B (2, 0), C (4, 4) and D (0, 4).

3810. $\int_{(0,\,0)}^{(\pi,\,2\pi)} -x\cos y\,dx + y\sin x\,dy$ along the segment connecting the points (0, 0) and (π, 2π).

3811. $\int_{(0,\,0)}^{(1,\,1)} xy\,dx + (y - x)\,dy$ along the curves (1) $y = x$; (2) $y = x^2$; (3) $y^2 = x$; (4) $y = x^3$.

3812. $\int_{(0,\,0)}^{(1,\,1)} 2xy\,dx + x^2\,dy$ along the curves (1) $y = x$; (2) $y = x^2$; (3) $y = x^3$; (4) $y^2 = x$.

3813. $\int\limits_L y\,dx + x\,dy$, where L is the quarter of the circle $x = R\cos t$, $y = R\sin t$, from $t_1 = 0$ to $t_2 = \frac{\pi}{2}$.

3814. $\int\limits_L y\,dx - x\,dy$, where L is the ellipse $x = a\cos t$, $y = b\sin t$, taken in the positive direction.

3815. $\int\limits_L \frac{y^2\,dx - x^2\,dy}{x^2 + y^2}$, where L is the semicircle $x = a\cos t$, $y = a\sin t$ from $t_1 = 0$ to $t_2 = \pi$.

3816. $\int\limits_L (2a - y)\,dx - (a - y)\,dy$, where L is the first (from the origin) arc of the cycloid $x = a(t - \sin t)$, $y = a(1 - \cos t)$.

3817. $\int\limits_L \frac{x^2\,dy - y^2\,dx}{x^{5/3} + y^{5/3}}$, where L is the quarter of the astroid $x = R\cos^3 t$, $y = R\sin^3 t$, from the point (R, 0) to the point (0, R).

3818. $\int\limits_L x\,dx + y\,dy + (x + y - 1)\,dz$, where L is the straight line segment from the point (1, 1, 1) to the point (2, 3, 4).

3819. $\int\limits_L yz\,dx + zx\,dy + xy\,dz$, where L is the arc of the helix $x = R\cos t$, $y = R\sin t$, $z = \frac{at}{2\pi}$ from the point of intersection of the curve with the plane $z = 0$ to the point of its intersection with the plane $z = a$.

3820. $\int_{(1,1,1)}^{(4,4,4)} \frac{x\,dx + y\,dy + z\,dz}{\sqrt{x^2 + y^2 + z^2 - x - y + 2z}}$ along a straight line.

3821. $\int_L y^2\,dx + z^2\,dy + x^2\,dz$, where L is the line of intersection of the sphere $x^2 + y^2 + z^2 = R^2$ and the cylinder $x^2 + y^2 = Rx$ $(R > 0, z \geq 0)$, integrated anticlockwise when viewed from the origin.

Green's formula

In Problems 3822 to 3823 transform the line integrals round the closed contours L taken in the positive direction into the double integrals over the domains bounded by these contours.

3822. $\int_L (1 - x^2)\,y\,dx + x\,(1 + y^2)\,dy.$

3823. $\int_L (e^{xy} + 2x\cos y)\,dx + (e^{xy} - x^2 \sin y)\,dy.$

3824. Evaluate the integral of Problem 3822 if the contour of integration L is the circle $x^2 + y^2 = R^2$, using two methods:

(1) directly,

(2) by Green's formula.

3825. Evaluate $\int_L (xy + x + y)\,dx + (xy + x - y)\,dy$, where L is (1) ellipse $\frac{x^2}{a^2} + \frac{y^2}{b^2} = 1$; (2) circle $x^2 + y^2 = ax$. The integration goes in the positive direction. Carry out the evolution by two methods:
(1) directly,

(2) with the aid of Green's formula.

3826. Prove that the integral

$$\int_L (yx^3 + e^y)\,dx + (xy^3 + xe^y - 2y)\,dy$$

equals zero if L is a closed curve symmetrical with respect to the origin.

3827. With the aid of Green's formula compute the difference between the integrals

$$I_1 = \int_{AmB} (x + y)^2\,dx - (x - y)^2\,dy$$

and $$I_2 = \int_{AnB} (x + y)^2\, dx - (x - y)^2\, dy,$$

where AmB is the straight line segment connecting the points A (0, 0) and B (1, 1), and AnB is the arc of the parabola $y = x^2$.

3828. Show that the integral

$$\int_L \{x \cos (N, x) + y \sin (N, x)\}\, ds,$$

where (N, x) is the angle between the external normal to the curve and the positive direction of the x-axis, taken round the closed contour L in the positive direction, is equal to twice the area of the figure bounded by the contour L.

3829. Prove that the integral $\int_L (2xy - y)\, dx + x^2\, dy$, where L is a closed contour, is equal to the area of the domain bounded by this contour.

3830. Prove that the integral $\int_L \varphi(y)\, dx + [x\varphi'(y) + x^3]\, dy$ equals the tripled moment of inertia, with respect to the y-axis, of a homogeneous plane figure, bounded by the contour L.

Path-independent line integrals. Finding the antiderivative

In Problems 3831 to 3835 check to see that the integrals taken round any closed contour are equal to zero irrespective of the kind of functions entering the integrand.

3831. $\int_L \varphi(x)\, dx + \psi(y)\, dy$.

3832. $\int_L f(xy)(y\, dx + x\, dy)$.

3833. $\int_L f\left(\frac{y}{x}\right) \frac{x\, dy - y\, dx}{x^2}$.

3834. $\int_L [f(x + y) + f(x - y)]\, dx + [f(x + y) - f(x - y)]\, dy$.

3835. $\int_L f(x^2 + y^2 + z^2)(x\, dx + y\, dy + z\, dz)$.

3836*. Prove that the integral $\int_L \frac{x\,dy - y\,dx}{x^2 + y^2}$, taken in the positive direction over any closed contour with the origin inside it is equal to 2π.

3837. Compute $\int_L \frac{x\,dy - y\,dx}{x^2 + 4y^2}$ round the circle $x^2 + y^2 = 1$ in the positive direction.

In Problems 3838 to 3844 evaluate the line integrals of the total differentials.

3838. $\int_{(-1,\,2)}^{(2,\,3)} y\,dx + x\,dy.$

3839. $\int_{(0,\,0)}^{(2,\,1)} 2xy\,dx + x^2\,dy.$

3840. $\int_{(3,\,4)}^{(5,\,12)} \frac{x\,dx + y\,dy}{x^2 + y^2}$ (the origin does not lie on the contour of integration).

3841. $\int_{(P_1)}^{(P_2)} \frac{x\,dx + y\,dy}{\sqrt{x^2 + y^2}}$, where the points P_1 and P_2 are situated on concentric circles with the origin as centre and radii equal respectively to R_1 and R_2 (the origin does not lie on the contour of integration).

3842. $\int_{(1,\,-1,\,2)}^{(2,\,1,\,3)} x\,dx - y^2\,dy + z\,dz.$

3843. $\int_{(0,\,2,\,3)}^{(3,\,2,\,1)} yz\,dx + zx\,dy + xy\,dz.$

3844. $\int_{(7,\,2,\,3)}^{(5,\,3,\,1)} \frac{zx\,dy + xy\,dz - yz\,dx}{(x - yz)^2}$ (the contour of integration does not intersect the surface $z = \frac{x}{y}$).

In Problems 3845 to 3852 find the functions given the total differentials.

3845. $du = x^2\,dx + y^2\,dy.$

3846. $du = 4\,(x^2 - y^2)\,(x\,dx - y\,dy).$

3847. $du = \frac{(x + 2y)\,dx + y\,dy}{(x + y)^2}.$

3848. $du = \frac{x}{y\sqrt{x^2 + y^2}}\,dx - \left(\frac{x^2 + \sqrt{x^2 + y^2}}{y^2\sqrt{x^2 + y^2}}\right) dy.$

3849. $du = \left[\frac{x-2y}{(y-x)^2} + x\right] dx + \left[\frac{y}{(y-x)^2} - y^2\right] dy.$

3850. $du = (2x\cos y - y^2 \sin x)\, dx + (2y\cos x - x^2 \sin y)\, dy.$

3851. $du = \frac{2x(1-e^y)}{(1+x^2)^2}\, dx + \left(\frac{e^y}{1+x^2} + 1\right) dy.$

3852. $du = \frac{(3y-x)\, dx + (y-3x)\, dy}{(x+y)^3}.$

3853. Choose the number n so that the expression $\frac{(x-y)\, dx + (x+y)\, dy}{(x^2+y^2)^n}$ becomes a total differential; find the corresponding function.

3854. Choose the constants a and b so that the expression $\frac{(y^2+2xy+ax^2)\, dx - (x^2+2xy+by^2)\, dy}{(x^2+y^2)^2}$ becomes a total differential; find the corresponding function.

In Problems 3855 to 3860 find the functions given total differentials.

3855. $du = \frac{dx + dy + dz}{x+y+z}.$

3856. $du = \frac{x\, dx + y\, dy + z\, dz}{\sqrt{x^2+y^2+z^2}}.$

3857. $du = \frac{yz\, dx + zx\, dy + xy\, dz}{1 + x^2y^2z^2}.$

3858. $du = \frac{2(zx\, dy + xy\, dz - yz\, dx)}{(x-yz)^2}.$

3859. $du = \frac{dx - 3\, dy}{z} + \frac{3y - x + z^3}{z^2}\, dz.$

3860. $du = e^{y/z}\, dx + \left(\frac{e^{y/z}(x+1)}{z} + ze^{yz}\right) dy + \left(-\frac{e^{y/z}(x+1)y}{z^2} + ye^{yz} + e^{-z}\right) dz.$

Applications of integrals

In Problems 3861 to 3868, using the line integral, compute the area of the figure enclosed by.

3861. Ellipse $x = a\cos t$, $y = b\sin t$.

3862. Astroid $x = a\cos^3 t$, $y = a\sin^3 t$.

3863. Cardioid $x = 2a\cos t - a\cos 2t$, $y = 2a\sin t - a\sin 2t$.

3864*. Loop of the folium of Descartes $x^3 + y^3 - 3axy = 0$.

3865. Loop of the curve $(x+y)^3 = xy$.

3866. Loop of the curve $(x+y)^4 = x^2y$.

3867*. Bernoulli's lemniscate $(x^2+y^2)^2 = 2a^2(x^2-y^2)$.

3868. Loop of the curve $(\sqrt{x} + \sqrt{y})^{12} = xy$.

Work

3869. At each point of a plane a material point is acted upon by a force having a constant magnitude F and directed along the positive x-axis. Find the work performed by this force as the point moves in the arc of the circle lying in the first quadrant.

3870. At each point of a plane a material point is acted upon by the force $\mathbf{F}$ whose projections on the coordinate axes are $X = xy$, $Y = x + y$. Compute the work performed by the force $\mathbf{F}$ as the point travels from the origin to the point (1, 1): (1) in the straight line $y = x$; (2) in the parabola $y = x^2$; (3) in the two-link polygonal line whose links are parallel to the axes of coordinates (two cases).

3871. Applied to each point M of the ellipse $x = a\cos t$, $y = b\sin t$ is a force $\mathbf{F}$ numerically equal to the distance between the point M and the centre of the ellipse and directed towards the centre of the ellipse. (a) Compute the work performed by the force $\mathbf{F}$ as the point moves in the arc of the ellipse located in the first quadrant. (b) Find the work if the point covers the whole length of the ellipse.

3872. The projections of a force on the coordinate axes are specified by the formulas $X = 2xy$ and $Y = x^2$. Show that the work of the force performed during displacement of a point depends on its initial and final positions only and is independent of the shape of the path. Compute the work performed as the point travels from the point (1, 0) to the point (0, 3).

3873. A force is inversely proportional to the distance of the point of its application from the xy-plane and is directed towards the origin. Compute the work performed as a point moves under the action of this force in the straight line $x = at$, $y = bt$, $z = ct$ from the point M (a, b, c) to the point N $(2a, 2b, 2c)$.

3874. A force is inversely proportional to the distance of the point of its application from the z-axis, perpendicular to this axis and is directed towards it. Find the work performed as a point moves under the action of this force in the circle $x = \cos t$, $y = 1$, $z = \sin t$ from the point M (1, 1, 0) to the point N (0, 1, 1).

3875. Prove that the work of the gravitational force of two mass points performed during the displacement of one of them is independent of the shape of the path. The gravitational force F is determined by Newton's law $F = \dfrac{km_1m_2}{r^2}$, where r is the distance between the points, m_1 and m_2 the masses concentrated at these points, k the gravitational constant.

3. Surface Integrals

Integrals over surfaces

In Problems 3876 to 3884 evaluate the integrals.

3876. $\iint\limits_S \left(z + 2x + \frac{4}{3}y\right) dq$, where S is the portion of the plane $\frac{x}{2} + \frac{y}{3} + \frac{z}{4} = 1$ lying in the first octant.

3877. $\iint\limits_S xyz\, dq$, where S is the portion of the plane $x + y + z = 1$ lying in the first octant.

3878. $\iint\limits_S x\, dq$, where S is the portion of the sphere $x^2 + y^2 + z^2 = R^2$ lying in the first octant.

3879. $\iint\limits_S y\, dq$, where S is the hemisphere $z = \sqrt{R^2 - x^2 - y^2}$.

3880. $\iint\limits_S \sqrt{R^2 - x^2 - y^2}\, dq$, where S is the hemisphere $z = \sqrt{R^2 - x^2 - y^2}$.

3881. $\iint\limits_S x^2y^2\, dq$, where S is the hemisphere $z = \sqrt{R^2 - x^2 - y^2}$.

3882. $\iint\limits_S \frac{dq}{r^2}$, where S is the cylinder $x^2 + y^2 = R^2$, bounded by the planes $z = 0$ and $z = H$ and r is the distance between a point on the surface and the origin.

3883. $\iint\limits_S \frac{dq}{r^n}$, where S is the sphere $x^2 + y^2 + z^2 = R^2$ and r is the distance between a point on the sphere and the fixed point $P\ (0, 0, c)\ (c > R)$.

3884. $\iint\limits_S \frac{dq}{r}$, where S is the portion of the surface of the hyperbolic paraboloid $z = xy$, cut off by the cylinder $x^2 + y^2 = R^2$ and r is the distance from a point on the surface to the z-axis.

3885*. Find the mass of a sphere if the surface density at each point equals the distance of this point from a certain fixed diameter of the sphere.

3886. Find the mass of a sphere if the surface density at each point is equal to the square of the distance of this point from a certain fixed diameter of the sphere.

Surface integrals with respect to coordinates

In Problems 3887 to 3893 evaluate the surface integrals.

3887. $\iint\limits_S x\,dy\,dz + y\,dx\,dz + z\,dx\,dy$, where S is the positive side of the cube formed by the planes $x = 0$, $y = 0$, $z = 0$, $x = 1$, $y = 1$, $z = 1$.

3888. $\iint\limits_S x^2y^2z\,dx\,dy$, where S is the positive side of the lower half of the sphere $x^2 + y^2 + z^2 = R^2$.

3889. $\iint\limits_S z\,dx\,dy$, where S is the external side of the ellipsoid

$$\frac{x^2}{a^2} + \frac{y^2}{b^2} + \frac{z^2}{c^2} = 1.$$

3890. $\iint\limits_S z^2\,dx\,dy$, where S is the outer side of the ellipsoid

$$\frac{x^2}{a^2} + \frac{y^2}{b^2} + \frac{z^2}{c^2} = 1.$$

3891. $\iint\limits_S xz\,dx\,dy + xy\,dy\,dz + yz\,dx\,dz$, where S is the outer side of the pyramid formed by the planes $x = 0$, $y = 0$, $z = 0$ and $x + y + z = 1$.

3892. $\iint\limits_S yz\,dx\,dy + xz\,dy\,dz + xy\,dx\,dz$, where S is the outer side of the surface situated in the first octant and formed by the cylinder $x^2 + y^2 = R^2$ and planes $x = 0$, $y = 0$, $z = 0$ and $z = H$.

3893. $\iint\limits_S y^2z\,dx\,dy + xz\,dy\,dz + x^2y\,dx\,dz$, where S is the outer side of the surface situated in the first octant and formed by the paraboloid of revolution $z = x^2 + y^2$; cylinder $x^2 + y^2 = 1$ and coordinate planes (Fig. 68).

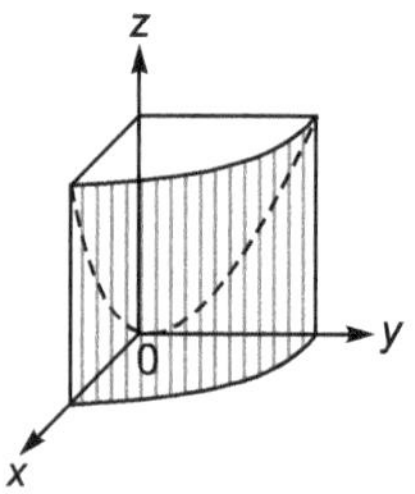

Fig. 68

Stokes' formula

3894. Using Stokes' formula, transform the integral $\int_L (y^2 + z^2)\,dx + (x^2 + z^2)\,dy + (x^2 + y^2)\,dz$ taken round a certain closed contour to the integral over the surface "pulled" on this contour.

3895. Evaluate the integral $\int_L x^2y^3\,dx + dy + z\,dz$, where L is the circle $x^2 + y^2 = R^2$, $z = 0$: (a) directly and (b) with the aid of Stokes' formula, taking the hemisphere $z = +\sqrt{R^2 - x^2 - y^2}$ as a surface. Integration round the circle in the *xy*-plane goes in the positive direction.

Ostrogradsky's formula

3896. Using Ostrogradsky's formula, transform the surface integral over a closed surface $\iint_S x^2\,dy\,dz + y^2\,dx\,dz + z^2\,dx\,dy$ to a triple integral for computing the volume of a solid. Integration is performed over the outer side of the surface S.

3897. Using Ostrogradsky's formula, transform the surface integral over a closed surface:

$$\iint_S \sqrt{x^2 + y^2 + z^2}\,\{\cos(N, x) + \cos(N, y) + \cos(N, z)\}\,d\sigma,$$

where N is an outer normal to the surface S, to a triple integral for computing the volume of a solid.

3898. Compute the integral of Problem 3897 if S is a sphere of radius R with the centre at the origin.

3899. Compute the integral

$$\iint_S [x^3 \cos(N, x) + y^3 \cos(N, y) + z^3 \cos(N, z)]\,d\sigma,$$

where S is a sphere of radius R with the origin as centre, and N is an outer normal.

3900. Compute the integrals of Problem 3891 to 3893, using Ostrogradsky's formula.

14

Differential Equations

1. Equations of the First Order

Equations with variables separable

In Problems 3901 to 3910 find the general solutions of the differential equations.

3901. $(xy^2 + x)\,dx + (y - x^2y)\,dy = 0.$ **3902.** $xyy' = 1 - x^2.$

3903. $yy' = \dfrac{1 - 2x}{y}.$ **3904.** $y' \tan x - y = a.$

3905. $xy' + y = y^2.$ **3906.** $y' + \sqrt{\dfrac{1 - y^2}{1 - x^2}} = 0.$

3907. $\sqrt{1 - y^2}\,dx + y\sqrt{1 - x^2}\,dy = 0.$ **3908.** $e^{-s}\left(1 + \dfrac{ds}{dt}\right) = 1.$

3909. $y' = 10^{x + y}.$ **3910.** $y' + \sin\dfrac{x + y}{2} = \sin\dfrac{x - y}{2}.$

3911. The relationship between the velocity of a projectile v and the path l covered by it in the bore of a barrel is established in ballistics by the following equation : $v = \dfrac{al^n}{b + l^n}$, where $v = \dfrac{dl}{dt}$ and $n < 1$. Find the relationship between the time t during which the projectile moves in the bore and the distance l covered.

3912. If x denotes the quantity of the hydriodic acid HI decomposed by the time t, then the decomposition rate $\left(\dfrac{dx}{dt}\right)$ is determined by the differential equation $\dfrac{dx}{dt} = k_1\left(\dfrac{1 - x}{v}\right)^2 - k_2\left(\dfrac{x}{v}\right)^2$, where k_1, k_2 and v are constants. Integrate this equation.

In Problems 3913 to 3916 find the particular solutions of the differential equations satisfying the given initial conditions.

3913. $y' \sin x = y \ln y;\ y|_{x=\frac{\pi}{2}} = e.$

3914. $y' = \dfrac{1+y^2}{1+x^2};\ y|_{x=0} = 1.$

3915. $\sin y \cos x\, dy = \cos y \sin x\, dx;\ y|_{x=0} = \dfrac{\pi}{4}.$

3916. $y - xy' = b(1 + x^2 y');\ y|_{x=1} = 1.$

3917. Find the curve which passes through the point (2, 3) and possesses the following property : the segment of any of its tangents contained between the coordinate axes is bisected at the point of tangency.

3918. Find the curve which passes through the point (2, 0) and possesses the following property : the segment of the tangent between the point of tangency and the y-axis has a constant length equal to two.

3919. Find all the curves possessing the following property : the segment of the tangent between the point of tangency and the x-axis is bisected at the point of intersection with the y-axis.

3920. Find all the curves whose subtangents are proportional to the abscissas of the points of tangency (the proportionality factor is equal to k).

3921. Find the curve which passes through the point $(a, 1)$ and has a subtangent with a constant length a.

3922. Find the curve the length of whose normal (its segment from a point on the curve to the x-axis) is a constant equal to a.

3923. Find the curve possessing the following property : the sum of the lengths of the tangent and subtangent at any of its points is proportional to the product of the coordinates of the point of tangency (the proportionality factor is equal to k).

3924. Find the curve $y = f(x)\ (f(x) \geq 0,\ f(0) = 0)$ bounding a curvilinear trapezoid with the base $[0, x]$, whose area is proportional to the $(n+1)$th power of $f(x)$. It is known that $f(1) = 1$.

3925. A material point, whose mass is equal to 1 g, performs rectilinear motion under the action of a force directly proportional to the time as measured from the time $t = 0$ and inversely proportional to the velocity of its motion. At the time $t = 10$ s the velocity was equal to 0.5 m/s, and the force to 4×10^{-5} N. What will the velocity be in a minute after the point started?

3926. A material point performs rectilinear motion so that its kinetic energy at the time t is directly proportional to the average velocity of motion in the time interval from zero to t. It is known that at $t = 0$ the path $s = 0$. Show that the motion is uniform.

3927. A motorboat moves in still water with a speed $v = 10$ km/h. At full speed its engine was cut off and in 20 seconds the speed was reduced to $v_1 = 6$ km/h. Assuming that the force of water resistance to the moving boat is proportional to its speed, find the speed of the boat in two minutes after the engine was shut off; find also the distance travelled by the boat during one minute with the engine dead.

3928. The bottom of a vertical cylindrical vessel with the cross-sectional area S is provided with a small circular hole whose area is q. The hole is covered with a diaphragm (like the objective of a camera). The vessel is filled with water to the height h. At the time $t = 0$ the diaphragm starts open, the area of the hole being proportional to the time, the hole opens completely during T seconds. What will the height H of the water in the vessel be in T seconds after the experiment began?

(See Problems 2701 to 2706).

3929. The rate of cooling of a body is proportional to the difference between the temperature of the body and the ambient temperature. In Problems 2710 and 2711 we assumed the proportionality factor to be constant. Sometimes it is supposed that it depends linearly on time, $k = k_0\,(1 + \alpha t)$. Find the relationship between the temperature of the body θ and time t if at $t = 0$, $\theta = \theta_0$ and the ambient temperature is θ_1.

3930*. The rate of growth of the area of a young victoria-regia leaf, which has the shape of a circle, is proportional to the length of its circumference and quantity of sunlight received by this leaf. The latter, in its turn, is proportional to the area of the leaf and cosine of the angle between the direction of sun rays and the vertical. Find the relationship between the area S of the leaf and time t if it is known that at 6 a.m. this area was equal to 1600 cm^2 and at 6 p.m. of the same day to 2500 cm^2. (Observation is supposed to have been carried out from the equator on the day of equinox when the angle between the direction of sun rays and the vertical may be taken equal to 90° at 6 a.m. and at 6 p.m. and to 0° at noon.)

In Problems 3931 to 3933, substituting the sought-for functions reduce the given equations to equations with separable variables and solve them.

3931. $y' = \cos(x - y)$ (put $u = x - y$).

3932. $y' = 3x - 2y + 5$.

3933. $y'\sqrt{1 + x + y} = x + y - 1$.

Homogeneous equations

In Problems 3934 to 3944 find general solutions to the following equations :

3934. $y' = \dfrac{y^2}{x^2} - 2.$

3935. $y' = \dfrac{x+y}{x-y}.$

3936. $x\,dy - y\,dx = y\,dy.$

3937. $y' = \dfrac{2xy}{x^2 - y^2}.$

3938. $y' = \dfrac{x}{y} + \dfrac{y}{x}.$

3939. $xy' - y = \sqrt{x^2 + y^2}.$

3940. $y^2 + x^2 y' = xyy'.$

3941. $y' = e^{y/x} + \dfrac{y}{x}.$

3942. $xy' = y \ln \dfrac{y}{x}.$

3943. $(3y^2 + 3xy + x^2)\,dx = (x^2 + 2xy)\,dy.$

3944. $y' = \dfrac{y}{x} + \dfrac{\varphi\left(\dfrac{y}{x}\right)}{\varphi'\left(\dfrac{y}{x}\right)}.$

In Problems 3945 to 3948 find particular solutions of the differential equations satisfying the given initial conditions.

3945. $(xy' - y) \arctan \dfrac{y}{x} = x;\ y|_{x=1} = 0.$

3946. $(y^2 - 3x^2)\,dy + 2xy\,dx = 0;\ y|_{x=0} = 1.$

3947. $y' = \dfrac{y^2 - 2xy - x^2}{y^2 + 2xy - x^2};\ y|_{x=1} = -1.$

3948. $y\left(\dfrac{dy}{dx}\right)^2 + 2x\dfrac{dy}{dx} - y = 0;\ y|_{x=0} = \sqrt{5}.$

3949. Bring the equation $y' = \dfrac{y}{x} + \varphi\left(\dfrac{x}{y}\right)$ to quadrature. What must the function $\varphi\left(\dfrac{x}{y}\right)$ be so that $y = \dfrac{x}{\ln|Cx|}$ is the general solution of the given equation?

3950. Find the curve such that the square of the intercept cut by any tangent off the y-axis is equal to the product of the coordinates of the point of tangency.

3951. Find the curve such that the initial ordinate of any tangent is equal to the corresponding subnormal.

3952. Find the curve such that the length of the polar radius of any point M equals the distance between the point of intersection of the tangent at the point M and the y-axis, and the origin.

3953*. The light rays emanating from a point source, when reflected from the mirror of a searchlight, are directed as a parallel beam. What surface of revolution is the mirror?

Linear equations

In Problems 3954 to 3964 find the general solutions of the given equations.

3954. $y' + 2y = 4x.$

3955. $y' + 2xy = xe^{-x^2}.$

3956. $y' + \dfrac{1-2x}{x^2}y = 1.$

3957. $(1+x^2)y' - 2xy = (1+x^2)^2.$

3958. $y' + y = \cos x.$

3959. $y' + ay = e^{mx}.$

3960. $2y\,dx + (y^2 - 6x)\,dy = 0.$

3961. $y' = \dfrac{1}{2x - y^2}.$

3962. $y' = \dfrac{y}{2y\ln y + y - x}.$

3963. $x(y' - y) = (1+x^2)e^x.$

3964. $y' + y\Phi'(x) - \Phi(x)\Phi'(x) = 0$, where $\Phi(x)$ is a given function.

In Problems 3965 to 3968 find the particular solutions of the equations satisfying the indicated initial conditions.

3965. $y' - y\tan x = \sec x;$ $\quad y|_{x=0} = 0.$

3966. $xy' + y - e^x = 0;$ $\quad y|_{x=a} = b.$

3967. $xy' - \dfrac{y}{x+1} = x;$ $\quad y|_{x=1} = 0.$

3968. $t(1+t^2)\,dx = (x + xt^2 - t^2)\,dt;\ x|_{t=1} = -\dfrac{\pi}{4}.$

3969. Let y_1 and y_2 are two different solutions of the equation

$$y' + P(x)\cdot y = Q(x).$$

(a) Prove that $y = y_1 + C(y_2 - y_1)$ is the general solution of the same equation (C is a constant).

(b) At what relationship between the constants α and β will the linear combination $\alpha y_1 + \beta y_2$ be a solution of the given equation?

(c) Prove that if y_3 is the third particular solution different from y_1 and y_2, then the ratio $\dfrac{y_2 - y_1}{y_3 - y_1}$ is constant.

3970. Prove the identity (see Problem 2345) :

$\int_0^x e^{zx - z^2}\,dz = e^{x^2/4}\int_0^x e^{-z^2/4}\,dz,$ deriving for the function $I(x) = \int_0^x e^{zx - z^2}\,dz$ a differential equation and solving it.

3971. Find the curve such that the initial ordinate of any tangent is less than the abscissa of the point of tangency by two scale units.

3972*. Find the curve such that the area of the rectangle constructed on the abscissa of any point and the initial ordinate of the tangent at this point is a constant ($= a^2$).

3973*. Find the curve for which the area of the triangle formed by the x-axis, tangent line and radius vector of the point of tangency is constant ($= a^2$).

3974. A mass point m performs a rectilinear motion under the action of a force proportional to the time (the proportionality factor equals k_1) passed from the instant when its velocity was zero. Besides, the point is acted upon by the medium resistance force which is proportional to the velocity (the proportionality factor is equal to k). Find the dependence of the velocity on time.

3975. A mass point m is in rectilinear motion under the action of a force proportional to the cube of the time elapsed from the instant when the velocity was v_0 (the proportionality factor is equal to k). Besides, the point is acted upon by the medium counterforce which is proportional to the product of the velocity by the time (the proportionality facator is equal to k_1). Find the dependence of the velocity on time.

3976. The initial temperature of a body θ_0°C equals the ambient temperature. The body receives heat from a heater (the rate of heat feeding is a specified function of the time : $c\varphi(t)$, where c is the constant heat capacity of the body). Besides, the body loses heat into the surrounding medium (the rate of cooling is proportional to the difference between the temperature of the body and the ambient temperature). Find the dependence of the temperature of the body on the time measured from the beginning of the experiment.

Solve Problems 3977 and 3978 taking into account that if alternating current $I = I(t)$ flows in the conductor with the inductance L and resistance R, then the voltage drop along the conductor will be equal to $L\dfrac{dI}{dt} + RI$.

3977. The potential difference across the terminals of a coil drops uniformly from $E_0 = 2$ V to $E_1 = 1$ V during 10 seconds. What will the current be in ten seconds if at the beginning of the experiment it was equal $16\frac{2}{3}$ A? The resistance of the coil is 0.12 ohm, the inductance 0.1 H.

3978. Find the current in a coil at the time t if its resistance is R, inductance L, initial current $I_0 = 0$, and the electromotive force varies according to the law $E = E_0 \sin \omega t$.

Miscellaneous problems
(Equations with separable variables, homogeneous and linear equations)

In Problems 3979 to 3997 find general solutions of the equations :

3979. $y' = \frac{x^2 + xy + y^2}{x^2}$.

3980. $x^2 dy + (3 - 2xy)\,dx = 0$.

3981. $x(x^2 + 1)\,y' + y = x(1 + x^2)^2$.

3982. $y' = \frac{y + 1}{x}$.

3983. $y' = \frac{1 + y^2}{xy(1 + x^2)}$.

3984. $(8y + 10x)\,dx + (5y + 7x)\,dy = 0$.

3985. $x^3 y' = y(y^2 + x^2)$.

3986. $\frac{xy' - y}{x} = \tan \frac{y}{x}$.

3987. $\left(x - y \cos \frac{y}{x}\right) dx + x \cos \frac{y}{x}\, dy = 0$.

3988. $y' = e^{2x} - e^x y$.

3989. $\frac{dx}{x^2 - xy + y^2} = \frac{dy}{2y^2 - xy}$.

3990. $\frac{dy}{dx} = \frac{1}{x \cos y + \sin 2y}$.

3991. $(x - 2xy - y^2)\,dy + y^2\,dx = 0$.

3992. $y' + y \cos x = \sin x \cos x$.

3993. $(x + 1)\,y' - ny = e^x (x + 1)^{n+1}$.

3994. $y\,dx = (y^3 - x)\,dy$.

3995. $\left(\frac{dy}{dx}\right)^2 - (x + y)\frac{dy}{dx} + xy = 0$.

3996*. $yy' \sin x = \cos x\,(\sin x - y^2)$.

3997. $y' = (x + y)^2$.

3998. Make sure that the integral curves of the equation $(1 - x^2)\,y' + xy = ax$ are ellipses and hyperbolas with the centres at the point $(0, a)$ and the axes parallel to the coordinate axes, each curve having one constant axis whose length is equal to 2.

In Problems 3999 to 4002 find the particular solutions of the given equations satisfying the indicated conditions.

3999. $\frac{y - xy'}{x + yy'} = 2$; $\quad y|_{x=1} = 1$.

4000. $y' - \frac{y}{1 - x^2} = 1 + x$; $\quad y|_{x=0} = 1$.

4001. $(1 + e^x)\,yy' = e^y$; $\quad y|_{x=0} = 0$.

4002. $y' = 3x^2 y + x^5 + x^2$; $\quad y|_{x=0} = 1$.

4003. Prove that only the straight lines $y = kx$ and hyperbolas $xy = m$ possess the following property : the length of the polar radius of any of their points is equal to the length of the tangent drawn at this point.

4004. Find the curve such that the length of the normal is proportional to the square of the ordinate. The proportionality factor is equal to k.

4005. Find the curve such that any tangent intersects with the y-axis at the point equidistant from the point of tangency and the origin.

4006. Find the equation of the curve intersecting with the x-axis at the point $x = 1$ and possessing the following property : the length of the subnormal at any point of the curve is equal to the arithmetic mean of the coordinates of this point.

4007. Find the curve such that the area of the trapezoid formed by the coordinate axes, ordinate of an arbitrary point and the tangent at this point equals half the square of its abscissa.

4008. The area of the figure bounded by a curve, the x-axis, and two ordinates, one of which is constant, the other variable, is equal to the ratio of the cube of the variable ordinate to the variable abscissa. Find the curve.

4009. Find the curve such that the area of the figure bounded by the x-axis, two ordinates and arc MM' of this curve is proportional to the arc length MM' at any choice of the points M and M'.

4010. Find the curve such that the abscissa of the centre of gravity of the curvilinear trapezoid formed by the coordinate axes straight line $x = a$ and the curve is equal to $\frac{3a}{4}$ for any a.

4011*. Find the curve all the tangents to which pass through a given point (x_0, y_0).

4012. Find the curve passing through the origin, all the normals to which pass through a given point (x_0, y_0).

4013. Find the curve such that the angle, formed with the x-axis by the tangent to the curve at any of its points, is twice the angle formed by the polar radius of the point of tangency with the same axis.

4014. A body whose mass is $m = 1$ is acted upon by a force proportional to the time (the proportionality factor is equal to k_1). Besides, the body experiences the counteraction of the medium which is proportional to the velocity of the body (the proportionality factor being equal to k_2). Find the law of body's motion (dependence of the path on time).

4015. A particle falls in a medium whose resistance is proportional to the square of the velocity of the particle. Show that the equation of this free fall is : $\frac{dv}{dt} = g - kv^2$, where k is a constant, and g is the gravitational acceleration. Integrate this equation and show that v tends to $\sqrt{\frac{g}{k}}$ as $t \to \infty$.

4016. The friction force decelerating the motion of a disk rotating in a liquid is proportional to the angular velocity of rotation.

(1) The disk which began to rotate with an angular velocity of 3 r.p.s. in a minute rotates at a rate of 2 r.p.s. What will its angular velocity be after three minutes of rotation?

(2) The disk which began to rotate with an angular velocity of 5 r.p.s. in two minutes rotates at a rate of 3 r.p.s. In what time after start will it roate with a velocity equal to 1 r.p.s.?

4017. A bullet enters a board $h = 0.1$ m thick with a velocity of $v_0 = 200$ m/s, pierces it, and leaves the board with a velocity of $v_1 = 80$ m/s. Assuming that the resistance of the board offered to the bullet is proportional to the square of its velocity, find the time during which the bullet pierced the board.

4018*. A drop of water, having the initial mass of M_0 g and evaporating uniformly at a rate of m g/s, moves by inertia with the initial velocity v_0 cm/s. The resistance force of the medium is proportional to the velocity of the drop and its radius. At the initial time ($t = 0$) it is equal to f_0 dynes. Find the dependence of the velocity of the drop on time.

4019*. A drop of water, having the initial mass M_0 g and evaporating at a rate of m g/s, falls freely in the air. The resistance force is proportional to the velocity of the drop (the proportionality factor is equal to k).

Find the velocity of the drop as a function of time elapsed from the instant the drop started falling, it at the initial time its velocity was equal to zero. Assume that $k \neq 2m$.

4020*. Solve the previous problem for a spherical drop assuming that the resistance force of the air is proportional to the product of the drop velocity by the area of its surface. The density of the liquid is γ. (Reduce to quadratures.)

4021*. If in a certain process one substance turns into another, and the rate of generation of the product is proportional to the available quantity of the original substance, then such a phenomenon is called a process (or reaction) of the first order.

A substance whose initial quantity is m_0 turns into another substance, and from the product thus obtained a second product begins to generate immediately. Both reactions are of the first order; the proportionality factors are known : k_1 for the first process and k_2 for the second.

What quantity of the second product will be generated in t time units after the beginning of the process?

4022. A reservoir whose volume is 100 l is filled with brine which contains 10 kg of dissolved salt. The reservoir is fed with water which enters it at a rate of 3 l/min, and the mixture is pumped over into the second reservoir whose capacity is also 100 litres and which is originally filled with pure water. As a result, the surplus quantity of the liquid is pouring out of the second reservoir. How much salt will the second reservoir contain in an hour's time? What is the maximum quantity of salt in the second reservoir and when is it reached? (The salt concentration in each of the reservoirs is maintained uniform by stirring up the mixture.)

4023. The voltage and resistance of a circuit vary uniformly during a minute from zero to 120 V and from zero to 120 ohms, respectively (see Problems 3977 and 3978). The inductance of the circuit is constant (1 henry), the initial current being equal to I_0. Find the relationship between the current and time during the first minute of the experiment.

4024*. A narrow horizontal cylindrical tube AB is hermetically filled with gas. The tube rotates uniformly with an angular velocity ω about the vertical axis OO_1 (Fig. 69) passing through one of its ends. The length of the tube is l cm, the cross-sectional area is S cm^2, the mass of the gas contained in it is M g, the pressure (which is constant throughout the entire length of the tube at rest) is p_0. Find the distribution of pressure along the rotating tube, i.e., express p as a function of x.

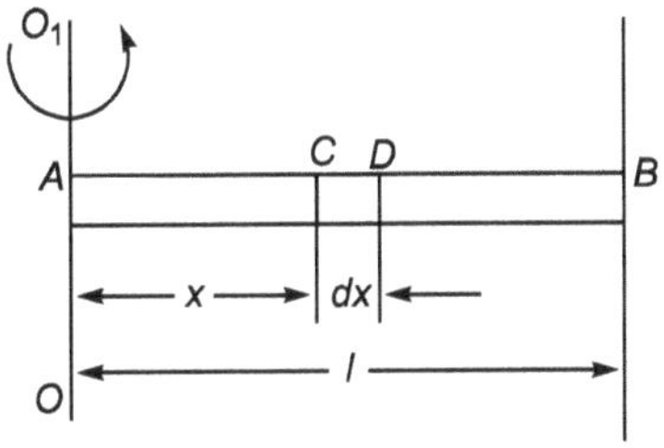

Fig. 69

Other examples of equations of the first order

In Problems 4025 to 4037 find general solutions of the equations reducing them to linear or homogeneous equations by changing the variables.

4025. $y' = \dfrac{2y - x - 5}{2x - y + 4}$.

4026. $y' = \dfrac{2x - y + 1}{x - 2y + 1}$.

4027. $(x + y + 1)\,dx = (2x + 2y - 1)\,dy$.

4028. $y' = \dfrac{2(y + 2)^2}{(x + y - 1)^2}$.

4029. $y' = \dfrac{y^2 - x}{2y(x + 1)}$.

4030. $y' = \dfrac{y^3}{2(xy^2 - x^2)}$.

4031. $(1 - xy + x^2y^2)\,dx = x^2\,dy$.

4032. $(x^2y^2 - 1)\,y' + 2xy^3 = 0$.

4033. $yy' + x = \frac{1}{2}\left(\frac{x^2 + y^2}{x}\right)^2$.

4034. $xy' + 1 = e^y$.

4035. $(x^2 + y^2 + 1)\,dy + xy\,dx = 0$.

4036. $x\,dx + y\,dy + x\,(x\,dy - y\,dx) = 0$.

4037. $(x^2 + y^2 + y)\,dx = x\,dy$.

In Problems 4038 to 4047 solve the given Bernoulli's equations.

4038. $y' + 2xy = 2x^3y^3$.

4039. $y' + \frac{y}{x+1} + y^2 = 0$.

4040. $y^{n-1}\,(ay' + y) = x$.

4041. $x\,dx = \left(\frac{x^2}{y} - y^3\right)dy$.

4042. $xy' + y = y^2 \ln x$.

4043. $y' - y \tan x + y^2 \cos x = 0$.

4044. $y' + \frac{2y}{x} = \frac{2\sqrt{y}}{\cos^2 x}$.

4045. $xy' - 4y - x^2\sqrt{y} = 0$.

4046. $y\,dy - \frac{ay^2}{x^2}\,dx = \frac{b\,dx}{x^2}$.

4047. $y' = \frac{y\varphi'(x) - y^2}{\varphi(x)}$, where $\varphi(x)$ is a specified function.

4048. Find the curve such that the y-intercept cut off by the tangent at an arbitrary point is

(1) proportional to the square of the ordinate of the point of tangency,

(2) proportional to the cube of the ordinate of the point of tangency.

4049. Find the curves specified by the equations of the form $\rho = f(\varphi)$ for which the area of the sectors bounded by the curve and the polar radii of a fixed point (ρ_0, φ_0) and a moving point (ρ, φ) of the curve is proportional to the product of the coordinates ρ and φ of this moving point. The proportionality factor is equal to k.

Exact differential equations

In Problems 4050 to 4057 find the general solutions of the given equations.

4050. $(2x^3 - xy^2)\,dx + (2y^3 - x^2y)\,dy = 0$.

4051. $\frac{x\,dy}{x^2 + y^2} = \left(\frac{y}{x^2 + y^2} - 1\right)dx$.

4052. $e^y\,dx + (xe^y - 2y)\,dy = 0$.

4053. $yx^{y-1}\,dx + x^y \ln x\,dy = 0.$

4054. $\dfrac{x\,dx + y\,dy}{\sqrt{x^2+y^2}} = \dfrac{y\,dx - x\,dy}{x^2}.$

4055. $\dfrac{y + \sin x \cdot \cos^2(xy)}{\cos^2(xy)}\,dx + \dfrac{x}{\cos^2(xy)}\,dy + \sin y\,dy = 0.$

4056. $(1 + x\sqrt{x^2+y^2})\,dx + (-1 + \sqrt{x^2+y^2})y\,dy = 0.$

4057. $\left(\dfrac{1}{y}\sin\dfrac{x}{y} - \dfrac{y}{x^2}\cos\dfrac{y}{x} + 1\right)dx + \left(\dfrac{1}{x}\cos\dfrac{y}{x} - \dfrac{x}{y^2}\sin\dfrac{x}{y} + \dfrac{1}{y^2}\right)dy = 0.$

Integrating factor

In Problems 4058 to 4062 find the integrating factor and the general solutions of the given equations.

4058. $(x^2 + y)\,dx - x\,dy = 0.$

4059*. $y(1 + xy)\,dx - x\,dy = 0.$

4060. $(x^2 + y^2 + 2x)\,dx + 2y\,dy = 0.$

4061. $\dfrac{y}{x}\,dx + (y^3 - \ln x)\,dy = 0.$

4062. $(x\cos y - y\sin y)\,dy + (x\sin y + y\cos y)\,dx = 0.$

4063. Make sure that the function $e^{\int P(x)\,dx}$ serves as the integrating factor of the linear equation $\dfrac{dy}{dx} + P(x)\,y = Q(x).$

4064. Find the integrating factor of Bernoulli's equation $y' + P(x)\,y = y^n Q(x).$

4065. Find the conditions at which the equation

$$X(x, y)\,dx + Y(x, y)\,dy = 0$$

allows for an integrating factor of the form $M = F(x + y).$

4066. Find the conditions at which the equation

$$X \cdot (x, y)\,dx + Y(x, y)\,dy = 0$$

allows for an integrating factor of the form $M = F(x \cdot y).$

Miscellaneous problems

In Problems 4067 to 4088 find the general solutions of the equations.

4067. $y' = ax + by + c.$

4068. $ay' + by + cy^m = 0.$

4069. $y' = \dfrac{x + y - 2}{y - x - 4}.$

4070. $y' = \dfrac{y^2 + xy - x^2}{y^2}.$

4071. $y' = \dfrac{a^2}{(x+y)^2}$.

4072. $y'(y^2 - x) = y$.

4073. $\dfrac{2x\,dx}{y^3} + \dfrac{y^2 - 3x^2}{y^4}\,dy = 0$.

4074. $(2y + xy^3)\,dx + (x + x^2y^2)\,dy = 0$.

4075. $\left(2xy + x^2y + \dfrac{y^3}{3}\right)dx + (x^2 + y^2)\,dy = 0$.

4076. $y' = \dfrac{(1+y)^2}{x(y+1) - x^2}$.

4077. $x\,dy + y\,dx + y^2(x\,dy - y\,dx) = 0$.

4078. $\left[\dfrac{1}{x} - \dfrac{y^2}{(x-y)^2}\right]dx + \left[\dfrac{x^2}{(x-y)^2} - \dfrac{1}{y}\right]dy = 0$.

4079. $y' = x\sqrt{y} + \dfrac{xy}{x^2 - 1}$.

4080. $y \sin x + y' \cos x = 1$.

4081. $y' - y + y^2 \cos x = 0$.

4082. $y' = \dfrac{\cos x \sin y + \tan^2 x}{\sin x \cdot \cos y}$.

4083. $xy' \cos \dfrac{y}{x} = y \cos \dfrac{y}{x} - x$.

4084. $\left(x \cos \dfrac{y}{x} + y \sin \dfrac{y}{x}\right) y\,dx + \left(x \cos \dfrac{y}{x} - y \sin \dfrac{y}{x}\right) x\,dy = 0$.

4085. $y' = \dfrac{x}{\cos y} - \tan y$.

4086. $y - y' \cos x = y^2 \cos x\,(1 - \sin x)$.

4087. $2yy' = e^{\frac{x^2+y^2}{x}} + \dfrac{x^2+y^2}{x} - 2x$.

4088. $(1 + e^{x/y})\,dx + e^{x/y}\left(1 - \dfrac{x}{y}\right)dy = 0$.

4089. Find the curve such that the ratio of the subnormal at any point to the sum of its abscissa and ordinate is equal to the ratio of the ordinate of this point to its abscissa.

4090. Find the curve such that the segment of the tangent at any point contained between the x-axis and the straight line $y = ax + b$ is bisected by the point of tangency.

4091. Find the curve such that the ratio of the distance between the normal at any of its points and the origin to the distance between the same normal and the point (a, b) is equal to the constant k.

4092. Find the curve such that the distance between the origin and the tangent at an arbitrary point is equal to the distance between the origin and the normal at the same point.

4093*. Find the curve such that the ordinate of any of its points is the proportional mean between the abscissa and the sum of the abscissa and subnormal at the same point.

4094. An electric circuit whose resistance $R = \frac{3}{2}$ ohms is fed with voltage which increases uniformly from zero to 120 V during two minutes. Also, inductance is introduced automatically so that its quantity in *henries* is numerically equal to the current in *amperes*. Find the dependence of the current on time during the first two minutes of the experiment.

2. General Differential Equations of the First Order

Field of directions. Isoclines

4095. Given the differential equation $y' = -\frac{x}{y}$. (a) Construct field of directions specified by this equation. (b) Find out the location of the field vector with respect to the polar radius of any point of the field. (c) Find out the form of integral curves of the equation proceeding from field of directions. (d) Find the integral curves solving the given equation by the usual method (separating the variables). (e) Indicate the family of isoclines of the given equation.

4096. Write the differential equation whose isoclines are :

(1) equilateral hyperbolas $xy = a$; (2) parabolas $y^2 = 2px$;

(3) circles $x^2 + y^2 = R^2$.

4097. Find the isoclines of the differential equation of a family of parabolas $y = ax^2$. Make a drawing. Interpret the result geometrically.

4098. Make sure that the isoclines of a homogeneous equation (and only of a homogeneous equation!) are straight lines passing through the origin.

4099. Indicate linear equations whose isoclines are straight lines.

4100. Let y_1, y_2, y_3 be the ordinates of any three isoclines of some linear equation corresponding to one abscissa. Make sure that the ratio $\frac{y_2 - y_1}{y_3 - y_1}$ retains one and the same value whatever this abscissa is.

Approximate integration of differential equations

4101. Given the equation $y' = \frac{x^2 + y^2}{10}$. Construct approximately the integral curve corresponding to the interval $1 \le x \le 5$ and passing through the point M (1, 1).

4102. Given the equation $y' = \frac{1}{x^2 + y^2}$. Construct approximately the integral curve corresponding to the interval $0.5 \le x \le 3.5$ and passing through the point (0.5, 0.5).

4103. Given the equation $y' = xy^3 + x^2$. Applying Euler's method, compute y for $x = 1$ if y is a particular solution satisfying the initial condition $y|_{x=0} = 0$. Compute y to within 0.01.

4104. Given the equation $y' = \sqrt{x} \cdot y^2 + 1$. Using Euler's method, compute y for $x = 2$ if y is a particular solution satisfying the initial condition $y|_{x=1} = 0$. Compute y with two decimal places.

4105. Given : the equation $y' = \frac{xy}{2}$ and the initial condition $y|_{x=0} = 1$. Find the exact solution of this equation and the value of y for $x = 0.9$. Then, find this value with the aid of the approximate method, subdividing the interval [0, 0.9] into 9 parts. Indicate the relative error of the latter result.

4106. Given : the equation $y' = \frac{3x^2}{x^3 + y + 1}$ and the initial condition $y|_{x=1} = 0$. Find the exact solution of the equation and, using one of the approximate methods for integrating equations, compute the value of x for $y = 1$ (compare with the value of x obtained in the exact solution).

4107. $y' = y^2 + xy + x^2$. Using the method of successive approximations, find the second approximation for the solution satisfying the initial condition $y|_{x=0} = 1$.

4108. $y' = xy^3 - 1$. For $x = 1$ find the value of the solution of the given equation which satisfies the initial condition $y|_{x=0} = 0$. Confine yourself to the third approximation in applying the method of successive approximations. Carry out the computations with two decimal places.

In Problems 4109 to 4116 find first several terms of the power series expansions of solutions of the equations with the indicated initial conditions.

4109. $y' = y^3 - x; y|_{x=0} = 1.$

4110. $y' = x^2y^2 - 1; y|_{x=0} = 1.$

4111. $y' = x^2 - y^2; y|_{x=0} = 0.$

4112. $y' = \frac{1 - x^2}{y} + 1; y|_{x=0} = 1.$

4113. $y' = \frac{xy}{1 + x + y}; y|_{x=0} = 0.$

4114. $y' = e^y + xy; y|_{x=0} = 0.$

4115. $y' = \sin y - \sin x; y|_{x=0} = 0.$

4116. $y' = 1 + x + x^2 0 - 2y^2; y|_{x=1} = 1.$

Singular solutions. Clairaut's Equations and Lagrange's Equations

In Problems 4117 to 4130 find the general and singular solutions of Clairaut's equations and Lagrange's equations.

4117. $y = xy' + y'^2$.

4118. $y = xy' - 3y'^3$.

4119. $y = xy' + \dfrac{1}{y'}$.

4120. $y = xy' + \sqrt{1 + y'^2}$.

4121. $y = xy' + \sin y'$.

4122. $xy' - y = \ln y'$.

4123. $y = y'^2 (x + 1)$.

4124. $2yy' = x (y'^2 + 4)$.

4125. $y = yy'^2 + 2xy'$.

4126. $y = x (1 + y') + y'^2$.

4127. $y' = \ln (xy' - y)$.

4128. $y = y' (x + 1) + y'^2$.

4129. $y = y' x + a\sqrt[3]{1 - y'^3}$.

4130. $x = y\left(\dfrac{1}{\sqrt{y'}} - \dfrac{1}{y'}\right)$.

In Problems 4131 to 4133 find the singular solutions of the equations using the same method as in Problems 4117 to 4128.

4131. $y'^2 - yy' + e^x = 0$.

4132. $x^2y'^2 - 2(xy - 2) y' + y^2 = 0$.

4133. $y' (y' - 2x) = 2(y - x^2)$.

4134. Prove the theorem : if a linear differential equation is a Clairaut's equation, then the family of its integral curves presents a pencil of straight lines.

4135. The area of a triangle formed by the tangent to the sought for curve and coordinate axes is a constant. Find the curve.

4136. Find the curve the tangents to which cut off the coordinate axes intercepts whose sum is equal to $2a$.

4137. Find the curve such that the product of the distances from any tangent to two given points is constant.

4138. Find the curve such that the area of the rectangle formed by the tangent and the normal at any point equals the area of the rectangle with the sides equal to the abscissa and ordinate of this point.

4139. Find the curve for which the sum of the normal and subnormal is proportional to the abscissa.

4140*. Find the curve such that the segment of the normal contained between the coordinate axes has a constant length a.

4141. The velocity of a material point at an arbitrary time differs from the average velocity (from the start to this instant) by a magnitude directly proportional to the kinetic energy of the point and inversely proportional to the time as measured from the beginning of motion. Find the dependence of the path on time.

Orthogonal and isogonal trajectories and evolvents

In Problems 4142 to 4147 find the trajectories orthogonal to

4142. Ellipses having a common major axis equal to $2a$.

4143. Parabolas $y^2 = 4(x - a)$.

4144. Circles $x^2 + y^2 = 2ax$.

4145. Cissoids $(2a - x)y^2 = x^3$.

4146. Equals parabolas touching a given straight line, the vertex being the point of tangency for each parabola.

4147. Circles of one and the same radius whose centres lie on a given straight line.

4148. Find the family of trajectories intersecting the curves $x^2 = 2a(y - x\sqrt{3})$ at an angle $\alpha = 60°$.

4149. Find the isogonal trajectories of the family of parabolas $y^2 = 4ax$; the angle of intersection $\alpha = 45°$.

4150*. Find the lines of sound propagation over a plane from a fixed source of sound lying in the same plane if along some direction a wind blows with a constant velocity a.

In Problems 4151 to 4154 find the evolvents of the

4151. Circle $x^2 + y^2 = R^2$.

4152. Catenary $y = a \cosh \dfrac{x}{a}$.

4153. Circle $x = a(\cos t + t \sin t)$, $y = a(\sin t - t \cos t)$.

4154. Semicubical parabola $y = 3t^2$, $x = -2t^3$.

3. Equations of the Second and Higher Orders

Particular cases of the second-order equations

In Problems 4155 to 4182 find general solutions of the given equations.

4155. $y'' = x + \sin x$.

4156. $y'' = \arctan x$.

4157. $y'' = \ln x$.

4158. $xy'' = y'$.

4159. $y'' = y' + x$.

4160. $y'' = \dfrac{y'}{x} + x$.

4161. $(1 + x^2)y'' + (y')^2 + 1 = 0$.

4162. $xy'' = y' \ln \dfrac{y'}{x}$.

4163. $(y'')^2 = y'$.

4164. $2xy'y'' = (y')^2 + 1$.

4165. $y'' - 2\cot x \cdot y' = \sin^3 x$.

4166. $1 + (y')^2 = 2yy''$.

4167. $(y')^2 = 2yy'' = 0$.

4168. $a^2y'' - y = 0$.

4169. $y'' = \dfrac{1}{4\sqrt{y}}$.

4170. $y'' + \dfrac{2}{1-y}(y')^2 = 0$.

4171. $yy'' + (y')^2 = 1$.

4172. $yy'' = (y')^2$.

4173. $2yy'' - 3(y')^2 = 4y^2$.

4174. $y(1 - \ln y)\,y'' + (1 + \ln y)(y')^2 = 0$.

4175. $y'' = 2yy'$.

4176. $\cos y \cdot \dfrac{d^2y}{dx^2} + \sin y \left(\dfrac{dy}{dx}\right)^2 = \dfrac{dy}{dx}$.

4177. $yy'' - (y')^2 = y^2y'$.

4178. $yy'' - yy' \ln y = (y')^2$.

4179. $y'' = y'\left(\dfrac{y'}{y} - 2\sqrt{\dfrac{y'}{y}} - 4\right)$.

4180. $(x + a)\,y'' + x(y')^2 = y'$.

4181*. $yy'y'' = (y')^3 + (y'')^2$.

4182. $xy'' - \dfrac{1}{4}(y'')^2 - y' = 0$.

In Problems 4183 to 4188 solve the given equations with the aid of a suitable substitution : $yy' = p$, $(y')^2 = p$, $xy' = p$, $\dfrac{y'}{y} = p$ and so on.

4183. $xyy'' + x(y')^2 = 3yy'$.

4184. $xy'' = y'(e^y - 1)$.

4185. $yy'' + (y')^2 = x$.

4186. $y'' + \dfrac{1}{x}y' - \dfrac{y}{x^2} = 0$.

4187. $x^2y\dfrac{d^2y}{dx^2} - \left(x\dfrac{dy}{dx} - y\right)^2 = 0$.

4188. $yy'' = y'(2\sqrt{yy'} - y')$.

In Problems 4189 to 4199 find the particular solutions of the given equations with the initial conditions indicated below.

4189. $y''(x^2 + 1) = 2xy'$; $\quad y|_{x=0} = 1,\ y'|_{x=0} = 3$.

4190. $xy'' + x(y')^2 - y' = 0$; $y|_{x=2} = 2,\ y|_{x=2} = 1$.

4191. $y'' = \dfrac{y'}{x} + \dfrac{x^2}{y'}$; $\quad y|_{x=2} = 0,\ y'|_{x=2} = 4$.

4192. $2y'' = 3y^2$; $\quad y|_{x=-2} = 1,\ y'|_{x=-2} = -1$.

4193. $yy'' = (y')^2 - (y')^3$; $\quad y|_{x=1} = 1,\ y'|_{x=1} = -1$.

4194. $y^3y'' = -1$; $\quad y|_{x=1} = 1,\ y'|_{x=1} = 0$.

4195. $y^4 - y^3y'' = 1$; $\quad y|_{x=0} = \sqrt{2},\ y'|_{x=0} = \dfrac{\sqrt{2}}{2}$.

4196. $y'' = e^{2y}$; $\quad y|_{x=0} = 0,\ y'|_{x=0} = 1$.

4197. $2(y')^2 = y''(y - 1)$; $\quad y|_{x=1} = 2,\ y'|_{x=1} = -1$.

4198*. $x^4y'' = (y - xy')^3$; $\quad y|_{x=1} = 1,\ y'|_{x=1} = 1$.

4199. $y'' = xy' + y + 1$; $\quad y|_{x=0} = 1,\ y'|_{x=0} = 0$.

4200*. What curve possesses the property that the radius of curvature at any of its points is proportional to the length of the normal? Put the proportionality factor $k = -1, +1, -2, +2$.

4201. Find the curve such that the projection of the radius of curvature onto the y-axis is a constant equal to a.

4202. Find the curve, passing through the origin, such that the ratio of the area of the triangle MTP (Fig. 70), formed by the tangent at some point M of the curve, ordinate of this point MP and x-axis, to the area of the curvilinear triangle OMP is equal to a constant number $k\left(k > \frac{1}{2}\right)$.

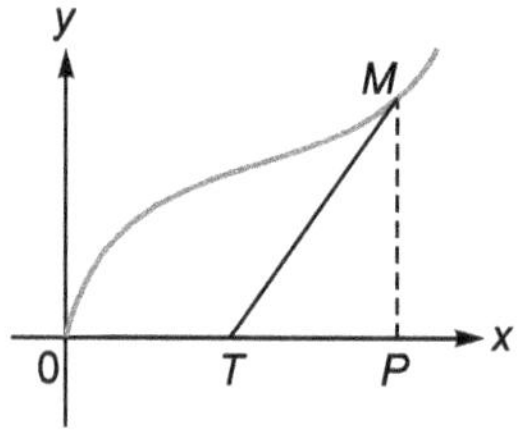

Fig. 70

4203. Find the curve whose arc length measured from some point is proportional to the slope of the tangent at the end-point of the arc.

4204. A mass point m is thrown up vertically with initial velocity v_0. The air resistance is equal to kv^2. Therefore, directing the y-axis vertically, we have the upward motion :

$$m\frac{d^2y}{dt^2} = -mg - kv^2,$$

and for the free fall :

$$m\frac{d^2y}{dt^2} = -mg + kv^2,$$

where $v = \frac{dy}{dt}$. Find the velocity of the mass point at the time it falls on the ground.

4205. A thin nonextensible flexible thread is suspended by its ends. What shape will the thread attain in equilibrium under the action of the load uniformly distributed along the projection of the thread on the horizontal plane? (The weight of the thread is neglected.)

4206. Find the law of a rectilinear motion of a mass point m if it is known that the work performed by the force acting in the direction of motion and depending on the path is proportional to the time elapsed from the starting time. The proportionality factor is equal to k.

4207*. A light ray penetrates at an angle of α_0 with the vertical from air (whose index of refraction is m_0) into a liquid with a variable index of refraction. The latter depends linearly on the depth and is constant in the plane parallel to the horizon; on the surface of the liquid it is equal to m_1, and at the depth h to m_2. Find the shape of the light ray in the liquid. (The index of refraction of a medium is inversely proportional to the velocity of light propagation.)

Particular cases of equations of higher orders

In Problems 4208 to 4217 find the general solutions of the given equations.

4208. $y''' = \frac{1}{x}$.

4209. $y''' = \cos 2x$.

4210. $y^{(X)} = e^{ax}$.

4211. $x^2 y''' = (y'')^2$.

4212. $xy^{(V)} = y^{(IV)}$.

4213. $y''' = (y'')^3$.

4214. $y' y''' = 3(y'')^2$.

4215. $yy''' = y'y'' = 0$.

4216. $y''' [1 + (y')^2] = 3y' (y'')^2$.

4217. $(y'')^2 - y'y''' = \left(\frac{y'}{x}\right)^2$.

Approximate solutions

4218. When investigating the vibration of a material system with one degree of freedom we come across a differential equation of the form $y'' = f_1(x) + f_2(y) + f_3(y')$.
Solve this equation graphically if :
(1) $f_1(x) = 0,\ f_2(y) = -\sqrt{y},\ f_3(y') = 0.5y'$ and $y|_{x=0} = y'|_{x=0} = 0$;
(2) $f_1(x) = -x,\ f_2(y) = 0,\ f_3(y') = -0.1\,y' - 0.1y'^3$ and $y|_{x=0} = y'|_{x=0} = 1$.

4219. $y'' = yy' - x^2;\ y|_{x=0} = 1,\ y'|_{x=0} = 1$.

(1) Solve the given equation graphically.

(2) Find first several terms of the expansion of the solution into a power series.

4220. Find the first six terms of the expansion into a series of the differential equation $y'' = \frac{y'}{y} - \frac{1}{x}$, satisfying the initial conditions $y|_{x=1} = 1,\ y'|_{x=1} = 0$.

4221. Find, in the form of a power series, the particular solution of the equation $y'' = x \sin y'$, satisfying the initial conditions $y|_{x=1} = 0$, $y'|_{x=1} = \frac{\pi}{2}$. (Confine yourself to the first six terms).

4222. Find, in the form of a power sereis, the particular solution $y = f(x)$ of the equation $y'' = xyy'$ satisyfing the initial conditions $f(0) = 1$, $f'(0) = 1$. If we confine ourselves to the first five terms of the expansion, then will it be sufficient to compute $f(-0.5)$ accurate to 0.001?

4223. Find the first seven terms of the series expansion of the solution of the differential equation $yy'' + y' + y = 0$ satisfying the initial conditions $y|_{x=0} = 1$, $y'|_{x=0} = 0$. Determine the order of smallness of the difference $y - (2 - x - e^{-x})$ as $x \to 0$.

4224. Find the first twelve terms of the series expansion of the solution of the differential equation $y'' + yy' - 2 = 0$ satisfying the initial conditions $y|_{x=0} = 0$, $y'|_{x=0} = 0$. Evaluate the integral $\int_0^1 y\,dx$ to within 0.001. Compute $y'|_{x=0.5}$ up to 0.00001.

4225*. An electric circuit consists of an inductance ($L = 0.4$ H) and an electrolytic bath connected in series. The bath contains one litre of water acidified with small quantity of sulphuric acid. Decomposition of water produced by a current leads to a change in the concentration, and hence, in the resistance of the solution. The voltage across the terminals is kept constant (20 V). According to the Faraday laws of electrolysis, the amount of any substance deposited or dissolved is proportional to the quantity (charge) of electricity passed, time and electrochemical equivalent of the substance. The electrochemical equivalent of water is equal to 0.000187 g/C. The resistance of the solution at the beginning of the experiment $R_0 = 2$ ohms, the initial current equals 10 A. Find the dependence (in the form of a power series) of the volume of the water contained in the bath on time.

4226*. An electric circuit consists of an inductance ($L = 0.4$ H) and an electrolytic bath connected in series. The initial resistance of the bath is 2 ohms. The bath contains a water solution of hydrogen chloride (10 g of HCl dissolved in one litre of water). The acid is decomposed by current which causes a change in the concentration of the solution (compare with the previous problem, where the amount of the dissolved substance remained unchanged, whereas the volume of the solvent varied). The voltage across the circuit terminals is 20 V, electrochemical equivalent k of hydrogen chloride is equal to 0.000381 g/C, the initial current is 10 A. Find the relationship (in the form of a power series) between the amount of the hydrochloric acid in the solution and time.

4. Linear Equations

4227. The functions x^3 and x^4 satisfy a homogeneous linear differential equaiton of the second order. Make sure that they form a fundamental system and derive the equation.

4228. The same for the functions e^x and x^2e^x.

4229. The functions x, x^3, e^x form a fundamental system of solutions of a linear homogeneous equation of the third order. Write this equation.

4230. The functions x^2 and x^3 form a fundamental system of solutions of a homogeneous equation of the second order. Find the solution of this equation satisfying the initial conditions $y|_{x=1} = 1$, $y'|_{x=1} = 0$.

4231. The functions $\cos^2 x$ and $\sin^2 x$ satisfy some linear homogeneous equation of the second order :

(a) check to see that they form a fundamental system of solutions;

(b) derive the equation;

(c) show that the other fundamental system of this equation is formed by the functions 1 and $\cos 2x$.

4232*. If y_1 is a particular solution of the equation $y'' + y'P(x) + yQ(x) = 0$, then

$$y_2 = Cy_1 \int e^{-\int P(x)\,dx} \frac{dx}{y_1^2} \quad (C \text{ constant})$$

is also a solution. Show this (1) by a direct check, (2) using the substitution $y = y_1 z$, (3) with the aid of Ostrogradsky's formula.

4233. Using the formula of Problem 4232, find the general solution of the equation $(1 - x^2)y'' - 2xy' + 2y = 0$, knowing its particular solution $y_1 = x$.

4234. Solve the equation $y'' + \frac{2}{x}y' + y = 0$, knowing its particular solution $y_1 = \frac{\sin x}{x}$.

4235. The equation $(2x - x^2)y'' + (x^2 - 2)y' + 2(1 - x)y = 0$ has a solution $y = e^x$. Find the solution of the equation satisfying the initial conditions $y|_{x=1} = 0$, $y'|_{x=1} = 1$.

4236*. Find the necessary and sufficient condition for the equation $y'' + y'P(x) - yQ(x) = 0$ to have two linearly independent solutions y_1 and y_2 satisfying the condition $y_1 y_2 = 1$.

4237*. Find the general solution of the equation

$$(1 - x^2)y'' - xy' + 9y = 0,$$

if its particular solution is a polynomial of the third degree.

In Problems 4238 to 4240 it is rather easy to choose one particular solution (to say nothing of the trivial solution $y = 0$) for the given equation. Find the general solutions of these equations.

4238. $y'' - \tan x \cdot y' + 2y = 0.$

4239. $y'' - y' + \dfrac{y}{x} = 0.$

4240. $y'' - \dfrac{2x}{x^2+1} y' + \dfrac{2y}{x^2+1} = 0.$

4241. Find the general solution of the equation

$$x^3 y''' - 3x^2 y'' + 6xy' - 6y = 0,$$

knowing the particular solutions $y_1 = x$ and $y_2 = x^2$.

In Problems 4242 to 4244 find the general solutions of the nonhomogeneous equations.

4242. $x^2 y'' - xy' + y = 4x^3.$

4243. $y'' - \dfrac{x}{x-1} y' + \dfrac{1}{x-1} y = x - 1.$

4244. $(3x + 2x^2)\, y'' - 6\,(1 + x)\, y' + 6y = 6.$

4245. The equation $(1 + x^2)\, y'' + 2xy' - 2y = 4x^2 + 2$ allows for the particular solution $y = x^2$. Find the solution of this equation satisfying the conditions $y|_{x=-1} = 0$, $y'|_{x=-1} = 0$.

4246. Find the first six terms of the power series expansion of the solution of the differential equation $y'' - (1 + x^2)\, y = 0$ satisfying the initial condition $y|_{x=0} = -2$, $y'|_{x=0} = 2$

4247. Find the first nine terms of the power series expansion of the solution of the differential equation $y'' = x^2 y - y'$ satisfying the initial conditions $y|_{x=0} = 1$, $y'|_{x=0} = 0$.

4248. Write in the form of a power series the particular solution of the equation $y'' - xy' + y - 1 = 0$; $y|_{x=0} = 0$, $y'|_{x=0} = 0$.

4249. Write in the form of a power series the general solution of the equation $y'' = y \cdot e^x$. (Confine yourself to the first six terms.)

4250. Write in the form of a power series the general solution of the equation $y'' + xy' - x^2 y = 0$. (Confine yourself to the first six terms.)

Equations with constant coefficients

In Problems 4251 to 4261 find the general solutions of the given equations.

4251. $y'' + y' - 2y = 0.$

4252. $y'' - 9y = 0.$

4253. $y'' - 4y' = 0.$

4254. $y'' - 2y' - y = 0.$

4255. $3y'' - 2y' - 8y = 0.$

4256. $y'' + y = 0.$

4257. $y'' + 6y' + 13y = 0.$

4258. $4y'' - 8y' + 5y = 0.$

4259. $y'' - 2y' + y = 0.$

4260. $4\dfrac{d^2x}{dt^2} - 20\dfrac{dx}{dt} + 25x = 0.$

4261. $2y'' + y' + 2\sin^2 15° \cos^2 15° \cdot y = 0.$

In Problems 4262 to 4264 find the solution of the given equation satisfying the indicated initial conditions.

4262. $y'' - 4y' + 3y = 0;$ $\quad y|_{x=0} = 6,\ y'|_{x=0} = 10.$

4263. $y'' + 4y' + 29y = 0;$ $\quad y|_{x=0} = 0,\ y'|_{x=0} = 15.$

4264. $4y'' + 4y' + y = 0;$ $\quad y|_{x=0} = 2,\ y'|_{x=0} = 0.$

4265. Given a particular solution of a homogeneous linear equation of the second order with constant coefficients $y_1 = e^{mx}$. The discriminant of the corresponding characteristic equation is equal to zero. Find the particular solution of this differential equation turning unity together with its derivative, at $x = 0$.

4266. Find the integral curve of the equation $y'' + 9y = 0$, passing through the point $M\ (\pi, -1)$ and touching the straight line $y + 1 = x - \pi$ at this point.

4267. Find the integral curve of the equation $y'' + ky = 0$, passing through the point $M\ (x_0, y_0)$ and touching the straight line $y - y_0 = a(x - x_0)$ at this point.

In Problems 4268 to 4282 give the general solutions of the nonhomogeneous equations, finding their particular solutions either by choice or by the method of variation of the arbitrary constants.

4268. $2y'' + y' - y = 2e^x.$

4269. $y'' + a^2y = e^x.$

4270. $y'' - 7y' + 6y = \sin x.$

4271. $y'' + 2y' + 5y = -\dfrac{17}{2}\cos 2x.$

4272. $y'' - 6y' + 9y = 2x^2 - x + 3.$

4273. $y'' - 2y' + 2y = 2x.$

4274. $y'' + 4y' - 5y = 1.$

4275. $y'' - 3y' + 2y = f(x)$, if $f(x)$ is equal to :

(1) $10e^{-x}$; (2) $3e^{2x}$; (3) $2\sin x$;

(4) $2x^3 - 30$; (5) $2e^x \cos\dfrac{x}{2}$; (6) $x - e^{-2x} + 1$;

(7) $e^x(3 - 4x)$; (8) $3x + 5\sin 2x$; (9) $2e^x - e^{-2x}$;

(10) $\sin x \sin 2x$; (11) $\sinh x$.

4276. $2y'' + 5y' = f(x)$ if $f(x)$ is equal to :

(1) $5x^2 - 2x - 1$; (2) e^x; (3) $29\cos x$;

(4) $\cos^2 x$; (5) $0.1\,e^{-2.5x} - 25\sin 2.5x$;

(6) $29\,x\sin x$; (7) $100x \cdot e^{-x}\cos x$; (8) $3 \cdot \cosh\dfrac{5}{2}x$.

4277. $y'' - 4y' + 4y = f(x)$ if $f(x)$ equals :

(1) 1; (2) e^{-x}; (3) $3e^{2x}$;
(4) $2(\sin 2x + x)$; (5) $\sin x \cos 2x$; (6) $\sin^3 x$;
(7) $8(x^2 + e^{2x} + \sin 2x)$; (8) $\sinh 2x$; (9) $\sinh x + \sin x$;
(10) $e^x - \sinh(x-1)$.

4278. $y'' + y = f(x)$ if $f(x)$ equals :

(1) $2x^3 - x + 2$; (2) $-8\cos 3x$; (3) $\cos x$; (4) $\sin x - 2e^{-x}$;
(5) $\cos x \cos 2x$; (6) $24\sin^4 x$; (7) $\cosh x$.

4279. $5y'' - 6y' + 5y = f(x)$ if $f(x)$ equals :

(1) $5e^{3x/5}$; (2) $\sin \frac{4}{5} x$; (3) $e^{2x} + 2x^3 - x + 2$;
(4) $e^{3x/5} \cdot \cos x$; (5) $e^{3x/5} \cdot \sin \frac{4}{5} x$; (6) $13e^x \cdot \cosh x$.

4280. $y'' + y + \cot^2 x = 0$. **4281.** $y'' - 2y' + y = \dfrac{e^x}{x^2+1}$.

4282. $y'' - y' = f(x)$ if $f(x)$ equals:

(1) $\dfrac{e^x}{1+e^x}$; (2) $e^{2x}\sqrt{1-e^{2x}}$; (3) $e^{2x} \cos e^x$.

In Problems 4283 to 4287 find the particular solutions of the equations satisfying the indicated initial conditions.

4283. $4y'' + 16y' + 15y = 4e^{-3x/2}$; $y|_{x=0} = 3$, $y|_{x=0} = -5.5$.

4284. $y'' - 2y' + 10y = 10x^2 + 18x + 6$; $y|_{x=0} = 1$, $y'|_{x=0} = 3.2$

4285. $y'' - y' = 2(1-x)$; $y|_{x=0} = 1$, $y'|_{x=0} = 1$.

4286. $y'' - 2y' = e^x(x^2 + x - 3)$; $y|_{x=0} = 2$, $y'|_{x=0} = 2$

4287. $y'' + y + \sin 2x = 0$; $y|_{x=\pi} = y'|_{x=\pi} = 1$.

4288*. Show that the particular solution y of the equation $a_0y'' + a_1y' + a_2y = Ae^{px}$ (a_0, a_1, a_2 constant coefficients, p and A real or complex numbers) has the form $\bar{y} = \dfrac{A}{\varphi(p)} e^{px}$ if p is not a root of the characteristic equation $\varphi(r) \equiv a_0r^2 + a_1r + a_2 = 0$; $\bar{y} = \dfrac{Ax}{\varphi'(p)} e^{px}$, if p is a simple root of the characteristic equation : $\bar{y} = \dfrac{Ax^2}{\varphi''(p)} e^{px}$, if p is a double root of the characteristic equation.

In Problems 4289 to 4292 find the general solutions of Euler's equations.

4289. $x^2y'' - 9xy' + 21y = 0$. **4290.** $x^2y'' + xy' + y = x$.

4291. $y'' - \dfrac{y'}{x} + \dfrac{y}{x^2} = \dfrac{2}{x}$.

4292. $x^2y'' - 2xy' + 2y + x - 2x^3 = 0.$

4293. If the axis of a turbine shaft occupies a horizontal position, and if the centre of gravity of the disk fitted on the shaft does not lie on the axis, then the bending deflection y of the axis (see Fig. 71), when the shaft is in rotation, satisfies the equation

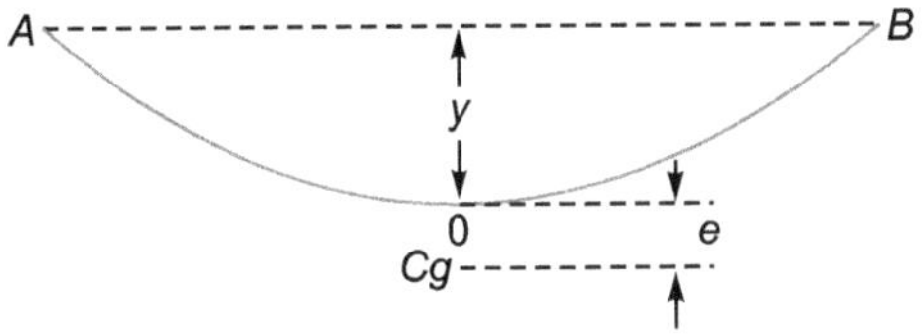

Fig. 71

$$\frac{d^2y}{dt^2} + \left(\frac{1}{m\alpha} - \omega^2\right) y = g \cos \omega t + \omega^2 e,$$

where m is the mass of the disk, α a constant depending on the mode of fastening the ends A and B; ω the angular velocity of rotation, e the eccentricity of the centre of gravity of the disk. Find the general solution of this equation.

4294. A material point whose mass is 1 g repels in a straight line from a certain centre with a force proportional to its distance from this centre (the proportionality factor is equal to 4). The resistance of the medium is proportional to the velocity of travel (the proportionality factor is equal to 3). At the beginning of motion the distance from the centre is equal to 1 cm, and the velocity to zero. Find the law of motion.

4295. A material point whose mass is 1 g travels in a straight line towards point A under the action of a certain attracting force which is proportional to its distance from the point A. At the distance of 1 cm the attracting force is equal to 0.1 dyne. The resistance of the medium is proportional to the velocity of travel and equals 0.4 dyne at a velocity of 1 cm/s. At the time $t = 0$ the mass point is found at a distance of 10 cm from the point A and its velocity is zero. Find the dependence of the distance on time and compute this distance for $t = 3$ s (accurate to 0.01 cm).

4296. A material point of mass m travels in a straight line from A to B under the action of a constant force F. The resistance of the medium is proportional to the distance of the point from B, and at the starting instant (at the point A) it is equal to f $(f < F)$. The initial velocity of the point is zero. How long will the point travel from A to B? $(AB = a)$.

4297. A body whose mass is 200 g is suspended by a spring and is deflected from rest by expanding the spring by 2 cm; then it is left alone (without an initial velocity). Find the equation of body's motion, assuming that the resistance of the medium is proportional to the velocity. If the body moves with a velocity of 1 cm/s, then the medium offers a resistance of 0.1 gf; the springy force counteracting to its extension by 2 cm is equal to 10 kgf. The weight of the spring is neglected.

4298. A cylindrical wooden block ($S = 100\ \text{cm}^2$, $h = 20$ cm, $\gamma = 0.5\,\text{g/cm}^3$) is completely plunged into water and is left alone without an initial velocity. Assuming that the friction force is proportional to the height of the submerged portion, find out what the proportionality factor k must be so that, as a result of the first emersion, exactly half the block is seen floating above the surface of the water.

How much time (t_1) will the first emersion last? Write the equation of motion for the first emersion.

4299*. A long narrow tube turns with a constant angular velocity ω round a vertical axis perpendicular to it. At the initial time a ball of mass m was found inside the tube at a distance of a_0 from the axis. Assuming that the ball's initial velocity with respect to the tube was equal to zero, find the law of motion of the ball with respect to the tube.

4300. Solve the previous problem in the assumption that the ball is attached to the point O by a spring. The force with which the spring acts on the ball is proportional to the strain of the spring, a force of k dynes causes a change in the length of the spring by 1 cm. The length of the unstrained spring is a_0.

Equations of higher orders

In Problems 4301 to 4311 find the general solutions of the equations.

4301. $y''' + 9y' = 0.$

4302. $y^{(IV)} - 13y'' + 36y = 0.$

4303. $y^{(IV)} = 8y'' - 16y.$

4304. $y^{(IV)} = 16y.$

4305. $y''' - 13y' - 12y = 0.$

4306. $y''' - 3y'' + 3y' - y = 0.$

4307. $y^{(IV)} + 2y''' + y'' = 0.$

4308. $y^{(n)} = y^{(n-2)}.$

4309. $y^{(IV)} + y = 0.$

4310. $64y^{(VIII)} + 48y^{(VI)} + 12y^{(IV)} + y'' = 0.$

4311. $y^{(n)} + \frac{n}{1}y^{(n-1)} + \frac{n(n-1)}{1 \times 2}y^{(n-2)} + \ldots + \frac{n}{1}y' + y = 0.$

4312. $y''' = -y'; \; y|_{x=0} = 2,\ y'|_{x=0} = 0,\ y''|_{x=0} = -1.$

4313. $y^{(V)} = y'$; $y|_{x=0} = 0,\ y'|_{x=0} = 1,\ y''|_{x=0} = 0,\ y'''|_{x-0} = 1,\ y^{(IV)}|_{x=0} = 2.$

In Problems 4314 to 4320 give the general solutions of nonhomogeneous equations, finding their particular solutions either by trial or by the method of variation of parameters.

4314. $y''' - 4y'' + 5y' - 2y = 2x + 3.$

4315. $y''' - 3y' + 2y = e^{-x}(4x^2 + 4x - 10).$

4316. $y^{(IV)} + 8y'' + 16y = \cos x.$

4317. $y^{(IV)} + 2a^2y'' + a^4y = \cos ax.$

4318. $y^{(V)} + y''' = x^2 - 1.$

4319. $y^{(IV)} - y = xe^x + \cos x.$

4320. $y^{(IV)} - 2y'' + y = 8(e^x + e^{-x}) + 4(\sin x + \cos x).$

4321. $y''' + 2y'' + y' + 2e^{-2x} = 0;\ y|_{x=0} = 2,$

$$y'|_{x=0} = 1,\ y''|_{x=0} = 1.$$

4322. $y''' - y' = 3(2 - x^2);\ y|_{x=0} = y'|_{x=0} = y''|_{x=0} = 1.$

4323. Solve the Euler equation $x^3y''' + xy' - y = 0.$

5. Systems of Differential Equations

4324.1. $\begin{cases} \dfrac{dx}{dt} = y - 7x, \\ \dfrac{dy}{dt} + 2x + 5y = 0. \end{cases}$

4324.2. $\begin{cases} \dfrac{dx}{dt} = 2x + y, \\ \dfrac{dy}{dt} = 3x + 4y. \end{cases}$

4324.3. $\begin{cases} \dfrac{dx}{dt} = x - 3y, \\ \dfrac{dy}{dt} = 3x + y. \end{cases}$

4324.4. $\begin{cases} \dfrac{dx}{dt} = x - y + z, \\ \dfrac{dy}{dt} = x + y - z, \\ \dfrac{dz}{dt} = 2x - y. \end{cases}$

4324.5. $\begin{cases} \dfrac{dx}{dt} = x - 2y - z, \\ \dfrac{dy}{dt} = -x + y + z, \\ \dfrac{dz}{dt} = x - z. \end{cases}$

4324.6. $\begin{cases} \dfrac{dx}{dt} = 3x - y + z, \\ \dfrac{dy}{dt} = x + y + z, \\ \dfrac{dz}{dt} = 4x - y + 4z. \end{cases}$

(the roots of the characteristic equation are $r_1 = 1,\ r_2 = 2,\ r_3 = 5$).

4324.7. $\begin{cases} \dfrac{dx}{dt} = 2x + y, \\ \dfrac{dy}{dt} = x + 3y + z, \\ \dfrac{dz}{dt} = 2y + 3z - x. \end{cases}$

(the roots of the characteristic equation are $r_1 = 2,\ r_{2,3} = 3 \pm i$).

4325. $\begin{cases} \dfrac{dx}{dt} = y, \\ \dfrac{dy}{dt} = x + e^t + e^{-t}. \end{cases}$

4326. $\begin{cases} \dfrac{dx}{dt} = 2y - 5x + e^t, \\ \dfrac{dy}{dt} = x - 6y + e^{-2t}. \end{cases}$

4327. $\begin{cases} yzy' = x \left(y' = \dfrac{dy}{dx} \right), \\ y^2 z' = x \left(z' = \dfrac{dz}{dx} \right). \end{cases}$

4328. $\begin{cases} y' = \dfrac{x + y}{z}, \\ z' = \dfrac{x - y}{y}. \end{cases}$

4329. $\begin{cases} xy' = y, \\ xzz' + x^2 + y^2 = 0. \end{cases}$

4330. $\begin{cases} y' = \dfrac{2xy}{x^2 - y^2 - z^2}, \\ z' = \dfrac{2xz}{x^2 - y^2 - z^2}. \end{cases}$

4331. $\begin{cases} z = y'(z - y)^2, \\ y = z'(z - y)^2. \end{cases}$

4332. $\begin{cases} 4\dfrac{dx}{dt} - \dfrac{dy}{dt} + 3x = \sin t, \\ \dfrac{dx}{dt} + y = \cos t. \end{cases}$

4333. $\begin{cases} \dfrac{d^2y}{dt^2} = x, \\ \dfrac{d^2x}{dt^2} = y. \end{cases}$

4334. $\begin{cases} \dfrac{d^2x}{dt^2} + \dfrac{dy}{dt} + x = e^t, \\ \dfrac{dx}{dt} + \dfrac{d^2y}{dt^2} = 1. \end{cases}$

4335. $\dfrac{dx}{z - y} = \dfrac{dy}{x - z} = \dfrac{dz}{y - x}.$

In Problems 4336 to 4339 find the particular solutions of the systems of differential equations satisfying the indicated initial conditions.

4336. $\begin{cases} \dfrac{dy}{dx} = \dfrac{y^2 - yz}{x^2 - yz}, \\ \dfrac{dz}{dx} = \dfrac{z(x + y)}{x^2 - yz}; \end{cases}$ $y|_{x=0} = 1,\ z|_{x=0} = -1.$

4337. $\begin{cases} \dfrac{dx}{dt} = 1 - \dfrac{2x}{t}, \\ \dfrac{dy}{dt} = x + y - 1 = \dfrac{2x}{t};\ x|_{t=1} = \dfrac{1}{3},\ \ y|_{t=1} = -\dfrac{1}{3}. \end{cases}$

4338. $\begin{cases} \dfrac{dx}{dt} = z + y - x, \\ \dfrac{dy}{dt} = z + x - y, \\ \dfrac{dz}{dt} = x + y + z;\ x|_{t=0} = 1,\ \ y|_{t=0} = z|_{t=0} = 0. \end{cases}$

4339. $\begin{cases} \dfrac{dx}{dt} = y + z, \\ \dfrac{dy}{dt} = z + x, \\ \dfrac{dz}{dt} = x + y;\ x|_{t=0} = -1,\ y|_{t=0} = 1,\ \ z|_{t=0} = 0. \end{cases}$

4340. Find a pair of curves such that : (a) the tangents drawn at points with equal abscissas intersect on the y-axis; (b) the normals drawn at points with equal abscissas intersect on the x-axis; (c) one of the curves passes through the point (1, 1), the other through the point (1, 2).

4341. Given two curves : $y = f(x)$ passing through the point (0, 1) and $y = \int_{-\infty}^{x} f(t)\,dt$ passing through the point $\left(0, \dfrac{1}{2}\right)$. The tangents drawn to both curves at the points with equal abscissas intersect on the x-axis. Find the curve $y = f(x)$.

4342. Find the space curve, passing through the point (0, 1, 1), such that : (a) the trace of the tangent on the plane Oxy describes the bisector of the angle between the positive directions of the x- and y-axes as the point of tangency displaces along the curve; (b) the distance of this trace from the origin is equal to the z-coordinate of the point of tangency.

4343. Two small balls each of mass m are joined by a very light spring whose elongation is proportional to the extending force. The length of the unextended spring is l_0. The spring is then extended to reach the length l_1, and at the time $t = 0$ both balls situated vertically one above the other begin to fall (the resistance of the medium is neglected). As the time T elapses the length of the spring is reduced to l_0. Find the law of motion for each of the balls.

4344. A horizontal tube turns about a vertical axis with an angular velocity of two radians per second. The tube contains two balls (300 g and 200 g) joined by an unextended weightless elastic spring 10 cm long, the heavier ball being located farther from the axis of rotation. A force of 0.24 N extends the spring by 1 cm, and the centre of gravity of the balls is 10 cm distant from the axis of rotation. the balls are held in the indicated position by a certain mechanism. At the time which is considered to be the time zero the mechanism ceases to operate and the balls start moving. Find the law of motion of each ball with respect to the tube. (Friction is neglected.)

4345. The rate of growth of a culture of microorganisms is proportional to their quantity and to the amount of nutrients (the proportioanlity factor is equal to k). The rate of reduction of the nutrients is proportional to the quantity of the microorganisms available (the proportionality factor is k_1). At the beginning of the experiment the vessel contained A_0 microorganisms and B_0 nutrients. Find the dependence of the quantity A of microorganisms and the amount B of nutrients on time ($k > 0,\ k_1 > 0$).

4346*. Suppose the bacteria are reproduced at a rate proportional to their available quantity (the proportionality factor is equal to a), but at the same time they generate poison destroying them at a rate proportional to the amount of the poison and the quantity of the bacteria (the proportionality factor is b). Let us then assume that the rate of generating the poison is proportional to the available quantity of the bacteria (the proportionality factor is equal to c). The number of bacteria first increases to a certain greatest value and then decreases tending to zero. Show that for any time t the number N of the bacteria is determined by the formula

$$N = \frac{4M}{(e^{kt} + e^{-kt})^2},$$

where M is the maximum number of bacteria and the time t is measured from the time when $N = M$, k is some constant.

4347. Two cylinders connected with a capillary at the bottom and whose bases lie in one plane are filled with liquid to different levels (H_1 and H_2). The volume of the liquid flown through the capillary per unit time is proportional to the difference of the levels, i.e., equal to $\alpha\ (h_1 - h_2)$, where α is the proportionality factor. Find the law of change in the liquid level in the vessels above the capillary. The cross-sectional areas of the vessels are S_1 and S_2.

6. Computational Problems

4348. One kilogram of water whose heat capacity is considered to be constant and the initial temperature is equal to θ_0 is warmed by an electric heater submerged into the water. The resistance of the heater depends linearly on temperature θ : $R = R_0\,(1 + 0.004\,\theta)$, where R_0 is the resistance at 0°C (the law valid for the majority of pure metals). The thermal insulation of the vessel is good enough to neglect heat emission.

Find the relationship between the temperature θ and time t in the interval $0 \le t \le T$ if :

(1) Voltage E is introduced uniformly from $E = 0$ to $E = E_1$ during T seconds. Compute (accurate to 1°C) by how many degrees the temperature of the water will increase after ten mintues of heating if $\theta_0 = 0°$, $E_1 = 110$ V, $R_0 = 10$ ohms and $T = 10$ min.

(2) The voltage varies according to the law $E = E_0 \sin 100\,\pi t$. Compute (accurate to 1°C) by how many degrees the temperature of the water will increase after ten minutes of heating if $\theta_0 = 0°$, $E_0 = 100$ V and $R_0 = 10$ ohms.

4349. One litre of water is warmed by a coil whose resistance is 24 ohms. At the same time the water is emitting heat to the surrounding medium whose temperature is 20°C (the rate of cooling is proportional to the difference between the temperatures of the water and medium). It is also known that if the current is cut off, the temperature of the water reduces from 40°C to 30°C during 10 minutes. The initial temperature of the water is 20°C. To what temperature will the water be warmed in ten minutes if :

(1) The voltage is introduced uniformly from $E_0 = 0$ to $E_1 = 120$ V during 10 min? Accuracy of computations is 0.1 °C.

(2) The current is alternating, and the voltage varies according to the formula $E = 110 \sin 100\,\pi t$? The accuracy of computations is 0.1°C.

4350. Given the equation $y' = \dfrac{x}{y} - x^2$. Compile the table of values of the solution satisfying the initial condition $y|_{x=1} = 1$, taking the values of x from 1 to 1.5 spaced at 0.05. Carry out the computations to the third decimal place.

4351. Compute for $x = 1$ the value of the particular solution of the differential equation $y' = y + x$ satisfying the initial condition $y|_{x=0} = 1$. Then, compute the first five approximations : y_1, y_2, y_3, y_4, y_5 (to the fourth decimal place), using the method of successive approximations. Compare the results.

4352. As is known, the integral $\int e^{-x^2}\,dx$ cannot be taken in elementary functions. Proceeding from the fact that the function $y = e^{x^2}\int_0^x e^{-t^2}\,dt$ is the solution of the equation $y' = 2xy + 1$, evaluate $\int_0^{0.5} e^{-x^2}\,dx$. Use the method of successive approximations, confining yourself to the fifth approximation. Compare the results with the approximate value computed by Simpson's rule.

4353. The function $y = f(x)$ is the solution of the differential equation $y' = y^2 - x$ with the initial condition $y|_{x=0} = 1$. Using the method of successive approximations, find the fourth approximation (y_4), confining yourself to such number of terms which is necessary to compute $y_4(0.3)$ with three decimal places. Find then first several terms of the expansion of $f(x)$ into a power series; compute also $f(0.3)$ with three decimal places and, considering $f(0.3)$ to be a more accurate result, estimate the error of the value $y_4(0.3)$.

4354. The function $y = f(x)$ is the solution of the differential equation $y'' = \frac{y'}{y} - \frac{1}{x}$ with the initial conditions $y|_{x=0} = 1$, $y'|_{x=0} = 0$. Find $f(1.6)$ to within 0.001.

4355*. The function $y = f(x)$ is the solution of the differential equation $y'' = y' - y + x$ with the initial conditions $y|_{x=1} = 1$, $y'|_{x=1} = 0$. Find $f(1.21)$ to within 0.000001.

4356*. The function $y = f(x)$ is the solution of the differential equation $y'' = xy' - y + e^x$ for the initial conditions $y|_{x=0} = 1$, $y'|_{x=0} = 0$. Find $f\left(\frac{1}{2}\right)$ to within 0.0001.

4357. A curve is specified by the equation $y = f(x)$. Find the series expansion of the function $f(x)$, knowing that it satisfies the differential equation $y'' = xy$ and the initial conditions $y|_{x=0} = 0$, $y'|_{x=0} = 1$. Compute (to within 0.0001) the curvature of the curve at the point with abscissa 1.

15

Trigonometric Series

1. Trigonometric Polynomials

4358. Using Euler's formulas $\cos x = \frac{e^{ix} + e^{-ix}}{2}$ and $\sin x = \frac{e^{ix} - e^{-ix}}{2i}$, prove that the functions $\sin^n x$ and $\cos^n x$ can be represented in the form of trigonometric polynomials of the nth degree.

4359. Prove the relationships

$$\int_0^{2\pi} \sin^n x \cos mx\, dx = \int_0^{2\pi} \sin^n x \sin mx\, dx = \int_0^{2\pi} \cos^n x \cos mx\, dx$$

$$= \int_0^{2\pi} \cos^n x \sin mx\, dx = 0 \text{ if } m > n \text{ (} m \text{ and } n \text{ integers).}$$

4360. Show that any trigonometric polynomial of the nth degree made up only of cosines can be represented in the form $P(\cos \varphi)$, where $P(x)$ is a polynomial of the nth degree with respect to x.

4361. With the aid of Euler's formulas (see Problem 4358) prove the relationship

$$\cos \varphi + \cos 2\varphi + \ldots + \cos n\varphi = \frac{\sin \frac{n\varphi}{2} \cos \frac{(n+1)\varphi}{2}}{\sin \frac{\varphi}{2}}.$$

4362. Prove the relationships:

(1) $\cos \varphi + \cos 3\varphi + \ldots + \cos (2n-1)\varphi = \frac{\sin 2n\varphi}{2 \sin \varphi}$;

(2) $\sin \varphi + \sin 2\varphi + \ldots + \sin n\varphi = \frac{\sin \frac{n\varphi}{2} \sin \frac{(n+1)\varphi}{2}}{\sin \frac{\varphi}{2}}$.

4363. Find the zeros of the trigonometric polynomials

$$\sin \varphi + \sin 2\varphi + \ldots + \sin n\varphi$$

and $$\cos \varphi + \cos 2\varphi + \ldots + \cos n\varphi$$

in the interval $[0, 2\pi]$.

4364. Show that the trigonometric polynomial

$$\sin \varphi + \frac{\sin 2\varphi}{2} + \ldots + \frac{\sin n\varphi}{n}$$

in the interval $[0, \pi]$ has maxima at the points $\frac{\pi}{n+1}, 3\frac{\pi}{n+1}, \ldots, (2q-1)\frac{\pi}{n+1}$ and minima at the points $\frac{2\pi}{n}, 2\frac{2\pi}{n}, \ldots, (q-1)\frac{2\pi}{n}$, where $q = \frac{n}{2}$ if n is even and $q = \frac{n+1}{2}$ if n is odd.

4365*. Prove that the trigonometric polynomial without a constant term,

$$\Phi_n(\varphi) = a_1 \cos \varphi + b_1 \sin \varphi + \ldots + a_n \cos n\varphi + b_n \sin n\varphi,$$

which is not identically equal to zero, cannot retain a constant sign for all values of φ.

2. Fourier Series

4366. Verify that the function $y = x^3 \sin \frac{1}{x}$ for $x \neq 0$ and $y = 0$ for $x = 0$ in the interval $[-\pi, \pi]$ is continuous together with its first derivative but does not satisfy the conditions of Dirichlet's theorem. Can it be expanded into a Fourier series in the interval $[-\pi, \pi]$?

Solve Problems 4367 to 4371 assuming that $f(x)$ is a continuous function.

4367. The function $f(x)$ satisfies the condition

$$f(x + \pi) = -f(x).$$

Prove that all its even Fourier coefficients are equal to zero $(a_0 = a_2 = b_2 = a_4 = b_4 = \ldots = 0)$.

4368. The function $f(x)$ satisfies the condition

$$f(x + \pi) = f(x).$$

Prove that all its odd Fourier coefficients are equal to zero.

4369. The function $f(x)$ satisfies the conditions $f(-x) = f(x)$ and $f(x+\pi) = -f(x)$.
Prove that $b_1 = b_2 = b_3 = \ldots = 0$ and $a_0 = a_2 = a_4 = \ldots = 0$.

4370. The function $f(x)$ satisfies the conditions

$$f(-x) = -f(x) \quad \text{and} \quad f(x+\pi) = -f(x).$$

Prove that $a_0 = a_1 = a_2 = \ldots = 0$ and $b_2 = b_4 = b_6 = \ldots = 0$.

4371. The function $f(x)$ satisfies the conditions:
(a) $f(-x) = f(x)$ and $f(x+\pi) = f(x)$;
(b) $f(-x) = -f(x)$ and $f(x+\pi) = f(x)$.
Which of its Fourier coefficients vanish?

4372. Expand into a Fourier series the function which is equal to -1 in the interval $(-\pi, 0)$ and to 1 in the interval $(0, \pi)$.

4373. Expand the function $y = \frac{\pi}{4} - \frac{x}{2}$ into a Fourier sine series in the interval $(0, \pi)$.

4374. Using the results of Problems 4372 and 4373, obtain the expansions for the functions $y = x$ and $y = \frac{\pi - x}{2}$. Indicate the intervals for which the obtained formulas are valid.

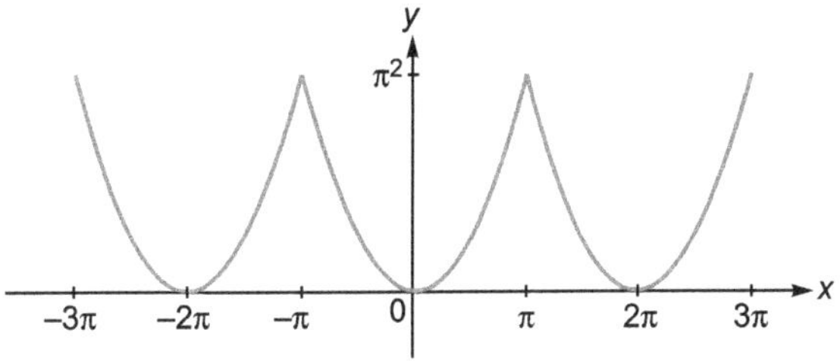

Fig. 72

4375. Expand the function $y = \frac{\pi}{4} - \frac{x}{2}$ into a Fourier cosine series in the interval $(0, \pi)$.

4376. Expand the function $y = x^2$ into a Fourier series:
(1) in the interval $(-\pi, \pi)$,
(2) in the interval $(0, 2\pi)$ (Figs. 72 and 73).
With the aid of the obtained expansions compute the sums of the series:

$$S_1 = 1 + \frac{1}{2^2} + \frac{1}{3^2} + \ldots + \frac{1}{n^2} + \ldots,$$

$$S_2 = 1 - \frac{1}{2^2} + \frac{1}{3^2} - \ldots + (-1)^{n-1}\frac{1}{n^2} + \ldots,$$

$$S_3 = 1 + \frac{1}{3^2} + \frac{1}{5^2} + \ldots + \frac{1}{(2n-1)^2} + \ldots$$

In Problems 4377 to 4390 expand the given functions into a Fourier series in the indicated intervals.

4377. The function $y = x^2$ into a sine series in the interval $(0, \pi)$.

4378. The function $y = x^3$ in the interval $(-\pi, \pi)$.

4379. The function $f(x)$ equal to 1 for $-\pi < x < 0$ and to 3 for $0 < x < \pi$.

4380. The function $f(x)$, equal to 1 in the interval $(0, h)$ and to 0 in the interval (h, π), into a cosine series $(0 < h < \pi)$.

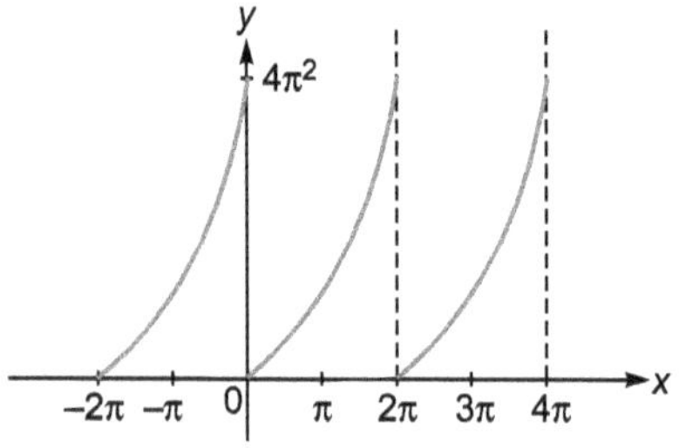

Fig. 73

4381. The continuous function $f(x)$, equal to 1 for $x = 0$, equal to 0 in the interval $(2h, \pi)$ and linear in the interval $(0, 2h)$, into a cosine series $\left(0 < h < \frac{\pi}{2}\right)$.

4382. The function $y = |x|$ in the interval $(-l, l)$.

4383. The function $y = e^x - 1$ in the interval $(0, 2\pi)$.

4384. The function $y = e^x$ in the interval $(-l, l)$.

4385. The function $y = \cos ax$ in the interval $(-\pi, \pi)$ (a is a nonintegral number).

4386. The function $y = \sin ax$ in the interval $(-\pi, \pi)$ (a is a nonintegral number).

4387. The function $y = \sin ax$ (a integral) in the interval $(0, \pi)$ into a cosine series.

4388. The function $y = \cos ax$ (a integral) in the interval $(0, \pi)$ into a sine series.

4389. The function $y = \sinh ax$ in the interval $(-\pi, \pi)$.

4390. The function $y = \cosh x$ in the interval $(0, \pi)$ into a cosine series and a sine series.

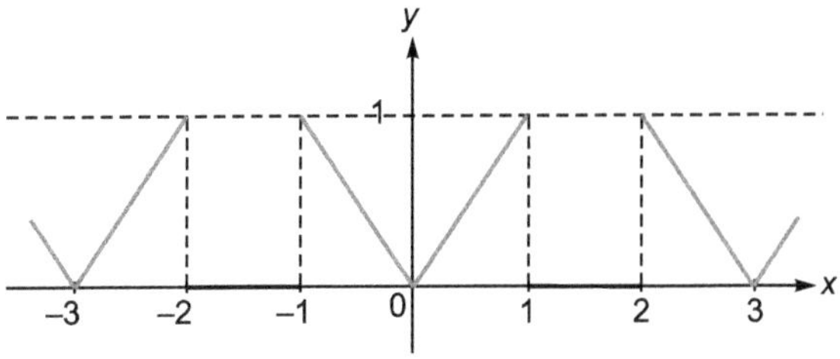

Fig. 74

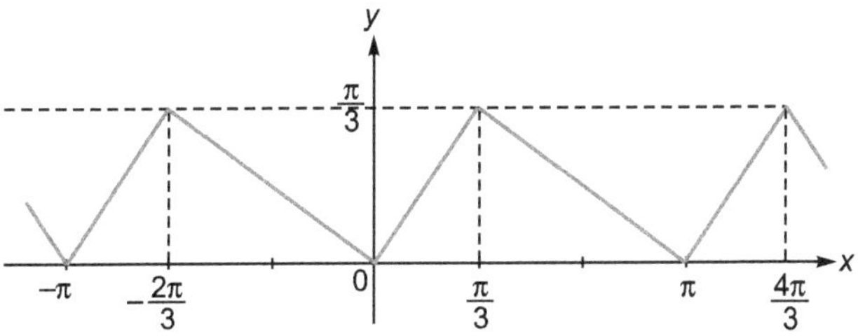

Fig. 75

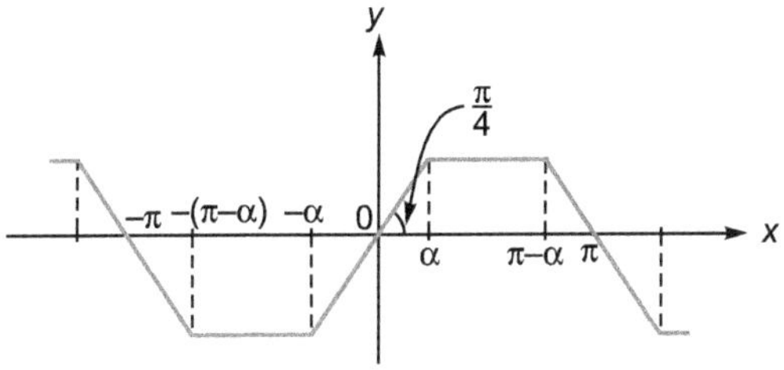

Fig. 76

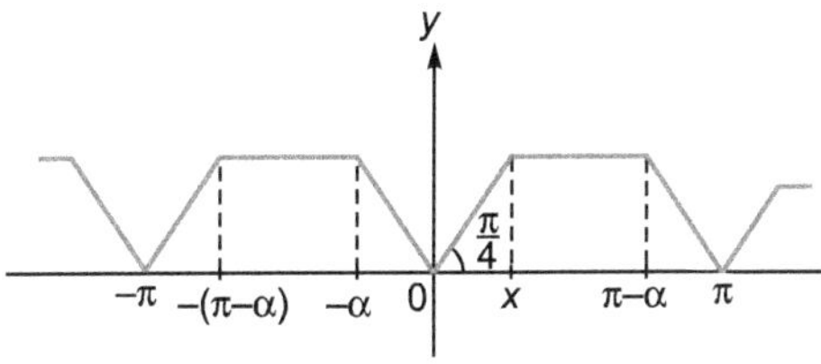

Fig. 77

4391. Expand into a Fourier series the function whose graph is shown in Fig. 74.

4392*. Expand into a Fourier series the function whose graph is given in Fig. 75.

4393*. Expand into Fourier series the functions whose graphs are shown in Figs. 76 and 77.

4394. Expand the function $y = x(\pi - x)$ into a sine series in the interval $(0, \pi)$. Use the obtained result for finding the sum of the series.

$$1 - \frac{1}{3^3} + \frac{1}{5^3} - \frac{1}{7^3} + \dots + \frac{(-1)^{n-1}}{(2n-1)^3} + \dots .$$

4395. Given a function $\varphi(x) = (\pi^2 - x^2)^2$.

(a) Make sure that the following equalities are valid:

$$\varphi(-\pi) = \varphi(\pi), \quad \varphi'(-\pi) = \varphi'(\pi) \quad \text{and} \quad \varphi''(-\pi) = \varphi''(\pi)$$

$$[\text{but } \varphi'''(-\pi) \neq \varphi'''(\pi)].$$

(b) Using the obtained equalities, expand the function $\varphi(x)$ into a, Fourier series in the interval $(-\pi, \pi)$.

(c) Compute the sum of the series

$$1 - \frac{1}{2^4} + \frac{1}{3^4} - \frac{1}{4^4} + \dots + \frac{(-1)^{n-1}}{n^4} + \dots .$$

3. Krylov's Method. Harmonic Analysis

In Problems 4396 to 4399 improve the convergence of the trigonometric series, bringing the coefficients to the order k indicated in parentheses.

4396*. $\sum\limits_{n=1}^{\infty} \frac{n^2}{n^3+1} \sin nx \ (k = 4).$

4397*. $\sum\limits_{n=1}^{\infty} (-1)^{n-1} \frac{n+1}{n^2+1} \sin nx \ (k = 2).$

4398*. $\sum\limits_{n=0}^{\infty} \frac{n^2+1}{n^4+1} \cos nx \ (k = 4).$

4399*. $\sum\limits_{n=2}^{\infty} \frac{n \sin \frac{n\pi}{2}}{n^2-1} \cos nx \ (k = 5).$

4400. The functions $f_i(x)$ $(i = 1, 2, 3)$ are specified in the interval $[0, 2\pi]$ by the following table:

x	0	$\frac{\pi}{6}$	$\frac{\pi}{3}$	$\frac{\pi}{2}$	$\frac{2\pi}{3}$	$\frac{5\pi}{6}$	π	$\frac{7\pi}{6}$	$\frac{4\pi}{3}$	$\frac{3\pi}{2}$	$\frac{5\pi}{3}$	$\frac{11\pi}{6}$
$f_1(x)$	27	32	35	30	26	20	18	22	26	30	32	36
$f_2(x)$	0.43	0.87	0.64	0.57	0.28	0	–0.30	–0.64	–0.25	0.04	0.42	0.84
$f_3(x)$	2.3	3.2	2.1	1.6	–0.4	–0.2	–0.4	0.3	0.7	0.9	1.2	1.6

Find the approximate expression of these functions in the form of a trigonometric polynomial of the second degree.

16

Elements of Field Theory

Vector field divergence and curl

4401. Find the vector lines of the homogeneous field $\mathbf{A}(P) = a\mathbf{i} + b\mathbf{j} + c\mathbf{k}$, where a, b and c are constants.

4402. Find the vector lines of the plane field $\mathbf{A}(P) = -\omega y\mathbf{i} + \omega x\mathbf{j}$, where ω is a constant.

4403. Find the vector lines of the field $\mathbf{A}(P) = -\omega y\mathbf{i} + \omega x\mathbf{j} + h\mathbf{k}$, where ω and h are constants.

4404. Find the vector lines of the field:

(1) $\mathbf{A}(P) = (y + z)\mathbf{i} - x\mathbf{j} - x\mathbf{k}$;

(2) $\mathbf{A}(P) = (z - y)\mathbf{i} + (x - z)\mathbf{j} + (y - x)\mathbf{k}$;

(3) $\mathbf{A}(P) = x(y^2 - z^2)\mathbf{i} - y(z^2 + x^2)\mathbf{j} + z(x^2 + y^2)\mathbf{k}$.

In Problems 4405 to 4408 compute the divergence and the curl of the given vector fields.

4405. $\mathbf{A}(P) = x\mathbf{i} + y\mathbf{j} + z\mathbf{k}$.

4406. $\mathbf{A}(P) = (y^2 + z^2)\mathbf{i} + (z^2 + x^2)\mathbf{j} + (x^2 + y^2)\mathbf{k}$.

4407. $\mathbf{A}(P) = x^2yz\mathbf{i} + xy^2z\mathbf{j} + xyz^2\mathbf{k}$.

4408. $\mathbf{A}(P) = \text{grad}\,(x^2 + y^2 + z^2)$.

4409. A vector field is created by a force which has a constant value F and is directed along the positive x-axis. Compute the divergence and curl of this field.

4410. A plane vector field is set up by a force inversely proportional to the square of the distance from the point of its application to the origin and directed towards the origin. (For instance, a plane electric field generated by a point charge). Find the divergence and curl of this field.

4411. Find the divergence and curl of a space field if the forces of the field are governed by the same conditions as in Problem 4410.

4412. A vector field is created by a force inversely proportional to the distance from the point of its application to the z-axis, perpendicular to this axis and directed towards it. Compute the divergence and curl of this field.

4413. A vector field is created by a force inversely proportional to the distance from the point of its application to the plane xOy and directed towards the origin. Compute the divergence of this field.

In Problem 4414 and furtherafter $\mathbf{r}$ denotes the radius vector and $r = |\mathbf{r}|$ is its absolute value.

4414. Compute div $(a\mathbf{r})$, where a is a constant scalar.

4415. Prove the relationship

$$\operatorname{div}(\varphi \mathbf{A}) = \varphi \operatorname{div} \mathbf{A} + (\mathbf{A} \operatorname{grad} \varphi),$$

where $\varphi = \varphi(x, y, z)$ is a scalar function.

4416. Compute div $\mathbf{b}(\mathbf{ra})$ and div $\mathbf{r}(\mathbf{ra})$, where $\mathbf{a}$ and $\mathbf{b}$ are constant vectors.

4417. Compute div $(\mathbf{a} \times \mathbf{r})$, where $\mathbf{a}$ is a constant vector.

4418. Without passing to coordinates, compute the divergence of the vector field:

(1) $\mathbf{A}(P) = \mathbf{r}(\mathbf{ar}) - 2\mathbf{a}\mathbf{r}^2$, (2) $\mathbf{A}(P) = \dfrac{\mathbf{r} - \mathbf{r}_0}{|\mathbf{r} - \mathbf{r}_0|^3}$,

(3) $\operatorname{grad} \dfrac{1}{|\mathbf{r} - \mathbf{r}_0|}$.

4419. Compute the divergence of the vector field

$$\mathbf{A}(P) = f(|\mathbf{r}|)\frac{\mathbf{r}}{|\mathbf{r}|}.$$

Prove that the divergence is equal to zero only when $f(|\mathbf{r}|) = \dfrac{C}{r^2}$, in case of a space field, and $f(|\mathbf{r}|) = \dfrac{C}{|\mathbf{r}|}$, in case of a plane field, where C is an arbitrary constant.

4420. Prove that

$$\operatorname{rot}[\mathbf{A}_1(P) + \mathbf{A}_2(P)] = \operatorname{rot} \mathbf{A}_1(P) + \operatorname{rot} \mathbf{A}_2(P).$$

4421. Compute $\operatorname{rot}[\varphi \mathbf{A}(P)]$, where $\varphi = \varphi(x, y, z)$ is a scalar function.

4422. Compute rot $\mathbf{ra}$, where $\mathbf{a}$ is a constant vector.

4423. Compute rot $(\mathbf{a} \times \mathbf{r})$, where $\mathbf{a}$ is a constant vector.

4424. A solid rotates with a constant angular velocity ω about its axis. Find the divergence and curl of the field of linear velocities.

4425. Prove the relationship

$$\mathbf{n}(\operatorname{grad}(\mathbf{An}) - \operatorname{rot}(\mathbf{A} \times \mathbf{n})) = \operatorname{div} \mathbf{A}$$

if $\mathbf{n}$ is a constant unit vector.

The fundamental notions of gradient, divergence and curl (grad, div, curl) introduced in vector analysis can be conveniently represented by means of a symbolic vector operator ∇ (introduced by W. R. Hamilton) called nabla or del or the Hamiltonian operator. It is defined by the formula

$$\nabla = \frac{\partial}{\partial x}\mathbf{i} + \frac{\partial}{\partial y}\mathbf{j} + \frac{\partial}{\partial z}\mathbf{k},$$

where $\frac{\partial}{\partial x}$, $\frac{\partial}{\partial y}$ and $\frac{\partial}{\partial z}$ symbolize the differentiation with respect to x, y and z. Operations involving the nabla operator are performed according to the ordinary rules of vector algebra under the convention that the multiplication of $\frac{\partial}{\partial x}$ by an expression (scalar or vector) is understood as the differentiation of this expression with respect to the corresponding variable. Then, grad $u = \nabla u$; div $\mathbf{A} = \nabla \mathbf{A}$; curl $\mathbf{A} = \nabla \times \mathbf{A}$.

Differential operations of the second order can also be written with the aid of the Hamiltonian operator.

$$\nabla\, \nabla u = \text{div grad}\, u;\ \ \nabla \times \nabla u = \text{curl grad}\, u;$$
$$\nabla(\nabla \mathbf{A}) = \text{grad div}\, \mathbf{A};\ \ \nabla(\nabla \times \mathbf{A}) = \text{div curl}\, \mathbf{A};$$
$$\nabla \times (\nabla \times \mathbf{A}) = \text{curl curl}\, \mathbf{A}.$$

4426. Prove that $\mathbf{r} \cdot \nabla r^n = nr^n$, where $\mathbf{r}$ is the radius vector.

4427. Prove the relationships:

(1) curl grad $u = 0$; (2) div curl $\mathbf{A} = 0$.

4428. Prove that

$$\text{div grad}\, u = \frac{\partial^2 u}{\partial x^2} + \frac{\partial^2 u}{\partial y^2} + \frac{\partial^2 u}{\partial z^2}.$$

(This expression is called the Laplacian operator and is usually designated Δu. With the aid of the Hamiltonian operator it can be written in the form $\Delta u = (\nabla\nabla)u = \nabla^2 u$.)

4429. Prove that

$$\text{curl curl}\, \mathbf{A}\,(P) = \text{grad div}\, \mathbf{A}\,(P) = -\Delta\, \mathbf{A}(P),$$

where $\Delta\, \mathbf{A}(P) = \Delta A_x \mathbf{i} + \Delta A_y \mathbf{j} + \Delta A_z \mathbf{k}$.

Potential

4430. A vector field is created by a constant vector $\mathbf{A}$. Verify that this field has a potential and find it.

4431. A vector field is generated by a force proportional to the distance of the point of application from the origin and directed towards the latter. Show that this is a conservative field and find its potential.

4432. The forces of a field are inversely proportional to the distances of the points of their application from the plane Oxy and are directed towards the origin. Is it a conservative field?

4433. The forces of a field are proportional to the square of the distance between the points of their application and the applicate axis and are directed towards the origin. Will this field be a conservative one?

4434. A vector field is generated by a force inversely proportional to the distance of the point of its application from the z-axis perpendicular to this axis and directed towards it. Show that this is a conservative field and find its potential.

4435. A vector field is set up by linear velocities of points of a solid rotating about its axis. Has this field a potential?

4436. The forces of a field are specified as follows: $\mathbf{A}(P) = f(\mathbf{r})\dfrac{\mathbf{r}}{r}$ (a so-called centred field). Show that the potential of this field is

$$u(x, y, z) = \int_a^r f(r)\,dr \ (r = \sqrt{x^2 + y^2 + z^2}),$$

wherefrom obtain (as a particular case) the potential of a field of forces attracting a mass point and also the potential of the field considered in Problem 4431.

4437. Find the work performed by the forces of the field $\mathbf{A}(P) = xy\mathbf{i} + yz\mathbf{j} + xz\mathbf{k}$ in displacing a mass point m round a closed line consisting of a segment of the straight line $x + z = 1$, $y = 0$; a quarter of the circle $x^2 + y^2 = 1$, $z = 0$ and a segment of the straight line $y + z = 1$, $x = 0$ (Fig. 78) in the direction indicated in the drawing. How will the amount of work change if the arc BA is replaced by the polygonal line BOA or by the segment BA?

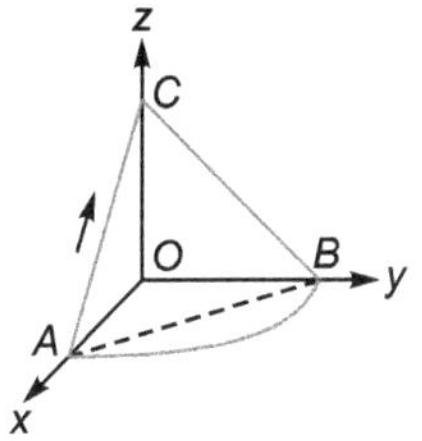

Fig. 78

Potential of an attracting force[1]

4438. Given in the plane $O\xi\eta$ is a homogeneous rod AB whose length is $2l$ and linear density δ. The rod is situated on the axis $O\xi$ symmetrically with respect to the origin (Fig. 79).

[1]Here (in Problems 4438 to 4449) Newton's force of gravity is meant. Instead of the expression 'the potential of a mass' located on (or in) a given geometrical object we use for brevity 'the potential of a given object'.

(a) Find the potential $u(x, y)$ of the rod.

(b) Show that the projections X and Y of the attracting force acting on point P of mass m with the coordinates $\xi = x, \eta = y$ are

$$X = mk\delta\left(\frac{1}{PA} - \frac{1}{PB}\right),\ Y = -\frac{mk\delta}{y}\left(\frac{CB}{PB} + \frac{AC}{PA}\right),$$

and the absolute value of the resultant force $R = \dfrac{2mk\delta}{y}\sin\dfrac{1}{2}\times(\alpha+\beta)$, where k is the gravitational constant, C the projection of the point P on the axis $O\xi$, α the angle APC and β the angle BPC.

4439. Find the potential of the circle $x^2 + y^2 = R^2$, $z = 0$ at the point $(R, 0, 2R)$ if the density at each point is equal to the absolute value of the sine of the angle between the radius vector of the point and the x-axis.

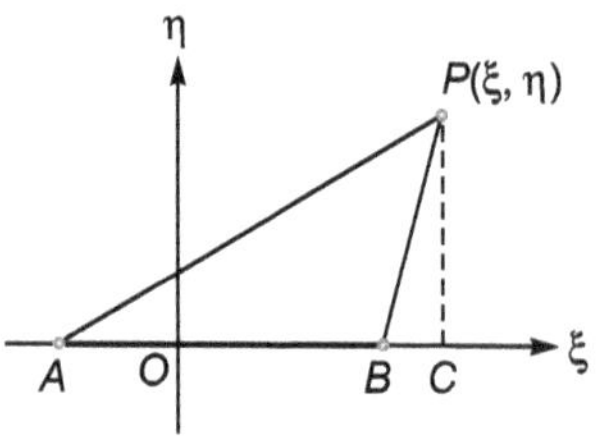

Fig. 79

4440. Find the potential of the first turn of a homogeneous (density δ) helix $x = a\cos t$, $y = a\sin t$, $z = bt$ at the origin.

4441. Find the potential of a homogeneous square with the side a (surface density δ) at one of its vertices.

4442. Distributed on the plane Oxy is a mass with the density δ decreasing with the distance ρ from the origin according to the law $\delta = \dfrac{1}{1+\rho^2}$. Find the potential at the point $(0, 0, h)$. (Consider three cases: $h < 1$, $h = 1$ and $h > 1$.)

4443*. Compute the potential of a homogeneous lateral surface of a circular cylinder:

(1) at the centre of its base.

(2) at the mid-point of its axis (the radius of the cylinder R, altitude H, surface density δ).

4444. Compute the potential of a homogeneous lateral surface of a right circular cone (the radius of the base R, altitude H) at its vertex.

4445. Given a homogeneous right circular cylinder (the radius of the base R, altitude H, density δ).

(1) Find the potential at the centre of its base.

(2) Find the potential at the mid-point of its axis.

4446. Given a homogeneous right circular cone (the radius of the base R, altitude H, density δ). Find the potential of the cone at its vertex.

4447. Find the potential of a homogeneous hemisphere $x^2 + y^2 + z^2 \leq R^2 (z \geq 0)$ whose density is δ at the point $A(0, 0, a)$. (Consider two cases: $a \geq R$ and $a \leq R$.)

4448*. Find the potential of a homogeneous solid bounded by two concentric spheres of the radii R and $r\,(R > r)$ and density δ at the point located at the distance a from the centre of the sphere. (Consider three cases: $a \geq R$, $a \leq r$ and $r \leq a \leq R$.) Show that if a point is found in the inner hollow of the solid, then the attracting force acting on this point is equal to zero.

4449. Find the potential of a homogeneous solid sphere $x^2 + y^2 + z^2 \leq R$ at the point $A(0, 0, a)\,(a > R)$ if the density $\delta = \lambda z^2$, i.e., is proportional to the square of the distance of the point from the plane Oxy.

Flux and circulation (in a plane)

4450. Compute the flux and circulation of a constant vector $\mathbf{A}$ along an arbitrary closed curve L.

4451. Compute the flux and circulation of vector $\mathbf{A}(P) = a\mathbf{r}$, where a is a constant scalar, and $\mathbf{r}$ the radius vector of point P, along an arbitrary closed curve L.

4452. Compute the flux and circulation of vector $\mathbf{A}(P) = x\mathbf{i} - y\mathbf{j}$ along an arbitrary closed curve L.

4453. Compute the flux and circulation of vector

$$\mathbf{A}(P) = (x^3 - y)\mathbf{i} + (y^3 + x)\mathbf{j}$$

round a circle of radius R with the centre at the origin.

4454. The potential of a velocity field of the particles of a flowing fluid is $u = \ln r$, where $r = \sqrt{x^2 + y^2}$. Determine the quantity of the fluid flowing out from a closed contour L surrounding the origin, per unit time (flux) and the amount of the fluid flowing along this contour per unit time (circulation). How will the result change if the origin lies outside the contour?

4455. The potential of a velocity field of the particles of a flowing fluid is $u = \varphi$, where $\varphi = \arctan \frac{y}{x}$. Determine the flux and circulation of the vector over a closed contour L.

4456. The potential of a velocity field of the particles of a flowing fluid is $u(x, y) = x(x^2 - 3y^2)$. Compute the quantity of the fluid flowing through a straight line segment joining the origin to the point $(1, 1)$.

Flux and circulation (in space)

4457. Prove that the flux of radius vector $\mathbf{r}$ through any closed surface is equal to the tripled volume of the solid bounded by this surface.

4458. Compute the flux of the radius vector through the lateral surface of a circular cylinder (the radius of the base R, the altitude H) if the axis of the cylinder passes through the origin.

4459. Using the results of Problems 4457 and 4458, find the flux of the radius vector through both bases of the cylinder of the previous problem.

4460. Compute the flux of the radius vector through the lateral surface of a circular cone whose base is contained in the plane xOy and the axis coincides with the z-axis. (The altitude of the cone is equal to 1, radius of the base to 2.)

4461. Find the flux of the vector $\mathbf{A}(P) = xy\mathbf{i} + yz\mathbf{j} + xz\mathbf{k}$ through the boundary of the part of the sphere $x^2 + y^2 + z^2 = 1$ contained in the first octant.

4462*. Find the flux of the vector $\mathbf{A}(P) = yz\mathbf{i} + xz\mathbf{j} + xy\mathbf{k}$ through the lateral surface of a pyramid with the vertex at the point $S(0, 0, 2)$ whose base is a triangle with the vertices $O(0, 0, 0)$, $A(2, 0, 0)$ and $B(0, 1, 0)$.

4463. Compute the circulation of the radius vector over one turn AB of the helix $x = a\cos t$, $y = a\sin t$, $z = bt$, where A and B are the points corresponding to the respective value of the parameter 0 and 2π.

4464. A solid rotates with a constant angular velocity ω about the z-axis. Compute the circulation of a linear velocity field over a circle of radius R whose centre lies on the axis of rotation and the plane containing the circle is perpendicular to the axis of rotation in the direction of rotation.

4465*. Compute the flux of the rotation of the field of vectors $\mathbf{A}(P) = y\mathbf{i} + z\mathbf{j} + x\mathbf{k}$ through the surface of the paraboloid of revolution $z = 2(1 - x^2 - y^2)$, cut off by the plane $z = 0$.

Answers

Chapter 1

1. All natural numbers n, except $n = 1$ and $n = 2$. If the sum of angles is S, and the number of sides is n, then $S = \pi (n - 2)$.

4. (a) For $x = -2$, $x = 1$, $x = 6$ the function vanishes;
   (b) for $x < -2$, $-2 < x < 1$, $x > 6$ the function is positive;
   (c) for $1 < x < 6$ the function is negative.

6. $r = \dfrac{1}{\sqrt{\pi h}}$. 7. $S = \dfrac{a^2 - b^2}{4} \tan \alpha$. 8. $b = \sqrt{25 - a^2}$.

9. $f(0) = -2$, $f(1) = -0.5$, $f(2) = 0$, $f(-2) = 4$, $f\left(-\dfrac{1}{2}\right) = -5$,

   $f(\sqrt{2}) = -0.242\ldots$, $\left|f\left(\dfrac{1}{2}\right)\right| = 1$; $\varphi(0) = 2$, $\varphi(1) = 0.5$, $\varphi(2) = 0$,

   $\varphi(-2) = -4$, $\varphi(4) = 0.4$. $f(-1)$ does not exist. $\varphi(-1)$ does not exist.

10. $f(1) = 0$, $f(a) = a^3 - 1$, $f(a + 1) = a^3 + 3a^2 + 3a$,
    $f(a - 1) = a^3 - 3a^2 + 3a - 2$, $2f(2a) = 16a^3 - 2$.

11. $F(0) = \dfrac{1}{4}$, $F(2) = 1$, $F(3) = 2$, $F(-1) = \dfrac{1}{8}$, $F(2.5) = \sqrt{2}$, $F(-1.5) = \dfrac{1}{\sqrt{128}}$,
    $\varphi(0) = \dfrac{1}{4}$, $\varphi(2) = 1$, $\varphi(-1) = \dfrac{1}{2}$. $\varphi(x) = 2^{x-2}$ for $x > 0$ and $\varphi(x) = 2^{-x-2}$ for $x < 0$; $\varphi(-1) + F(1) = 1$.

12. $\psi(0) = 0$, $\psi(1) = a$, $\psi(-1) = -\dfrac{1}{a}$, $\psi\left(\dfrac{1}{a}\right) = a^{\frac{1-a}{a}}$, $\psi(a) = a^{a+1}$,
    $\psi(-a) = -a^{1-a}$.

13. $\varphi(t^2) = t^6 + 1$; $[\varphi(t)]^2 = t^6 + 2t^3 + 1$.

20. $\dfrac{f(b) - f(a)}{b - a}$ is equal to the tangent of the angle between the secant passing through the points $(a, f(a))$ and $(b, f(b))$, and the positive x-axis.

22. (a) $x_1 = 0$, $x_2 = 2$; (b) $x_1 = -1$, $x_2 = 3$.

23. $x_1 = -2$, $x_2 = 5$, $x_3 = -\dfrac{1}{2}$.

24. $x = a$ is always one of the roots.

25. 4 and -2; -2, 2, 4, 10.

26. $x_1 = -3$, $x_2 = -2$, $x_3 = 2$, $x_4 = 3$.

27. $x \le -1$ and $x \ge 2$.

28. $a = 4, b = -1.$

29. $a = -\dfrac{1}{2 \sin 0.5} \approx -1.04$ (putting $\sin 0.5 \approx 0.48$); $b = 1$; $c = -\dfrac{1}{2} + 2k\pi$ or

$a = \dfrac{1}{2 \sin 0.5} \approx 1.04; b = -1;\ c = \dfrac{1}{2} + (2k + 1)\pi\ (k = 0, \pm 1, \pm 2, \dots).$

30. $y = (x + 1)^2.$ **31.** $y = \left|\dfrac{1}{\cos x}\right|.$ **32.** $y = \sqrt[3]{(a^t + 1)^2}.$

33. $u = \sqrt{1 + (\log_{10} \sin x)^2}.$ **34.** $v = \sin (1 + x).$

35. (1) $y = v^3, v = \sin x$; (2) $y = \sqrt[3]{v}, v = u^2, u = x + 1$;

(3) $y = \log_{10} v, v = \tan x$; (4) $y = u^3, u = \sin v, v = 2x + 1$;

(5) $y = 5^u, u = v^2, v = 3x + 1.$

36. (a) $-\dfrac{3}{8}$; (b) 0; (c) $\sin 12$; (d) $-\sin 2x \cos^2 2x$;

(e) $x^9 - 3x^7 + 3x^5 - 2x^3 + x$; (f) 0; (g) $\sin (2 \sin 2x)$.

38. (1) $y = \pm \sqrt{1 - x^2}$; (2) $y = \pm \dfrac{b}{a}\sqrt{x^2 - a^2}$; (3) $y = \sqrt[3]{a^3 - x^3}$;

(4) $y = \dfrac{C}{x}$; (5) $y = \dfrac{\log_2 5}{x}$; (6) $y = \dfrac{10000}{x} - 1$;

(7) $y = \log_2 (x^3 + 7) - \log_2 (x^2 - 2) - x$; (8) $y = \arccos \dfrac{x^2}{1 + x}$.

39*. Let $x > 0$ and $y > 0$, then $y + y - x - x = 0$; $y = x$ (the graph is the bisector of the first quadrant). Let $x > 0$ and $y < 0$, then $y - y - x - x = 0$, $x = 0$ (the graph is the negative y-axis). Let $x < 0$ and $y > 0$, then $y + y - x + x = 0$; $y = 0$ (the graph is the negative x-axis). Let $x < 0$ and $y < 0$, then $y - y - x + x = 0$ is the identity (the graph is a set of all interior points of the third quadrant).

40.

x	1	2	3	4	5	6
y	1	$\frac{1}{2}$	$\frac{1}{6}$	$\frac{1}{24}$	$\frac{1}{120}$	$\frac{1}{720}$

41.

n	1	2	3	4	5	6	7	8	9	10	11	12	13	14	15	16	17	18	19	20
u	0	1	2	2	3	3	4	4	4	4	5	5	6	6	6	6	7	7	8	8

42.

n	1	2	3	4	5	6	7	8	9	10	11	12	13	14	15	16	17	18	19	20
u	0	0	0	1	0	2	0	2	1	2	0	4	0	2	2	3	0	4	0	4

43. If $f(x)$ is the weight of the segment AM, then $f(x) = 2x$ for $0 \le x \le 1$, $f(x) = 2 + \dfrac{3}{2}(x - 1)$ for $1 < x \le 3$, $f(x) = x + 2$ for $3 < x \le 4$. The function is defined for $0 \le x \le 4$.

44. For $0 \le x \le R$ $S = \pi (2R - x)^2$; for $R \le x \le 3R$ $S = \pi R^2$; for $3R \le x \le 4R$ $S = \pi (6Rx - x^2 - 8R^2)$. Outside the interval $[0, 4R]$ the function $S = f(x)$ is not defined.

45. $V = \pi x\left(R^2 - \frac{x^2}{4}\right); 0 < x < 2R.$ **46.** $S = \frac{\pi x^2}{2R}\sqrt{4R^2 - x^2}; 0 < x < 2R.$

47. (1) $x > 0$; (2) $x > -3$; (3) $x \leq \frac{5}{2}$; (4) $-\infty < x \leq 0$; (5) the whole number scale, except for the points $x = \pm 1$; (6) the whole number scale; (7) not defined only for $x = 0, x = -1, x = 1$; (8) the whole number scale, except for the points $x = 1$ and $x = 2$; (9) $-1 \leq x \leq 1$; (10) $-\infty < x < 0$ and $4 < x < \infty$; (11) $-\infty < x \leq 1$ and $3 \leq x < \infty$, on the interval (1, 3) the function is not defined; (12) $-\infty < x < 1$ and $2 < x < \infty$, on the interval [1, 2] the function is not defined; (13) $-4 \leq x \leq 4$; (14) $1 \leq x \leq 3$;

(15) $0 \leq x \leq 1$; (16) $-\frac{3}{2} \leq x \leq \frac{5}{2}$; (17) $0 \leq x \leq \frac{1}{2}$; (18) $-1 \leq x \leq 1$;

(19) $-\infty < x < 0$; (20) meaningless; (21) $1 \leq x \leq 4$;

(22) $2k\pi < x < (2k + 1)\pi$, where k is an integer;

(23) $2k\pi \leq x \leq (2k + 1)\pi$, where k is an integer;

(24) $0 < x < 1$ and $1 < x < \infty$.

48. (1) $-2 \leq x < 0$ and $0 < x < 1$; (2) $-1 \leq x \leq 3$; (3) $1 \leq x < 4$; (4) $\frac{3}{2} < x < 2$ and $2 < x < \infty$; (5) the domain of definition consists only of one point $x = 1$; (6) $-1 < x < 0$ and $1 < x < 2; 2 < x < \infty$;

(7) $3 - 2\pi < x < 3 - \pi, 3 < x \leq 4$; (8) $-4 \leq x \leq -\pi$ and $0 \leq x \leq \pi$;

(9) $2k\pi < x < (2k + 1)\pi$, where k is an integer, (10) $4 < x < 5$ and $6 < x < \infty$;

(11) defined nowhere; (12) $-1 < x \leq 1$ and $2 \leq x < 3$; (13) the whole number scale; (14) $4 \leq x \leq 6$; (15) $2 < x < 3$.

49. (1) Yes;

(2) identical on any interval not containing the point $x = 0$;

(3) identical on the interval $[0, \infty)$; (4) identical on the interval $(0, \infty)$.

50. (1) For instance, $y = \sqrt{4 - x^2}$; (2) for instance, $y = \frac{1}{x\sqrt{4 - x^2}}$;

(3) for instance, $y = \frac{1}{x - 2} + \frac{1}{x - 3} + \frac{1}{x - 4}$.

51. (1) $1 < x \leq 3$;

(2) $0 \leq x < +\infty$ for two branches and $1 \leq x < +\infty$ for the other two branches.

52. $-\infty < x < \infty$

53. (1) $y > 0$ for $x > 2$, $y < 0$ for $x < 2$, $y = 0$ y for $x = 2$;

(2) $y > 0$ for $x < 2$ and $x > 3$, $y < 0$ for $2 < x < 3$, $y = 0$ for $x_1 = 2$ and $x_2 = 3$;

(3) $y > 0$ in the interval $(-\infty, \infty)$, the function has no zeros;

(4) $y > 0$ in the intervals (0, 1) and $(2, +\infty)$, $y < 0$ in the intervals $(-\infty, 0)$ and (1, 2); $y = 0$ for $x_1 = 0, x_2 = 1, x_3 = 2$;

(5) $y > 0$ for $x \neq 0$, $y = 0$ for $x = 0$.

54. (1), (3), (8), (10), (11), (15) – even; (5), (6), (9), (12), (14), (17)–odd; (2), (4), (7), (13), (16)–neither even nor odd.

55. (1) $y = (x^2 + 2) + 3x$; (2) $y = (1 - x^4) + (-x^3 - 2x^5)$;

(3) $y = (\sin 2x + \tan x) + \cos\dfrac{x}{2}$.

57. (1) $y = \dfrac{a^x + a^{-x}}{2} + \dfrac{a^x - a^{-x}}{2}$;

(2) $y = \dfrac{(1+x)^{100} + (1-x)^{100}}{2} + \dfrac{(1+x)^{100} - (1-x)^{100}}{2}$.

59. Functions (1), (5), (6), (8).

60. The graphs see on Figs. 80 and 81.

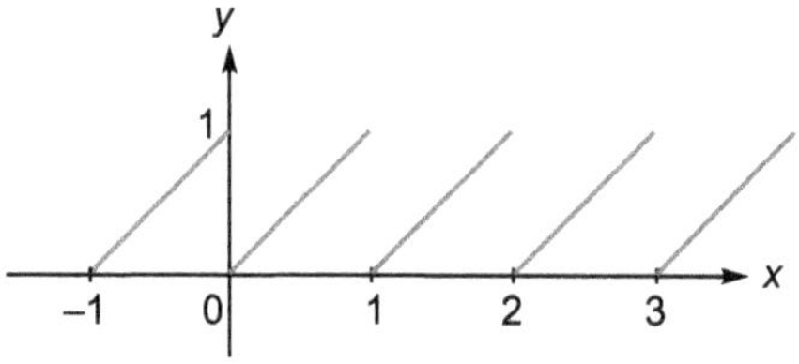

Fig. 80

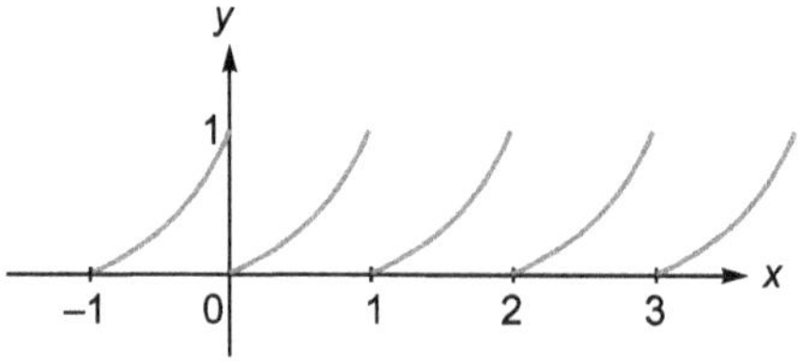

Fig. 81

61. (1) Decreases on the interval $(-\infty, 0)$, increases on the interval $(0, +\infty)$;
(2) decreases on the interval $(-\infty, 0)$, on the interval $(0, +\infty)$ retains constant value-zero.

62. (1) The greatest value 1, least 0; (2) greatest 1, least -1;
(3) greatest 2, least 0; (4) no greatest value, least 1.

65. $I = \dfrac{E}{3}$.

66. (a) $p = 0.727h$; (b) 10.5 g/cm^2; (c) 36.4 cm.

67. $F = \dfrac{8}{45}w$.

68. (1) $y = \dfrac{2}{3}x + 4$; (2) $y = 1.195x + 1.910$; (3) $y = -0.57x + 8.63$.

69. (a) $V = 100 + 0.35t$; (b) 100 cm^3.

70. $S = 16.6 + 1.34t$.

71. $V = 12 - 0.7t$.

72. $\Delta y = 6$.

73. $\Delta y = -6$.

74. $\Delta x = 4$.

75. The terminal value of the argument $x_2 = 2a$.

76. $x = 3$; when graphically finding the roots look for the point of intersection of the graphs $y = \varphi(x)$ and $y = 2x - 4$.

78*. Pay attention to the fact that in the hypothesis the sign of equality is excluded from the always true relationship $|f(x) + \varphi(x)| \le |f(x)| + |\varphi(x)|$. A strict inequality will be valid for $x < 3$ and $x > 4$. The problem can be solved by constructing the graphs of the functions $\Phi(x) = |f(x) + \varphi(x)|$ and $\psi(x) = |f(x)| + |\varphi(x)|$.

79. $x < 2$. See the hint for solving Problem 78*.

82. $y = \begin{cases} 0 \text{ on the interval } (-\infty, -3); \\ -\frac{5}{9}x^2 + 5 \text{ on the interval } [-3, 3]; \\ \frac{2}{3}x - 2 \text{ on the interval } [3, 6]. \end{cases}$

83. (1) $y = -\frac{7}{8}$ for $x = \frac{1}{4}$; (2) $y = \frac{17}{4}$ for $x = -\frac{3}{2}$; (3) $y = 5$ for $x = 0$;
(4) $y = -\frac{7a^2}{8}$ for $x = \frac{a}{4}$; (5) $y = \frac{a^4}{4b^2}$ for $x = \frac{a^2}{2b^2}$.

84. (1) $y = -6$ for $x = -2$; (2) $y = 0.31875$ for $x = \frac{3}{8}$; (3) $y = \frac{5}{8}$ for $x = \frac{1}{4}$;
(4) $y = a^4$ for $x = 0$; (5) $y = -\frac{9}{4}b^2$ for $x = \frac{b}{2a}$.

85. $a = \frac{a}{2} + \frac{a}{2}$. **86.** $a = \frac{a}{2} + \frac{a}{2}$. **87.** 4 m. **88.** Each 50 cm long.

89. The one whose axial section is a square.

90. The smaller the altitude of the cone the larger its lateral surface; the function approaches the greatest value for the radius of the base circle equal to $\frac{P}{4}$, i.e., when the cone degenerates into a planar disk.

91. 12.5 cm.

92. The altitude of the rectangle must equal half the altitude of the triangle.

93. The radius of the cylinder must equal half the radius of the cone.

94. For $H > 2R$ the radius of the cylinder must be equal to $\frac{RH}{2(H-R)}$; for $H \leq 2R$ the total surface area of the inscribed cylinder will be directly proportional to the radius of its base circle.

95. $\frac{P}{2}$. **96.** $a = \frac{P}{6 - \sqrt{3}}$. **97.** $\frac{4}{\pi + 4}$.

98. The side must be equal to 10 cm.

99. The side of the base and the lateral edges must be 10 cm long.

100. The side of the triangle must be equal to $\frac{3a}{9 + 4\sqrt{3}}$.

101. The sought-for point is $\left(\frac{b}{6}, \frac{b}{6}\right)$. **102.** The sought-for point is $\left(\frac{15}{11}, \frac{37}{11}\right)$.

104. (1) $x_1 \approx -1.1$, $x_2 \approx 2.1$; (2) $x_1 = -1$, $x_2 = \frac{5}{2}$; (3) $x_1 \approx 0.5$, $x_2 \approx 4.1$;
(4) $x_1 = x_2 = \frac{3}{2}$; (5) has no real roots.

105. $x_1 = -3$, $x_2 = 8$. When graphically solving the problem seek for the point of intersection of the graphs of the function $y = \varphi(x)$ and the parabola $y^2 = 7x + 25$.

106. If $b^2 - 4ac > 0$ and $a > 0$, then the function is defined throughout the number scale except for the interval $x_1 \leq x \leq x_2$, where x_1 and x_2 are the roots of the trinomial. If $b^2 - 4ac > 0$ and $a < 0$, then the function is defined only for $x_1 < x < x_2$. If $b^2 - 4ac < 0$ and $a > 0$, then the function is defined throughout the number scale. If $b^2 - 4ac < 0$ and $a < 0$, then the function is defined nowhere. Finally, if $b^2 - 4ac = 0$, then the function will be defined throughout the number scale, except for one of its points : $x = -\frac{b}{2a}$ if $a > 0$, and is defined nowhere if $a < 0$.

107. $f(x+1) = 2x^2 + 5x + 3$.

108*. Let $\frac{x^2 + 2x + c}{x^2 + 4x + 3c} = m$, where m is an arbitrary real number, then $(m-1)x^2 + 2(2m-1)x + c(3m-1) = 0$. The argument x must be a real number, hence, $(2m-1)^2 - (m-1)(3mc - c) \geq 0$ or $(4-3c)m^2 + 4(c-1)m - (c-1) \geq 0$, but since m is a real number, this inequality, in its turn, is valid only under the condition that

$$\begin{cases} 4 - 3c > 0, \\ 4(c-1)^2 + (4-3c)(c-1) \leq 0, \end{cases}$$

whence $0 \leq c \leq 1$, but by hypothesis $c \neq 0$, hence, $0 < c \leq 1$.

109. $pv = 1748$.

110. The variable x is inversely proportional to v.

111. The variable x is directly proportional to v.

112. The amount of substance deposited is inversely proportional to the volume of the solvent.

114. (1) for $x = 1$, $y = 4$ is the greatest value,
for $x = 5$, $y = \frac{4}{5}$ is the least value;
(2) for $x = -1$, $y = \frac{1}{7}$ is the greatest value,
for $x = 2$, $y = -2$ is the least value;
(3) for $x = 0$, $y = 1$ is the greatest value,
for $x = 4$, $y = -\frac{3}{5}$ is the least value.

117. (1) $y = x$; (2) $y = \frac{x}{2}$; (3) $y = \frac{1-x}{3}$; (4) $y = \pm\sqrt{x-1}$; (5) $y = \frac{1}{x}$;
(6) $y = \frac{x-1}{x}$; (7) $y = 1 \pm \sqrt{x+1}$; (8) $y = \pm\sqrt{x^3-1}$; (9) $y = \log_{10}\frac{x}{10}$;
(10) $y = -2 + 10^{x-1}$; (11) $y = 2^{1/x}$; (12) $y = \log_2\frac{x}{1-x}$;
(13) $y = \frac{1}{2}\log_{10}\frac{x}{2-x}$; (14) $y = \frac{1}{3}\arcsin\frac{x}{2}$;
(15) $y = \dfrac{1 + \arcsin\frac{x-1}{2}}{1 - \arcsin\frac{x-1}{2}}$; (16) $y = \pm\cos\frac{x}{4}$ $(0 \leq x \leq 2\pi)$.

119. $d = -a$. **122.** $1 < x \leq 3$; $y = 1 + 2^{1-x^2}$. **123.** $y = \arcsin\sqrt[3]{x - x^2 - 2}$.

125. $x_1 \approx -0.5$, $x_2 = 1$, $x_3 \approx 54.5$.

126*. (1) $x_1 = 1.4$, the rest of the roots being imaginary; x_1 is the abscissa of the point of intersection of the graphs of the cubic and linear functions : $y = x^3$ and $y = -x + 4$;
(2) $x_1 = 1, x_2 = -1, x_3 = 3$; it is useful to substitute the variable $x = x' + \alpha$ and to choose α such that the coefficient of x'^2 vanishes; then as in (1); (3) $x_1 = 4, x_2 = x_3 = 1$; see the hint to (2); (4) $x_1 = -1$, the remaining roots are imaginary; see the hint to (2).

127. (1) 1.465 ...; (2) $\approx$ 14.26 cm; (3) about 6.8 cm.

128. If $y_1 = x^n, y_2 = \sqrt[n]{x}$, then

for $n > 1$	for $0 < x < 1$	$y_1 < y_2$, and	for $1 < x < \infty$ $y_1 > y_2$,
for $0 < n < 1$	for $0 < x < 1$	$y_1 > y_2$, and	for $1 < x < \infty$ $y_1 < y_2$,
for $-1 < n < 0$	for $0 < x < 1$	$y_1 < y_2$, and	for $1 < x < \infty$ $y_1 > y_2$,
for $n < -1$	for $0 < x < 1$	$y_1 > y_2$, and	for $1 < x < \infty$ $y_1 < y_2$.

133. $x_1 = 1, \ x_2 = 2$.

134. The points of intersection (1, 2); (3, 8); $\left(3, \frac{4}{3}\right)$; (– 1.5, 0.3). **135.** $n = 15$.

136. Proceeding from the definition of hyperbolic functions one can prove that sinh (– x) = – sinh x, tanh (– x) = – tanh x, cosh (– x) = cosh x. These functions are not periodic.

140. $y_{\text{least}} \approx 0.8$ for $x \approx 0.4$.

141. The graph of the function is symmetric about the origin, since the function is odd $y = \frac{a^x - a^{-x}}{2}$.

143. (1) $A = 1, T = \frac{2}{3}\pi$; (2) $A = 5, T = \pi$; (3) $A = 4, T = 2$;
(4) $A = 2, T = 4\pi$; (5) $A = 1, T = \frac{8}{3}$; (6) $A = 3, T = \frac{16}{3}\pi$.

144. (1) $2, \frac{2\pi}{3}, \frac{3}{2\pi}, 5$; (2) $1, 4\pi, \frac{1}{4\pi}, \frac{3\pi - 1}{2}$; (3) $\frac{1}{3}, 1, 1, -\frac{\pi}{3}$; (4) $1, 6\pi^2, \frac{1}{6\pi^2}, \frac{1}{2\pi}$.

146. The domain of definition is $(0, \pi)$. The area will be the greatest for $x = \frac{\pi}{2}$.

147. $x = R \sin\left(\frac{vt}{R} + \frac{\pi}{2} + \arccos\frac{a}{R}\right)$.

148. $y = \sin\left[\frac{t - t_0}{t_1 - t_0}(\arcsin y_1 - \arcsin y_0) + \arcsin y_0\right]$;

$$T = \frac{2\pi (t_1 - t_0)}{\arcsin y_1 - \arcsin y_0}; \ \varphi_{\text{initial}} = \frac{t_1 \arcsin y_0 - t_0 \arcsin y_1}{t_1 - t_0}.$$

149. $x = R(1 - \cos\varphi) + a - \sqrt{a^2 - R^2 \sin^2\varphi}$, where $\varphi = 2\pi nt$.

151. (1) $x_1 = 0, x_{2,3} \approx \pm 1.9$; (2) $x = 0; \pm 4.5; \pm 7.72$; then rather accurately we can put $x \approx \pm \frac{(2n+1)\pi}{2}$ $(n > 3)$; (3) $x \approx 0.74$; (4) $x_1 = 0.9, x_2 = 2.85, x_3 = 5.8$; (5) an infinite set of roots; $x_1 = 0$, x_2 is slightly smaller than $\frac{\pi}{2}$, x_3 is slightly greater than $\frac{3\pi}{2}$, and so on.

152. (1) 2π; (2) 2π; (3) 24; (4) 2.

153. (1) $y = \sqrt{2}\sin\left(x + \frac{\pi}{4}\right)$;

(2) $y = \sqrt{5 + 2\sqrt{3}}\sin(x + \varphi_0)$, where $\varphi_0 = \arcsin\frac{1}{\sqrt{5 + 2\sqrt{3}}}$.

155*. (1) Period $\frac{\pi}{2}$. On the interval $[0, 2\pi]$ the function can be represented as follows:

$$y = \sin x + \cos x \text{ on the interval } \left[0, \frac{\pi}{2}\right],$$

$$y = \sin x - \cos x \text{ on the interval } \left[\frac{\pi}{2}, \pi\right],$$

$$y = -\sin x - \cos x \text{ on the interval } \left[\pi, \frac{3\pi}{2}\right],$$

$$y = -\sin x + \cos x \text{ on the interval } \left[\frac{3\pi}{2}, 2\pi\right].$$

(2) Period 2π. On the interval $[0, 2\pi]$ the function can be represented as follows:

$$y = \tan x \text{ on the interval } \left[0, \frac{\pi}{2}\right),$$

$$y = 0 \text{ on the interval } \left(\frac{\pi}{2}, \pi\right],$$

$$y = -\tan x \text{ on the interval } \left[\pi, \frac{3}{2}\pi\right),$$

$$y = 0 \text{ on the interval } \left(\frac{3}{2}\pi, 2\pi\right].$$

156. (1) The domain of definition consists of an infinite set of intervals of the form $(2n\pi, (2n + 1)\pi)$, where $n = 0, \pm 1, \pm 2, \ldots$; neither even nor odd; periodic , period 2π. In the interval $\left(0, \frac{\pi}{2}\right)$ sine increases from 0 to 1, hence, $\log \sin x$, remaining negative, increases to become zero. In the interval $\left(\frac{\pi}{2}, \pi\right)$ sine decreases from 1 to 0, hence, $\log \sin x$ also decreases. On the interval $(\pi, 2\pi)$ sine takes on negative values, hence, the function $\log \sin x$ is not defined. (2) The domain of definition consists of separate points, $x = \frac{\pi}{2} + 2\pi n$, where $n = 0, \pm 1, \pm 2, \ldots$ At these points $y = 0$. The graph consists of separate points on the x-axis. (3) The function is defined throughout the number scale except for the points $x = \pi n$, where $n = 0, \pm 1, \pm 2, \ldots$.

158. $\omega = 2\arcsin\frac{\alpha}{2\pi}$. **159.** $\gamma = \arctan\frac{a(l\cos\varphi + b\sin\varphi)}{b^2 + l^2 + a(b\cos\varphi - l\sin\varphi)}$.

160. $\alpha = \arccos\left[1 - \frac{x(2a - x)}{2R(a + R - x)}\right]$.

161. (1) $-1 \le x \le 1$; (2) $0 \le x \le 1$; (3) $0 \le x \le 1$; (4) $-1 \le x \le 0$; (5) $0 < x < \infty$; (6) $-\infty < x < 0$; (7) $0 \le x < \infty$; (8) $-\infty < x \le 0$; (9) $-\infty < x < 1$; (10) $1 < x < \infty$.

162. (1) $-1 \le x \le 1$; (2) $0 \le x \le 1$; (3) $-\infty < x < \infty$;
(4) defined everywhere except for $x = 0$.

163*. Period 2π. For the graph see Fig. 82. *Hint.* On the interval $-\frac{\pi}{2} \le x \le \frac{\pi}{2}$ we have $y = \arcsin(\sin x) \equiv x$ by definition of the function arcsin x.

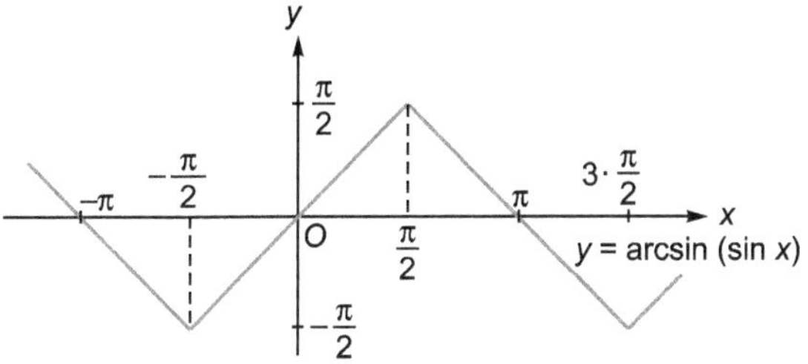

Fig. 82

To obtain the graph of the function on the interval $\frac{\pi}{2} \le x \le 3\frac{\pi}{2}$ put $z = x - \pi$, then $x = \pi + z$, $-\frac{\pi}{2} \le z \le \frac{\pi}{2}$,
$y = \arcsin(\sin x) = \arcsin \sin(z + \pi) = -\arcsin(\sin z) = -z$;
$y = \pi - x$ and so on.

167. $y_{\text{greatest}} \approx 15$, $y_{\text{least}} \approx 5.5$; the function passes from increasing to decreasing at $x = -2$. Zero of the function : $x \approx -3.6$.

169. $y = \frac{1}{32}(267 - 10x - x^2)$ or $y = -0.0312x^2 - 0.3125x + 8.344$; zeros of the function : $x_1 \approx -22.09$, $x_2 \approx 12.09$. To get the roots accurate to 0.01 take the coefficients accurate to 0.0001.

170. $x_1 \approx 2.60$ cm, $x_2 \approx 7.87$ cm.

171. $x_1 \approx -2.3$, $x_2 \approx 3$; the remaining roots are imaginary.

172*. Choose α such that the coefficient of x'^3 vanishes; $x_1 \approx -3.6$, $x_2 \approx -2.9$, $x_3 \approx 0.6$, $x_4 \approx 4.8$.

173. $x_1 \approx 0.59$, $x_2 \approx 3.10$, $x_3 \approx 6.29$, $x_4 \approx 9.43$; in general $x \approx \pi n$ $(n > 2)$.

174. $x_1 \approx -0.57$, $y_1 \approx -1.26$; $x_2 \approx -0.42$, $y_2 \approx 1.19$; $x_3 \approx 0.46$, $y_3 \approx 0.74$, $x_4 \approx 0.54$, $y_4 \approx -0.68$.

Chapter 2

176. $\lim\limits_{n\to\infty} u_n = 1$, $n \ge 4$. **177.** $\lim\limits_{n\to\infty} u_n = 0$; $n > \frac{1}{\sqrt{\varepsilon}}$.

178. $n = 19999$.

179. $\lim\limits_{n\to\infty} v_n = 0$, $n \ge 1000$. The magnitude v_n can be greater or smaller than its limit, or equal to it (the latter happens when $n = 2k + 1$, where $k = 0, 1, 2, \ldots$).

180. $\lim_{n\to\infty} u_n = 1$, $n \ge 14$; $n \ge \log_2 \frac{1}{\varepsilon}$.

181. $n \ge \frac{1}{3}\sqrt{\frac{5-6\varepsilon}{\varepsilon}}$ if $\varepsilon \le \frac{5}{6}$; $n = 0$ if $\varepsilon > \frac{5}{6}$.

182. $n \ge \frac{a}{\sqrt{\varepsilon(2+\varepsilon)}}$; u_n is a decreasing sequence.

183. $\lim_{n\to\infty} v_n = 0$; v_n reaches its limit when $n = m + 1$, since beginning with this value of n, $v_n = 0$.

185. 0. **186.** (1) No; (2) Yes.

189. For $a = 0$ this limit can equal any number or not exist at all.

190. $\delta < \sqrt{4+\varepsilon} - 2$; $\delta < 0.00025$. **191.** $\delta < 2 - \sqrt{3}$. **192.** $\delta < \frac{2}{13}$.

193. $\left|x - \frac{\pi}{2}\right| < \frac{\pi}{2} - \arcsin 0.99 \approx 0.136$. **194.** $N \ge \sqrt{\frac{1}{\varepsilon} - 1}$ if $\varepsilon \le 1$; $N = 0$ if $\varepsilon > 1$.

195. $N \ge \sqrt{\frac{4}{\varepsilon} - 3}$ if $\varepsilon \le \frac{4}{3}$; $N = 0$ if $\varepsilon > \frac{4}{3}$. **196.** $n > \frac{N-1}{2}$.

197. u_n is a positive infinitely large magnitude if the difference of the progression $d > 0$, and a negative one if $d < 0$. For a geometric progression this assertion is valid only when the ratio of the progression exceeds unity in its absolute value.

198. $-\frac{1}{10^4+2} < x < \frac{1}{10^4-2}$. **199.** $\frac{3000}{1001} < x < \frac{3000}{999}$.

200. $\delta < \frac{1}{\sqrt{N}} = 0.01$. **201.** $\log_2 0.99 < x < \log_2 1.01$. **202.** $M \ge 10^N = 10^{100}$.

203. $\sin x$, $\cos x$ and all inverse trigonometric functions. **205.** No. Yes.

206. No. **207.** (1) For instance, $x_n = \frac{\pi}{2} + 2n\pi$ and $x_n = 2\pi n$; (2) No.

209. If $a > 0$, then the function is not bounded (but is not infinitely large) as $x \to +\infty$; as $x \to -\infty$, it tends to zero. If $0 < a < 1$, the function is not bounded (but is not infinitely large) as $x \to -\infty$; as $x \to +\infty$ it tends to zero. For $a = 1$ the function is bounded throughout the number scale.

210. (1), (3) and (5) No.; (2) and (4) Yes. **213.** $\frac{-1}{10001} < x < \frac{1}{9999}$.

214. $N \ge \left(\frac{1-\varepsilon^2}{2\varepsilon}\right)^2$.

215. (1) $y = 1 + \frac{1}{x^3-1}$; (2) $y = \frac{1}{2} + \frac{-1}{2(2x^2+1)}$; (3) $y = -1 + \frac{2}{1+x^2}$.

216*. Compare u_n with the sum of the terms of the geometric progression $\frac{1}{3}, \frac{1}{9}, \frac{1}{27}, \ldots, \frac{1}{3^n}$.

220. 3. **221.** Yes.

222. $f(x) = 9\pi$ for $0 \le x \le 5$; $f(x) = 4\pi$ for $5 < x \le 10$; $f(x) = \pi$ for $10 < x \le 15$. The function is discontinuous at $x = 5$ and at $x = 10$.

223. $a = 1$. **224.** $A = -1$, $B = 1$. **225.** $x = 2$; $x = -2$. **226.** 2/3.

227. The function $y = \frac{\sin x}{x}$ has a removable discontinuity at the point $x = 0$, $y = \frac{\cos x}{x}$ is a discontinuity of the second kind (infinite).

228. The function is discontinuous at $x = 0$.

229. The function has three points of discontinuity. At $x = 0$ a removable discontinuity, at $x = \pm 1$ a discontinuity of the second kind (infinite).

230. No. If $x \to 0$ from the right, then $f(x) \to \frac{\pi}{2}$, if $x \to 0$ from the left, then $f(x) \to -\frac{\pi}{2}$. **231.** The function is discontinuous at $x = 0$. **232.** 0.

234. No. If $x \to 1$ from the right, then $y \to 1$; if $x \to 1$ from the left, then $y \to 0$.

235. If $x \to 0$ from the right, then $y \to 1$; if $x \to 0$ from the left, then $y \to -1$.

236. The function is discontinuous at $x = 0$ (a discontinuity of the first kind).

237. The function has discontinuities of the first kind at the points

$$x = \frac{\pi}{2}(2k + 1).$$

238. For $x = 0$ the function is continuous, for $x \neq 0$ the function is discontinuous.

239. All three functions are discontinuous when x is an integer (positive or negative) or zero.

241*. Write the polynomial in the form $x^n\left(a_0 + \frac{a_1}{x} + \dots + \frac{a_n}{x^n}\right)$ and investigate its behaviour as $x \to \pm\infty$.

244*. Sketch the graph of the function $y = \frac{a_1}{x - \lambda_1} + \frac{a_2}{x - \lambda_2} + \frac{a_3}{x - \lambda_3}$ on having investigated its behaviour in the vicinity of the points λ_1, λ_2 and λ_3.

245. 1. **246.** $\frac{1}{2}$. **247.** 3. **248.** ∞. **249.** 0.

250. 0. **251.** $\frac{15}{17}$. **252.** 1. **253.** 0. **254.** 4.

255. 1. **256.** 0. **257.** 0. **258.** 0. **259.** 1. **260.** $\frac{4}{3}$.

261. $\frac{1}{2}$. **262.** $-\frac{1}{2}$. **263.** -1. **264*.** 1. Note that $\frac{1}{(n-1)n} = \frac{1}{n-1} - \frac{1}{n}$.

265. $\frac{1}{2}$. **266.** 1. **267.** 0. **268.** 9. **269.** $\frac{3}{4}$. **270.** ∞.

271. 0. **272.** 0. **273.** $-\frac{2}{5}$. **274.** $\frac{1}{2}$. **275.** 6. **276.** ∞.

277. -1. **278.** ∞. **279.** 0. **280.** $\frac{m}{n}$. **281.** 0. **282.** ∞.

283. $\frac{1}{2}$. **284.** -1. **285.** 0. **286.** $\frac{1}{4}$. **287.** $-\frac{1}{2}$.

288. 100. **289.** -1. **290.** 1. **291.** ∞. **292.** 0.

293. 0. **294.** ∞. **295.** 4. **296.** $\frac{1}{4}$. **297.** 3.

298. $\frac{1}{2\sqrt{x}}$ if $x > 0$; ∞ if $x = 0$. **299.** $\frac{1}{3}$. **300.** $\frac{2}{3}$. **301.** $\frac{1}{4a\sqrt{a-b}}$. **302.** $\frac{m}{n}$.

303*. $\frac{1}{2}$. Add unity to, and subtract from the numerator. **304.** $-\frac{1}{4}$.

305. One root tends to $-\frac{c}{b}$, the other to ∞.

306. 0. **307.** 0. **308.** 0 if $x \to +\infty$; ∞ if $x \to -\infty$.

309. $\frac{1}{2}$ if $x \to \infty$; $-\infty$ if $x \to -\infty$. **310.** $\frac{a+b}{2}$ if $x \to +\infty$, ∞ if $x \to -\infty$.

311. $\pm\frac{5}{2}$. **312.** 0. **313.** 1. **314.** 3. **315.** k.

316. $\frac{\alpha}{\beta}$. **317.** $\frac{2}{5}$. **318.** 0 if $n > m$, 1 if $n = m$, ∞ if $n < m$.

319. 2/3. **320.** 1/3. **321.** 1/2. **322.** 3/4. **323.** ∞.
324. -1. **325.** 1/2. **326.** ∞. **327.** 0. **328.** 1/2.
329. ∞. **330.** $-3/2$. **331.** 1. **332.** $\pi/2$. **333.** $2/\pi$.

334. $-\frac{a}{\pi}$. **335.** $\frac{\sqrt{2}}{2}$. **336.** 2. **337.** $\frac{\sqrt{2}}{2}$. **338.** -2.

339. $-2\sin a$. **340.** $\frac{\beta^2-\alpha^2}{2}$. **341.** $\cos^3\alpha$. **342.** $\frac{\sin 2\beta}{2\beta}$.

343. $-\sin\alpha$. **344.** $\frac{2\sin a}{\cos^3 a}$. **345.** $\frac{\sqrt{2}}{8}$. **346.** 1. **347.** 6.

348. $\frac{3}{2}$. **349.** -1. **350*.** $\frac{1}{\sqrt{2\pi}}$. Put $\arccos x = y$. **351.** $\frac{1}{e}$.

352. $\frac{1}{e}$. **353.** 1. **354.** e^{mk}. **355.** e^6. **356.** $e^{-2/3}$.

357. e^2. **358.** 0 if $x \to +\infty$, ∞ if $x \to -\infty$. **359.** ∞ if $x \to +\infty$, 0 if $x \to -\infty$.

360. 1. **361.** ∞ if $x \to +\infty$, 0 if $x \to -\infty$. **362.** e^2. **363.** e. **364.** $\sqrt{e}$.

365. k. **366.** $1/a$. **367.** a. **368.** $1/e$. **369.** $\ln a$. **370.** 2/3. **371.** e.

372*. 3/2; add unity to, and subtract from, the numerator.

373. 2. **374.** 1. **375.** $a - b$. **376.** 1.

377. 0 if $x \to +\infty$, ∞ if $x \to -\infty$. **378.** 1 if $x \to +\infty$, -1 if $x \to -\infty$.

379. (1) a^n; (2) 0 if $A \neq 0$, a^n if $A = 0$ and $a \neq 0$, and ∞, if $A = a = 0$; (3) $\frac{1}{1+A}$.

380. 0 if $x \to +\infty$; $-\infty$ if $x \to -\infty$.

381. For $a > 1$ the limit equals 1 if $x \to +\infty$, and 0 if $x \to -\infty$. For $a < 1$ the limit equals 0 if $x \to +\infty$, and 1 if $x \to -\infty$. For $a = 1$ the limit is equal to 1/2.

382. For $a > 1$ the limit equals 1 if $x \to +\infty$, and -1 if $x \to -\infty$. For $a < 1$ vice versa. For $a = 1$ the limit equals 0.

383. 0. **384.** 0. **385.** 1. **386.** 0. **387.** $-\cos a$. **388.** 1/12.

389. 1/8. **390*.** $\frac{\sin x}{x}$. Multiply and divide by $\sin\frac{x}{2^n}$. **391.** 1/2. **392.** 0.

393*. $-1/2$. Use the formula $\arctan b - \arctan a = \arctan\frac{b-a}{1+ab}$. **394.** $\frac{1}{2}$.

395*. $\frac{1}{2}$. Replace $\arcsin x$ by $\arctan\frac{x}{\sqrt{1-x^2}}$ and take advantage of the hint to Problem 393. **396.** ∞ if $n < 1$; e if $n = 1$; 1 if $n > 1$.

397*. 1. Take the expression $1 - (1 - \cos x)$ instead of $\cos x$.

398. $-1/2$. **399.** $1/e$. **400.** e. **401.** e^{ab}. **402.** v_n is of higher order.

403. u_n and v_n are equivalent infinitesimals. **405.** Of the same order.

406. For $x = 0$ the order of smallness is different. For $x = \pm \frac{\sqrt{3}}{3}$ Δy and Δx are equivalent. **407.** No. **408.** Of the 3rd order.

409. (1) 2; (2) 1/2; (3) 1; (4) 10. **410.** $x = \frac{1}{2}\sqrt[3]{\frac{a^2}{2b^2}}$. **411.** $a = k$. **412.** No.

414. (1) $\frac{1}{3}$; (2) $\frac{1}{2}$; (3) $\frac{1}{2}$; (4) an equivalent infinitesimal;
(5) an equivalent infinitesimal; (6) 1;
(7) an equivalent infinitesimal; (8) 2; (9) 2; (10) 1;
(11) 2/3; (12) 2. **415.** $a^2\sqrt{3}$. **416.** $2\pi R^2$, $4R^2$.

418. From the fact that the polygonal line approaches infinitely the straight line (in the sense of bringing their points together) it does not follow that the length of the polygonal line tends to the length of the segment.

419. a. **420.** a, $\frac{\pi a}{2}$. **421.** $2\pi\,(R + r)$.

422. Both the segment and the angle have the order $\frac{1}{2}$.

425. (1) 10.25; (2) 30.2; (3) 16.125; (4) 40.4; (5) 0.558; (6) 0.145.

426. (1) 10.16; (2) 20.12; (3) 1.02; (4) 4.04.

427. $\ln 1.01 \approx 0.01$; $\ln 1.02 \approx 0.02$; $\ln 1.1 \approx 0.1$; $\ln 1.2 \approx 0.2$.

Chapter 3

428. (a) 5; (b) 5. **429.** (a) $v = 0.25\,\frac{\text{m}}{\text{s}}$; (b) $v = 0.55\,\frac{\text{m}}{\text{s}}$; (c) $\frac{t_1 + t_2}{1200}\,\frac{\text{m}}{\text{s}}$.

430. 75.88, 60.85, 49.03, 48.05.

431. $53.9\,\frac{\text{m}}{\text{s}}$, $49.49\,\frac{\text{m}}{\text{s}}$, $49.25\,\frac{\text{m}}{\text{s}}$, $49.005\,\frac{\text{m}}{\text{s}}$, $v_5 = 49.0\,\frac{\text{m}}{\text{s}}$, $v_{10} = 98.0\,\frac{\text{m}}{\text{s}}$, $v = 9.8t\,\frac{\text{m}}{\text{s}}$.

432. (a) $4\,\frac{\text{g}}{\text{cm}}$; (b) $40\,\frac{\text{g}}{\text{cm}}$; (c) $4l\,\frac{\text{g}}{\text{cm}}$, where l is the length of the segment AM.

433. (1) $95\,\frac{\text{g}}{\text{cm}}$; (2) (a) $35\,\frac{\text{g}}{\text{cm}}$; (b) $5\,\frac{\text{g}}{\text{cm}}$; (c) $185\,\frac{\text{g}}{\text{cm}}$.

434. (1) $1.002\,\frac{\text{cal}}{\text{g}\cdot\text{deg}} = 4198\,\frac{\text{J}}{\text{kg}\cdot\text{deg}}$; (2) $1.013\,\frac{\text{cal}}{\text{g}\cdot\text{deg}}$.

435*. Introduce the mean angular velocity, then, passing to the limit, get the required quantity.

438. $k = \frac{f'(t)}{f(t)}$, where k is the linear expansion coefficient. **439.** $k = S\,\frac{\varphi'(P)}{\varphi(P)}$.

440. (1) 56; (2) 19; (3) 7.625; (4) 1.261. **441.** (1) 4.52; (2) – 0.249; (3) 0.245.

442. (a) 6.5; (b) 6.1; (c) 6.01; (d) 6.001.

443. $f'(5) = 10$, $f'(-2) = -4$, $f'\left(-\frac{3}{2}\right) = -3$. **444.** 3, 0, 6, $\frac{1}{3}$.

445. $x_1 = 0, x_2 = 2.$ **446.** For the function $f(x) = x^3$ it is not. **447.** 1.

448. 0.4343. **449.** 2.303. **454.** (1) 0; (2) 6; (3) –4; (4) $k_1 = 2, k_2 = 4.$

455. (1, 1); (– 1, – 1). **456.** (1) (0, 0); (2) (1/2, 1/4). **457.** No.

458. $\alpha_1 = \arctan\frac{1}{7}, \alpha_2 = \arctan\frac{1}{13}.$ **459.** $\alpha_1 = \frac{\pi}{2}, \alpha_2 = \arctan\frac{3}{4}.$ **460.** arctan 3.

461. $y = 12x - 16, x + 12y - 98 = 0$; the subtangent equals $\frac{2}{3}$, the subnormal equals 96. **462.** For $x = 0$ and for $x = 2/3$.

463. (1) (2, 4); (2) (– 3/2, 9/4); (3) (– 1, 1) and (1/4, 1/16).

466. (1) $6x - 5$; (2) $4x^3 - x^2 + 5x - 0.3$; (3) $2ax + b$; (4) $\frac{1}{3\sqrt[3]{x^2}}$;

(5) $\frac{1}{\sqrt{x}} + \frac{1}{x^2}$; (6) $\frac{0.2}{\sqrt[4]{y^3}} - 10y^2 - \frac{0.4}{y^3}$; (7) $\frac{1}{n} - \frac{n}{x^2} + \frac{2x}{m^2} - \frac{2m^2}{x^3}$;

(8) $\frac{3}{2}m\sqrt{x} + \frac{7}{6}n\sqrt[6]{x} + \frac{1}{2}p\frac{1}{\sqrt{x^3}}$; (9) $\frac{2mz + n}{p + q}$;

(10) $-\frac{1}{15}t^{-5/3} + 7.28\,t^{-2.4} - \frac{0.5}{t\sqrt[5]{t}}$; (11) $2x - 1$;

(12) $3.5\,x^2\sqrt{x} - 1 + \frac{1}{2\sqrt{x}}$; (13) $3v^2 + 2v - 1$; (14) $6(a - x)$;

(15) $\frac{2ax}{a+b} + \frac{b}{a+b} - \frac{c}{(a+b)x^2}$; (16) $\frac{3m(mu+n)^2}{p^3}$.

467. $f(1) = 1, f'(1) = 2, f(4) = 8, f'(4) = 2.5, f(a^2) = 3a^2 - 2|a|, f'(a^2) = 3 - \frac{1}{|a|}.$

468. $f(-1) = -5, f'(-1) = -8, f'(2) = \frac{19}{16}, f'\left(\frac{1}{a}\right) = 3a^4 + 10a^3 - a^2.$

469. 13. **471.** (1) $4x^3 - 3x^2 - 8x + 9$; (2) $7x^6 - 10x^4 + 8x^3 - 12x^2 + 4x + 3$;

(3) $-\frac{1}{2\sqrt{x}}\left(1 + \frac{1}{x}\right)$; (4) $\frac{1}{9}\left(\frac{60}{\sqrt[6]{x}} - \frac{5}{x\sqrt[6]{x^5}} + \frac{\sqrt{3}}{x\sqrt[3]{x}} - 48\sqrt[6]{27x^2}\right)$;

(5) $\frac{1 + 12x}{3\sqrt[3]{x^2}} + \frac{9\sqrt[3]{x^2} + 10x\sqrt[3]{x} + 36x\sqrt[3]{x^2}}{3\sqrt[3]{x^2}}$; (6) $2x(3x^4 - 28x^2 + 49)$;

(7) $\frac{1 + \sqrt{2} + \sqrt{3} + 2\sqrt{2x} + 2\sqrt{3x} + 2\sqrt{6x} + 3x\sqrt{6}}{2\sqrt{x}}$.

472. $-\frac{2}{(x-1)^2}$. **473.** $\frac{1 - x^2}{(1 + x^2)^2}$. **474.** $\frac{3t^2 - 6t - 1}{(t-1)^2}$.

475. $\frac{v^4 + 2v^3 + 5v^2 - 2}{(v^2 + v + 1)^2}$. **476.** $\frac{ad - bc}{(cx + d)^2}$. **477.** $-\frac{4x}{3(x^2 - 1)^2} + 1 + 2x - 3x^2$.

478. $\frac{2v^4(v^3 - 5)}{(v^3 - 2)^2}$. **479.** $-\frac{6x^2}{(x^3 + 1)^2}$. **480.** $-\frac{6x^2}{(x^3 - 1)^2}$. **481.** $\frac{2v - 1}{a^2 - 3}$.

482. $-\frac{3x^2}{\sqrt{\pi}}$. **483.** $-\frac{2t + 1}{(t^2 + t + 1)^2}$. **484.** $\frac{3 - 2t}{(t^2 - 3t + 6)^2}$. **485.** $\frac{4x^3(2b^2 - x^2)}{(b^2 - x^2)^2}$.

486. $\frac{1 + 2x + 3x^2 - 2x^3 - x^4}{(1 + x^3)^2}$. **487.** $\frac{6x(1 + 3x - 5x^3)}{(1 - x^2)^2(1 - 2x^3)^2}$. **488.** $\frac{a + 2bx}{m(a + bm)}$.

489. $-\dfrac{a^2b^2c^2\,[(x-b)(x-c)+(x-c)(x-a)+(x-a)(x-b)]}{(x-a)^2\,(x-b)^2\,(x-c)^2}$.

490. $f'(0)=0,\ f'(1)=6$. **491.** $F'(0)=11,\ F'(1)=2,\ F'(2)=-1$.

492. $F'(0)=-\dfrac{1}{4},\ F'(-1)=\dfrac{1}{2}$. **493.** $s'(0)=\dfrac{3}{25},\ s'(2)=\dfrac{17}{15}$.

494. $y'(1)=16,\ y'(a)=15a^2+\dfrac{2}{a^3}-1$. **495.** $\rho'(2)=\dfrac{5}{9},\ \rho'(0)=1$.

496. $\varphi'(1)=-\dfrac{a+1}{4}$. **497.** $z'(0)=1$.

498. (1) $4x^3-3x^2(a+b+c+d)+2x(ab+ac+ad+bc+db+cd)$
$-(abc+abd+acd+bcd)$;
(2) $8x(x^2+1)^3$; (3) $-20(1-x)^{19}$; (4) $60(1+2x)^{29}$;
(5) $-20x(1-x^2)^9$; (6) $5(15x^2+2x)(5x^3+x^2-4)^4$;
(7) $6(3x^2-1)(x^3-x)^5$; (8) $6\left(14x+\dfrac{4}{x^2}\right)\left(7x^2-\dfrac{4}{x}+6\right)^5$;
(9) $4\left(3t^2+\dfrac{3}{t^4}\right)\left(t^3-\dfrac{1}{t^3}+3\right)^3$; (10) $-\dfrac{4(x+1)}{(x-1)^3}$;
(11) $\dfrac{5(x^2+2x-1)(1+x^2)^4}{(1+x)^6}$; (12) $24(x^2+x+1)(2x^3+3x^2+6x+1)^3$.

499. $\dfrac{(s+2)(s+4)}{(s+3)^2}$. **500.** $\dfrac{(3-t)\,t^2}{(1-t)^3}$. **501.** $\dfrac{1-\sqrt{2}}{2\sqrt{x}\,(1+\sqrt{2x})^2}$.

502. $-\dfrac{4}{3\sqrt[3]{4x^2}\,(1+\sqrt[3]{2x})^2}$. **503.** $-\dfrac{x}{\sqrt{1-x^2}}$. **504.** $-\dfrac{4(1-2\sqrt{x})^3}{\sqrt{x}}$.

505. $\dfrac{mv^{m-1}}{(1-v)^{m+1}}$. **506.** $-\dfrac{4(2x-1)}{(x^2-x+1)^3}$. **507.** $\dfrac{x}{\sqrt{(a^2-x^2)^3}}$.

508. $-\dfrac{2x}{3\sqrt[3]{(1+x^2)^4}}$. **509.** $\dfrac{2x^3+4x^7}{\sqrt{(1-x^4-x^8)^3}}$. **510.** $\dfrac{3-x}{3\sqrt{(1-x)^3}}$.

511. $\dfrac{x(x^2+2a^2)}{\sqrt{(x^2+a^2)^3}}$. **512.** $-\dfrac{v+\sqrt{a^2+v^2}}{a^2\sqrt{a^2+v^2}}$. **513.** $-\dfrac{2}{3\sqrt[3]{(2x-1)^4}}-\dfrac{15x}{2\sqrt[4]{(x^2+2)^7}}$.

514. $u'(1)=9$. **515.** $y'(2)=-\dfrac{\sqrt{3}}{3}$. **516.** 0. **517.** $\cos x-\sin x$.

518. $\dfrac{1-\cos x-x\sin x}{(1-\cos x)^2}$. **519.** $\dfrac{x-\sin x\cdot\cos x}{x^2\cos^2 x}$. **520.** $\varphi\cos\varphi$.

521. $(\alpha\cos\alpha-\sin\alpha)\left(\dfrac{1}{\alpha^2}-\dfrac{1}{\sin^2\alpha}\right)$. **522.** $\dfrac{1}{1+\cos t}$.

523. $\dfrac{\sin x+\cos x+x(\sin x-\cos x)}{1+\sin 2x}$.

524. $\dfrac{(1+\tan x)(\sin x+x\cos x)-x\sin x\sec^2 x}{(1+\tan x)^2}$. **525.** $-\sin 2x$.

526. $\tan^3 x\sec^2 x$. **527.** $-\sin^3 x$. **528.** $\dfrac{3}{2}\sin 2x(2-\sin x)$. **529.** $\tan^4 x$.

530. $2x\dfrac{\sin x}{\cos^3 x}$. **531.** $-\dfrac{16\cos 2x}{\sin^3 2x}$. **532.** $3\cos 3x$. **533.** $-\dfrac{a}{3}\sin\dfrac{x}{3}$.

534. $9\cos(3x+5)$. **535.** $\dfrac{1}{2\cos^2\dfrac{x+1}{2}}$. **536.** $\dfrac{1}{\sqrt{1+2\tan x}\cdot\cos^2 x}$. **537.** $-\dfrac{\cos\dfrac{1}{x}}{x^2}$.

538. $\cos(\sin x)\cdot\cos x$. **539.** $-12\cos^2 4x\sin 4x$. **540.** $\dfrac{1}{4\sqrt{\tan\dfrac{x}{2}}\cdot\cos^2\dfrac{x}{2}}$.

541. $\dfrac{x\cos\sqrt{1+x^2}}{\sqrt{1+x^2}}$. **542.** $-\dfrac{2x}{3\sin^2\sqrt[3]{1+x^2}\cdot\sqrt[3]{(1+x^2)^2}}$.

543. $4(1+\sin^2 x)^3\sin 2x$.

544. $\dfrac{x^2-1}{2x^2\cos^2\left(x+\dfrac{1}{x}\right)\sqrt{1+\tan\left(x+\dfrac{1}{x}\right)}}$. **545.** $\dfrac{\sin 2\left(\dfrac{1-\sqrt{x}}{1+\sqrt{x}}\right)}{\sqrt{x}(1+\sqrt{x})^2}$.

546. $-3\sin 3x\sin(2\cos 3x)$. **548.** $\arcsin x+\dfrac{x}{\sqrt{1-x^2}}$.

549. $\dfrac{\pi}{2(\arccos x)^2\sqrt{1-x^2}}$. **550.** $\dfrac{2\arcsin x}{\sqrt{1-x^2}}$.

551. $\arcsin x$. **552.** $-\dfrac{1}{(\arcsin x)^2\sqrt{1-x^2}}$.

553. $\sin x\cdot\arctan x+x\cos x\cdot\arctan x+\dfrac{x\sin x}{1+x^2}$.

554. $-\dfrac{x+\arccos x\sqrt{1-x^2}}{x^2\sqrt{1-x^2}}$. **555.** $\dfrac{\arctan x}{2\sqrt{x}}+\dfrac{\sqrt{x}}{1+x^2}$. **556.** 0.

557. $\dfrac{1}{x\sqrt{x^2-1}}$. **558.** $-\dfrac{2x^2}{(1+x^2)^2}$. **559.** $\dfrac{\sqrt{1-x^2}+x\arcsin x}{\sqrt{(1-x^2)^3}}$.

560. $\dfrac{2x}{\arctan x}-\dfrac{x^2}{(1+x^2)(\arctan x)^2}$. **561.** $\dfrac{1}{\sqrt{2x-x^2}}$.

562. $-\dfrac{\sqrt{2}}{\sqrt{1+2x-2x^2}}$. **563.** $\dfrac{2x}{1+x^4}$. **564.** $-\dfrac{2}{|x|\sqrt{x^2-4}}$.

565. $\dfrac{\cos x}{|\cos x|}$. **566.** $-\dfrac{2\arctan\dfrac{1}{x}}{1+x^2}$. **567.** $\dfrac{\arccos x}{\sqrt{1-x^2}\cdot\sqrt{1-(\arccos x)^2}}$.

568. $-\dfrac{1}{(1+x)\sqrt{2x(1-x)}}$.

569. $\dfrac{x+1}{8\sqrt[4]{(\arcsin\sqrt{x^2+2x})^3}\sqrt{(1-2x-x^2)(x^2+2x)}}$.

570. $\dfrac{\sin\alpha}{1-\cos\alpha\cos x}$. **571.** $\dfrac{\sqrt{a^2-b^2}}{a+b\cos x}$. **572.** $\dfrac{1}{2(1+x^2)}$.

573. $2x\log_3 x+\dfrac{x}{\ln 3}$. **574.** $\dfrac{2\ln x}{x}$. **575.** $\dfrac{\ln x+1}{\ln 10}$. **576.** $\dfrac{1}{2x\sqrt{\ln x}}$.

577. $\dfrac{x\ln x - x + 1}{x\ln^2 x}\ln 2$. **578.** $\sin x \ln x + x\cos x \ln x + \sin x$. **579.** $-\dfrac{1}{x\ln^2 x}$.

580. $\dfrac{1 - n\ln x}{x^{n+1}}$. **581.** $\dfrac{2}{x(1+\ln x)^2}$. **582.** $\dfrac{1 + x^2 - 2x^2\ln x}{x(1+x^2)^2}$.

583. $x^{n-1}(n\ln x + 1)$. **584.** $\dfrac{\ln x}{x\sqrt{1+\ln^2 x}}$. **585.** $-\dfrac{2}{1-2x}$.

586. $\dfrac{2x-4}{x^2-4x}$. **587.** $\cot x$. **588.** $\dfrac{2x}{(x^2-1)\ln 3}$.

589. $\dfrac{2}{\sin 2x}$. **590.** $-\dfrac{2}{\arccos 2x\sqrt{1-4x^2}}$. **591.** $4\ln^3 \sin x \cdot \cot x$.

592. $\dfrac{a}{(ax+b)[1+\ln^2(ax+b)]}$. **593.** $n(1+\ln\sin x)^{n-1}\cot x$.

594. $\dfrac{1}{x\log_5 x \log_3(\log_5 x)\ln 2\ln 3\ln 5}$.

595. $\dfrac{x}{\arctan\sqrt{1+x^2}\,(2+x^2)\sqrt{1+x^2}}$. **596.** $\dfrac{6x^2\arcsin[\ln(a^3+x^3)]}{(a^3+x^3)\sqrt{1-\ln^2(a^3+x^3)}}$.

597. $\dfrac{\cot\dfrac{x+3}{4}}{12\sqrt[3]{\ln^2\sin\dfrac{x+3}{4}}}$. **598.** $2^x\ln 2$. **599.** $10^x\ln 10$. **600.** $-\dfrac{\ln 3}{3^x}$.

601. $4^{-x}(1 - x\ln 4)$. **602.** $10^x(1 + x\ln 10)$. **603.** $e^x(1+x)$.

604. $\dfrac{1-x}{e^x}$. **605.** $\dfrac{2^x(\ln 2 - 1) + 3x^2 - x^3}{e^x}$. **606.** $e^x(\cos x - \sin x)$.

607. $\dfrac{e^x}{\sin^2 x}(\sin x - \cos x)$. **608.** $-\dfrac{\sin x + \cos x}{e^x}$. **609.** $\dfrac{(\ln x - 1)\ln 2}{\ln^2 x}2^{x/\ln x}$.

610. $3x^2 - 3^x\ln 3$. **611.** $\dfrac{e^x}{2\sqrt{1+e^x}}$. **612.** $e^x(x^2+1)$. **613.** $\dfrac{2e^x}{(1-e^x)^2}$.

614. $-\dfrac{2\cdot 10^x\ln 10}{(1+10^x)^2}$. **615.** $\dfrac{e^x(x-1)^2}{(x^2+1)^2}$. **616.** $e^x(\cos x + \sin x + 2x\cos x)$.

617. $-e^{-x}$. **618.** $2\cdot 10^{2x-3}\ln 10$. **619.** $\dfrac{e^{\sqrt{x+1}}}{2\sqrt{x+1}}$. **620.** $2^x\ln 2\cdot\cos(2^x)$.

621. $3^{\sin x}\cos x\cdot\ln 3$. **622.** $3\sin^2 x\cos x\cdot a^{\sin^3 x}\ln a$.

623. $\dfrac{2e^{\arcsin 2x}}{\sqrt{1-4x^2}}$. **624.** $2^{3x}\cdot 3^x\ln 2\cdot\ln 3$. **625.** $\dfrac{e^{\sqrt{\ln x}}}{2x\sqrt{\ln x}}$.

626. $\cos(e^{x^2+3x-2})\,e^{x^2+3x-2}(2x+3)$.

627. $-12\cdot 10^{1-\sin^4 3x}\ln 10\cdot\sin^3 3x\cos 3x$.

628. $\dfrac{(2ax+b)\,e^{\sqrt{\ln(ax^2+bx+c)}}}{2(ax^2+bx+c)\sqrt{\ln(ax^2+bx+c)}}$.

629. $\dfrac{\cot\sqrt[3]{\arctan(e^{3x})}\cdot e^{3x}}{(1+e^{6x})\sqrt[3]{[\arctan(e^{3x})]^2}}$. **630.** $-2ab^2xe^{-b^2x^2}$. **631.** $\dfrac{2}{a^2}xe^{-x^2/a^2}(a^2-x^2)$.

632. $Ae^{-k^2x}\,[\omega\cos(\omega x+\alpha)-k^2\sin(\omega x+\alpha)]$. **633.** $a^x x^a\left(\frac{a}{x}+\ln a\right)$.

634. $3\sinh^2 x\cosh x$. **635.** $\tanh x$. **636.** $\frac{1}{\cosh 2x}$.

637. $-\frac{2x}{\cosh^2(1-x^2)}$. **638.** $2\sinh 2x$. **639.** $\sinh(\sinh x)\cosh x$.

640. $\frac{\sinh x}{2\sqrt{\cosh x}}$. **641.** $e^{\cosh^2 x}\sinh 2x$. **642.** $\frac{1}{x\cosh^2(\ln x)}$. **643.** $x\cosh x$.

644. $\frac{3\tanh x}{2\cosh^2 x\sqrt[4]{1+\tanh^2 x}}$. **645.** $\frac{1}{4\cosh^4\frac{x}{2}}$. **646.** $\frac{1}{2\sqrt{\cosh x-\sinh x}}$.

647. $\frac{1}{1-\sinh^4 x}$. **648.** $\frac{x(4+\sqrt{x})\sinh 2x+2(2x^2\sqrt{x}-1)\cosh 2x}{2x^2}$.

649. $\frac{xe^{3x}}{\sinh^2 x}[(3x+2)\sinh x-x\cosh x]$. **650.** $x^{x^2+1}(2\ln x+1)$.

651. $x^{x^x}\cdot x^x\left(\ln^2 x+\ln x+\frac{1}{x}\right)$. **652.** $(\sin x)^{\cos x}\left(\frac{\cos^2 x}{\sin x}-\sin x\ln\sin x\right)$.

653. $(\ln x)^x\left(\frac{1}{\ln x}+\ln\ln x\right)$. **654.** $2\sqrt[x]{(x+1)^2}\left[\frac{1}{x(x+1)}-\frac{\ln(x+1)}{x^2}\right]$.

655. $x^2e^{x^2}\sin 2x\,(3+2x^2+2x\cot 2x)$. **656.** $-\frac{2(x-2)(x^2+11x+1)}{3(x-5)^4\sqrt[3]{(x+1)^2}}$.

657. $2x^{\ln x-1}\ln x$. **658.** $\frac{57x^2-302x+361}{20(x-2)(x-3)}\cdot\frac{(x+1)^2\sqrt[4]{x-2}}{\sqrt[5]{(x-3)^2}}$.

659. $\frac{1}{2}\sqrt{x\sin x\sqrt{1-e^x}}\left(\frac{1}{x}+\cot x-\frac{1}{2}\cdot\frac{e^x}{1-e^x}\right)$.

660. $\frac{1}{\sqrt{1-x^2}\,[(\arcsin x)^2-1]}\sqrt{\frac{1-\arcsin x}{1+\arcsin x}}$. **661.** $x^{\frac{1}{x}-2}(1-\ln x)$.

662. $x^{\sin x}\left(\cos x\ln x+\frac{\sin x}{x}\right)$. **663.** $\left(\frac{x}{x+1}\right)^x\left(\frac{1}{x+1}+\ln\frac{x}{x+1}\right)$.

664. $x^{\sqrt{x}-\frac{1}{2}}(2+\ln x)$. **665.** $(x^2+1)^{\sin x}\left[\frac{2x\sin x}{x^2+1}+\cos x\ln(x^2+1)\right]$.

666. $\frac{x^4+6x^2+1}{3x(1-x^4)}\sqrt[3]{\frac{x(x^2+1)}{(x^2-1)^2}}$. **667.** $\frac{(1+\sqrt[3]{x})^2}{\sqrt[3]{x^2}}$. **668.** $\frac{a}{k\cos^2\left(\frac{x}{k}+b\right)}$.

669. $\frac{p}{2\sqrt{1+\sqrt{2px}}\sqrt{2px}}$. **670.** $\frac{2x-3}{1+(x^2-3x+2)^2}$. **671.** $\frac{1+\sin x}{(x-\cos x)\ln 10}$.

672. $\frac{3}{2}\sin 2x\,(\cos x-2)$. **673.** $\sec^2\frac{x}{5}$. **674.** $-\frac{1+2\sqrt{x}}{6\sqrt{x}\sqrt[3]{(x+\sqrt{x})^4}}$.

675. $2\sin\frac{x}{2}\cos 2x+\frac{1}{2}\cos\frac{x}{2}\sin 2x$. **676.** $e^{\cos x}(\cos x-\sin^2 x)$.

677. $\frac{x^4(7x^6-40)}{\sqrt[3]{(x^6-8)^2}}$. **678.** $e^{-x^2}\left(\frac{1}{x}-2x\ln x\right)$.

679. $\frac{5(x-1)}{x\sqrt{x}}\left(\sqrt{x}+\frac{1}{\sqrt{x}}\right)^9$. **680.** $-\frac{1}{1+x^2}$. **681.** $2x^2e^{2x+3}$.

682. $\frac{2\sin 2x}{\cos^2 2x}$. **683.** $\frac{1+x^2}{1+x^2+x^4}$. **684.** $-\frac{2(x\cos x+\sin x)}{x^2\sin^2 x}$.

685. $\frac{1}{3}\cot\frac{x}{2}\sin\frac{2x}{3}-\frac{1}{2}\sin^2\frac{x}{3}\cos^2\frac{x}{2}$. **686.** $-\frac{4(31x^5+18)}{27x^5\sqrt[9]{(4x^5+2)^8}}$.

687. $\frac{1}{\sqrt{x^2+a^2}}$. **688.** $\arctan\sqrt{x}+\frac{\sqrt{x}}{2(1+x)}$.

689. $\frac{\tan x(1+2\tan^2 x)}{\cos^2 x\sqrt{1+\tan^2 x+\tan^4 x}}$. **690.** $\frac{\cos 2x}{x}-2\sin 2x\ln x$.

691. $\frac{1+x^4}{1+x^6}$. **692.** $\frac{n\cos x}{\sqrt{1-n^2\sin^2 x}}$. **693.** $\frac{\cos x}{2\sqrt{\sin x-\sin^2 x}}$.

694. $\sin^5 3x\cos^3 3x$. **695.** $\frac{x\arcsin x}{\sqrt{1-x^2}}$.

696. $-\frac{1}{2}\sin\frac{\arcsin x}{2}\frac{1}{\sqrt{1-x^2}}$. **697.** $\frac{1+2\sqrt{x}+4\sqrt{x+\sqrt{x}}}{8\sqrt{x}\sqrt{x+\sqrt{x}}\sqrt{x+\sqrt{x+\sqrt{x}}}}$.

698. $\frac{3}{2\sqrt{3x-9x^2}}$. **699.** $\frac{\ln x-2}{x^2}\sin\left[2\left(\frac{1-\ln x}{x}\right)\right]$.

700. $\frac{2x-\cos x}{(x^2-\sin x)\ln 3}$. **701.** $-\frac{1}{2\sqrt{1-x^2}}$.

702. $-\frac{1}{x\sqrt{1-x^2}(x+\sqrt{1-x^2})}$. **703.** $\arcsin(\ln x)+\frac{1}{\sqrt{1-\ln^2 x}}$.

704. $-\frac{2e^x}{(1+e^x)^2}\sec^2\left(\frac{1-e^x}{1+e^x}\right)$. **705.** $-\frac{2\sin^3 x}{\sqrt{1+\sin^2 x}}$.

706. $-0.8\left(\cos\frac{2x+1}{2}-\sin 0.8x\right)\left(\sin\frac{2x+1}{2}+0.8\cos 0.8x\right)$.

707. $10^{\sqrt{x}}\left(1+\frac{\sqrt{x}}{2}\ln 10\right)$. **708.** $-\frac{4}{\tan 2x\sin^2 2x}$.

709. $-\frac{1}{(x^2+2x+2)\arctan\frac{1}{1+x}}$. **710.** $-\frac{1}{\sqrt{x^2-1}}$.

711. $\frac{x+2}{2\sqrt{x+3}\sqrt[3]{(1+x\sqrt{x+3})^2}}$. **712.** $\frac{x(8+9\sqrt{x})}{4\sqrt{1+\sqrt{x}}}$. **713.** $-\frac{\sin 2x}{2\sqrt{(1+\sin^2 x)^3}}$.

714. $3x^2\arctan x^3+\frac{3x^5}{1+x^6}$. **715.** $\frac{\cot x\ln\cos x+\tan x\ln\sin x}{\ln^2\cos x}$. **716.** $\sqrt{\frac{1-x}{1+x}}$.

717. $\frac{4}{(1-4x)^2}\left(\sqrt{\frac{1-4x}{1+4x}}+\arcsin 4x\right)$. **718.** $-\frac{e^{1/\ln x}}{x\ln^2 x}$.

719. $\frac{1}{e^x-1}$. **720.** $10^{x\tan x}\ln 10\left(\tan x+\frac{x}{\cos^2 x}\right)$.

721. $2\sin x\,(x\sin x\cos x^2 + \cos x\sin x^2)$. **722.** $\dfrac{2\sin x}{\cos 2x\sqrt{\cos 2x}}$.

723. $\dfrac{2-3x-x^2}{2(1-x)(1+x^2)}\sqrt{\dfrac{1-x}{1+x^2}}$. **724.** $\dfrac{x^2}{1-x^4}$. **725.** $2^{x/\ln x}\,\dfrac{\ln x-1}{\ln^2 x}\ln 2$.

726. $\sqrt{\dfrac{a-x}{x-b}}$. **727.** $-\dfrac{2(2\cos^2 x+1)}{\sin^2 2x}$. **728.** $-\dfrac{1}{(1+x)\sqrt{1-x^2}}\,e^{\sqrt{\frac{1-x}{1+x}}}$.

729. $\sqrt{\dfrac{a-x}{a+x}}$. **730.** $\dfrac{\sqrt{x^2+1}}{x}$. **731.** $-\cos 2x$. **732.** $\dfrac{x^2}{\sqrt{(x^2-1)^3}}$.

733. $(a^2+1)\sin x e^{ax}$. **734.** $e^{1-\cos x}(1+x\sin x)$. **735.** $\dfrac{2e^{-2x}}{(1+e^{-4x})(\arctan e^{-2x})^2}$.

736. $10e^x\sin 3x$. **737.** $9x^2\arcsin x$. **738.** $\dfrac{e^{-\sqrt{x}}}{4\sqrt{x}\sqrt{(1+e^{-\sqrt{x}})^3}}$. **739.** $\dfrac{x}{\sqrt{2+4x-x^2}}$.

740. $\dfrac{(\cos x-\sin x)(e^x+e^{-x})}{e^x\cos x+e^{-x}\sin x}$. **741.** $\dfrac{\arctan x}{\sqrt{(1+x^2)^3}}$.

742. $\dfrac{\sin(x-\cos x)(1+\sin x)}{\cos^2(x-\cos x)}$. **743.** $e^x\sin x\cos^3 x\,(1+\cot x-3\tan x)$.

744. $\dfrac{54\sqrt[5]{x^4}}{55\sqrt[11]{(9+6\sqrt[5]{x^9})^{10}}}$. **745.** $\dfrac{1}{\sqrt{e^{2x}+4e^x+1}}$.

746. $\dfrac{e^{\arctan\sqrt{1+\ln(2x+3)}}}{(2x+3)[2+\ln(2x+3)]\sqrt{1+\ln(2x+3)}}$.

747. $\dfrac{e^{x^2}}{(e^x+e^{-x})^2}[2x(e^x+e^{-x})-(e^x-e^{-x})]$. **748.** $\dfrac{\ln(1+\sin x)}{\sin^2 x}$.

749. $\dfrac{40}{2x-3\sqrt{1-4x^2}}$. **750.** $\dfrac{x^5+1}{x^4(x^2+1)}$. **751.** $\dfrac{x^2}{\sqrt{1-2x-x^2}}$.

752. $\dfrac{1}{x}-\dfrac{x}{1-x^2}+\cot x$. **753.** $\dfrac{(1+2x^2)\sin x+x(1+x^2)\cos x}{\sqrt{1+x^2}}$.

754. $\dfrac{(x^2-32x-73)(3-x)^3}{2(x+1)^6\sqrt{x+2}}$. **755.** $\dfrac{3e^{\sqrt{x}}(2+\sqrt{x})}{10\sqrt[5]{(1+xe^{\sqrt{x}})^2}}$.

756. $\left(2x-\dfrac{1}{1+x^2}\right)\dfrac{e^{x^2-\arctan x+\frac{1}{2}\ln x+1}}{\sqrt{x}}$. **757.** $\dfrac{1}{\cos^5 x}$.

758. $\dfrac{e^x\arctan x}{\ln^5 x}\left[1+x+\dfrac{1}{(1+x^2)\arctan x}-\dfrac{5}{\ln x}\right]$.

759. $\dfrac{(1-x^2)e^{3x-1}\cos x}{(\arccos x)^3}\left[\dfrac{3-2x-3x^2}{1-x^2}-\tan x+\dfrac{3}{\sqrt{1-x^2}\arccos x}\right]$.

760. $4\sqrt{(x^2+a^2)^3}$. **761.** $(\arcsin x)^2$. **762.** $\dfrac{e^{-x}-e^x}{e^{-x}+e^x}$.

763. $\dfrac{1}{ae^{mx}+be^{-mx}}$. **764.** $\dfrac{1}{x^3+1}$. **765.** $\dfrac{1}{x}\sqrt{\dfrac{1-x}{1+x}}$.

766. $(\tan 2x)^{\cot\frac{x}{2}}\left(\dfrac{4\cot\frac{x}{2}}{\sin 4x}-\dfrac{\ln\tan 2x}{2\sin^2\frac{x}{2}}\right)$. **767.** $\dfrac{3x^2+10x+20}{15(x^2+4)\sqrt[3]{(x-5)^2}\sqrt[5]{x^2+4}}$.

768. $\dfrac{1}{x^4+x^2+1}$. **769.** $-\dfrac{2nx^{n-1}}{x^{2n}+1}$ if n is even, and $-\dfrac{2nx^n}{|x|(x^{2n}+1)}$, if n is odd.

770. $\dfrac{24x^3}{(1+8x^3)^2}$. **774.** (a) $\dfrac{1-(n+1)x^n+nx^{n+1}}{(1-x)^2}$;

(b) $\dfrac{2-n(n+1)x^{n-1}+2(n^2-1)x^n-n(n-1)x^{n+1}}{(1-x)^3}$.

Hint : Use the value of the sum $x+x^2+\ldots+x^n$.

776. $\sqrt{1-y^2}\,e^{-\arcsin y}$ and $\dfrac{\cos\ln x}{x}$. **777.** $\dfrac{1}{3(s^2-1)}$. **779.** $\dfrac{1}{2\sqrt{x-x^2}}$.

780. $\alpha'(x)=\dfrac{1}{x[1+\ln\alpha(x)]}$.

781. $(\sinh^{-1}x)'=\dfrac{1}{\sqrt{1+x^2}}$, $(\cosh^{-1}x)'=\dfrac{1}{\sqrt{x^2-1}}$, $(\tanh^{-1}x)'=\dfrac{1}{1-x^2}$.

782. $\dfrac{e^t}{1-t}$. **783.** $\dfrac{-(1+x^4)^2}{8x^3}$, $-\dfrac{1}{2\sqrt[4]{(1-y)^3(1+y)^5}}$. **784.** $\dfrac{1}{3y^2-4}$.

785. $\dfrac{1}{2^s\ln 2}\sqrt{1-2^{2s}}$, $\dfrac{1}{\ln 2}\cot t$. **789.** $-\sqrt{2}$. **790.** $-\dfrac{1}{a}$. **791.** $-\dfrac{1}{4}$. **792.** $-\dfrac{b^2x}{a^2y}$.

793. $-\sqrt{\dfrac{y}{x}}$. **794.** $\dfrac{ay-x^2}{y^2-ax}$. **795.** $\dfrac{3a^2\cos 3x+y^2\sin x}{2y\cos x}$. **796.** $\dfrac{2a}{3(1-y^2)}$.

797. $\dfrac{y}{y-x}$. **798.** $\dfrac{x}{y}\cdot\dfrac{y^2-2x^2}{2y^2-x^2}$. **799.** $-\dfrac{3x^2+2axy+by^2}{ax^2+2bxy+3y^2}$.

800. $-\dfrac{y\cos^2(x+y)(\cos(xy)-\sin(xy))-1}{x\cos^2(x+y)(\cos(xy)-\sin(xy))-1}$. **801.** $2^{x-y}\dfrac{2^y-1}{1-2^x}$.

802. $\dfrac{1}{2(1+\ln y)}$. **803.** $\dfrac{\sqrt{1-y^2}(1-\sqrt{1-x^2})}{\sqrt{1-x^2}(1-\sqrt{1-y^2})}$. **804.** $\dfrac{y^2-xy\ln y}{x^2-xy\ln x}$.

805. $-\dfrac{\sin(x+y)}{1+\sin(x+y)}$. **806.** $-\dfrac{1+y\sin(xy)}{x\sin(xy)}$. **807.** $-\sqrt[3]{\dfrac{y}{x}}$. **808.** $\dfrac{e^y}{2-y}$.

809. $\dfrac{\sin y}{2\sin 2y-\sin y-x\cos y}$. **810.** $\dfrac{\sqrt{1-k^2}}{1+k\cos x}$. **811.** $\dfrac{y\cos x+\sin(x-y)}{\sin(x-y)-\sin x}$.

812. $\dfrac{1+y^2}{y^2}$. **814.** (2, 4).

816. $y+4x+4=0$, $8y-2x+15=0$; the subtangent is equal to $\dfrac{1}{2}$; the subnormal to -8. **819.** (a) $t_1=0$, $t_2=8$; (b) $t_1=0$, $t_2=4$, $t_3=8$.

820. $181.5\cdot 10^3$ ergs. **821.** $\omega=13\,\dfrac{\text{rad}}{\text{s}}$. **822.** $\omega=2\pi\,\dfrac{\text{rad}}{\text{s}}$.

823. $\omega=(2at-b)\,\dfrac{\text{rad}}{\text{s}}$; ω vanishes at $t=\dfrac{b}{2a}$ s. **824.** 23 A.

825. (0, 0), (1, 1), (2, 0). **827.** (1, 0), (−1, −4).

828. $y=2x-2$, $y=2x+2$. **829.** $3x+y+6=0$.

830. Tangent $y - y_0 = (x - x_0)\cos x_0$, normal $y - y_0 = -(x - x_0)\sec x_0$.
831. Tangent $x_0(y - y_0) = x - x_0$, normal $(y - y_0) + x_0(x - x_0) = 0$.
832. Tangent $x + 2y = 4a$, normal $y = 2x - 3a$.
833. Tangent $y - y_0 = \frac{x_0^2(3a - x_0)}{y_0(2a - x_0)^2}(x - x_0)$,

normal $y - y_0 = -\frac{y_0(2a - x_0)^2}{x_0^2(3a - x_0)}(x - x_0)$.

835. The subtangents are equal to $x/3$, $2x/3$ and $-2x$, the subnormals, to $-3x^5$, $-3x^2/2$ and $1/2\,x^2$, respectively.
836. $y = \frac{x_0}{2a}(x - x_0/2)$; $y - y_0 = -\frac{2a}{x_0}(x - x_0)$.
837. $2x - y + 1 = 0$. **838.** $27x - 3y - 79 = 0$. **839.** $2x - y - 1 = 0$.
840. $4x - 4y - 21 = 0$. **842.** 3.75. **844.** $x + 25y = 0$, $x + y = 0$.
845. $(0, 1)$. **846.** $y = x$. **848.** $x - y - 3e^{-2} = 0$. **849.** $2/\sqrt{5}$.
850. $(1 + \sqrt{3}/2, 1)$. **857.** $2x - y \pm 1 = 0$.
858. If $y = f(x)$ is the equation of the given curve, then the equation of the required locus will be $y = xf'(x)$.
(a) The parabola $y^2 = \frac{1}{2}px$;
(b) the straight line parallel to the x-axis, $y = \frac{1}{\ln b}$;
(c) $y\sqrt{a^2 - x^2} + x^2 = 0$; (d) the circle $x^2 + y^2 = a$.
859. (1) $\varphi_1 = 0$, $\varphi_2 = \arctan\frac{18}{31}$; (2) $\arctan\frac{8}{15}$.
860. (1) arctan 3; (2) 45°. **861.** 90°. **862.** 45° and 90°.
863. arctan 3. **864.** $\arctan(2\sqrt{2})$.
865. For an odd n the tangent is $\frac{x}{a} + \frac{y}{b} = 2$, the normal $ax - by = a^2 - b^2$. For an even n the tangents are $\frac{x}{a} \pm \frac{y}{b} = 2$, the normals $ax \pm by = a^2 - b^2$.
879. $\Delta y = 1.461$, $dy = 1.4$. **880.** $\Delta y = 0.1012$, $dy = 0.1$, $\frac{dy}{\Delta y} = 0.9880$.
881. 4. **882.** -2.
883. $\Delta y = 1.91$, $dy = 1.9$, $\Delta y - dy = 0.01$, $\frac{\Delta y - dy}{\Delta y} = 0.0052$.
884. $\Delta y = 0.1$, $dy = 0.1025$, $\Delta y - dy = -0.0025$, $\frac{\Delta y - dy}{\Delta y} = 0.025$.
885.

Δx	$= 1$	0.1	0.01
Δy	$= 18$,	1.161,	0.110601
dy	$= 11$,	1.1,	0.11
$\Delta y - dy$	$= 7$,	0.061,	0.000601,
$\delta = \frac{\Delta y - dy}{\Delta y}$	$= 0.39$,	0.0526,	0.0055.

886. $\Delta y \approx 1.3$, $dy \approx 1.1$, $\Delta y - dy \approx 0.2$, $\delta = \frac{\Delta y - dy}{\Delta y} \approx 0.15$.
887. (a) $dy = 16$, $\frac{\Delta y - dy}{\Delta y}\,\% = 5.88\%$; (b) $dy = 8$, $\frac{\Delta y - dy}{\Delta y}\,\% = 3.03\%$;
(c) $dy = 1.6$, $\frac{\Delta y - dy}{\Delta y}\,\% = 0.62\%$.

888. (a) $dy = 4.8\text{ cm}^2$; (b) $dy = 6.0\text{ cm}^2$; (c) $dy = 9.6\text{ cm}^2$.

889. (1) $\frac{0.125}{\sqrt{x}}dx$; (2) $\frac{5dx}{3\sqrt[3]{x^2}}$; (3) $-\frac{4dx}{x^3}$; (4) $-\frac{dx}{x^5}$; (5) $-\frac{dx}{4x\sqrt{x}}$;

(6) $-\frac{dx}{3nx\sqrt[3]{x}}$; (7) $\frac{dx}{2(a+b)\sqrt{x}}$; (8) $-\frac{p\ln q}{q^x}dx$;

(9) $-\frac{0.2(m-n)}{x^{1.2}}dx$; (10) $-\frac{(m+n)\,dx}{2x\sqrt{x}}$;

(11) $\left[(2x+4)(x^2-\sqrt{x})+(x^2+4x+1)\left(2x-\frac{1}{2\sqrt{x}}\right)\right]dx$;

(12) $-\frac{6x^2\,dx}{(x^3-1)^2}$; (13) $\frac{2t\,dt}{(1-t^2)^2}$; (14) $3(1+x-x^2)^2(1-2x)\,dx$;

(15) $\frac{2\tan x}{\cos^2 x}dx$; (16) $5^{\ln\tan x}\frac{2\ln 5}{\sin 2x}dx$; (17) $-2^{-\frac{1}{\cos x}}\ln 2\frac{\sin x}{\cos^2 x}dx$;

(18) $-\frac{dx}{2\sin\frac{x}{2}}$; (19) $\frac{(x^2-1)\sin x+2x\cos x}{(1-x^2)^2}dx$;

(20) $\left(\frac{1}{2\sqrt{\arcsin x}\sqrt{1-x^2}}+\frac{2\arctan x}{1+x^2}\right)dx$; (21) $\left(\frac{5}{\sqrt{1-x^2}}-\frac{1}{1+x^2}\right)\frac{dx}{2}$;

(22) $\left(3^{-\frac{1}{x^2}}\cdot\frac{2}{x^3}\cdot\ln 3+9x^2-\frac{2}{\sqrt{x}}\right)dx$. **890.** (1) – 0.0059; (2) – 0.0075;

(3) 0.0086; (4) 0; (5) 0.00287. **891.** $\Delta y \approx 0.00025$, $\sin 30°\,1' \approx 0.50025$.

892. 0.00582. **893.** – 0.0693. **894.** $d\rho = -\frac{k\sin 2\varphi}{\sqrt{\cos 2\varphi}}d\varphi$. **895.** 0.3466.

896. $\sin 60°03' = 0.8665$; $\sin 60°\,18' = 0.8686$. **899.** 0.995.

900. $\arctan 1.02 \approx 0.795$; $\arctan 0.97 \approx 770$. **901.** 0.355. **902.** 0.52164.

903. (a) Change in the length of the thread : $2ds = \frac{8f}{3l}df$;

(b) change in the sag $df = \frac{3l}{4f}ds$.

904. The error of determining the angle by its sine : $\Delta x_3 = \tan x\cdot\Delta y$; the error in determining the angle by its tangent : $\Delta x_T = \frac{1}{2}\sin 2x\cdot\Delta z$ (where Δy and Δz are the errors in the given magnitudes y and z respectively); $\frac{\Delta x_S}{\Delta x_T} = \frac{1}{\cos^2 x}$; the accuracy of determining the angle by the logarithm of its tangent is higher than that of determining by the logarithm of its sine.

905. 0.3%. **906.** (1) $dy = \frac{(2t^3+4t+7)(3t^2+2)\,dt}{3\sqrt[3]{[(t^3+2t+1)(t^3+2t+6)]^2}}$;

(2) $ds = -\frac{t}{2}\sin\frac{t^2-1}{2}dt$; (3) $dz = -ds$;

(4) $dv = \frac{2\ln 3}{3^{\frac{1}{\ln\tan s}}\ln^2\tan s}\frac{ds}{\sin 2s}$; (5) $ds = \frac{(4u-3)\,du}{2\sqrt{2u^2-3u+1}}$;

(6) $dy = -\frac{2\,ds}{\cos 2s}$. **908.** Continuous and differentiable.

909. $f(x)$ is continuous everywhere except for the points $x = 0$ and $x = 2$; $f'(x)$ exists and is continuous everywhere except for the points $x = 0, 1, 2$ for which it is nonexistent.

910. For $x = k\pi$ where k is an arbitrary integer.

911. Continuous but nondifferentiable. **912.** $f'(0) = 0$.

913. Continuous but nondifferentiable.

914. Δy and Δx are infinitesimals of different orders.

915. Continuous but nondifferentiable. **916.** Yes, no. **917.** a. **918.** $a\omega e^{a\varphi}$.

919. Abscissa changes at the rate $v_x = -2r\omega \sin 2\varphi$, ordinate $v_y = -2r\omega \cos 2\varphi$.

920. The rate of change in the abscissa $v_x = v(1 + \cos\varphi)$; the rate of change in the ordinate $v_y = v \sin\varphi$ (φ is the angle between the y-axis and polar radius of the point). **921.** $-\dfrac{p \ln 2}{5540} \approx -0.000125\,p$.

922. $2\,\dfrac{\text{unit}}{\text{s}}$ at the point (3, 6) and $-2\,\dfrac{\text{unit}}{\text{s}}$ at the point (3, – 6).

923. $2\,\dfrac{\text{cm}}{\text{s}}$ at the point (3, 4) and $-2\,\dfrac{\text{cm}}{\text{s}}$ at the point (– 3, 4).

924. At the points (3, 16/3) and (– 3, – 16/3). **925.** $4v$ and $2av$.

926. $2\pi v$ and $2\pi rv$. **927.** $4\pi r^2 v$ and $8\pi rv$.

928. For $x = 2\pi k \pm \dfrac{\pi}{3}$ and for $x = 2\pi k \pm \dfrac{2\pi}{3}$. **929.** For $x = 2\pi k$.

930. $1/n^2$ times. **932.** (a) Yes; (b) no.

934. (1) $x^2 - 18x + 9y = 0$; (2) $y^2 = 4x^2(1 - x^2)$; (3) $y^3 = (x-1)^2$;
(4) $x = \arccos(1 - y) \mp \sqrt{2y - y^2}$; (5) $y = \dfrac{2(1 + x - x^2)}{1 + x^2}$.

935. (1) $t = (2k+1)\pi$; (2) $t = 1$; (3) $t = \pi/4 + \pi k$; (4) $t_1 = 1$, $t_2 = -1$.

936. $-\dfrac{b}{a}\cot\varphi$. **937.** $-\dfrac{b}{a}\tan\varphi$. **938.** $\cot\dfrac{\varphi}{2}$. **939.** $\dfrac{3t^2 - 1}{2t}$.

940. -1. **941.** $\dfrac{t}{2}$. **942.** $\dfrac{\cos\varphi - \varphi\sin\varphi}{1 - \sin\varphi - \varphi\cos\varphi}$. **943.** $\dfrac{1 + t^2}{t(2 + 3t - t^3)}$.

944. $\dfrac{1 - \tan t}{1 + \tan t}$. **945.** $\dfrac{t(2 - t^3)}{1 - 2t^3}$. **946.** $-\dfrac{4}{3}$. **947.** 0 and $\dfrac{1}{3}$.

948. Does not exist. **949.** $\sqrt{3}/6$.

950. (1) $t = \pi/2 + \alpha$; (2) $t = \pi - \alpha$;
(3) $t = \pi/6 + \alpha/3$, where α is the angle formed by the tangent with the x-axis.

956. (1) The curves intersect at two points at the angles $\alpha_1 = \alpha_2 = \arctan\dfrac{41}{2} \approx 87°21'$;
(2) the curves intersect at three points at the angles $\alpha_1 = \alpha_2 = 30°$ and $\alpha_3 = 0°$.

958. The length of the tangent $T = \left|\dfrac{y}{\sin\frac{3}{2}t}\right|$, the length of the normal $N = \left|\dfrac{y}{\cos\frac{3}{2}t}\right|$, the length of the subtangent $S_T = \left|y \cot\dfrac{3}{2}t\right|$, the length of the subnormal $S_N = \left|y \tan\dfrac{3}{2}t\right|$.

959. $\left|\frac{y}{\cos t}\right|, \left|\frac{y}{\sin t}\right|, |y \tan t|$ and $|y \cot t|$.

961. $\left|\frac{y}{\sin t}\right|, \left|\frac{y}{\cos t}\right|, |y \cot t|$ and $|y \tan t|$.

963. $x + 2y - 4 = 0,\ 2x - y - 3 = 0$.

964. $4x + 2y - 3 = 0,\ 2x - 4y + 1 = 0$. **965.** $y = 2,\ x = 1$.

966. (1) $4x + 3y - 12a = 0,\ 3x - 4y + 6a = 0$;
(2) $x + y = \frac{x^2\sqrt{2}}{16},\ y - x = \frac{\pi\sqrt{2}}{2}$; (3) $y = 1 + x \ln a$.

969. $p = 2a \cos t$. **970.** $\theta = \varphi,\ \alpha = 2\varphi$. **974.** 3, – 3.

975. (1) 0; (2) 0, $\sqrt{3}, -\sqrt{3}$. **977.** $\frac{f_1(t) f_2'(t)}{f_1'(t)} = \tan\theta$.

978. $\arctan \frac{2}{3} bt^2 = \arctan \frac{2}{3}\varphi$.

979. $\rho = \sqrt{a^2 \cos^2 t + b^2 \sin^2 t},\ \varphi = \arctan\left(\frac{b}{a}\tan t\right)$ tangent of the angle between the tangent line and polar radius equals $\frac{2ab}{(b^2 - a^2)\sin 2t}$.

980. The polar subtangent $S_T = \frac{\rho^2}{\frac{d\rho}{d\varphi}}$, the polar subnormal $S_N = \frac{d\rho}{d\varphi}$.

983. $\frac{\rho}{\ln a}$. **984.** $\rho \ln a$. **985.** $\sqrt{1 + a^2}$. **986.** $\frac{r}{\sqrt{r^2 - x^2}} = \frac{r}{y}$.

987. $\frac{\sqrt{b^4x^2 + a^4y^2}}{b^2x}$. **988.** $\sqrt{1 + \frac{p}{2x}}\,dx$ or $\frac{\sqrt{y^2 + p^2}}{y}\,dx$. **989.** $\sqrt{1 + \frac{4}{9ax}}$.

990. $\sqrt{1 + \cos^2 x}\,dx$. **991.** $\frac{e^x + e^{-x}}{2} = y$. **992.** r. **993.** $2a \sin\frac{t}{2}$.

994. $3a \cos t \sin t\,dt$. **995.** $a\sqrt{1 + t^2}\,dt$. **996.** $4a \sin\frac{t}{2}\,dt$. **997.** $a \cot t\,dt$.

998. at. **999.** $a\sqrt{\cosh 2t}\,dt$.

1000. $\frac{3}{2}$ m/min, the velocity is directed vertically downwards.

1001. $10\sqrt{26} \approx 51$ km/h, the velocity vector is parallel to the hypotenuse of the right-angled triangle one side of which is horizontal and equal to 50 km, the other being vertical and equalling 10 km.

1002. 14.63 km/h. **1003.** 40 km/h.

1004. $R_\omega\left(\sin\alpha + \frac{R\sin 2\alpha}{2\sqrt{l^2 - R^2\sin^2\alpha}}\right)$. **1005.** 9.43 m/s. **1006.** 2.

1007. $-24x$. **1008.** 207 360. **1009.** 360.

1010. $6(5x^4 + 6x^2 + 1)$. **1011.** $4 \sin 2x$. **1012.** $\frac{4}{e}$. **1013.** $-\frac{1}{2}$.

1014. $\frac{5!}{(1 - x)^6}$. **1015.** $\frac{6}{x}$. **1016.** $\frac{an(n + 1)}{x^{n+2}}$. **1017.** $16a \sin 2\varphi$.

1018. $\frac{2(-1)^n n!}{(1 + x)^{n+1}}$. **1019.** $2e^{x^2}(3x + 2x^3)$. **1020.** $\frac{6x(2x^3 - 1)}{(x^3 + 1)^3}$.

1021. $\frac{2x}{1+x^2} + 2\arctan x$. **1022.** $-\frac{a^2}{\sqrt{(a^2-x^2)^3}}$. **1023.** $-\frac{x}{(\sqrt{1+x^2})^3}$.

1024. $\frac{a+3\sqrt{x}}{4x\sqrt{x}(a+\sqrt{x})^3}$. **1025.** $\frac{e^{\sqrt{x}}(\sqrt{x}-1)}{4x\sqrt{x}}$.

1026. $-\frac{\arcsin x + x\sqrt{1-x^2}}{\sqrt{(1-x^2)^3}}$. **1027.** $\frac{a(a^2-1)\sin x}{\sqrt{(1-a^2\sin^2 x)^3}}$.

1028. $x^x\left[(\ln x+1)^2 + \frac{1}{x}\right]$. **1029.** $a^n e^{ax}$. **1030.** $(-1)^n e^{-x}$.

1031. $a^n \sin\left(ax + n\frac{\pi}{2}\right) + b^n \cos\left(bx + n\frac{\pi}{2}\right)$.

1032. $2^{n-1}\sin\left[2x + (n-1)\frac{\pi}{2}\right]$. **1033.** $e^x(x+n)$.

1034. $(-1)^n\frac{(n-2)!}{x^{n-1}}\,(n \geq 2)$. **1035.** $\frac{(-1)^n a^n n!}{(ax+b)^{n+1}}$.

1036. $\frac{(-1)^{n-1}a^n(n-1)!}{(ax+b)^n}$. **1037.** $(-1)^{n-1}\frac{(n-1)!}{x^n \ln a}$.

1038. $(-1)^n\frac{n!}{2}\left[\frac{1}{(x+1)^{n+1}} + \frac{1}{(x-1)^{n+1}}\right]$.

1039. $(-1)^n n!\left[\frac{1}{(x-2)^{n+1}} - \frac{1}{(x-1)^{n+1}}\right]$.

1040. $4^{n-1}\cos\left(4x + n\frac{\pi}{2}\right)$. **1054.** $\frac{d^2x}{dy^2} = -\frac{\frac{d^2y}{dx^2}}{\left(\frac{dy}{dx}\right)^3}$. **1056.** $-\frac{b^4}{a^2y^3}$.

1057. $-\frac{3r^3x}{y^5}$. **1058.** $-\frac{2(3y^4+8y^2+5)}{y^8}$. **1059.** $\frac{(3-s)e^{2s}}{(2-s)^3}$.

1060. $-\frac{2a^3xy}{(y^2-ax)^3}$. **1061.** $-\frac{y}{[1-\cos(x+y)]^3}$.

1062. $-\frac{y[(x-1)^2+(y-1)^2]}{x^2(y-1)^3}$. **1063.** $\frac{d^2x}{dy^2} = \frac{\frac{d^2y}{dx^2}}{\left(\frac{dy}{dx}\right)^3}$. **1064.** $\frac{1}{e^2}$.

1065. $-\frac{p^2}{\sqrt{(y^2+p^2)^3}}$. **1069.** $-\frac{2a}{9b^2t^4}$. **1070.** $-\frac{a^2}{y^3} = -\frac{1}{a\sin^3 t}$. **1071.** $-\frac{3b\cos t}{a^3\sin^5 t}$.

1072. $-\frac{1}{a(1-\cos\varphi)^2}$. **1073.** (1) $\frac{\cos^2 t - 4\sin^2 t}{9a^2\cos^7 t\sin^3 t}$; (2) 0, since $x + y = 0$.

1074. (1) $4t^2$; (2) $-\frac{2}{1-t^2}$. **1075.** $\frac{2+t^2}{a(\cos t - t\sin t)^3}$. **1080.** 16 m/s^2.

1081. $v = 2t - 4$, $a = 2$. **1082.** $-\pi^2/18$ cm/s^2. **1084.** -0.0015 m/s^2.

1085. $-1/8$ m/s^2.

1088. (1) $(x^2 - 379)\sin x - 40x\cos x$; (2) $e^x\sum_{k=0}^{n} C_n^k\left(x + k\frac{\pi}{2}\right)$;

$$(3)\ \alpha^n x^3 \sin\left(\alpha x + n\frac{\pi}{2}\right) + 3n\alpha^{n-1}x^2 \sin\left[\alpha x + (n-1)\frac{\pi}{2}\right] + 3n(n-1)\times\alpha^{n-2}x\sin\left[\alpha x + (n-2)\frac{\pi}{2}\right] + n(n-1)(n-2)\alpha^{n-3}\sin\left[\alpha x + (n-3)\frac{\pi}{2}\right].$$

1093. $y^{(2n)}(0) = 0,\ y^{(2n+1)}(0) = [1\cdot 3\cdot 5 \ldots (2n-1)]^2.$

1095. $y^{(2n-1)}(0) = 0,\ y^{(2n)}(0) = 2[2\cdot 4\cdot 6 \ldots (2n-2)]^2.$

1096. $-\dfrac{2dx^2}{9x\sqrt[3]{x}}.$ **1097.** $m(m-1)(m-2)x^{m-3}dx^3.$

1098. $4(x+1)(5x^2-2x-1)dx^2.$ **1099.** $4^{-x^2}\cdot 2\ln 4\cdot(2x^2\ln 4 - 1)dx^2.$

1100. $\dfrac{ab(a^2-b^2)\sin 2x\, dx^2}{(a^2\cos^2 x + b^2\sin^2 x)^2}.$ **1101.** $\dfrac{4\ln x - 4 - \ln^3 x}{x^2\sqrt{(\ln^2 x - 4)^3}}dx^2.$

1102. $-4\sin 2x\, dx^3.$ **1103.** $\pm\dfrac{3a\sec^2\varphi}{4\sqrt{\tan\varphi}}(1+5\tan^2\varphi)\,d\varphi^2.$ **1104.** $\dfrac{a^{2/3}dx^2}{3x^{3/4}y^{1/2}}.$

1105. (1) $d^2y = \dfrac{4x}{x^4-1}d^2x - \dfrac{4(1+3x^4)}{(x^4-1)^2}dx^2$; (2) $d^2y = -4\sec^2 2t\, dt^2.$

1106. (1) $d^2y = \cos z\, d^2z - \sin z\, dz^2$;
(2) $d^2y = a^x\cos(a^x)\ln a\, d^2x - a^x\ln^2 a\,(a^x\sin a^x - \cos a^x)\,dx^2$;
(3) $d^2y = a^{t^3}\ln a\,[\cos a^{t^3}(6t + 9t^4\ln a) - a^{t^3}\sin a^{t^3}\, 9t^4\ln a]\,dt^2.$

Chapter 4

1110. (1) Point of maximum; (2) decreases; (3) increases; (4) point of minimum; (5) point of maximum; (6) point of minimum; (7) point of minimum; (8) point of maximum; (9) point of minimum.

1112. Increases at the point $x_1 = 0$, decreases at $x_2 = 1$; increases at $x_3 = -\dfrac{\pi}{2}$, and decreases at $x_4 = 2$.

1113. Decreases at $x_1 = \dfrac{1}{2}$, increases at $x_2 = 2$ and $x_3 = e$, $x_4 = 1$ is a point of minimum.

1114. Increases at $x_1 = 1$, decreases at $x_2 = -1$, $x_3 = 0$ is a point of minimum.

1115. Decreases at $x_1 = \dfrac{1}{2}$, increases at $x_2 = -\dfrac{1}{2}$, $x_3 = 0$ is a point of maximum.

1125. Three roots belonging respectively to the intervals (1, 2), (2, 3) and (3, 4).

1127. $\sin 3x_2 - \sin 3x_1 = 3(x_2 - x_1)\cos 3\xi$, where $x_1 < \xi < x_2$.

1128. $a(1-\ln a) - b(1-\ln b) = (b-a)\ln\xi$, where $a < \xi < b$.

1129. $\arcsin[2(x_0 + \Delta x)] - \arcsin 2x_0 = \dfrac{2\Delta x}{\sqrt{1-4\xi^2}}$, where $x_0 < \xi < x_0 + \Delta x$.

1135. As $x \to 0$ ξ tends to zero assuming not all the intermediate values but only such a sequence at which $\cos\dfrac{1}{\xi}$ tends to zero.

1136. 0.833. **1137.** 0.57. **1138.** 1.0414.
1139. 0.1990. **1140.** 0.8449. **1141.** 1.7853.

1149*. The required inequality follows from the increasing of the function $y = \frac{\tan x}{x}$ in the interval $\left(0, \frac{\pi}{2}\right)$.

1150. $(-\infty, -1)$ increases, $(-1, 3)$ decreases, $(3, \infty)$ increases.

1151. $(-\infty, -1)$ decreases, $(-1, 0)$ increases, $(0, 1)$ decreases, $(1, \infty)$ increases.

1152. $(-\infty, -1/2)$ increases, $(-1/2, 11/18)$ decreases, $(11/18, \infty)$ increases.

1153. $\left(-\infty, \frac{2}{3}a\right)$ increases, $\left(\frac{2}{3}a, a\right)$ decreases, (a, ∞) increases.

1154. $(-\infty, -1)$ increases, $(-1, 1)$ decreases, $(1, \infty)$ increases.

1155. $(-\infty, 0)$ decreases, $\left(0, \frac{1}{2}\right)$ decreases, $\left(\frac{1}{2}, 1\right)$ increases, $(1, \infty)$ decreases.

1156. $(-\infty, 0)$ increases, $(0, \infty)$ decreases.

1157. $(-\infty, 0)$ decreases $(0, 2)$ increases, $(2, \infty)$ decreases.

1158. $(0, 1)$ decreases, $(1, e)$ decreases, (e, ∞) increases.

1159. $\left(0, \frac{1}{2}\right)$ decreases, $\left(\frac{1}{2}, \infty\right)$ increases.

1160. $\left(0, \frac{\pi}{3}\right)$ decreases, $\left(\frac{\pi}{3}, \frac{5\pi}{3}\right)$ increases, $\left(\frac{5\pi}{3}, 2\pi\right)$ decreases.

1161. $\left(0, \frac{\pi}{6}\right)$ increases, $\left(\frac{\pi}{6}, \frac{\pi}{2}\right)$ decreases, $\left(\frac{\pi}{2}, \frac{5\pi}{6}\right)$ increases, $\left(\frac{5\pi}{6}, \frac{3\pi}{2}\right)$ decreases, $\left(\frac{3\pi}{2}, 2\pi\right)$ increases.

1162. Increases monotonically.

1163. Increases monotonically.

1164. $\left(0, \frac{3}{4}a\right)$ increases, $\left(\frac{3}{4}a, a\right)$ decreases.

1165. $y_{max} = 0$ at $x = 0$, $y_{min} = -1$ at $x = 1$.

1166. $y_{max} = 17$ at $x = -1$, $y_{min} = -47$ at $x = 3$.

1167. $y_{max} = 4$ at $x = 0$, $y_{min} = \frac{8}{3}$ at $x = -2$.

1168. $y_{max} = 2$ at $x = 0$, $y_{min} = \sqrt[3]{4}$ at $x = 2$.

1169. $y_{max} = \frac{2}{\ln 3}$ at $x = -3$. **1170.** $y_{max} = 0$ at $x = 0$.

1171. $y_{max} = 0$ at $x = 0$, $y_{min} = -\frac{2}{3}$ at $x = 1$. **1172.** $y_{min} = 2$ at $x = \frac{2}{3}$.

1173. $y_{max} = \frac{\sqrt{205}}{10}$ at $x = \frac{12}{5}$.

1174. $y_{max} = \sqrt[3]{a^4}$ at $x = 0$, $y_{min} = 0$ at $x = \pm a$.

1175. $y_{min} = 0$ at $x = 0$. **1176.** Increases monotonically.

1177. $y_{max} = \frac{81}{8}\sqrt[3]{18}$ at $x = \frac{1}{2}$, $y_{min} = 0$ at $x = -1$ and at $x = 5$.

1178. $y_{max} = 2.5$ at $x = 1$, $y_{min} = \frac{e(4-e)}{2} \approx 1.76$ at $x = e$.

1179. $y_{max} = \frac{1}{2}$ at $x = 0$, $y_{min} = \frac{\pi}{8}$ at $x = 1$.

1180. $y_{max} = 0$ at $x = 0$, $y_{min} = \dfrac{3\sqrt{3} - 2\pi}{48}$ at $x = \dfrac{1}{2}$.

1181. $y_{max} = \dfrac{6\pi\sqrt{3} - \pi^2 + 18}{36} \approx 1.13$ at $x = \pm\dfrac{\pi}{3}$, $y_{min} = 1$ at $x = 0$.

1182. $y_{max} = \sin\dfrac{1}{2} + \dfrac{1}{16}$ at $x = \dfrac{1}{2}$,

$y_{min} = \dfrac{36\sqrt{3} - 12\pi\sqrt{3} + 72 - \pi^2 + 6\pi}{144}$ at $x = \dfrac{\pi}{6}$.

1183. $y_{max} = \dfrac{1}{\pi}$ at $x = 1$, $y_{min} = -\dfrac{1}{\pi}$ at $x = 3$.

1184. If $ab \le 0$, there is no extremum. If $ab > 0$ and $a > 0$, then $y_{min} = 2\sqrt{ab}$ at $x = \dfrac{1}{2p}\ln\dfrac{b}{a}$; if $ab > 0$ and $a < 0$, then $y_{max} = -2\sqrt{ab}$ at $x = \dfrac{1}{2p}\ln\dfrac{b}{a}$.

1185. 13 and 4. **1186.** 8 and 0. **1187.** 2 and –10.

1188. 2 and – 12. **1189.** 10 and 6. **1190.** 1 and $\dfrac{3}{5}$.

1191. $\dfrac{3}{5}$ and – 1.

1192. The least value is equal to $(a + b)^2$, no greatest value.

1193. $\dfrac{\pi}{2}$ and $-\dfrac{\pi}{2}$.

1194. The greatest value is equal to 1, no least value.

1195. The least value is equal to $\left(\dfrac{1}{e}\right)^{1/e}$, no greatest value.

1196. $\sqrt[3]{9}$ and 0. **1197.** $\dfrac{\pi}{4}$ and 0. **1208.** 4 and 4. **1209.** 1.

1210. 6 and 6. **1211.** 3, 6 and 4 cm. **1212.** 3 cm. **1213.** 1 cm.

1214. $\sqrt[3]{4v}$. **1215.** The radius of the base is equal to the altitude $= \sqrt[3]{\dfrac{v}{\pi}}$.

1216. $H = 2R$. **1217.** $\dfrac{20\sqrt{3}}{3}$ cm. **1218.** $2\pi\sqrt{\dfrac{2}{3}} \approx 293°56'$.

1219. The lateral side $= \dfrac{3p}{4}$, the base $= \dfrac{p}{2}$.

1220. The lateral side $= \dfrac{3p}{5}$, the base $= \dfrac{4p}{5}$.

1221. $\dfrac{2R\sqrt{3}}{3}$. **1222.** $\dfrac{4}{3}R$. **1223.** $\dfrac{2m_0}{3k}$ s, $\dfrac{2}{27}\,\dfrac{m_0^3 g^2 \cdot \text{cm}^2}{k^2 s^2}$.

1224. $\sqrt{\dfrac{2aP}{k}}$. **1225.** 20 km/h, 720 rub. **1226.** In $1\dfrac{27}{43}$ h $\approx$ 1 h 38 min.

1227. The distance between the chord and point A must equal $\dfrac{3}{4}$ of the diameter.

1228. $\dfrac{4R\sqrt{5}}{5}$ and $\dfrac{R\sqrt{5}}{5}$.

1229. The height of the rectangle is equal to $\frac{\sqrt{8R^2+h^2}-3h}{4}$, where h is the distance from the mid point of the chord subtending the arc of the segment and R is the radius of the circle.

1230. The radius of the base circle of the cone must be 1.5 times the radius of the cylinder.

1231. $4R$. **1232.** $\approx 49°$. **1233.** $60°$. **1234.** $R\sqrt{3}$.

1235. $\frac{4}{3}R$. **1237.** $\frac{x}{3}+\frac{y}{6}=1$. **1238.** $a\sqrt{2}$ and $b\sqrt{2}$.

1239. The area of the rectangle $= \frac{2}{\pi} \times$ the area of the ellipse.

1240. Through the point (2, 3). **1241.** $C(-\sqrt{6}, -\sqrt{6})$.

1242. $x = a - p$ if $a > p$, $x = 0$ if $a \le p$.

1243. The cross section of the trough must have the shape of a semicircle.

1244. The length of the timber $= 13\frac{1}{3}$ m, the side of the cross section $= \frac{2\sqrt{2}}{3}$ m.

1245. The required value is equal to the arithmetic mean of the results of the measurements :

$$x = \frac{x_1 + x_2 + \ldots + x_n}{n}.$$

1246. 3 km from the camp. **1247.** At a height of $\frac{R\sqrt{2}}{2}$.

1248. The distance from the source I_1 equals $\frac{l\sqrt[3]{I_1}}{\sqrt[3]{I_1}+\sqrt[3]{I_2}}$; in other words, the distance l is divided by the required point in the ratio $\sqrt[3]{I_1} : \sqrt[3]{I_2}$.

1249. 2.4 m. **1250.** $F_{\text{least}} = \frac{kP}{\sqrt{1+k^2}}$ at $\varphi = \arctan k$. **1251.** ≈ 4.5.

1252. $2b + \sqrt{\frac{Sb}{a}}$ and $2a + \sqrt{\frac{Sa}{b}}$.

1253*. $\frac{RHL}{(L-R)(L+2R)}$, where L is the generatrix of the cone. Take into consideration that the difference between the distance from the centre of the sphere to the vertex of the cone and the radius of the sphere is equal to the difference between the altitude of the cone and the submerged segment.

1254. $\frac{R}{4}$. **1255.** $\frac{R}{2}$. **1256.** $P(p, \pm p\sqrt{2})$.

1263*. $\frac{3}{4}$. Since, the function is a constant ($y' = 0$), the value of this constant is equal to that of the given function for any value of x, say $x = 0$.

1264. π. **1265.** 0. **1267.** $y_{\max} = \frac{4}{27}a^3$ at $x = \frac{a}{3}$, $y_{\min} = 0$ at $x = a$.

1268. $y_{\max} = \frac{a^4}{16}$ at $x = \frac{a}{2}$, $y_{\min} = 0$ at $x = 0$ and at $x = a$.

1269. $y_{max} = -2a$ at $x = -a$, $y_{min} = 2a$ at $x = a$. **1270.** $y_{max} = \frac{5}{4}$ at $x = \frac{3}{4}$.

1271. $y_{max} = 1$ at $x = 1$, $y_{min} = -1$ at $x = -1$. **1272.** $y_{min} = 1$ at $x = 0$.

1273. $y_{max} = \frac{4}{e^2}$ at $x = 2$, $y_{min} = 0$ at $x = 0$. **1274.** $y_{min} = e$ at $x = e$.

1275. $y_{max} = \sqrt[e]{e}$ at $x = e$. **1276.** Maximum at $a = 2$.

1277. $a = -\frac{2}{3}$, $b = -\frac{1}{6}$.

1278. Convex in the neighbourhood of the point (1, 11), concave in the vicinity of the point (3, 3).

1279. Convex in the neighbourhood of the point $\left(1, \frac{\pi}{4}\right)$, concave in the vicinity of the point $\left(-1, -\frac{\pi}{4}\right)$.

1280. Convex in the vicinity of the point $\left(\frac{1}{e^2}, -\frac{2}{e^4}\right)$, concave in the neighbourhood of the point (1, 0).

1287. A point of inflection $\left(\frac{5}{3}, -\frac{250}{27}\right)$. Intervals : of convexity $\left(-\infty, \frac{5}{3}\right)$, of concavity $\left(\frac{5}{3}, \infty\right)$.

1288. There is no point of inflection, the graph is concave.

1289. Points of inflection (2, 62) and (4, 206). Intervals : of concavity $(-\infty, 2)$ of convexity (2, 4), of concavity $(4, \infty)$.

1290. Points of inflection (– 3, 294) and (2, 114). Intervals : of convexity $(-\infty, -3)$, of concavity (– 3, 2), of convexity $(2, \infty)$.

1291. Point of inflection (1, – 1). Intervals : of convexity $(-\infty, 1)$, of concavity $(1, \infty)$.

1292. There is no point of inflection. The graph is concave.

1293. Points of inflection $\left(-3a, -\frac{9a}{4}\right)$, (0, 0), $\left(3a, \frac{9a}{4}\right)$. Intervals : of concavity $(-\infty, -3a)$, of convexity $(-3a, 0)$, of concavity $(0, 3a)$, of convexity $(3a, \infty)$.

1294. Point of inflection (b, a). Intervals : of convexity $(-\infty, b)$, of concavity (b, ∞).

1295. Point of inflection $\left(\arcsin\frac{\sqrt{5}-1}{2}, e^{\frac{\sqrt{5}-1}{2}}\right)$. Intervals : of concavity $\left(-\frac{\pi}{2}, \arcsin\frac{\sqrt{5}-1}{2}\right)$, of convexity $\left(\frac{\sqrt{5}-1}{2}, \frac{\pi}{2}\right)$.

1296. Points of inflection $(\pm 1, \ln 2)$. Intervals : of convexity $(-\infty, -1)$, of concavity $(-1, 1)$, of convexity $(1, \infty)$.

1297. Point of inflection $\left(ae^{3/2}, \frac{3}{2}e^{-3/2}\right)$. Intervals : of convexity $(0, ae^{3/2})$, of concavity $(ae^{3/2}, \infty)$.

1298. There is no inflection point. The graph is concave.

1299. Point of inflection $\left(\frac{1}{2}, e^{\arctan\frac{1}{2}}\right)$. Intervals : of concavity $\left(-\infty, \frac{1}{2}\right)$, of convexity $\left(\frac{1}{2}, \infty\right)$.

1300. Point of inflection $(1, -7)$. Intervals : of convexity $(0, 1)$, of concavity $(1, \infty)$.

1305. $a = -\frac{3}{2},\ b = \frac{9}{2}$.

1306. $\alpha = -\frac{20}{3}, \beta = \frac{4}{3}$. The points $(-2, -2.5)$ and $(0, 0)$ are also points of inflection.

1307. For $a \le -\frac{e}{6}$ and for $a > 0$. **1316.** Points of inflection $(1, 4)$ and $(1, -4)$.

1317. Points of inflection at $t = \frac{3\pi}{4} \pm k\pi\ (k = 0, 1, 2, \ldots)$.

1318. $\dfrac{\sin b - \sin a}{\ln \frac{b}{a}} = \xi \cos \xi$, where $a < \xi < b$.

1319. $e^b + e^a = 2e^{\xi}$, where $a < \xi < b$. **1324.** $\dfrac{2}{3\sqrt[6]{a}}$. **1325.** 0.

1326. 1. **1327.** $\frac{\alpha}{\beta}$. **1328.** $\frac{1}{3}$. **1329.** $\frac{a}{\sqrt{b}}$. **1330.** $-\frac{1}{2}$.

1331. 2. **1332.** $\frac{m}{n}a^{m-n}$. **1333.** $\dfrac{\ln \frac{a}{b}}{\ln \frac{c}{d}}$. **1334.** -2.

1335. 2. **1336.** $\ln \frac{a}{b}$. **1337.** $\cos a$. **1338.** 2. **1339.** 1.

1340. 1. **1341.** $\frac{1}{128}$. **1342.** 16. **1343.** 1. **1344.** 1.

1345. -2. **1346.** 0. **1347.** 0. **1348.** a. **1349.** $\frac{1}{2}$.

1350. $\frac{4a^2}{\pi}$. **1351.** -1. **1352.** 0. **1353.** ∞.

1354. $\frac{a+b+c}{3}$. **1355.** 1. **1356.** ∞. **1357.** 1.

1358. 1. **1359.** e. **1360.** 1. **1361.** e^2. **1362.** e^{π}.

1363. 1. **1364.** $\frac{1}{2}$. **1366.** The values of x^x exceed those of $a^x x^a$.

1367. The values of $f(x)$ exceed those of $\ln f(x)$.

1374. $f(115) \approx 1520990$, $f(120) \approx 1728120$, $\delta_{x=100} \approx 0.03$ (absolute error).

1375. $y = \pm \frac{b}{a}x$. **1376.** $x = 0, y = 0$. **1377.** $y = 0$.

1378. $x = b, y = c$. **1379.** $x = -1, y = \frac{1}{2}x - 1$. **1380.** $x + y = 0$.

1381. $y = x + 2$. **1382.** $y = \pm x$. **1383.** $x = 0, y = 0, x + y = 0$.

1384. $x = b;\ x = 2b;\ y = x + 3(b - a)$. **1385.** $y + 1 = 0, 2x + y + 1 = 0$.

1386. $x = -\frac{1}{e}, y = x + \frac{1}{e}$. **1387.** $x = 0, y = x$. **1388.** $x = 0, y = x + 3$.

1389. $y = \frac{\pi}{2}x - 1$. **1390.** $y = 2x \pm \frac{\pi}{2}$. **1391.** $y = x$ if $f(x)$ is not an identity constant.

1392. If $\lim_{t \to t_0} \varphi(t) = \infty$ and $\lim_{t \to t_0} \psi(t) = b$, then $y = b$ is an asymptote; if $\lim_{t \to t_0} \psi(t) = \infty$ and $\lim_{t \to t_0} \varphi(t) = a$, then $x = a$ is an asymptote.

1393. $x = -1, y = 0$. **1394.** $y = \frac{1}{2}x + e$. **1395.** $y = \pm\frac{1}{2}x - \frac{1}{2}$.

1396. $x + y + a = 0$. **1397.** $x = 2$; $2x + 8y + 1 = 0$; $6x - 40y + 9 = 0$.

1398. Defined everywhere. The graph is symmetric about the origin. $y_{max} = \frac{1}{2}$ at $x = 1$, $y_{min} = -\frac{1}{2}$ at $x = -1$. Points of inflection of the graph $\left(-\sqrt{3}, -\frac{\sqrt{3}}{4}\right)$, (0, 0) and $\left(\sqrt{3}, \frac{\sqrt{3}}{4}\right)$. Asymptote $y = 0$.

1399. Defined everywhere, except for the values of $x = \pm 1$. The graph is symmetric about the y-axis. No maxima. $y_{min} = 1$ at $x = 0$. No poitns of inflection. Asymptotes : $x = \pm 1, y = 0$.

1400. Defined everywhere, except for the values of $x = \pm 1$. The graph is symmetric about the origin. No extrema. Point of inflection (0, 0). Asymptotes : $x = -1$, $x = 1$, $y = 0$.

1401. Defined everywhere, except for the values of $x = 1$, $x = 2$ and $x = 3$. $y_{max} \approx -2.60$ at $x \approx 2.58$; $y_{min} \approx 2.60$ at $x \approx 1.42$. No points of inflection. Asymptotes : $x = 1$, $x = 2$, $x = 3$, $y = 0$.

1402. Not defined for $x = \pm 1$. The graph is symmetric about the y-axis. $y_{max} = 0$ at $x = 0$. No minima. Increases for $x < -1$, decreases for $x > 1$. The graph has no points of inflection. Asymptotes : $x = \pm 1$, $y = 1$.

1403. Defined everywhere. The graph is symmetric about the y-axis. $y_{min} = -1$ at $x = 0$; (1, 0) and (– 1, 0) are the points of inflection of the graph with a horizontal tangent line; $\left(\pm\frac{\sqrt{5}}{5}, -\frac{64}{125}\right)$ are the points of inflection. No asymptotes.

1404. Defined everywhere; the graph is symmetric about the y-axis. $y_{max} = 0$ at $x = 0$, $y_{min} = -\frac{27}{8}$ at $x = \pm\frac{1}{2}$. Points of inflection of the graph with a horizontal tangent line (± 1, 0). Four more points of inflection of the graph : at $x \approx \pm 0.7$ and $x \approx \pm 0.26$. No asymptotes.

1405. Defined everywhere, except at $x = 0$. $y_{min} = 3$ at $x = \frac{1}{2}$. No maxima. Point of inflection of the graph : $\left(-\frac{\sqrt[3]{2}}{2}, 0\right)$. Asymptote : $x = 0$.

1406. Defined everywhere, except at $x = 0$. The graph is symmetric about the y-axis. $y_{min} = 2$ at $x = \pm 1$. No maxima. The graph has no points of inflection. Asymptote: $x = 0$.

1407. Defined everywhere, except at $x = 1$. $y_{min} = -1$ at $x = 0$. No maxima. Point of inflection of the graph : $\left(-\frac{1}{2}, -\frac{8}{9}\right)$. Asymptotes : $x = 1$ and $y = 0$.

1408. Defined everywhere, except at $x = \pm\sqrt{3}$. The graph is symmetric about the origin. $y_{max} = -4.5$ at $x = 3$, $y_{min} = 4.5$ at $x = -3$. Point of inflection of the graph : (0, 0). Asymptotes : $x = \pm\sqrt{3}$ and $x + y = 0$.

1409. Defined everywhere, except at $x = -1$. No minima. $y_{max} = -3\frac{3}{8}$ at $x = -3$. Point of inflection of the graph : (0, 0). Asymptotes : $x = -1$ and $y = \frac{1}{2}x - 1$.

1410. Defined everywhere, except at $x = 1$. No maxima. $y_{min} = \frac{27}{4}$ at $x = \frac{3}{2}$. Point of inflection of the graph : (0, 0). Asymptote : $x = 1$.

1411. Defined everywhere, except at $x = 1$. $y_{max} = 0$ at $x = 0$, $y_{min} = \frac{4}{3}\sqrt[3]{4}$ at $x = \sqrt[3]{4}$. Point of inflection of the graph : $\left(-\sqrt[3]{2}, -\frac{2}{3}\sqrt[3]{2}\right)$. Asymptotes : $x = 1$ and $y = x$.

1412. Defined everywhere, except at $x = -1$. $y_{max} = \frac{2}{27}$ at $x = 5$, $y_{min} = 0$ at $x = 1$. Abscissas of the points of inflection of the graph : $5 \pm 2\sqrt{3}$. Asymptotes : $x = -1$ and $y = 0$.

1413. Defined everywhere, except at $x = 0$. $y_{max} = \frac{7}{2}$ at $x = 1$. $y_{max} = -\frac{11}{6}$ at $x = -3$, $y_{min} = \frac{27}{8}$ at $x = 2$. Abscissa of the point of inflection of the graph : $\frac{9}{7}$. Asymptotes : $x = 0$ and $y = \frac{1}{2}x + 1$.

1414. Defined everywhere, except at $x = 0$. No maxima. $y_{min} \approx -0.28$ at $x \approx 1.46$. Abscissa of the point of inflection of the graph : $-\sqrt[3]{2}$. Asymptote : $x = 0$.

1415. Defined everywhere, except at $x = 0$. $y_{max} = -2.5$ at $x = -2$; no minima. The graph has no points of inflection. Asymptotes : $x = 0$ and $y = x$.

1416. Defined everywhere, $y_{max} = \frac{1}{e}$ at $x = 1$. No minima. Point of inflection of the graph : $\left(2, \frac{2}{e^2}\right)$. Asymptote : $y = 0$.

1417. Defined everywhere. $x_{max} = \frac{4}{e^2}$ at $x = 2$, $y_{min} = 0$ at $x = 0$. Abscissas of the points of inflection of the graph : $2 \pm \sqrt{2}$. Asymptote : $y = 0$.

1418. Defined everywhere except at $x = 0$. $y_{min} = e$ at $x = 1$. No. maxima. The graph has no points of inflection. Asymptotes : $x = 0$, $y = 0$.

1419. Defined for $x > -1$. $y_{min} = 0$ at $x = 0$. No maxima. The graph has no points of inflection. Asymptote : $x = -1$.

1420. Defined everywhere. The graph is symmetric about the y-axis. $y_{min} = 0$ at $x = 0$. No maxima. Points of inflection of the graph : $(\pm 1, \ln 2)$. No asymptotes.

1421. Defined everywhere. The graph is symmetric about the y-axis. $y_{max} = \frac{1}{e}$ at $x = \pm 1$, $y_{min} = 0$ at $x = 0$. Abscissas of the points of inflection of the grpah : $\pm \frac{\sqrt{5 \pm \sqrt{17}}}{2}$. Asymptote : $y = 0$.

1422. Defined everywhere. $y_{max} = \frac{27}{e^3}$ at $x = 3$. No minima. The abscissas of the points of inflection 0 and $3 \pm \sqrt{3}$. Asymptote : $y = 0$.

1423. Defined everywhere. The graph is symmetric about the origin. $y_{max} = \frac{1}{\sqrt{e}}$ at $x = 1$, $y_{min} = -\frac{1}{\sqrt{e}}$ at $x = -1$. Points of inflection of the graph $(0, 0)$, $(\sqrt{3}, \sqrt{3}\, e^{-3/2})$ and $(-\sqrt{3}, -3e^{-3/2})$. Asymptote : $y = 0$.

1424. Defined everywhere except at $x = 0$. No extrema. The graph has no points of inflection. Asymptotes : $x = 0$, $y = 0$ and $y = -1$.

1425. Defined for $x > 0$. No extrema. Point of inflection of the graph :

$$\left(e^{3/2}, e^{3/2} + \frac{3}{2} e^{-3/2}\right).$$ Asymptotes : $x = 0$ and $y = x$.

1426. The function is defined for $-\infty < x < -1$ and for $0 < x < \infty$. In the interval $(-\infty, -1)$ it increases from e to ∞, in the interval $(0, +\infty)$ from 1 to e. The graph consists of two separate branches. Asymptotes : $y = e$ and $x = -1$.

1427. Defined everywhere. No extrema. For $x = \pm k\pi$ $(k = 1, 3, 5, \ldots)$ it is stationary. The graph is symmetric about the origin, has no asymptotes. Points of inflection : $(k\pi, k\pi)$ $(k = 0, \pm 1, \pm 2, \ldots)$; at the points of inflection the graph intersects the straight line $y = x$.

1428. Defined everywhere. The graph is symmetric about the y-axis. The points of extremum satisfy the equation $\tan x = -x$. Abscissas of the points of inflection satisfy the equation $x \tan x = 2$. No asymptotes.

1429. Defined on the intervals $\left(-\frac{\pi}{2} + 2k\pi, \frac{\pi}{2} + 2k\pi\right)$, where $k = 0, \pm 1, \pm 2, \ldots$. Period 2π. The graph is symmetric about the y-axis. $y_{max} = 0$ at $x = 2k\pi$. The graph has no points of inflection. Asymptotes : $x = \frac{\pi}{2} + k\pi$.

1430. Defined on the intervals $\left(-\frac{\pi}{2} + 2k\pi, \frac{\pi}{2} + 2k\pi\right)$, where $k = 0, \pm 1, \pm 2, \ldots$. Period 2π. The graph is symmetric about the y-axis. $y_{min} = 1$ at $x = 2k\pi$. The graph has no points of inflection. Asymptotes : $x = \frac{\pi}{2} + k\pi$.

1431. Defined everywhere. The graph is symmetric about the origin. $y_{max} = \frac{\pi}{2} - 1$ at $x = -1$, $y_{min} = 1 - \frac{\pi}{2}$ at $x = 1$. Point of inflection : $(0, 0)$. Asymptotes : $y = x \pm \pi$.

1432. Defined everywhere, except at $x = 1$ and $x = 3$. $y_{max} = \frac{1}{e}$ at $x = 2$. No minima. Asymptotes : $x = 1$, $x = 3$ and $y = 1$.

1433. Defined everywhere. Period 2π. $y_{min} = 1$ at $x = k\pi$, where $k = 0, \pm 1, \pm 2, \ldots$; $y_{max} = e - 1$ at $x = \frac{\pi}{2} + 2k\pi$ and $y_{max} = 1 + \frac{1}{e}$ at $x = \frac{3\pi}{2} + 2k\pi$. No asymptotes.

1434. Defined everywhere. $y_{max} = \frac{4}{27}$ at $x = \frac{8}{27}$, $y_{min} = 0$ at $x = 0$. The graph has neither points of inflection, nor asymptotes.

1435. Defined everywhere. The graph is symmetric about the y-axis. $y_{max} = 0$ at $x = 0$, $y_{min} = -3$ at $x = \pm 1$. The graph has neither points of inflection, nor asymptotes.

1436. Defined everywhere. The graph is symmetric about the origin. $y_{max} = \frac{2}{3}$ at $x = 1$, $y_{min} = -\frac{2}{3}$ at $x = -1$. Point of inflection : $(0, 0)$. No asymptotes.

1437. Defined everywhere. $y_{max} = 2$ at $x = 0$, $y_{min} = 0$ at $x = -1$. Point of inflection : $\left(-\frac{1}{2}, 1\right)$. Asymptote : $y = 1$.

1438. Defined everywhere. $y_{max} \approx 2.2$ at $x = \frac{7}{11}$, $y_{min} = 0$ at $x = 1$. Abscissas of the points of inflection of the graph : -1 and $\frac{7 \pm 3\sqrt{3}}{11}$. No asymptotes.

1439. Defined everywhere. $y_{max} = 2\sqrt[3]{4}$ at $x = 4$, $y_{min} = 0$ at $x = 0$. Point of inflection : $(6, 0)$. Asymptote : $x + y = 2$.

1440. The function is defined for $x \geq 0$, double-valued. The function $y = x + \sqrt{x^5}$ (the upper branch of the graph) increases monotonically. The function $y = x - \sqrt{x^5}$ (the lower branch of the graph) has a maximum at $x = \frac{\sqrt[3]{20}}{5}$. The graph has neither points of inflection, nor asymptotes.

1441. Defined for $x \geq 0$, double-valued. The function $y = x^2 + \sqrt{x^5}$ (the upper branch of the graph) increases monotonically. The function $y = x^2 - \sqrt{x^5}$ (the lower branch of the graph) has a maximum at $x = \frac{16}{25}$. Abscissa of the point of inflection of the lower branch of the graph : $\frac{64}{225}$. No asymptotes.

1442. Defined for $x \geq -1$, double-valued. No extrema. The graph is symmetric about the x-axis and has points of inflection $(0, 1)$ and $(0, -1)$. No asymptotes.

1443. Defined on the intervals $[-1, 0]$ and $(1, \infty)$, double-valued. The graph is symmetric about the x-axis. $|y|_{max} = \frac{\sqrt[4]{12}}{3}$ at $x = \frac{-\sqrt{3}}{3}$. Abscissa of the points of inflection of the graph : $\sqrt{1 + \frac{\sqrt{12}}{3}}$. No asymptotes.

1444. Defined for $x \geq 0$, double-valued. The graph is symmetric about the x-axis. $|y|_{max} = \frac{\sqrt{12}}{9}$ at $x = \frac{1}{3}$. The graph has no points of inflection. No asymptotes.

1445. Defined for $x = 0$ and for $x \geq 1$. The origin is an isolated point. The graph is symmetric about the x-axis. No extrema. Points of inflection of the graph : $\left(\frac{4}{3}, \pm \frac{4\sqrt{3}}{9}\right)$. No asymptotes.

1446. Defined for $x < 0$ and for $x \geq \sqrt[3]{2}$, double-valued. The graph is symmetric about the x-axis. $|y|_{max} = 1$ at $x = -1$. The graph has no points of inflection. Asymptotes : $x = 0$ and $y = \pm \frac{x\sqrt{3}}{3}$.

1447. Defined for $x \leq -2$ and for $x > 0$, double-valued. The graph is symmetric about the straight line $y = x$. $y_{max} = -2$ at $x = 1$. The graph has no points of inflection. Asymptotes ; $x = 0$, $y = 0$ and $x + y = 0$.

1448. Defined for $-a \leq x < a$, double-valued. The graph is symmetric with respect to the x-axis. $|y|_{max} = a\sqrt{\frac{5\sqrt{5} - 11}{2}}$ at $x = -\frac{a}{2}(\sqrt{5} - 1)$. There are no points of inflection. Asymptote : $x = a$.

1449. Defined for $0 \leq x \leq 4$, double-valued. The graph is symmetric with respect to the x-axis. $|y|_{max} = \sqrt{3}$ at $x = 3$. Abscissa of the points of inflection of the graph : $3 - \sqrt{3}$. No asymptotes.

1450. Defined for $-2 \leq x \leq 2$, double-valued. The graph is symmetric with respect to the axes of coordinates. $|y|_{max} = \frac{3\sqrt{3}}{5}$ at $x = \pm 1$. Points of inflection : $(0, 0)$ and $\left(\pm\sqrt{3}, \pm\frac{\sqrt{3}}{5}\right)$. No asymptotes.

1451. Defined for $-1 \leq x \leq 1$, double-valued. The graph is symmetric with respect to the axes of coordinates. $|y|_{max} = \frac{1}{2}$ at $x = \pm\frac{\sqrt{2}}{2}$. Point of inflection : $(0, 0)$. No asymptotes.

1452. Defined for $x \geq 1$, double-valued. The graph is symmetric with respect to the x-axis. $|y|_{max} = 1$ at $x = 2$. Abscissa of the points of inflection : $\frac{6 + 2\sqrt{3}}{3}$. Asymptote $y = 0$.

1453. Defined for $0 \leq x < 2a$, double-valued. The graph is symmetric about the x-axis. No extrema. No points of inflection. Asymptote $x = 2a$.

1454. Defined for $x < 0$, for $0 < x \leq 1$ and for $x \geq 2$, double-valued. The graph is symmetric with respect to the x-axis, has asymptotes $x = 0$ and $y = \pm 1$ and two points of inflection. No extrema.

1455. Defined for $-a \leq x < 0$ and for $0 < x \leq a$, double-valued. The graph is symmetric about the x-axis. No extrema. Points of inflection : $\left[(a\sqrt{3} - 1), \pm a\sqrt[4]{\frac{27}{2}}\right]$. Asymptote $x = 0$.

1456. Defined for $-1 \leq x \leq 1$ and for $x = \pm 2$, double-valued. The graph is symmetric about the axes of coordinates and has two isolated points : $(\pm 2, 0)$. $y|_{max} = 1$ at $x = 0$. No points of inflection and no asymptotes.

1457. Defined for $-1 \le x \le 1$, double-valued. The graph is symmetric about the axes of coordinates. $|y|_{max} = 1$ at $x = 0$. Points of inflection $\left(\pm \frac{\sqrt{2}}{2}, \pm \frac{\sqrt{2}}{4}\right)$. No asymptotes.

1458. Defined for $x \le -1$ and for $x \ge 1$, double-valued. The graph is symmetric about the axes of coordinates. No extrema. Points of inflection $\left(\pm \sqrt{2}, \pm \frac{1}{2}\right)$. Asymptotes $y = \pm x$.

1459. Defined for $x \ge 0$, double-valued. The graph is symmetric about the x-axis. $|y|_{max} = 1$ for $x = \frac{1}{2}$. Abscissa of the points of inflection of the graph $\frac{1+\sqrt{2}}{2}$. Asymptote $y = 0$.

1460. Defined everywhere, except at $x = 0$. No extrema. Points of inflection $\left(-\frac{1}{2}, e^{-2} + \frac{1}{2}\right)$. Asymptotes $x = 0$ and $x + y = 1$.

1461. Defined everywhere, except at $x = \frac{\pi}{2} + k\pi$, where $k = 0, \pm 1, \pm 2, \ldots$ period π. No extrema. The graph has no points of inflection. Asymptotes $x = \frac{\pi}{2} + k\pi$.

1462. Defined everywhere. The graph is symmetric about the y-axis. Points of extremum satisfy the equation $y = \tan x$. Asymptote $y = 0$.

1463. Defined everywhere. No extrema. The graph has no points of inflection. For $x \le 0$ the function is identically equal to the linear function $y = 1 - x$. Asymptote $x + y = 3$. $(0, 1)$ is a corner point of the graph with two different tangents.

1464. Defined everywhere. The graph is symmetric about the y-axis. $y_{max} = 3$ at $x = 0$, $y_{min} = -1$ at $x = \pm 2$. The graph has no points of inflection, no asymptotes, and its right-hand curve is a portion of the parabola $y = x^2 - 4x + 3$ lying on the right of the y-axis. $(0, 3)$ is a corner point of the graph with two different tangent lines.

1465. $x(t)$ and $y(t)$ are defined for all t, and $y(x)$ for all x. $(-3, 3)$ is a point of maximum, $(5, -1)$, a point of minimum, $(1, 1)$, a point of inflection. No asymptotes. As $x \to \infty$, the angle of inclination of the line to the x-axis tends to $45°$.

1466. $x(t)$ and $y(t)$ are defined for all t and $y(x)$ for all x. Asymptotes $y = x$ and $y = x + 6\pi$; $\left(-1 - 3\pi, -1 + \frac{3\pi}{2}\right)$ is a point of maximum, $\left(1 - 3\pi, 1 - \frac{3\pi}{2}\right)$ a point of minimum, $(-3\pi, 0)$ a point of inflection.

1467. $x(t)$ and $y(t)$ are defined for all t, except for $t = -1$. Asymptote : $x + y + 1 = 0$. $(0, 0)$ is a double point, at which the curve crosses itself, the axes of coordinates being tangent to the graph at this point. No points of inflection. A closed loop of the curve is found in the first quadrant.

1468. $x(t)$ and $y(t)$ are defined for all t. The function $y(x)$ is not defined for $x < -\frac{1}{e}$, it is double-valued for $-\frac{1}{e} < x < 0$ and single-valued for $x > 0$. The curve is symmetric with respect to the straight line $x + y = 0$. $\left(e, \frac{1}{e}\right)$ is a point of maximum. There are two inflection points. The axes of coordinates serve as asymptotes.

1469. A closed curve symmetric about the x-axis with a cusp $(a, 0)$.

1470. A closed three-leafed rose. The function is defined on the intervals : $\left[0, \frac{\pi}{3}\right]$, $\left[\frac{2}{3}\pi, \pi\right]$, $\left[\frac{4}{3}\pi, \frac{5}{3}\pi\right]$. Extrema at $\varphi = \frac{\pi}{6}$, $\varphi = \frac{5\pi}{6}$ and $\varphi = \frac{3\pi}{2}$.

1471. The function is defined on the intervals $\left[0, \frac{\pi}{2}\right)$, $\left[\pi, \frac{3\pi}{2}\right)$. Its graph is symmetric about the pole. The straight lines $x = a$ and $x = -a$ are asymptotes[1].

1472. The function is defined on the intervals $\left[0, \frac{\pi}{2}\right)$, $\left[\frac{3\pi}{4}, \frac{3\pi}{2}\right)$, $\left[\frac{7\pi}{4}, 2\pi\right]$. Its graph is symmetric about the pole. Asymptotes : $x = a$ and $x = -a$. At the pole the curve touches the straight line $\varphi = \frac{3\pi}{4}$.

1473. Exists for all values of φ. At $\varphi = 0$ a maximum is equal to $2a$, at $\varphi = \pi$ a minimum is equal to 0. The line is closed and symmetric about the polar axis. The pole is a cusp.

1474. The function is defined on the intervals $\left[0, \frac{\pi}{2} + \arccos\frac{1}{b}\right]$, $\left[\frac{3\pi}{2} - \arccos\frac{1}{b}, 2\pi\right]$. At the point $\varphi = 0$ it has a maximum equal to $a(1 + b)$, at the points $\varphi = \frac{\pi}{2} + \arccos\frac{1}{b}$ and $\varphi = \frac{3\pi}{2} - \arccos\frac{1}{b}$, a minimum equal to 0. The graph of the function is symmetric with respect to the polar axis.

1475. Exists for $\varphi > 0$. $(\sqrt{2\pi}, 0.5)$ is an inflection point. The polar axis serves as an asymptote. The curve is spirally wound round the pole, asymptotically approaching it.

1476. Exists for $\varphi \geq 0$. The graph is a spiral emanating from the pole and asymptotically approaching the circle $\rho = 1$.

1477. Exists for $-1 \leq t \leq 1$, the whole curve is situated to the right of the y-axis. A closed curve. A maximum at $t = 0$ ($\varphi = 1$ radian, $\rho = 1$). No points of inflection. Touches the y-axis at $t = \pm 1$.

1478. A four-leafed rose. The origin is the point at which the curve touches itself twice.

[1]Here and henceforward asymptotes are given in Cartesian coordinates with a polar axis as the x-axis and a perpendicular to the polar axis passing through the pole as the y-axis.

1479. The whole curve lies on the strip $-\dfrac{a\sqrt{2}}{2} \le x \le \dfrac{a\sqrt{2}}{2}$ and is symmetric with respect to the origin. Asymptote : $x = 0$. (0, 0) is an inflection point with the x-axis as a tangent. There are two more points of inflection.

1480. A closed curve with four cusps : $(a, 0), (0, a), (-a, 0)$ and $(0, -a)$; it is symmetric about the four axes : $x = 0$, $y = 0$, $y = x$, $y = -x$. The origin is an isolated point.

1481. A curve symmetric with respect to the axes of coordinates and the bisectors of the quadrants. Asymptotes : $(x \pm y)^2 = \dfrac{1}{2}$. The origin is a quadruple point at which the curve crosses itself; at this point the branches of the curve touch the axes of coordinates. The graph has the shape of a "mill".

1485. The rest of the roots are simple. **1486.** $0.1 < x < 0.2$.

1487. $-0.7 < x_1 < -0.6$ and $0.8 < x_2 < 0.9$. **1488.** $0.32 < x < 0.33$.

1489. $-3.11 < x_1 < -3.10$, $0.22 < x_2 < 0.23$ and $2.88 < x_3 < 2.89$.

1490. $0.38 < x_1 < 0.39$ and $1.24 < x_2 < 1.25$. **1491.** $-0.20 < x < -0.19$.

1492. $0.84 < x < 0.85$. **1493.** $1.63 < x < 1.64$. **1494.** $1.537 < x < 1.538$.

1495. $0.826 < x < 0.827$. **1496.** $1.096 < x < 1.097$.

1497. $0.64 < x < 0.65$. For $0 < a < 1$ there exists only one real number equal to its logarithm which is less than 1. For $1 < a < e^{1/e}$ there are two different numbers equal to their logarithms : one from the interval $(1, e)$ the other from the interval $(e, +\infty)$. For $a = e^{1/e}$ the only number equal to its logarithm will be the number e (which is the double root of the equation $\log_a x = x$). For $e^{1/e} < a < \infty$ there are no real numbers equal to their logarithms.

1498. $(x-4)^4 + 11(x-4)^3 + 37(x-4)^2 + 21(x-4) - 56$.

1499. $(x+1)^3 - 5(x+1) + 8$.

1500. $$(x-1)^{10} + 10(x-1)^9 + 45(x-1)^8 + 120(x-1)^7 + 210(x-1)^6 + 249(x-1)^5 + 195(x-1)^4 + 90(x-1)^3 + 15(x-1)^2 - 5(x-1) - 1.$$

1501. $x^6 - 9x^5 + 30x^4 - 45x^3 + 60x^2 - 9x + 1$.

1502. $f(-1) = 143$, $f'(0) = -60$, $f''(1) = 26$.

1503. $$-1 - (x+1) - (x+1)^2 - \ldots - (x+1)^n + (-1)^{n+1} \frac{(x+1)^{n+1}}{[-1 + \theta(x+1)]^{n+2}},$$ where $0 < \theta < 1$.

1504. $$x + \frac{x^2}{1} + \frac{x^3}{2!} + \ldots + \frac{x^n}{(n-1)!} + \frac{x^{n+1}}{(n+1)!}(\theta x + n + 1)\, e^{\theta x}$$ where $0 < \theta < 1$.

1505. $$2 + \frac{x-4}{4} - \frac{(x-4)^2}{64} + \frac{(x-4)^3}{512} - \ldots + (-1)^{n-1} \frac{(2n-2)!\,(x-4)^n}{n!\,(n-1)!\,2^{4n-2}} + \frac{(-1)^n\,(2n)!\,(x-4)^{n+1}}{2^{2n+1}\, n!\,(n+1)!\,\sqrt{[4 + \theta(x-4)]^{2n+1}}},$$ where $0 < \theta < 1$.

1506. $$1 + \frac{x^2}{2!} + \frac{4^4}{4!} + \ldots + \frac{x^{2n}}{(2n)!} + \frac{x^{2n+1}}{(2n+1)!} \frac{e^{\theta x} - e^{-\theta x}}{2},$$ where $0 < \theta < 1$.

1507. $(x-1)+\frac{5}{2!}(x-1)^2+\frac{11}{3!}(x-1)^3+\frac{6}{4!}(x-1)^4+\ldots+$
$$+\frac{(-1)^n 6(x-1)^n}{(n-3)(n-2)(n-1)n}+\frac{(-1)^{n+1} 6(x-1)^{n+1}}{(n-2)(n-1)n(n+1)[1+\theta(x-1)]^{n-2}},$$
where $0<\theta<1$.

1508. $\frac{2x^2}{2!}-\frac{2^3x^4}{4!}+\frac{2^5x^6}{6!}-\frac{2^7x^8}{8!}+\ldots+(-1)^{n-1}$
$\frac{2^{2n-1}x^{2n}}{(2n)!}+\frac{(-1)^n 2^{2n} x^{2n+1}}{(2n+1)!}\times\sin 2\theta x$, where $0<\theta<1$.

1509. $2-(x-2)+(x-2)^2-(x-2)^3+\frac{(x-2)^4}{[1+\theta(x-2)]^5}$, where $0<\theta<1$.

1510. $x+\frac{x^3}{3}\cdot\frac{1+2\sin^3\theta x}{\cos^4\theta x}$, where $0<\theta<1$.

1511. $x+\frac{x^3}{6}+\frac{x^4}{4!}\frac{9\theta x+6\theta^3x^3}{(1-\theta^2x^2)^{7/2}}$, where $0<\theta<1$.

1512. $1-\frac{1}{2}(x-1)+\frac{1\cdot 3}{2^2\cdot 2}(x-1)^2-\frac{1\cdot 3\cdot 5}{2^3\cdot 3!}(x-1)^3+\frac{1\cdot 3\cdot 5\cdot 7}{2^4\cdot 4!}$
$\frac{(x-1)^4}{\sqrt{[1+\theta(x-1)]^9}}$, where $0<\theta<1$.

1513*. By virtue of existence of the third derivative, we have
$$f(a+h)=f(a)+hf'(a)+\frac{h^2}{2!}f''(a)+\frac{h^3}{3!}f'''(a+\theta_1 h).$$
Comparing with the expression in the text, we get
$$\frac{h^2}{2!}[f''(a+\theta h)-f''(a)]=\frac{h^3}{3!}f'''(a+\theta_1 h),$$
i.e., $\frac{f''(a+\theta h)-f''(a)}{h}=\theta$
$$\frac{f''(a+\theta h)-f''(a)}{\theta h}=\frac{1}{3}f'''(a+\theta_1 h).$$
Finally, pass to the limit as $h\to 0$.

1514. The function decreases. (0, 3) is the point of inflection of the graph.

1515. The function has a minimum equal to 1.

1516. The function has a minimum equal to 2.

1517. The function has a maximum equal to – 11.

1518. The function increases. (0, 0) is the point of inflection of the graph.

1519. The function increases. (0, 4) is the point of inflection of the graph.

1520. $f(x)=1-6(x-1)+(x-1)^2+\ldots$, $f(1.03)\approx 0.82$.

1521. $f(x)=321+1087(x-2)+1648(x-2)^2+\ldots$,
$f(2.02)\approx 343.4$, $f(1.97)\approx 289.9$.

1522. $f(x)=1+60(x-1)+2570(x-1)^2+\ldots$, $f(1.005)\approx 1.364$.

1523. $f(x)=-6+21(x-2)+50(x-2)^2+\ldots$,
$f(2.1)\approx -3.4$, $f(2.1)=-3.36399$; $\delta=0.036$; $\delta'\approx 0.011=1.1\%$.

1524. 1.65. **1525.** 0.78, $\delta<0.01$. **1526.** 0.342020.

1527. 0.985. **1528.** 0.40, $\delta<0.01$. **1529.** $\frac{\sqrt{2}}{4}$. **1530.** $\frac{a}{b^2};\frac{b}{a^2}$.

1531. 36. **1532.** 0.128. **1533.** $\frac{\sqrt{2}}{4}$. **1534.** 0. **1535.** 1.

1536. $\frac{8\sqrt{2}}{3a}$. **1537.** $\frac{6|x|}{(1+9x^4)^{3/2}}$. **1538.** $\frac{a^4b^4}{(b^4x^2+a^4y^2)^{3/2}}$.

1539. $|\cos x|$. **1540.** $\frac{1}{3\sqrt[3]{a|xy|}}$. **1541.** $\frac{|(m-1)(ab)^{2m}(xy)^{m-2}|}{(b^{2m}x^{2m-2}+a^{2m}y^{2m-2})^{3/2}}$.

1542. $\frac{1}{a\cosh^2\frac{x}{a}}$. **1543.** $\frac{1}{6}$. **1544.** $\frac{2}{3a|\sin 2t_1|}$. **1545.** $\frac{2}{\pi a}$.

1546. $\frac{3}{8a\left|\sin\frac{t}{2}\right|}$. **1547.** $\frac{1}{\sqrt{1+\ln^2 a}}$. **1548.** $\frac{2+\varphi^2}{a(\varphi+1^2)^{3/2}}$.

1549. $\frac{\varphi^2+k^2+k}{a\varphi^{k-1}(\varphi^2+k^2)^{3/2}}$. **1550.** $\frac{(a^2+b^2)^{3/2}}{2ab\sqrt{2}}$.

1554. $(x+4)^2+\left(y-\frac{7}{2}\right)^2=\frac{125}{4}$. **1555.** $(x-2)^2+(y-2)^2=2$.

1556. $(x+2)^2+(y-3)^2=8$. **1557.** $\left(x-\frac{\pi-10}{4}\right)^2+\left(y-\frac{9}{4}\right)^2=\frac{125}{16}$.

1558. $\left(x+\frac{7}{3}a\right)^2+\left(y-\frac{8}{3}a\right)^2=\frac{125}{9}a^2$. **1559.** $\left(\frac{a}{4},\frac{a}{4}\right)$.

1560. $\left(\frac{\sqrt{2}}{2},-\frac{1}{2}\ln 2\right)$. **1561.** $\left(-\frac{1}{2}\ln 2,\frac{\sqrt{2}}{2}\right)$. **1562.** At $t=k\pi$.

1563. $\frac{3}{4}a$. **1566.** $a=3, b=-3, c=1$.

1567. $y=-x^5-0.6x^4+4.5x^3+0.1x^2$.

1568. $\xi=x-\frac{[1+n^2x^{2(n-1)}]x}{n-1}, \eta=x^n+\frac{1+n^2x^{2(n-1)}}{n(n-1)x^{n-2}}$.

1569. $\xi=\frac{(a^2+b^2)x^3}{a^4}, \eta=-\frac{(a^2+b^2)y^3}{b^4}; (a\xi)^{2/3}-(b\eta)^{2/3}=(a^2+b^2)^{2/3}$.

1570. $\xi=x+3x^{1/3}y^{2/3}, \eta=y+3x^{2/3}y^{1/3}; (\xi+\eta)^{2/3}+(\xi-\eta)^{2/3}=2a^{2/3}$.

1571. $\xi=\pm\frac{4}{3}\sqrt{\frac{y}{a}}(3y+a), \eta=-\frac{9y^2+2ay}{2a}$.

1572. $\xi=-\frac{4}{3}t^3, \eta=3t^2-\frac{3}{2}, \xi^2=\frac{16}{243}\left(\eta+\frac{3}{2}\right)^3$.

1573. $\left(\frac{3\eta}{8}\right)^4+6a^2\left(\frac{3\eta}{8}\right)^2+3a^3\xi=0$. **1574.** $\xi^{2/3}+\eta^{2/3}=(2a)^{2/3}$.

1576. Yes. **1579.** $2p\left[\sqrt{\left(\frac{x+p}{3p}\right)^3}-1\right]$. **1580.** $\frac{4(a^3-b^3)}{ab}$. **1581.** $6a$.

1582*. $16a$. Transform the obtained parametric equations of the evolute to the new coordinates and parameter, putting $x=-x_1$, $y=-y_1$, $t=t_1+\pi$.

1583*. Take advantage of the relation between the length of the evolute and the increase in the curvature radius.

1584. 0.785. **1585.** 0.073. **1586.** (3.00, 2.46).

1587. (– 0.773, – 0.841). **1588.** (1.38, 4.99). **1589.** (0.57, – 3.62).

1590. 0.78. **1591.** (2.327, 0.845).

Chapter 5

1592. (1) $\int_0^3 (x^2 + 1)\,dx$; (2) $\int_a^b (e^x + 2)\,dx$; (3) $\int_0^\pi \sin x\,dx$;

(4) $\int_{-2}^2 (8 - 2x^2)\,dx$; (5) $\int_0^1 (\sqrt{x} - x^2)\,dx$; (6) $\int_1^e (\ln x - \ln^2 x)\,dx$.

1593. $20 - \dfrac{4}{n}$ and $20 + \dfrac{4}{n}$; $\alpha = \dfrac{4}{n}$, $\sigma = \dfrac{1}{5n}$.

1594. $\alpha = \dfrac{149}{600} \approx 0.248$, $\delta \approx 0.039$. **1595.** 31.5. **1596.** $10\dfrac{2}{3}$.

1597. $\dfrac{2}{3}ah = 40\text{ cm}^2$. **1598.** $10\dfrac{2}{3}$. **1599.** 8. **1600.** $21\dfrac{1}{3}$. **1601.** $2\dfrac{7}{8}$.

1602. 140 cm. **1603.** ≈ 122.6 m. **1604.** $20\dfrac{5}{6}$ cm. **1605.** 625 J. **1606.** 4 cm.

1607. (a) $m_n = \sum\limits_{i=0}^{n-1} v(\xi_i)(t_{i+1} - t_i)$, $t_0 = T_0$, $t_n = T_1$; (b) $m = \int_{T_0}^{T_1} v(t)\,dt$.

1608. (a) $\theta_n = \sum\limits_{i=0}^{n-1} \psi(\xi_i)(t_{i+1} - t_i)$, $t_0 = T_0$, $t_n = T_1$; (b) $\theta = \int_{T_0}^{T_1} \psi(t)\,dt$.

1609. $Q_n = \sum\limits_{i=0}^{n-1} I(\xi_i)(t_{i+1} - t_i)$, $t_0 = 0$, $t_n = T$; $Q = \int_0^T I(t)\,dt$.

1610. (a) $A_n = \sum\limits_{i=0}^{n-1} \varphi(\xi_i)\psi(\xi_i)(t_{i+1} - t_i)$, $t_0 = T_0$, $t_n = T_1$; (b) $A = \int_{T_0}^{T_1} \varphi(t)\psi(t)\,dt$.

1611. 1500 C. **1612.** ≈ 67600 J. **1613.** 2880 J.

1614. (a) $P_n = \sum\limits_{i=0}^{n-1} a\xi_i(x_{i+1} - x_i)$, $x_0 = 0$, $x_n = b$; (b) $P = \int_0^b ax\,dx$.

1615. (a) $\dfrac{ab^2}{2} = 18.75$ kgf;

(b) the straight line must be drawn at a distance $\dfrac{b}{\sqrt{2}} \approx 17.7$ cm from the surface.

1616. $e - 1$. **1617.** $\dfrac{b^{k+1} - a^{k+1}}{k+1}$.

1618. (1) 50; (2) $4a$; (3) $\dfrac{7a^3}{24}$; (4) $\dfrac{7}{3}ab^2$; (5) $a\left(a^2 - \dfrac{a}{2} + 1\right)$; (6) $\dfrac{4}{3}m$;

(7) 31.5; (8) $\dfrac{(a-b)^3}{6}$; (9) $\dfrac{a^2}{3}$; (10) $\dfrac{a(a^2 - 3ab + 3b^2)}{3(a-b)^2}$; (11) 4;

(12) $16\dfrac{2}{15}$; (13) 0.

1619*. $\dfrac{1}{k+1}$; $\approx 1.67 \times 10^{11}$. Write the expression whose limit is sought for in the form of the nth integral sum of a certain function.

1620. ln 2. **1621.** ln 2. **1622*.** ln a, ln 3 ≈ 1.1. See Problems 1620 and 1621.

1623*. (1) $ae^a - e^a + 1$; (2) $a \ln a - a + 1$; (3) $\frac{(\ln b)^2 - (\ln a)^2}{2}$.

The expression $q + 2q^2 + \ldots + nq^n$ is found by differentiating the sum of terms of the geometric progression.

1624. $\int_0^{2\pi} |\sin x|\, dx = 2\int_0^{\pi} \sin x\, dx$. **1625.** $\frac{1}{2}$. **1626.** $\frac{64}{3}$. **1627.** $\frac{8}{5}$.

1630. $8 < I < 9.8$. **1631.** $3 < I < 5$. **1632.** $\pi < I < 2\pi$.

1633. $\frac{20}{29} < I < 1$. **1634.** $\frac{\pi}{9} < I < \frac{2\pi}{3}$. **1635.** $\frac{e^2 - 1}{e^{e^2 - 1}} < I < \frac{e^2 - 1}{e^2}$.

1636. (1) First, (2) second. **1637.** (1) First, (2) second, (3) first, (4) second.

1640. $0.85 < I < 0.90$.

1641. (a) $1 < I < \sqrt{2} \approx 1.414$; (b) $1 < I < \frac{1 + \sqrt{2}}{2} \approx 1.207$; (c) $1 < I \sqrt{\frac{6}{5}} \approx 1.095$.

1642. $y_{\text{mean}} = \frac{k(x_1 + x_2)}{2} + b$; $\frac{x_1 + x_2}{2}$.

1643. $y_{\text{mean}} = \frac{a}{3}(x_1^2 + x_1x_2 + x_2^2)$. If $x_1x_2 \geq 0$, then at one point; if $x_1 < 0$ and $x_2 > 0$, then at two points provided the inequalities $-\frac{x_1}{2} \leq x_2 \leq -2x_1$ are satisfied, otherwise at one.

1644. 24.5. **1645.** $\frac{\pi a}{4}$. **1646.** 0. **1647.** $\frac{2}{3}h = 1$ m. **1648.** 11 A.

1649. ~1558 W. **1650.** (1) $\frac{x^3}{3}$; (2) $\frac{x^6 - a^6}{9}$; (3) $\frac{x^4 - x^5}{20}$. **1651.** $s = \frac{2}{3}t^3$.

1652. $A = 100\,s + 25s^2$ J, s path in m.

1653. $A = \frac{1}{R}\left(\frac{\alpha^2}{3}t^3 + \alpha\beta t^2 + \beta^2 t\right)$, where $\alpha = \frac{E_2 - E_1}{t_2 - t_1}$, $\beta = \frac{E_1t_2 - E_2t_1}{t_2 - t_1}$.

1654. $Q = c_0t + \frac{\alpha}{2}t^2 + \frac{\beta}{3}t^3$. **1655.** $dS = 10$, $\Delta S = 10.10033 \ldots$ **1656.** $dS = 1$.

1657.

Δx	ΔS	dS	α	δ
1	92.25	64	28.25	0.442
0.1	6.644	6.4	0.244	0.382
0.01	0.6424	0.64	0.0024	0.00376

1658. $\frac{1}{3}$. **1659.** 0, $\frac{\sqrt{2}}{2}$, 1. **1660.** $\frac{d}{dx}\int_x^a f(x)\,dx = -f(x)$.

1661. $-1, -\frac{5}{4}$. **1662.** $\frac{\sin 2x}{x}$. **1663.** (1) x; (2) $-4x \ln x$.

1664*. $2\ln^2 2x - \ln^2 x$. Transform the integral $\int_x^{2x} \ln^2 x\, dx$ to a sum of the integrals $\int_x^a \ln^2 x\, dx + \int_a^{2x} \ln^2 x\, dx$, where $a > 0$.

1665. $y' = -\frac{\cos x}{e^y}$. **1666.** (1) $\frac{dy}{dx} = \cot t$; (2) $\frac{dy}{dx} = -t^2$. **1667.** -2.

1668. Minimum at $x = 0$. $I(0) = 0$. **1669.** 1.

1670. $y_{max} = 5/6$ at $x = 1$, $y_{min} = 2/3$ at $x = 2$. The point of inflection (3/2, 3/4).

1672. (1) $\frac{3}{4}$; (2) $-\frac{15}{32}$; (3) 52; (4) $4\frac{5}{6}$; (5) $45\frac{1}{6}$; (6) ≈ 0.08;

(7) $2-\sqrt{2}$; (8) $6\frac{2}{3}$; (9) $3\left(\frac{1}{\sqrt[3]{a}}-\frac{1}{\sqrt[3]{b}}\right)$;

(10) $\frac{z_1^2 - z_0^2}{2} - \frac{4}{3}(\sqrt{z_1^3} - \sqrt{z_0^3}) + z_1 - z_0$.

1673. (1) 2; (2) 0; (3) $e^3 - 1$; (4) 1; (5) $\pi/4$; (6) $\pi/6$.

1674. 0. **1675.** $1-\sqrt{3}$; -1.

Chapter 6

1676. $\frac{2}{3}\sqrt{x^3} + C$. **1677.** $\frac{mx^{\frac{n}{m}+1}}{n+m} + C$. **1678.** $C - \frac{1}{x}$.

1679. $\approx 0.4343 \times 10^x + C$. **1680.** $\frac{(ae)^x}{1+\ln a} + C$. **1681.** $\sqrt{x} + C$. **1682.** $\sqrt{\frac{2h}{g}} + C$.

1683. $\approx 4.1\, x^{0.83} + C$. **1684.** $u - u^2 + C$. **1685.** $\frac{2}{5}x^2\sqrt{x} + x + C$.

1686. $C - \frac{2}{3x\sqrt{x}} - e^x + \ln|x|$. **1687.** $C - 10x^{-0.2} + 15x^{0.2} - 3.62x^{1.38}$.

1688. $z - 2\ln|z| - \frac{1}{z} + C$. **1689.** $\frac{2x^2 - 12x - 6}{3\sqrt{x}} + C$.

1690. $\frac{3}{2}\sqrt[3]{x^2} + \frac{18}{7}x\sqrt[6]{x} + \frac{9}{5}x\sqrt[3]{x^2} + \frac{6}{13}x^2\sqrt[6]{x} + C$. **1691.** $\frac{6}{7}\sqrt[6]{x^7} - \frac{4}{3}\sqrt[4]{x^3} + C$.

1692. $\frac{1}{\sqrt{3}}\arcsin x + C$. **1693.** $3x - \frac{2\,(1.5)^x}{\ln 1.5} + C$. **1694.** $\frac{1}{2}(\tan x + x) + C$.

1695. $C - \cot x - \tan x$. **1696.** $\tan x - x + C$. **1697.** $C - \cot x - x$.

1698. $x - \sin x + C$. **1699.** $\arctan x - \frac{1}{x} + C$.

1700. $\ln|x| + 2\arctan x + C$. **1701.** $\tan x + C$. **1702.** $\frac{\pi}{2}x + C$.

1703. $\frac{\sin^2 x}{2} + C$. **1704.** $\frac{\tan^4 x}{4} + C$. **1705.** $2\sqrt{1+x^2} + C$.

1706. $\frac{(x+1)^{16}}{16} + C$. **1707.** $C - \frac{1}{8(2x-3)^4}$. **1708.** $\frac{(a+bx)^{1-c}}{b(1-c)} + C$.

1709. $C - \frac{5}{33}(8-3x)^{11/5}$. **1710.** $C - \frac{\sqrt{(8-2x)^3}}{3}$. **1711.** $\frac{3m}{b}\sqrt[3]{a+bx} + C$.

1712. $\frac{2}{3}\sqrt{(x^2+1)^3} + C$. **1713.** $C - \frac{1}{3}\sqrt{(1-x^2)^3}$. **1714.** $\frac{5}{18}\sqrt[5]{(x^3+2)^6} + C$.

1715. $\sqrt{x^2+1} + C$. **1716.** $\frac{2}{5}\sqrt{4+x^5} + C$. **1717.** $\frac{3}{8}\sqrt[3]{(x^4+1)^2} + C$.

1718. $\sqrt{3x^2 - 5x + 6} + C$. **1719.** $\frac{1}{4}\sin^4 x + C$.

1720. $\sec x + C$. **1721.** $3\sqrt[3]{\sin x} + C$. **1722.** $C - \frac{2}{5}\cos^5 x$. **1723.** $\frac{2}{3}\sqrt{(\ln x)^3} + C$.

1724. $\frac{(\arctan x)^3}{3} + C$. **1725.** $C - \frac{1}{2(\arcsin x)^2}$. **1726.** $2\sqrt{1 + \tan x} + C$.

1727. $\sin 3x + C$. **1728.** $\tan(1 + \ln x) + C$. **1729.** $\frac{1}{3}\sin 3x + C$.

1730. $x\cos\alpha - \frac{1}{2}\sin 2x + C$. **1731.** $C - \frac{1}{2}\cos(2x - 3)$. **1732.** $C - \frac{1}{2}\sin(1 - 2x)$.

1733. $\frac{1}{2}\tan\left(2x - \frac{\pi}{4}\right) + C$ or $\frac{1}{2}(\tan 4x - \sec 4x) + C$.

1734. $C - \cos(e^x)$. **1735.** $\ln(1 + x^2) + C$. **1736.** $\ln|\arcsin x| + C$.

1737. $\ln(x^2 - 3x + 8) + C$. **1738.** $\frac{1}{2}\ln|2x - 1| + C$. **1739.** $\frac{1}{c}\ln|cx + m| + C$.

1740. $\frac{1}{2}\ln(x^2 + 1) + C$. **1741.** $\frac{1}{2}\ln|x^3 + 1| + C$. **1742.** $\ln(e^x + 1) + C$.

1743. $\frac{1}{2}\ln(e^{2x} + a^2) + C$. **1744.** $C - \ln|\cos x|$. **1745.** $\ln|\sin x| + C$.

1746. $C - \frac{1}{3}\ln|\cos 3x|$. **1747.** $\frac{1}{2}\ln|\sin(2x + 1)| + C$. **1748.** $C - \ln(1 + \cos^2 x)$.

1749. $\ln|\ln x| + C$. **1750.** $\frac{\ln^{m+1} x}{m + 1} + C$ if $m \neq -1$ and $\ln|\ln x| + C$ if $m = -1$.

1751. $e^{\sin x} + C$. **1752.** $e^{\sin x} + C$. **1753.** $\frac{a^{3x}}{3\ln a} + C$.

1754. $C - \frac{a^{-x}}{\ln a}$. **1755.** $C - \frac{e^{1-3x}}{3}$. **1756.** $0.5e^{x^2} + C$.

1757. $C - \frac{1}{3}e^{-x^3}$. **1758.** $\arcsin\frac{x}{3} + C$. **1759.** $\frac{1}{5}\arcsin 5x + C$.

1760. $\frac{1}{3}\arctan 3x + C$. **1761.** $\arcsin\frac{x}{2} + C$.

1762. $\frac{1}{3\sqrt{2}}\arctan\frac{\sqrt{2}}{3}x + C$. **1763.** $\frac{1}{3}\arcsin\frac{3x}{2} + C$.

1764. $\frac{1}{2}\arctan x^2 + C$. **1765.** $\frac{1}{2}\arcsin\frac{x^2}{a} + C$. **1766.** $\frac{1}{6}\arctan\frac{x^3}{2} + C$.

1767. $\frac{1}{4}\arcsin x^4 + C$. **1768.** $\frac{1}{2}\arctan\frac{e^x}{2} + C$. **1769.** $\frac{\arcsin 2^x}{\ln 2} + C$.

1770. $\frac{1}{a}\arctan\frac{\sin\alpha}{a} + C$. **1771.** $e^x + e^{-x} + C$.

1772. $\frac{1}{3}e^{3x} + \frac{3}{2}e^{2x} + 3e^x + x + C$. **1773.** $\arcsin x - \sqrt{1 - x^2} + C$.

1774. $\frac{3}{2}\ln(x^2 + 9) - \frac{1}{3}\arctan\frac{x}{3} + C$. **1775.** $\arcsin x + \sqrt{1 - x^2} + C$.

1776. $\frac{1}{2}\arctan x^2 - \frac{1}{4}\ln(x^4 + 1) + C$. **1777.** $\arcsin x + \frac{1}{\sqrt{1 - x^2}} + C$.

1778. $\frac{2}{3}[x^3 - \sqrt{(x^2 - 1)^3}] - x + C$. **1779.** $C - 2\sqrt{1 - x^2} - \frac{2}{3}\sqrt{(\arcsin x)^3}$.

1780. $C - \frac{1}{9}[\sqrt{1-9x^2} + (\arccos 3x)^3]$. **1781.** $x - 4\ln|x+4| + C$.
1782. $\frac{1}{2}\left[x - \frac{1}{2}\ln|2x+1|\right] + C$. **1783.** $\frac{A}{b}\left[x - \frac{a}{b}|bx+a|\right] + C$.
1784. $C - x - 6\ln|3-x|$. **1785.** $2x + 3\ln|x-2| + C$.
1786. $\frac{1}{2}x + \frac{5}{4}\ln|2x-1| + C$. **1787.** $x + \ln(x^2+1) + C$.
1788. $x - 2\arctan x + C$. **1789.** $C - \frac{1}{4}x^4 - \frac{1}{3}x^3 - \frac{1}{2}x^2 - x - \ln|1-x|$.
1790. $\frac{x^3}{3} - x + \arctan x + C$. **1791.** $\ln\left|\frac{x-1}{x}\right| + C$. **1792.** $\ln\left|\frac{x}{x+1}\right| + C$.
1793. $\frac{1}{5}\ln\left|\frac{2x-3}{x+1}\right| + C$. **1794.** $\frac{1}{b-a}\ln\left|\frac{b-x}{a-x}\right| + C$.
1795. $x + \ln\left|\frac{x-1}{x+1}\right| + C$. **1796.** $\frac{1}{3}\ln\left|\frac{x-5}{x-2}\right| + C$. **1797.** $\frac{1}{7}\ln\left|\frac{x-2}{x+5}\right| + C$.
1798. $\frac{1}{12}\ln\left|\frac{2x-3}{2x+3}\right| + C$. **1799.** $\frac{1}{2\sqrt{6}}\ln\left|\frac{\sqrt{2}+x\sqrt{3}}{\sqrt{2}-x\sqrt{3}}\right| + C$.
1800. $\frac{1}{2}\arctan\frac{x-1}{2} + C$. **1801.** $\frac{1}{\sqrt{2}}\arctan\frac{x+1}{\sqrt{2}} + C$.
1802. $\frac{2}{3}\arctan\frac{1-2x}{3} + C$. **1803.** $\frac{1}{4}\arctan\frac{2x+1}{2} + C$.
1804. $\frac{1}{2}\arcsin(2x+3) + C$. **1805.** $\arcsin(x-2) + C$.
1806. $\frac{1}{3}\arcsin\frac{3x-1}{3} + C$. **1807.** $\frac{1}{3}\arcsin\frac{3x+1}{\sqrt{3}} + C$.
1808. $\frac{x}{2} + \frac{\sin 2x}{4} + C$. **1809.** $\frac{x}{2} - \frac{\sin 2x}{4} + C$. **1810.** $C - \cot\frac{x}{2}$.
1811. $\tan\left(\frac{x}{2} - \frac{\pi}{4}\right) + C$. **1812.** $2\tan\frac{x}{2} - x + C$.
1813. $2\tan\left(\frac{x}{2} + \frac{\pi}{4}\right) - x + C$. **1814.** $\frac{1}{3}\tan^3 x + C$.
1815. $\ln(2 + \sin 2x) + C$. **1816.** $C - \frac{1}{4}\left(\frac{\cos 4x}{2} + \cos 2x\right)$.
1817. $\frac{1}{10}\sin 5x + \frac{1}{2}\sin x + C$. **1818.** $\frac{1}{6}\sin 3x - \frac{1}{14}\sin 7x + C$.
1819. $\frac{1}{8}\left(2x + \sin 2x + \frac{1}{2}\sin 4x + \frac{1}{3}\sin 6x\right) + C$. **1820.** $\ln\left|\tan\left(\frac{\pi}{4} + \frac{x}{2}\right)\right| + C$.
1821. $\ln(1 + \sin x) + C$. **1822.** $\frac{\cos^2 x}{2} - \ln|\cos x| + C$. **1823.** $\frac{1}{\sin x} - \frac{1}{3\sin^3 x} + C$.
1824. $2\sqrt{\cos\alpha}\left(\frac{\cos^2\alpha}{5} - 1\right) + C$. **1825.** $\tan x + \frac{1}{3}\tan^3 x + C$.
1826. $\sin x - \frac{\sin^3 x}{3} + C$. **1827.** $\frac{1}{3}\tan^3 x - \tan x + x + C$.
1828. $C - \cos x + \frac{2}{3}\cos^3 x - \frac{1}{5}\cos^5 x$. **1829.** $\frac{3}{8}x - \frac{1}{4}\sin 2x + \frac{1}{32}\sin 4x + C$.
1830. $\frac{1}{2}\tan^2 x + \ln|\cos x| + C$. **1831.** $C - \cot x - \frac{2}{3}\cot^3 x - \frac{1}{5}\cos^5 x$.

1832. $\frac{1}{4}\sin 2x - \frac{1}{2}x\cos 2x + C$. **1833.** $x\sin x + \cos x + C$. **1834.** $C - e^{-x}(x+1)$.

1835. $\frac{3x}{\ln^2 3}(x\ln 3 - 1) + C$. **1836.** $\frac{x^{n+1}}{n+1}\left(\ln x - \frac{1}{n+1}\right) + C$.

1837. $\frac{x^2+1}{2}\arctan x - \frac{x}{2} + C$. **1838.** $x\arccos x - \sqrt{1-x^2} + C$.

1839. $x\arctan\sqrt{x} - \sqrt{x} + \arctan\sqrt{x} + C$.

1840. $2\sqrt{x+1}\arcsin x + 4\sqrt{1-x} + C$. **1841.** $x\tan x - \frac{x^2}{2} + \ln|\cos x| + C$.

1842. $\frac{x^2}{4} + \frac{1}{4}x\sin 2x + \frac{1}{8}\cos 2x + C$. **1843.** $C - \frac{1}{2x^2}\log(x\sqrt{e})$.

1844. $\sqrt{1+x^2}\arctan x - \ln(x + \sqrt{1+x^2}) + C$.

1845. $2(\sqrt{x} - \sqrt{1-x}\arcsin\sqrt{x}) + C$. **1846.** $x\ln(x^2+1) - 2x + 2\arctan x + C$.

1847. $C - \frac{x}{2(1+x^2)} + \frac{1}{2}\arctan x$. **1848.** $x^2\sqrt{1+x^2} - \frac{2}{3}\sqrt{(1+x^2)^3} + C$.

1849. $\frac{(x^3+1)\ln(1+x)}{2} - \frac{x^3}{9} + \frac{x^2}{6} - \frac{x}{3} + C$. **1850.** $C - e^{-x}(2 + 2x + x^2)$.

1851. $e^x(x^3 - 3x^2 + 6x - 6) + C$. **1852.** $a^x\left(\frac{x^2}{\ln a} - \frac{2x}{\ln^2 a} + \frac{2}{\ln^3 a}\right) + C$.

1853. $C - x^3\cos x + 3x^2\sin x + 6x\cos x - 6\sin x$.

1854. $\frac{1}{6}x^3 + \frac{1}{4}x^2\sin 2x + \frac{1}{4}x\cos 2x - \frac{1}{8}\sin 2x + C$.

1855. $x(\ln^2 x - 2\ln x + 2) + C$. **1856.** $C - \frac{1}{x}(\ln^3 x + 3\ln^2 x + 6\ln x + 6)$.

1857. $C - \frac{8}{27\sqrt{x^3}}\left(\frac{9}{x}\ln^2 x + 3\ln x + 2\right)$.

1858. $x(\arcsin x)^2 + 2\arcsin x\cdot\sqrt{1-x^2} - 2x + C$.

1859. $\frac{x^2+1}{2}(\arctan x)^2 - x\arctan x + \frac{1}{2}\ln(1+x^2) + C$.

1860. $\frac{e^x(\sin x - \cos x)}{2} + C$. **1861.** $\frac{e^{3x}}{13}(\sin 2x - 5\cos 2x) + C$.

1862. $\frac{e^{ax}}{a^2+n^2}(n\sin nx + a\cos nx) + C$. **1863.** $\frac{x}{2}(\sin\ln x - \cos\ln x) + C$.

1864. $\frac{x}{2}(\cos\ln x + \sin\ln x) + C$.

1865*. $C - \frac{x}{2}\sqrt{1-x^2} + \frac{1}{2}\arcsin x$. (Put $dv = \frac{x\,dx}{\sqrt{1-x^2}}$ and then, reduce $\int\sqrt{1-x^2}\,dx$ to the form $\int\frac{1-x^2}{\sqrt{1-x^2}}\,dx$.)

1866*. $\frac{x}{2}\sqrt{a^2+x^2} + \frac{a^2}{2}\ln(x + \sqrt{a^2+x^2}) + C$. (Put $u = \sqrt{a^2+x^2}$.)

1867. $\frac{x-2}{x+2}e^x + C$. **1868.** $\frac{1}{2}[(x^2-1)\sin x - (x-1)^2\cos x]e^x + C$.

1869. $2[\sqrt{x+1} - \ln(1 + \sqrt{x+1})] + C$.

1870. $\frac{2\sqrt{x-1}}{35}(5x^3 + 6x^2 + 8x + 16) + C$. **1871.** $C - \frac{11}{2(x-2)^2} - \frac{4}{x-2}$.

1872. $\ln\left|\dfrac{\sqrt{x+1}-1}{\sqrt{x+1}+1}\right| + C.$ **1873.** $2\sqrt{x-2} + \sqrt{2}\arctan\sqrt{\dfrac{x-2}{2}} + C.$

1874. $2[\sqrt{x} - \ln(1+\sqrt{x})] + C.$ **1875.** $2\arctan\sqrt{x} + C.$

1876. $2(\sqrt{x} - \arctan\sqrt{x}) + C.$

1877. $\dfrac{3}{2}(x+1)^{2/3} - 3(x+1)^{1/3} + 3\ln|1+\sqrt[3]{x+1}| + C.$

1878. $\dfrac{2}{a}[\sqrt{ax+b} - m\ln|\sqrt{ax+b}+m|] + C.$

1879. $x + \dfrac{6\sqrt[6]{x^5}}{5} + \dfrac{3\sqrt[3]{x^2}}{2} + 2\sqrt{x} + 3\sqrt[3]{x} + 6\sqrt[6]{x} + 6\ln|\sqrt[6]{x}-1| + C.$

1880. $3\sqrt[3]{x} + 3\ln|\sqrt[3]{x}-1| + C.$ **1881.** $2\sqrt{x} - 4\sqrt[4]{x} + 4\ln(1+\sqrt[4]{x}) + C.$

1882. $\dfrac{6}{5}[\sqrt[6]{x^5} + 2\sqrt[12]{x^5} + 2\ln|\sqrt[12]{x^5}-1|] + C.$

1883. $\dfrac{4}{21}(3e^x - 4)\sqrt[4]{(e^x+1)^3} + C.$ **1884.** $\ln\dfrac{\sqrt{1+e^x}-1}{\sqrt{1+e^x}+1} + C.$

1885. $2\sqrt{1+\ln x} - \ln|\ln x| + 2\ln|\sqrt{1+\ln x}-1| + C.$

1886. $0.4\sqrt{(1+\cos^2 x)^3}\,(3 - 2\cos^2 x) + C.$

1887. $\dfrac{1}{2}\ln^2(\tan x) + C.$ **1888.** $C - \dfrac{2}{9}\sqrt{a^3 - x^3}\,(2a^3 + x^3).$

1889. $\dfrac{x^2-4}{2} + \dfrac{8}{x^2-4} + 4\ln|x^2-4| + C.$ **1890.** $C - \dfrac{\sqrt{x^2+a^2}}{a^2 x}.$

1891. $\dfrac{a^2}{2}\arcsin\dfrac{x}{a} - \dfrac{x}{2}\sqrt{a^2-x^2} + C.$ **1892.** $C - \dfrac{1}{a}\arcsin\dfrac{a}{|x|}.$

1893. $C - \dfrac{\sqrt{(1+x^2)^3}}{3x^3}.$ **1894.** $C - \dfrac{\sqrt{1-x^2}}{x} - \arcsin x.$

1895. $\dfrac{x}{a^2\sqrt{x^2+a^2}} + C.$ **1896.** $C - \dfrac{\sqrt{(9-x^2)^5}}{45x^5}.$ **1897.** $\dfrac{\sqrt{x^2-9}}{9x} + C.$

1898. $\ln\dfrac{|x|}{1+\sqrt{x^2+1}} + C.$ **1899.** $C - \dfrac{x}{a^2\sqrt{x^2-a^2}}.$

1900. $\dfrac{x}{4}(x^2-2)\sqrt{4-x^2} + 2\arcsin\dfrac{x}{2} + C.$

1901. $\dfrac{1}{4\sqrt{15}}\ln\left|\dfrac{x\sqrt{15}+2\sqrt{4x^2+1}}{x\sqrt{15}-2\sqrt{4x^2+1}}\right| + C.$

1902*. $\arccos\dfrac{1}{|x|} - \dfrac{\sqrt{x^2-1}}{x} + C.$ (The substitution $x = \dfrac{1}{z}$ is useful.)

1903*. $2\arcsin\sqrt{x} + C.$ (The substitution $x = \sin^2 z$ is useful.)

1904*. $\ln\left|\dfrac{xe^x}{1+xe^x}\right| + C.$ (Multiply both the numerator and denominator by e^x and put $xe^x = z$.)

1905. $2e^{\sqrt{x}}(\sqrt{x}-1) + C.$ **1906.** $3[(2-\sqrt[3]{x^2})\cos\sqrt[3]{x} + 2\sqrt[3]{x}\sin\sqrt[3]{x}] + C.$

1907. $\frac{x \arcsin x}{\sqrt{1-x^2}} + \frac{1}{2}\ln(1-x^2) + C.$

1908. $x \arctan x - \frac{1}{2}\ln(1+x^2) - \frac{1}{2}(\arctan x)^2 + C.$

1909. $\ln\frac{|x|}{\sqrt{1+x^2}} - \frac{1}{x}\arctan x - \frac{1}{2}(\arctan x)^2 + C.$

1910. $\frac{1}{3}\sqrt{(x^2+2x)^3} + C.$ **1911.** $\frac{1}{9}(1+e^{3x})^3 + C.$ **1912.** $2e^{\sqrt{x}} + C.$

1913. $e^{-\cos x} + C.$ **1914.** $C - \frac{2}{3}(1-e^x)^{3/2}.$ **1915.** $\frac{1}{2}\sin x^2 + C.$

1916. $C - \frac{5}{24}(2-3x^{4/3})^{6/5}.$ **1917.** $C - \frac{1}{3}\ln|1+3x^3-x^6|.$

1918. $\frac{2}{3}\ln(1+x^{3/2}) + C.$ **1919.** $C - \ln(3+e^{-x}).$ **1920.** $C - \arcsin e^{-x}.$

1921. $2\sqrt{1+x^2} + 3\ln(x+\sqrt{1+x^2}) + C.$

1922. $\frac{1}{9}[2\sqrt{9x^2-4} - 3\ln|3x+\sqrt{9x^2-4}|] + C.$ **1923.** $2\sin\sqrt{x} + C.$

1924. $\arcsin\frac{\ln x}{\sqrt{3}} + C.$ **1925.** $C - \frac{1}{2}\ln|1-\ln^2 x|.$

1926. $\frac{1}{\sqrt{x^2+1}} + \ln(x+\sqrt{x^2+1}) + C.$

1927. $\frac{(\arctan x)^{n+1}}{n+1} + C$ if $n \neq -1$ and $\ln|\arctan x|$ if $n = -1.$

1928. $C - 2\cot 2\varphi.$ **1929.** $2x - \tan x + C.$ **1930.** $\frac{1}{5}\tan^5 x + C.$

1931. $\frac{2}{45}\sqrt{\tan^5 x}\,(5\tan^2 x + 9) + C.$ **1932.** $\frac{1}{3}[\tan 3x + \ln(\cos^2 3x)] + C.$

1933. $\frac{x^3}{3} - \frac{x^2}{2} + x - \ln|x+1| + C.$ **1934.** $C - \frac{1}{x-1} - \frac{1}{2(x-1)^2}.$

1935. $\frac{\sqrt{2+4x}\,(x-1)}{6} + C.$ **1936.** $x\sqrt{1+2x} - \frac{1}{3}\sqrt{(1+2x)^3} + C.$

1937. $\frac{2}{15}(3x-2a)\sqrt{(a+x)^3} + C.$

1938. $\frac{x}{2} + \frac{1}{4}\sin 2x + \frac{4}{3}\sqrt{\sin^3 x} - \cos x + C.$ **1939.** $\frac{a^{mx}b^{nx}}{m\ln a + n\ln b} + C.$

1940. $C - \ln(1-x+\sqrt{5-2x+x^2}).$

1941. $\frac{1}{3}\ln(3x-1+\sqrt{9x^2-6x+2}) + C.$ **1942.** $\frac{1}{3}\arcsin\frac{3x-2}{\sqrt{2}} + C.$

1943. $C - 8\sqrt{5+2x-x^2} - 3\arcsin\frac{x-1}{\sqrt{6}}.$

1944. $\frac{1}{2}\ln(x^2+2x+2) + \arctan(x+1) + C.$

1945. $C - \sqrt{3-2x-x^2} - 4\arcsin\frac{x+1}{2}.$

1946. $\frac{3}{8}\left[\ln(4x^2-4x+17)+\frac{1}{6}\arctan\frac{2x-1}{4}\right]+C.$

1947. $3\sqrt{x^2+2x+2}-4\ln(x+1+\sqrt{x^2+2x+2})+C.$ **1948.** $\ln\frac{(x-4)^2}{|x-3|}+C.$

1949. $\frac{2}{9}\sqrt{9x^2+6x+2}+\frac{13}{9}\ln(3x+1+\sqrt{9x^2+6x+2})+C.$

1950. $C-\ln|2x^2-3x+1|.$

1951. $\frac{29}{45}\arctan\frac{5x+3}{9}-\frac{3}{10}\ln(5x^2+6x+18)+C.$

1952. $\frac{61}{16}\ln|8x+9+4\sqrt{4x^2+9x+1}|-\frac{5}{4}\sqrt{4x^2+9x+1}+C.$

1953. $\frac{1}{3}\sqrt{3x^2-11x+3}+\frac{11}{6\sqrt{3}}\ln\left|x-\frac{11}{6}+\sqrt{x^2-\frac{11}{3}x+\frac{2}{3}}\right|+C.$

1954. $\frac{1}{2}\sqrt{2x^2+3x}-\frac{3}{4\sqrt{2}}\ln\left(x+\frac{3}{4}\sqrt{x^2+\frac{3x}{2}}\right)+C.$

1955. $\sqrt{(a-x)(x-b)}-(a-b)\arctan\sqrt{\frac{a-x}{x-b}}+C.$

1956. $x\arctan x-\frac{1}{2}\ln(1+x^2)+C.$ **1957.** $\frac{1}{8}\sin 2x-\frac{1}{4}x\cos 2x+C.$

1958. $\frac{1}{\omega^3}[(\omega^2x^2-2)\sin\omega x+2\omega x\cos\omega x]+C.$

1959. $e^{2x}\left(\frac{1}{2}x^3-\frac{3}{4}x^2+\frac{3}{4}x-\frac{3}{8}\right)+C.$

1960. $\tan x\cdot\ln(\cos x)+\tan x-x+C.$ **1961.** $\ln|\ln(\sin x)|+C.$

1962. $\frac{1}{4}\left[\ln(1+x^4)+\frac{1}{1+x^4}\right]+C.$ **1963.** $\frac{1}{3}\left(\ln\left|\tan\frac{3x}{2}\right|+\cos 3x\right)+C.$

1964. $\frac{1}{3}\tan\left(\frac{\pi}{4}+\frac{3x}{2}\right)+C.$ **1965.** $C-\frac{1}{8}\ln\frac{2+\cos 2x}{2-\cos 2x}.$

1966. $\ln\frac{e^x}{e^x+1}+C.$ **1967.** $2\ln(e^{x/2}+e^{-x/2})+C.$

1968. $e^{e^x}+C.$ **1969.** $\frac{1}{4}e^{2x^2}+C.$

1970. $\frac{1}{\sqrt{2}}[3\ln(x+\sqrt{1+x^2})+\frac{1}{3}(x^2-2)\sqrt{1+x^2}]+C.$

1971. $x-\sqrt{1-x^2}\arcsin x+C.$ **1972.** $C-\frac{1}{2}\left(\frac{x}{\sin^2 x}+\cot x\right).$

1973. $\frac{e^x}{2}\left(1-\frac{2\sin 2x+\cos 2x}{5}\right)+C.$ **1974.** $\frac{1}{2}(\tan x+\ln|\tan x|)+C.$

1975. $\ln|\sin x+\cos x|+C.$ **1976.** $\frac{1}{2}\ln\left|\tan\left(\frac{\varphi}{2}+\frac{\pi}{6}\right)\right|+C.$

1977. $\sec x-\tan x+x+C.$ **1978.** $\sin x-\arctan\sin x+C.$

1979. $\sqrt{2}\ln\left|\tan\frac{x}{4}\right|+C.$ **1980.** $\ln x\cdot\ln(\ln x)-\ln x+C.$

1981. $\dfrac{e^{x^2}(x^2-1)}{2}+C.$ **1982.** $C-\dfrac{1}{2}e^{-x^2}(x^4+2x^2+2).$

1983. $\dfrac{1}{6}(x^2-1)\sqrt{1+2x^2}+C.$ **1984.** $C-\dfrac{x(x^2-3)}{2\sqrt{1-x^2}}-\dfrac{3}{2}\arcsin x.$

1985. $\dfrac{1}{5}\sqrt{(x^2-a^2)^5}-\dfrac{a^2}{3}\sqrt{(x^2-a^2)^3}+a^4\sqrt{x^2-a^2}+a^5\arcsin\dfrac{a}{|x|}+C.$

1986. $\dfrac{\sqrt{4+x^2}\,(x^2-2)}{24x^3}+C.$ **1987.** $\dfrac{\sqrt{(x^2-8)^3}}{24x^3}+C.$

1988. $\dfrac{\sqrt{(4+x^2)^3}\,(x^2-6)}{120x^5}+C.$ **1989.** $\dfrac{\sqrt{x^2-3}\,(2x^2+3)}{27x^3}+C.$

1990. $\dfrac{4}{3}[\sqrt[4]{x^3}-\ln(\sqrt[4]{x^3}+1)]+C.$

1991. $x+4\sqrt{x+1}+4\ln(\sqrt{1+x}-1)+C.$ **1992.** $2\arctan\sqrt{1+x}+C.$

1993. $\ln\dfrac{x}{(\sqrt[6]{x}+1)^6}+C.$ **1994.** $\sqrt{x^2+2x}+\ln|x+1+\sqrt{x^2+2x}|+C.$

1995*. $\dfrac{x^8}{8(1-x^2)^4}+C.$ (The substitution $x=\sin u$ is useful.)

1996. $\dfrac{2}{\sqrt{ab}}\arctan\sqrt{\dfrac{ax}{b}}+C.$ **1997.** $C-\dfrac{(1+x^8)^{3/2}}{12x^{12}}.$ **1998.** $\dfrac{x^2}{2\sqrt{1-x^4}}+C.$

1999. $\dfrac{1}{4}x^2\sqrt{x^4+4}-\ln(x^2+\sqrt{x^4+4})+C.$ **2000.** $\ln\left|\dfrac{\sqrt{x}-1}{\sqrt{x}+1}\right|+C.$

2001. $C-\dfrac{2}{3}\sqrt{\dfrac{1-x^3}{x^3}}-\dfrac{2}{3}\arcsin\sqrt{x^3}.$

2002. $C-\dfrac{x^3}{4(1+x^2)^2}-\dfrac{3x}{8(1+x^2)}+\dfrac{3\arctan x}{8}.$

2003. $\dfrac{(x^2+1)\arctan x}{\sqrt{x}}-2\sqrt{x}+C.$ **2004.** $\arcsin e^x-\sqrt{1-e^{2x}}+C.$

2005. $2\sqrt{e^x-1}-2\arctan\sqrt{e^x-1}+C.$

2006*. $C-\dfrac{1}{2}\ln^2\left(1+\dfrac{1}{x}\right)$ $\left(\text{use the substitution } u=1+\dfrac{1}{x}.\right)$

2007. $\arctan x+\dfrac{1}{x}-\dfrac{1}{3x^3}+C.$

2008. $x\arccos\sqrt{\dfrac{x}{x+1}}+\sqrt{x}-\arctan\sqrt{x}+C.$

2009. $x\ln(x+\sqrt{1+x^2})-\sqrt{1+x^2}+C.$ **2010.** $\dfrac{3}{55}\sqrt[3]{\tan^5 x}\,(5\tan^2 x+11)+C.$

2011. $\dfrac{\sqrt{2}}{5}(\tan^2 x+5)\sqrt{\tan x}+C.$ **2012.** $\ln\dfrac{|x+1|}{\sqrt{2x+1}}+C.$

2013. $\dfrac{1}{5}\ln[(x-2)^2\sqrt{2x+1}]+C.$ **2014.** $\ln\left|\dfrac{(x-1)^4(x-4)^5}{(x+3)^7}\right|+C.$

2015. $\dfrac{3}{11}\ln|3x+1|+\dfrac{2}{33}\ln|2x-3|-\dfrac{1}{3}\ln|x|+C.$

2016. $\frac{x^3}{3} + \frac{x^2}{2} + 4x + \ln\left|\frac{x^2(x-2)^5}{(x+2)^3}\right| + C.$

2017. $\frac{1}{4}x + \ln|x| - \frac{7}{16}\ln|2x-1| - \frac{9}{16}\ln|2x+1| + C.$

2018. $\ln|2x-1| - 6\ln|2x-3| + 5\ln|2x-5| + C.$

2019. $\ln\sqrt{\frac{x^2-2}{x^2-1}} + C.$ **2020.** $\frac{1}{2\sqrt{2}}\ln\left|\frac{x-\sqrt{2}}{x+\sqrt{2}}\right| + \frac{1}{2\sqrt{3}}\left|\frac{x-\sqrt{3}}{x+\sqrt{3}}\right| + C.$

2021. $\frac{x^2}{2} + \ln\left|\frac{x(x-2)\sqrt{(x-1)(x+1)^3}}{x+2}\right| + C.$ **2022.** $\ln\left|\frac{x^2}{x+1}\right| + \frac{6}{x+1} + C.$

2023. $4\ln|x| - 3\ln|x-1| - \frac{9}{x-1} + C.$ **2024.** $\frac{4}{x+2} + \ln|x+1| + C.$

2025. $x + \frac{1}{x} + \ln\frac{(x-1)^2}{|x|} + C.$ **2026.** $C - \frac{1}{3(x-2)^3} + \frac{1}{2(x-2)^2} + \ln|x-2|.$

2027. $\frac{1}{x} + \frac{1}{2}\ln\left|\frac{x-1}{x+1}\right| + C.$ **2028.** $2\ln\left|\frac{x+4}{x+2}\right| - \frac{5x+12}{x^2+6x+8} + C.$

2029. $\frac{3}{2(x-2)^2} + \ln|x-5| + C.$ **2030.** $\frac{x}{8} - \ln|x+1| - \frac{9x^2+12x+5}{3(x+1)^3} + C.$

2031. $\frac{(x+2)^2}{2} - \frac{1}{4(x-1)^2} - \frac{9}{4(x-1)} + \frac{31}{8}\ln|x-1| + \frac{1}{8}\ln|x+1| + C.$

2032. $\frac{1}{x-1} + \ln\frac{\sqrt{(x-1)(x-3)}}{|x|} + C.$

2033. $\frac{3}{2x} - \frac{5}{4}\ln|x| + 20\ln|x-3| - \frac{47}{4}\ln|x-2| + C.$

2034. $\frac{1}{4}\ln\left|\frac{x}{x-2}\right| - \frac{1}{x}\left(1 + \frac{1}{2x}\right) - \frac{1}{2(x-2)} + C.$

2035. $C - \frac{x}{(x^2-1)^2}.$ **2036.** $\ln\frac{|x|}{\sqrt{x^2+1}} + C.$

2037. $\frac{1}{6}\ln\frac{(x+1)^2}{x^2-x+1} + \frac{1}{\sqrt{3}}\arctan\frac{2x-1}{\sqrt{3}} + C.$

2038. $\frac{1}{3}\ln\frac{|x-1|}{\sqrt{x^2+x+1}} + \frac{1}{\sqrt{3}}\arctan\frac{2x+1}{\sqrt{3}} + C.$

2039. $\ln\frac{\sqrt{(x^2-2x+5)^3}}{|x-1|} + \frac{1}{2}\arctan\frac{x-1}{2} + C.$

2040. $\frac{(x+1)^2}{2} + \ln\frac{|x-1|}{\sqrt{x^2+1}} - \arctan x + C.$ **2041.** $\frac{1}{4}\ln\left|\frac{1+x}{1-x}\right| - \frac{1}{2}\arctan x + C.$

2042. $\frac{1}{4}\ln\frac{x^4}{(x+1)^2(x^2+1)} - \frac{1}{2}\arctan x + C.$

2043. $\frac{1}{2}\ln|x+1| - \frac{1}{4}\ln(x^2+1) - \frac{1}{2(x+1)} + C.$

2044. $\frac{1}{4}\left[\ln\frac{\sqrt{x^2+1}}{|x-1|} + \arctan x - \frac{7}{(x-1)^2}\right] + C.$

2045. $\frac{x^2}{2} - 2x - \frac{2}{x} + 2\ln(x^2 + 2x + 2) - 2\arctan(x+1) + C.$

2046. $\ln\frac{x^2+4}{\sqrt{x^2+2}} + \frac{3}{2}\arctan\frac{x}{2} - \frac{3\sqrt{2}}{2}\arctan\frac{x\sqrt{2}}{2} + C.$

2047*. $\frac{1}{4\sqrt{2}}\ln\frac{x^2 + x\sqrt{2} + 1}{x^2 - x\sqrt{2} + 1} + \frac{\sqrt{2}}{4}\arctan\frac{x\sqrt{2}}{1 - x^2} + C.$
(Add $2x^2$ to and subtract from the denominator of the integrand.)

2048. $\frac{2-x}{4(x^2+2)} + \frac{\ln(x^2+2)}{2} - \frac{1}{4\sqrt{2}}\arctan\frac{x}{\sqrt{2}} + C.$

2049. $\frac{1}{16}\ln|x| - \frac{1}{18}\ln(x^2+1) + \frac{7}{288}\ln(x^2+4) - \frac{1}{24(x^2+4)} + C.$

2050. $\frac{13x - 159}{8(x^2 - 6x + 13)} + \frac{53}{16}\arctan\frac{x-3}{2} + C.$

2051. $\frac{3}{8}\arctan(x+1) - \frac{5x^3 + 15x^2 + 18x + 8}{8(x^2 + 2x + 2)^2} + C.$

2052. $\frac{x}{216(x^2+9)} + \frac{x}{36(x^2+9)^2} + \frac{1}{648}\arctan\frac{x}{3} + C.$

2053. $\frac{x-1}{2(x^2+1)} - \frac{1}{2}\ln|x+1| + \frac{1}{4}\ln(1+x^2) + C.$

2054. $\frac{15x^5 + 40x^3 + 33x}{48(1+x^2)^3} + \frac{15}{48}\arctan x + C.$

2055. $\frac{1}{4}\left(\frac{2x^6 - 3x^2}{x^4 - 1} + \frac{3}{2}\ln\left|\frac{x^2-1}{x^2+1}\right|\right) + C.$

2056. $\frac{x}{x^2+x+1} + \frac{2}{\sqrt{3}}\arctan\frac{2x+1}{\sqrt{3}} - 2\ln(x^2+x+1) + \frac{x^4}{4} - \frac{2x^3}{3} + \frac{x^2}{2} + 2x + C.$ **2057.** $\frac{3x^2 - x}{(x-1)(x^2+1)} + \ln\frac{(x-1)^2}{x^2+1} + \arctan x + C.$

2058. $C - 6\ln\left|\frac{x-1}{x}\right| - \frac{12x^2 - 5x - 1}{2(x^3 - x^2)}.$ **2059.** $\frac{1}{x^2(x^2+1)} + \ln\sqrt{x^2+1} + C.$

2060. $\frac{1}{2}\cdot\frac{1+x}{(1+x^2)^2} + \frac{1}{4}\cdot\frac{x-2}{x^2+1} + \frac{1}{4}\arctan x + C.$

2061. $\frac{2}{3}\ln\left|\frac{x^3+1}{x^3}\right| - \frac{1}{3x^3} - \frac{1}{3(x^3+1)} + C.$

2062. $\frac{1}{648}\left[\arctan\frac{x+1}{3} + \frac{3(x+1)}{x^2+2x+10} + \frac{18(x+1)}{(x^2+2x+10)^2}\right] + C.$

2063. $\frac{3}{8}\arctan(x+1) + \frac{3}{8}\cdot\frac{x+1}{x^2+2x+2} + \frac{x}{4(x^2+2x+2)^2} + C.$

2064. $C - \frac{x}{8(x^2+4)} - \frac{2x+5}{2(x^2+4x+5)} - \frac{1}{16}\arctan\frac{x}{2} - \arctan(x+2).$

2065. $C - \frac{57x^4 + 103x^2 + 32}{8x(x^2+1)^2} - \frac{57}{8}\arctan x.$

2066. $\frac{3 - 7x - 2x^2}{2(x^3 - x^2 - x + 1)} + \ln\frac{|x-1|}{(x+1)^2} + C.$

2067. $\left(-\frac{1}{2}x^4+\frac{5}{4}x^2-\frac{3}{5}\right)\frac{1}{x(3-2x^2)^2}+\frac{1}{8\sqrt{6}}\ln\left|\frac{\sqrt{3}+x\sqrt{2}}{\sqrt{3}-x\sqrt{2}}\right|+C.$

2068. $\ln\frac{x}{(1+\sqrt[10]{x})^{10}}+\frac{10}{\sqrt[10]{x}}-\frac{5}{\sqrt[5]{x}}+\frac{10}{3\sqrt[10]{x^3}}-\frac{5}{2\sqrt[5]{x^2}}+C.$

2069. $2\sqrt{x}-3\sqrt[3]{x}-8\sqrt[4]{x}+6\sqrt[6]{x}+48\sqrt[12]{x}+3\ln(1+\sqrt[12]{x})$
$+\frac{33}{2}\ln(\sqrt[6]{x}-\sqrt[12]{x}+2)-\frac{171}{\sqrt{7}}\arctan\frac{2\sqrt[12]{x}-1}{\sqrt{7}}+C.$

2070. $6\left[\frac{1}{9}(x+1)^{3/2}-\frac{1}{8}(x+1)^{4/3}+\frac{1}{7}(x+1)^{7/6}-\frac{1}{6}(x+1)\right.$
$\left.+\frac{1}{5}(x+1)^{5/6}-\frac{1}{4}(x+1)^{2/3}\right]+C.$

2071. $\ln\left|\frac{\sqrt{x+1}-\sqrt{1-x}}{\sqrt{1+x}+\sqrt{1-x}}\right|+2\arctan\sqrt{\frac{1-x}{1+x}}+C.$

2072. $(\sqrt{x}-2)\sqrt{1-x}-\arcsin\sqrt{x}+C.$

2073. $6\sqrt[3]{(1+x)^2}\left[\frac{(1+x)^2}{16}-\frac{1+x}{5}+\frac{\sqrt{1+x}}{7}+\frac{1}{4}\right]+C.$

2074. $\ln\frac{|u^2-1|}{\sqrt{u^4+u^2+1}}+\sqrt{3}\arctan\frac{1+2u^2}{\sqrt{3}}+C$, where $u=\sqrt[3]{\frac{1-x}{1+x}}$.

2075*. $\frac{4}{3}\sqrt[4]{\frac{x-1}{x+2}}+C$. Multiply both the numerator and denominator by $\sqrt[4]{x-1}$ and take the factors outside the radical.

2076. $\frac{2}{3}x\sqrt{x}+\frac{24}{11}x\sqrt[6]{x^5}+\frac{36}{13}x^2\sqrt[6]{x}+\frac{8}{5}x^2\sqrt{x}+\frac{6}{17}x^2\sqrt[6]{x^5}+C.$

2077. $3\left[\ln\left|\frac{\sqrt[3]{x}}{1+\sqrt[3]{x}}\right|+\frac{2\sqrt[3]{x}+3}{2(1+\sqrt[3]{x})^2}\right]+C.$

2078. $\frac{1}{2}\ln(\sqrt[3]{x^2+1}-1)-\frac{1}{4}\ln[\sqrt[3]{(x^2+1)^2}$
$+\sqrt[3]{x^2+1}+1]+\frac{\sqrt{3}}{2}\arctan\frac{2\sqrt[3]{x^2+1}+1}{\sqrt{3}}+C.$

2079. $\frac{1}{8}\sqrt[3]{(1+x^3)^8}-\frac{1}{5}\sqrt[3]{(1+x^3)^5}+C.$

2080. $\frac{1}{6}\ln\frac{u^2+u+1}{(u-1)^2}-\frac{1}{\sqrt{3}}\arctan\frac{2u+1}{\sqrt{3}}+C$, where $u=\frac{\sqrt[3]{x^3+1}}{x}$.

2081. $\frac{1}{4}\ln\frac{\sqrt[4]{1+x^4}+x}{\sqrt[4]{1+x^4}-x}-\frac{1}{2}\arctan\frac{\sqrt[4]{1+x^4}}{x}+C.$

2082. $\frac{1}{4}\ln\frac{\sqrt{1-x^4}+1}{x^2}-\frac{1}{4}\frac{\sqrt{1-x^4}}{x^4}+C.$

2083. $\frac{3}{7}(4\sqrt{x}+\sqrt[4]{x}-3)\sqrt[3]{1+\sqrt[4]{x}}+C.$

2084. $6u+2\ln\frac{u-1}{\sqrt{u^2+u+1}}-2\sqrt{3}\arctan\frac{2u+1}{\sqrt{3}}+C$, where $u=\sqrt[3]{1+\sqrt{x}}$.

2085. $\frac{1}{5}\ln\frac{|u-1|}{\sqrt{u^2+u+1}}+\frac{\sqrt{3}}{5}\arctan\frac{1+2u}{\sqrt{3}}+C$, where $u=\sqrt[3]{1+x^5}$.

2086. $C-\frac{\sqrt[3]{1+x^3}}{x}+\frac{1}{\sqrt{3}}\arctan\frac{2\sqrt[3]{1+x^3}+x}{x\sqrt{3}}$

$$-\frac{1}{3}\ln\left|\frac{\sqrt[3]{1+x^3}+x}{\sqrt{\sqrt[3]{(1+x^3)^2}+x\sqrt[3]{1+x^3}+x^2}}\right|.$$

2087. $C-\frac{1}{10}\sqrt{\left(\frac{1+x^4}{x^4}\right)^5}+\frac{1}{3}\sqrt{\left(\frac{1+x^4}{x^4}\right)^3}-\frac{1}{2}\sqrt{\frac{1+x^4}{x^4}}$.

2088. $\frac{u}{2(u^3+1)}-\frac{1}{6}\ln\frac{u+1}{\sqrt{u^2-u+1}}-\frac{1}{2\sqrt{3}}\arctan\frac{2u-1}{\sqrt{3}}+C$, where $u=\sqrt[3]{\frac{1-x^2}{x^2}}$.

2089. $12\left[\frac{\sqrt[3]{u^{13}}}{13}-\frac{3\sqrt[3]{u^{10}}}{10}+\frac{3\sqrt[3]{u^7}}{7}-\frac{\sqrt[3]{u^4}}{4}\right]+C$, where $u=1+\sqrt[4]{x}$.

2090. $\frac{1}{15}\cos^3 x\,(3\cos^2 x-5)+C$.

2091. $\frac{1}{3\cos^3 x}-\frac{1}{\cos x}+C$.

2092. $\ln|\tan x|-\frac{1}{2\sin^2 x}+C$.

2093. $\tan x+\frac{1}{4}\sin 2x-\frac{3}{2}x+C$.

2094. $\frac{1}{2}(\tan^2 x-\cot^2 x)+2\ln|\tan x|+C$.

2095. $\frac{(\tan^2 x-1)(\tan^4 x+10\tan^2 x+1)}{3\tan^3 x}+C$.

2096. $\frac{1}{\cos x-1}+C$.

2097. $\frac{1}{2}\cot\frac{x}{2}-\frac{1}{6}\cot^3\frac{x}{2}+C$.

2098. $\frac{5}{16}x+\frac{1}{12}\sin 2x\left(\cos^4 x+\frac{5}{4}\cos^2 x+\frac{15}{8}\right)+C$.

2099. $x-\frac{1}{3}\cot^3 x+\cot x+C$.

2100. $\frac{1}{4}\tan^4 x-\frac{1}{2}\tan^2 x-\ln|\cos x|+C$.

2101. $x-\frac{1}{7}\cot^7 x+\frac{1}{5}\cot^5 x-\frac{1}{3}\cot^3 x+\cot x+C$.

2102. $C-\frac{\cos x}{2\sin^2 x}+\frac{1}{2}\ln\left|\tan\frac{x}{2}\right|$.

2103. $\frac{1}{4}\ln\left|\frac{1+\tan x}{1-\tan x}\right|+\frac{1}{2}\sin x\cos x+C$.

2104. $C-\frac{1}{1+\tan x}$.

2105. $\frac{\sqrt{2}}{2}\ln\left|\tan\left(\frac{\pi}{8}+\frac{x}{2}\right)\right|+C$.

2106. $\frac{1}{\sqrt{a^2+b^2}}\ln\left|\tan\frac{x+\arctan\frac{a}{b}}{2}\right|+C$.

2107. $\ln\frac{|C\sin x|}{\sqrt{\cos 2x}}$.

2108. $\ln\frac{|C\sin x|}{\sqrt{1-4\sin^2 x}}$.

2109. $\frac{1}{x}(x+\ln|\sin x+\cos x|)+C$.

2110. $\frac{1}{2}\arctan\left(2\tan\frac{x}{2}\right)+C.$ **2111.** $\frac{2}{3}\arctan\frac{5\tan\frac{x}{2}+4}{3}+C.$

2112. $\ln(2+\cos x)+\frac{4}{\sqrt{3}}\arctan\left(\frac{1}{\sqrt{3}}\tan\frac{x}{2}\right)+C.$

2113. $\frac{\cos x(\cos x-\sin x)}{4}-\frac{1}{4}\ln|\cos x-\sin x|+C.$

2114. $\frac{4}{25}x-\frac{3}{25}\ln|\tan x+2|+\frac{2}{5(\tan x+2)}-\frac{3}{25}\ln|\cos x|+C.$

2115. $\frac{\cos 2x-15}{15(4+\sin 2x)}+\frac{4}{15\sqrt{15}}\arcsin\frac{4\sin 2x+1}{4+\sin 2x}+C.$

2116. $\frac{1}{2-\tan\frac{x}{2}}+C.$ **2117.** $\frac{1}{3}\arctan(3\tan x)+C.$

2118. $\frac{1}{\sqrt{2}}\arctan(\sqrt{2}\tan x)+C.$ **2119.** $\frac{1}{2}\tan x+\frac{1}{2\sqrt{2}}\arctan(\sqrt{2}\tan x)+C.$

2120. $\frac{1}{ab}\arctan\frac{a\tan x}{b}+C.$ **2121.** $C-\frac{1}{2}\left[\cot x+\frac{1}{\sqrt{2}}\arctan\left(\frac{\tan x}{\sqrt{2}}\right)\right].$

2122. $\ln\frac{|\sqrt[3]{\tan x}-1|}{\sqrt[6]{\tan^2 x+\tan x+1}}-\frac{\sqrt{3}}{3}\arctan\frac{2\tan x+1}{\sqrt{3}}+C.$

2123. $2\left(\sin\frac{x}{2}-\cos\frac{x}{2}\right)+C$, for the values of x satisfying the inequality $\sin\frac{x}{2}+\cos\frac{x}{2}\geq 0$ and $-2\left(\sin\frac{x}{2}-\cos\frac{x}{2}\right)+C$, for those satisfying the inequality $\sin\frac{x}{2}+\cos\frac{x}{2}\leq 0$.

2124. $2\sqrt{\tan x}+C.$ **2125*.** $C-\frac{4\sqrt{2}}{5}\sqrt{\cot^5 x}$. (Put, $u=\cot x$).

2126. $4\sqrt[4]{\tan x}+C.$

2127. $\frac{1}{\sqrt{2}}\ln(\sqrt{2}\tan x+\sqrt{1+2\tan^2 x})+C.$ **2128.** $2\arcsin\sqrt{\sin x}+C.$

2129. $C-\frac{1}{3}\tan x(2+\tan^2 x)\sqrt{4-\cot^2 x}.$

2130. $\frac{4}{\sqrt{\cos\frac{x}{2}}}+2\arctan\sqrt{\cos\frac{x}{2}}-\ln\frac{1+\sqrt{\cos\frac{x}{2}}}{1-\sqrt{\cos\frac{x}{2}}}+C.$

2131. $\frac{1}{\sqrt{2}}[\ln(\sin x+\cos x-\sqrt{\sin 2x})+\arcsin(\sin x-\cos x)]+C.$

2132. $\sinh x+C.$ **2133.** $\cosh x+C.$ **2134.** $\tanh x+C.$

2135. $x+C.$ **2136.** $\frac{1}{2a}\sinh 2ax+C.$ **2137.** $\frac{\sinh x\cdot\cosh x-x}{2}+C.$

2138. $x-\tanh x+C.$ **2139.** $x-\coth x+C.$

2140. $\frac{1}{3}\cosh^3 x - \cosh x + C.$ **2141.** $\sinh x + \frac{1}{3}\sinh^3 x + C.$

2142. $x - \tanh x - \frac{1}{3}\tanh^3 x + C.$ **2143.** $\frac{1}{3}\sinh^3 x + \frac{1}{5}\sinh^5 x + C.$

2144. $\ln|\sinh x| - \frac{1}{2}\coth^2 x - \frac{1}{4}\coth^4 x + C.$ **2145.** $\ln|\tanh x| + C.$

2146. $\ln\left|\tanh\frac{x}{2}\right| + C.$ **2147.** $\frac{1}{2}\tanh\frac{x}{2} - \frac{1}{6}\tanh^3\frac{x}{2} + C.$

2148. $\frac{1}{2}\ln\frac{1+\sqrt{\tanh x}}{|1-\sqrt{\tanh x}|} - \arctan\sqrt{\tanh x} + C.$

2149. $x\tanh x - \ln\cosh x + C.$ **2150.** $C - \frac{e^{3x}}{3\sinh^3 x}.$

2151*. $\ln\frac{|Cx|}{2+x+2\sqrt{x^2+x+1}}$. (Apply, for instance, the substitution $x = \frac{1}{z}$).

2152. $\frac{1}{2}\arccos\frac{2-x}{x\sqrt{2}} + C.$ **2153.** $\arcsin\frac{x-1}{x\sqrt{2}} + C.$

2154. $C - \frac{1}{\sqrt{2}}\ln\left|\frac{\sqrt{2+x-x^2}+\sqrt{2}}{x} + \frac{1}{2\sqrt{2}}\right|.$

2155. $\ln|x+1+\sqrt{2x+x^2}| - \frac{4}{x+\sqrt{2x+x^2}} + C.$

2156. $C - \frac{1}{\sqrt{3}}\ln\left|\frac{3+3x+2\sqrt{3(x^2+x+1)}}{x-1}\right|.$

2157. $C - \frac{1}{\sqrt{15}}\ln\left|\frac{x+6+\sqrt{60x-15x^2}}{2x-3}\right|.$

2158. $\frac{1}{2}(x-1)\sqrt{x^2-2x-1} - \ln|x-1+\sqrt{x^2-2x-1}| + C.$

2159. $\frac{1}{2}\left(x-\frac{1}{2}\right)\sqrt{3x^2-3x-1} + \frac{1}{8\sqrt{3}}\ln\left|\sqrt{3x^2-3x+1}+\frac{\sqrt{3}}{2}(2x-1)\right| + C.$

2160. $\frac{1}{2}\left[(x+2)\sqrt{1-4x-x^2} + 5\arcsin\frac{x+2}{\sqrt{5}}\right] + C.$

2161. $C - \frac{3}{2(2x-1-2\sqrt{x^2-x+1})} - \frac{3}{2}\ln|2x-1-2\sqrt{x^2-x+1}|$
$+ 2\ln|x-\sqrt{x^2-x+1}|.$

2162. $\ln\left|\frac{x+\sqrt{x^2+1}}{x}\right| - \frac{\sqrt{1+x^2}}{x} + C.$

2163. $\frac{1-\sqrt{x^2+2x+2}}{x+1} + \ln(x+1+\sqrt{x^2+2x+2}) + C.$

2164. $\frac{1}{2}(3-x)\sqrt{1-2x-x^2} + 2\arcsin\frac{x+1}{\sqrt{2}} + C.$

2165. $x\sqrt{x^2-2x+5} - 5\ln(x-1+\sqrt{x^2-2x+5}) + C.$

2166. $C - \frac{1}{2}(3x-19)\sqrt{3-2x-x^2} + 14\arcsin\frac{x+1}{2}.$

2167. $(x^2 - 5x + 20)\sqrt{x^2 + 4x + 5} - 15 \ln (x + 2 + \sqrt{x^2 + 4x + 5}) + C.$

2168. $\left(\frac{1}{3}x^2 - \frac{5}{6}x + \frac{1}{6}\right)\sqrt{x^2 + 2x + 2} + \frac{5}{2}\ln (x + 1 + \sqrt{x^2 + 2x + 2}) + C.$

2169. $(x^2 + 5x + 36)\sqrt{x^2 - 4x - 7} + 112 \ln |x - 2 + \sqrt{x^2 - 4x - 7}| + C.$

2170. $\left(\frac{1}{4}x^3 - \frac{7}{6}x^2 + \frac{95}{24}x - \frac{145}{12}\right)\sqrt{x^2 + 4x + 5}$

$$+ \frac{35}{8}\ln (x + 2 + \sqrt{x^2 + 4x + 5} + C.$$

2171. $\frac{\sqrt{x^2 + 2x - 3}}{8(x+1)^2} + \frac{1}{16}\arccos \frac{2}{x+1} + C.$

2172. $\frac{1}{2\sqrt{2}}\ln \frac{\sqrt{2 + 2x^2} - x}{\sqrt{2 + 2x^2} + x} + \ln (x + \sqrt{x^2 + 1}) + C.$ **2173.** $\frac{\sqrt{2x^2 - 2x + 1}}{x} + C.$

2174. $\ln \frac{\sqrt{x^2 + 2x + 4} - 1}{\sqrt{x^2 + 2x + 4} + 1} - \frac{1}{\sqrt{2}}\arctan \frac{\sqrt{2(x^2 + 2x + 4)}}{x + 1} + C.$

2175. $C - \frac{1}{8(x-1)^8} - \frac{1}{3(x-1)^9} - \frac{3}{10(x-1)^{10}} - \frac{1}{11(x-1)^{11}}.$

2176. $\frac{1}{3}[x^3 + \sqrt{(x^2 - 1)^3}] + C.$ **2177.** $\frac{3(4x - 3a)\sqrt[3]{(a + x)^4}}{28} + C.$

2178. $\frac{1}{m\sqrt{ab}}\arctan \left(e^{mx}\sqrt{\frac{a}{b}}\right) + C.$ **2179.** $\frac{1}{2}\arcsin x - \frac{x + 2}{2}\sqrt{1 - x^2} + C.$

2180. $\frac{x^2}{2} - 2x + \frac{1}{6}\ln \frac{|x-1|(x + 2)^{32}}{|x + 1|^3} + C.$ **2181.** $\frac{1}{4}\ln \left|\frac{1 + x}{1 - x}\right| + \frac{1}{2}\arctan x + C.$

2182. $\frac{3}{8}\arctan x - \frac{x}{4(x^4 - 1)} - \frac{3}{16}\ln \left|\frac{x - 1}{x + 1}\right| + C.$

2183. $2\sqrt{x + 1}(\ln |x + 1| - 2) + C.$

2184. $\left(\frac{1}{2}x + \frac{3}{4}\right)\cos 2x + \left(\frac{1}{2}x^2 + \frac{3}{2}x + \frac{9}{4}\right)\sin 2x + C.$

2185. $x^2 \cosh x - 2x \sinh x + 2 \cosh x + C.$

2186. $x \arctan (1 + \sqrt{x}) - \sqrt{x} + \ln |x + 2\sqrt{x} + 2| + C.$

2187. $\ln \left|\frac{1 - \sqrt{1 - x^2}}{x}\right| - \frac{\arcsin x}{x} + C.$ **2188.** $3e^{\sqrt[3]{x}}(\sqrt[3]{x^2} - 2\sqrt[3]{x} + 2) + C.$

2189. $3e^{\sqrt[3]{x}}(\sqrt[3]{x^5} - 5\sqrt[3]{x^4} + 20x - 60\sqrt[3]{x^2} + 120\sqrt[3]{x} - 120) + C.$

2190. $e^{3x}\left(\frac{1}{3}x^3 - x^2 + \frac{2}{3}x + \frac{13}{9}\right) + C.$ **2191.** $2(\sin \sqrt{x} - \sqrt{x}\cos \sqrt{x}) + C.$

2192. $\frac{\sqrt{x - 1}(3x + 2)}{4x^2} + \frac{3}{4}\arctan \sqrt{x - 1} + C.$

2193. $\frac{x^2}{2} + \frac{x}{2}\sqrt{x^2 - 1} - \frac{1}{2}\ln |x + \sqrt{x^2 - 1}| + C.$

2194. $\ln(x + \sqrt{1 + x^2}) - \dfrac{\sqrt{(1 + x^2)^5}}{5x^5} - \dfrac{\sqrt{(1 + x^2)^3}}{3x^3} - \dfrac{\sqrt{1 + x^2}}{x} + C.$

2195. $\left(\dfrac{1}{4}x^3 - \dfrac{3}{8}x\right)\sqrt{x^2 + 1} + \dfrac{3}{8}\ln(x + \sqrt{x^2 + 1}) + C.$

2196. $3[\ln|u| - \ln(1 + \sqrt{1 - u^2}) - \arcsin u] + C$, where $u = \sqrt[3]{x}$.

2197. $\dfrac{15x^2 + 5x - 2}{4x^2\sqrt{1 + x}} + \dfrac{15}{8}\ln\left|\dfrac{\sqrt{1 + x} - 1}{\sqrt{1 + x} + 1}\right| + C.$

2198. $C - \dfrac{\sqrt{2x + 1}}{x} + \ln\left|\dfrac{\sqrt{2x + 1} - 1}{\sqrt{2x + 1} + 1}\right|.$

2199. $\dfrac{1}{15}\left[\dfrac{1}{2}\ln\dfrac{(z - 1)^2}{z^2 + z + 1} - \sqrt{3}\arctan\dfrac{2z + 1}{\sqrt{3}}\right] + C$, where $z = x^5$.

2200. $C - \dfrac{1}{4}\ln\left|\tan\dfrac{x}{2}\right| + \dfrac{1}{8\sin^2\dfrac{x}{2}}.$ **2201.** $\dfrac{1}{\sqrt{2}}\arctan\dfrac{\tan x}{\sqrt{2}} + C.$

2202. $\dfrac{2}{b^2\sin 2\alpha}\ln\left|\dfrac{\sin(\alpha - x)}{\sin(\alpha + x)}\right| + C$, where $\alpha = \arccos\dfrac{a}{b}$ if $a^2 < b^2$;

$\dfrac{1}{a^2\sin\alpha}\arctan\dfrac{\tan x}{\sin\alpha} + C$, where $\alpha = \arccos\dfrac{b}{a}$ if $a^2 > b^2$.

2203. $\dfrac{1}{2}x^2\ln(1 + x^3) - \dfrac{3}{4}x^2 + \dfrac{1}{4}\ln(x^2 - x + 1)$

$- \dfrac{1}{2}\ln(x + 1) + \dfrac{\sqrt{3}}{2}\arctan\dfrac{2x - 1}{\sqrt{3}} + C.$

2204. $\dfrac{x}{\ln x} + C.$ **2205.** $\arctan\sqrt{x^2 - 1} - \dfrac{\ln x}{\sqrt{x^2 - 1}} + C.$

2206. $\dfrac{1}{2}e^x[(x^2 - 1)\cos x + (x - 1)^2\sin x] + C.$ **2207.** $\dfrac{x^2e^{x^2}}{2} + C.$

2208. $\dfrac{2}{3}\dfrac{\tan^2 x - 3}{\sqrt{\tan x}} + C.$

2209. $\dfrac{1}{4}(\tan^4 x - \cot^4 x) + 2(\tan^2 x - \cot^2 x) + 6\ln|\tan x| + C.$

2210. $\arctan(\tan^2 x) + C.$ **2211.** $\ln\left|1 + \tan\dfrac{x}{2}\right| + C.$

2212. $\arctan\dfrac{\tan x}{\sqrt{2 + \tan^2 x}} + \ln(\sqrt{2 + \tan^2 x} + \tan x) + C.$

2213. $\ln\dfrac{x^2 + 1 + \sqrt{x^4 + 3x^2 + 1}}{x} + C.$ **2214.** $C - \dfrac{1}{\sqrt{15}}\ln\left|\dfrac{x + 6 + \sqrt{60x - 15x^2}}{2x - 3}\right|.$

2215. $\dfrac{e^x}{1 + x} + C.$ **2216.** $2x\sqrt{1 + e^x} - 4\sqrt{1 + e^x} - 2\ln\dfrac{\sqrt{1 + e^x} - 1}{\sqrt{1 + e^x} + 1} + C.$

2217. $\dfrac{1}{6}\ln\dfrac{1 + x^2}{x^2} - \dfrac{\arctan x}{3x^3} - \dfrac{1}{6x^2} + C.$

2218. $C - \frac{\arctan x}{2(1+x^2)} + \frac{\arctan x}{4} + \frac{x}{4(1+x^2)}$.

2219. $\frac{1}{4}\ln\frac{|x+1|}{\sqrt{x^2+1}} - \frac{\arctan x}{2(x+1)^2} - \frac{1}{4(x+1)} + C$.

2220. $x - \log_2|1-2^x| + \frac{1}{\ln 2}\left[\frac{1}{1-2^x} + \frac{1}{2(1-2^x)^2} + \frac{1}{3(1-2^x)^3}\right] + C$.

2221. $\arctan(e^x - e^{-x}) + C$. **2222.** $\ln\frac{1+e^x-\sqrt{1+e^x+e^{2x}}}{1-e^x+\sqrt{1+e^x+e^{2x}}} + C$.

2223. $x - \frac{2}{\sqrt{3}}\arctan\frac{1+2\tan x}{\sqrt{3}} + C$.

2224. $\frac{35}{128}x - \frac{1}{4}\sin 2x + \frac{7}{128}\sin 4x + \frac{1}{24}\sin^3 2x + \frac{1}{1024}\sin 8x + C$.

2225. $\frac{1}{2}x^2 + \frac{3}{2}\ln(1+x^2) + \frac{1}{(1+x^2)^2} + C$.

2226. $\frac{8}{49(x-5)} - \frac{27}{49(x+2)} + \frac{30}{343}\ln\left|\frac{x-5}{x+2}\right| + C$.

2227. $C - \frac{\sqrt{2}}{2}\arctan(\sqrt{2}\cot 2x)$. **2228.** $x\tan\frac{x}{2} + C$.

2229*. $\frac{1}{\sqrt{2}}\arccos\frac{x\sqrt{2}}{x^2+1} + C$. (Divide both the numerator and denominator by x^2 and apply the substitution $x + \frac{1}{x} = z$).

2230. $e^{\sin x}(x - \sec x) + C$.

Chapter 7

2231. $\frac{2}{3}(\sqrt{8}-1)$. **2232.** $\frac{7}{72}$. **2233.** $-5(\sqrt[5]{16}-1)$. **2234.** $7\frac{2}{3}$.

2235. $\frac{T}{\pi}\cos\varphi_0$. **2236.** 12. **2237.** $0.2(e-1)^5$. **2238.** $3\ln\frac{b}{b-a}$.

2239. $\frac{1}{4}$. **2240.** $\frac{\pi}{2}$. **2241.** $1 + \frac{1}{2}\log e$. **2242.** $e - \sqrt{e}$.

2243. $\frac{\pi}{6n}$. **2244.** 2. **2245.** $\frac{4}{3}$. **2246.** $\ln\frac{3}{2}$. **2247.** $0.2\ln\frac{4}{3}$.

2248. $\arctan\frac{1}{7}$. **2249.** $\frac{1}{2}\ln\frac{8}{5}$. **2250.** $\frac{\pi}{6}$. **2251.** 2.

2252. $\frac{2}{7}$. **2253.** $\frac{4}{3}$. **2254.** $\frac{\pi}{2\omega}$. **2255.** $-0.083\ldots$.

2256. $\frac{2}{3} + \frac{\pi}{4} - \alpha + \frac{\cot^3\alpha}{3} - \cot\alpha$. **2257.** 1. **2258.** $-\sqrt{2}/3$.

2259. $1 - 2/e$. **2260.** $\pi/2 - 1$. **2261.** $\frac{\pi(9-4\sqrt{3})}{36} + \frac{1}{2}\ln\frac{3}{2}$.

2262. $\pi^3 - 6\pi$. **2263.** $2 - \frac{3}{4\ln 2}$. **2264.** 1. **2265.** $\frac{141a^3\sqrt[3]{a}}{20}$.

2266. $\frac{\pi a^2}{4}$. **2267.** $\frac{e^\pi - 2}{5}$. **2268.** $6 - 2e$.

2269. (a) $\frac{8}{15}$; (b) $\frac{7\times 5\times 3\times 1}{8\times 6\times 4\times 2}\cdot\frac{\pi}{2}\approx 0.429$; (c) $\frac{10\times 8\times 6\times 4\times 2}{11\times 9\times 7\times 5\times 3}=\frac{256}{693}$.

2270. $J_{m,n}=\frac{n-1}{m+n}J_{m,n-2}=\frac{m-1}{m+n}J_{m-2,n}$

If n is odd, then

$$J_{m,n}=\frac{(n-1)(n-3)\dots 4\cdot 2}{(m+n)(m+n-2)\dots(m+3)(m+1)};$$

If m is odd, then

$$J_{m,n}=\frac{(m-1)(m-3)\dots 4\cdot 2}{(m+n)(m+n-2)\dots(n+3)(n+1)};$$

If m is even and n is even, then

$$J_{m,n}=\frac{(n-1)(n-3)\dots 3\times 1\cdot(m-1)(m-3)\dots 3\times 1}{(m+n)(m+n-2)(m+n-4)\dots 4\cdot 2}\cdot\frac{\pi}{2}.$$

2271. $(-1)^n n!\left[1-\frac{1}{e}\left(\frac{1}{n!}+\frac{1}{(n-1)!}+\dots+\frac{1}{1!}+1\right)\right]$. **2272.** $\frac{11}{48}+\frac{5\pi}{64}$.

2274*. $\frac{p!\,q!}{(p+q+1)!}$. Put $x=\sin^2 z$ and take advantage of the result of problem 2270.

2275. $7+2\ln 2$. **2276.** $2-\frac{\pi}{2}$. **2277.** $\frac{32}{3}$. **2278.** $\frac{5}{3}-2\ln 2$.

2279. $\ln\frac{e+\sqrt{1+e^2}}{1+\sqrt{2}}$. **2280.** $8+\frac{3\sqrt{3}}{2}\pi$.

2281*. $\frac{5}{16}\pi$. Putting $x=2z$, transform the given integral to $2\int_0^{\pi/2}\sin^6 z\,dz$.

2282*. $\frac{8}{35}$. Put $x=\frac{z}{2}$. **2283.** $\frac{\pi}{32}$. **2284.** $\sqrt{2}-\frac{2}{\sqrt{3}}+\ln\frac{2+\sqrt{3}}{1+\sqrt{2}}$.

2285. $\frac{8}{15}$. **2286.** $\sqrt{3}-\frac{\pi}{3}$. **2287.** $\frac{1}{32}\left(\pi+\frac{7\sqrt{3}}{2}-8\right)$. **2288.** $\frac{3}{16}\pi$.

2289. $\frac{\pi}{16}$. **2290.** $\frac{\sqrt{3}}{2}+\ln(2-\sqrt{3})$. **2291.** $\frac{\pi}{4}$. **2292.** $\frac{\sqrt{3}}{24}$.

2293. $\frac{\pi}{3}$. **2294.** $\arctan\frac{1}{2}$. **2295.** $\frac{\sqrt{6}}{27}+\frac{\pi\sqrt{2}}{48}$. **2296.** $\frac{20}{9}$.

2297. $2\ln\frac{6}{5}\approx 0.365$. **2298.** $\frac{2}{\pi},\frac{1}{2}$. **2299.** $2+\ln\frac{2}{e^2+1}$.

2300. For $a=e$. **2301.** $\frac{1}{2}\ln\frac{8}{5}$. **2302.** $\frac{2}{45}$.

2303. $8\ln 3-15\ln 2+\frac{13}{8}$. **2304.** $\frac{5}{192}(5+7\sqrt[5]{5^3})$. **2305.** $\frac{\pi}{6}$.

2306. $a^2[\sqrt{2}-\ln(\sqrt{2}+1)]$. **2307.** $\sqrt{3}-\frac{1}{2}\ln(2+\sqrt{3})$. **2308.** $\frac{848}{105}$.

2309. $4-\pi$. **2310.** $\ln\frac{7+2\sqrt{7}}{9}$. **2311.** $\frac{\pi}{4}-\frac{1}{2}$.

2312. $\frac{2}{\sqrt{5}}\arctan\frac{1}{\sqrt{5}}$. **2313.** $\frac{\pi}{2}\sqrt{\frac{6}{7}}$.

2314. $\dfrac{\pi^4}{16} - 3\pi^2 + 24.$

2315. $\dfrac{16\pi}{3} - 2\sqrt{3}.$ **2316.** $\dfrac{19}{27} - \dfrac{5}{6\sqrt{6}}.$ **2317.** $\dfrac{1}{a^2 - b^2} \ln \left|\dfrac{a}{b}\right|.$

2319. $x = 2.$ **2320.** $x = \ln 4.$

2322*. Use the relationships $4 - x^2 \geq 4 - x^2 - x^3 \geq 4 - 2x^2$, valid for $0 \leq x \leq 1$.

2323*. Take advantage of the inequlities $\sqrt{1 - x^2} \leq \sqrt{1 - x^{2n}} \leq 1$, where $-1 \leq x \leq 1$ and $n \geq 1$.

2324. $1.098 < I < 1.110.$

2325*. To estimate the integral from below use the inequality $1 + x^4 < (1 + x^2)^2$, the Bunyakovsky inequality being used for estimating it from above.

2326. $I\,(1) \approx 1.66$ - the greatest value, $I\left(-\dfrac{1}{2}\right) \approx -0.11$ – the least value.

2327. Minimum at $x = 1 \left(y = -\dfrac{17}{12}\right)$, points of inflection $\left(2, -\dfrac{4}{3}\right)$ and $\left(\dfrac{4}{3}, -\dfrac{112}{81}\right)$.

2332*. (a) Substitute $t = -x$, subdivide the interval $[-a, -x]$ into $[-a, a]$ and $[a, -x]$, and take into consideration that the integral of an odd function on the interval $[-a, a]$ is equal to zero.

(b) No if $a \neq 0$; yes if $a = 0$.

2333*. Put $t = \dfrac{1}{z}$.

2338. Each of the integrals equals $\dfrac{\pi}{4}$.

2339*. Put $x = \pi - z$. The integral is equal to $\dfrac{\pi^2}{4}$.

2340*. Subdivide the interval of integration $[a, a + T]$ into the intervals $[a, 0]$, $[0, T]$ and $[T, a + T]$, and then, taking advantage of the property $f(x) = f(x + T)$, show that $\int_0^a f(x)\,dx = \int_T^{a+T} f(x)\,dx$.

2341*. The equality required for the proof is equivalent to the equality $\int_x^{x+T} f(z)\,dz = 0$.

Make sure that the integral in the left-hand side of this equality is independent of x, and then, put $x = -\dfrac{T}{2}$.

2342. $\dfrac{2 \times 4 \times 6 \ldots 2n}{1 \times 3 \times 5 \ldots (2n + 1)}$.

2343. The substitution $z = \tan \dfrac{x}{2}$ is not applicable, since the function $\tan \dfrac{x}{2}$ is discontinuous at $x = \pi$.

2344*. In estimating I_n take advantage of the fact that I_n decreases with an increase in n.

2345*. Change the variable by the formula $z = \frac{x+t}{2}$ and exploit the property of an integral of an even function.

2346*. Change the variable by the formula $z = k\omega^2 x^2$, and then, apply L'Hospital's rule.

2347. By the rectangle rule $\pi \approx 2.904$ (with deficit) and $\pi \approx 3.305$ (with excess). By the trapezoid rule $\pi = 3.104$. By Simpson's formula $\pi = 3.127$.

2348. By the rectangle rule $\pi = 3.04$ (with deficit) and $\pi = 3.24$ (with excess). By the trapezoid rule $\pi \approx 3.140$. By Simpson's formula $\pi \approx 3.1416$ (with all correct digits).

2349. $\ln 10 \approx 2.31$, $M = \frac{1}{\ln 10} \approx 0.433$. **2350.** ≈ 0.837. **2351.** ≈ 1.09.

2352. ≈ 2.59. **2353.** ≈ 0.950. **2354.** ≈ 1.53. **2355.** ≈ 0.985.

2356. ≈ 0.957. **2357.** $\approx$ 239 m^2 (by Simpson's formula).

2358. $\approx$ 5.7 m^2 (by Simpson's formula). **2359.** $\approx$ 1950 mm^2.

2360. ≈ 10.9. **2361.** ≈ 36.2. **2362.** ≈ 98.2. **2363.** ≈ 9.2.

2364. $\approx$ 569 mm^2. **2365.** $\approx$ 138 mm^2. **2366.** 1/3.

2367. Diverges. **2368.** $1/a$. **2369.** Diverges. **2370.** π.

2371. Diverges. **2372.** $1 - \ln 2$. **2373.** $\frac{1}{2}$. **2374.** $\frac{\pi}{4}$.

2375. $n \frac{\sqrt{a^4+1}+1}{a^2}$. **2376.** $\frac{1}{2}$. **2377.** $\frac{1}{2}$. **2378.** Diverges.

2379. 2. **2380.** 1/2. **2381.** $\frac{a}{a^2+b^2}$ if $a > 0$, diverges if $a \le 0$.

2382. $\frac{\pi}{4} + \frac{1}{2}\ln 2$. **2383.** $\frac{2\pi}{3\sqrt{3}}$. **2384.** $\frac{\pi}{2}$. **2385.** $\frac{1}{2} + \frac{\pi}{4}$.

2386. Converges. **2387.** Diverges. **2388.** Converges.

2389. Diverges. **2390.** Converges. **2391.** Diverges. **2392.** Diverges.

2393. Converges. **2394.** $\frac{\pi}{2}$. **2395.** Diverges. **2396.** $\frac{8}{3}$.

2397. $-\frac{1}{4}$. **2398.** 1. **2399.** Diverges. **2400.** 2. **2401.** π.

2402. $\frac{1}{2}\pi(a+b)$. **2403.** $\frac{33\pi}{2}$. **2404.** $\frac{\pi}{3\sqrt{3}}$. **2405.** $\frac{\pi}{\sqrt{3}}$.

2406. $14\frac{4}{7}$. **2407.** $\frac{10}{7}$. **2408.** Diverges. **2409.** $6 - \frac{9}{2}\ln 3$.

2410. $-\frac{2}{e}$. **2411.** Diverges. **2412.** Converges. **2413.** Diverges.

2414. Converges. **2415.** Converges. **2416.** Diverges.

2417. Converges. **2418.** No.

2419. For $k < -1$ converges, for $k \ge -1$ diverges.

2420. (1) For $k > 1$ converges for $k \le 1$ diverges;

(2) $I = \frac{1}{(k-1)(\ln 2)^{k-1}}$ if $k > 1$; diverges if $k \le 1$.

2421. For $k < 1$ converges, for $k \ge 1$ diverges.

2422. Diverges for any k.

2423. Converges if both inequalities $k > -1$ and $t > k + 1$ hold true.

2424. For $m < 3$ converges, for $m \geq 3$ diverges.

2425. For $k < 1$ converges, for $k \geq 1$ diverges.

2426. π. **2427*.** $\frac{5\pi}{3}$. Put $x = \cos\varphi$ and integrate by parts.

2428. $\frac{3+2\sqrt{3}}{4}\pi - \frac{3}{2}\ln 2$. **2429.** $\frac{1\times 3\times 5\ldots(2n-3)}{2\times 4\times 6\ldots(2n-2)}\frac{\pi}{2a^{2n-1}}$.

2430. $n!$. **2431.** $\frac{n!}{2}$. **2432.** $(-1)^n\, n!$.

2433*. (a) $\frac{(m-1)(m-3)\ldots 3\times 1}{m(m-2)\ldots 4\times 2}\frac{\pi}{2}$;

(b) $\frac{(m-1)(m-3)\ldots 4\times 2}{m(m-2)\ldots 3\times 1}$. Put $x = \sin\varphi$.

2434*. $2\frac{2n(2n-2)\ldots 4\times 2}{(2n+1)(2n-1)\ldots 3\times 1}$. Put $x = \sin^2\varphi$.

2435. $\frac{\pi-\alpha}{\sin\alpha}$ ($I = 1$ for $\alpha = \pi$).

2436*. To prove the equality of the integrals put in one of them $x = \frac{1}{z}$.

Then, compute their sum using the identity

$$\frac{1+x^2}{1+x^4} = \frac{1}{2}\left(\frac{1}{1+x^2+x\sqrt{2}} + \frac{1}{1+x^2-x\sqrt{2}}\right).$$

2437*. Represent the integral in the form of a sum of two integrals : $\int_0^\infty = \int_0^1 + \int_1^\infty$; in the second integral put $x = \frac{1}{y}$.

2438. 0. **2439.** $\frac{1}{2}\sqrt{\frac{\pi}{a}}$. **2440.** $\sqrt{\pi}$. **2441*.** $\frac{\sqrt{\pi}}{4}$. Integrate by parts.

2442. $\frac{1\times 3\times 5\ldots(2n-1)}{2^n}\frac{\sqrt{\pi}}{2}$. **2443.** $\frac{\pi}{2}$.

2444. $\frac{\pi}{2}$ if $a > 0$; 0 if $a = 0$; $-\frac{\pi}{2}$ if $a < 0$.

2445. $\frac{\pi}{2}$ if $a > b$; $\frac{\pi}{4}$ if $a = b$; 0 if $a < b$.

2446*. $\frac{\pi}{2}$. Integrate by parts.

2447*. $\frac{\pi}{4}$. Represent the numerator in the form of a difference of the sines of multiple arcs.

2448*. $\frac{\pi}{4}$. Apply the methods used in solving Problems 2446 and 2447.

2449*. Putting $y = \frac{\pi}{2} - z$, reduce $\varphi(x)$ to the form $\varphi(x) = \int_{\pi/2}^{\pi/2-x} \ln \sin z\, dz$. According to the formula $\sin z = 2\sin\frac{z}{2}\cos\frac{z}{2}$, break the integral into three integrals, one of which is found directly. The remaining two are reduced to integrals of the same type as the initial one by change of the variable; $\varphi\left(\frac{\pi}{2}\right) = \frac{\pi}{2}\ln 2$.

2450. $-\frac{\pi}{2}\ln 2$. **2451.** $-\frac{\pi^2}{2}\ln 2$.

2452*. $\frac{\pi}{2}\ln 2$. Integrate by parts.

2453*. $\frac{\pi}{2}\ln 2$. Reduced to the previous problem by change of the variable.

2454. $-\frac{\pi}{2}\ln 2$.

Chapter 8

2455. $\frac{16}{3}$. **2456.** $\frac{9}{4}$. **2457.** $\frac{16}{3}p^2$. **2458.** $\frac{1}{3}$. **2459.** $\frac{32}{3}\sqrt{6}$.

2460. $2\frac{1}{4}$. **2461.** $2\pi + \frac{4}{3}$ and $6\pi - \frac{4}{3}$.

2462. $\frac{4}{3}(4\pi + \sqrt{3})$ and $\frac{4}{3}(8\pi - \sqrt{3})$.

2464. $\frac{b^2c}{a} - ab\ln\frac{c+b}{a} = b\left[\varepsilon b - a\ln\left(\varepsilon + \sqrt{\varepsilon^2 - 1}\right)\right]$, where ε is an eccentricity.

2465. $a^2\left[\frac{\pi}{6} - \frac{\sqrt{2}}{8}\ln(\sqrt{3}+\sqrt{2})\right]$; $a^2\left[\frac{\pi}{6} - \frac{\sqrt{2}}{8}\ln(\sqrt{3}+\sqrt{2})\right]$ and $a^2\left[\frac{2\pi}{3} + \frac{\sqrt{2}}{4}\ln(\sqrt{3}+\sqrt{2})\right]$.

2466. $S_1 = S_3 = \pi - \frac{\sqrt{2}}{2}\ln 3 - 2\arcsin\sqrt{\frac{2}{3}} \approx 0.46$; $S_2 = 2(\pi - S_1)$.

2467. $\frac{\pi}{2} - \frac{1}{3}$. **2468.** $\frac{1}{12}$.

2470. $\left|\frac{m-n}{m+n}\right|$; $4\left|\frac{m-n}{m+n}\right|$ if both m and n are even; $2\left|\frac{m-n}{m+n}\right|$ if both m and n are odd; $\left|\frac{m-n}{m+n}\right|$ if m and n are of opposite signs.

2471. (a) $\frac{3}{14}$; (b) $73\frac{1}{7}$. **2472.** 1 (the figure consists of two equal portions.)

2473. $\frac{8}{15}$. **2474.** $\frac{3}{4}\pi$. **2475.** $\frac{4}{3}$. **2476.** $\frac{\pi a^2}{8}$.

2477. $8\left(\sqrt{1+\frac{2}{3}\sqrt{3}} - \arctan\sqrt{1+\frac{2}{3}\sqrt{3}}\right)$. **2478.** $e + \frac{1}{e} - 2$. **2479.** 4.

2480. $\frac{3}{e}(e^3 - 4)$. **2481.** $\frac{18}{e^2} - 2$.

2482. (a) $b(\ln b - 1) - a(\ln a - 1)$; (b) $b - a$. **2483.** $3 - e$.

2484. $\frac{3 - 2\ln 2 - 2\ln^2 2}{16}$. **2485.** $2 - \sqrt{2}$. **2486.** $\frac{1}{3} + \ln\frac{\sqrt{3}}{2}$.

2487. $\frac{5}{3}\sqrt{2}$. **2488.** $\sqrt{2} - 1$. **2489.** $\frac{\pi}{4}$. **2490.** $3\pi a^2$. **2491.** $\frac{3}{8}\pi a^2$. **2492.** $6\pi a^2$.

2493. (1) $\frac{\pi R^2}{n^2}(n+1)(n+2)$; (2) $\frac{\pi R^2}{n^2}(n-1)(n-2)$.

2494. (1) $\frac{72}{5}\sqrt{3}$; (2) $\frac{8}{15}$. **2495.** (1) $\frac{4}{3}\pi^3 a^2$; (2) $\frac{76a^2\pi^3}{3}$.

2496. $\frac{\pi a^2}{4}$ (two-leafed rose). **2497.** $\frac{\pi a^2}{4}$. **2498.** $18\pi a^2$.

2499. $\frac{a^2}{8}(4 - \pi)$. **2500.** $\frac{37\pi}{6} - 5\sqrt{3}$. **2501.** $\frac{51\sqrt{3}}{16}$. **2502.** a^2.

2505*. $a^2\frac{5\pi + 18\sqrt{3}}{32}$. For constructing the curve consider the variation of φ from 0 to 3π.

2506. $\frac{\pi}{4}$. **2507.** a^2. **2508.** $a^2\left(1 + \frac{\pi}{6} - \frac{\sqrt{3}}{2}\right)$. **2509.** $\frac{\pi}{2}(a^2 + b^2)$. **2510.** a^2.

2511. $\pi\sqrt{2}$. **2512.** π. **2513.** 2. **2514.** $3\pi a^2$. **2515.** 4π.

2516*. (1) $\sqrt{\pi}/2$.

(2) $\sqrt{\pi}$. Take advantage of the fact that $\int_0^\infty e^{-x^2}\,dx = \frac{\sqrt{\pi}}{2}$ (Poisson's integral).

2517. $\frac{\pi a^2}{2}$. **2518.** $2 - \frac{\pi}{2}$ and $2 + \frac{\pi}{2}$. **2519.** $a\sinh\frac{b}{a}$.

2520. $\frac{y}{2p}\sqrt{y^2 + p^2} + \frac{p}{2}\ln\frac{y + \sqrt{y^2 + p^2}}{p}$. **2521.** $1 + \frac{1}{2}\ln\frac{3}{2}$. **2522.** $\ln 3 - \frac{1}{2}$.

2523. $\ln\frac{e^b - e^{-b}}{e^a - e^{-a}}$. **2524.** $\frac{8}{9}\left(\frac{5}{2}\sqrt{\frac{5}{2}} - 1\right)$. **2525.** $4\frac{26}{27}$. **2526.** $4a\sqrt{3}$.

2527. $\frac{\pi}{2} + 2\ln\left(\tan\frac{3\pi}{8}\right) = \frac{\pi}{2} + 2\ln(\sqrt{2} + 1)$. **2528.** $\frac{1}{6} + \frac{1}{4}\ln 3$.

2529. 2. **2530.** 8. **2531.** For $t = \frac{2\pi}{3}$; $\left[x = a\left(\frac{2\pi}{3} - \frac{\sqrt{3}}{2}\right), y = \frac{3a}{2}\right]$.

2532. For $t = \frac{\pi}{6}$, $\left(x = \frac{3\sqrt{3}}{8}R,\ y = \frac{R}{8}\right)$.

2533*. $4\frac{a^2 + ab + b^2}{a + b}$. Put $x = a\cos^3 t$, $y = b\sin^3 t$.

2534. $5a\left[1 + \frac{1}{2\sqrt{3}}\ln(2 + \sqrt{3})\right]$. **2535.** $a\ln\frac{a}{y}$. **2536.** $\frac{\pi^2}{2}R$.

2537. $\pi^3/3$. **2538.** $4\sqrt{3}$. **2541.** $2(e^t - 1)$.

2543. $\pi a\sqrt{1 + 4\pi^2} + \frac{a}{2}\ln(2\pi + \sqrt{1 + 4\pi^2})$. **2545.** $\ln\frac{3}{2} + \frac{5}{12}$.

2546. $8a$. **2547.** $\frac{3}{2}\pi a$.

2549. k must have the form $\frac{2N+1}{2N}$ or $\frac{2N}{2N-1}$, where N is an integer.

2550. 4. **2551.** $\ln \frac{\pi}{2}$.

2554*. Prove that the length of the ellipse can be written in the form $L = 4\int_0^{\pi/4} (\sqrt{a^2\cos^2 t + b^2 \sin^2 t} + \sqrt{a^2 \sin^2 t + b^2 \cos^2 t})\,dt$ and apply the theorem on estimating an integral.

2555. 2π. **2556.** (1) $\frac{4}{3}\pi ab^2$; (2) $\frac{4}{3}\pi a^2 b$. **2557.** $\frac{8}{15}\pi h^2 a$.

2558. $\frac{\pi h^2}{3}(3a+h)$. **2559.** $\frac{\pi}{4}(e^2-1)$.

2560. $\frac{\pi}{4}\left[\frac{e^{2b}-e^{-2b}}{2} - \frac{e^{2a}-e^{-2a}}{2} + 2(b-a)\right]$. **2561.** $\frac{3\pi}{10}$.

2562. $\frac{\pi}{2}(15 - 16\ln 2)$. **2563.** $\pi\left(\frac{\pi^2}{4} - 2\right)$. **2564.** $\frac{8\pi}{3}$. **2565.** $2\pi^2$.

2566. $\frac{\pi a^3}{4}\left[\sqrt{2}\ln(1+\sqrt{2}) - \frac{2}{3}\right]$. **2567.** (1) $\frac{2}{3}\pi a^3$; (2) $\frac{\pi^2}{16}$.

2568. $5\pi^2 a^3$. **2569.** $\pi a^3\left(\frac{3\pi^2}{2} - \frac{8}{3}\right)$. **2570.** $\frac{32}{105}\pi a^3$.

2571. $\frac{16\pi c^6}{105ab^2}$. **2572.** $\frac{\pi^2}{2}$. **2573.** $\frac{\pi e}{2}$.

2574*. (1) π; (2) $\pi\sqrt{\frac{\pi}{2}}$. See the point to Problem 2516.

2575*. $\frac{3\pi\sqrt{2\pi}}{32}$. See the hint to Problem 2516.

2576*. π^2. Use the Dirichlet integral $\int_0^\infty \frac{\sin x}{x}\,dx = \frac{\pi}{2}$.

2577*. $2\pi^2 a^3$. It is advisable to represent the function parametrically, putting $x = 2a\sin^2 t$, $y = \frac{2a\sin^3 t}{\cos t}$.

2578. $\frac{2}{3}\pi a^3$.

2579. $\frac{4}{3}\pi abc$. Apply the formula $V = \int_{x_1}^{x_2} S(x)\,dx$, where $S(x)$ is the cross-sectional area.

2580. (1) $\pi\sqrt{2}$; (2) 36π.

2581. $v_1 = \pi\sqrt{2}\left(2\sqrt{6} - \frac{11}{3}\right)$, $v_2 = \pi\sqrt{2}\left(2\sqrt{6} + \frac{11}{3}\right)$.

2582. $v_1 = v_3 = 4\pi(\sqrt{6} + \sqrt{3} - 4)$, $v_2 = 8\pi(4 - \sqrt{3})$.

2583. $\frac{8\pi\sqrt{6}}{3}$. **2584.** 8π.

2585*. $\frac{2}{3}R^2H = 400\ \text{cm}^3$. Take the axis of symmetry of the base as the x-axis.

2586. $\frac{4}{15}ahH = 128\ \text{cm}^3$. **2587.** $\frac{2}{3}abH = 133\frac{1}{3}\ \text{cm}^3$.

2588*. $\frac{2}{3}\pi R^2H$. The area of the symmetric parabolic segment equals $\frac{2}{3}ah$, where a is its base and h, the altitude.

2589*. $\frac{R^2H}{6}\left(\pi + \frac{4}{3}\right)$ and $\frac{R^2H}{6}\left(\pi - \frac{4}{3}\right)$. (See the hint to Problem 2588).

2590. $\frac{8}{3}a^3$. **2591.** $\frac{8}{3}\pi r^3$. **2592.** $\frac{16}{3}R^3$. **2593.** $\frac{4}{3}R^2H$.

2594. $\frac{56}{3}\pi a^2$. **2595.** $\frac{\pi}{9}(\sqrt{(1+a^4)^3} - 1)$. **2596.** $\frac{\pi a^2}{4}(e^2 - e^{-2} + 4)$.

2597. $2\pi b^2 + \frac{2\pi ab}{\varepsilon}\arcsin\varepsilon$ and $2\pi a^2 + \frac{\pi b^2}{\varepsilon}\ln\frac{1+\varepsilon}{1-\varepsilon}$, where ε is eccentricity of the ellipse.

2598. $2\pi[\sqrt{2} + \ln(1+\sqrt{2})]$. **2599.** $\pi\left[\sqrt{5} - \sqrt{2} + \ln\frac{2\sqrt{2}+2}{\sqrt{5}+1}\right]$.

2600. $3\pi a^2$. **2601.** $\pi a^2\sqrt{2}\left(2 - \frac{\pi}{2}\right)$. **2602.** $\frac{2\pi\sqrt{2}}{5}(e^\pi - 2)$.

2603. $\frac{12}{5}\pi a^2$. **2604.** $8\pi a^2\left(\pi - \frac{4}{3}\right)$. **2605.** $\frac{32}{5}\pi a^2$. **2606.** $4\pi^2r^2$.

2607. $2\pi a^2(2-\sqrt{2})$. **2608.** $\pi[\sqrt{2} + \ln(1+\sqrt{2})]$. **2609.** $4\pi a^2$.

2610. $\frac{ah^2}{2}$. **2611.** $\frac{a^3}{6}, \frac{a^3}{6}, \frac{a^2\sqrt{2}}{12}$.

2613. The centre of gravity lies on the axis of symmetry of the segment at the distance $\frac{2}{5}h$ from the base.

2614. For $S_1 : \xi = \frac{3}{5}a$, $\eta = \frac{3}{8}b$; for $S_2 : \xi = \frac{3}{10}a$, $\eta = \frac{3}{4}b$.

2615. $\xi = 0$, $\eta = \frac{2r}{\pi}$. **2616.** $\xi = 0$, $\eta = \frac{4r}{3\pi}$.

2617. The centre of gravity lies on the bisector of the central angle subtended by the arc at the distance $2r\frac{\sin\frac{\alpha}{2}}{\alpha}$ from the centre.

2618. $\xi = \frac{a}{5}$, $\eta = \frac{a}{5}$. **2619.** $\xi = \frac{4a}{3\pi}$, $\eta = \frac{4b}{3\pi}$.

2620. $\frac{b^2}{2} + \frac{ab}{2\varepsilon}\arcsin\varepsilon$, where ε is eccentricity of the ellipse.

2621. $\xi = \frac{\pi}{2}$, $\eta = \frac{\pi}{8}$. **2622.** $\frac{\pi}{2} + \frac{4}{5}$. **2623.** $\frac{\pi}{12} + \frac{\sqrt{3}}{8}$. **2624.** $\frac{3}{20}$.

2625. $\xi = \frac{5}{8}a, \eta = 0.$ **2626.** $\xi = 0, \eta = a\frac{e^4 + 4e^2 - 1}{4e(e^2 - 1)}.$

2628. $\xi = \pi a, \eta = \frac{4}{3}a.$ **2629.** $\xi + \pi a, \eta = \frac{5}{6}a.$

2630. $\xi = \frac{2}{5}a, \eta = \frac{2}{5}a.$ **2631.** $\xi = \frac{256a}{315\pi}, \eta = \frac{256a}{315\pi}.$

2633. $\xi = \frac{6a(4 - \pi^2)}{\pi^3}, \eta = \frac{2a(\pi^2 - 6)}{\pi^2}.$

2634. The centre of gravity lies on the axis of symmetry of the sector at the distance $\frac{2}{3}\frac{r \sin\alpha}{\alpha}$ from the centre of the circle.

2635. $\xi = \frac{5}{6}a, \eta = 0.$ **2636.** $\xi = \frac{\sqrt{2}}{8}\pi a, \eta = 0.$

2638. $\xi = -\frac{a}{5}\frac{2e^{2\pi} + e^{\pi}}{e^{\pi} - e^{\pi/2}}, \eta = \frac{a}{5}\frac{e^{2\pi} - 2e^{\pi}}{e^{\pi} - e^{\pi/2}}.$ **2639.** $\xi = \frac{4}{5}a, \eta = \frac{4}{5}a.$

2640. $\frac{3}{8}R.$

2641. The centre of gravity lies on the axis of symmetry at the distance $\frac{R}{2}$ from the centre.

2642. $\frac{H}{3}, \frac{H\sqrt{R^2 + H^2}}{3(R + \sqrt{R^2 + H^2})}, \frac{H}{4}.$ **2643.** $\frac{h}{3}.$ **2644.** $\frac{l}{3}(a^2 + ab + b^2).$

2645. $\frac{\pi R^3}{2} = M\frac{R^2}{2}$ (M mass of the semicircle.) **2646.** $\frac{\sqrt{(1 + e)^3} - 2\sqrt{2}}{3}.$

2647. $I_x = \frac{256}{15}a^3, I_y = 16a^3\left(\pi^2 - \frac{128}{45}\right).$ **2648.** $\frac{ab^3}{3}.$

2649. (1) $\frac{bh^3}{12}$; (2) $\frac{bh^3}{4}$; (3) $\frac{bh^3}{36}.$ **2650.** $\frac{\pi R^4}{8}.$ **2651.** $\frac{\pi R^4}{2}.$

2652. $\frac{\pi}{4}ab^3$ and $\frac{\pi}{4}ba^3.$ **2653.** $\frac{1}{2}\pi R^4 H.$ **2654.** $\frac{1}{10}\pi R^4 H.$

2655. $\frac{8}{15}\pi R^5.$ **2656.** $\frac{8}{15}\pi ab^4$, where $2a$ is the length of the axis of revolution.

2657. $\frac{1}{6}\pi R^4 H.$ **2658.** $\frac{56\pi}{15}.$

2659. (1) $I_x = \frac{\pi(e^4 - 1)}{8}$; (2) $I_y = 4\pi(3 - e).$

2660. MR^2, where M is the mass of the lateral surface of the cylinder.

2661. $\frac{1}{2}MR^2.$ **2662.** $\frac{2}{3}MR^2.$ **2663.** $\frac{9}{2}\pi a^3.$ **2664.** $6\pi^2 ab^2.$

2665. Volume $\frac{3\sqrt{2}}{8}\pi^2 a^3$, surface $6\sqrt{2}\pi a^2.$

2666. Volume $12\pi^3 a^3$, surface $32\pi^2 a^2.$

2667. The axis of rotation must be perpendicular to the diagonal of the square; the axis of rotation must be perpendicular to the median.

2668. ≈ 23.7 m. **2669.** $x_2 = x_1 + \sin\left(\frac{2\pi t_2}{T} + \varphi_0\right) - \sin\left(\frac{2\pi t_1}{T} + \varphi_0\right)$.

2670. $\frac{kmM}{a(a+1)}, \frac{a+l}{a}M, \frac{kmM}{l}\ln\frac{r_1(r_2+l)}{r_2(r_1+l)}$. **2671.** $\frac{2kmM}{\pi r^2}$.

2672. $\frac{km\ Ma}{\sqrt{(R^2+a^2)^3}} = \frac{km\ M\cos^3\varphi}{a^2}$, where φ is the angle between the straight lines joining the point C to the centre of the ring and to any point on the ring, $\frac{kmM}{R}$.

2673. $\frac{2km\ M}{R^2}\left(1 - \frac{a}{a^2+R^2}\right)$. **2674.** $2\pi km\sigma$.

2675*. $2\pi km\gamma h\left(1 - \frac{h}{\sqrt{h^2+(R-r)^2}}\right) = 2\pi km\gamma h\,(1-\cos\alpha)$, where α is the angle between the generatrix of the cone and its axis. Use the solution of problem 2673.

2676. $2km\gamma$.

2678*. $\frac{kM^2}{l^2}\ln\frac{4}{3}$. First compute the force of interaction between the element ds of the first rod and the second rod (take advantage of the result of Problem 2670) and then, find the total force of interaction.

2679. $\frac{g^2M^3}{6m^2}$. **2680.** $\frac{\pi H^2 d}{12}(R^2 + 2Rr + 3r^2)$. **2681.** $\approx 1.63\cdot 10^{11}$ kgf-m.

2682. 353 250 kgf-m.

2683. $\frac{\pi\ dR^2H^2}{12}, \frac{\pi\ dR^2H^2}{4}$. Amount of work given in the answers to Problems 2683-2686 wil be in kgf-m, if distance is taken in metres and specific weight in kgf/m^3.

2684. $\frac{\pi dR^4}{4} \approx 101.8$ kgf-m. **2685.** $\frac{\pi\ d\ R^2H^2}{6} \approx 26\ 800$ kfg-m.

2686. $\frac{4}{15}\ dabH^2 = 240$ kgf-m. **2687.** $\frac{Sl^3\omega^2\gamma}{6} \approx 0.418$ kgf-m ≈ 4.2 J.

2688. $\frac{ab^3\ d\gamma\omega^2}{6} \approx 1.16$ kgf-m. **2689.** $\frac{ah^3\ d\omega^2\gamma}{24} \approx 0.05$ kgf-m.

2690. $\frac{ha^3\ d\omega^2\gamma}{60} \approx 0.015$ kgf-m. **2691.** $\frac{\pi R^4\ H\omega^2\gamma}{4}$.

2692. $\frac{MR^2\pi^2n^2}{3600}; \frac{M\ R^2\,(3\pi-8)\ \pi n^2}{3600}$. **2693.** (a) $\frac{ah^2}{6}$; (b) twice.

2694. $\frac{a^3\sqrt{2}}{2}$. **2695.** 22.2 tons. **2696.** $\frac{2}{3}\ da^2b$.

2697. $abd\left(h + \frac{b}{2}\sin\alpha\right)$.

2699. (a) $\frac{d^2H^2S}{2} = 32$ kgf-m; (b) $\frac{1}{2}\ SH^2\,(1-d)^2 = 2$ kgf-m. **2700.** $\frac{4}{3}\ \pi R^4$.

2701. ≈ 0.206 cm^2. **2702.** (a) ≈ 33.2 s; (b) ≈ 64.6 s. **2703.** ≈ 1 h 6 min 53 s.

2704. $\dfrac{2bL\sqrt{2a}}{3S\sqrt{g}}(2\sqrt{2}-1)$.

2705. $\dfrac{2b\sqrt{2g}}{3}[(H+h)^{3/2}-H^{3/2}]$; at $H=0:\dfrac{2b\sqrt{2g}}{3}h^{3/2}=\dfrac{2\sqrt{2g}}{3}S\sqrt{h}$, where S is the area of the slit.

2706. (a) $\approx$ 2.4 s; (b) $\approx$ 6.3 s; (c) $\approx$ 53 s; (d) at $t\to\infty$.

2707. $\approx$ 3.4 kgf-m.

2708. (1) (a) $\approx$ 7.16 kgf-m; (b) $\approx$ 16.6 kgf-m; (c) $\approx$ 23.8 kgf-m;
(2) with the gas expanding infinitely the work increases infinitely.

2709. $\approx$ 1600 kgf-m. **2710.** $\approx$ 82 min. **2711.** Somewhat more than 5°.

2712. $\dfrac{\sigma}{2a\pi\varepsilon_0}$. **2713.** (a) $4\cdot10^{-6}$ J; (b) $6\cdot10^{-6}$ J. **2714.** 5 cm.

2715. $\approx$ 946 C. **2716.** $\approx$ 1092 C. **2717.** $\approx$ 5110 C.

2718. $\dfrac{E_0^2}{2}$. Effective voltage of alternating current equals $\dfrac{E_0}{\sqrt{2}}$.

2719. $\dfrac{E_0I_0}{2}T\cos\varphi_0$. **2720.** $\approx$ 7 min. **2721.** $\approx$ 2.915 I.

2722. (a) $H_1=H\dfrac{\ln a-\ln c}{\ln a-\ln b}\approx 15$ cm. (b) $\approx$ 0.125%.

2723. $\dfrac{1}{1024}$ of the initial amount. **2724.** $\approx$ 2.49 g.

2725. $\dfrac{8}{9}$ g. **2726.** $\approx$ 37.3 min.

Chapter 9

2727*. $S_n=1-\dfrac{1}{n+1}$, $S=1$. Represent each term of the series as a sum of two addends.

2728. $S_n=\dfrac{1}{2}\left(1-\dfrac{1}{2n+1}\right)$, $S=\dfrac{1}{2}$. **2729.** $S_n=\dfrac{1}{3}\left(1-\dfrac{1}{3n+1}\right)$, $S=\dfrac{1}{3}$.

2730. $S_n=\dfrac{1}{3}\left(1+\dfrac{1}{2}+\dfrac{1}{3}-\dfrac{1}{n+1}-\dfrac{1}{n+2}-\dfrac{1}{n+3}\right)$, $S=\dfrac{11}{18}$.

2731. $S_n=\dfrac{1}{6}\left(1+\dfrac{1}{3}+\dfrac{1}{5}-\dfrac{1}{2n+1}-\dfrac{1}{2n+3}-\dfrac{1}{2n+5}\right)$, $S=\dfrac{23}{90}$.

2732. $S_n=\dfrac{1}{2}\left[\dfrac{1}{2}-\dfrac{1}{(n+1)(n+2)}\right]$, $S=\dfrac{1}{4}$.

2733. $S_n=1+\dfrac{1}{2}-\dfrac{1}{2^n}-\dfrac{1}{2\cdot3^n}$, $S=\dfrac{3}{2}$. **2734.** $S_n=1-\dfrac{1}{(n+1)^2}$, $S=1$.

2735. $S_n=\dfrac{1}{8}\left[1-\dfrac{1}{(2n+1)^2}\right]$, $S=\dfrac{1}{8}$.

2736. $S_n = \arctan \frac{n}{n+1}$, $S = \frac{\pi}{4}$. **2737.** Converges. **2738.** Converges.

2739. Diverges. **2740.** Converges. **2741.** Diverges.
2742. Diverges. **2743.** Converges. **2744.** Diverges.
2745. Diverges. **2746.** Converges. **2747.** Converges.
2748. Diverges. **2749.** Converges. **2750.** Diverges.
2751. Converges. **2752.** Converges. **2753.** Diverges.
2767. Converges. **2768.** Diverges. **2769.** Converges.
2770. Converges. **2771.** Converges. **2772.** Diverges.
2773. Diverges. **2774.** Converges. **2775.** Diverges.
2776. Diverges. **2777.** Diverges. **2778.** Converges.
2779. Converges. **2780.** Diverges. **2781.** Converges.
2782. Diverges. **2783.** Converges.

2784*. Diverges. Use the formula

$$\sin\alpha + \sin 2\alpha + \ldots + \sin k\alpha = \frac{\sin\frac{k+1}{2}\alpha \, \sin\frac{k}{2}\alpha}{\sin\frac{\alpha}{2}}$$

or the inequality $\sin x > \frac{2}{\pi} x$ if $0 < x < \frac{\pi}{2}$.

2790. Conditionally convergent. **2791.** Absolutely convergent.
2792. Conditionally convergent. **2793.** Absolutely convergent.
2794. Absolutely convergent. **2795.** Divergent.
2796. Conditionally convergent. **2797.** Absolutely convergent.
2798. Conditionally convergent. **2799.** Divergent.

2802. $-1 < x < 1$. **2803.** $\frac{1}{e} < x < e$. **2804.** $-1 < x < 1$.

2805. $-1 \le x \le 1$. **2806.** $-1 \le x < 1$. **2807.** $x < -1$ and $x > 1$.
2808. $-1 < x < 1$. **2809.** $-1 \le x < 1$. **2810.** $x \neq \pm 1$.
2811. For any x. **2812.** $-2 < x < 2$. **2813.** For any x.

2814. $x > 0$. **2815.** $x > 0$. **2816.** $x \ge 0$. **2822.** 11 terms.

2823*. Use the inequality $\ln(1+\alpha) \le \alpha$.

2825. $f(0) = \frac{1}{9}$, $f\left(\frac{\pi}{2}\right) = -\frac{1}{101}$, $f\left(\frac{\pi}{3}\right) = \frac{44}{1001}$, $f(1) = 0.049$, $f(-0.2) = 0.108$.

2827. $\frac{1}{4}\ln\frac{1+x}{1-x} - \frac{1}{2}\arctan x$. **2828.** $\frac{1}{2}\arctan x + \frac{1}{4}\ln\frac{1+x}{1-x}$.

2829. $(x+1)\ln(x+1) - x$. **2830.** $\frac{1}{2}$. **2831.** 0.2.

2832*. $\ln\frac{3}{2}$. Use the relation $\cos\frac{x}{2}\cos\frac{x}{4}\ldots\cos\frac{x}{2^n}\ldots = \frac{\sin x}{x}$.

2833*. $\frac{\pi^3}{12}$. Use the formula $\sum_{n=1}^{\infty}\frac{1}{n^2} = \frac{\pi^2}{6}$.

2834. (1) $\frac{1}{3}\left(\ln 2+\frac{\pi}{\sqrt{3}}\right)$; (2) $\frac{1}{2\sqrt{2}}\left[\ln(1+\sqrt{2})+\frac{\pi}{2}\right]$.

2835. ln 2. **2836.** $\frac{2-\sqrt{2}}{2}$.

2837. The given series cannot be differentiated termwise in any interval. Indeed, the general term of the series of derivatives has the form $\pi\cos(2^n\pi x)$. No matter how small the interval (α, β) is and where on the number scale it lies, there will always be found numbers of the form $\frac{k}{2^N}$ within it, where k is an integer and N is a sufficiently large whole positive number. But at $x=\frac{k}{2^N}$ the series of derivatives is divergent, since for all $n>N$ its terms become equal to π.

2838. $\frac{1}{(1-x)^2}$ and $\frac{1}{(1-x)^3}$.

2841. $(x-1)-\frac{(x-1)^2}{2}+\ldots+(-1)^{n+1}\frac{(x-n)^n}{n}+\ldots.$

2842. $1+\frac{3}{2}\left[(x-1)+\frac{1}{2}\frac{(x-1)^2}{2!}-\frac{1}{2^2}\frac{(x-1)^3}{3!}+\ldots+(-1)^n\frac{1\times 3\ldots(2n-5)}{2^{n-1}}\frac{(x-1)^n}{n!}+\ldots\right].$

2843. $\frac{1}{3}-\frac{x-3}{9}+\frac{(x-3)^2}{27}-\ldots+(-1)^{n+1}\frac{(x-3)^{n-1}}{3^n}+\ldots.$

2844. $1-\left(\frac{\pi}{4}\right)^2\frac{(x-2)^2}{2!}+\ldots+(-1)^{n+1}\left(\frac{\pi}{4}\right)^{2n-2}\frac{(x-2)^{2n-2}}{(2n-2)!}+\ldots.$

2845. $1+\frac{x^2}{2!}+\ldots+\frac{x^{2n-2}}{(2n-2)!}+\ldots.$

2846. $x^2+\frac{x^3}{1!}+\frac{x^4}{2!}+\ldots+\frac{x^{n+1}}{(n-1)!}+\ldots.$

2847. $\cos\alpha\left[1-\frac{x^2}{2!}+\frac{x^4}{4!}+\ldots+(-1)^{n+1}\frac{x^{2n-2}}{(2n-2)!}+\ldots\right]-\sin\alpha\left[x-\frac{x^3}{3!}+\frac{x^5}{5!}+\ldots+(-1)^{n+1}\frac{x^{2n-1}}{(2n-1)!}+\ldots\right].$

2848. $x+x^2+\frac{2x^3}{3!}-\frac{4x^5}{5!}+\ldots+\sqrt{2^n}\sin\frac{\pi n}{4}\cdot\frac{x^n}{n!}+\ldots.$

2849. $1-\frac{4x^4}{4!}+\frac{4^2x^8}{8!}+\ldots+(-1)^{n+1}\frac{4^{n-1}x^{4(n-1)}}{(4n-4)!}+\ldots.$

2850. $\ln 2+\frac{x}{2}+\frac{x^2}{8}-\frac{x^4}{192}+\ldots.$ **2851.** $e\left(1-\frac{x^2}{2}+\frac{x^4}{6}-\ldots\right).$

2852. $1-\frac{nx^2}{2}+\frac{3n^2-2n}{24}x^4+\ldots.$ **2853.** $\frac{x^2}{2}+\frac{x^4}{12}+\ldots.$

2854. $1+x^2-\frac{x^3}{2}+\frac{5x^4}{6}+\ldots.$ **2855.** $1+2x+\frac{(2x)^2}{2!}+\ldots+\frac{(2x)^{n-1}}{(n-1)!}+\ldots.$

2856. $1 - x^2 + \frac{x^4}{2!} - \ldots + (-1)^{n+1}\frac{x^{2(n-1)}}{(n-1)!} + \ldots.$

2857. $1 + \frac{x}{2!} + \frac{x^2}{3!} + \ldots + \frac{x^{n-1}}{n!} + \ldots.$ **2858.** $1 + \frac{x^6}{3!} + \frac{x^{12}}{5!} + \ldots + \frac{x^{6(n-1)}}{(2n-1)!} + \ldots.$

2859. $\frac{x}{2} - \frac{x^3}{2^3 \times 3!} + \ldots + (-1)^{n+1}\frac{x^{2n-1}}{2^{2n-1}(2n-1)!} + \ldots.$

2860. $1 - \left[x^2 - \frac{(2x)^4}{2 \times 4!} + \ldots + (-1)^{n+1}\frac{2^{2n-1}x^{2n}}{(2n)!} + \ldots\right].$

2861. $1 - \frac{x^2}{3!} + \ldots + (-1)^{n+1}\frac{x^{2(n-1)}}{(2n-1)!} + \ldots.$

2862. $-\frac{2x^3}{3!} + \frac{4x^5}{5!} - \ldots + (-1)^n\frac{2nx^{2n+1}}{(2n+1)!} + \ldots.$

2863. $\ln 10 + \left[\frac{x}{10} - \frac{x^2}{2 \times 10^2} + \ldots + (-1)^{n+1}\frac{x^n}{n \times 10^n} + \ldots\right].$

2864. $x^2 - \frac{x^3}{2} + \ldots + (-1)^n\frac{x^{n+1}}{n} + \ldots.$

2865. $1 + \left[\frac{x^2}{2} - \frac{1}{2} \times \frac{x^4}{4} + \ldots + (-1)^{n+1}\frac{1 \times 3 \ldots (2n-3)x^{2n}}{2 \times 4 \ldots (2n-2)2n} + \ldots\right].$

2866. $2 - 2\left[\frac{1}{3}\left(\frac{x}{2}\right)^3 + \frac{2}{3^2 \times 2!}\left(\frac{x}{2}\right)^6 + \ldots + \frac{2 \times 5 \ldots (3n-4)}{3^n \times n!}\left(\frac{x}{2}\right)^{3n} + \ldots\right].$

2867. $1 - \left[\frac{1}{3}x^3 - \frac{1 \times 4}{3^2 2!}x^6 + \ldots + (-1)^{n+1}\frac{1 \cdot 4 \ldots (3n-2)}{3^n \times n!}x^{3n} + \ldots\right].$

2868. $x^2 + \left[\frac{1}{2}x^4 + \frac{1 \times 3}{2 \times 4}x^6 + \ldots + \frac{1 \cdot 3 \ldots (2n-1)}{2^n \cdot n!}x^{2n+2} + \ldots\right].$

2869. $1 + 2^2x + \ldots + n^2x^{n-1} + \ldots$, $S = 12$.

2870. (1) $-7!$; (2) $\frac{105}{16}$; (3) $\frac{10!}{4!}$ and (4) $\frac{8}{3}$.

2871. $\frac{1}{6}$. **2872.** $\frac{1}{4}$. **2873.** 1. **2874.** $\frac{1}{2}$. **2875.** $\frac{2}{3}$.

2876. $\frac{1}{3}$. **2877.** $\frac{1}{60}$. **2878.** $\frac{-1}{10} < x < \frac{1}{10}$. **2879.** $-1 < x \le 1$.

2880. $-10 \le x < 10$. **2881.** $x = 0$. **2882.** $-\frac{\sqrt{2}}{2} < x < \frac{\sqrt{2}}{2}$.

2883. $-\infty < x < \infty$. **2884.** $-\frac{1}{3} < x < \frac{1}{3}$. **2885.** $-1 \le x \le 1$.

2886. $-\frac{1}{e} \le x < \frac{1}{e}$. **2887.** $x = 0$. **2888.** $-1 \le x < 1$. **2889.** $-\frac{1}{e} < x < \frac{1}{e}$.

2890. $x - \frac{1}{2}\frac{x^3}{3} + \frac{1 \times 3}{2 \times 4}\frac{x^5}{5} - \ldots + (-1)^{n+1}\frac{1 \times 3 \ldots (2n-3)}{2^{n-1}(n-1)!}\frac{x^{2n-1}}{2n-1}$
$+ \ldots (-1 \le x \le 1).$

2891. $x + \frac{x^3}{3} + \ldots + \frac{x^{2n+1}}{2n+1} + \ldots (-1 < x < 1).$

2892. $x^2 + \frac{x^4}{2\times 3} + \ldots + \frac{x^{2n}}{n(2n-1)} + \ldots (-1 \le x \le 1)$.

2893. $4\left(\frac{x^3}{3!} + \frac{2x^5}{5!} + \ldots + \frac{nx^{2n+1}}{(2n+1)!} + \ldots\right)(-\infty < x < \infty), \frac{1}{2e}$.

2894. 1.39, error 0.01. **2895.** 0.3090, error 0.0001.
2896. 2.154, error 0.001. **2897.** 7.389. **2898.** 1.649.
2899. 0.3679. **2900.** 0.7788. **2901.** 0.0175. **2902.** 1.000.
2903. 0.17365. **2904.** 0.9848. **2905.** 3.107. **2906.** 4.121.
2907. 7.937. **2908.** 1.005. **2909.** 3.017. **2910.** 5.053.
2911. 2.001. **2912.** 1.0986. **2913.** 0.434294. **2914.** 0.6990.

2915. $1 + 2x + \frac{5}{2}x^2 + \ldots + \left[2 + \frac{1}{2!} + \frac{1}{3!} + \ldots + \frac{1}{(n-1)!}\right]x^{n-1} + \ldots$.

2916. $x - \frac{3}{2}x^2 + \frac{11}{6}x^3 - \ldots + (-1)^{n+1}\left[1 + \frac{1}{2} + \frac{1}{3} + \ldots + \frac{1}{n}\right]x^n + \ldots$.

2917. $1 - \frac{x}{3} + \frac{x^3}{81} + \ldots$. **2918.** $-\frac{x}{2} + \frac{5x^3}{32} + \ldots$.

2919. $x - x^2 + 2x^3 + \ldots$.

2920. $C + x - \frac{x^3}{3\times 3!} + \ldots + (-1)^{n+1}\frac{x^{2n-1}}{(2n-1)(2n-1)!} + \ldots (-\infty < x < \infty)$.

2921. $C + \ln|x| - \frac{x^2}{2\times 2!} + \frac{x^4}{4\times 4!} - \ldots + (-1)^n\frac{x^{2n}}{2n(2n)!} + \ldots$
$(-\infty < x < 0$ and $0 < x < \infty)$.

2922. $C + \ln|x| + x + \frac{x^2}{2\times 2!} + \ldots + \frac{x^n}{n\times n!} + \ldots$ $(-\infty < x < 0$ and $0 < x < \infty)$.

2923. $C - \frac{1}{x} + \ln|x| + \frac{x}{2} + \frac{x^2}{2\times 3!} + \ldots + \frac{x^n}{n(n+1)!} + \ldots$
$(-\infty < x < 0$ and $0 < x < \infty)$.

2924. $x - \frac{x^3}{3} + \frac{x^5}{5\times 2!} - \ldots + (-1)^{n+1}\frac{x^{2n-1}}{(2n-1)(n-1)!} + \ldots (-\infty < x < \infty)$.

2925. $x - \frac{x^3}{3^2} + \frac{x^5}{5^2} - \ldots + (-1)^{n+1}\frac{x^{2n-1}}{(2n-1)^2} + \ldots (-1 \le x \le 1)$.

2926. $x + \frac{1}{2}\frac{x^5}{5} + \frac{1\times 3}{2\times 4}\frac{x^9}{9} + \ldots + \frac{1\times 3\ldots(2n-3)}{2^{n-1}(n-1)!}\frac{x^{4n-3}}{4n-3} + \ldots (-1 \le x \le 1)$.

2927. $x + \frac{1}{2}\frac{x^4}{4} - \frac{1}{2\times 4}\frac{x^7}{7} + \ldots + (-1)^n\frac{1\times 3\ldots(2n-5)}{2^{n-1}(n-1)!}\frac{x^{3n-2}}{3n-2} + \ldots$
$(-1 \le x \le 1)$.

2928. $x + \frac{x^{10}}{10} + \frac{x^{19}}{19} + \ldots + \frac{x^{9n-8}}{9n-8} (-1 \le x < 1)$.

2929. $\frac{1}{4}\frac{x^3}{3} - \frac{3}{4\times 8}\frac{x^7}{7} + \ldots + (-1)^{n+1}\frac{3\times 7\ldots(4n-5)}{4^n\times n!}\frac{x^{4n-1}}{4n-1} + \ldots$
$(-1 \le x \le 1)$.

2930. 0.3230, error 0.0001. **2931.** 0.24488, error 0.00001.
2932. 0.4971, error 0.0001. **2933.** 3.518, error 0.001.

2934. 0.012, error 0.001. **2935.** 32.831. **2936.** 0.487.

2937. 0.006. **2938.** 0.494. **2940.** 3.141592654.

2941. $x + \frac{2}{1 \times 3} x^3 + \frac{2^2}{1 \times 3 \times 5} x^5 + \ldots + \frac{2^{n-1}}{1 \times 3 \times 5 \ldots (2n-1)} x^{2n-1} + \ldots.$

2942*. $1 - \frac{1}{2^2} + \frac{1}{3^3} - \ldots + (-1)^{n+1} \frac{1}{n^n} + \ldots.$ Express x^x in the form $e^{x \ln x}$, expand into a series in powers of $x \ln x$ and integrate the expressions of the form $x^n \ln^n x$.

2943. 0.6449. **2944.** 0.511. **2945.** 1.015.

2946*. 3.71. It is inconvenient to compute the area by the formula $S = 4\int_0^1 \sqrt[4]{1 - x^4}\, dx$, since at $x = 1$ the corresponding series converges slowly.

Compute the area of the sector bounded by the curve, the y-axis and the bisector of the first quadrant. This yields a rapidly convergent series.

2947. 0.2505. **2948.** 3.821. **2949.** 0.119. **2950.** 1.225.

2951. (0.347, 2.996).

2952. (1.71, 0.94).

Chapter 10

2953. $z = \frac{\pi}{3}(x^2y - y^3).$

2954. $S = \frac{1}{4}\sqrt{(x + y + z)(x + y - z)(x - y + z)(y + z - x)}.$

2955.

y \ x	0	1	2	3	4	5
0	1	3	5	7	9	11
1	–2	0	2	4	6	8
2	–5	–3	–1	1	3	5
3	–8	–6	–4	–2	0	2
4	–11	–9	–7	–5	–3	–1
5	–14	–12	–10	–8	–6	–4

2956.

y \ x	0	0.1	0.2	0.3	0.4	0.5	0.6	0.7	0.8	0.9	1
0	0.00	0.10	0.20	0.30	0.40	0.50	0.60	0.70	0.80	0.90	1.00
0.1	0.10	0.14	0.22	0.32	0.41	0.51	0.61	0.71	0.81	0.90	1.00
0.2	0.20	0.22	0.28	0.36	0.45	0.54	0.63	0.73	0.82	0.92	1.01
0.3	0.30	0.32	0.36	0.42	0.50	0.58	0.67	0.76	0.85	0.95	1.04
0.4	0.40	0.41	0.45	0.50	0.57	0.64	0.72	0.81	0.89	0.98	1.08
0.5	0.50	0.51	0.54	0.58	0.64	0.71	0.78	0.86	0.94	1.03	1.12
0.6	0.60	0.61	0.63	0.67	0.72	0.78	0.85	0.92	1.00	1.08	1.16
0.7	0.70	0.71	0.73	0.76	0.81	0.86	0.92	0.99	1.06	1.14	1.22
0.8	0.80	0.81	0.82	0.85	0.89	0.94	1.00	1.06	1.13	1.20	1.28
0.9	0.90	0.91	0.92	0.95	0.98	1.03	1.08	1.14	1.20	1.27	1.34
1	1.00	1.00	1.02	1.04	1.08	1.12	1.16	1.22	1.28	1.34	1.41

2957. (1) $\frac{9}{16}$; (2) 1; (3) 16, 2, 2. **2958.** $\dfrac{\varphi(a)\,\psi\left(\frac{1}{a}\right)-\psi(a)\,\varphi\left(\frac{1}{a}\right)}{\varphi(1)\,\psi(1)}$; $a-\frac{1}{a}$.

2959. The second function changes at a higher rate.

2960. A parabola of the second order ; (1) no; (2) no.

2961. Put $m=\frac{1}{x}$. **2965.** The function will not be single-valued.

2966. (1) 1; (2) 1; (3) $\frac{1}{5}$; (4) not defined; (5) 1.

2967. $z=(x+y)^{x-y}+(x+y)^{y-x}$, $(x+y>0)$; z will be a rational function of u and v but not of w, t, x and y.

2968. $z=(x+y)^{xy}+(xy)^{2x}$.

2969. $u=(x^2+y^2+z^2)^2-\dfrac{x^2+y^2+z^2}{4}[(x^2+y^2+z^2)^2+3(x+y+z)^4]$ is an integral rational function with respect to ξ and η, x, y and z, but not with respect to ω and φ.

2970. $z=\left(\dfrac{u+v}{u-v}\right)^v+u$, $u=x^2+y^2$, $v=xy$.

2971. $x=$ const, parabola, $y=$ const, parabola, $z=$ const $\neq 0$, hyperbola, $z=0$, a pair of straight lines.

2972. $x=$ const, $y=$ const, straight lines, $z=$ const $\neq 0$, hyperbola, $z=0$, a pair of straight lines.

2973. $x=$ const, parabola, $y=$ const, cubical parabola, $z=$ const $\neq 0$, 3rd order curve, $z=0$, semicubical parabola.

2974. $z=$ const >0, ellipse, $x=$ const and $y=$ const, 3rd order curves (for $x=0$ and $y=0$, semicubical parabolas).

2975. $0<y<2$, $-1<y-\frac{1}{2}x<0$. **2976.** $x^2\le y\le\sqrt{x}$.

2977. $0<y<x\sqrt{3}$, $y<(a-x)\sqrt{3}$.

2978. $(x-a)^2+(y-b)^2<R^2$, $-\infty<z<\infty$.

2979. $(x-a)^2+(y-b)^2+(z-c)^2 \le R^2$. **2980.** $x^2+y^2<4R^2$.

2981. $v=\frac{1}{6}xy\,(2R \pm \sqrt{4R^2-x^2-y^2})$; the function is not single-valued. The domain of definition of the function $x^2+y^2 \le 4R^2$, $x>0$, $y>0$.

2982. For $0\le x\le 1$, $0\le y\le 1$ $S=xy$;
for $0\le x\le 1$, $1\le y$ $S=x$;
for $1\le x$, $0\le y\le 1$ $S=y$;
for $1\le x\le 2$, $1\le y\le 2$ $S=xy-x-y+2$;
for $1\le x\le 2$, $2\le y$ $S=x$;
for $2\le x$, $1\le y\le 2$ $S=y$;
for $2\le x$, $2\le y$ $S=2$.

2983. $\frac{x^2}{a^2}+\frac{y^2}{b^2}\le 1$. **2984.** $y^2>4x-8$.

2985. The entire plane except for the points of the circle $x^2+y^2=R^3$.

2986. The interior portion of the right-hand vertical angle formed by the bisectors of the quadrant including the bisectors themselves $x+y\ge 0$, $x-y\ge 0$.

2987. Same as in Problem 2986, but without boundaries.

2988. The inside portion of the right and left-hand vertical angles formed by the straight lines $y=1+x$ and $y=1-x$, including these lines, but without the point of their intersection:

$$1-x\le y\le 1+x \quad (x>0),$$
$$1+x\le y\le 1-x \quad (x<0)$$

(for $x=0$ the function is not defined).

2989. The portion of the plane lying inside the first and third quadrants (without the boundaries).

2990. A closed domain lying between the positive x-axis and parabola $y=x^2$ (including the boundary) : $x\ge 0, y\ge 0$; $x^2\ge y$.

2991. An annulus formed by the circles $x^2+y^2=1$ and $x^2+y^2=4$ including the circles themselves $1\le x^2+y^2=4$.

2992. The portion of the plane lying inside the parabola $y^2=4x$, between the parabola and the circle $x^2+y^2=1$, including the arc of the parabola, except for its vertex, and excluding the arc of the circle.

2993. The portion of the plane lying outside the circles of the unit radii, with the points $(-1, 0)$ and $(1, 0)$ as centres. The points of the first circle belong to the domain, those of the second one do not belong to it.

2994. Only the points of the circle $x^2+y^2=R^2$.

2995. The entire plane except for the straight lines $x+y=n$ (n is an arbitrary whole number, positive, negative or zero).

2996. The interior of the circle $x^2+y^2=1$ and the rings $2n\le x^2+y^2\le 2n+1$ (n an integer), the boundaries included.

2997. If $x\ge 0$, then $2n\pi\le y\le(2n+1)\pi$; if $x<0$, then $(2n+1)\pi\le y\le(2n+2)\pi$ (n an integer).

2998. $x>0$; $2n\pi<y<2(n+1)\pi$ (n an integer).

2999. The open domain cross-hatched in Fig. 83. For $x>0$, $y>x+1$, for $x<0$, $x<y<x+1$.

3000. The portion of the plane contained between the curve $y = \dfrac{1}{1+x^2}$ and its asymptote including the boundary.

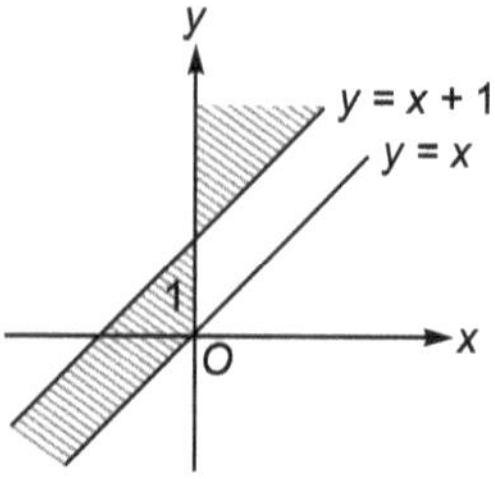

Fig. 83

3001. $x > 0, y > 0, z > 0$.

3002. The space contained between the spheres $x^2 + y^2 + z^2 = r^2$ and $x^2 + y^2 + z^2 = R^2$, including the surface of the outer sphere and excluding the surface of the inner sphere.

3003. 2. **3004.** 0. **3005.** 0.

3006. The function possesses no limit as $x \to 0, y \to 0$. **3007.** 0. **3008.** 1.

3009. (a) $y = 0$ or $y = x^{\alpha}$ $(\alpha > 1)$, $x \to 0$ arbitrarily; (b) $y = \dfrac{x}{3}$, $x \to 0$ arbitrarily.

3010. The point (0, 0); near it the function can take on arbitrarily large positive values.

3011. All the points with integral coordinates.

3012. On the straight line $y = x$.

3013. On the straight lines $x = m$, $y = n$ (m and n integers).

3014. On the parabola $y^2 = 2x$.

3015. (1) Continuous; (2) discontinuous; continuous with respect to x and y separately; (3) continuous; (4) discontinuous; (5) discontinuous; (6) discontinuous. Pass over to polar coordinates.

3016. The circles with the origin as centre and the radii $1, \dfrac{\sqrt{2}}{2}, \dfrac{\sqrt{3}}{3}, \dfrac{1}{2}$, respectively.

3017. Circles passing through the points A and B.

3025. The straight lines $y = ax + b$, where $a = \ln b$.

3026. Concentric spheres with point A as centre and the radii equal to 1, 2, 3, 4.

3027. Ellipsoids of revolution with the points A and B as foci:

$$\sqrt{(x - x_1)^2 + (y - y_1)^2 - (z - z_1)^2} + \sqrt{(x - x_2)^2 + (y - y_2)^2 + (z - z_2)^2} = \text{const.}$$

3028. Spheres $x^2 + y^2 + z^2 = \left(\dfrac{c-1}{c+1}\right)^2$, where $c = e^u$.

3029. Paraboloids of revolution $x^2 + y^2 = cz$.

3030. (1) Planes $2x + 3y - z = C$; (2) hyperboloids of revolution or a cone $x^2 + y^2 - 2z^2 = C$.

3032. $\dfrac{1}{v}\dfrac{\partial v}{\partial T}$ at $T = T_0$.

3033. $\frac{\partial\theta}{\partial t}$ is the rate of change in temperature at the given point; $\frac{\partial\theta}{\partial x}$ is the rate of change in temperature along the rod at the given time.

3034. $\frac{\partial S}{\partial h} = b$ is the rate of change in the area depending on the height of the rectangle; $\frac{\partial S}{\partial b} = h$ is the rate of change in the area depending on the base of the rectangle.

3036. $\frac{\partial z}{\partial x} = 1, \frac{\partial z}{\partial y} = -1.$ **3037.** $\frac{\partial z}{\partial x} = 3x^2y - y^3, \frac{\partial z}{\partial y} = x^3 - 3y^2x.$

3038. $\frac{\partial\theta}{\partial x} = ae^{-t}, \frac{\partial\theta}{\partial t} = -axe^{-t} + b.$ **3039.** $\frac{\partial z}{\partial u} = \frac{1}{v} - \frac{v}{u^2}, \frac{\partial z}{\partial v} = -\frac{u}{v^2} + \frac{1}{u}.$

3040. $\frac{\partial z}{\partial x} = \frac{x^4 + 3x^2y^2 - 2xy^3}{(x^2 + y^2)^2}, \frac{\partial z}{\partial y} = \frac{y^4 + 3x^2y^2 - 2x^3y}{(x^2 + y^2)^2}.$

3041. $\frac{\partial z}{\partial x} = 30xy(5x^2y - y^3 + 7)^2, \frac{\partial z}{\partial y} = 3(5x^2y - y^3 + 7)^2(5x^2 - 3y^2).$

3042. $\frac{\partial z}{dx} = \sqrt{y} - \frac{y}{3\sqrt[3]{x^4}}, \frac{\partial z}{\partial y} = \frac{x}{2\sqrt{y}} + \frac{1}{\sqrt[3]{x}}.$

3043. $\frac{\partial z}{\partial x} = \frac{1}{\sqrt{x^2 + y^2}}, \frac{\partial z}{\partial y} = \frac{y}{x^2 + y^2 + x\sqrt{x^2 + y^2}}.$

3044. $\frac{\partial z}{\partial x} = \frac{y}{x^2 + y^2}, \frac{\partial z}{\partial y} = -\frac{x}{x^2 + y^2}.$

3045. $\frac{\partial z}{\partial x} = \frac{y}{(x^2 + y^2)\left(\arctan \frac{y}{x}\right)^2}, \frac{\partial z}{\partial y} = -\frac{x}{(x^2 + y^2)\left(\arctan \frac{y}{x}\right)^2}.$

3046. $\frac{\partial z}{\partial x} = ux^{y-1}, \frac{\partial z}{\partial y} = x^y \ln x.$ **3047.** $\frac{\partial z}{\partial x} = \frac{2x}{x^2 + y^2}, \frac{\partial z}{\partial y} = \frac{2y}{x^2 + y^2}.$

3048. $\frac{\partial z}{\partial x} = -\frac{2}{\sqrt{x^2 + y^2}}, \frac{\partial z}{\partial y} = \frac{2x}{y\sqrt{x^2 + y^2}}.$

3049. $\frac{\partial z}{\partial x} = \frac{xy\sqrt{2}}{(x^2 + y^2)\sqrt{x^2 - y^2}}, \frac{\partial z}{\partial y} = -\frac{x^2\sqrt{2}}{(x^2 + y^2)\sqrt{x^2 - y^2}}.$

3050. $\frac{\partial z}{\partial x} = \frac{2}{y \sin \frac{2x}{y}}, \frac{\partial z}{\partial y} = -\frac{2x}{y^2 \sin \frac{2x}{y}}.$ **3051.** $\frac{\partial z}{\partial x} = -\frac{1}{y} e^{-\frac{x}{y}}, \frac{\partial z}{\partial y} = \frac{x}{y^2} e^{-\frac{x}{y}}.$

3052. $\frac{\partial z}{\partial x} = \frac{1}{x + \ln y}, \frac{\partial z}{\partial y} = \frac{1}{y(x + \ln y)}.$

3053. $\frac{\partial u}{\partial v} = -\frac{w}{v^2 + w^2}, \frac{\partial u}{\partial w} = \frac{v}{v^2 + w^2}.$

3054. $\frac{\partial z}{\partial x} = \frac{1}{y} \cos \frac{x}{y} \cos \frac{y}{x} + \frac{y}{x^2} \sin \frac{x}{y} \sin \frac{y}{x};$

$\frac{\partial z}{\partial y} = -\frac{x}{y^2} \cos \frac{x}{y} \cos \frac{y}{x} - \frac{1}{x} \sin \frac{x}{y} \sin \frac{y}{x}.$

3055. $\frac{\partial z}{\partial x} = \frac{y}{x^2} 3^{-\frac{y}{x}} \ln 3, \frac{\partial z}{\partial y} = -\frac{1}{x} 3^{-\frac{y}{x}} \ln 3.$

3056. $\frac{\partial z}{\partial x} = y^2(1 + xy)^{y-1}, \frac{\partial z}{\partial y} = xy(1 + xy)^{y-1} + (1 + xy)^y \ln(1 + xy).$

3057. $\frac{\partial z}{\partial x} = y \ln(x + y) + \frac{xy}{x + y}, \frac{\partial z}{\partial y} = x \ln(x + y) + \frac{xy}{x + y}.$

3058. $\frac{\partial z}{\partial x} = x^{x^y} x^{y-1} (y \ln x + 1), \frac{\partial z}{\partial y} = x^y x^{x^y} \ln^2 x.$

3059. $\frac{\partial u}{\partial x} = yz, \frac{\partial u}{\partial y} = xz, \frac{\partial u}{\partial z} = xy.$ **3060.** $\frac{\partial u}{\partial x} = y + z, \frac{\partial u}{\partial y} = x + z, \frac{\partial u}{\partial z} = x + y.$

3061. $\frac{\partial u}{\partial x} = \frac{x}{\sqrt{x^2 + y^2 + z^2}}, \frac{\partial u}{\partial y} = \frac{y}{\sqrt{x^2 + y^2 + z^2}}, \frac{\partial u}{\partial z} = \frac{z}{\sqrt{x^2 + y^2 + z^2}}.$

3062. $\frac{\partial u}{\partial x} = 3x^2 + 3y - 1, \frac{\partial u}{\partial y} = z^2 + 3x, \frac{\partial u}{\partial z} = 2yz + 1.$

3063. $\frac{\partial w}{\partial x} = yz + vz + vy, \frac{\partial w}{\partial y} = xz + zv + vx, \frac{\partial w}{\partial z} = xy + yv + vx,$
$\frac{\partial w}{\partial v} = yz + xz + xy.$

3064. $\frac{\partial u}{\partial x} = (3x^2 + y^2 + z^2) e^{x(x^2 + y^2 + z^2)}, \frac{\partial u}{\partial y} = 2xye^{x(x^2 + y^2 + z^2)},$
$\frac{\partial u}{\partial z} = 2xze^{x(x^2 + y^2 + z^2)}.$

3065. $\frac{\partial u}{\partial x} = 2x \cos(x^2 + y^2 + z^2), \frac{\partial u}{\partial y} = 2y \cos(x^2 + y^2 + z^2),$
$\frac{\partial u}{\partial z} = 2z \cos(x^2 + y^2 + z^2).$

3066. $\frac{\partial u}{\partial x} = \frac{\partial u}{\partial y} = \frac{\partial u}{\partial z} = \frac{1}{x + y + z}.$

3067. $\frac{\partial u}{\partial x} = \frac{y}{z} x^{\frac{y}{z} - 1}, \frac{\partial u}{\partial y} = \frac{1}{z} x^{\frac{y}{z}} \ln x, \frac{\partial u}{\partial z} = -\frac{y}{z^2} x^{\frac{y}{z}} \ln x.$

3068. $\frac{\partial u}{\partial x} = y^z x^{y^z - 1}, \frac{\partial u}{\partial y} = zy^{z-1} x^{y^z} \ln x, \frac{\partial u}{\partial z} = y^z x^{y^z} \ln x \ln y.$

3069. $\frac{2}{5}, \frac{1}{5}.$ **3070.** $0, \frac{1}{4}.$ **3071.** $\frac{\partial z}{\partial x} = 2(2x + y)^{2x + y} [1 + \ln(2x + y)],$
$\frac{\partial z}{\partial y} = (2x + y)^{2x + y} [1 + \ln(2x + y)].$

3072. $\frac{\partial z}{\partial x} = \frac{3}{x \ln y} \left(1 + \frac{\ln x}{\ln y}\right)^2, \frac{\partial z}{\partial y} = -\frac{3 \ln x}{y \ln^2 y} \left(1 + \frac{\ln x}{\ln y}\right)^2.$

3073. $\frac{\partial z}{\partial x} = ye^{\sin \pi xy} (1 + \pi xy \cos \pi xy), \frac{\partial z}{\partial y} = xe^{\sin \pi xy} (1 + \pi xy \cos \pi xy).$

3074. $\frac{\partial z}{\partial x} = \frac{1 - x^2 - y^2 - \sqrt{x^2 + y^2}}{(1 + \sqrt{x^2 + y^2})^2} 2x, \frac{\partial z}{\partial y} = \frac{1 - x^2 - y^2 - \sqrt{x^2 + y^2}}{(1 + \sqrt{x^2 + y^2})^2} 2y.$

3075. $\frac{\partial z}{\partial x} = \frac{y\sqrt{x^y}}{2x(1 - x^y)}, \frac{\partial z}{\partial y} = \frac{\sqrt{x^y} \ln x}{2(1 + x^y)}.$

3076. $\dfrac{\partial z}{\partial x} = -\dfrac{y}{(1+\sqrt{xy})\sqrt{xy - x^2y^2}}, \dfrac{\partial z}{\partial y} = -\dfrac{x}{(1+\sqrt{xy})\sqrt{xy - x^2y^2}}.$

3077. $\dfrac{\partial z}{\partial x} = \dfrac{y^2 + 2xy}{\sqrt{1 + (xy^2 + yx^2)^2}}, \dfrac{\partial z}{\partial y} = \dfrac{x^2 + 2xy}{\sqrt{1 + (xy^2 + yx^2)^2}}.$

3078. $\dfrac{\partial z}{\partial x} = -\dfrac{1}{x^2}\sqrt{\dfrac{xy - x - y}{xy + x + y}}, \dfrac{\partial z}{\partial y} = -\dfrac{1}{y^2}\sqrt{\dfrac{xy - x - y}{xy + x + y}}.$

3079. $\dfrac{\partial z}{\partial x} = \dfrac{y\left[\left(1 + \arctan^2 \dfrac{y}{x}\right)^2 + 2\arctan^3 \dfrac{y}{x}\right]}{(x^2 + y^2)\left(1 + \arctan^2 \dfrac{y}{x}\right)\left(1 + \arctan \dfrac{y}{x}\right)^2},$

$\dfrac{\partial z}{\partial y} = -\dfrac{x\left[\left(1 + \arctan^2 \dfrac{y}{x}\right)^2 + 2\arctan^3 \dfrac{y}{x}\right]}{(x^2 + y^2)\left(1 + \arctan^2 \dfrac{y}{x}\right)\left(1 + \arctan \dfrac{y}{x}\right)^2}.$

3080. $\dfrac{\partial u}{\partial x} = -\dfrac{4kx}{(x^2 + y^2 + z^2)^3}, \dfrac{\partial u}{\partial y} = -\dfrac{4ky}{(x^2 + y^2 + z^2)^3}, \dfrac{\partial u}{\partial z} = -\dfrac{4kz}{(x^2 + y^2 + z^2)^3}.$

3081. $\dfrac{\partial u}{\partial x} = \dfrac{z(x - y)^{z-1}}{1 + (x - y)^{2z}}, \dfrac{\partial u}{\partial y} = -\dfrac{z(x - y)^{z-1}}{1 + (x - y)^{2z}}, \dfrac{\partial u}{\partial z} = \dfrac{(x - y)^z \ln(x - y)}{1 + (x - y)^{2z}}.$

3082. $\dfrac{\partial u}{\partial x} = yz\,(\sin x)^{yz-1} \cos x, \dfrac{\partial u}{\partial y} = z(\sin x)^{yz} \ln \sin x;$

$\dfrac{\partial u}{\partial z} = y\,(\sin x)^{yz} \ln \sin x.$

3083. $\dfrac{\frac{\partial u}{\partial x}}{x} = \dfrac{\frac{\partial u}{\partial y}}{y} = \dfrac{\frac{\partial u}{\partial z}}{z} = \dfrac{2}{r(r^2 - 1)}$, where $r = \sqrt{x^2 + y^2 + z^2}$.

3084. $\dfrac{\partial w}{\partial x} = (2xy^2 - yzv)\tan^3\alpha, \dfrac{\partial w}{\partial y} = (2x^2y - xzv)\tan^3\alpha,$

$\dfrac{\partial w}{\partial z} = (2zv^2 - xyv)\tan^3\alpha, \dfrac{\partial w}{\partial v} = (2z^2v - xyz)\tan^3\alpha,$

where $\alpha = x^2y^2 + z^2v^2 - xyzv$.

3085. 4. **3086.** $\left(\dfrac{\partial u}{\partial z}\right)_{\substack{z=b\\t=a}} = \dfrac{3b}{2}\sqrt{\dfrac{ab}{b^2 - a^2}}, \left(\dfrac{\partial u}{\partial t}\right)_{\substack{z=b\\t=a}} = -\dfrac{3a}{2}\sqrt{\dfrac{ab}{b^2 - a^2}}.$

3087. 1 and –1. **3088.** $\dfrac{\sqrt{2}}{2}$. **3089.** $\dfrac{3}{2}$. **3090.** $-\dfrac{13}{22}$. **3091.** 45°. **3092.** 30°.

3093. $\arctan \dfrac{4}{7}$. **3094.** $d_x z = (y^3 - 6xy^2)\,dx, d_y z = (3xy^2 - 6x^2y + 8y^3)\,dy.$

3095. $d_x z = \dfrac{x\,dx}{\sqrt{x^2 + y^2}}, d_y z = \dfrac{y\,dy}{\sqrt{x^2 + y^2}}.$

3096. $d_x z = \dfrac{y(y^2 - x^2)\,dx}{(x^2 + y^2)^2}, d_y z = \dfrac{x(x^2 - y^2)\,dy}{(x^2 + y^2)^2}.$

3097. $d_x u = \dfrac{3x^2\,dx}{x^3 + 2y^3 - z^3}, d_y u = \dfrac{6y^2\,dy}{x^3 + 2y^3 - z^3}, d_z u = \dfrac{-3z^2\,dz}{x^3 + 2y^3 - z^3}.$

3098. $\frac{1}{270}$. **3099.** ≈ 0.0187. **3100.** $\frac{97}{600}$.

3101. $xy[(2y^3 - 3xy^2 + 4x^2y)\,dx + (4y^2x - 3yx^2 + 2x^3)\,dy]$.

3102. $\frac{x\,dx + y\,dy}{x^2 + y^2}$. **3103.** $\frac{2(x\,dy - y\,dx)}{(x - y)^2}$. **3104.** $\frac{y\,dx - x\,dy}{y\sqrt{y^2 - x^2}}$.

3105. $(x\,dy + y\,dx)\cos(xy)$. **3106.** $\frac{dx}{1 + x^2} + \frac{dy}{1 + y^2}$. **3107.** $\frac{4xy(x\,dy - y\,dx)}{(x^2 - y^2)^2}$.

3108. $\frac{x\,dy + y\,dx}{1 + x^2y^2}$. **3109.** $x^{zy-1}(yz\,dx + zx\ln x\,dy + xy\ln x\,dz)$. **3110.** 0.08.

3111. $0.25e$. **3112.** $\frac{1}{36}$. **3113.** ≈ 7.5. **3114.** ≈ 0.005.

3115. ≈ 1.08. **3116.** 5. **3117.** 1.8 ± 0.2. **3118.** 4730 ± 100.

3119. $2\delta_a + \frac{\delta_B B \sin C}{\sin B \sin(B + C)} + \frac{\delta_C C \sin B}{\sin C \sin(B + C)}$.

3120. Increases at the rate of 444 cm^2/s. **3121.** By ≈ 2575 cm^3.

3123. $dr = \frac{s}{p}\,ds + \left(\frac{1}{2} - \frac{s^2}{2p^2}\right)dp = 0.16$ cm, i.e., about 1%.

3124. $e^{\sin t - 2t^3}(\cos t - 6t^2)$. **3125.** $\sin 2t + 2e^{2t} + e^t(\sin t + \cos t)$.

3126. $\frac{3 - 12t^2}{\sqrt{1 - (3t - 4t^3)^2}}$.

3127. $\frac{\partial z}{\partial u} = 3u^3 \sin v \cos v(\cos v - \sin v)$, $\frac{\partial z}{\partial v} = u^3(\sin v + \cos v)(1 - 3\sin v \cos v)$.

3128. $\frac{\partial z}{\partial u} = 2\frac{u}{v^2}\ln(3u - 2v) + \frac{3u^2}{v^2(3u - 2v)}$,
$\frac{\partial z}{\partial v} = -\frac{2u^2}{v^3}\ln(3u - 2v) - \frac{2u^2}{v^2(3u - 2v)}$.

3129. $\frac{\partial u}{\partial x} = \frac{e^x}{e^x + e^y}$, $\frac{du}{dx} = \frac{e^x + 3e^{x^3}x^2}{e^x + e^{x^3}}$. **3130.** $\frac{dz}{dx} = \frac{e^x(x + 1)}{1 + x^2e^{2x}}$. **3131.** $\frac{du}{dx} = \frac{1}{1 + x^2}$.

3132. $\frac{dz}{dt} = \left(3 - \frac{4}{t^3} - \frac{1}{2\sqrt{t}}\right)\sec^2\left(3t + \frac{2}{t^2} - \sqrt{t}\right)$. **3133.** $\frac{du}{dx} = e^{ax}\sin x$.

3134. $dz = \frac{y^2\,dx + x^2\,dy}{(x + y)^2}\arctan(xy + x + y) + \frac{xy[(y + 1)\,dx + (x + 1)\,dy]}{(x + y)[1 + (xy + x + y)^2]}$.

3135. $\frac{e^{\frac{x^2 + y^2}{xy}}}{x^2y^2}[(y^4 - x^4 + 2xy^3)x\,dy + (x^4 - y^4 + 2x^3y)y\,dx]$.

3136. $\frac{\partial z}{\partial x} = 2x\frac{\partial f}{\partial u} + ye^{xy}\frac{\partial f}{\partial v}$, $\frac{\partial z}{\partial y} = -2y\frac{\partial f}{\partial u} + xe^{xy}\frac{\partial f}{\partial v}$; $u = x^2 - y^2$; $v = e^{xy}$. **3145.** $\frac{3x^2y - y^3}{3xy^2 - x^3}$.

3146. $\frac{x(y^2 - 2x^2)}{y(2y^2 - x^2)}$. **3147.** $\frac{ye^{xy} - ye^x - e^y}{xe^y + e^x - xe^{xy}}$. **3148.** $-\frac{x}{y}\cdot\frac{2(x^2 + y^2) - a^2}{2(x^2 + y^2) + a^2}$.

3149. $\frac{y}{x}\cdot\frac{2x + e^{xy} - \cos xy}{\cos xy - e^{xy} - x}$. **3150.** $-\sqrt[3]{\frac{y}{x}}$. **3151.** $\frac{y^2}{1 - xy}$. **3152.** $\frac{a^2}{(x + y)^2}$.

3153. $\frac{2y}{x(y-1)}$. **3154.** $\frac{y}{y-1}$. **3155.** $\frac{y^2}{x^2}\frac{\ln x-1}{\ln y-1}$.

3157. $\left(\frac{\partial y}{\partial x}\right)_{\substack{x=6\\y=2}}=\frac{4}{3}, \left(\frac{\partial y}{\partial x}\right)_{\substack{x=6\\y=8}}=-\frac{4}{3}$. **3158.** -1.

3161. $\frac{\partial z}{dx}=-\frac{c^2x}{a^2z}, \frac{\partial z}{dy}=-\frac{c^2y}{b^2z}$. **3162.** $\frac{\partial z}{\partial x}=\frac{2-x}{z+1}, \frac{\partial z}{\partial y}=\frac{2y}{z+1}$.

3163. $\frac{\partial z}{\partial x}=-\frac{yz}{xy+z^2}, \frac{\partial z}{\partial y}=-\frac{xz}{xy+z^2}$. **3164.** $\frac{\partial z}{\partial x}=\frac{z}{x(z-1)}, \frac{\partial z}{\partial y}=\frac{z}{y(z-1)}$.

3167. $\partial z=-\frac{\sin 2x\, dx+\sin 2y\, dy}{\sin 2z}$. **3168.** $z=\frac{x^2-y^2}{4}$.

3169. $z=\frac{3xy-x^3}{2}$. **3170.** $z=k\arctan\frac{y}{x}$. **3171.** $dz=\frac{x\,dx}{z}-\frac{y\,dy}{z}$.

3172. $dz=\frac{x\,dx}{a}+\frac{y\,dy}{a}$. **3173.** $dz=\sqrt{z}(x\,dx-y\,dy)$.

3174. $2(x\,dx+y\,dy)$. **3175.** $2(x\,dx+y\,dy)$.

3176. $dz=e^{-u}[(v\cos v-u\sin v)\,dx+(u\cos v+v\sin v)\,dy]$.

3185. $\frac{\partial^2 z}{\partial x^2}=\frac{2x^2+y^2}{\sqrt{x^2+y^2}}, \frac{\partial^2 z}{\partial y^2}=\frac{x^2+2y^2}{\sqrt{x^2+y^2}}, \frac{\partial^2 z}{\partial x\,\partial y}=\frac{xy}{\sqrt{x^2+y^2}}$.

3186. $\frac{\partial^2 z}{\partial x^2}=-\frac{x}{(x^2+y^2)^{3/2}}, \frac{\partial^2 z}{\partial y^2}=\frac{x^3+(x^2-y^2)\sqrt{x^2+y^2}}{(x^2+y^2)^{3/2}(x+\sqrt{x^2+y^2})^2}$,

$\frac{\partial^2 z}{\partial x\,\partial y}=-\frac{y}{(x^2+y^2)^{3/2}}$.

3187. $\frac{\partial^2 z}{\partial x^2}=-\frac{2x}{(1+x^2)^2}, \frac{\partial^2 z}{\partial y^2}=-\frac{2y}{(1+y^2)^2}, \frac{\partial^2 z}{\partial x\,\partial y}=0$.

3188. $\frac{\partial^2 z}{\partial x^2}=2a^2\cos 2(ax+by), \frac{\partial^2 z}{\partial y^2}=2b^2\cos 2(ax+by)$;

$\frac{\partial^2 z}{\partial x\,\partial y}=2ab\cos 2(ax+by)$.

3189. $\frac{\partial^2 z}{\partial x^2}=e^{xe^y+2y}, \frac{\partial^2 z}{\partial y^2}=x(1+xe^y)\,e^{xe^y+y}, \frac{\partial^2 z}{\partial x\,\partial y}=(1+xe^y)e^{xe^y+y}$.

3190. $\frac{\partial^2 z}{\partial x^2}=-\frac{4y}{(x+y)^3}, \frac{\partial^2 z}{\partial y^2}=\frac{4x}{(x+y)^3}, \frac{\partial^2 z}{\partial x\,\partial y}=\frac{2(x-y)}{(x+y)^3}$.

3191. $\frac{\partial^2 z}{\partial x^2}=\frac{\ln y(\ln y+1)}{x^2}e^{\ln x\ln y}, \frac{\partial^2 z}{\partial y^2}=\frac{\ln x(\ln x-1)}{y^2}e^{\ln x\ln y}$,

$\frac{\partial^2 z}{\partial x\,\partial y}=\frac{\ln x\ln y+1}{xy}e^{\ln x\ln y}$.

3192. $\frac{\partial^2 z}{\partial x^2}=\frac{xy^3}{\sqrt{(1-x^2y^2)^3}}, \frac{\partial^2 z}{\partial y^2}=\frac{x^3y}{\sqrt{(1-x^2y^2)^3}}, \frac{\partial^2 z}{\partial x\,\partial y}=\frac{1}{\sqrt{(1-x^2y^2)^3}}$.

3193. $\frac{(x-z)y}{\sqrt{(x^2+y^2+z^2-2xz)^3}}$. **3194.** $2y^3(2+xy^2)\,e^{xy^2}$. **3195.** $\frac{4x(3y^2-x^2)}{(x^2+y^2)^3}$.

3196. $-x(2\sin xy+xy\cos xy)$. **3197.** $(x^2y^2z^2+3xyz+1)\,e^{xyz}$.

3198. $mn(n-1)(n-2)p(p-1)x^{m-1}y^{n-3}z^{p-2}$. **3204.** $a=-3$.

3209. $$\frac{\partial^2 y}{\partial x^2} = -\frac{\dfrac{\partial^2 f}{\partial x^2}\left(\dfrac{\partial f}{\partial y}\right)^2 - 2\dfrac{\partial^2 f}{\partial x\,\partial y}\dfrac{\partial f}{\partial x}\dfrac{\partial f}{\partial y} + \dfrac{\partial^2 f}{\partial y^2}\left(\dfrac{\partial f}{\partial x}\right)^2}{\left(\dfrac{\partial f}{\partial y}\right)^3}$$

$$= \left(\frac{\partial f}{\partial y}\right)^2 \begin{vmatrix} 0 & \dfrac{\partial f}{\partial x} & \dfrac{\partial f}{\partial y} \\ \dfrac{\partial f}{\partial x} & \dfrac{\partial^2 f}{\partial x^2} & \dfrac{\partial^2 f}{\partial x\,\partial y} \\ \dfrac{\partial f}{\partial y} & \dfrac{\partial^2 f}{\partial x\,\partial y} & \dfrac{\partial^2 f}{\partial y^2} \end{vmatrix}.$$

3219. $-2y\,dx^2 + 4(y - x)\,dx\,dy + 2x\,dy^2$. **3220.** $-\dfrac{(dx - dy)^2}{(x - y)^2}$.

3221. $\dfrac{(3x^2 - y^2)\,dx^2 + 8xy\,dx\,dy + (3y^2 - x^2)\,dy^2}{(x^2 + y^2)^3}$.

3222. $2\sin 2y\,dx\,dy + 2x\cos 2y\,dy^2$. **3223.** $e^{xy}[(y\,dx + x\,dy)^2 + 2\,dx\,dy]$.

3224. $2(z\,dx\,dy + y\,dx\,dz + x\,dy\,dz)$.

3225. $-\cos(2x + y)(2\,dx + dy)^3$, $(2\,dx + dy)^3$; 0.

3226. $-\sin(x + y + z)(dx + dy + dz)^2$.

3227. $-\dfrac{c^4}{z^3}\left[\left(\dfrac{x^2}{a^2} + \dfrac{z^2}{c^2}\right)\dfrac{dx^2}{a^2} + \dfrac{2xy}{a^2b^2}\,dx\,dy + \left(\dfrac{y^2}{b^2} + \dfrac{z^2}{c^2}\right)\dfrac{dy^2}{b^2}\right]$.

3228. $-\dfrac{2z\,[xy^3\,dx^2 + (x^2y^2 + 2xyz^2 - z^4)\,dx\,dy + x^3y\,dy^2]}{(z^2 - xy)^3}$.

3229. $-31.5\,dx^2 + 206\,dx\,dy - 306\,dy^2$. **3230.** $\dfrac{d^2y}{dt^2} + y$.

3231. $y'' - 5y' + y$. **3232.** $\dfrac{d^2y}{dt^2} + ay$. **3233.** $y - x''$. **3234.** $-\dfrac{x'''}{x'^5}$.

3235. $-\dfrac{v'' + 2v}{v^3}$. **3236.** $\dfrac{d\rho}{d\varphi} = \rho$. **3237.** $\dfrac{2\rho'^2 - \rho\rho'' + \rho^2}{(\rho'^2 + \rho^2)^{3/2}}$. **3238.** $-\dfrac{\partial z}{\partial v}$.

3239. $\dfrac{\partial^2 u}{\partial \rho^2} + \dfrac{1}{\rho^2}\dfrac{\partial^2 u}{\partial \varphi^2} + \dfrac{1}{\rho}\dfrac{\partial u}{\partial \rho}$. **3240.** $\omega''(\rho) + \dfrac{1}{\rho}\omega'(\rho) + k\omega(\rho)$. **3241.** $-4\dfrac{\partial^2 w}{\partial u^2} + 2$.

Chapter 11

3242. $x^3 + 2y^3 - xy + h(3x^2 - y) + k(6y^2 - x) + 3xh^2 - hk + 6yk^2 + h^3 + 2k^3$.

3243. $\Delta z = 15h^2 - 6hk + k^2 + h^3$.

3244. $\Delta z = -2h + 7k - 4h^2 + 4hk + 2k^2 - 2h^3 - h^2k + \dfrac{5}{2}hk^2 + \dfrac{1}{4}k^3 - h^3k + \dfrac{1}{2}h^2k^2 + \dfrac{1}{4}hk^3$, $f(1.02, 2.03) \approx 2.1726$.

3245. $Ax^2 + By^2 + Cz^2 + Dxy + Eyz + Fzx + (2Ax + Dy + Fz)h + (2By + Dx + Ez)k + (2Cz + Ey + Fx)l + Ah^2 + Bk^2 + Cl^2 + Dhk + Ekl + Fhl$.

3246. $z = \frac{1}{2} + \frac{1}{2}\left(x - \frac{\pi}{4}\right) + \frac{1}{2}\left(y - \frac{\pi}{4}\right) - \frac{1}{4}\left[\left(x - \frac{\pi}{4}\right)^2 - 2\left(x - \frac{\pi}{4}\right)\left(y - \frac{\pi}{4}\right) + \left(y - \frac{\pi}{4}\right)^2\right] - \frac{1}{6}\left[\cos\xi\cos\eta\left(x - \frac{\pi}{4}\right)^3 + 3\sin\xi\cos\eta\left(x - \frac{\pi}{4}\right)^2\left(y - \frac{\pi}{4}\right) + 3\cos\xi\sin\eta\left(x - \frac{\pi}{4}\right)\left(y - \frac{\pi}{4}\right)^2 + \sin\xi\cos\eta\left(y - \frac{\pi}{4}\right)^3\right].$

3247. $z = 1 + (x-1) + (x-1)(y-1) + \frac{1}{2}(x-1)^2(y-1) + \ldots, z_1 \approx 1.1021.$

3248. $e^x\left[\sin y + h\sin y + k\cos y + \frac{1}{2}(h^2\sin y + 2hk\cos y - k^2\sin y) + \frac{1}{6}(h^3\sin y + 3h^2k\cos y - 3hk^2\sin y - k^3\cos y)\right] + \ldots, z_1 \approx 1.1051.$

3249. $y + xy + \frac{1}{2}x^2y - \frac{1}{6}y^3 + \ldots.$

3250. $y + \frac{1}{2!}(2xy - y^2) + \frac{1}{3!}(3x^2y - 3xy^2 + 2y^3) + \ldots.$

3251. $1 + (x + y) + \ldots + \frac{x^{n+1} - y^{n+1}}{x - y} + \ldots.$

3252*. $x - y - \frac{1}{3}(x^3 - y^3) + \frac{1}{5}(x^5 - y^5) - \ldots + \frac{(-1)^n}{2n+1}(x^{2n+1} - y^{2n+1}) + \ldots$

Note that $\arctan\frac{x - y}{1 + xy} = \arctan x - \arctan y.$

3253. $\left(\sum_{n=1}^{\infty}\frac{x^n}{n}\right)\left(\sum_{n=1}^{\infty}\frac{y^n}{n}\right) = \sum_{n=1}^{\infty}\sum_{m=1}^{\infty}\frac{x^ny^m}{nm}.$ **3254.** $\sum_{n=2}^{\infty}\frac{(x+y)^n - x^n - y^n}{n}.$

3255. $\sum_{n=0}^{\infty}(-1)^n\frac{(x^2+y^2)^{2n+1}}{(2n+1)!}.$

3256. $\sum_{m=0}^{\infty}\frac{x^m}{m!}\sum_{n=0}^{\infty}(-1)^n\frac{y^{2n}}{(2n)!} = \sum_{m=0}^{\infty}\sum_{n=0}^{\infty}(-1)^n\frac{x^my^{2n}}{m!(2n)!}.$

3257. $z = 1 + (x-1) + \frac{1}{4}(y-1) - \frac{1}{8}(x-1)(y-1) + \frac{9}{64}(y-1)^2 + \ldots.$

3259. $(0, 0), \left(-\frac{5}{3}, 0\right), (-1, 2), (-1, -2).$ **3260.** $\left(\frac{1}{2}, -1\right).$

3261. $(0, 0), (0, a), (a, 0), \left(\frac{a}{3}, \frac{a}{3}\right).$

3262. $(0, 0), (0, 2b), (a, b), (2a, 0), (2a, 2b).$ **3263.** $\left(\frac{\pi}{6}, \frac{\pi}{6}\right).$

3264. $\left(\frac{b}{a}, \frac{c}{a}\right).$ **3265.** $\left(-\frac{2}{3}, -\frac{2}{3}\right).$ **3266.** $(2, 1, 7).$ **3267.** $(6, 4, 10).$

3268. A and C maxima, B minimum; in the neighbourhood of D the surface has the shape of a saddle, along EF the function retains the constant value.

3269. $(-2, 0), \left(\frac{16}{7}, 0\right)$, each of the points will be stationary for one of the branches of the function.

3270. (1, 1), (–1, –1).

3271*. (0, 0). To make sure that the found point is a point of maximum it is sufficient to represent the function in the form:

$$z = 10 - (x - y)^2 - 2x^2 - y^2.$$

3272. (2, –2). **3273.** (–1, 1). **3277.** (6, 4) is a point of maximum.

3278. There is no extremum at the point (0, 0). (1, 1) is a point of minimum.

3279. The greatest and the least values lie on the boundary of the domain; the greatest value $z = 4$ is at the points (2, 0) and (–2, 0); the least value $z = -4$ at the points (0, 2) and (0, –2). The stationary point (0, 0) yields no extremum.

3280. The greatest value $z = 17$ is at the point (1, 2); the least value $z = -3$ at the point (1, 0); the stationary point (–4, 6) lies outside the given domain.

3281. The greatest value $z = 4$ is at the stationary point (2, 1) (this point being thus a point of maximum). The least value $z = -64$ is at the point (4, 2), i.e., on the boundary.

3282. The least value of the function $z = 0$ is at the point (0, 0). The greatest value $z = \frac{3}{e}$ is at the points $(0, \pm 1)$.

3283. $z_{\text{greatest}} = \frac{3}{2}\sqrt{3}$ at the point $\left(\frac{\pi}{3}, \frac{\pi}{3}\right)$ (maximum). $z_{\text{least}} = 0$ at the point (0, 0) (on the boundary).

3284. All the summands are equal to one another.

3285. All the factors are equal to one another. **3286.** $\left(\frac{8}{5}, \frac{16}{5}\right)$.

3287. $\frac{x}{a} + \frac{y}{b} + \frac{z}{c} = 3$. **3288.** $x = \frac{\sum_{i=1}^{n} x_i}{n}$, $y = \frac{\sum_{i=1}^{n} y_i}{n}$.

3289. $(3, \sqrt{39}, 0)$; $(3, -\sqrt{39}, 0)$. **3290.** Cube.

3291. At the point (1, 1), minimum $z = 2$.

3292. (a, a) or $(-a, -a)$, $z = a^2$ (maximum), $(a, -a)$ or $(-a, a)$, $z = -a^2$ (minimum).

3293. $(-a\sqrt{2}, -a\sqrt{2})$, $z = -\frac{\sqrt{2}}{a}$ (minimum), $(a\sqrt{2}, a\sqrt{2})$, $z = \frac{\sqrt{2}}{a}$ (maximum).

3294. Stationary points $x = -\frac{1}{2}\arctan\frac{b}{a}$, $y = \frac{1}{2}\arctan\frac{a}{b}$.

3295. (3, 3, 3), $u = 9$ (minimum).

3296. Each of the two of the variables is equal to 2, the third being equal to 1 (minimum equal to 4); two of the variables are equal to $\frac{4}{3}$ (each), the third to $\frac{7}{3}$ $\left(\text{maximum equal to } \frac{112}{27}\right)$.

3297*. Investigate for minimum the function $\frac{x_1^2 + x_2^2 + \ldots + x_n^2}{n}$ if $x_1 + x_2 + \ldots + x_n = A$. In general, the relationship $\frac{\sum x_i^k}{n} \geq \left(\frac{\sum x_i}{n}\right)^k$ is valid if $k \geq 1$ and $x_i \geq 0$.

3299. $u_{\min} = \dfrac{abc}{bc + ca + ab}$ at $x = \dfrac{bc}{bc + ca + ab}$; $y = \dfrac{ac}{bc + ac + ab}$;

$z = \dfrac{ab}{bc + ac + ab}$.

3300. $u_{\text{greatest}} = 1, u_{\text{least}} = -\dfrac{1}{2}$. **3301.** $\left(\dfrac{21}{13}, 2, \dfrac{63}{26}\right)$. **3302.** $(3, -1, 1)$.

3303. (a) $(-2, 0, 0)$; (b) $(2, 0, 0)$. **3304.** Cube. **3305.** Cube.

3306. $\dfrac{8abc}{3\sqrt{3}}$.

3307. If R is the radius of the tent base; H, the height of the cylindrical portion; h, the height of the conical top, then the following relations must be valid:

$$R = \frac{h\sqrt{5}}{2},\ H = \frac{h}{2}.$$

3308. If l is the lateral side of the trapezoid; b the base and x the angle of inclination of the lateral side, then the following relations must be valid : $i = b = \dfrac{2\sqrt{A}}{\sqrt[4]{3^3}}, \alpha = \dfrac{\pi}{3}$, where A is the given cross-sectional area. And the surface $u = 2\sqrt[4]{3} \cdot \sqrt{A} \approx 2.632\sqrt{A}$.

3309. Cube.

3310. Each side of the base is equal to $2\alpha + \sqrt[3]{2v}$, the altitude being equal to half the side: $\left(\alpha + \dfrac{1}{2}\sqrt[3]{2v}\right)$.

3311. a^3 (cube). **3312.** The least area is equal to $3\sqrt{-ab}$.

3313. $\left(\dfrac{4}{\sqrt{5}}, \dfrac{3}{\sqrt{5}}\right)$ and $\left(-\dfrac{4}{\sqrt{5}}, -\dfrac{3}{\sqrt{5}}\right)$. **3314.** $\left(-\dfrac{5}{9}, -\dfrac{1}{9}\right)$. **3315.** $(3, 5)$.

3316. $z_{\text{greatest}} = 2$. **3317.** The side of the triangle $\sqrt{2S}$, $\sqrt{2S}$ and $2\sqrt{S}$.

3318. Altitude $\dfrac{H}{3}$, sides of the base $\dfrac{2a\sqrt{2}}{3}$ and $\dfrac{2a\sqrt{2}}{3}$, volume $V = \dfrac{8}{27}abH$.

3319. Tetrahedron.

3320. The normal to the ellipse at the required point must be perpendicular to the line joining the given points.

3321. Draw the normal at the points $\left(\pm a\sqrt{\dfrac{a}{a+b}}, \pm b\sqrt{\dfrac{b}{a+b}}\right)$.

3322. $\left(9, \dfrac{1}{8}, \dfrac{3}{8}\right), \left(-9, -\dfrac{1}{8}, -\dfrac{3}{8}\right)$. **3323.** $2\sqrt{2}$. **3324.** $x + y = 2, y = x$.

3325. $x - y + a = 0, x + y - 3a = 0$.

3326. $x + 2y - 1 = 0, 2x - y - 2 = 0$.

3327. $x - y + 2 = 0, x + y - 2 = 0$. **3328.** $(0, 0)$. **3329.** $(0, 0)$.

3330. $(0, 0)$. **3331.** $(a, 0)$. **3332.** $(0, a), (0, -a), (a, 0), (-a, 0)$.

3333. $(2, 0), (-2, 0)$. **3334.** $(0, 3), (-3, 0), (-6, 3)$.

3335. $(0, 0)$ double point. **3336.** $(0, 0)$ isolated point.

3338. $k\pi; k = 0, 1, 2, \ldots$, cusps. **3339.** $(a, 0)$ cusp. **3340.** $(0, 0)$.

3341. $x = -f'(a), y = f(a) - af'(a); y = x \arcsin x + \sqrt{1 - x^2}$.

3342. $16y^3 + 27x^4 = 0$. **3343.** $y^2 = 4ax$.

3344. $y = \frac{x}{2}$ and $y = -\frac{x}{2}$. **3345.** $y = -\frac{x^4}{4}$. **3346.** $y = 0$ and $16y = x^4$.

3347. $y = x$ and $y = x - \frac{4}{27}$. The former is a locus of singular points, the latter is an envelope.

3348. $x^2 + \frac{2}{3\sqrt{3}} y^2 = 0$ and $x^2 - \frac{2}{3\sqrt{3}} y^3 = 0$.

3349. $x^{2/3} + y^{2/3} = d^{2/3}$. **3350.** Four straight lines $x \pm y = \pm R$.

3351. $2by(x^2 + y^2) + x^2 = 0$. **3352.** Parabola $\sqrt{x} + \sqrt{y} = \sqrt{a}$.

3353. Cycloid $x = \frac{R}{2}(t - \sin t)$, $y = \frac{R}{2}(1 - \cos t)$.

3354. Ellipse $x^2 + \frac{y^2}{2} = R^2$. **3355.** Hyperbola $xy = \frac{a}{4}$.

3357. Evolute of parabola $y^2 = \frac{8}{27p}(x - p)^3$.

3359. Hyperbolas $xy = \frac{1}{2}$ and $xy = -\frac{1}{2}$.

3361. (a) $2r \cdot \frac{d\mathbf{r}}{dt} = 2|\mathbf{r}| \cdot \frac{d|\mathbf{r}|}{dt}$; (b) $\left(\frac{d\mathbf{r}}{dt}\right)^2 + \mathbf{r}\,\frac{d^2r}{dt^2}$; (c) $\mathbf{r} \times \frac{d^2\mathbf{r}}{dt^2}$; (d) $\left(\mathbf{r}\,\frac{d\mathbf{r}}{dt}\,\frac{d^3\mathbf{r}}{dt^3}\right)$.

3362. From the equality $\frac{d\mathbf{r}}{dt} = \alpha(t)\mathbf{r}$ it follows that

$$\frac{d^2\mathbf{r}}{dt^2} = \frac{d\alpha}{dt}\mathbf{r} + \alpha\,\frac{d\mathbf{r}}{dt} = \left(\frac{d\alpha}{dt} + \alpha^2\right)\mathbf{r} = \beta(t) \cdot \mathbf{r} \text{ and so on.}$$

3363. Differentiating the equality $\mathbf{r}^2 = \text{const}$ (see Problem 3361), we obtain: $\mathbf{r} \cdot \frac{d\mathbf{r}}{dt} = 0$. The tangent to the spherical line, i.e., to the line located on the sphere, is perpendicular to the radius of the sphere drawn to the point of tangency. The converse is also true.

3368. $\frac{d\mathbf{r}}{dx} = \frac{d\mathbf{r}}{du}\varphi'$, $\frac{d^2\mathbf{r}}{dx^2} = \frac{d^2\mathbf{r}}{du^2}\varphi'^2 + \frac{d\mathbf{r}}{du}\varphi''$,

$$\frac{d^3\mathbf{r}}{dx^3} = \frac{d^3\mathbf{r}}{du^3}\varphi'^3 + 3\,\frac{d^2\mathbf{r}}{du^2}\varphi'\varphi'' + \frac{d\mathbf{r}}{du}\varphi'''.$$

3370. From the equality $\mathbf{a}\,\frac{d\mathbf{r}(\tau)}{dt} = 0$, where $t_1 < \tau < t_2$, it follows that on a closed (by virtue of the equality $\mathbf{r}(t_1) = \mathbf{r}(t_2)$) curve we can always find a point at which the tangent is perpendicular to any pressigned direction.

3371. The hodograph of velocity $\mathbf{v}\ \{a \cos t, a \sin t, 2bt\}$ is a helix; the hodograph of acceleration $\mathbf{w}\{-a \sin t, a \cos t, 2b\}$ is a circle.

3372. Scalar multiplication by $\mathbf{a}$ and $\mathbf{r}$ yields : $\mathbf{a}\frac{d\mathbf{r}}{dt} = 0$, $\mathbf{r}\,\frac{d\mathbf{r}}{dt} = 0$. Hence, $\mathbf{ar} = \text{const}$ is the equation of a plane and $\mathbf{r}^2 = \text{const}$ is the equation of a sphere. The required path is a circle whose plane is perpendicular to the vector $\mathbf{a}$.

3374. Ellipse. Velocity will be maximum at the time when the material point is at the end of the minor semiaxis, and it will be minimum when the point is at the end of the major semiaxis. Acceleration will be maximum (minimum) at the time when velocity is minimum (maximum).

3375. Velocity components : $\frac{d\rho}{dt}, \rho\frac{d\varphi}{dt}, \rho \sin\varphi \frac{d\theta}{dt}$. *Hint:* Find the scalar products: $\frac{d\mathbf{r}}{dt}\mathbf{e}_\rho, \frac{d\mathbf{r}}{dt}\mathbf{e}_\varphi, \frac{d\mathbf{r}}{dt}\mathbf{e}_\theta$.

3376. $\dfrac{x-\frac{t^4}{4}}{t^2} = \dfrac{y-\frac{t^3}{3}}{t} = \dfrac{z-\frac{t^2}{2}}{1}$; $t^2x + ty + z = \frac{t^6}{4} + \frac{t^4}{3} + \frac{t^2}{2}$.

3377. $\dfrac{x-\frac{a\sqrt{2}}{2}}{-a\sqrt{2}} = \dfrac{y-\frac{a\sqrt{2}}{2}}{a\sqrt{2}} = \dfrac{z-\frac{k}{8}}{\frac{k}{\pi}}$; $-x + y + \frac{k}{\pi a\sqrt{2}}$; $z = \frac{k^2}{8\pi a\sqrt{2}}$.

3378. $x - 6a = \frac{y-18a}{6} = \frac{z-72a}{36}$; $x + 6y + 36z = 2706a$.

3379. $\dfrac{x-\frac{\pi}{2}+1}{1} = \dfrac{y-1}{1} = \dfrac{z-2\sqrt{2}}{\sqrt{2}}$; $x + y + \sqrt{2}\cdot z = \frac{\pi}{2} + 4$.

3380. $\frac{x-1}{12} = \frac{y-3}{-4} = \frac{z-4}{3}$; $12x - 4y + 3z - 12 = 0$.

3381. $\frac{x+2}{27} = \frac{y-1}{28} = \frac{z-6}{4}$; $27x + 28y + 4z + 2 = 0$.

3382. $\frac{x-x_0}{z_0} = \frac{y-y_0}{z_0} = \frac{z-z_0}{y_0+x_0}$; $\frac{x+y}{x_0+y_0} + \frac{z}{z_0} = 2$.

3383. $\frac{x-x_0}{y_0^2z_0^2} = \frac{y-y_0}{x_0^2z_0^2} = \frac{z-z_0}{-x_0^2y_0^2}$; $\frac{x-x_0}{x_0^2} + \frac{y-y_0}{y_0^2} - \frac{z-z_0}{z_0^2} = 0$.

3384. $\mathbf{r}_0\left\{\frac{\sqrt{3}}{2}, \frac{1}{2}, e^{\pi/6}\right\}$.

3385. $6x - 8y - z + 3 = 0$; $\frac{x-1}{6} = \frac{y-1}{-8} = \frac{z-1}{-1}$; $\frac{x-1}{31} = \frac{y-1}{26} = \frac{z-1}{-22}$.

3386. $\sqrt{b}(x-x_0) - \sqrt{a}(y-y_0) = 0$; $\frac{x-x_0}{\sqrt{b}} = \frac{y-y_0}{-\sqrt{a}} = \frac{z-z_0}{0}$;

$\frac{x-x_0}{\sqrt{2az_0}} = \frac{y-y_0}{\sqrt{2bz_0}} = \frac{z-z_0}{-(a+b)}$.

3387. $\frac{1}{e}x - ey - \sqrt{2}z + 2 = 0$; $\dfrac{x-e}{-\frac{1}{e}} = \dfrac{y-\frac{1}{e}}{e} = \dfrac{z-\sqrt{2}}{\sqrt{2}}$;

$\dfrac{x-e}{1} = \dfrac{y-\frac{1}{e}}{1} = \dfrac{z-\sqrt{2}}{-\sqrt{2}\sinh 1}$.

3389. $\frac{x-1}{2} = \frac{y}{-1} = \frac{z-1}{3}$; $2x - y + 3z - 5 = 0$;

$\frac{x-1}{3} = \frac{y}{3} = \frac{z-1}{-1}$; $3x + 3y - z - 2 = 0$; $\frac{x-1}{8} = \frac{y}{-11} = \frac{z-1}{-9}$;

$8x - 11y - 9z + 1 = 0$.

3390. $\frac{x-1}{1}=\frac{y-1}{-1}=\frac{z-1}{0}$; $x-y=0$; $\frac{x-1}{0}=\frac{y-1}{0}=\frac{z-1}{1}$; $z=1$;
$\frac{x-1}{1}=\frac{y-1}{1}=\frac{z-1}{0}$; $x+y-2=0$.

3391. $\frac{x-\frac{\sqrt{2}}{2}}{\sqrt{2}}=\frac{y-\frac{\sqrt{2}}{2}}{-\sqrt{2}}=\frac{z-1}{4}$; $\sqrt{2}x-\sqrt{2}y+4z=4$;
$\frac{x-\frac{\sqrt{2}}{2}}{\sqrt{2}}=\frac{y-\frac{\sqrt{2}}{2}}{3\sqrt{2}}=\frac{z-1}{1}$; $\sqrt{2}x+3\sqrt{2}y+z-5=0$;
$\frac{x-\frac{\sqrt{2}}{2}}{13}=\frac{y-\frac{\sqrt{2}}{2}}{-3}=\frac{z-1}{-4\sqrt{2}}$; $-13x+3y+4\sqrt{2}z+\sqrt{2}=0$.

3392. $\frac{x+1}{2}=\frac{y-13}{3}=\frac{z}{6}$; $2x+3y+6z=37$; $\frac{x+1}{6}=\frac{y-13}{2}=\frac{z}{-3}$;
$6x+2y-3z=20$; $\frac{x+1}{3}=\frac{y-13}{-6}=\frac{z}{2}$; $3x-6y+2z=-81$.

3393. For any point of the curve the equation of the touching plane is $3x-2y-11=0$, i.e., the curve entirely lies in this plane.

3394. A touching plane is one and the same for all points of the curve. Its equation is

$$\begin{vmatrix} x & y & z \\ a_1 & a_2 & a_3 \\ b_1 & b_2 & b_3 \end{vmatrix} = \begin{vmatrix} a_1 & a_2 & a_3 \\ b_1 & b_2 & b_3 \\ c_1 & c_2 & c_3 \end{vmatrix}.$$

3395. $\frac{\cosh^2 t}{\sinh t}$. **3396.** $R=\sqrt{2}\operatorname{cosec} 2t$. **3398.** $k=\sqrt{\frac{(y'z''-z'y'')^2+y''^2+z''^2}{(1+y'^2+z'^2)^3}}$.

3399. $\tau_1=\frac{\mathbf{r}'}{|\mathbf{r}'|}, \beta_1=\frac{\mathbf{r}'\times\mathbf{r}''}{|\mathbf{r}'\times\mathbf{r}''|}, \mathbf{v}_1=\frac{(\mathbf{r}'\times\mathbf{r}'')\times\mathbf{r}'}{|\mathbf{r}'|\cdot|\mathbf{r}'\times\mathbf{r}''|}$.

3400. $\tau_1=v_1\times\beta_1$; $v_1=\beta_1\times\tau_1$; $\beta_1=\tau_1\times v_1$.

3401. The required vector ω (if any) can be represented in the form

$$\omega=(\omega\tau_1)\tau_1+(\omega v_1)v_1+(\omega\beta_1)\beta_1 \qquad (1)$$

From the hypothesis it follows that

$$\omega\times\tau_1=kv_1; \omega\times v_1=-k\tau_1+T\beta_1; \quad \omega\times\beta_1=-Tv_1 \qquad (2)$$

Performing scalar multiplication by v_1, β_1, τ_1, we find respectively that $\omega\tau_1=T, \omega v_1=0, \omega\beta_1=k$ and hence, $\omega=T\tau_1+k\beta_1$. Substitution into formulas (2) shows that this vector satisfies the conditions of the problem.

3402. $99+\ln 10\approx 101.43$. **3403.** $a\ln(1+\sqrt{2})=a\ln\left(\tan\frac{3\pi}{8}\right)$. **3404.** $\sqrt{3}(e^t-1)$.

3405. 5. **3406.** $4a$. **3407.** $z\sqrt{2}$. **3408.** $a\ln\frac{\sqrt{2a}+\sqrt{x}}{\sqrt{2a}-\sqrt{x}}$. **3409.** $\frac{a}{2}\left(1+\frac{1}{2}\ln 3\right)$.

3410. $8x-8y-z=4$; $\frac{x-2}{8}=\frac{y-1}{-8}=\frac{z-4}{-1}$.

3411. $x + y - z - 1 = 0; \dfrac{x-1}{1} = \dfrac{y-1}{1} = \dfrac{z-1}{-1}$.

3412. $z + a = 0, x = a, y = a$.

3413. $17x + 11y + 5z = 60; \dfrac{x-3}{17} = \dfrac{y-4}{11} = \dfrac{z+7}{5}$.

3414. $x - y + 2z - \dfrac{\pi}{2} = 0; \dfrac{x-1}{1} = \dfrac{y-1}{-1} = \dfrac{z - \frac{\pi}{2}}{2}$.

3415. $\dfrac{x}{a} + \dfrac{y}{b} + \dfrac{z}{c} = \sqrt{3}; a\left(x - \dfrac{a\sqrt{3}}{3}\right) = b\left(y - \dfrac{b\sqrt{3}}{3}\right) = c\left(z - \dfrac{c\sqrt{3}}{3}\right)$.

3416. $x + 11y + 5z - 18 = 0; \dfrac{x-1}{1} = \dfrac{y-2}{11} = \dfrac{z+1}{5}$.

3417. $3x - 2y - 2z + 1 = 0; \dfrac{x-1}{3} = \dfrac{y-1}{-2} = \dfrac{z-1}{-2}$.

3418. $2x + y + 11z - 25 = 0; \dfrac{x-1}{2} = \dfrac{y-1}{1} = \dfrac{z-2}{11}$.

3419. $5x + 4y + z - 28 = 0; \dfrac{x-2}{5} = \dfrac{y-3}{4} = \dfrac{z-6}{1}$.

3421. $x - y + 2z = \sqrt{\dfrac{11}{2}}$ and $x - y + 2z = -\sqrt{\dfrac{11}{2}}$.

3422. $x + y + z = \sqrt{a^2 + b^2 + c^2}$.

3424. All the planes pass through the origin.

3425. $x_0x + y_0y + z_0z = a^2; \dfrac{x}{x_0} = \dfrac{y}{y_0} = \dfrac{z}{z_0}$.

3426. $\dfrac{xx_0}{a^2} - \dfrac{yy_0}{b^2} = 2(z + z_0); \dfrac{a(x-x_0)}{bx_0} = -\dfrac{b(y-y_0)}{ay_0} = \dfrac{z-z_0}{-2ab}$.

3428. $\dfrac{9}{2}a^2$. **3430.** $2x + y - z = 2$. **3434.** $4x - 2y - 3z = 3$.

3435. Parallel to the plane xOy at the points (0, 3, 3) and (0, 3, –7); to the plane yOz at the points (5, 3, –2) and (–5, 3, –2); to the plane xOz at the points (0, – 2, – 2) and (0, 8, – 2).

3436. (a) $6u_0v_0x - 3(u_0 + v_0)y + 2z + (u_0 + v_0)(u_0^2 - 4u_0v_0 + v_0^2) = 0$.

(b) $3(x_0^2 - y_0)x - 3x_0(y + y_0) + 2z + 4z_0 = 0$.

3437. $2z(x^2 + y^2 + z^2) + p(x^2 + y^2) = 0$.

3438. $(x^2 + y^2 + z^2)^3 = 27a^3xyz$.

3439. (1) $\{-2, 1\}$; (2) $\{10xy - 3y^3, 5x^2 - 9xy^2 + 4y^3\}$.

3440. (1) $6\mathbf{i} + 4\mathbf{j}$; (2) $\dfrac{1}{3}(2\mathbf{i} + \mathbf{j})$; (3) $\dfrac{-y_0\mathbf{i} + x_0\mathbf{j}}{x_0^2 + y_0^2}$.

3441. (1) $\tan\varphi \approx 0.342, \varphi \approx 18°52'$; (2) $\tan\varphi \approx 4.87, \varphi \approx 78°24'$.

3442. Negative y-axis.

3443. (1) $\cos\alpha \approx 0.99, \alpha = 8°$; (2) $\cos\alpha \approx -0.199, \alpha \approx 101°30'$.

3444. (1) $\left(-\frac{1}{3}, \frac{3}{4}\right), \left(\frac{7}{3}, -\frac{3}{4}\right)$; (2) Points on the circle $x^2 + y^2 = \frac{2}{3}$.

3447. (1) $\{3x_0^2 y_0^2 z_0, 2x_0^3 y_0 z_0, x_0^3 y_0^2\}$;

(2) $\frac{x\mathbf{i} + y\mathbf{j} + z\mathbf{k}}{\sqrt{x^2 + y^2 + z^2}} = \frac{\mathbf{r}}{|\mathbf{r}|}$, where $\mathbf{r}$ is a radius vector.

3450. (1) $2\mathbf{r}$; (2) $2\frac{\mathbf{r}}{|\mathbf{r}|}$; (3) $2\mathbf{F}'(\mathbf{r}^2)\mathbf{r}$; (4) $\mathbf{a}(\mathbf{br}) + \mathbf{b}(\mathbf{ar})$; (5) $\mathbf{a} \times \mathbf{b}$.

3451. (1) 0; (2) $\frac{\sqrt{2}}{2}$; (3) $-\sqrt{5}$; (4) $\frac{\cos\alpha + \sin\alpha}{2}$. **3452.** $\frac{\sqrt{2}}{3}$.

3453. $\frac{1}{2}$. **3455.** (1) 5; (2) $\frac{98}{13}$. **3456.** -22. **3459.** $\frac{1}{\mathbf{r}^2}$.

Chapter 12

3460. $M = \iint\limits_D \gamma(x, y)\, d\sigma$. **3461.** $\iint\limits_D \sigma(x, y)\, d\sigma$.

3462. $T = \frac{1}{2}\omega^2 \iint\limits_D y^2 \gamma(x, y)\, d\sigma$. **3463.** $Q = (t_2 - t_1) \iint\limits_D c(x, y)\, \gamma(x, y) d\sigma$.

3464. $M = \iiint\limits_\Omega \gamma(x, y, z)\, dv$. **3465.** $E = \iiint\limits_\Omega \delta(x, y, z)\, dv$.

3466. $8\pi(5 - \sqrt{2}) < I < 8\pi(5 + \sqrt{2})$. **3467.** $36\pi < I < 100\pi$.

3468. $2 < I < 8$. **3469.** $-8 < I < \frac{2}{3}$. **3470.** $0 < I < 64$.

3471. $4 < I < 36$. **3472.** $4 < I < 8(5 - 2\sqrt{2})$. **3473.** $4\pi < I < 22\pi$.

3474. $0 < I < \frac{4}{3}\pi R^5$. **3475.** $24 < I < 72$. **3476.** $28\pi\sqrt{3} < I < 52\pi\sqrt{3}$.

3477. 1. **3478.** $(e - 1)^2$. **3479.** $\frac{\pi}{12}$. **3480.** $\ln\frac{4}{3}$.

3481. $\ln\frac{2 + \sqrt{2}}{1 + \sqrt{3}}$. **3482.** $\pi - 2$. **3483.** 2. **3484.** $-\frac{\pi}{16}$.

3485. $\int_3^5 dx \int_{\frac{3x+1}{2}}^{\frac{3x+4}{2}} f(x, y)\, dy$. **3486.** $\int_0^2 dx \int_0^{2-x} f(x, y)\, dy$.

3487. $\int_0^1 dx \int_0^{\sqrt{1-x^2}} f(x, y)\, dy$.

3488. $\int_0^1 dx \int_{x-1}^{1-x} f(x, y)\, dy$.

3489. $\int_{-\sqrt{2}}^{\sqrt{2}} dx \int_{x^2}^{4-x^2} f(x, y)\, dy.$

3490. $\int_{-2}^{2} dx \int_{-3/2\sqrt{4-x^2}}^{3/2\sqrt{4-x^2}} f(x, y)\, dy.$

3491. $\int_{0}^{4} dx \int_{2-\sqrt{4x-x^2}}^{3+\sqrt{4x-x^2}} f(x, y)\, dy.$

3492. $\int_{0}^{1} dx \int_{x^2}^{\sqrt{x}} f(x, y)\, dy.$

3493. $\int_{0}^{2} dx \int_{x}^{2x} f(x, y)\, dy + \int_{2}^{3} dx \int_{x}^{6-x} f(x, y)\, dy.$

3494. $\int_{-2/3}^{1/3} dx \int_{1-2x}^{x+3} f(x, y)\, dy + \int_{1/3}^{2/3} dx \int_{x}^{x+3} f(x, y)\, dy$

$+ \int_{2/3}^{5/3} dx \int_{x}^{5-2x} f(x, y)\, dy.$

3495. $\int_{0}^{1} dx \int_{x/2}^{2x} f(x, y)\, dy + \int_{1}^{2} dx \int_{x/2}^{2/x} f(x, y)\, dy.$

3496. $\int_{0}^{2} dx \int_{-2\sqrt{2x}}^{2x} f(x, y)\, dy + \int_{2}^{9/2} dx \int_{-2\sqrt{2x}}^{2\sqrt{2x}} f(x, y)\, dy$

$+ \int_{9/2}^{8} dx \int_{-2\sqrt{2x}}^{24-4x} f(x, y)\, dy.$

3497. $\int_{-3}^{-2} dx \int_{-\sqrt{9-x^2}}^{\sqrt{9-x^2}} f(x, y)\, dy + \int_{-2}^{2} dx \int_{-\sqrt{1+x^2}}^{\sqrt{1+x^2}} f(x, y)\, dy$

$+ \int_{2}^{3} dx \int_{-\sqrt{9-x^2}}^{\sqrt{9-x^2}} f(x, y)\, dy.$

3498. $\int_{0}^{1} dx \int_{x^2}^{x} f(x, y)\, dy.$

3499. $\int_{0}^{1} dy \int_{-\sqrt{1-y^2}}^{\sqrt{1-y^2}} f(x, y)\, dx.$

3500. $\int_{0}^{r} dy \int_{r-\sqrt{r^2-y^2}}^{y} f(x, y)\, dx.$

3501. $\int_{-\sqrt{2}}^{\sqrt{2}} dy \int_{-\sqrt{4-2y^2}}^{\sqrt{4-2y^2}} f(x, y)\, dx.$

3502. $\int_{1}^{2} dy \int_{1}^{y} f(x, y)\, dx + \int_{2}^{4} dy \int_{y/2}^{2} f(x, y)\, dx.$

3503. $\int_0^4 \partial y \int_0^{y/2} f(x, y)\, dx + \int_4^6 dy \int_0^{6-y} f(x, y)\, dx.$

3504. (1) $\int_0^1 dy \int_y^{2-y} f(x, y)\, dx;$

(2) $\int_0^1 dy \int_{\sqrt{y}}^{3-2y} f(x, y)\, dx;$

(3) $\int_0^1 dy \int_{y^{3/2}}^{2-\sqrt{2y-y^2}} f(x, y)\, dx.$

3505. (1) $\int_0^2 dy \int_{y/2}^{2y} f(x, y)\, dx + \int_2^4 dy \int_{2y-3}^{y+6/2} f(x, y)\, dx;$

(2) $\int_1^3 dy \int_{y+1/2}^{9-y/2} f(x, y)\, dx;$

(3) $\int_{-1}^3 dx \int_0^{1+\sqrt{3+2x-x^2}} f(x, y)\, dy;$

(4) $\int_0^1 dy \int_{1-\sqrt{1-y^2}}^{3+\sqrt{1-y^2}} f(x, y)\, dx + \int_1^2 dy \int_{2-\sqrt{2y-y^2}}^{2+\sqrt{2y-y^2}} f(x, y)\, dx.$

3506. (1) $\frac{2}{3} a^{3/2}$; (2) 9; (3) $\frac{1}{2}$. **3507.** 0. **3508.** $\frac{33}{140}$.

3509. $\frac{9}{4}$. **3510.** – 2. **3511.** $\frac{\pi}{6}$. **3512.** $\frac{4}{135}$. **3513.** 4.

3514. 3. **3515.** $12\frac{2}{3}$. **3516.** $\frac{2}{3}R$. **3517.** 6.

3518. $\frac{abc\,(a+b+c)}{2}$. **3519.** $\frac{a^6}{48}$. **3520.** $\frac{a^{11}}{110}$. **3521.** $2e - 5$.

3522. $\frac{1}{2}\left(\ln 2 - \frac{5}{8}\right)$. **3523.** $\frac{1}{180}$. **3524.** $\frac{\pi^2}{16} - \frac{1}{2}$.

3525. (1) $\int_0^{2\pi} d\varphi \int_0^R f(\rho\cos\varphi, \rho\sin\varphi)\, \rho\, d\rho;$

(2) $\int_{-\pi/2}^{\pi/2} d\varphi \int_0^{a\cos\varphi} f(\rho\cos\varphi, \rho\sin\varphi)\, \rho\, d\rho;$

(3) $\int_0^{\pi} d\varphi \int_0^{b\sin\varphi} f(\rho\cos\varphi, \rho\sin\varphi)\, \rho\, d\rho.$

3526. $\int_{\pi/4}^{\arctan 2} d\varphi \int_{4\cos\varphi}^{8\cos\varphi} f(\rho\cos\varphi, \rho\sin\varphi)\, \rho\, d\rho.$

3527. $\int_0^{\arctan\frac{a}{b}} d\varphi \int_0^{b\sin\varphi} f(\rho\cos\varphi, \rho\sin\varphi)\,\rho\, d\rho$

$$+ \int_{\arctan\frac{a}{b}}^{\pi/2} d\varphi \int_0^{a\cos\varphi} f(\rho\cos\varphi, \rho\sin\varphi)\,\rho\, d\rho.$$

3528. $\int_0^{\pi/4} d\varphi \int_0^{\sec\varphi} f(\rho\cos\varphi, \rho\sin\varphi)\,\rho\, d\rho.$

3529. $\int_0^{\pi/2} d\varphi \int_{\sqrt{2}\sec\left(\varphi-\frac{\pi}{4}\right)}^{2} f(\rho\cos\varphi, \rho\sin\varphi)\,\rho\, d\rho.$

3530. $\int_{-\pi/4}^{\pi/4} d\varphi \int_0^{a\sqrt{\cos 2\varphi}} f(\rho\cos\varphi, \rho\sin\varphi)\,\rho\, d\rho.$

3531. $\int_0^{\pi/2} d\varphi \int_0^{a\sin 2\varphi} f(\rho\cos\varphi, \rho\sin\varphi)\,\rho\, d\rho.$

3532. $\int_0^{\pi/2} d\varphi \int_0^{R} f(\rho\cos\varphi, \rho\sin\varphi)\,\rho\, d\rho.$

3533. $\int_{\pi/6}^{\pi/2} d\varphi \int_{R/2\sin\varphi}^{2R\sin\varphi} f(\rho\cos\varphi, \rho\sin\varphi)\,\rho\, d\rho.$

3534. $\frac{\pi}{2}\int_0^R f(\rho^2)\,\rho\, d\rho.$

3535. $\frac{R^2}{2}\int_0^{\arctan R} f(\tan\varphi)\, d\varphi.$

3536. $\frac{\pi}{4}[(1+R^2)\ln(1+R^2) - R^2].$

3537. $\frac{\pi(\pi-2)}{8}.$

3538. $\pi R^2 h.$

3539. $\frac{R^3}{3}\left(\pi - \frac{4}{3}\right).$

3540. $\frac{\pi^2}{6}.$

3542. $x = 2\rho\cos\varphi$, $y = 3\rho\sin\varphi$; $I = 6\int_0^{2\pi} d\varphi \int_0^1 f(2\rho\cos\varphi, 3\rho\sin\varphi)\,\rho\, d\rho.$

3543. $x = \rho\cos\varphi$, $y = \sqrt{3}\,\rho\sin\varphi$;

$$I = \sqrt{3} \int_0^{\pi} d\varphi \int_0^{\sqrt{3}\cos^2\varphi \sin\varphi} f(\rho\cos\varphi, \sqrt{3}\rho\sin\varphi)\,\rho\, d\rho.$$

3544. $x = a\rho\cos\varphi$, $y = b\rho\sin\varphi$; $I = ab\int_0^{\pi/2} d\varphi \int_1^2 f(\sqrt{4-\rho^2})\,\rho\, d\rho.$

3545. $\dfrac{a^2b^2}{8}$.

3546. $\dfrac{1}{\sqrt[4]{6}}$.

3547. $\int_0^1 dz \int_{\pi/4}^{\pi/3} d\varphi \int_0^R f(\rho\cos\varphi, \rho\sin\varphi, z)\,\rho\, d\rho.$

3548. $\int_{-\pi/2}^{\pi/2} d\varphi \int_0^{2\cos\varphi} \rho\, d\rho \int_0^{\rho^2} f(\rho\cos\varphi, \rho\sin\varphi, z)\, dz.$

3549. $\int_0^{\pi/2} \sin\theta\, d\theta \int_0^{\pi/2} d\varphi \int_0^R f(\rho\cos\varphi\sin\theta, \rho\sin\varphi\sin\theta, \rho\cos\theta)\,\rho^2\, d\rho.$

3550. $\int_{-\pi/4}^{\pi/4} d\varphi \int_0^{R\sqrt{\cos 2\varphi}} \rho\, d\rho \int_{-\sqrt{R^2-\rho^2}}^{\sqrt{R^2-\rho^2}} f(\rho\cos\varphi, \rho\sin\varphi, z)\, dz.$

3551. $\int_0^{2\pi} d\varphi \int_0^{R\sqrt{3}/2} \rho\, d\rho \int_{R-\sqrt{R^2-\rho^2}}^{\sqrt{R^2-\rho^2}} f(\rho\cos\varphi, \rho\sin\varphi, z)\, dz$

or $\int_0^{2\pi} d\varphi \int_0^{\pi/3} \sin\theta\, d\theta \int_0^R f(\rho\cos\varphi\sin\theta, \rho\sin\varphi\sin\theta, \rho\cos\theta)\,\rho^2\, d\rho$

$+ \int_0^{2\pi} d\varphi \int_{\pi/3}^{\pi/2} \sin\theta\, d\theta \int_0^{2R\cos\theta} f(\rho\cos\varphi\sin\theta, \rho\sin\varphi\sin\theta, \rho\cos\theta)\,\rho^2\, d\rho.$

3552. $\dfrac{\pi a}{2}$.

3553. $\dfrac{8}{9}a^2$.

3554. $\dfrac{4}{15}\pi R^5$.

3555. $\dfrac{\pi}{8}$.

3556. $\dfrac{4}{15}\pi(R^5 - r^5)$.

3557. $\dfrac{2\pi}{3}$.

3558. $\pi\left[3\sqrt{10} + \ln\dfrac{\sqrt{2}-1}{\sqrt{10}-1} - \sqrt{2} - 8\right]$.

3559. $186\dfrac{2}{3}$.

3560. $\frac{ab}{6}\left(\frac{a^2}{p}+\frac{b^2}{q}\right)$. **3561.** $\frac{abc}{6}$. **3562.** 12.

3563. $\frac{1}{6}$. **3564.** $78\frac{15}{32}$. **3565.** $\frac{48}{5}\sqrt{6}$. **3566.** 16. **3567.** 45.

3568. $13\frac{1}{3}$. **3569.** $16\frac{1}{5}$. **3570.** $ar^2\left(\frac{\pi}{4}-\frac{1}{3}\right)$. **3571.** 2π.

3572. $\frac{16}{3}R^3$. **3573.** $12\frac{4}{21}$. **3574.** $\frac{4R^5}{15a^2}$. **3575.** 27. **3576.** $\frac{3}{8}$.

3577. $\frac{88}{105}$. **3578.** $\frac{1}{3}abc$. **3579.** $\frac{\pi a^3}{4}$. **3580.** $2\left(e^2-\frac{2e^3+1}{9}\right)$.

3581. $3e-8$. **3582*.** $4e-e^2-1$. The solid is symmetrical about the plane $y=x$.

3583. $2\left(\pi^2-\frac{35}{9}\right)$. **3584.** $\frac{1}{45}$. **3585.** $\frac{16}{9}$. **3586.** $\frac{\pi}{4}$.

3587. 40π. **3588.** 2π. **3589.** $\frac{5}{2}\pi R^3$. **3590.** $\frac{3}{2}\pi a^3$.

3591. $\frac{4}{3}a^3\left(\frac{\pi}{2}-\frac{2}{3}\right)$. **3592.** $\frac{a^3}{24}$. **3593.** $\frac{15}{8}\left(\frac{3\pi}{8}+1\right)$. **3594.** $\frac{3}{2}\left(\frac{\pi}{2}-1\right)$.

3595. $\frac{\pi\sqrt{2}}{24}$. **3596.** $\frac{\pi^2R^2h}{16}$. **3597.** $\frac{1}{2}$. **3598.** 2. **3599.** πab.

3600. $\frac{ab}{6}$. **3601.** $\frac{16}{3}$. **3602*.** $\frac{5}{8}\pi a^2$. Pass over to polar coordinates.

3603. $\frac{3}{4}\pi$. **3604.** $2a^2$. **3605.** $\frac{2}{3}$. **3606.** $\frac{1}{60}$. **3607.** $\frac{1}{1260}$.

3608*. (1) $\frac{a^2b^2}{2c^2}$; (2) $\frac{39}{25}\pi$. Make use of the result of Problem 3541.

3609. 8. **3610.** $\frac{7}{12}$. **3611.** $\frac{3}{35}$. **3612.** $4(4-3\ln 3)$.

3613*. $\frac{\pi}{2}$. The projection of the solid on the plane Oxy is a circle.

3614. $\frac{\pi}{8}$. Transfer the origin to the point $\left(\frac{1}{2},\frac{1}{2},0\right)$.

3615*. $\frac{19}{6}\pi$ and $\frac{15}{2}\pi$. Pass over to cylindrical coordinates.

3616. $\frac{5}{12}\pi R^3$. **3617.** $\frac{\pi}{96}$. **3618.** $\frac{92}{75}\pi R^3$.

3619*. $\frac{1}{3}\pi a^3$. Pass over to spherical coordinates. **3620.** $\frac{a^3}{360}$. **3621.** $\frac{4}{21}\pi a^3$.

3622. $\frac{4}{3}\pi a^3$. **3623.** $\frac{64}{105}\pi a^3$. **3624.** $\frac{\pi^2a^3}{6}$. **3625.** $\frac{21(2-\sqrt{2})}{4}\pi$.

3626. 14. **3627.** 36. **3628.** 8π. **3629.** $2\sqrt{2}\,\pi p^2$.

3630*. $2\pi R^2$. Project the surface on the plane Oyz.

3631. $8\sqrt{2}ab$. **3632.** $\frac{16}{3}(\sqrt{8}-1)$. **3633.** $\frac{2\pi}{3}\{(1+R^2)^{3/2}-1\}$.

3634. $\frac{2\pi}{3}(\sqrt{8}-1)$. **3635.** $4\pi a\left(a-\sqrt{a^2-R^2}\right)$. **3636.** $2R^2(\pi-2)$.

3637. $2R^2(\pi+4-4\sqrt{2})$.

3638. $\frac{\pi}{4}\left\{3\sqrt{2}-\sqrt{3}-\frac{\sqrt{2}}{2}\ln 2+\sqrt{2}\ln(\sqrt{3}+\sqrt{2})\right\}$. **3639.** $\frac{2a^2}{\sin 2\alpha}$.

3640*. $\frac{\pi R^2}{12}(\sqrt{3}-\sqrt{2}) \approx 3.42\cdot 10^8$ km^2. Pass over to spherical coordinates.

3641. $\frac{16}{3}\pi a^2$. **3642.** $8R^2$. **3643.** $\frac{ab^2}{2}$. **3644.** $\frac{2}{3}R^3$.

3645. πR^3. **3646.** $\frac{9}{4}a^3$. **3647.** Static moment is equal to $\frac{ah^2}{6}$.

3648. The centre of gravity lies on the minor axis at the distance $\frac{4b}{3\pi}$ from the major axis (b minor semiaxis).

3649. $\xi=\left(1-\frac{\pi}{4}\right)(\sqrt{2}+1)$, $\eta=\frac{1}{8}\left(\frac{\pi}{2}-1\right)(2+\sqrt{2})$.

3650. The centre of gravity lies on the bisector of the angle α at the distance $\frac{4}{3}R\frac{\sin\frac{\alpha}{2}}{\alpha}$ from the centre of the circle.

3651. The centre of gravity lies on the bisector of the angle α at the distance $\frac{4}{3}R\frac{\sin^3\frac{\alpha}{2}}{\alpha-\sin\alpha}$ from the centre of the circle.

3652. $\xi=\frac{3\pi}{16}$, $\eta=0$. **3653.** $\frac{5}{4}\pi R^4$. **3654.** $\frac{2}{3}a^4$.

3655. $\frac{\pi ab}{4}(a^2+b^2)$. **3656.** $\frac{ab(a^2+b^2)}{12}$. **3657.** $\frac{ah}{48}(a^2+12h^2)$.

3658. $\frac{3\pi R^4}{2}$. **3659.** $ah\left(\frac{2h^2}{7}+\frac{a^2}{30}\right)$.

3662*. Choose a system of coordinates such that its origin coincides with the centre of gravity of the figure and one of the coordinate axes is parallel to the axis about which the moment of inertia is sought for.

3663. $\frac{a^2bc}{2}$, $\frac{ab^2c}{2}$ and $\frac{abc^2}{2}$. **3664.** $\frac{\pi R^2H^2}{4}$. **3665.** $\frac{\pi abc^2}{4}$.

3666. $\xi=\frac{14}{15}$, $\eta=\frac{26}{15}$, $\zeta=\frac{8}{3}$. **3667.** $\xi=\frac{3}{8}a$, $\eta=\frac{3}{8}b$, $\zeta=\frac{3}{8}c$.

3668. $\xi=\frac{6}{5}$, $\eta=\frac{12}{5}$, $\zeta=\frac{8}{5}$. **3669.** $\xi=\frac{18}{7}$, $\eta=\frac{15}{16}\sqrt{6}$, $\zeta=\frac{12}{7}$.

3670. $\xi=0$, $\eta=0$, $\zeta=\frac{5a}{83}(6\sqrt{3}+5)$. **3671.** $\xi=0$, $\eta=0$, $\zeta=\frac{3R}{8}(1+\cos\alpha)$.

3672. $\xi=0$, $\eta=0$, $\zeta=\frac{9a}{20}$. **3673.** $\xi=\frac{R}{2}$, $\eta=\frac{R}{2}$, $\zeta=\frac{R}{2}$.

3674. $\xi=0$, $\eta=0$, $\zeta=\frac{55+9\sqrt{3}}{130}$.

3675. $\frac{1}{3}M(b^2+c^2)$, $\frac{1}{3}M(c^2+a^2)$, $\frac{1}{3}M(a^2+b^2)$ and $\frac{1}{12}M(a^2+b^2+c^2)$.

3676. $\frac{7}{5}MR^2$. **3677.** $\frac{1}{5}M(b^2+c^2)$, $\frac{1}{5}M(c^2+a^2)$, $\frac{1}{5}M(a^2+b^2)$.

3678. $M\left(\frac{R^2}{4}+\frac{H^2}{3}\right)$ and $\frac{M}{12}(H^2+3R^2)$. **3679.** $\frac{2}{5}M\frac{R^5-r^5}{R^3-r^3}$.

3680. $\frac{1}{36}\pi R^2H(3R^2+H^2)$. **3681.** $\frac{1}{2}M\left(R^2+\frac{1}{6}H^2\right)$.

3682. $\frac{55+9\sqrt{3}}{65}Mc^2$. **3683.** $\frac{M}{2}(R^2+r^2)$. **3684.** $\frac{4}{3}a^2$. **3685.** $2\pi r(R-r)$.

3686. $\frac{4}{3}\gamma ab^2$. **3687.** $2\pi\gamma(R^2-r^2)$. **3688.** $\frac{\pi R^2H}{6}(3R^2+2H^2)$.

3689*. $\frac{\pi\gamma h^{n+3}tg^2\alpha}{n+3}$. If the axis of the cone is taken as the z-axis its vertex as the origin, then the equation of the cone will be $x^2+y^2-z^2\tan^2\alpha=0$.

3690. $\frac{2}{3}\pi\gamma R^6$. **3691.** $\frac{\pi a^5}{5}\left(18\sqrt{3}-\frac{97}{6}\right)$.

3692*. $\xi=0,\ \eta=0,\ \zeta=\frac{5}{4}R$. Pass over to cylindrical coordinates.

3693*. $\frac{59}{480}\pi R^5$. See the hint to the previous problem.

3694*. Choose a system of coordinates such that its origin coincides with the centre of gravity of the solid and one of the axes is parallel to the axis with respect to which moment of inertia is sought for.

3695. $\frac{kMm}{a^2}$, where M is the mass of the sphere and k is the gravity constant.

3696*. Take advantage of the result of the previous problem.

3697. $\frac{17}{56}\frac{kM}{R^2}$, k is the gravity constant.

3699. The centre of pressure lies on the axis of symmetry of the rectangle perpendicular to the side a at a distance of $\frac{2}{3}b$ from the side lying on the surface. In the second case (the side a is situated at a depth h) the distance between the centre of gravity and the upper side will be equal to $\frac{2b}{3}\frac{b+\frac{3}{2}l}{b+2i}$, where $l=\frac{h}{\sin a}$. (For $l \gg b$ the centre of pressure coincides approximately with the centre of the rectangle).

3700. (a) $\frac{h}{2}\sin\alpha$; (b) $\frac{3}{4}h\sin\alpha$.

3701. The centre of pressure lies on the major axis of the ellipse at a distance $a+\frac{a^2}{4(a+h)}$ from its upper end-point.

3702*. Choose a system of coordinates such that one of the coordinate planes coincides with the plane of the plate, and one of the axes with the line of intersection of the surface of the liquid and the plane of the plate.

3703. Diverges. **3704.** 2π. **3705.** $\frac{\pi}{4a^2}$. **3706.** 4. **3707.** 2. **3708.** $\frac{1}{4}$.

3709*. $\dfrac{\alpha}{2\sin\alpha}$. Pass over to polar coordinates.

3710*. $\dfrac{1}{2}$. Change the order of integration.

3711. $\dfrac{1}{16}$. See the hint to the previous problem. **3712.** Converges. **3713.** Diverges.

3714. Converges. **3715.** Diverges. **3716.** No. **3717.** $\dfrac{8}{15}$. **3718.** $\dfrac{\pi}{16}$.

3719*. $\pi\sqrt{\pi}$; use the Poisson integral $\int_0^\infty e^{-x^2}\,dx = \dfrac{\sqrt{\pi}}{2}$.

3720. Diverges. **3721.** Converges. **3722.** Diverges.

3723. $\dfrac{8}{3}\pi R^3\left(\ln R - \dfrac{1}{3}\right)$. **3724.** π. (See the hint to Problem 3719).

3725. $\dfrac{\pi}{4}$. **3726.** $\dfrac{\sqrt{\pi}}{2}$.

3727. $2\pi km\gamma\,(R + H - \sqrt{R^2 + H^2})$. The force is directed along the axis of the cylinder, k is the gravity constant.

3728. $\dfrac{2\pi km\gamma H}{l}(l - H)$, where l is the generatrix of the cone. The force is directed along the axis of the cone.

3729. (a) $a = 4\gamma_{\text{mean}} - 3\gamma_0$, $b = \dfrac{4}{R}(\gamma_{\text{mean}} - \gamma_0)$; (b) $\dfrac{4}{3}\pi kR\gamma_{\text{mean}} = \dfrac{kMm}{R^2}$.

3730. Defined everywhere, except for $x = 0$. **3731.** 3π.

3733. $\dfrac{b}{8a^4}\left\{\dfrac{5a^2 + 3b^2}{(a^2 + b^2)^2} + \dfrac{3}{ab}\arctan\dfrac{b}{a}\right\}$.

3734. $\dfrac{1\times 3\times 5\ldots(2n-3)}{2\times 4\times 6\ldots(2n-2)}\,\dfrac{\pi}{2a^{2n-1}}$ $(n > 1)$. **3735.** $\dfrac{(n-1)!}{a^n}$.

3736*. $\dfrac{\pi(a^2 + b^2)}{4|ab|^3}$. Differentiate with respect to a and b and add the results.

3737. $\ln(1 + a)$. **3738.** $\dfrac{1}{2}\ln(1 + a)$. **3739.** $\dfrac{\pi}{2}\ln(a + \sqrt{1 + a^2})$.

3740. $\pi(\sqrt{1 - a^2} - 1)$.

3741. $\dfrac{\pi}{2}\ln(1 + a)$, if $a \geq 0$; $-\dfrac{\pi}{2}\ln(1 - a)$, if $a \leq 0$. **3742.** $\pi\ln\dfrac{1 + \sqrt{1 - a^2}}{2}$.

3743. $\pi\arcsin a$. **3744.** $\pi\arcsin a$. **3745.** $\sqrt{\pi a}$.

3746*. $\sqrt{\pi}(\sqrt{b} - \sqrt{a})$. Differentiate with respect to a or to b.

3747*. $\arctan\dfrac{b}{a} - \arctan\dfrac{c}{a} = \arctan\dfrac{a(b - c)}{a^2 + bc}$. Differentiate with respect either to b or to c.

3748. $\dfrac{1}{2}\ln\dfrac{a^2 + b^2}{a^2 + c^2}$. **3749*.** $\pi\ln\dfrac{a + b}{2}$. Differentiate with respect either to a or to c.

3750. $\dfrac{\pi}{2}\ln(1 + a)$ for $a > 0$; $-\dfrac{\pi}{2}\ln(1 - a)$ for $a < 0$; $\int_0^{\pi/2}\dfrac{x}{\tan x}\,dx = \dfrac{\pi}{2}\ln 2$.

3751*. $\ln \dfrac{1+\beta}{1+\alpha}$. Integrate with respect to the parameter n within the limits from α to β.

3752. $\sqrt{\pi}\,(b-a)$. **3753.** $\displaystyle\int_0^{\infty} \frac{\cos x\,dx}{\sqrt{x}} = \int_0^{\infty} \frac{\sin x\,dx}{\sqrt{x}} = \sqrt{\frac{\pi}{2}}$.

3755. $\dfrac{\pi}{2} \ln \dfrac{a}{b}$. **3756.** $\dfrac{1}{n} \ln \dfrac{b}{a}$.

3757*. $$I = \lim_{\varepsilon \to 0}\left[\int_{\varepsilon}^{\infty} \frac{f(ax) - f(bx)}{x}\,dx\right] = \lim_{\varepsilon \to 0}\left[\int_{\varepsilon}^{\infty} \frac{f(ax)}{x}\,dx - \int_{\varepsilon}^{\infty} \frac{f(bx)}{x}\,dx\right]$$
$$= \lim_{\varepsilon \to 0} \int_0^{\infty} \frac{f(x)}{x}\,dx.$$

Estimate the last integral replacing $f(x)$ by its greatest and least values in the interval $(a\varepsilon, b\varepsilon)$ and pass to the limit.

3758. $\ln \dfrac{b}{a}$. **3759.** $\ln \dfrac{b}{a}$. **3760.** $\dfrac{1}{2} \ln \left|\dfrac{a+b}{a-b}\right|$. **3761.** $ab \ln \dfrac{b}{a}$.

3762. $\dfrac{3}{4} \ln 3$. Representing $\sin^3 x$ as the difference of sines of multiple arcs, reduce the problem to the previous one (at the appropriate choice of a and b).

3763*. The given relationships can be proved by two methods:

(1) integration by parts;

(2) change in the order of integration in the double integral obtained as the result of substitution of an integral instead of $\Phi(az)$.

3764*. See the hint to Problem 3763.

3765*. Use the second method of solving Problem 3763. When proving the second relationship it is necessary to investigate the integral.

$$\int_0^{\infty} \frac{\sin ax \cos(x \sin\theta)}{x}\,dx$$

for $|a| > 1$ and $|a| \le 1$. To this end transform the expression found in the numerator, and take into account that

$$\int_0^{\infty} \frac{\sin x}{x}\,dx = \frac{\pi}{2} \quad \text{(Dirichlet's integral).}$$

3767*. Substitute in the left-hand member of the equality the expression for y' and y'' obtained by differentiating the integral y with respect to the parameter. Integrate by parts one of the obtained addends.

3768*. See the hint to Problem 3767.

3769*. See the hint to Problem 3767.

Chapter 13

3770. $\sqrt{5} \ln 2$. **3771.** 24. **3772.** $\dfrac{p^2}{3}(5\sqrt{5} - 1)$.

3773. $2\pi a^{2n+1}$. **3774.** $\dfrac{ab(a^2 + ab + b^2)}{3(a+b)}$. **3775.** $4\pi a\sqrt{a}$.

3776. $\int_{\varphi_1}^{\varphi_2} F(\rho\cos\varphi, \rho\sin\varphi)\sqrt{\rho^2+\rho'^2}\,d\varphi$. **3777*.** $\frac{\pi a^2}{2}$. Pass over to polar coordinates.

3778. $\frac{2a^3\sqrt{2}}{3}$. **3779.** $\frac{1}{12}\left[(R^2+4)^{\frac{3}{2}}-8\right]$. **3780.** $\frac{8a\pi^3\sqrt{2}}{3}$.

3781. $\frac{R^4\sqrt{3}}{32}$. **3782.** $\frac{2\sqrt{2}}{3}\left[(1+2\pi^2)^{\frac{3}{2}}-1\right]$. **3783.** $R^2\sqrt{2}$.

3784. $\frac{1}{3}\left\{(x_2^2+1)^{\frac{3}{2}}-(x_1^2+1)^{\frac{3}{2}}\right\}$. **3785.** δa.

3786. $\frac{b^2}{2}+\frac{ab}{2\varepsilon}\arcsin\varepsilon$, where ε is the eccentricity of the ellipse.

3787. $\left(2\pi a^2+\frac{8\pi^3b^2}{3}\right)\sqrt{a^2+b^2}$. **3788.** $(1-e^{-t})\sqrt{3}$.

3789. $\left(0, \frac{2a}{\pi}, \frac{b\pi}{2}\right)$. **3790.** $\frac{8k\sqrt{2}}{15}\left[(3\pi^2-1)(2\pi^2+1)^{\frac{3}{2}}+1\right]$.

3791. $J_x = I_y = \left(\frac{a^2}{2}+\frac{h^2}{3}\right)\sqrt{4\pi^2a^2+h^2}$, $I_z = a^2\sqrt{4\pi^2a^2+h^2}$.

3792. $3\pi R^2$. **3793.** $\frac{\pi p^2}{4}$. **3794.** $\frac{11}{3}$. **3795.** R^2.

3796. $ka\left(a+\frac{b^2}{2c}\ln\frac{a+c}{a-c}\right)$, where $c=\sqrt{a^2-b^2}$. For $a=b$ $S=2ka^2$.

3797. $\frac{98}{81}p^2$. **3798.** $8R^2$. **3799.** $4R^2$. **3800.** $\frac{2Im}{a}$.

3801. $\frac{8mI\sqrt{2}}{a}$. **3803.** $\frac{2\pi\, mIa}{b^2}$, where a and b are semiaxes of the ellipse.

3804. $\frac{2\pi\, mI}{p}$. **3805.** $\frac{2\pi\, mIR^2}{(h^2+R^2)^{\frac{3}{2}}}$. For $R=h\sqrt{2}$. **3806.** 3.

3807. $\frac{ab}{2}$. **3808.** $-\frac{56}{15}$. **3809.** $37\frac{1}{3}$. **3810.** 4π.

3811. (1) $\frac{1}{3}$; (2) $\frac{1}{12}$; (3) $\frac{17}{30}$; (4) $-\frac{1}{20}$.

3812. In all the four cases the integral is equal to 1.

3813. 0. **3814.** $-2\pi ab$. **3815.** $-\frac{4}{3}a$. **3816.** πa^2.

3817. $\frac{3}{16}\pi R\sqrt[3]{R}$. **3818.** 13. **3819.** 0. **3820.** $3\sqrt{3}$.

3821. $-\frac{\pi R^3}{4}$. **3822.** $\iint_D (x^2+y^2)\,dx\,dy$. **3823.** $\iint_D (y-z)e^{xy}\,dx\,dy$.

3824. $\frac{\pi R^4}{2}$. **3825.** (1) 0; (2) $-\frac{\pi a^3}{8}$. **3827.** $\frac{1}{3}$.

3836*. Apply Green's formula to the doubly connected domain bounded by the contour L and an arbitrary circle with the origin as centre which does not intersect the contour L.

3837. π. **3838.** 8. **3839.** 4. **3840.** $\ln\frac{13}{5}$. **3841.** $R_2 - R_1$.

3842. $\frac{10}{3}$. **3843.** 0. **3844.** $-\frac{9}{2}$. **3845.** $u = \frac{x^3+y^3}{3} + C$.

3846. $u = (x^2 - y^2)^2 + C$. **3847.** $u = \ln|x+y| - \frac{y}{x+y} + C$.

3848. $u = \frac{\sqrt{x^2+y^2}+1}{y} + C$. **3849.** $u = \ln|x-y| + \frac{y}{x-y} + \frac{x^2}{2} - \frac{y^3}{3} + C$.

3850. $u = x^2\cos y + y^2\cos x + C$. **3851.** $u = \frac{e^y - 1}{1+x^2} + y + C$.

3852. $u = \frac{x-y}{(x+y)^2} + C$. **3853.** $n = 1, u = \frac{1}{2}\ln(x^2+y^2) + \arctan\frac{y}{x} + C$.

3854. $a = b = -1, u = \frac{x-y}{x^2+y^2} + C$. **3855.** $u = \ln|x+y+z| + C$.

3856. $u = \sqrt{x^2+y^2+z^2} + C$. **3857.** $\arctan xyz + C$.

3858. $u = \frac{2x}{x-yz} + C$. **3859.** $u = \frac{x-3y}{z} + \frac{z^2}{2} + C$.

3860. $u = e^{\frac{y}{z}}(x+1) + e^{yz} - e^{-z}$. **3861.** πab **3862.** $\frac{3}{8}\pi a^2$.

3863. $6\pi a^2$. **3864*.** $\frac{3}{2}a^2$. Represent it parametrically, putting $y = tx$. **3865.** $\frac{1}{60}$.

3866. $\frac{1}{210}$. **3867*.** $2a^2$. Put $y = x\tan t$. **3868*.** $\frac{1}{30}$. Put $y = xt^2$. **3869.** FR.

3870. (1) $\frac{4}{3}$; (2) $\frac{17}{12}$; (3) $\frac{3}{2}$ and 1. **3871.** (a) $\frac{a^2-b^2}{2}$; (b) 0. **3872.** 0.

3873. $\frac{k\sqrt{a^2+b^2+c^2}}{c}\ln 2$, where k is the factor of proportionality.

3874. $0.5\,k\ln 2$, where k is the factor of proportionality.

3876. $4\sqrt{61}$. **3877.** $\frac{\sqrt{3}}{120}$. **3878.** $\frac{\pi R^3}{4}$. **3879.** 0.

3880. πR^3. **3881.** $\frac{2\pi R^6}{15}$. **3882.** $2\pi\arctan\frac{H}{R}$.

3883. $\frac{2\pi R}{c(n-2)}\left[\frac{1}{(c-R)^{n-2}} - \frac{1}{(c+R)^{n-2}}\right]$ for $n \neq 2$; $\frac{2\pi R}{c}\ln\frac{c+R}{c-R}$ for $n = 2$.

3884. $\pi[R\sqrt{R^2+1} + \ln(R + \sqrt{R^2+1})]$.

3885*. π^2R^3. Use spherical coordinates. **3886.** $\frac{8}{3}\pi R^4$. **3887.** 3. **3888.** $\frac{2\pi R^7}{105}$.

3889. $\frac{4}{3}\pi abc$. **3890.** 0. **3891.** $\frac{1}{8}$. **3892.** $R^2H\left(\frac{2R}{3} + \frac{\pi H}{8}\right)$. **3893.** $\frac{\pi}{8}$.

3894. $2\iint\limits_S (x-y)\,dx\,dy + (y-z)\,dy\,dz + (z-x)\,dx\,dz.$

3895. $-\frac{\pi R^6}{8}.$ **3896.** $2\iiint\limits_\Omega (x+y+z)\,dx\,dy\,dz.$

3897. $\iiint\limits_\Omega \frac{x+y+z}{\sqrt{x^2+y^2+z^2}}\,dx\,dy\,dz.$ **3898.** 0. **3899.** $\frac{12}{5}\pi R^5.$

Chapter 14

3901. $1+y^2 = C(1-x^2).$ **3902.** $x^2+y^2 = \ln Cx^2.$ **3903.** $y = \sqrt[3]{C+3x-3x^2}.$

3904. $y = C\sin x - a.$ **3905.** $Cx = \frac{y-1}{y}.$ **3906.** $x\sqrt{1-y^2} + y\sqrt{1-x^2} = C.$

3907. $\sqrt{1-y^2} = \arcsin x + C.$ **3908.** $e^t = C(1-e^{-S}).$

3909. $10^x + 10^{-y} = C.$ **3910.** $\ln\left|\tan\frac{y}{4}\right| = C - 2\sin\frac{x}{2}.$

3911. $t = \frac{1}{a}\left(l + \frac{b\cdot l^{1-n}}{1-n}\right).$ **3912.** $t = \frac{v^2}{2\sqrt{k_1k_2}}\ln\frac{\sqrt{k_1}(1-x)+x\sqrt{k_2}}{\sqrt{k_1}(1-x)-x\sqrt{k_2}}.$

3913. $y = e^{\tan\frac{x}{2}}.$ **3914.** $y = \frac{1+x}{1-x}.$ **3915.** $\cos x = \sqrt{2}\cos y.$

3916. $y = \frac{b+x}{1+bx}.$ **3917.** Hyperbola $xy = 6.$

3918. Tractrix $y = \sqrt{4-x^2} + 2\ln\left|\frac{2-\sqrt{4-x^2}}{x}\right|.$ **3919.** Parabolas $y^2 = Cx.$

3920. $y^k = Cx.$ **3921.** $y = e^{\frac{x-a}{a}}.$ **3922.** $(x-C)^2 + y^2 = a^2.$

3923. $y = \frac{1}{k}\ln|C(k^2x^2-1)|.$ **3924.** $x = y^n.$ **3925.** $\approx 2.7\ \frac{\text{m}}{\text{s}}.$

3927. $0.467\ \frac{\text{km}}{\text{h}}$; 85.2 m. **3928.** $H = \left[\sqrt{h} - \frac{\sqrt{2g}}{4S}qT\right]^2.$

3929. $\ln\left|\frac{\theta_0-\theta_1}{\theta-\theta_1}\right| = \frac{k_0}{2}(2t+\alpha t^2).$

3930*. If t is the time counted off from midnight in hours, then the differential equation of the problem has the form.

$$\frac{dS}{S\sqrt{S}} = k\cos\frac{\pi(t-12)}{12}\,dt, \text{ hence, } S = \frac{160\,000}{\left[9-\sin\frac{\pi(t-12)}{12}\right]^2}.$$

The function $S(t)$ is defined for $6 \le t \le 18$.

3931. $\pi + \cot\frac{\pi - y}{2} = C.$ **3932.** $4y - 6x - 7 = Ce^{-2x}.$

3933. $x + C = 2u + \frac{2}{3}\ln|u-1| - \frac{8}{3}\ln(u+2)$, where $u = \sqrt{1+x+y}.$

3934. $y - 2x = Cx^3(y+x).$ **3935.** $\arctan\frac{y}{x} = \ln C\sqrt{x^2+y^2}.$

3936. $\ln|y| + \frac{x}{y} = C.$ **3937.** $x^2 + y^2 = Cy.$ **3938.** $y = \pm x\sqrt{2\ln|Cx|}.$

3939. $x^2 = C^2 + 2Cy$. **3940.** $e^{\frac{y}{x}} = Cy$. **3941.** $\ln|Cx| = -e^{-\frac{y}{x}}$.

3942. $y = xe^{1+Cx}$. **3943.** $(x+y)^2 = Cx^3 e^{-\frac{x}{x+y}}$. **3944.** $Cx = \varphi\left(\frac{y}{x}\right)$.

3945. $\sqrt{x^2+y^2} = e^{\frac{y}{x}\arctan\frac{y}{x}}$. **3946.** $y^3 = y^2 - x^2$. **3947.** $y = -x$.

3948. $y^2 = 5 \pm 2\sqrt{5}x$.

3949. If $\frac{y}{x} = u$, then $\ln|x| = \int \frac{du}{\varphi\left(\frac{1}{u}\right)}$; $\varphi(u) = -\frac{1}{u^2}$ or $\varphi\left(\frac{x}{y}\right) = -\frac{y^2}{x^2}$.

3950. $x = Ce^{\pm 2\sqrt{\frac{y}{x}}}$. **3951.** $x = y\ln|Cy|$. **3952.** $x^2 = 2Cy + C^2$.

3953*. Paraboloid of revolution. Let the plane Oxy be a meridian plane of the mirror surface, the required line lies in this plane. The needed differential equation is derived by equating the tangents of the angles of incidence and reflection expressed in terms of x, y, y'.

3954. $y = Ce^{-2x} + 2x - 1$. **3955.** $y = e^{-x^2}\left(C + \frac{x^2}{2}\right)$.

3956. $y = Cx^2 e^{\frac{1}{x}} + x^2$. **3957.** $y = (x + C)(1 + x^2)$.

3958. $y = Ce^{-x} + \frac{1}{2}(\cos x + \sin x)$.

3959. If $m \neq -a$, then $y = Ce^{-ax} + \frac{e^{mx}}{m+a}$; if $m = -a$, then $y = (C + x)e^{mx}$.

3960. $y^2 - 2x = Cy^3$. **3961.** $x = Ce^{2y} + \frac{1}{2}y^2 + \frac{1}{2}y + \frac{1}{4}$.

3962. $x = y\ln y + \frac{C}{y}$. **3963.** $y = e^x\left(\ln|x| + \frac{x^2}{2}\right) + Ce^x$.

3964. $y = Ce^{-\Phi(x)} + \Phi(x) - 1$. **3965.** $y = \frac{x}{\cos x}$. **3966.** $y = \frac{e^x + ab - e^a}{x}$.

3967. $y = \frac{x}{x+1}(x - 1 + \ln|x|)$. **3968.** $x = -t\arctan t$.

3969. (b) $\alpha + \beta = 1$. **3971.** $y = Cx - x\ln|x| - 2$.

3972*. $y = Cx \pm \frac{a^2}{2x}$. The differential equation derived for solution $xy - x^2y'| = a^2$.

3973*. $x = Cy \pm \frac{a^2}{y}$. The differential equation derived for solution $\left|xy - y^2\frac{dx}{dy}\right| = 2a^2$.

3974. $v = \frac{k_1}{k}\left[t - \frac{m}{k} + \frac{m}{k}e^{-\frac{kt}{m}}\right]$.

3975. $v = (v_0 + b)e^{-at^2} + b(at^2 - 1)$, where $a = \frac{k_1}{2m}$; $b = \frac{2km}{k_1^2}$.

3976. $\theta - \theta_0 = e^{-kt}\int_0^t \varphi(t)\,e^{kt}\,dt$. **3977.** 9.03A.

3978. $I = \dfrac{E_0}{R^2 + \omega^2 L^2} \cdot \left[\omega L e^{-\frac{Rt}{L}} + R \sin \omega t - \omega L \cos \omega t \right]$.

3979. $x = Ce^{\arctan \frac{y}{x}}$. **3980.** $y = Cx^2 + \dfrac{1}{x}$.

3981. $y = \dfrac{C}{x}\sqrt{x^2+1} + \dfrac{(1+x^2)^2}{3x}$. **3982.** $y = Cx - 1$.

3983. $(1 + x^2)(1 + y^2) = Cx^2$. **3984.** $(x + y)^2 (2x + y)^3 = C$.

3985. $x = Ce^{-\frac{x^2}{2y^2}}$. **3986.** $\sin \dfrac{y}{x} = Cx$. **3987.** $\sin \dfrac{y}{x} + \ln |x| = C$.

3988. $y = Ce^{-e^x} + e^x - 1$. **3989.** $y(y - 2x)^3 = C(y - x)^2$.

3990. $x = Ce^{\sin y} - 2(1 + \sin y)$. **3991.** $x = y^2 \left(1 + Ce^{\frac{1}{y}}\right)$.

3992. $y = Ce^{-\sin x} + \sin x - 1$. **3993.** $y = (C + e^x)(1 + x)^n$.

3994. $x^4 = 4xy + C$. **3995.** $y = Ce^x$ and $y = C + \dfrac{x^2}{2}$.

3996*. $y^2 = \dfrac{2}{3}\sin x + \dfrac{C}{\sin^2 x}$. Reduce to an equation linear with respect to $z = y^2$.

3997. $\arctan(x + y) = x + C$. **3999.** $\arctan \dfrac{y}{x} + \ln(x^2 + y^2) = \dfrac{\pi}{4} + \ln 2$.

4000. $y = \dfrac{1}{2}\sqrt{\dfrac{1+x}{1-x}}\,[2 + x\sqrt{1-x^2} + \arcsin x]$.

4001. $(1 + y)e^{-y} = \ln \dfrac{1+e^x}{2} + 1 - x$. **4002.** $y = \dfrac{5}{3}e^{x^3} - \dfrac{1}{3}(2 + x^3)$.

4004. $y = \dfrac{1}{2k}[e^{kx + C} + e^{-(kx + C)}]$. **4005.** $x^2 + y^2 = Cx$.

4006. $(y - x)^2 (x + 2y) = 1$. **4007.** Parabolas $y = x + Cx^2$.

4008. $(2y^2 - x^2)^3 = Cx^2$. **4009.** Catenary **4010.** $y = Cx^2$.

4011. A pencil of straight lines $y - y_0 = C(x - x_0)$. The differential equation $y - y_0 = y'(x - x_0)$.

4012. A circle with the point (x_0, y_0) as centre: $x^2 + y^2 = 2(xx_0 + yy_0)$.

4013. Any circle with the centre on the y-axis and tangent to the x-axis.

4014. If the path is S and time t, then $S = S_0 + Ce^{-k_2 t} - \dfrac{k_1}{k_2^2}t + \dfrac{k_1}{2k_2} - t^2$, where S_0 is the initial path and k_1 and k_2 are the factors of proportionality.

4016. (1) $\dfrac{8}{9}$ revolution per second; (2) in 6 min 18 s. **4017.** 0.00082 s.

4018*. $v = v_0\left(1 - \dfrac{m}{M_0}t\right)^{-1} e^{-\frac{3f_0}{mv_0}\left(1 - \sqrt[3]{1 - \frac{m}{M_0}t}\right)}$. The acting force F is equal to $\dfrac{d(mv)}{dt}$. In solving Problems 4018 to 4020 take into consideration that the mass m is a variable depending on time t; velocity v being the required function.

4019*. $v = \frac{g}{2m-k}(M_0 - mt)\left[\left(1 - \frac{m}{M_0}t\right)^{\frac{k}{m}-2} - 1\right].$

4020*. $v = \frac{g}{\mu}e^{k_1\mu^{2/3}}\int_0^t \mu e^{-k_1\mu^{2/3}}\,dt$, where $\mu = M_0 - mt$, $k_1 = \frac{3k}{M}\sqrt[3]{\frac{9\pi}{2\gamma^2}}$. See the hint to solution of Problem 4018.

4021*. $y = m_0 + \frac{m_0}{k_1 - k_2}(k_2 e^{-k_1 t} - k_1 e^{-k_2 t})$, where t is the time and y is the quantity of the second product. If x is the quantity of the first product generated during t time units, then $\frac{dx}{dt} = k_1(m_0 - x)$, whence $x = x(t)$. The rate $\frac{dy}{dt}$ of appearing of the second product is proportional to the magnitude $x - y$.

4022. 2.97 kg of salt. The maximum is achieved at $t = 33\frac{1}{3}$ min and is equal to 3.68 kg.

4023. $I = 1 + (I_0 - 1)e^{-t^2}$.

4024*. $p = \frac{p_0 l e^{k\omega^2 x^2}}{\int_0^l e^{k\omega^2 x^2}dx}$, where $k = \frac{M}{2p_0 lS}$.

Of practical importance in the case when ω is very large (as with centrifuges). Instead of computing the integral in the denominator at a given ω (it cannot be expressed in elementary functions), $\lim_{\omega\to\infty} p$ (see Problem 2439) is usually evaluated. The differential equation for this problem has the form

$$S\,dp = \omega^2 x\,dm,$$

where dm is the mass of the element CD. Further, $\gamma = 2kp$(one of the forms of the Boyle-Meriotte law; the factor of proportionality is denoted by $2k$ to simplify the notation involved); $dm = \gamma S\,dx = 2\,kp\,S\,dx$. As a result, an equation with separable variables, $\frac{dp}{p} = 2k\omega^2 x\,dx$, is obtained. Its integration yields $p = Ce^{k\omega^2 x^2}$. Then, $M = \int_0^M dm = C2kS\int_0^l e^{k\omega^2 x^2}dx$, wherefrom C is found. We have

$$p = \frac{Me^{k\omega^2 x^2}}{2kS\int_0^l e^{k\omega^2 x^2}dx}, \text{ but } \gamma_0 = 2\,kp_0 = \frac{M}{lS},\ k = \frac{M}{2p_0 lS}$$

and finally

$$p = \frac{p_0 l e^{k\omega^2 x^2}}{\int_0^l e^{k\omega^2 x^2}dx}.$$

4025. $(x + y - 1)^3 = C(x - y + 3)$. **4026.** $x^2 - xy + y^2 + x - y = C$.

4027. $x - 2y + \ln|x + y| = C$. **4028.** $e^{-2\arctan\frac{y+2}{x-3}} = C(y + 2)$.

4029. $y^2 = x + (x + 1)\ln\frac{C}{x+1}$. **4030.** $y^2 e^{-\frac{y^2}{x}} = C$.

4031. $y = \frac{1}{x}\tan(\ln|Cx|)$. **4032.** $x^2y^2 + 1 = Cy$.

4033. $Cx = 1 - \frac{x}{x^2 + y^2}$. **4034.** $(1 + Cx)e^y = 1$.

4035. $y^4 + 2x^2y^2 + 2y^2 = C$. **4036.** $x^2 + y^2 = C(y - 1)^2$.

4037. $y = x\tan(x + C)$. **4038.** $\frac{1}{y^2} = Ce^{2x^2} + x^2 + \frac{1}{2}$.

4039. $y = \frac{1}{(1 + x)(C + \ln|1 + x|)}$. **4040.** $ny^n = Ce^{\frac{-nx}{a}} + nx - a$.

4041. $x^2 = y^2(C - y^2)$. **4042.** $y(1 + \ln x + Cx) = 1$.

4043. $y(x + C) = \sec x$. **4044.** $y = \left(\frac{C + \ln|\cos x|}{x} + \tan x\right)^2$.

4045. $y = \frac{x^4}{4}\ln^2|Cx|$. **4046.** $y^2 = Ce^{\frac{-2a}{x}} - \frac{b}{a}$. **4047.** $y = \frac{\varphi(x)}{x + C}$.

4048. (1) $\frac{a}{x} + \frac{b}{y} = 1$; (2) $\frac{a}{x^2} + \frac{b}{y^2} = 1$. **4049.** $\frac{\rho - k}{\rho} = \frac{(\rho_0 - k)\varphi}{\rho_0\varphi_0}$.

4050. $x^4 - x^2y^2 + y^4 = C$. **4051.** $x + \arctan\frac{y}{x} = C$.

4052. $xe^y - y^2 = C$. **4053.** $x^y = C$. **4054.** $\sqrt{x^2 + y^2} + \frac{y}{x} = C$.

4055. $\tan(xy) - \cos x - \cos y = C$. **4056.** $\frac{1}{3}\sqrt{(x^2 + y^2)^3} + x - \frac{1}{2}y^2 = C$.

4057. $\sin\frac{y}{x} - \cos\frac{x}{y} + z - \frac{1}{y} = C$.

4058. $x - \frac{y}{x} = C$. The integrating factor $\mu(x) = \frac{1}{x^2}$.

4059*. $x^2 + \frac{2x}{y} = C$. Look for the integrating factor in the form of the function $\mu(y)$.

4060. $(x^2 + y^2)e^x = C$. **4061.** $\frac{y^2}{2} + \frac{\ln x}{y} = C$.

4062. $(x\sin y + y\cos y - \sin y)e^x = C$. **4064.** $\mu = y^{-n}e^{-(n-1)\int P(x)\,dx}$.

4065. The expression $\frac{Y'_x - X'_y}{X - Y}$ must be a function of $(x + y)$.

4066. The expression $\frac{Y'_x - Y'_y}{xX - yY}$ must be a function of xy.

4067. $abx + b^2y + a + bc = Ce^{bx}$. **4068.** $y = \left[Ce^{\frac{(m-1)bx}{a}} - \frac{c}{b}\right]^{\frac{1}{1-m}}$.

4069. $x^2 + 2xy - y^2 - 4x + 8y = C$. **4070.** $\frac{2x}{x - y} + \ln|x + y| + 3\ln|y - x| = C$.

4071. $x + y = a\tan\left(C + \frac{y}{a}\right)$. **4072.** $y^3 - 3xy = C$. **4073.** $x^2 - y^2 = Cy^3$.

4074. $3x^2y + x^3y^3 = C$. **4075.** $y\left(x^2 + \frac{1}{3}y^2\right) = Ce^{-x}$.

4076. $\ln|1+y| - \frac{1+y}{x} = C$. **4077.** $y^2 - 1 + Cxy = 0$. **4078.** $\frac{xy}{x-y} + \ln\left|\frac{x}{y}\right| = C$.

4079. $3\sqrt{y} = C\sqrt[4]{x^2-1} + x^2 - 1$. **4080.** $y = \sin x + C\cos x$.

4081. $y = \frac{2e^x}{C + e^x(\cos x + \sin x)}$. **4082.** $\tan x - \frac{\sin y}{\sin x} = C$.

4083. $xe^{\sin\frac{y}{x}} = C$. **4084.** $xy\cos\frac{y}{x} = C$. **4085.** $\sin y = x - 1 + Ce^{-x}$.

4086. $y = \frac{\tan x + \sec x}{C + \sin x}$. **4087.** $\ln|Cx| = -e^{-\frac{x^2+y^2}{x}}$.

4088. $x + ye^{\frac{x}{y}} = C$. **4089.** $y = x\ln|Cx|$. **4090.** $y^2 - by - axy = C$.

4091. Circle $x^2 + y^2 - \frac{2k}{k+1}(ax + by) = C\ (k \neq -1)$ or the circle $x^2 + y^2 - \frac{2k}{k-1}(ax + by) = C\ (k \neq 1)$; if $k = -1$ or $k = 1$, then a straight line $ax + by = C$. **4092.** Logarithmic spirals $\sqrt{x^2 + y^2} = Ce^{\pm\arctan\frac{y}{x}}$.

4093*. $y^2 = \frac{x^4 + C^4}{2x^2}$. The differential equation is $y^2 = x(x - yy')$. **4094.** $I = \frac{t}{2}$.

4095. The field vector at each point is perpendicular to the polar radius of the point. Integral curves—a family of concentric circles with the origin as centre. The equation of the family is $x^2 + y^2 = C$. Isoclines—a family of straight lines passing through the origin.

4096. (1) $y' = f(xy)$; (2) $y' = f\left(\frac{y^2}{x}\right)$; (3) $y' = f(x^2 + y^2)$.

4097. Straight lines $y = Cx$. The result can be stated in the form of the following geometrical theorem: if a family of coaxial parabolas having a common axis and a common vertex are intersected by a straight line passing through the vertex, then the tengents to various parabolas at the points of their intersection with the straight line will be parallel to one another.

4099. $y' = \frac{ay + b}{x} + C$; $y' = ay + bx + C$. **4103.** With $\Delta x = 0.05$ $y \approx 0.31$.

4104. With $\Delta x = 0.05$ $y \approx 1.68$.

4105. The exact solution $y = e^{\frac{x^2}{4}} = f(x)$; $f(0.9) = 1.2244$. Approximate solution: $f(0.9) = 11942$. Relative error is $\sim 2.5\%$.

4106. The exact solution $x = \sqrt[3]{3(e-1)} \approx 1.727$; numerical integration with the interval divided into 4 parts yields $x \approx 1.72$.

4107. $y_2 = 1 + x + \frac{3}{2}x^2 + \frac{4}{3}x^3 + \frac{13}{24}x^4 + \frac{1}{4}x^5 + \frac{1}{18}x^6 + \frac{1}{63}x^7$.

4108. -1.28. **4109.** $y = 1 + x + x^2 + 2x^3 + \frac{13}{4}x^4 + \ldots$.

4110. $y = 1 - x + \frac{x^3}{3} - \frac{x^4}{2} + \frac{x^5}{5} + \dots$.

4111. $y = \frac{1}{3}x^3 - \frac{1}{7\times 9}x^7 - \frac{2}{7\times 11\times 27}\times x^{11} - \dots$.

4112. $y = 1 + 2x - x^2 + \frac{4}{3}x^3 - \frac{3}{2}x^4 + \dots$. **4113.** $y = 0$.

4114. $y = x + \frac{x^2}{2} + \frac{2x^3}{3} + \frac{11x^4}{2\times 3\times 4} + \dots$. **4115.** $y = \frac{x^2}{2!} - \frac{x^3}{3!} - \frac{x^6}{6!} - \dots$.

4116. $y = 1 + (x-1) - \frac{(x-1)^2}{2!} + \frac{2(x-1)^3}{3!} + \frac{4(x-1)^4}{4!} - \frac{60(x-1)^5}{5!} + \dots$.

4117. $y = Cx - C^2$; singular integral $x^2 + 4y = 0$.

4118. $y = Cx - 3C^3$; singular integral $9y \pm 2x\sqrt{x} = 0$.

4119. $y = Cx + \frac{1}{C}$; singular integral $y^2 = 4x$.

4120. $y = Cx + \sqrt{1 + C^2}$; singular integral $x^2 + y^2 = 1$.

4121. $y = Cx + \sin C$; singular solution $y = x(\pi - \arccos x) + \sqrt{1 - x^2}$.

4122. $y = Cx - \ln C$; singular solution $y = \ln x + 1$.

4123. $y = (\sqrt{x+1} + C)^2$; singular solution $y = 0$.

4124. $y = Cx^2 + \frac{1}{C}$; singular integral $y^2 - 4x^2 = 0$.

4125. $2Cx = C^2 - y^2$; no singular integral.

4126. $x = Ce^{-p} + 2(1 - p)$, $y = x(1 + p) + p^2$; no singular integral.

4127. $y = Cx - e^C$; singular solution $y = x(\ln x - 1)$.

4128. $y = Cx + C + C^2$; singular solution $y = -\frac{1}{4}(x+1)^2$.

4129. $y = Cx + a\sqrt[3]{1 - C^3}$; singular integral $\sqrt{y^3} - \sqrt{x^3} = \sqrt{a^3}$.

4130. $(C - x)y = C^2$; singular solution $y = 4x$.

4131. $y^2 - 4e^x = 0$. **4132.** $xy = 1$. **4133.** $2y - x^2 = 0$.

4135. Equilateral hyperbola $2xy = \pm a^2$, where a^2 is the area of the triangle; trivial solution–any straight line of the family $y = \pm \frac{C^2}{2}x + aC$.

4136. $(y - x - 2a)^2 = 8ax$. **4137.** Ellipses and hyperbolas.

4138. $x = \frac{Ce^{-\frac{1}{2p^2}}(1 + p^2)}{p^2}$, $y = \frac{Ce^{-\frac{1}{2p^2}}}{p}$ or $x = \frac{(p^2+1)C}{\sqrt{p}\sqrt[4]{(p^2+2)^3}}$, $y = \frac{-C\sqrt{p}}{\sqrt[4]{(p^2+2)^3}}$.

4139. $y^2 = Cx^{-\frac{1}{k}} + \frac{k^2x^2}{2k+1}$.

4140*. $\begin{cases} y = \cos\alpha\left(C + \frac{a}{2}\sin\alpha\right), \\ x = \sin\alpha\left(a - C - \frac{a}{2}\sin^2\alpha\right) \end{cases}$ In the obtained differential equation put

$\frac{dy}{dx} = \tan\alpha$, then express x in terms of y and parameter α, find dx, replace dx by $\frac{dy}{\tan\alpha}$ and solve the obtained differential equation considering y as a function of α.

4141. $S = at^2$, where a is a specific constant. **4142.** $x^2 + y^2 = 2a^2 \ln |Cx|$.

4143. $y = Ce^{-\frac{x}{2}}$. **4144.** $y = C(x^2 + y^2)$. **4145.** $(x^2 + y^2)^2 = C(y^2 + 2x^2)$.

4146. If the parameter of the parabolas is equal to $2p$ and a straight line is chosen as the y-axis, then the required equations will be: $y = C + \frac{2}{3}\sqrt{\frac{2x^3}{p}}$.

4147. Tractrices.

4148. Measuring the angle α in one of the two possible directions, we get the equation of the family $xy - \frac{\sqrt{3}}{2}(x^2 + y^2) = C$.

4149. Measuring the angle α in one of the two possible directions, we get the equation of the family

$$\ln(2x^2 + xy + y^2) + \frac{6}{\sqrt{7}} \arctan \frac{x + 2y}{x\sqrt{7}} = C.$$

4150*. Let us assume, for instance, that the wind blows along the x-axis. The lines of sound propagation over the plane Oxy are orthogonal paths of the family of circles $(x - at)^2 + y^2 = (v_0 t)^2$, where t is the time elapsed from the moment the sound wave started from the source of sound, and v_0 is the speed of sound in motionless air.

For any fixed t the differential equation of the sought-for orthogonal paths is $y' = \frac{y}{x - at}$ together with the equation of the family of circles.

Eliminating t, we get a Lagrange's equation. Its general solution is

$x = C(\cos\varphi + b)\left(\tan\frac{\varphi}{2}\right)^{\frac{1}{b}}$, $y = C\sin\varphi\left(\tan\frac{\varphi}{2}\right)^{\frac{1}{b}}$, where $b = \pm\frac{a}{v_0}$, φ, a parameter.

4151. $x = C\sin t + R(\cos t + t\sin t)$, $y = -C\cos t + R(\sin t - t\cos t)$.

4152. $x = \frac{C}{\cosh t} + a(t - \tanh t)$, $y = C\tanh t + \frac{a}{\cosh t}$.

4153. $x = a(\cos t + t\sin t) - \cos t\left(\frac{at^2}{2} + C\right)$,

$y = a(\sin t + t\cos t) - \sin t\left(\frac{at^2}{2} + C\right)$.

4154. $x = C\sin t + 2\tan t$, $y = \tan^2 t - C\cos t - 2$.

4155. $y = \frac{x^3}{6} - \sin x + C_1 x + C_2$.

4156. $y = \frac{\arctan x}{2}(x^2 - 1) - \frac{x}{2}\ln(1 + x^2) + C_1 x + C_2$.

4157. $y = \frac{x^2}{2}\left[\ln x - \frac{3}{2}\right] + C_1 x + C_2$. **4158.** $y = C_1 x^2 + C_2$.

4159. $y = C_1e^x + C_2 - x - \frac{x^2}{2}$. **4160.** $y = \frac{1}{3}x^3 + C_1x^2 + C_2$.

4161. $y = (1 + C_1^2)\ln|x + C_1| - C_1x + C_2$. **4162.** $y = (C_1x - C_1^2)e^{\frac{x}{C_1}+1} + C_2$.

4163. $y = \frac{1}{12}(x + C_1)^3 + C_2$. **4164.** $y = \frac{2}{3C_1}\sqrt{(C_1x-1)^3} + C_2$.

4165. $y = -\frac{1}{3}\sin^3 x + C_1\left(\frac{x}{2} - \frac{\sin 2x}{4}\right) + C_2$.

4166. $(x + C_2)^2 = 4C_1(y - C_1)$. **4167.** $y = C_1(x + C_2)^{\frac{2}{3}}$.

4168. $y = C_1e^{\frac{x}{a}} + C_2e^{-\frac{x}{a}}$. **4169.** $x = \frac{4}{3}\left(y^{\frac{1}{2}} - 2C_1\right)\sqrt{y^{\frac{1}{2}} + C_1} + C_2$.

4170. $y = \frac{x + C_1}{x + C_2}$. **4171.** $(x + C_2)^2 - y^2 = C_1$. **4172.** $y = C_1e^{C_2x}$.

4173. $y\cos^2(x + C_1) = C_2$. **4174.** $(x + C_2)\ln y = x + C_1$.

4175. If the orbitrary constant introduced by the first integration is positive $(+C_1^2)$, then $y = C_1\tan(C_1x + C_2)$; and if it is negative $(-C_1^2)$, then $y = C_1\frac{1 + e^{2(C_1x + C_2)}}{1 - e^{2(C_1x + C_2)}} = -C_1\coth(C_1x + C_2)$; if $C_1 = 0$, then $y = -\frac{1}{x + C_2}$.

4176. $x = C_1 + \cos C_2 \ln\left|\tan\frac{y + C_2}{2}\right|$. **4177.** $C_1x + C_2 = \ln\left|\frac{y}{y + C_1}\right|$.

4178. $\frac{x + C_2}{2} = C_1\arctan(C_1\ln y)$, $C_1 > 0$. **4179.** $\ln|C_1y| = 2\tan(2x + C_2)$.

4180. $y = \ln|x^2 + C_1| + \frac{1}{\sqrt{-C_1}}\ln\left|\frac{x - \sqrt{-C_1}}{x + \sqrt{-C_1}}\right| + C_2$ for $C_1 < 0$, and $y = \ln|x^2 + C_1| + \frac{2a}{\sqrt{C_1}} + \arctan\frac{x}{\sqrt{C_1}}\, C_2$ for $C_1 > 0$.

4181*. On substituting $y' = p$ the equation decomposes into two, one of which is of the Clairaut type. Its general solution is

$$y = C_1 + C_2e^{C_1x}, \text{ and singular solutions } y = \frac{4}{C - x}.$$

The other equation is $y' = 0$.

4182. $y = C_1x(x - C_1) + C_2$ and singular solutions $y = \frac{x^3}{3} + C$.

4183. $y^2 = C_1x^4 + C_2$. **4184.** $x = \ln\left|\frac{C_1x^{C_1}}{C_2 - x^{C_1}}\right|$. **4185.** $y = \sqrt{\frac{1}{3}x^3 + C_1x + C_2}$.

4186. $y = C_1x + \frac{C_2}{x}$. **4187.** $y = C_1xe^{\frac{C_2}{x}}$. **4188.** $\ln|y + C_1| + \frac{C_1}{y + C_1} = x + C_2$.

4189. $y = x^3 + 3x + 1$. **4190.** $y = 2 + \ln\frac{x^2}{4}$. **4191.** $y = \frac{2}{5}x^2\sqrt{2x} - \frac{16}{5}$.

4192. $y = \frac{4}{(x + 4)^2}$.

4193. $y - x = 2\ln|y|$. **4194.** $y = \sqrt{2x - x^2}$. **4195.** $y = \sqrt{1 + e^{2x}}$.

4196. $y = -\ln|1-x|$. **4197.** $y = \dfrac{x+1}{x}$.

4198*. $y = x$. Make the substitution $y = ux$. **4199.** $y = 2e^{\frac{1}{2}x^2} - 1$.

4200*. Differential equation of the curve $dx = \dfrac{dy}{\sqrt{(C_1 y)^{\frac{2}{k}} - 1}}$, where k is the factor of proportionality. If $k = 1$, then $y = \dfrac{1}{2C_1}[e^{C_1 x + C_2} + e^{-(C_1 x + C_2)}]$ $= \dfrac{\cosh(C_1 x + C_2)}{C_1}$; this is a catenary. If $k = -1$, then $(x + C_2)^2 + y^2 = C_1^2$; this is a circle. If $k = 2$, then $(x + C_2)^2 = 4C(y - C_1)$; this is a parabola. If $k = -2$, then $dx = \sqrt{\dfrac{C_1 y}{1 - C_1 y}}\,dy$; this is a differential equation of a cycloid.

4201. $e^{\frac{y}{a}} = C_2 \sec\left(\dfrac{x}{a} + C_1\right)$. **4202.** $Cx = y^{2k-1}$. **4203.** Catenary.

4204. $v = \sqrt{\dfrac{mgv_0^2}{mg + kv_0^2}}$. **4205.** Parabola.

4206. $S = \dfrac{m}{3k}\left[\sqrt{\left(\dfrac{2k}{m}t + C\right)^3} - \sqrt{C^3}\right]$.

4207*. Let the x-axis be directed vertically downwards, the origin of coordinates be located on the surface of the liquid, the equation of the light beam $y = f(x)$. At a depth x, we have $\dfrac{\sin\alpha}{\sin(\alpha + d\alpha)} = \dfrac{m + dm}{m}$, where m is the index of refraction for the depth x, and α is the angle between the vertical and the tangent to the light beam. Obviously, $\tan\alpha$ is equal to y'. From the equation $m\sin\alpha = (m + dm)(\sin\alpha\cos d\alpha + \cos\alpha\sin d\alpha)$, by removing brackets and neglecting the infinitesimals of higher orders (leaving only those of the first order), we obtain $m\,d\alpha = -dm\tan\alpha$, whence $\dfrac{dm}{m} = -\dfrac{dy'}{y'(1 + y'^2)}$. Integrating this equation, find y' as a function of m. Replacing m by its expression in terms of x and integrating for the second time, we get the solution

$$y = \frac{m_0 h \sin\alpha_0}{m_2 - m_1}\ln\left|m + \sqrt{m^2 - m_0^2\sin^2\alpha_0}\right| + C,$$

Where $m = \dfrac{(m_2 - m_1)x + m_1 h}{h}$.

4208. $y = x^2\ln\sqrt{x} + C_1 x^2 + C_2 x + C_3$.

4209. $y = -\dfrac{1}{8}\sin 2x + C_1 x^2 + C_2 x + C_3$.

4210. $y = \dfrac{e^{ax}}{a^{10}} + P_9$ (P_9 is a polynomial of the 9th degree with respect to x with arbitrary coefficients).

4211. $y = C_1\dfrac{x^2}{2} + C_2 x + C_3 - C_1^2(x + C_1)\ln|x + C_1|$.

4212. $y = C_1x^5 + C_2x^3 + C_3x^2 + C_4x + C_5$.

4213. $y = \frac{1}{3}(C_1 - 2x)^{\frac{3}{2}} + C_2x + C_3$. **4214.** $x = C_1y^2 + C_2y + C_3$.

4215. The solutions can be written in three forms : $y = C_1 \sin(C_2x + C_3)$ or $y = C_1 \sinh(C_2x + C_3)$ or $y = C_1 \cosh(C_2x + C_3)$.

4216. $(x + C_2)^2 + (y + C_3)^2 = C_1^2$. **4217.** $y = C_2\left(xe^{C_1x} - \frac{1}{C_1}e^{C_1x}\right) + C_3$.

4219. (2) $y = 1 + x + \frac{x^2}{2!} + \frac{2x^3}{3!} + \frac{3x^4}{4!} + \frac{14x^5}{5!} + \ldots$.

4220. $y = 1 - \frac{(x-1)^2}{2!} - \frac{2(x-1)^4}{4!} + \frac{3(x-1)^5}{5!} + \ldots$.

4221. $y = \frac{\pi}{2}(x-1) + \frac{(x-1)^2}{2!} + \frac{(x-1)^3}{3!} + \frac{(x-1)^4}{4!} + \frac{4(x-1)^5}{5!} + \ldots$.

4222. $y = 1 + x + \frac{x^3}{3!} + \frac{2x^4}{4!} + \frac{3x^5}{5!} + \ldots$. If $f(x) \approx 1 + x + \frac{x^3}{3!} + \frac{2x^4}{4!}$, then for $x = -0.5$ an alternating numerical series is obtained, and the value of the first of the rejected terms is smaller than 0 . 001.

4223. $y = 1 - \frac{x^2}{2!} + \frac{x^3}{3!} - \frac{x^4}{4!} + \frac{4x^5}{5!} - \frac{14x^6}{6!} + \ldots$; of the fifth order.

4224. $y = x^2 - \frac{1}{10}x^5 + \frac{1}{80}x^8 - \frac{7}{4400}x^{11} + \ldots$; 0.318; 0.96951.

4225*. The differential equation is $E = L\frac{d^2Q}{dt^2} + \frac{dQ}{dt}\frac{V_0 - kQ}{k_1}$, where Q is the charge flown through the circuit during the interval of time from the beginning of the experiment till the time t. Expressing Q in terms of V (V is the amount of water available in the vessel at the time t) and determining (from the conditions of the problem) the coefficients, we obtain the equation

$V'' + aVV' + b = 0$, where $a = \frac{1}{k_1L} = 0.005$, $b = \frac{kE}{L} = 0.00935$. Integrating it for the initial conditions: $V_0 = 1000\ \text{cm}^3$, $V_0' = -kI_0 = -0.00187\ \text{cm}^3/\text{s}$, we get the following series:

$V = 1000 - 0.00187t - 10^{-9}\cdot[2.91t^3 - 3.64t^4 + 3.64t^5 - 3.04t^6 + 2.17t^7 \ldots]$.

This is an alternating series; the coefficients, beginning with the sixth, decrease tending to zero which is convenient for the computations.

4226*. The differential equation for this problem has the form

$$L\frac{d^2Q}{dt^2} + \frac{dQ}{dt}\cdot\frac{k_1}{M_0 - kQ} = E.$$

Taking the quantity of hydrogen chloride not decomposed by the time t as the required function, we reduce the equation to the form $yy'' + ay' + by = 0$, where $a = \frac{k_1}{L} = 50$, $b = \frac{kE}{L} = 0.0191$. Integrating this equation with the initial conditions $y_0 = M_0 = 10$; $y_0' = -kI_0 = -0.00381$, we get the series $y = 10 - 0.00381t + 10^{-10}t^3(1.21 - 1.52t + \ldots)$.

4227. $x^2y'' - 6xy' + 12y = 0$. **4228.** $xy'' - (2x+1)y' + (x+1)y = 0$.

4229. $(x^3 - 3x^2 + 3x)y''' - (x^3 - 3x + 3)y'' - 3x(1-x)y' + 3(1-x)y = 0$.

4230. $y = 3x^2 - 2x^3$. **4231.** (a) $\dfrac{\sin^2 x}{\cos^2 x} \neq$ const; (b) $y'' \sin 2x - 2y' \cos 2x = 0$.

4232*. (3) By Ostrogradsky's formula $\begin{vmatrix} y_1 & y_2 \\ y_1' & y_2' \end{vmatrix} = C \cdot e^{-\int P(x)\,dx}$,

or developing the Wronskian determinant; $y_1 y_2' - y_1' y_2 = Ce^{-\int P(x)dx}$. Divide both members of the equation by y_1^2, then $\dfrac{d}{dx}\left(\dfrac{y_2}{y_1}\right) = \dfrac{C}{y_1^2} e^{-\int P(x)dx}$, where from there follows the required relationship.

4233. $y = C_1 x \ln \left|\dfrac{1+x}{1-x}\right| - 2C_1 + C_2 x$. **4234.** $y = C_1 \dfrac{\sin x}{x} + C_2 \dfrac{\cos x}{x}$.

4235. $y = x^2 - e^{x-1}$.

4236*. Functions P and Q must be related as follows : $Q' + 2P \cdot Q = 0$. Substitute $y_1 = \dfrac{1}{y_2}$ into the formula (following from Ostrogradsky's formula) of Problem 4232, differentiate the obtained relationship twice and substitute y_2', y_2'' into the given equation.

4237*. $y = C_1(4x^3 - 3x) + C_2\sqrt{1 - x^2}\,(4x^2 - 1)$. By hypothesis, put $y_1 = Ax^3 + Bx^2 + Cx + D$. Substituting y_1 in the given equation, we get $B = 0$, $D = 0, \dfrac{A}{C} = \dfrac{4}{-3}$ or $A = 4k, C = -3k$. Consequently, the particular solution will be $y_1 = k\,(4x^3 - 3x)$. In conformity with the property of a linear equation we can assume $k = 1$, then $y_1 = 4x^3 - 3x$. Knowing one particular solution, we find a second particular solution and finally obtain the general solution.

4238. $y = C_1 \sin x + C_2 \left[1 - \sin x \ln \left|\tan\left(\dfrac{\pi}{4} - \dfrac{\pi}{2}\right)\right|\right]$.

4239. $y = C_1 x + C_2 x \int \dfrac{e^x\,dx}{x^2}$. **4240.** $y = C_1 x + C_2 (x^2 - 1)$.

4241. $y = C_1 x + C_2 x^2 + C_3 x^3$. **4242.** $y = x^3 + x\,(C_1 + C_2 \ln|x|)$.

4243. $y = C_1 e^x + C_2 x - x^2 - 1$. **4244.** $y = C_1 x^3 + C_2(x + 1) - x$.

4245. $y = 2 + 3x + x\left(\dfrac{\pi}{2} + 2 \arctan x\right) + x^2$.

4246. $y = -2 + 2x - x^2 + \dfrac{x^3}{3} - \dfrac{x^4}{4} + \dfrac{7x^5}{60} - \ldots$.

4247. $y = 1 + \dfrac{2x^4}{4!} - \dfrac{2x^5}{5!} + \dfrac{2x^6}{6!} - \dfrac{2x^7}{7!} + \dfrac{62x^8}{8!} - \ldots$.

4248. $y = \dfrac{x^2}{2} + \left[\dfrac{x^4}{4!} + \dfrac{3x^6}{6!} + \dfrac{5x^8}{8!} + \ldots + \dfrac{(2n-1)\,x^{2n+2}}{(2n+2)!} + \ldots\right]$.

4249. $y + C_1\left(1 + \dfrac{x^2}{2} + \dfrac{x^3}{6} + \dfrac{x^4}{12} + \dfrac{x^5}{24} + \ldots\right) + C_2\left(x + \dfrac{x^3}{6} + \dfrac{x^4}{12} + \dfrac{x^5}{30} + \ldots\right)$.

4250. $y = C_1\left(1 + \frac{x^4}{12} + \dots\right) + C_2\left(x - \frac{x^3}{6} + \frac{3x^5}{40} + \dots\right)$.

4251. $y = C_1e^{x} + C_2e^{-2x}$. **4252.** $y = C_1e^{3x} + C_2e^{-3x}$.

4253. $y = C_1e^{4x} + C_2$. **4254.** $y = C_1e^{(1+\sqrt{2})x} + C_2e^{(1-\sqrt{2})x}$.

4255. $y = C_1e^{2x} + C_2e^{-\frac{4}{3}x}$. **4256.** $y = C_1 \cos x + C_2 \sin x$.

4257. $y = e^{-3x}(C_1 \cos 2x + C_2 \sin 2x)$. **4258.** $y = e^{x}\left(C_1 \cos \frac{x}{2} + C_2 \sin \frac{x}{2}\right)$.

4259. $y = e^{x}(C_1 + C_2x)$. **4260.** $x = (C_1 + C_2t)\, e^{2.5t}$.

4261. $y = (C_1 + C_2x)e^{-\frac{1}{4}x}$. **4262.** $y = 4e^{x} + 2e^{3x}$.

4263. $y = 3e^{-2x} \sin 5x$. **4264.** $y = e^{-\frac{x}{2}}(2 + x)$.

4265. $y = [1 + (1 - m)\, x]\, e^{mx}$. **4266.** $y = \cos 3x - \frac{1}{3} \sin 3x$.

4267. If $k > 0$, then $y = \frac{a}{\sqrt{k}} \sin[\sqrt{k}\,(x - x_0)] + y_0 \cos[\sqrt{k}\,(x - x_0)]$; if $k < 0$, then $y = \frac{1}{2\sqrt{k_1}}[(y_0\sqrt{k_1} + a)e^{\sqrt{k_1}(x - x_0)} + (y_0\sqrt{k_1} - a)e^{-\sqrt{k_1}(x - x_0)}]$, where $k_1 = -k$.

4268. $y = C_1e^{-x} + C_2e^{\frac{x}{2}} + e^{x}$. **4269.** $y = C_1 \cos ax + C_2 \sin ax + \frac{e^x}{a^2 + 1}$.

4270. $y = C_1e^{6x} + C_2e^{x} + \frac{5 \sin x + 7 \cos x}{74}$.

4271. $y = e^{-x}(C_1 \cos 2x + C_2 \sin 2x) - \frac{1}{2} \cos 2x - 2 \sin 2x$.

4272. $y = (C_1 + C_2x)\, e^{3x} + \frac{2}{9}x^2 + \frac{5}{27}x + \frac{11}{27}$.

4273. $y = e^{x}(C_1 \cos x + C_2 \sin x) + x + 1$. **4274.** $y = C_1e^{x} + C_2e^{-5x} - 0.2$.

4275. $y = C_1e^{x} + C_2e^{2x} + \bar{y}$, where $\bar{y}$ equals:

(1) $\frac{5}{3}e^{-x}$; (2) $3xe^{2x}$; (3) $\frac{3}{5} \cos x + \frac{1}{5} \sin x$; (4) $x^3 + \frac{9}{2}x^2 + \frac{21}{2}x - \frac{15}{4}$;

(5) $-\frac{8}{5}e^{x}\left[\cos \frac{x}{2} + 2 \sin \frac{x}{2}\right]$; (6) $\frac{1}{2}x + \frac{5}{4} - \frac{1}{12}e^{-2x}$; (7) $e^{x}(2x^2 + x)$;

(8) $\frac{3}{2}x + \frac{1}{4}(9 + 3 \cos 2x - \sin 2x)$; (9) $-2xe^{x} - \frac{1}{12}e^{-2x}$;

(10) $\frac{1}{20} \cos x - \frac{3}{20} \sin x + \frac{7}{260} \cos 3x + \frac{9}{260} \sin 3x$;

(11) $-\frac{1}{12}e^{-x} - \frac{1}{2}xe^{x}$.

4276. $y = C_1 + C_2e^{-\frac{5}{2}x} + \bar{y}$, where $\bar{y}$ equals:

(1) $\frac{1}{3}x^3 - \frac{3}{5}x^2 + \frac{7}{25}x$; (2) $\frac{1}{7}e^{x}$; (3) $5 \sin x - 2 \cos x$;

(4) $\frac{1}{10}x + \frac{5}{164} \sin 2x - \frac{1}{41} \cos 2x$; (5) $\cos 2.5x + \sin 2.5x - 0.02xe^{-2.5x}$;

(6) $\left(-5x - \frac{16}{29}\right)\cos x - \left(2x - \frac{185}{29}\right)\sin x$;

(7) $e^{-x}[(10x + 18)\sin x - (20x + 1)\cos x]$; (8) $\frac{3}{10}\left(\frac{1}{5}e^{\frac{5}{2}x} - xe^{-\frac{5}{2}x}\right)$.

4277. $y = e^{2x}(C_1 + C_2x) + \bar{y}$, where $\bar{y}$ equals:

(1) $\frac{1}{4}$; (2) $\frac{1}{9}e^{-x}$; (3) $\frac{3}{2}x^2e^{2x}$; (4) $\frac{1}{4}\cos 2x + \frac{1}{2}x + \frac{1}{2}$;

(5) $\frac{1}{169}\left(\frac{-5}{2}\sin 3x + 6\cos 3x\right) - \frac{1}{50}(3\sin x + 4\cos x)$;

(6) $\frac{3}{100}(3\sin x + 4\cos x) + \frac{1}{676}(5\sin 3x - 12\cos 3x)$;

(7) $2x^2 + 4x + 3 + 4x^2e^{2x} + \cos 2x$; (8) $\frac{1}{4}\left(x^2e^{2x} - \frac{1}{8}e^{-2x}\right)$;

(9) $\frac{1}{2}\left(e^x - \frac{1}{9}e^{-x}\right) + \frac{1}{25}(3\sin x + 4\cos x)$; (10) $e^x - \frac{1}{2}e^{x-1} + \frac{1}{18}e^{1-x}$.

4278. $y = C_1\cos x + C_2\sin x + \bar{y}$, where $\bar{y}$ equals:

(1) $2x^3 - 13x + 2$; (2) $\cos 3x$; (3) $\frac{1}{2}x\sin x$; (4) $-\frac{1}{2}x\cos x - e^{-x}$;

(5) $\frac{1}{4}\left(x\sin x - \frac{1}{4}\cos 3x\right)$; (6) $9 + 4\cos 2x - 0.2\cos 4x$;

(7) $0.5\cosh x$; (8) $0.5 + 0.1\cosh 2x$.

4279. $y = e^{\frac{3}{5}x}\left(C_1\cos\frac{4}{5}x + C_2\sin\frac{4}{5}x\right) + \bar{y}$, where $\bar{y}$ equals:

(1) $\frac{25}{16}e^{\frac{3}{5}x}$; (2) $\frac{15}{219}\sin\frac{4}{5}x + \frac{40}{219}\cos\frac{4}{5}x$;

(3) $\frac{1}{13}e^{2x} + \frac{1}{5}\left(2x^3 + \frac{36}{5}x^2 + \frac{107}{25}x - \frac{908}{125}\right)$;

(4) $-\frac{5}{9}\cos x\cdot e^{\frac{3}{5}x}$; (5) $-\frac{1}{8}xe^{\frac{3}{5}x}\cos\frac{4}{5}x$; (6) $0.5e^{2x} + 1.3$.

4280. $y = 2 + C_1\cos x + C_2\sin x + \cos x\ln\left|\tan\frac{x}{2}\right|$.

4281. $y = e^x\left(C_1 + C_2x - \ln\sqrt{x^2+1} + x\arctan x\right)$.

4282. (1) $y = e^x(x + C_1) - (e^x + 1)\ln(e^x + 1) + C_2$;

(2) $y = \frac{1}{2}e^x\left[\arctan e^x + e^x\sqrt{1 - e^{2x}} + C_1\right] + \frac{1}{3}\sqrt{(1 - e^{2x})^3} + C_2$;

(3) $y = C_1e^x - \cos e^x + C_2$.

4283. $y = (1 + x)e^{-\frac{3}{2}} + 2e^{-\frac{5}{2}x}$.

4284. $x = e^x(0.16\cos 3x + 0.28\sin 3x) + x^2 + 2.2x + 0.84$.

4285. $y = e^x + x^2$. **4286.** $y = e^x(e^x - x^2 - x + 1)$.

4287. $y = \frac{1}{3}\sin 2x - \frac{1}{3}\sin x - \cos x$.

4288*. Differentiate twice the expressions for y; substitute y, y' and y'' into the given equation; in all the three cases, we get an identity.

4289. $y = x^3 (C_1 + C_2x^4)$. **4290.** $y = \frac{x}{2} + C_1 \cos \ln|x| + C_2 \sin \ln|x|$.

4291. $y = x[C_1 + C_2 \ln|x| + \ln^2|x|]$. **4292.** $y = x\ln|x| + C_1 x + C_2x^2 + x^3$.

4293. If $\frac{1}{m\alpha} > \omega^2$, then $y = C_1 \cos kt + C_2 \sin kt + \frac{g}{k^2 - \omega^2} \cos \omega t + \frac{e\omega^2}{k^2}$, where $k^2 = \frac{1}{m\alpha} - \omega^2$. If $\frac{1}{m\alpha} < \omega^2$, then $y = C_1 e^{kt} + C_2 e^{-kt} - \frac{g}{k^2 + \omega^2} \cos \omega t - \frac{e\omega^2}{k^2}$, where $k^2 = \omega^2 - \frac{1}{m\alpha}$.

4294. $s = \frac{1}{5} (4e^t + e^{-4t})$.

4295. $s = e^{-0.2t} [10 \cos (0.245t) + 8.16 \sin (0.245t)]$; $s|_{t=3} \approx 7.07$ cm.

4296. $t = \sqrt{\frac{am}{f}} \ln \frac{F + \sqrt{f(2F - f)}}{F - f}$.

4297. $s = e^{-0.245t}[2 \cos (156.6t) + 0.00313 \sin (156.6t)]$.

4298*. $k = 33\frac{1}{3}$ g/cm $= 33\frac{1}{3} \cdot g$ dyne/cm; $t = 0.38$ s; the height of the immersed portion of the block $x = 5[3 + \cos (8.16t)]$. Consider $g = 1000$ cm/s^2.

4299*. $r = \frac{a_0}{2} (e^{\omega t} + e^{-\omega t})$. Rotation occurs as if the tube were motionless, but the ball is acted upon by the force $m\omega^2\mathbf{r}$, where $\mathbf{r}$ is the distance from the axis of rotation to the ball.

4300. If $k > m\omega^2$, then $\mathbf{r} = \frac{a_0}{k - m\omega^2}\left[k - m\omega^2 \cos\left(t\sqrt{\frac{k}{m} - \omega^2}\right)\right]$;

If $k = m\omega^2$, then $r = a_0\left(1 + \frac{k}{2m}t^2\right)$;

If $k < m\omega^2$, then $r = \frac{a_0}{m\omega^2 - k}\left[m\omega^2 \cosh\left(t\sqrt{\omega^2 - \frac{k}{m}}\right) - k\right]$.

4301. $y = C_1 \cos 3x + C_2 \sin 3x + C_3$. **4302.** $y = C_1e^{2x} + C_2e^{-2x} + C_3e^{3x} + C_4e^{-3x}$.

4303. $y = (C_1 + C_2x)\, e^{2x} + (C_3 + C_4x)\, e^{-2x}$.

4304. $y = C_1e^{2x} + C_2e^{-2x} + C_3\cos 2x + C_4 \sin 2x$.

4305. $y = C_1e^{-x} + C_2e^{-3x} + C_3e^{4x}$. **4306.** $y = C_1e^x + C_2xe^x + C_3x^2e^x$.

4307. $y = C_1 + C_2x + C_3e^{-x} + C_4xe^{-x}$.

4308. $y = C_1e^x + C_2e^{-x} + C_3x^{n-3} + C_4x^{n-4} + \ldots + C_{n-1}x + C_n$.

4309. $y = e^{\frac{x}{\sqrt{2}}}\left(C_1 \cos\frac{x}{\sqrt{2}} + C_2 \sin\frac{x}{\sqrt{2}}\right) + \ldots + e^{-\frac{x}{\sqrt{2}}}\left(C_3 \cos\frac{x}{\sqrt{2}} + C_4 \sin\frac{x}{\sqrt{2}}\right)$.

4310. $y = (C_1 + C_2x + C_3x^2) \cos\frac{x}{2} + (C_4 + C_5x + C_6x^2) \sin\frac{x}{2} + C_7x + C_8$.

4311. $y = e^{-x} (C_1 + C_2x + C_3x^2 + \ldots + C_nx^{n-1})$.

4312. $y = 1 + \cos x$. **4313.** $y = e^x + \cos x - 2$.

4314. $y = (C_1 + C_2x)\, e^x + C_3e^{2x} - x - 4$.

4315. $y = (C_1 + C_2x)\, e^x + C_3e^{-2x} + (x^2 + x - 1)\, e^{-x}$.

4316. $y = (C_1 + C_2x) \cos 2x + (C_3 + C_4x) \sin 2x + \frac{1}{9} \cos x$.

4317. $y = (C_1 + C_2x)\cos ax + (C_3 + C_4x)\sin ax - \dfrac{x^2 \cos ax}{8a^2}.$

4318. $y = \dfrac{1}{60}x^5 - \dfrac{1}{2}x^3 + C_1x^2 + C_2x + C_3 + C_4 \cos x + C_5 \sin x.$

4319. $y = C_1e^x + C_2e^{-x} + C_3 \sin x + C_4 \cos x + \dfrac{x^2 - 3x}{8}e^x - \dfrac{1}{4}x \sin x.$

4320. $y = (C_1 + C_2x + x^2)e^x + (C_3 + C_4x + x^2)e^{-x} + \sin x + \cos x.$

4321. $y = 4 - 3e^{-x} + e^{-2x}.$ **4322.** $y = e^x + x^3.$

4323. $y = x(C_1 + C_2 \ln|x| + C_3 \ln^2|x|).$

4324.1. $\begin{cases} x = e^{-6t}(C_1 \cos t + C_2 \sin t), \\ y = e^{-6t}[(C_2 + C_1)\cos t + (C_2 - C_1)\sin t]. \end{cases}$

4324.2. $\begin{cases} x = C_1e^t + C_2e^{5t}, \\ y = -C_1e^t + 3C_2e^{5t}. \end{cases}$ **4324.3.** $\begin{cases} x = e^t(C_1 \cos 3t + C_2 \sin 3t), \\ y = e^t(C_1 \sin 3t - C_2 \cos 3t). \end{cases}$

4324.4. $\begin{cases} x = C_1e^t + C_2e^{2t} + C_3e^{-t}, \\ y = C_1e^t - 3C_3e^{-t}, \\ z = C_1e^t + C_2e^{2t} - 5C_3e^{-t}. \end{cases}$ **4324.5.** $\begin{cases} x = C_1 + 3C_2e^{2t}, \\ y = -2C_2e^{2t} + C_3e^{-t}, \\ z = C_1 + C_2e^{2t} - 2C_3e^{-t}. \end{cases}$

4324.6. $\begin{cases} x = C_1e^t + C_2e^{2t} + C_3e^{5t}, \\ y = C_1e^t - 2C_2e^{2t} + C_3e^{5t}, \\ z = -C_1e^t - 3C_2e^{2t} + 3C_3e^{5t}. \end{cases}$

4324.7. $\begin{cases} x = C_1e^{2t} + e^{3t}(C_2 \cos t + C_3 \sin t), \\ y = e^{3t}[(C_2 + C_3)\cos t + (C_3 - C_2)\sin t], \\ z = C_1e^{2t} + e^{3t}[(2C_2 - C_3)\cos t + (C_2 + 2C_3)\sin t]. \end{cases}$

4325. $\begin{cases} x = C_1e^t + C_2e^{-t} + t \sinh t, \\ y = C_1e^t - C_2e^{-t} + \sinh t + t \cosh t. \end{cases}$

4326. $\begin{cases} x = C_1e^{-4t} + C_2e^{-7t} + \dfrac{7}{40}e^t + \dfrac{1}{5}e^{-2t}, \\ y = \dfrac{1}{2}C_1e^{-4t} - C_2e^{-7t} + \dfrac{1}{40}e^t + \dfrac{3}{10}e^{-2t}. \end{cases}$

4327. $\begin{cases} z = C_1y; \\ zy^2 - \dfrac{3}{2}x^2 = C_2. \end{cases}$ **4328.** $\begin{cases} y = \dfrac{\sqrt{C_1 + x^2}}{\ln\left|\dfrac{C_2}{x + \sqrt{x^2 + C_1}}\right|}, \\ y = \sqrt{C_1 + x^2}\,\ln\left|\dfrac{C_2}{x + \sqrt{x^2 + C_1}}\right|. \end{cases}$

4329. $\begin{cases} \dfrac{y}{x} = C_1; \\ x^2 + y^2 + z^2 = C_2. \end{cases}$ **4330.** $\begin{cases} x^2 + y^2 + z^2 = C_1 y; \\ z = C_2 y. \end{cases}$

4331. $\begin{cases} y^2 - z^2 = C_1; \\ yz - y^2 - x = C_2. \end{cases}$ **4332.** $\begin{cases} x = C_1 e^{-t} + C_2 e^{-3t}; \\ y = C_1 e^{-t} + 3C_2 e^{-3t} + \cos t. \end{cases}$

4333. $\begin{cases} x = C_1 e^t + C_2 e^{-t} + C_3 \cos t + C_4 \sin t, \\ y = C_1 e^t + C_2 e^{-t} - C_3 \cos t - C_4 \sin t. \end{cases}$

4334. $\begin{cases} x = C_1 + C_2 t + C_3 t^2 - \dfrac{1}{6} t^3 + e^t, \\ y = C_4 - (C_1 + 2C_3)\, t - \dfrac{1}{2}(C_2 - 1)\, t^2 - \dfrac{1}{3} C_3 t^3 + \dfrac{t^4}{24} - e^t. \end{cases}$

4335. $\begin{cases} x + y + z = C_1; \\ x^2 + y^2 + z^2 = C_2. \end{cases}$ **4336.** $\begin{cases} z = x - y; \\ y(y - 2x)^3 = (x - y)^2. \end{cases}$

4337. $\begin{cases} x = \dfrac{t}{3}, \\ y = -\dfrac{t}{3}. \end{cases}$ **4338.** $\begin{cases} x = \dfrac{1}{3} e^{-t} + \dfrac{1}{6} e^{2t} + \dfrac{1}{2} e^{-2t}, \\ y = \dfrac{1}{3} e^{-t} + \dfrac{1}{6} e^{2t} - \dfrac{1}{2} e^{-2t}, \\ z = -\dfrac{1}{3} e^{-t} + \dfrac{1}{3} e^{2t}. \end{cases}$ **4339.** $\begin{cases} x = -e^{-t}, \\ y = e^{-t}, \\ z = 0. \end{cases}$

4340. The curves $y_1 = \dfrac{C_1 x^2 - C_2}{2x}$ and $y_2 = -\dfrac{C_1 x^2 + C_2}{2x}$. Under the given initial conditions, we get the hyperbolas $y_1 = \dfrac{3 - x^2}{2x}$, $y_2 = \dfrac{3 + x^2}{2x}$.

4341. $y = e^{2x}$. **4342.** The plane curve $\begin{cases} x - y + z = 0; \\ x = \pm \dfrac{z \ln|z|}{\sqrt{2}}. \end{cases}$

4343. $\begin{cases} x = \dfrac{1}{2}\left[gt^2 + (l_1 - l_0)\left(1 - \cos \dfrac{\pi t}{2T}\right)\right], \\ y = \dfrac{1}{2}\left[gt^2 + l_0 + l_1 + (l_1 - l_0) \cos \dfrac{\pi t}{2T}\right]. \end{cases}$

4344. $\begin{cases} x = 10 \cosh 2t - \dfrac{4}{49} \cos 14t + \dfrac{200}{49}, \\ y = 10 \cosh 2t + \dfrac{6}{49} \cos 14t - \dfrac{300}{49}. \end{cases}$

Here x is the path of the heavier ball and y, of the lighter one.

4345. $A = \dfrac{k\alpha^2}{2k_1}\left[1 - \left(\dfrac{1 - \beta e^{\alpha k t}}{1 + \beta e^{\alpha k t}}\right)^2\right]$, $B = \alpha \dfrac{1 - \beta e^{\alpha k t}}{1 + \beta e^{\alpha k t}}$, where

$\alpha = \sqrt{B_0^2 + \dfrac{2k_1}{k} A_0}$, $\beta = \dfrac{\alpha - B_0}{\alpha + B_0}$.

4346*. If T is the amount of the poison, then $\frac{dN}{dt} = aN - bNT$, $\frac{dT}{dt} = cN$ and $\frac{dN}{dt} = 0$ at the time when $N = M$.

4347. $h_1 = \frac{S_1H_1 + S_2H_2}{S_1 + S_2} + \frac{S_2}{S_1 + S_2}(H_1 - H_2)\, e^{-\alpha \frac{S_1 + S_2}{S_1 S_2}}$,

$h_2 = \frac{S_1H_1 + S_2H_2}{S_1 + S_2} - \frac{S_1}{S_1 + S_2}(H_1 - H_2)\, e^{-\alpha \frac{S_1 + S_2}{S_1 S_2}}$.

4348. (1) $\theta - \theta_0 + 0.002\,(\theta^2 - \theta_0^2) = 0.00008\,\frac{E_1^2 t^3}{R_0 T^2}$; by 53°;

(2) $\theta - \theta_0 + 0.002\,(\theta^2 - \theta_0^2) = \frac{6E_0^2}{\pi R_0 \cdot 10^7} \cdot (200\pi t - \sin 200\pi t)$; by 76°.

4349. (1) 44.5°; (2) 46.2°.

4350.

x	1.00	1.05	1.10	1.15	1.20	1.25
y	1.000	1.000	0.997	0.992	0.984	0.973

x	1.30	1.35	1.40	1.45	1.50
y	0.959	0.942	0.923	0.901	0.876

4351. $y\,|_{x=1} = 3.43656\ldots$

y_1	y_2	y_3	y_4	y_5
2.5	3.16667	3.37500	3.42500	3.43472

y_5 yields a relative error of the order of 0.1 %.

4352. 0.46128; the same is obtained by Simpson's formula for $2n = 10$. All signs are true.

4353. $y_4 = 1 + x + \frac{x^2}{2} + \frac{2x^3}{3} + \frac{7x^4}{12} + \frac{5x^5}{12} + \frac{16x^6}{75} +$ and so on; $y_4(0.3) \approx 1.543$;

$f(x) = 1 + x + \frac{x^2}{2} + \frac{2x^3}{3} + \frac{7x^4}{12} + \frac{11x^5}{20} + \frac{22x^6}{45}$ and so on; $f(0.3) \approx 1.545$.

The error is less than 0.2%.

4354. 0.808.

4355*. 1.001624. The result is obtained most quickly if the required function is sought for directly in the form of a power series.

4356*. 1.0244. See the hint to the previous problem.

4357. $y = x + \frac{2}{4!}x^4 + \frac{2.5}{7!}x^7 + \ldots + \frac{2.5 \ldots (3n-1)}{(3n+1)!}x^{3n+1} + \ldots$; $k = 0.2297$.

Chapter 15

4358. $\sin^{2k} x = \frac{C_{2k}^k}{2^{2k}} + \frac{(-1)^k}{2^{2k-1}} [\cos 2kx - C_{2k}^1 \cos (2k-2) x$

$+ C_{2k}^2 \cos (2k-4) x - \dots + (-1)^{k-1} C_{2k}^{k-1} \cos 2x]$;

$\sin^{2k+1} x = \frac{(-1)^k}{2^{2k}} [\sin (2k+1) x - C_{2k+1}^1 \sin (2k-1)x$

$+ C_{2k+1}^2 \sin (2k-3)x - \dots + (-1)^k C_{2k+1}^k \sin x]$;

$\cos^{2k} x = \frac{C_{2k}^k}{2^{2k}} + \frac{1}{2^{2k-1}} [\cos 2kx + C_{2k}^1 \cos (2k-2) x$

$+ C_{2k}^k \cos (2k-4) x + \dots + C_{2k}^{k-1} \cos 2x]$;

$\cos^{2k+1} x = \frac{1}{2^{2k}} [\cos(2k+1) x + C_{2k+1}^1 \cos (2k-1) x$

$+ C_{2k+1}^2 \cos(2k-3) x + \dots + C_{2k+1}^k \cos x]$.

4360. $\cos nx = \cos^n x - C_n^2 \cos^{n-2} x \sin^2 x + C_n^4 \cos^{n-4} x \sin^4 x \dots$

Since, $\sin x$ appears raised only to even powers, $\cos nx$ can be rationally expressed in terms of $\cos x$.

4363. (1) $\varphi = \nu \frac{2\pi}{n}$ and $\varphi = \nu \frac{2\pi}{n+1}$, where $\nu = 0, 1, 2, \dots, n$;

(2) $\varphi = \nu \frac{2\pi}{n}$, where $\nu = 1, 2, \dots, n-1$ for an odd n, and $\nu = 1, 2, \dots, n$ for an even n, and $\varphi = (2\nu - 1) \frac{\pi}{n+1}$, where $\nu = 1, 2, \dots, n+1$.

4365*. Note that $\int_0^{2\pi} \Phi_n(\varphi)\, d\varphi = 0$.

4366. Yes.

4371. (a) $b_1 = b_2 = b_3 = \dots = 0$ and $a_1 = a_3 = a_5 = \dots = 0$;

(b) $a_0 = a_1 = a_2 = \dots = 0$ and $b_1 = b_3 = b_5 = \dots = 0$.

4372. $\frac{4}{\pi} \sum_{n=0}^{\infty} \frac{\sin (2n+1)x}{2n+1}$.

4373. $\sum_{n=1}^{\infty} \frac{\sin 2nx}{2n}$.

4374. $x = 2 \sum_{n=1}^{\infty} (-1)^{n-1} \frac{\sin nx}{n} (-\pi, \pi)$; $\frac{\pi - x}{2} = \sum_{n=1}^{\infty} \frac{\sin nx}{n} (0.2\pi)$.

4375. $\frac{2}{\pi} \sum_{n=0}^{\infty} \frac{\cos (2n+1)x}{(2n+1)^2}$.

4376. (1) $\frac{\pi^2}{3} + 4 \sum_{n=1}^{\infty} (-1)^n \frac{\cos nx}{n^2}$;

(2) $\frac{4\pi^2}{3} + 4 \sum_{n=1}^{\infty} \frac{\cos nx}{n^2} - 4\pi \sum_{n=1}^{\infty} \frac{\sin nx}{n}$; $S_1 = \frac{\pi^2}{6}$, $S_2 = \frac{\pi^2}{12}$, $S_3 = \frac{\pi^2}{8}$.

4377. $\frac{2}{\pi}\sum_{n=1}^{\infty}(-1)^{n+1}\left\{\frac{\pi^2}{n}+\frac{2}{n^3}[(-1)^n-1]\right\}\sin nx.$

4378. $\sum_{n=1}^{\infty}(-1)^n\left(\frac{12}{n^3}-\frac{2\pi^2}{n}\right)\sin nx.$ **4379.** $2+\frac{4}{\pi}\sum_{n=0}^{\infty}\frac{\sin(2n+1)x}{2n+1}.$

4380. $\frac{2h}{\pi}\left[\frac{1}{2}+\sum_{n=1}^{\infty}\frac{\sin nh}{nh}\cos nx\right].$ **4381.** $\frac{2h}{\pi}\left[\frac{1}{2}+\sum_{n=1}^{\infty}\left(\frac{\sin nh}{nh}\right)^2\cos nx\right].$

4382. $\frac{l}{2}-\frac{4l}{\pi^2}\sum_{n=0}^{\infty}\frac{\cos\left[\frac{(2n+1)\pi x}{l}\right]}{(2n+1)^2}.$

4383. $\frac{e^{2\pi}-1}{\pi}\left[\frac{1}{2}+\sum_{n=1}^{\infty}\left(\frac{\cot nx}{1+n^2}-\frac{n\sin nx}{1+n^2}\right)\right]-1.$

4384. $\frac{e^l-e^{-l}}{2l}+l(e^l-e^{-l})\sum_{n=1}^{\infty}\frac{(-1)^n\cos\frac{n\pi x}{l}}{l^2+n^2\pi^2}$

$$+\pi(e^l-e^{-l})\sum_{n=1}^{\infty}\frac{(-1)^{n-1}\,n\sin\frac{n\pi x}{l}}{l^2+n^2\pi^2}$$

$$=\sinh l\left[\frac{1}{l}+2\sum_{n=1}^{\infty}(-1)^n\frac{l\cos\frac{n\pi x}{l}-\pi n\sin\frac{n\pi x}{l}}{l^2+n^2\pi^2}\right].$$

4385. $\frac{2\sin\pi a}{\pi}\left(\frac{1}{2a}+\frac{a\cos x}{1-a^2}-\frac{a\cos 2x}{2^2-a^2}+\dots\right).$

4386. $\frac{2\sin\pi a}{\pi}\left(\frac{\sin x}{1-a^2}-\frac{2\sin 2x}{2^2-a^2}+\frac{3\sin 3x}{3^2-a^2}-\dots\right).$

4387. $\sin ax=\begin{cases}\frac{4a}{\pi}\left[\frac{\cos x}{a^2-1}+\frac{\cos 3x}{a^2-3^2}+\frac{\cos 5x}{a^2-5^2}+\dots\right](a\text{ even});\\[2ex] \frac{4a}{\pi}\left[\frac{1}{2a^2}+\frac{\cos 2x}{a^2-2^2}+\frac{\cos 4x}{a^2-4^2}+\dots\right](a\text{ odd}).\end{cases}$

4388. $\cos ax=\begin{cases}-\frac{4}{\pi}\left[\frac{\sin x}{a^2-1^2}+\frac{3\sin 3x}{a^2-3^2}+\frac{5\sin 5x}{a^2-5^2}+\dots\right](a\text{ even});\\[2ex] -\frac{4}{\pi}\left[\frac{2\sin 2x}{a^2-2^2}+\frac{4\sin 4x}{a^2-4^2}+\frac{6\sin 6x}{a^2-6^2}+\dots\right](a\text{ odd}).\end{cases}$

4389. $\frac{2\sin a\pi}{\pi}\sum_{n=1}^{\infty}(-1)^{n-1}\frac{n}{a^2+n^2}\sin nx.$

4390. $\frac{\sinh \pi}{\pi}\left[1+2\sum_{n=1}^{\infty}(-1)^n\frac{\cos nx}{1+n^2}\right]$; $\frac{2}{\pi}\sum_{n=1}^{\infty}\frac{1-(-1)^n\cosh\pi}{1+n^2}n\sin nx.$

4391. $$f(x)=\frac{1}{3}+\frac{2}{\pi}\sum_{n=1}^{\infty}\left[\frac{\sin\frac{2\pi n}{3}}{n}-\frac{3\left(1-\cos\frac{2\pi n}{3}\right)}{2\pi n^2}\right]\cos\frac{2\pi nx}{3}$$

$$=\frac{1}{3}+\frac{\sqrt{3}}{\pi}\left(\frac{\cos\frac{2\pi x}{3}}{1}-\frac{\cos\frac{4\pi x}{3}}{2}+\frac{\cos\frac{8\pi x}{3}}{4}-\ldots\right)$$

$$-\frac{9}{2\pi^2}\left(\frac{\cos\frac{2\pi x}{3}}{1^2}+\frac{\cos\frac{4\pi x}{3}}{2^2}+\frac{\cos\frac{8\pi x}{3}}{4^2}+\ldots\right).$$

4392*. $$f(x)=\frac{\pi}{6}+\frac{3}{2\pi}\sum_{n=1}^{\infty}\frac{\sin\frac{n\pi}{3}}{n^2}\left(\cos\frac{n\pi}{3}\sin 2nx-\sin\frac{n\pi}{3}\cos 2nx\right)$$

$$=\frac{\pi}{6}+\frac{3\sqrt{3}}{8\pi}\left(\frac{\sin 2x}{1^2}-\frac{\sin 4x}{2^2}+\frac{\sin 8x}{4^2}-\frac{\sin 10x}{5^2}+\ldots\right)$$

$$-\frac{9}{8\pi}\left(\frac{\cos 2x}{1^2}+\frac{\cos 4x}{2^2}+\frac{\cos 8x}{4^2}+\frac{\cos 10x}{5^2}+\ldots\right).$$

Make use of the result of Problem 4368.

4393*. (1) $f(x)=\frac{4}{\pi}\left(\frac{\sin\alpha\cdot\sin x}{1^2}+\frac{\sin 3\alpha\cdot\sin 3x}{3^2}+\ldots\right)$;

(2) $$f(x)=\frac{\alpha(\pi-\alpha)}{\pi}-\frac{1}{\pi}\sum_{n=1}^{\infty}\frac{1-\cos 2n\alpha}{n^2}\cos 2nx$$

$$=\frac{\alpha(\pi-\alpha)}{\pi}-\frac{2}{\pi}\left(\frac{\sin^2\alpha\cdot\cos 2x}{1^2}+\frac{\sin^2 2\alpha\cdot\cos 4x}{2^2}+\ldots\right).$$

Make use of the result of Problem 4371.

4394. $\frac{8}{\pi}\sum_{n=1}^{\infty}\frac{\sin(2n-1)x}{(2n-1)^3}$; $\frac{\pi^3}{32}$.

4395. $\frac{8}{15}\pi^4-48\sum_{n=1}^{\infty}(-1)^n\frac{\cos nx}{n^4}$; (c) $\frac{7}{720}\pi^4$.

4396*. $\frac{\pi-x}{2}-\sum_{n=1}^{\infty}\frac{\sin nx}{n(n^3+1)}$ (see Problem 4374).

4397*. $\frac{x}{2}+\sum_{n=1}^{\infty}(-1)^{n-1}\frac{n-1}{n(n^2+1)}\sin nx$ (see Problem 4374).

4398*. $\frac{(\pi - x)^2}{4} - \frac{\pi^2}{12} + \sum_{n=1}^{\infty} \frac{n^2 - 1}{n^2(n^4 + 1)} \cos nx.$

Differentiate the series and use the solution of Problem 4374, remembering, that $\sum_{n=1}^{\infty} \frac{1}{n^2} = \frac{\pi^2}{6}$ (see Problem 4376).

4399. $\frac{\pi^3}{32} + \frac{\pi}{4} - \frac{\pi x^2}{8} - 2\cos x + \sum_{n=2}^{\infty} \frac{\sin n\frac{\pi}{2}}{n^3(n^2 - 1)} \cos nx \left(-\frac{\pi}{2} < x < \frac{\pi}{2}\right);$

make use of the series $\frac{\pi}{4} = \sum_{n=1}^{\infty} \frac{\sin\frac{\pi n}{2}}{n} \cos nx$ (see Problem 4380 for $h = \frac{\pi}{2}$), remembering that $\Sigma \frac{(-1)^{n-1}}{n^3} = \frac{\pi^3}{32}$ (see Problem 4394).

4400. $f_1(x) \approx 27.8 + 6.5 \cos x - 01 \sin x - 3.2 \cos 2x + 01 \sin 2x;$
$f_2(x) \approx 0.24 + 0.55 \cos x + 0.25 \sin x - 0.08 \cos 2x - 0.13 \sin 2x;$
$f_3(x) \approx 012 + 1.32 \cos x + 0.28 \sin x - 0.07 \cos 2x + 0.46 \sin 2x.$

Chapter 16

4401. Straight lines parallel to vector A $\{a, b, c\}$: $\frac{x - x_0}{a} = \frac{y - y_0}{b} = \frac{z - z_0}{c}.$

4402. Circles with the origin as centre $x^2 + y^2 = R^2$.

4403. Helices with a pitch $\frac{2\pi h}{\omega}$, located on cylinders whose axes coincide with the z-axis; $x = R\cos(\omega t + \alpha)$, $y = R\sin(\omega t + \alpha)$, $z = ht + z_0$, where Rs α and z_0 are arbitrary constants.

4404. (1) Circles formed as lines of intersection of spheres with the origin as centre and planes parallel to the bisector plane $y - z = 0$; $x^2 + y^2 + z^2 = R^2$, $y - z + C$, where R and C are arbitrary constants.

(2) Circles formed as lines of intersection of spheres with the origin as centre and planes cutting off the coordinate axes segments equal in magnitude and sign : $x^2 + y^2 + z^2 = R^2$, $x + y + z = C$.

(3) Lines of intersection of spheres $x^2 + y^2 + z^2 = R^2$ and hyperbolic paraboloids $zy = Cx$.

4405. div **A** = 3, curl **A** = 0.

4406. div **A** = 0, curl **A** = $2[(y - z)\mathbf{i} + (z - x)\mathbf{j} + (x - y)\mathbf{k}]$.

4407. div **A** = $6xyz$, curl **A** = $x(z^2 - y^2)\mathbf{i} + y(x^2 - z^2)\mathbf{j} + z(y^2 - x^2)\mathbf{k}]$.

4408. div **A** = 6, curl **A** = 0. **4409.** div **A** = 0, curl **A** = 0.

4410. div **A** = $\frac{k}{r^3}$, where k is the factor of proportionality, r is the distance between the point of force application and the origin of coordinates, curl **A** = 0.

4411. div **A** = 0, curl **A** = 0.

4412. div **A** = 0, curl **A** = 0. At the points of z-axis the field is not defined.

4413. div $\mathbf{A} = -\frac{k}{z\sqrt{x^2+y^2+z^2}}$, where k is the factor of proportionality.

At the points of the plane Oxy the field is not defined.

4414. $3a$. **4416.** div $\mathbf{b}$ $(\mathbf{ra}) = (\mathbf{ab})$, div $\mathbf{r}$ $(\mathbf{ra}) = 4\,(\mathbf{ra})$.

4417. 0. **4418.** (1) 0, (2) 0, (3) 0.

4419. div $\mathbf{A} = \frac{2f(r)}{r} + f'(r)$, for a three-dimensional field, div $\mathbf{A} = \frac{f(r)}{r} + f'(r)$, for a plane field.

4421. φ curl $\mathbf{A}$ + (grad $\varphi \times \mathbf{A}$). **4422.** $\frac{\mathbf{r}\times\mathbf{a}}{|\mathbf{r}|}$. **4423.** $2a$.

4424. $2\omega\mathbf{n}^0$, where $\mathbf{n}^0$ is a unit vector parallel to the axis of rotation.

4431. $u = -\frac{1}{2}k(x^2+y^2+z^2) + C$. **4432.** No. **4433.** No.

4434. $u = -\frac{1}{2}\ln(x^2+y^2) + C$. **4435.** No. **4437.** $\frac{2}{3}, \frac{1}{3}, \frac{1}{2}$.

4438. $k\delta \ln \frac{\sqrt{(l-x)^2+y^2}+l-x}{\sqrt{(l+x)^2+y^2}-l-x}$. **4439.** [1] $4k(\sqrt{2}-1)$.

4440. $\frac{k\delta\sqrt{a^2+b^2}}{b}\ln\frac{2\pi b+\sqrt{a^2+4\pi^2b^2}}{a}$. **4441.** $2k\delta a\ln(1+\sqrt{2})$.

4442. $\frac{2\pi k}{\sqrt{1-h^2}}\arccos h$ for $h<1$, $2\pi k$ for $h=1$

$\frac{2\pi k}{\sqrt{h^2-1}}\ln(h+\sqrt{h^2-1})$ for $h>1$.

4443*. (1) $2k\pi R\delta\ln\frac{H+\sqrt{H^2+R^2}}{R}$

(2) $4k\pi R\delta\ln\frac{H+\sqrt{H^2+4R^2}}{2R}$. Halve the cylinder by a cutting plane parallel to the base and compute the potential of the lateral surface of the cylinder as the sum of the potentials of the lateral surfaces of its halves, using the result of item (1).

4444. $2k\pi R\delta$.

4445*. (1) $k\pi\delta\left[R\sqrt{R^2+H^2}-H^2+R^2\ln\frac{H+\sqrt{R^2+H^2}}{R}\right]$,

(2) $\frac{k\pi\delta}{2}\left[H\sqrt{4R^2+H^2}-H^2+4R^2\ln\frac{H+\sqrt{4R^2+H^2}}{2R}\right]$;

See the hint to Problem 4443.

4446. $\pi k\delta H(l-H)$, where l is the generatrix of the cone.

4447. $u = \frac{2}{3}k\frac{\pi R^3\delta}{a}\left[\left(1+\frac{a^2}{R^2}\right)^{\frac{3}{2}} - \left(\frac{a}{R}\right)^3 - \frac{3n}{2R} + 1\right]$ for $a \geq R$;

[1] In the answers to Problem 4439 to 4449 k is the gravity constant.

$$u = \frac{2}{3} k\pi a^2\delta \left[\left(1 + \frac{R^2}{a^2}\right)^{\frac{3}{2}} - \left(\frac{R}{a}\right)^3 + \frac{3}{2}\left(\frac{R}{a}\right)^2 - 2\right] \text{ for } a \le R;$$

$$u = \frac{k\pi R^2\delta}{3}(4\sqrt{2} - 3) \text{ for } a = R.$$

4448*. $u = \frac{4k\pi\delta}{3a}(R^3 - r^3) = \frac{kM}{a}$ (M mass of the solid) for $a \ge R$;

$u = 2k\pi\delta(R^2 - r^2)$ for $a \le r$;

$u = \frac{4k\pi\delta}{3a}(a^3 - r^3) + 2k\pi\delta(R^2 - a^2)$ for $r \le a \le R$.

Pass a concentric sphere of radius a and use the results of the first two examples.

4449. $\frac{kM}{a}\left[1 + \frac{2}{7}\left(\frac{R}{a}\right)^2\right]$, where M is the mass of the sphere.

4450. Both the flux and circulation are equal to zero.

4451. The flux is equal to $2aS$, where S is the area of the domain bounded by the contour L. The circulation is equal to zero.

4452. Both the flux and circulation are equal to zero.

4453. The flux $\frac{3}{2}\pi R^4$, circulation $2\pi R^2$.

4454. If the origin lies inside the contour, then the flux is 2π, otherwise it is zero. The circulation in both cases is equal to zero.

4455. Circulation is equal to 2π if the origin lies inside the contour and is equal to zero if outside it. In both cases the flux is zero.

4456. 2. **4458.** $2\pi R^2 H$. **4459.** $\pi R^2 H$.

4460. 4π. Compute the flux through the base of the cone and make use of the result of Problem 4457.

4461. $\frac{3\pi}{16}$.

4462*. $\frac{1}{6}$. Use the Ostrogradsky formula and compute the flux through the base of the pyramid.

4463. $2\pi^2 b^2$. **4464.** $2\pi\omega R^2$.

4465. $-\pi$. Apply Stokes' theorem, taking the line of intersection of the paraboloid with the plane Oxy for the contour L.

Appendix

Tables of Basic Elementary Functions

1. Trigonometric functions

$\alpha°$	$\sin\alpha$	$\tan\alpha$	$\cot\alpha$	$\cos\alpha$	
0	0.0000	0.0000	—	1.000	90
1	0.0175	0.0175	57.3	1.000	89
2	0.0349	0.0349	28.6	0.999	88
3	0.0523	0.0524	19.1	0.999	87
4	0.0697	0.0699	14.3	0.998	86
5	0.0872	0.0875	11.4	0.996	85
6	0.1045	0.1051	9.51	0.995	84
7	0.1219	0.1228	8.14	0.993	83
8	0.139	0.141	7.11	0.990	82
9	0.156	0.158	6.31	0.988	81
10	0.174	0.176	5.67	0.985	80
11	0.191	0.194	5.145	0.982	79
12	0.208	0.213	4.705	0.978	78
13	0.225	0.231	4.331	0.974	77
14	0.242	0.249	4.011	0.970	76
15	0.259	0.268	3.732	0.966	75
16	0.276	0.287	0.487	0.961	74
17	0.292	0.306	0.271	0.956	73
18	0.309	0.325	3.078	0.951	72
19	0.326	0.344	2.904	0.946	71
20	0.342	0.364	2.747	0.940	70
21	0.358	0.384	0.605	0.934	69
22	0.375	0.404	0.475	0.927	68
23	0.391	0.424	0.356	0.921	67
24	0.407	0.445	0.246	0.914	66
25	0.423	0.466	2.145	0.906	65
26	0.438	0.488	2.050	0.899	64
27	0.454	0.510	1.963	0.891	63
28	0.469	0.532	1.881	0.883	62
29	0.485	0.554	1.804	0.875	61
30	0.500	0.577	1.732	0.866	60
31	0.515	0.601	1.664	0.857	59
32	0.530	0.625	1.600	0.848	58
33	0.545	0.649	1.540	0.839	57
34	0.559	0.675	1.483	0.829	56
35	0.574	0.700	1.428	0.819	55
36	0.588	0.727	1.376	0.809	54
37	0.601	0.754	1.327	0.799	53
38	0.616	0.781	1.280	0.788	52
39	0.629	0.810	1.235	0.777	51
40	0.643	0.839	1.192	0.766	50
41	0.656	0.869	1.150	0.755	49
42	0.669	0.900	1.111	0.743	48
43	0.682	0.933	1.072	0.731	47
44	0.695	0.966	1.036	0.719	46
45	0.707	1.000	1.000	0.707	45
	$\cos\alpha$	$\cot\alpha$	$\tan\alpha$	$\sin\alpha$	$\alpha°$

$\alpha°$	α radians	$\sin\alpha$	$\tan\alpha$
0.0	0.0	0.000	0.000
5.73	0.1	0.100	+ 0.100
11.5	0.2	0.199	+ 0.203
17.2	0.3	0.296	+ 0.310
22.9	0.4	0.389	+ 0.422
28.7	0.5	0.480	+ 0.547
34.4	0.6	0.564	+ 0.684
40.1	0.7	0.644	+ 0.842
45.0	$\frac{\pi}{4}$	0.707	+ 1.000
45.8	0.8	0.717	+ 1.028
51.6	0.9	0.784	+1.260
57.3	1.0	0.842	+ 1.558
63.0	1.1	0.891	+ 1.963
68.8	1.2	0.932	+ 2.579
74.5	1.3	0.964	+ 3.602
80.2	1.4	0.985	+ 5.798
86.0	1.5	0.997	+ 14.10
90.0	$\frac{\pi}{2}$	1.000	—
91.7	1.6	0.999	- 33.75
97.4	1.7	0.992	- 7.695
103.1	1.8	0.974	- 4.292
108.9	1.9	0.946	- 2.921
114.6	2.0	0.909	- 2.184
120.3		0.863	-1.711
126.1	2.1	0.808	- 1.373
131.8	2.2	0.745	- 1.118
	2.3		
135.0	$\frac{3\pi}{4}$	0.707	- 1.000
137.5		0.676	- 0.916
143.2	2.4	0.599	- 0.748
149.0	2.5	0.515	- 0.602
154.7	2.6	0.428	- 0.472
160.4	2.7	0.336	- 0.356
166.1	2.8	0.240	- 0.247
171.9	2.9	0.141	- 0.142
177.6	3.0	0.042	- 0.042
180.0	3.1	0.000	- 0.000
	π		

$$\sin\frac{\pi}{6} = \frac{1}{2},\quad \cos\frac{\pi}{6} = \frac{\sqrt{3}}{2},$$

$$\tan\frac{\pi}{6} = \frac{1}{\sqrt{3}},\quad \cot\frac{\pi}{6} = \sqrt{3},$$

$$\sin\frac{\pi}{4} = \cos\frac{\pi}{4} = \frac{1}{\sqrt{2}},$$

$$\tan\frac{\pi}{4} = \cot\frac{\pi}{4} = 1.$$

2. Hyperbolic functions

x	$\sinh x$	$\cosh x$	x	$\sinh x$	$\cosh x$
0	0	1			
0.1	0.100	1.005	2.1	4.022	4.144
0.2	0.201	1.020	2.2	4.457	4.568
0.3	0.305	1.045	2.3	4.937	5.037
0.4	0.411	1.081	2.4	5.466	5.557
0.5	0.521	1.128	2.5	6.050	6.132
0.6	0.637	1.185	2.6	6.695	6.769
0.7	0.759	1.255	2.7	7.407	7.474
0.8	0.888	1.337	2.8	8.192	8.253
0.9	1.026	1.433	2.9	9.060	9.115
1.0	1.175	1.543	3.0	10.02	10.07
1.1	1.336	1.669	3.1	11.08	11.12
1.2	1.509	1.811	3.2	12.25	12.29
1.3	1.698	1.971	3.3	13.54	13.58
1.4	1.904	2.151	3.4	14.97	15.00
1.5	2.129	2.352	3.5	16.54	16.57
1.6	2.376	2.578	3.6	18.29	18.31
1.7	2.646	2.828	3.7	20.21	20.24
1.8	2.942	3.107	3.8	22.34	22.36
1.9	3.268	3.418	3.9	24.69	24.71
2.0	3.627	3.762	4.0	27.29	27.31

For $x > 4$ assume that $\sinh x \approx \cosh x \approx \frac{e^x}{2}$ (accurate to 0.01).

$$\sinh x = \frac{e^x - e^{-x}}{2}; \quad \cosh x = \frac{e^x + e^{-x}}{2};$$

$$e^x = \sinh x + \cosh x; \quad e^{x\,i} = \cos x + i \sin x \,.$$

3. Inverse quantities, square and cubic roots, logarithms, exponential function

x	$\frac{1}{x}$	$\sqrt{x}$	$\sqrt{10x}$	$\sqrt[3]{x}$	$\sqrt[3]{10x}$	$\sqrt[3]{100x}$	$\log_{10} x$	$\ln x$	e^x	x
1.0	1.000	1.00	3.16	1.00	2.15	4.64	0.000	0.000	2.72	1.0
1.1	0.909	1.05	3.32	1.03	2.22	4.79	0.041	0.095	3.00	1.1
1.2	0.833	1.10	3.46	1.06	2.29	4.93	0.079	0.182	3.32	1.2
1.3	0.769	1.14	3.61	1.09	2.35	5.07	0.114	0.262	3.67	1.3
1.4	0.714	1.18	3.74	1.12	2.41	5.19	0.146	0.336	4.06	1.4
1.5	0.667	1.22	3.87	1.14	2.47	5.31	0.176	0.405	4.48	1.5
1.6	0.625	1.26	4.00	1.17	2.52	5.43	0.204	0.470	4.95	1.6
1.7	0.588	1.30	4.12	1.19	2.57	5.54	0.230	0.530	5.47	1.7
1.8	0.556	1.34	4.24	1.22	2.62	5.65	0.255	0.588	6.05	1.8
1.9	0.526	1.38	4.36	1.24	2.67	5.75	0.279	0.642	6.69	1.9

x	$\frac{1}{x}$	$\sqrt{x}$	$\sqrt{10x}$	$\sqrt[3]{x}$	$\sqrt[3]{10x}$	$\sqrt[3]{100x}$	$\log_{10} x$	$\ln x$	e^x	x
2.0	0.500	1.41	4.47	1.26	2.71	5.85	0.301	0.693	7.39	2.0
2.1	0.476	1.45	4.58	1.28	2.76	5.94	0.322	0.742	8.17	2.1
2.2	0.455	1.48	4.69	1.30	2.80	6.03	0.342	0.789	9.03	2.2
2.3	0.435	1.52	4.80	1.32	2.84	6.13	0.362	0.833	9.97	2.3
2.4	0.417	1.55	4.90	1.34	2.88	6.21	0.380	0.875	11.0	2.4
2.5	0.400	1.58	5.00	1.36	2.92	6.30	0.398	0.916	12.2	2.5
2.6	0.385	1.61	5.10	1.38	2.96	6.38	0.415	0.955	13.5	2.6
2.7	0.370	1.64	5.20	1.39	3.00	6.46	0.431	0.993	14.9	2.7
2.8	0.357	1.67	5.29	1.41	3.04	6.54	0.447	1.030	16.4	2.8
2.9	0.345	1.70	5.39	1.43	3.07	6.62	0.462	1.065	18.2	2.9
3.0	0.333	1.73	5.48	1.44	3.11	6.69	0.477	1.099	20.1	3.0
3.1	0.323	1.76	5.57	1.46	3.14	6.77	0.491	1.131	22.2	3.1
3.2	0.313	1.79	5.66	1.47	3.18	6.84	0.505	1.163	24.5	3.2
3.3	0.303	1.81	5.75	1.49	3.21	6.91	0.519	1.194	27.1	3.3
3.4	0.294	1.84	5.83	1.50	3.24	6.98	0.532	1.224	30.0	3.4
3.5	0.286	1.87	5.92	1.52	3.27	7.05	0.544	1.253	33.1	3.5
3.6	0.278	1.90	6.00	1.53	3.30	7.11	0.556	1.281	36.6	3.6
3.7	0.270	1.92	6.08	1.55	3.33	7.18	0.568	1.308	40.4	3.7
3.8	0.263	1.95	6.16	1.56	3.36	7.24	0.580	1.335	44.7	3.8
3.9	0.256	1.98	6.25	1.57	3.39	7.31	0.591	1.361	49.4	3.9
4.0	0.250	2.00	6.33	1.59	3.42	7.37	0.602	1.386	54.6	4.0
4.1	0.244	2.03	6.40	1.60	3.45	7.43	0.613	1.411	60.3	4.1
4.2	0.238	2.05	6.48	1.61	3.48	7.49	0.623	1.435	66.7	4.2
4.3	0.233	2.07	6.56	1.63	3.50	7.55	0.634	1.458	73.7	4.3
4.4	0.227	2.10	6.63	1.64	3.53	7.61	0.644	1.482	81.5	4.4
4.5	0.222	2.12	6.71	1.65	3.56	7.66	0.653	1.504	90.0	4.5
4.6	0.217	2.15	6.78	1.66	3.58	7.72	0.663	1.526	99.5	4.6
4.7	0.213	2.17	6.86	1.68	3.61	7.78	0.672	1.548	110	4.7
4.8	0.208	2.19	6.93	1.69	3.63	7.83	0.681	1.569	121	4.8
4.9	0.204	2.21	7.00	1.70	3.66	7.88	0.690	1.589	134	4.9
5.0	0.200	2.24	7.07	1.71	3.68	7.94	0.699	1.609	148	5.0
5.1	0.196	2.26	7.14	1.72	3.71	7.99	0.708	1.629	164	5.1
5.2	0.192	2.28	7.21	1.73	3.73	8.04	0.716	1.649	181	5.2
5.3	0.189	2.30	7.28	1.74	3.76	8.09	0.724	1.668	200	5.3
5.4	0.185	2.32	7.35	1.75	3.78	8.14	0.732	1.686	221	5.4
5.5	0.182	2.35	7.42	1.77	3.80	8.19	0.740	1.705	244	5.5
5.6	0.179	2.37	7.48	1.78	3.83	8.24	0.748	1.723	270	5.6
5.7	0.175	2.39	7.55	1.79	3.85	8.29	0.756	1.740	299	5.7
5.8	0.172	2.41	7.62	1.80	3.87	8.34	0.763	1.758	330	5.8
5.9	0.170	2.43	7.68	1.81	3.89	8.39	0.771	1.775	365	5.9
6.0	0.167	2.45	7.75	1.82	3.92	8.43	0.778	1.792	403	6.0
6.1	0.164	2.47	7.81	1.83	3.94	8.48	0.785	1.808	446	6.1
6.2	0.161	2.49	7.87	1.84	3.96	8.53	0.792	1.825	493	6.2
6.3	0.159	2.51	7.94	1.85	3.98	8.57	0.799	1.841	545	6.3
6.4	0.156	2.53	8.00	1.86	4.00	8.62	0.806	1.856	602	6.4

x	$\frac{1}{x}$	$\sqrt{x}$	$\sqrt{10x}$	$\sqrt[3]{x}$	$\sqrt[3]{10x}$	$\sqrt[3]{100x}$	$\log_{10} x$	$\ln x$	e^x	x
6.5	0.154	2.55	8.06	1.87	4.02	8.66	0.813	1.872	665	6.5
6.6	0.152	2.57	8.12	1.88	4.04	8.71	0.820	1.887	735	6.6
6.7	0.149	2.59	8.19	1.89	4.06	8.75	0.826	1.902	812	6.7
6.8	0.147	2.61	8.25	1.90	4.08	8.79	0.833	1.918	898	6.8
6.9	0.145	2.63	8.31	1.90	4.10	8.84	0.839	1.932	992	6.9
7.0	0.143	2.65	8.37	1.91	4.12	8.88	0.845	1.946	1097	7.0
7.1	0.141	2.67	8.43	1.92	4.14	8.92	0.851	1.960	1212	7.1
7.2	0.139	2.68	8.49	1.93	4.16	8.96	0.856	1.974	1339	7.2
7.3	0.137	2.70	8.54	1.94	4.18	9.00	0.863	1.988	1480	7.3
7.4	0.135	2.72	8.60	1.95	4.20	9.05	0.869	2.001	1636	7.4
7.5	0.133	2.74	8.66	1.96	4.22	9.09	0.875	2.015	1808	7.5
7.6	0.132	2.76	8.72	1.97	4.24	9.13	0.881	2.028	1998	7.6
7.7	0.130	2.78	8.78	1.98	4.25	9.17	0.887	2.041	2208	7.7
7.8	0.128	2.79	8.83	1.98	4.27	9.21	0.892	2.054	2440	7.8
7.9	0.127	2.81	8.89	1.99	4.29	9.24	0.898	2.067	2697	7.9
8.0	0.125	2.83	8.94	2.00	4.31	9.28	0.903	2.079	2981	8.0
8.1	0.124	2.85	9.00	2.01	4.33	9.32	0.909	2.092	3294	8.1
8.2	0.122	2.86	9.06	2.02	4.34	9.36	0.914	2.104	3641	8.2
8.3	0.121	2.88	9.11	2.03	4.36	9.40	0.919	2.116	4024	8.3
8.4	0.119	2.90	9.17	2.03	4.38	9.44	0.924	2.128	4447	8.4
8.5	0.118	2.92	9.22	2.04	4.40	9.47	0.929	2.140	4914	8.5
8.6	0.116	2.93	9.27	2.05	4.41	9.51	0.935	2.152	5432	8.6
8.7	0.115	2.95	9.33	2.06	4.43	9.55	0.940	2.163	6003	8.7
8.8	0.114	2.97	9.38	2.07	4.45	9.58	0.945	2.175	6634	8.8
8.9	0.112	2.98	9.43	2.07	4.47	9.62	0.949	2.186	7332	8.9
9.0	0.111	3.00	9.49	2.08	4.48	9.66	0.954	2.197	8103	9.0
9.1	0.110	3.02	9.54	2.09	4.50	9.69	0.959	2.208	8955	9.1
9.2	0.109	3.03	9.59	2.10	4.51	9.73	0.964	2.219	9897	9.2
9.3	0.108	3.05	9.64	2.10	4.53	9.76	0.969	2.230	10938	9.3
9.4	0.106	3.07	9.69	2.11	4.55	9.80	0.973	2.241	12088	9.4
9.5	0.105	3.08	9.75	2.12	4.56	9.83	0.978	2.251	13360	9.5
9.6	0.104	3.10	9.80	2.13	4.58	9.87	0.982	2.263	14765	9.6
9.7	0.103	3.11	9.84	2.13	4.60	9.90	0.987	2.272	16318	9.7
9.8	0.102	3.13	9.90	2.14	4.61	9.93	0.991	2.282	18034	9.8
9.9	0.101	3.15	9.95	2.15	4.63	9.97	0.996	2.293	19930	9.9
10.0	0.100	3.16	10.00	2.15	4.64	10.00	1.000	2.303	22026	10.0

Given in the column "$\log_{10} x$" are mantissas of common logarithms. Natural logarithms of numbers greater than 10 or less than 1 are to be found by the formula

$$\ln (x \cdot 10^k) = \ln x + k \ln 10$$

$$\ln 10 = 2.303; \qquad \ln 10^2 = 4.605;$$

$$\log_{10} x = 0.4343 \ln x; \quad \ln x = 2.303 \log_{10} x .$$

Formulas for approximate taking of roots:

$$(1)\ \sqrt[n]{1+x} \approx 1 + \frac{x}{n} + \frac{1-n}{2n^2} x^2 \quad \text{for } |x| < 1.$$

$$(2)\ \sqrt[n]{a^n + b} \approx a\left(1 + \frac{b}{na^n} + \frac{1-n}{2n^2} \cdot \frac{b^2}{a^{2n}}\right) \quad \text{for } \left|\frac{b}{a^n}\right| < 1.$$

4. Conversion of degrees to radians

α degrees	1	2	3	4	5	6	7	8	9
a radians	0.017	0.035	0.052	0.070	0.087	0.105	0.122	0.140	0.157
1 radian = 57 °17′45″									

TO THE READER

Mir Publishers welcome your comments on the content, translation and design of this book.
We would also be pleased to receive any proposals you care to make about our futrue publications.

Our address is:
USSR, 129820, Moscow I-110, GSP
Pervy Rizhsky Pereulok, 2
Mir Publishers

Ingram Content Group UK Ltd.
Milton Keynes UK
UKHW020733060623
422954UK00015B/771

9 789388 127325